FIGHTING AIRCRAFT OF WORLD WARS ONE AND TWO

169 Wardour Street
London W1A 2JX
This material first appeared in Purnell's Histories of the World Wars © 1966/72 BPC Publishing Limited and Purnell's History of the World Wars Specials © 1974/75 Phoebus Publishing Company

Made and printed in Belgium by
H. Proost & Cie p.v.b.a., Turnhout
ISBN 0 7026 0007 5

and went on to contribute on a freelance basis to many technical magazines. Since then his work for Purnell's Histories of the World Wars and Purnell's History of the World Wars Specials has established him as one of the most outstanding artists in his field.

ABOUT THIS BOOK

At the outbreak of World War I, the aircraft ranged against each other resembled flying kites, and they were regarded, above all, as aids to reconnaissance rather than weapons. But by 1945 these frail structures had developed into sleek machines, packed with sophisticated equipment and capable of delivering a shattering blow to any enemy on land, at sea, or in the air.

The story of these aircraft, and their development as a new weapon of war, is a fascinating one. The improvements in performance and capability of the early planes were soon reflected in refinement of their use. Strategic bombing, aerial photography and ground and sea support were evolved, while the staggering technical progress of World War II saw the passing of comparatively primitive planes and the advent of the first jet fighters.

This volume presents to the general reader a comprehensive account of these developments: aircraft design and armament, combat techniques and military applications used in air warfare by both Allied and Axis powers. It also includes some vivid first-hand accounts of missions and discusses the moral implications of war methods that wreaked an unprecedented amount of death and destruction.

CONTENTS

After hundreds, perhaps even thousands, of years of experiment and speculation man first took to the skies on the morning of December 17, 1903. On that momentous day, at Kitty Hawk, North Carolina, the brothers Orville and Wilbur Wright piloted their motor-powered aircraft the staggering distance of 852 feet in just 59 seconds.

Progress followed rapidly on this breakthrough, and by October 5, 1905, continued improvement and experiment had made possible a circular flight of 24½ miles in 38 minutes by the Wright brothers at Dayton, Ohio. In 1908 – by now complete with patented flying-machine – the brothers arrived in France to give a series of exhibition flights, and, on the last day of that year, to take the Michelin Trophy with a flight of 124 kilometres (78 miles) in a time of 2 hours and 20 minutes.

Perhaps inspired by the Americans' visit, on July 25 of the following year Louis Blériot further captured the public imagination with a flight over the Channel from Calais to Dover.

By then – in the space of only six years – flying had become not just possible but merely a question of mechanical reliability and technical resources. As such it had moved rapidly from the garden sheds and drawing boards of eccentrics and pioneer designers into the thrill-hungry, sporting world of rich young men with an eye for adventure and social glamour. Interestingly, this image of affluent daring which was soon to surround the young pilots of the Royal Flying Corps on the Western Front was to persist and find its reflection in the handlebar moustaches and silk cravats of Second World War RAF fame.

Nonetheless, it was Italian aviators who first realised the

HEAVIER THAN AIR CRAFT:

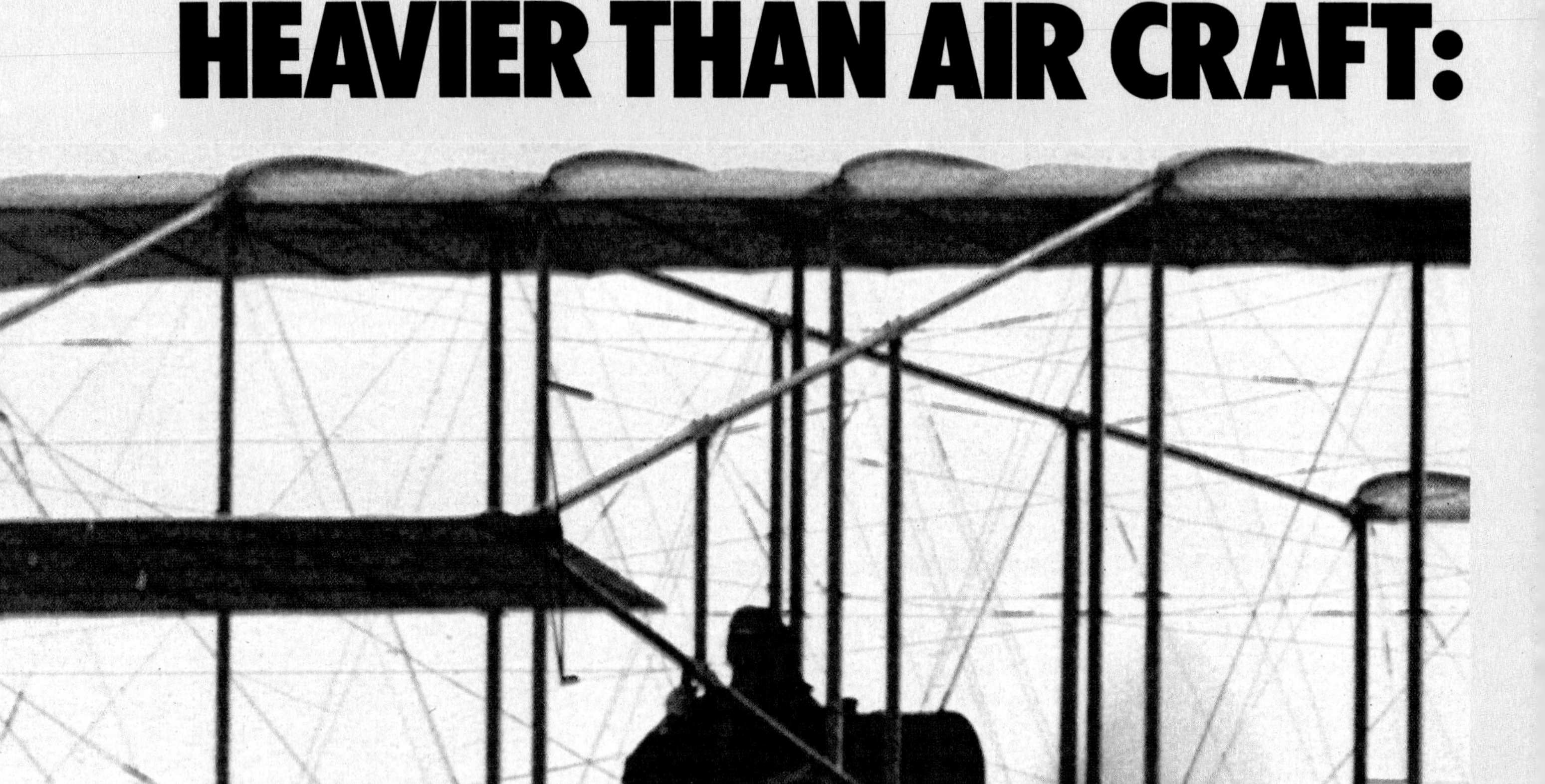

Jack Pia

A modern reconstruction of a typical 1910 aircraft of the wire and canvas era – a **Bristol Box-kite**

military potential of aircraft. On November 1, 1911, in fact, a certain Lieutenant Cavotti dropped four grenades, each weighing 4·4 pounds, on Turkish positions at Ain Zara in Libya. Despite the fact that Italian warships had bombarded the same positions with 152 heavy shells only a few days previously, it was the grenades that caused a furore. Words like 'ethics' and 'inhumane' were bandied hopelessly around the world press . . . but still the bombing went on.

The debate, of course, was irrelevant to the inevitable military application of aircraft, but it serves to clearly illustrate the total newness of a dimension which – like Space in the Seventies – naïve idealists hoped to preserve from the competing ambitions of their leaders.

Those leaders were, however, slow to realise that air-to-air warfare itself offered yet another realm for their activities. Even as war broke out in 1914, the French General Foch was to be heard offering the view that 'aviation is a good sport, but for the army it is useless'. He, like many of his senior contemporaries, could only visualise aircraft as components of land or sea operations – operating to provide intelligence or as spotters for the guns. It was to be a matter of years on the Western Front before military opinion accepted the inevitable facts: that if air space was worth having for whatever reason, then that air space itself was going to become a battleground.

Further, if the air was to become a battleground, then aircraft specifically designed and equipped to destroy other aircraft were needed – not simply as armed spotters or reconnaissance machines but as fighters, first and foremost.

STATE OF THE ART TO 1914

Above: Skipping and stumbling gaily across the shingle, these post-Edwardian holidaymakers greet the arrival of a flying-machine. Over-water flights, of course, placed great emphasis on the development of reliable and powerful motors. *Left, below:* Gustav Hamel, whose brilliant exhibition flights did much to popularise flying

Centre, below: The winner of the 1913 Aerial Derby. In the pre-war years racing gave great impetus to high performance flights. *Bottom left:* Flying boats and floatplanes, at first novel playthings of the wealthy, were soon to prove useful in the maritime reconnaissance rôle. *Below right:* A primitive German anti-aircraft early warning device

Bibliothek für Zeitgeschichte

The considerable advance in aeronautics since 1909 is reflected in the **Bristol Scout A**, designed in late 1913. Astonishingly clean and trim for its day, it was able to attain 95 mph on the 80 hp of its Gnome rotary engine

Below: Designed by the first Geoffrey de Havilland and built by the Royal Aircraft Factory, the **BE2a** was the basic military aircraft of the RFC at the outbreak of war. It had been ineligible for the 1912 Military Trials on Salisbury Plain, but flying *hors concours* it had been clearly the best all-round performer at the trials, this being reflected in the orders placed for this type but not for the winner of the competition. This particular aircraft was the first RFC machine to land in France

△Based on the design for the 1914 'Round Britain' race, the military **Sopwith 'Folder'** was typical of civilian machines adapted by the armed forces

▽The **Sopwith Tabloid** made its first appearance in 1913 as a sporting biplane. Apart from its very clean design, especially in the cowling of the rotary engine, it was remarkable in the placing of the two occupants side by side

BE2a. *Engine:* Renault V-8 in-line water-cooled engine, 70 hp *Maximum speed:* 70 mph. *Climb rate:* 9 minutes to 3,000 feet. *Ceiling:* 10,000 feet. *Endurance:* 3 hours. *Loaded weight:* 1,600 lbs. *Span:* 38 feet 7½ inches. *Length:* 29 feet 9½ inches

Left: The **Sopwith Gordon Bennett Racer,** pressed by the Admiralty on the outbreak of war, was one of the best pre-war designs. Very clean, and with a fully cowled 80-hp Gnôme rotary engine, it was capable of 105 mph

Right: The **Breguet AG4,** nicknamed the 'Whitebait', was an example of the sometimes rather odd designs which were built in fairly large numbers and developed quite considerably

Imperial War Museum

Right: The **Caudron G III,** adopted by the French air force as a reconnaissance aircraft, was obsolescent by the beginning of the war and was soon reduced to training duties

Right: The **Aviatik B I** was one of the prototype German two-seater reconnaissance aircraft of World War One. This sort of design—two-bay biplane with an in-line tractor engine and two crew—remained common up to the war's end

Right: The original version of the **SE2**, shown here, was built by the Royal Aircraft Factory, Farnborough, and foreshadowed to a remarkable degree the first aircraft built for the single-seat scouting rôle. It was capable of 92 mph

Imperial War Museum

In January 1912 a seaplane took off from an improvised staging on the forecastle of HMS *Africa*, the first time this had been done from a British warship

Imperial War Museum

Above: The **Bristol Box-kite.** The first mass-produced British aircraft, this type was much used in the development of RFC tactics and for training both military and civilian pilots. *Engine:* Gnôme rotary, 50 hp. *Maximum speed:* 40 mph. *Loaded weight:* 900 lbs. *Span* 33 feet *Length:* 38 feet 6 inches

Right: The **Maurice Farman M.F.7 'Longhorn'.** Despite its flimsy appearance, this 1913 type served as a trainer well into the war after starting out as a general duties and reconnaissance aircraft. *Engine:* Renault, 70 hp. *Speed:* 59 mph. *Ceiling:* 13,123 feet. *Endurance:* 3 hours 30 minutes. *Weight:* 1,885 lbs. *Span:* 51 feet. *Length:* 37 feet 2⅞ inches

A type much favoured by the Germans was the **Taube** (dove), so called because of the shape of the wings, which possessed large trailing portions at their outboard ends. Lateral control on this type of aircraft was effected by differential warping of these trailing portions. The *Taube* type, here represented by the Austrian-designed Etrich *Taube,* was used mainly for reconnaissance. Although superseded by faster, stronger and more manoeuvrable biplane types, *Tauben* continued in service up to 1916. *Engine:* Mercedes 6-cylinder in-line water-cooled engine, 120 hp. *Maximum speed:* 62.5 mph. *Ceiling:* 8,705 feet. *Loaded weight:* 1,914 lbs. *Span:* 47 feet 0⅝ inches. *Length:* 32 feet 3¾ inches

3 AUGUST, 1914: OUTBREAK OF WAR IN THE AIR

When war broke out between Britain, France and Germany in August 1914 the art and science of air warfare were not merely new, they were non-existent. It was only 11 years since the Wright brothers' first successful aeroplane flight at Kitty Hawk, and a bare five since Louis Blériot's crossing of the English Channel had destroyed the United Kingdom's island status, although the airships with which both France and Germany had been experimenting since the turn of the century had long been capable of making a return trip.

Prophets and scaremongers had long foreseen a 'Zeppelin menace'. Aeroplanes were taken less seriously. Although there had been many experimenters with heavier-than-air craft it was not until the arrival of Wilbur Wright at Le Mans in 1908 that European sportsmen—for flying was primarily a sport in those days—learned to make and fly properly controllable aeroplanes. The French learned fast, and although their experiments led at first in many directions it was not long before two main types of aeroplane became dominant: the 'tractor' which had a fuselage of more or less modern appearance, with the engine in front of the pilot and driving a propeller in the nose; and the 'pusher', in which the airscrew was mounted behind a bath-like nacelle for pilot and passenger, and the tail was carried on outrigger booms. Both types found a use in warfare; the pusher because pilot and observer, seated in the nose, had an excellent view of the ground, the tractor because its cleaner aerodynamic shape provided a better performance. Types were made in monoplane and biplane form, the former having the advantage of speed and the latter of structural strength.

The French army, although possessing a few airships, at once saw the value of aeroplanes for reconnaissance and built up a sizeable fleet. This frightened the Germans (hitherto secure in their superiority in airships) into emulation, and soon their machines, both in number and performance, had overtaken the French. By 1914 the German and Austro-Hungarian empires had many aeroplane factories and two main types had been more or less standardised: monoplanes known, from their back-swept wings and spreading tail, as *Tauben* (doves) and a biplane series also notable for a back-swept trailing edge known, for this reason, as 'arrows'. The wing plan in each case was based on the work of Etrich and Wels in Austria, who had discovered that such a

Right: The **Morane-Saulnier Type 'L'.** This French 'parasol' scouting monoplane was produced in an effort to combine the speed potential of the monoplane with the strength and reconnaissance capabilities of the biplane. The result was in fact so successful that the German authorities ordered several firms to build copies—a not unusual practice at the time. *Engine:* Gnôme or Le Rhône rotary, 80hp. *Maximum speed:* 71 mph. *Ceiling:* 13,100 feet. *Endurance:* 4 hours. *Loaded weight:* 1,499 lbs. *Span:* 33 feet 9½ inches. *Length:* 20 feet 9 inches

Below: The grisly result of an early wartime duel in the air

wing form produced inherent stability, providing a steady platform for aerial observation. The need for rapid manoeuvring in aerial combat had not been foreseen.

The Germans had only one 'pusher' type in service, the Otto biplane. They did, however, possess many excellent aero-engines, based on motor-racing engines. The *Kaiserpreis* race of 1907 for the Emperor's Cup, and the series of ostensibly sporting trials during 1909, 1910 and 1911 sponsored by Prince Henry, the Kaiser's brother, produced motorcars powered by remarkably efficient engines, made by Mercedes, Benz, Opel and Austro-Daimler. Water-cooled engines, on the motorcar principle, were popular because it was realised that a big, powerful engine could support a large airframe, thus fulfilling two of the army's demands: a high ceiling and long range. By the outbreak of war Germany held the altitude record at 27,500 feet, and the endurance record at 24 hours.

In aeronautics, as elsewhere, the French approach was directly opposed to the German. The French had been the first Europeans to fly, and because at first the problem had been to rise from the ground at all, they evolved relatively flimsy aeroplanes and the lightest possible engines. At the outbreak of war they had only one make of water-cooled engine, the Canton-Unné (Salmson) radial, but they had two kinds of air-cooled engine, based on the now forgotten rotary principle: the Gnôme and the Le Rhône. The rotary layout appears so improbable at this range in time that a short explanation is due. The crankshaft was held stationary and the rest of the engine—crank-case and radially disposed cylinders—revolved round it, carrying the airscrew with them.

The **Albatros BII** was in service with the German air services from before the war well into 1915 as a first line aircraft. In common with other Albatros reconnaissance types, it had an immensely strong fuselage made up of plywood skinning on a basic wooden rectangular framework. Despite the exposed engine, it is clear that some thought has been given to streamlining in the design of the relatively pointed nose. *Engine:* Mercedes 6-cylinder in-line, 100 hp. *Maximum speed:* 66 mph. *Climb:* About 260 feet per minute. *Ceiling:* 9,840 feet. *Endurance:* 4 hours. *Loaded weight:* 2,356 lbs. *Span:* 42 feet. *Length:* 25 feet

The 80 hp Gnôme was frail and temperamental, but it was the lightest of all for its power, and extremely compact. It was to make possible the first single-seater fighters – although anything so specialised as a fighter lies outside the period of this article. In 1914 all aeroplanes were used primarily for scouting.

Britain began late, and in a very small way. The authorities had always adopted a repressive and suspicious attitude to flying, and, just as motor racing was forbidden on the roads (in sharp contrast with France, Germany and Italy) so pioneer aviators were 'warned off', A. V. Roe being threatened with prosecution if he persisted in trying to fly from Hackney Marshes. Enthusiasts like the Hon C. S. Rolls and J. T. C. Moore-Brabazon learned their flying in France, and until the government-owned Aircraft Factory at Farnborough undertook the design and development of aeroplanes, such few machines as the Royal Flying Corps possessed were French. The Royal Navy, too, took an interest in flying, but the Navy, in contrast to the army, who patronised the Factory, encouraged private constructors such as Avro, Sopwith and Short Brothers. The British authorities had done little to foster the design of indigenous engines, and apart from a Factory copy of the Renault which began to emerge by the end of 1914, most service engines were French. The Belgian air force, too, relied entirely on France for both airframes and engines. Only Russia cast her net wide, to include machines from France, Britain, Germany, Austria and the United States.

Airmen distrusted

Aerial reconnaissance flights could, with advantage, have begun before the war. France's Lebaudy airships could have discovered German mobilisation plans and troop concentrations. The air was a new dimension, however, and as events were quickly to show, senior officers on each side proved more ready to believe their own preconceptions than the reports of their aerial observers. It was, however, purely as long-range scouts that aeroplanes were regarded, a means of 'seeing over the hill'. This does not mean that the air arm was universally accepted. Cavalrymen thought it might frighten their horses, gunners resented the need for increased camouflage, soldiers of the old school distrusted airmen on principle and the infantry fired at everything that flew. Nor were airmen regarded as heroes; they were more often suspected of 'dodging the column'.

However, in the early months of the war German machines flew 200-mile reconnaissance flights over the French positions daily, bringing back valuable information to corps headquarters, as the Germans, unlike the French and the British, had aircraft at corps level, landing with their messages beside corps' HQs.

The French air force had been slow to mobilise, but by this time it was in action, having bombed the German airship sheds at Metz on August 14. The British Royal Flying Corps, meanwhile, had arrived at Amiens, and by the 17th its four squadrons were installed alongside General French's HQ at Maubeuge, a dozen miles south-west of Mons. Their aeroplanes were supposedly unarmed. Officially they were regarded purely as scouts, although it was suggested that should enemy aircraft be encountered it might be possible to drop hand-grenades upon them from above, or possible *fléchettes,* pointed steel darts which had been issued for anti-personnel bombing. Nobody took these weapons seriously, although a senior German officer, General von Meyer, was to be fatally wounded by *fléchettes* from a French aeroplane on December 6. Far more effective were the weapons which pilots and observers improvised. Some carried service revolvers, some carbines, some the standard Lee Enfield rifle. Véry pistols were also employed, and sporting-guns firing chain-shot. A German aeroplane flew over Maubeuge on August 22, and amongst the machines unsuccessful in intercepting it was an Henri Farman of 5 Squadron in which Lieutenants L. A. Strange and Penn-Gaskell had rigged a Lewis machine gun on an improvised mounting, the first machine gun in the RFC. The same day the British army suffered its first casualty of the war, when an observer in 2 Squadron, Sergeant-Major Jillings, was wounded.

Riddled with bullets

'On the 23rd August,' wrote Major McCudden, VC, who at that time was an air mechanic, 'things began to hum.' It was the Battle of Mons. Continuous sorties were flown, and aeroplanes returned riddled with bullets, for everyone shot at anything that flew, friend or foe, and it was not until November, when the RFC adopted tricolour roundels like the French (but with colours reversed), that identification was more certain. It is thought that Blériots of 3 Squadron brought news of the German attempt to outflank the British army, which made possible the successful retreat from Mons. Infantry fire was the worst danger at this period, although the Germans already had effective 65-mm, 70-mm, 75-mm and 105-mm anti-aircraft guns on mobile mountings. Allied pilots returning from patrol made an easy mark when flying against the prevailing west wind; the maximum speed of a Farman or Blériot was barely 65 mph, so that ground speed against the wind could be very low indeed.

During the retreat RFC ground staffs managed every day to keep ahead of the Germans, although pilots sometimes returned from patrol to find the aerodrome from which they had taken off in German hands. Air mechanics flew on with their pilots, servicing engine and aircraft before sleeping under a wing; McCudden and one other fitter kept four machines in the air, using only the tools carried on board. At this time the armament of the single-seater Blériot Parasol flown by Captain Conran, a pilot of McCudden's squadron, was made up as follows: 16 hand grenades, two shrapnel bombs, each in a rack outside the fuselage, to be thrown by hand, and a 26-pound Melinite bomb (made from a French shell) tied to an upper fuselage longeron, to be dropped by cutting the string. 'Pilots landed,' wrote Maurice Baring, General Henderson's Intelligence officer at RFC HQ, 'with their maps showing long black lines of German troops on every road.' Message-dropping was tried but landing was better. In addition, wireless was being developed and was to prove very useful for directing artillery fire once the lines became stabilised. It was used, sparingly, at the Battle of the Marne but increasingly at that of the Aisne and during the First Battle of Ypres, when the RFC advanced once more to take up permanent quarters at Saint-Omer.

Much had been learned during the first three months. Reconnaissance machines, competing with the enemy in the same air space, had to fight for their information, and here the 'pusher' machines had the advantage because the observer had a clear field of fire forward, unmasked by the propeller. Until 1915 neither side developed a means of firing a machine gun forwards through the propeller-disc and aiming the machine as a whole. The nearest they came to it was rigging carbines on a Bristol Scout to fire obliquely forwards at 45 degrees, missing the propeller. This did not make an effective fighter but it was the best the RFC had, as the Bristol, with its 80 hp Gnôme, was one of the fastest machines in France, with a maximum speed of over 90 mph. The Vickers FB 5 'Gun Bus', the first *ad hoc* fighter aeroplane, was not operational before 1915.

Between August 16 and the final halt at Melun on September 4, the RFC occupied ten separate aerodromes, most of them improvised. Machines were pegged out in the open, and when stormy weather blew up, at Fère-en-Tardenois on the Aisne, after the return northward had begun, McCudden recalls seeing a Blériot 'absolutely stand vertically on its tail, poise for a second and then fall over on its back with a resounding crash'. An Henri Farman also blew over, and 5 Squadron had four Farmans completely wrecked. From Fère-en-Tardenois the RFC moved north, with the BEF, to what Raleigh, the official historian, calls their 'natural' position near the Channel ports, at St Omer, where they took up permanent quarters on October 12, in time for the First Battle of Ypres, in which the Belgian air force, after escaping the German invaders, played a useful part.

The light-hearted clublike atmosphere which united all ranks in the RFC was notably lacking in the French *Aviation Militaire*. Aerial reconnaissance was regarded as an Intelligence matter, and observers were therefore staff officers, billeted at army HQ, and having no social contact with the squadrons. Many non-commissioned pilots were used, by France and also by Germany. These were at a disadvantage *vis à vis* their observers and, indeed, their maintenance crews. It was hard for pilots holding the rank of private to reason with a technical NCO. In some units observers regarded the pilot as a mere chauffeur, and this was especially true in the German air force, as Manfred von Richthofen recorded in his memoirs *The Red Air Fighter*; indeed, a ludicrous incident took place during the first Battle of Ypres when the officer observer of a German two-seater driven down by the RFC, whose life had been saved by a brilliant forced landing, was seen to belabour his pilot for his incompetence!

Prying airmen

In the French service all aerial reconnaissance reports were forwarded by army HQs to the *Deuxième Bureau* for analysis; this was a clumsy arrangement. Sometimes observers' reports were disbelieved, and sometimes they were simply pigeon-holed. This also happened to a German dispatch reporting the presence of the BEF at Mons; but *coups* there were in plenty, both tactical and strategic. It was an aerial report that told the size of the German forces massing against Belgium, and which pointed the gap between the armies of Generals von Bülow and Kluck at the Marne. Ground forces, especially the gunners, learned to mislead the prying airman. False tracks were laid and imitation guns put out, with fireworks to add verisimilitude. This confused the other side and gave friendly aircraft an opportunity to plot enemy batteries when the latter fired on supposed positions.

Some excellent bombing was done by the French, as, for example, when the destruction of a railway tunnel at Soissons kept an ammunition train from the front and thus halted a barrage; the same pilot and observer, Roeckel and Châtelain, in the course of ten hours' artillery spotting near Vaubécourt on September 8, silenced half the artillery of the German *XVI Corps* during the First Battle of the Marne. By the end of the year the French, like the British, were using wireless-equipped aeroplanes, and had inspired the British to follow their lead in aerial photography. Both sides were using observation balloons, and the French had a section of man-carrying kites under Captain Saconney, which made a notable five-hour artillery observation on December 1. It was not until October 5, however, that the French claimed their first victim in aerial combat, an Aviatik biplane brought down by Sergeant Frantz and his mechanic in a Voisin pusher. They used a Hotchkiss *mitrailleuse* as their offensive weapon.

Ramshackle equipment

Imperial Russia cannot be said to have taken aviation very seriously. By 1913 she is said to have purchased about 250 miscellaneous aeroplanes, of which 150 were still optimistically described as modern. They included aircraft of the following makes: Albatros, Aviatik, Bristol, Curtiss, Deperdussin, Farman, Nieuport and Rumpler. To these in 1914 were added a few experimental machines by Sikorsky. Flying schools existed at Moscow, Odessa, Omsk and Tashkent, but when the Russian armies advanced upon East Prussia almost simultaneously with the German invasion of Belgium, she could muster only 72 military pilots, plus a reserve of 36 qualified civilians. Bad roads and overloaded railways made support an almost impossible task.

On the German side aeroplanes made valuable reconnaissance flights, as they were doing on the Western Front, and there were some casualties. Russian gun-fire brought down a German machine during the Battle of Lemberg on September 5, while on the following day the Germans made the mistake they had already made twice in the West: they employed a Zeppelin on low-level tactical work. Airship *L V* was brought down and captured, complete with its crew of 30. During the same fighting the Russians lost their most brilliant and picturesque pilot, Nesterov, the first man to loop the loop. This feat Nesterov achieved while the better known Pégoud was still nerving himself for the attempt; he was court-martialled for hazarding military property and sentenced to the equivalent of a month's confinement to barracks. His death was heroic but unnecessary. Encountering a German aeroplane and having no guns, he deliberately rammed the enemy and brought both machines down in flames.

At the end of 1914 air warfare was still at the 'experimental' stage. The initiative in making developments in tactics was still in the hands of the individual pilots. During the bad weather of the winter months there was bound to be a certain slackening of air activity, and not until the spring of 1915 were the lessons of 1914 to bear fruit.

The **Pfalz AI** reconnaissance machine used in the first few months of the war was merely a German-built copy of the French Morane-Saulnier Type 'L'

Bibliothek für Zeitgeschichte

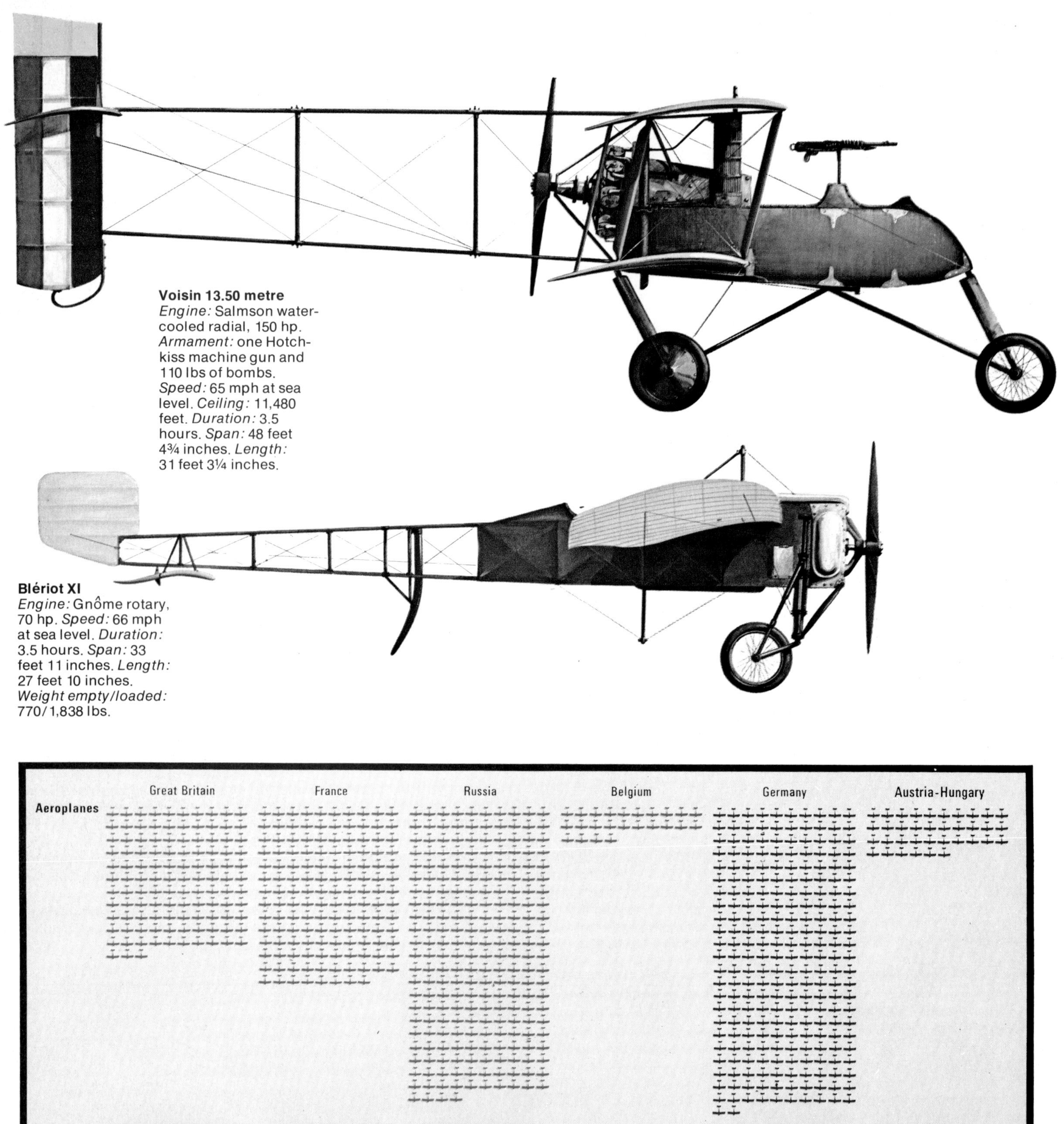

Voisin 13.50 metre
Engine: Salmson water-cooled radial, 150 hp. *Armament:* one Hotchkiss machine gun and 110 lbs of bombs. *Speed:* 65 mph at sea level. *Ceiling:* 11,480 feet. *Duration:* 3.5 hours. *Span:* 48 feet 4¾ inches. *Length:* 31 feet 3¼ inches.

Blériot XI
Engine: Gnôme rotary, 70 hp. *Speed:* 66 mph at sea level. *Duration:* 3.5 hours. *Span:* 33 feet 11 inches. *Length:* 27 feet 10 inches. *Weight empty/loaded:* 770/1,838 lbs.

Short Folder Seaplane
Engine: Gnôme rotary, 160 hp. *Speed:* 78 mph. *Armament:* Bombs or one 14-inch torpedo. *Endurance:* 5 hours. *Span:* 67 feet. *Length:* 39 feet. *Weight empty/loaded:* 2,000/3,040 lbs.

Austrian Lohner B I
Engine: Austro-Daimler, 120 hp. *Armament:* none. *Speed:* 81 mph. *Ceiling:* 8,500 feet. *Span:* 44 feet 2 inches. *Length:* 25 feet 11 inches. *Weight empty/loaded:* 1,368/1,940 lbs.

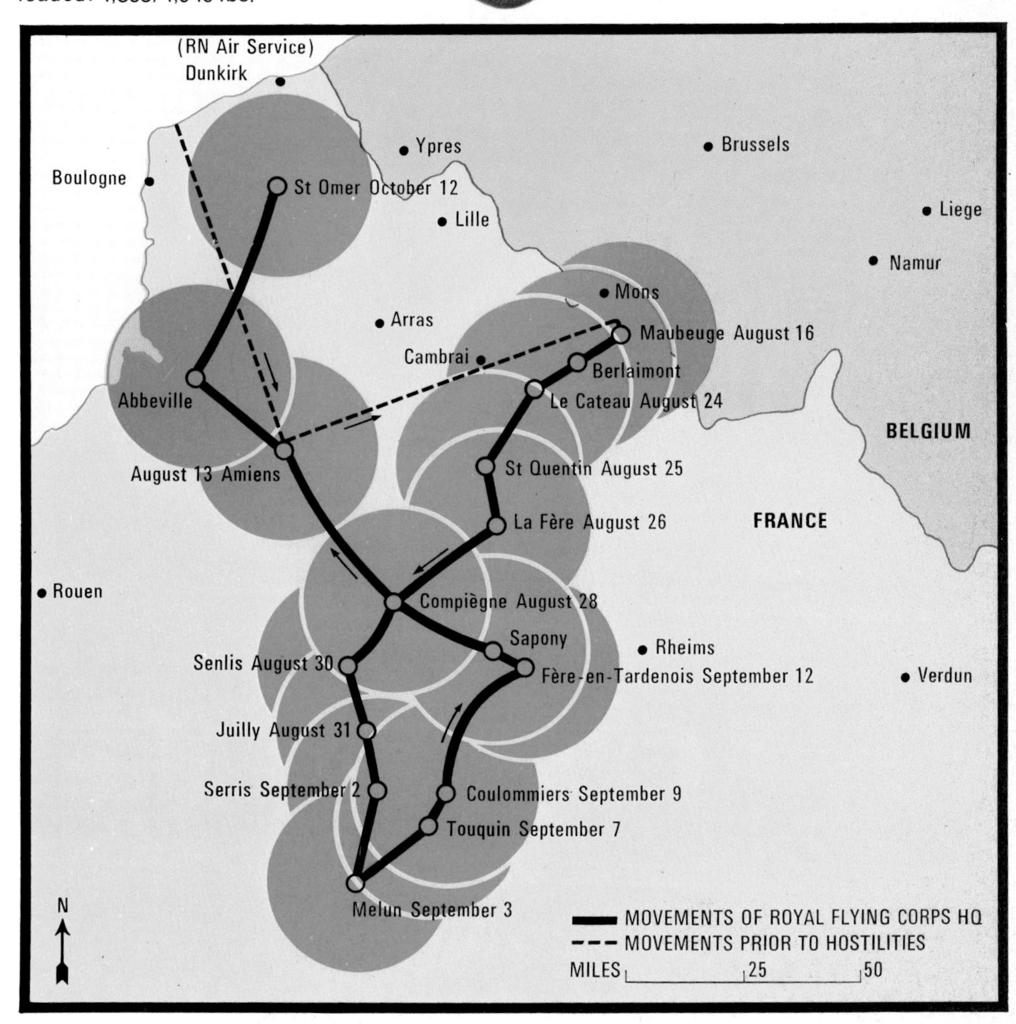

Far left: The aerial balance of forces at the beginning of the war. In many cases, for example Russia, a seemingly large air force lacked adequate backing and was composed of obsolete aircraft. *Left:* The movements of the RFC up to the end of 1914. *Above:* An improvised high angle mounting for a German machine gun in use as a primitive form of anti-aircraft defence.

1914: THE RETREAT IN THE AIR

A first-hand account of war in the air

On August 24 German shells fell quite close to our aerodrome. The battle of Mons was drawing to its close and the famous retreat had begun; but we were not the least downhearted. Our transport had to bustle off in a hurry before daybreak, but it was well towards the middle of the morning before we flew off to Le Cateau, where an emergency aerodrome had been prepared. I remember that one Henri Farman developed engine trouble at the last moment and had to be left behind; the smoke arising when it was burnt to prevent it falling into the enemy's hands was our last sight of Maubeuge aerodrome.

There were no quarters for us; we slept in our valises near the machines. The next day we soon realised that great events were taking place. We were under fire; shells were bursting in unexpected places and we constantly saw troops on the move. We made a number of reconnaissances, and when I dropped low, it came as a shock to me to sight the grey-green uniforms of German forces in localities which had been held by our own men the day before. The Germans blazed away whenever they saw me, but my machine took no damage. Up in the air I constantly saw fierce fights going on in isolated places when I looked down on one side, while a mile away on the other were transport, troops, and guns, all mixed up in the commencement of the historic retreat.

When I returned from my dawn reconnaissance to the field that was our aerodrome at Le Cateau, I could see no signs of machines or transport. A great battle was in progress; the only thing to do was to fly on southward and look for signs of our Squadron. Our eyes searched the roads until at last Number 5 Squadron's dear old red Bovril lorry hove into sight; I then landed my Henri Farman by the roadside and waited until the transport came along. When it did, I received orders to do another reconnaissance and report to an aerodrome near St Quentin.

This new job took me in the direction of Valenciennes and Maubeuge. While flying over the latter place, I was surprised to find heavy firing going on round the old forts, as I had imagined them to be in German hands by then. When I finally returned to St Quentin, I discovered our new aerodrome to be a cornfield that had only just been cut. A big L, fashioned of wheat-sheaves, told us where to land.

We were lucky enough to get a really good dinner in St Quentin that night, but beds were unattainable luxuries, and so we were once more compelled to sleep in our valises on the aerodrome. We stacked up sheaves round the machines and used others for bedding.

I fell asleep to the sound of distant firing, and it turned my last conscious thoughts to those forts round Maubeuge, which I pictured as rocks surrounded by the incoming tide. Dimly wondering how long the French reservists who manned them would be able to hold out, I found it almost impossible to realise that only a few days previously we had basked peacefully in warm sunshine in that same Maubeuge. Our impromptu couches seemed comfortable enough, but we woke up with sore bodies and sighed regretfully for the cosy beds in Maubeuge Town Hall, where we had been billeted, and the glorious omelettes that Renée, our waitress, gave us for breakfast.

August 27 was a day of great anxiety for our forces as fresh masses of Germans were reported to be working round to westward in order to turn our left flank. Smith Dorrien's cavalry won much distinction in the rearguard action, as they charged into the advancing foemen time after time in the dashing way that was so characteristic of their leader. From aloft I could see horse artillery galloping back, while often enough guns were fired at point-blank range. Meanwhile our few feeble aeroplanes did their best to keep headquarters informed of all that went on, while every now and then we found a chance to lend a hand to the ground forces in some hard-fought skirmish or to harass the thickest hordes of the enemy by dropping petrol bombs, hand grenades and the steel arrows that were known as flechettes.

After a hard and busy day's work, we settled down to another night on our cornfield. The fine weather had broken; thunderstorms were succeeded by a steady drizzle, which did not promise a comfortable night. But before we had time to think of supper, shells began to make our wheat-sheaves fly about, and all machines beat a hasty retreat to La Fère. No aerodrome had been arranged there, with the result that our machines landed just where they could in fields on the outskirts of the town. As No 5 Squadron had no chance of reuniting, I spent the night helping a staff officer to direct stragglers to collecting stations. We stood at the junction of four crossroads, sending the men of various divisions to their proper rallying points.

We heard many stories that night—grim tales of whole regiments wiped out, while it was a terrible sight to watch the return of those splendid troops who had marched up to Mons so recently. Some were minus weapons, tunics and boots, with their puttees wrapped round their feet. All were utterly worn out with ceaseless marching and fighting, but if they were not exactly what one might term orderly, at least they were obedient and glad to listen to the voice of authority. The memory of that night is still fresh in my mind, as there were so many alarms and the situation still remained so uncertain; but I see from my diary that August 28 was more hopeful. The entry I have is as follows:

August 28—Messenger for the day. Flew all day from La Fère with messages. Weather bad, heavy thunderstorms, machine waterlogged, cannot climb at all well. Hasty but orderly retreat; many stragglers and some confusion along the line of retirement, but perfect discipline and order extending back to the fighting line, which is very difficult to define, as so many little separate battles are going on in isolated spots, some so forlorn that they are obviously only desperate last stands far out of reach and without any hope of retirement. Saw a British cavalry regiment ride down two squadrons of Uhlans, *whom they caught unawares and completely cut up. Meals anyhow and any time. No letters from home yet.*

That night I could only manage a meagre dinner of bread and chocolate, but I had a wonderful bed at the *maire's* house. No rest for the weary, however, as about 0200 hours rifle fire in the street outside woke me up. I got out by the back garden and went off to my machine, where I stood by till dawn, when Captain Bonham-Carter turned up and we went off for an early-morning reconnaissance, feeling much safer as soon as we were in the air. That night we landed on the race-course at Compiègne, which was a treat after the fields which had been our aerodromes.

I spent the morning of August 28 fixing up a new type of petrol bomb to my Henri Farman, and in the afternoon Penn Gaskell and I went to try it out. We dropped two bombs on either side of the road north of St Quentin, where we found a lot of German transport; returning ten minutes later to have another go at the same lot, we found them moving south, so we dropped down to a low height and flew along over the road, where we managed to plant our third bomb right on to a lorry, which took fire and ran into a ditch. The lorry behind it caught fire as well, and both were well ablaze when we left. It was not a serious loss to the German army, but it sent us home very well pleased with ourselves.

That same evening a German machine dropped three bombs on our aerodrome, and one fell fairly close to our transport, but luckily it did not burst. We all made a rush to the spot to grab bits of the bombs as souvenirs and found that they were full of shrapnel bullets.

A successful bluff

I cannot remember whether this machine was the Albatross [sic] that Spratt brought down. He flew a Sopwith Tabloid and forced the enemy to land by circling round above him and making pretence to attack him. As a matter of fact, he had run out of ammunition, but the bluff succeeded and the occupants of the German machine were taken prisoner.

On August 30 we took another step backward, landing at Senlis.

We did not stop long in Senlis, but moved on that same night to Juilly, where we had a most exciting time that all old members of the RFC will never forget, as they were kept up all night, making an improvised stockade around the field in which the machines were parked on account of the rumours of a large force of *Uhlans* in the neighbouring woods. It was even suggested that we should fly our machines away in the dark, which at that time would have been somewhat of a feat if we had managed it successfully, as night flying was still a great adventure. However, with the aid of a squadron of the Irish Light Horse we kept watch all night. There were a number of false alarms, but the only invaders of our aerodrome were a number of refugees.

We left before dawn and flew to landing grounds farther south, some of our machines going to Serris, a little place not far from Paris, while others made for Pezarches. As a matter of fact, we departed none too soon; a Henri Farman of No 3 Squadron that had developed engine trouble had to be left behind and burnt, but the mechanics were told to salve the engine. They got it on to a tender and just got away in time, with the bullets of the Germans whizzing round their ears.

As usual, the German airmen spotted our new aerodrome at Serris and paid us a visit. They had an uncanny knack of finding out where we were located almost as soon as we arrived, so that we were not at all surprised to see them there. Norman Spratt went up to have a go at one of these disturbers of our peace and managed to fire 30 rounds at him from his revolver at close range, but the enemy remained apparently undamaged. Spratt landed in desperation and tied a hand grenade on to the end of a long piece of control cable; he had the bright idea of flying over the Hun and hitting his propeller with the grenade, but I felt very sceptical about his chances of bagging a victim that way, and I do not think he ever did.

Gordon Bell, on his Bristol Scout, was another pilot who distinguished himself during the retreat. Like Spratt, he flew a machine that was very light about the undercarriage, and I always admired the way these two pilots landed and took off from small rough fields without damaging their machines. Bell was wounded soon afterwards and had to return to England. He got a shot in his engine which forced him to come down where he could, with the result that he landed in a tree but was thrown out of the machine and escaped with a few bruises. When he picked himself up, however, he discovered that he had been wounded slightly in the knee, and from subsequent investigations it seems likely that he was fired on by our own or French troops. Some infantrymen could never resist the temptation to take a pot shot at an aeroplane without bothering to ascertain its nationality, and more than one airman got his baptism of fire from his own side. It was most certainly a case of 'save me from my friends' with a vengeance.

Gordon Bell had a great sense of humour and a bad stutter when angry. On this occasion a staff officer galloped up and asked if he had crashed. Bell explained, with much stuttering and profanity, that he always landed like that.

The Germans pushed on towards Paris at a very fast rate. On September 4 we received orders to move to Melun, and beat a most undignified retreat, as we had to clear out in a great hurry. The Germans were at that time within 20 miles of the French capital.

Our first day at Melun proved most exciting, however, as from the first reconnaissance we were able to see Kluck's army streaming east instead of south, while the British troops were moving in a southerly direction instead of the northerly one in which we expected to find them. It took many confirmatory reports to convince the Higher Command that this was so, because the sudden break off of the German advance seemed almost a miracle, while I fear that there were still a number of old-fashioned officers who did not yet quite trust the efficiency of aeroplanes, and so credited us with virtually no powers of observation.

During the night we heard the guns booming away to the north of us, and wondered what was happening. As it was a very warm evening, and for once in a way the whole of our transport had turned up, we did not bother to go and look for billets, but just rolled into our valises. Later in the night we had cause to regret this, as a fierce thunderstorm burst upon us. Some of us decided to stick it out and remained in the open, hoping that the rain would not penetrate our valises; while others packed themselves into the overcrowded, stifling transport lorries. The result was that we were all either drenched or suffocated.

The next day, however, we quickly forgot these discomforts in our joy at learning the definite news that the British army was advancing for the first time since the battle of Mons. The retreat was over; our spirits rose again, and all traces of weariness disappeared in the excitement and anticipation of at last getting back a bit of our own.

[*From* Recollections of an Airman *by L. A. Strange.*]

The eyes of the German advance, and the Allied retreat

Sopwith Tabloid
Engine: Gnôme rotary, 80 hp. *Armament:* small arms chosen by the pilot or one .303-inch Lewis gun. *Maximum speed:* 92 mph at ground level. *Initial climb rate:* 1,200 feet-per-minute. *Endurance:* 3½ hours. *Weights empty/loaded:* 730/1,120 lbs. *Span:* 25 feet 6 inches. *Length:* 20 feet 4 inches

Hansa-Brandenburg D
An orthodox two-seater, only about 12 examples were built for the German army. The fuselage was of steel tube construction covered with ply, and the rest of the structure was of the normal wooden construction with fabric covering. *Engine:* Benz Bz II, 110 hp. *Span:* 43 feet 0⅞ inches. *Length:* 27 feet 8⅞ inches

Avro 504
Engine: Gnôme rotary, 80 hp. *Armament:* small arms as chosen by the pilot, one .303-inch Lewis gun or a few small bombs. *Maximum speed:* 82 mph at ground level. *Climb rate:* 7 minutes to 3,500 feet. *Endurance:* 3½ hours. *Weights empty/loaded:* 924/1,574 lbs. *Span:* 36 feet. *Length:* 29 feet 5 inches

Aviatik BI
This aircraft first appeared in 1914, and was derived from the prewar P 15A. As it appeared originally, it lacked the fixed fin shown here, and possessed struts bracing the ends of the upper mainplane from the outer pairs of interplane struts. Its power was provided by a 100 hp Mercedes D I engine. The type was only produced in very small numbers

John Batchelor

CAPRONI Ca 42

Gross weight: 16,535 lb **Span**: 98 ft 1 in **Length**: 49 ft 6 in **Engine**: 3×270 hp Fiat, Isotta-Fraschini, or American Liberty **Armament**: 4 machine-guns **Crew**: 5 **Speed**: 87 mph at ground level **Ceiling**: 9,840 ft **Range**: 7 hr **Bomb load**: 3,910 lb

HOW THE BOMBER WAS BORN

'Aviation is good sport, but for the army it is useless.' This comment, attributed to General Foch, one of the more enlightened of military leaders, typified the prevailing attitude to an innovation which was to play an increasingly important role in warfare . . .

German ground crew member loading a 25-kg bomb

Like so many concepts of modern warfare, aerial bombing on a large scale was first developed during the First World War. The two main ingredients – bombs and a means of delivering them – were already in existence. The bombs were simple metal shells containing explosives and a detonator, which could be set off by a time fuse, and with fins to give more stable and accurately predictable flight. Such weapons had been conceived of since the earliest days of flight, but use of aeroplanes for bombing came about only when it was found how vulnerable airships were to defensive fire from the ground, and to attacks in the air.

Although several types of aeroplane were available in 1914, and experimental bombing from aeroplanes had been carried out before the war, their military potential was not generally appreciated by the strategists of the combatant nations. Considering the flimsy nature of these craft, mostly two seaters, it was understandable. Most were unable to fly higher than a few thousand feet and their average speed of about 60 miles per hour could be reduced to a crawl by strong headwinds. They were not only vulnerable to ground fire but their performance was also seriously affected by carrying the added weight of bombs or machine-guns.

For the most part, the military leaders of all the major powers saw the main function of aircraft as reconnoitring for the infantry and spotting the fall of shot for the artillery – merely an extension of the observation balloon. It was the pilots and observers who showed the fighting potential of their machines by taking pot-shots at enemy planes with hand-guns. This eventually led to the development of specifically designed single-seat fighters armed with fixed forward-firing machine-guns.

In a similar way, the use of early reconnaissance aircraft for dropping bombs led to the evolution of the true bomber – that is, an aeroplane designed to carry and deliver bombs in level flight, against a specific target, over medium or long range distances.

The main production model of Caproni's Ca 4 series of huge triplanes was brought into service in 1918. It was used by the British RNAS and air units of the Italian army and navy

The true beginning

At the start, just as reconnaissance aircraft were armed only with pistols, many of the first bombs dropped were simply grenades or canisters filled with gasoline, dropped over the sides of open cockpits. The French even threw down steel darts (*fléchettes*) in the hope of disrupting German infantry and cavalry formations.

The first aircraft used for both fighting and bombing were the general purpose types which were already in existence when war broke out. In fact, a Voisin III, the type most widely used for bombing by the French in the early days of the war, was also the first to shoot down an enemy aircraft in aerial combat. And it was with an Avro 504, the first British bomber, and the type to make the first organised raid in history, that some of the earliest experiments were made in fitting a machine-gun, leading to the development of the true fighter.

Two basic configurations were predominant at that time: the tractor aeroplane, with the engine and propeller in front, and the pusher type, like the Voisin, in which the engine and propeller were mounted behind a tub-like nacelle seating the pilot and observer, the tail being carried on booms. Both were made in biplane and monoplane form, biplanes being the more common. The pusher type soon became obsolete, but it was the most successful in the early days since the observer in front had a much better field of vision. (In two-seater tractor aircraft the second crew member invariably sat in front but since his view and ability to fire were restricted by the propeller and wing struts, the positions were later reversed.)

Using the experience with these general purpose types, different classes of aircraft were developed to meet specific requirements. An account of bombers might well be limited to the type defined as 'an aircraft designed to drop bombs in level flight'. These have been built in great variety up to the present day and indeed are the ones mainly dealt with here. But there have been others such as dive-bombers, torpedo-bombers and fighter-bombers combining a dual role. These, with aircraft designed primarily for a ground attack role in support of infantry, might be grouped separately as strike aircraft. However, the most important examples are included in this book. In fact, as we have implied, almost every basic tactical and strategic use of bombers was first tried out during the First World War.

Combined role

The fighter-bomber is a particular case in point. Like the Voisin, the earliest bombers combined both roles, but thereafter, the development of bombers took a separate course from that of the fighters designed to intercept them. Except for a period in the 1930s when a few notable bombers actually flew faster than the fighters of the day, they generally had to make up for their lack of speed by carrying heavier armament. This, together with the need to carry the largest possible bomb load, necessitated a continual compromise in design between weight, size and range on the one hand, and speed and altitude on the other. Although some remarkable engineering advances were made by bomber designers, such as the geodetic form of construction, for the most part they had to make use of the materials currently available. And most of the pioneering effort, in terms of speed at any rate, went into fighter design. For example, a number of exceptional engines were specifically designed for fighters whereas bombers usually had to make use of the same type of engines.

In more recent times however, with the development of small but powerful atomic missiles – as well as the atom bomb itself – there has not been the same need to consider weight of bomb load as the measure of a bomber's capability. The development of sophisticated defence systems, including supersonic fighters, has meant that bombers must be able to compete on an equal footing in both armament and speed. Largely because of the enormous costs involved the future of the true bomber was at one time in some doubt. This has been partly resolved by the American decision to go ahead with the B-1 strategic bomber, capable of three times the speed of sound. However, for reasons of cost and modern strategic planning, the fighter-bomber is one of the most common types now in service with the air forces of the world. The wheel has turned full circle back to the kind of aeroplane first used offensively sixty years ago.

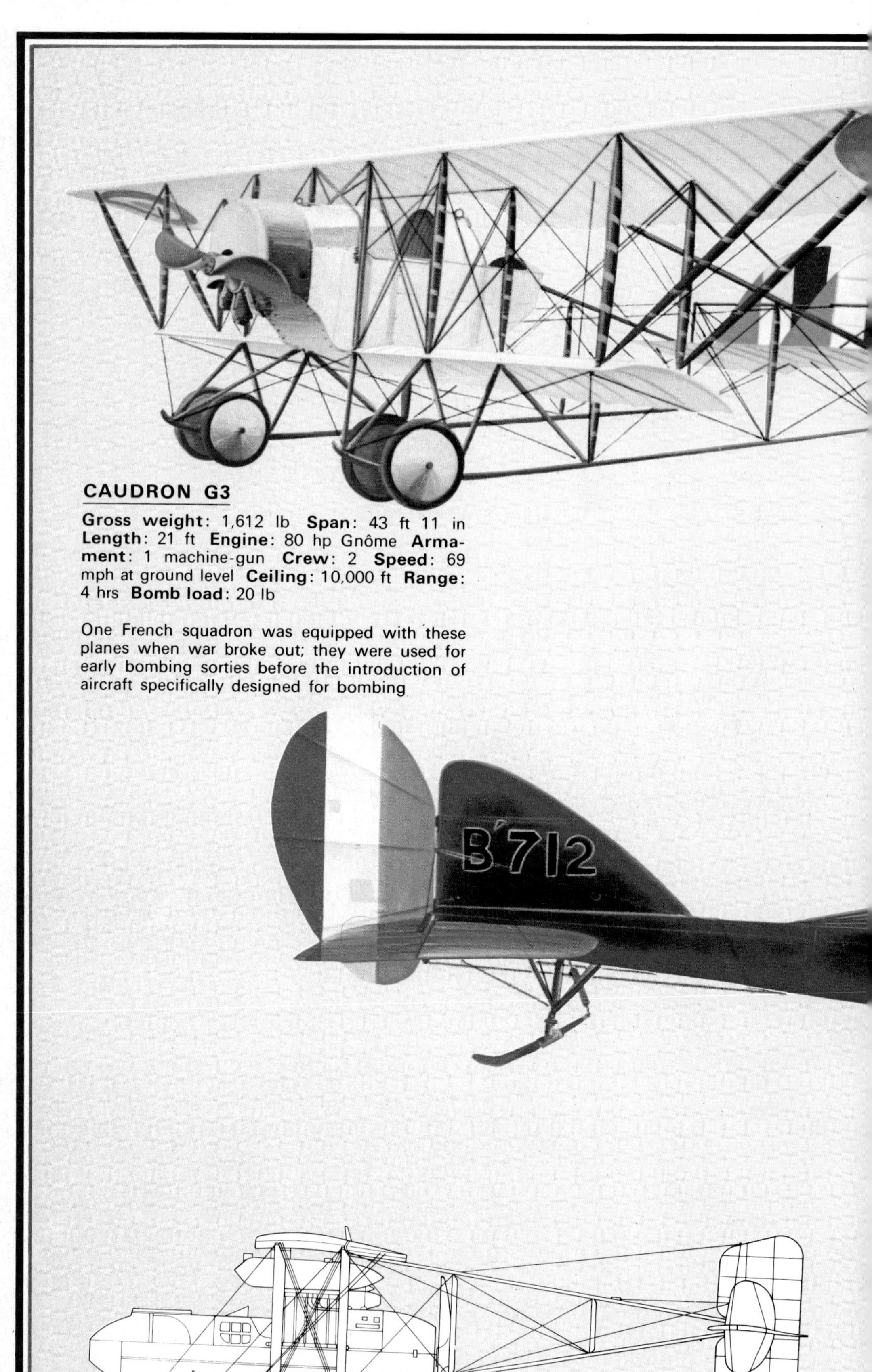

CAUDRON G3

Gross weight: 1,612 lb **Span**: 43 ft 11 in **Length**: 21 ft **Engine**: 80 hp Gnôme **Armament**: 1 machine-gun **Crew**: 2 **Speed**: 69 mph at ground level **Ceiling**: 10,000 ft **Range**: 4 hrs **Bomb load**: 20 lb

One French squadron was equipped with these planes when war broke out; they were used for early bombing sorties before the introduction of aircraft specifically designed for bombing

BREGUET-MICHELIN 5

Gross weight: 4,235 lb **Span**: 57 ft 8 in **Length**: 26 ft 1 in **Engine**: 220 hp Renault **Armament**: 1 machine-gun and 1×37-mm cannon **Crew**: 2 **Speed**: 86 mph at ground level **Ceiling**: NA **Range**: 5 hrs **Bomb load**: 660 lb

Problems with the Renault engine held back large-scale production until 1917, by which time it was neither fast nor manoeuvrable enough to be used as a day bomber

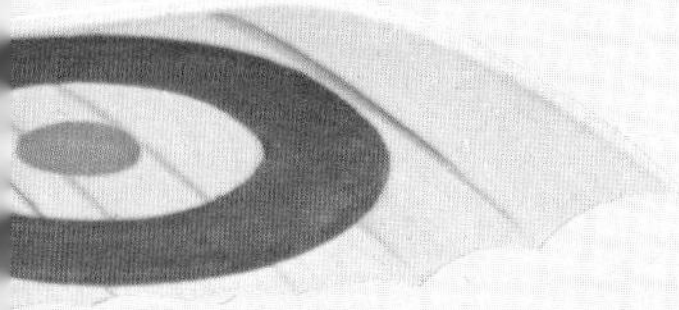

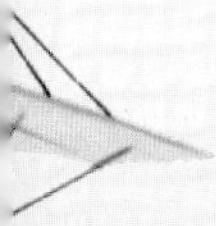

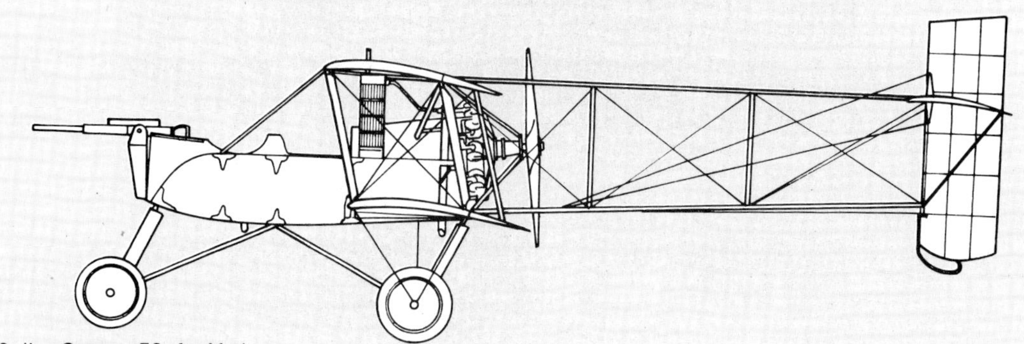

VOISIN 5

Gross weight: 3,240 lb **Span**: 52 ft 4½ in **Length**: 31 ft 6½ in **Engine**: 150 hp Canton-Unné **Armament**: 1 machine-gun **Crew**: 2 **Speed**: 74 mph **Ceiling**: 1,500 ft **Range**: 3½ hrs **Bomb load**: 130 lb

The Voisin pusher biplane, which equipped four of the French squadrons at the outbreak of war, was the most widely used bomber during the first two years of operations. The Voisin 5 variant was introduced at the end of 1915

BE 2e

Gross weight: 2,142 lb **Span**: 37 ft **Length**: 27 ft 3 in **Engine**: 90 hp RAF 1a **Armament**: 1–4 Lewis machine-guns **Crew**: 2 **Speed**: 72 mph at 6,500 ft **Ceiling**: 10,000 ft **Range**: NA **Bomb load**: 112–224 lb

Introduced into RFC service in the summer of 1916, in time to take part in the Battle of the Somme, but showed little improvement on previous BE2 types; the observer had to be left at home when a maximum bomb load was carried

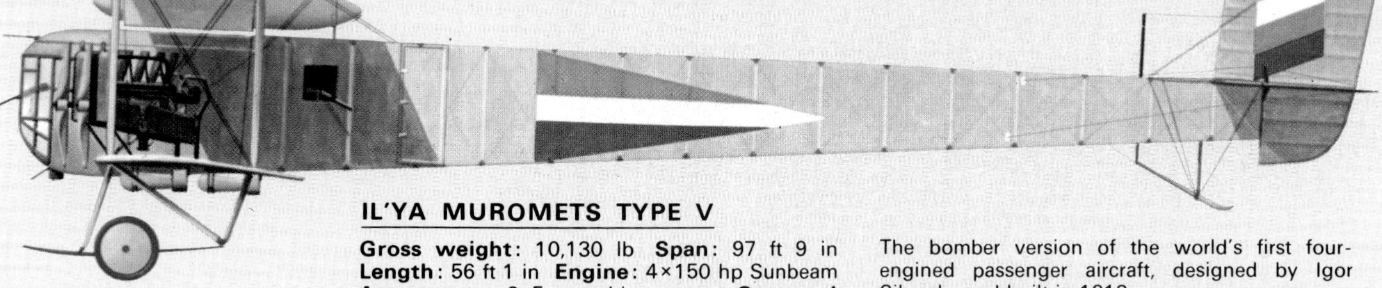

IL'YA MUROMETS TYPE V

Gross weight: 10,130 lb **Span**: 97 ft 9 in **Length**: 56 ft 1 in **Engine**: 4×150 hp Sunbeam **Armament**: 3–5 machine-guns **Crew**: 4 **Speed**: 75 mph **Ceiling**: 9,840 ft **Range**: 5 hrs **Bomb load**: 650 lb

The bomber version of the world's first four-engined passenger aircraft, designed by Igor Sikorsky and built in 1913

UP THERE, A NEW KIND OF WAR WAS BEGINNING

Though several countries had shown interest in military aviation in the years before the war, this quickly lapsed, and most of the early experiments in bombing were carried out through individual enterprise rather than official policy. Many of these early experiments were to prove of value as the war progressed

Even though bomber aircraft as such did not exist at the beginning of the First World War, the threat of bombing was well recognised. Visionaries like H. G. Wells had foreseen the destruction that might some day rain from the skies. As early as 1670 a Jesuit monk, Francesco de Lana, produced the first known design for a lighter-than-air craft. It did not work, but from his writings, it is clear that de Lana saw the possibilities of airborne invasion and bombing, and indeed referred to the destruction of cities and ships by fireballs hurled down from the sky.

The difficulties of bombing from balloons were self-evident for they could only travel where the wind took them. Nevertheless, such attempts were frequently made in the latter half of the 19th century, one of the first being by the Austrians in 1849 when unmanned hot air balloons carrying 30-lb time-fused bombs were launched against Venice.

It was the invention of the dirigible (steerable) airship at the turn of the century that made bombing a practical and a frightening possibility. Although such craft were also developed in Britain, France, the United States and Italy, it was in Germany, with the pioneering work of Count Ferdinand von Zeppelin, that the rigid airship made its greatest strides. At the beginning of the war the Germans possessed more and better airships than any other nation. These, rather than planes, were intended to provide Germany's primary means of bombing.

Until a few years before the war Britain had largely neglected aviation development, but government indifference and indecision between lighter- and heavier-than-air machines gave way under the threat of Zeppelin attack to a belated attempt to develop defensive aeroplanes.

Meanwhile, the first experiments at dropping bombs from aircraft were carried out in the United States, by the great pioneering designer/constructor Glenn Curtiss in 1910, using dummy bombs. The following year, live bombs were dropped during a military exercise by Lt M. S. Crissy from a Wright biplane. Both the US Army and the US Navy showed some initial interest. In fact, in 1908 the US Army had been the first combat service in the world to buy an aeroplane for evaluation. But the authorities lost enthusiasm for military aviation and although the US Army and Navy both established aeronautical divisions, the US Army Air Arm had only 20 planes on its strength when war broke out in Europe, all of them obsolete, and the Naval Air Arm was almost non-existent. While the Americans later built thousands of French and British aircraft under licence, no aeroplane of American design fought in France during the First World War. The only American aircraft used in combat were Curtiss flying-boats, employed by the British Royal Naval Air Service for anti-submarine patrols.

However, one result of those early bombing experiments was the evident necessity for some kind of aiming device to enable bombs to be dropped accurately. This led Lt Riley Scott to invent the first bomb-sight in 1912. It was installed in a Wright biplane of the US Army, and was a simple device of wires and nails. Of particular interest was the fact that the bomb-aimer lay in a prone position in the nose of the aircraft and viewed the ground through a mica window, anticipating the bombing method of many years later. Also, the bombs were carried horizontally underneath the aeroplane, also common practice years later, instead of being dropped over the side or carried vertically in racks.

Italy was the first country in the field of military aeronautics, having established an Army Aeronautical Section equipped with balloons as early as 1884, and it was also the first country to drop bombs on an enemy during war. This was on 1 November 1911, during the Italo-Turkish war, when Lt Gavotti dropped four grenades of 4.4 lb each on Turkish troops in Libya. Further raids followed, causing more consternation than damage. Then the Turks protested that an Italian aircraft had bombed a military hospital at Ain Zara and an immediate controversy arose in the Italian, Turkish and neutral Press. There was no independent way at that time of establishing whether a hospital had actually been bombed and the Italians reasonably pointed out that no similar protest had been made when their warships shelled Ain Zara a few days earlier. But many felt there was something particularly inhuman about aerial bombs, and the controversy about the subject has continued ever since.

When Italy entered the war in May 1915 against Austria and Hungary, her Army Air Service was perhaps more highly trained than any other and in an excellent state of readiness. This was offset to some extent by the fact that most of her 150 aircraft were French types such as Nieuport and Blériot monoplanes and Maurice-Farman pusher biplanes, already out-dated. An exception, however, was the Caproni Ca 30/33 series which, together with the Russian Il'ya Muromets, were the first very large planes built. These certainly gave Italy the lead in heavy bombing during the early part of the war.

The series began in 1913 with the Ca 30 powered by three Gnôme rotary engines, one of which was mounted as a pusher in the central nacelle while the other two drove, indirectly, two tractor propellers in twin fuselage booms. The indirect drive was not successful and was abandoned in the Ca 31, the outer pair of engines being re-located at the front of the booms. This became the standard configuration for the series. The first bomber to be built in quantity for the Italian Army Air Service was the Ca 32, in which the rotary engines were replaced by three Fiat inline water-cooled engines of 100 hp each. Deliveries began within three months of Italy's declaration of war and went into action almost immediately. They were easy to handle, had an excellent range, and could carry up to 1,000 lb of bombs.

The Ca 33 version was put into production the following year. It had a multi-wheel landing gear for operations from rough ground and included, for the first time, two gun positions – one in the front cockpit, ahead of the two pilots who sat side by side, and another at the rear. This type was so successful that it was also built under licence in France.

France moves in

France had made greater headway in aviation than any other country before the war, with the result that the French Army possessed the widest range of flying machines – about 138 in all. An Army Air Arm had been established by 1914 and with the approval of General Joffre, one of the few military leaders to see a potential for aircraft in the war beyond mere reconnaissance, this force began to explore various offensive possibilities. The smaller single-seat tractor scouts like the Nieuport biplane and Morane-Saulnier monoplane were formed into fighter squadrons (*escadrilles de chasse*) which were attached to each army for the purpose of harrying German reconnaissance craft. And within weeks of the outbreak of war, the larger two-seater pusher biplanes were formed into a bomber group (*l'ère Groupe de Bombardement*) consisting of three six-machine squadrons, under Commandant Göys.

The French bomber group, quickly joined by another two, was equipped with various Henri and Maurice Farman types, the twin-engined Caudron, the Bréguet-Michelin and the Voisin 13.50 (so named from its 13.50 metre wingspan). These pusher biplanes were completely blind from the rear, and as the idea of aerial combat did not exist before the war and since the bomb-aimer/gunner in front enjoyed a wide range of vision, they had things very much their own way to begin with, being sturdy and dependable. The Voisin was the most widely used for bombing in the early days. It could carry a bomb load of about 200 lb for three hours at a maximum speed of 55 mph and could take off and land on the roughest ground. More than 2,000 IIIs were built and supplied not only to France but also to Britain, Belgium, Italy and Russia.

Caproni Ca 41 triplanes used by the Royal Naval Air Service in Italy for a short period towards the end of the war

Caproni, Milan

In Germany, both the army and navy had established aviation corps before the war in which the pride of place was given to Zeppelins. Compared to the planes of that period, the dirigible airship was a formidable weapon. It had a speed of about 50 mph, barely less than that of most aircraft, and a much greater ceiling and range. It could cruise far behind the front lines and carry bomb loads of around 1,000 lb – impossible with aircraft until the development of multi-engined types like the Caproni. The Military Aviation Service, formed in 1912, had a fleet of six large airships and three smaller ones, to which were added three airships from a commercial airline service. The German Naval Air Service was primarily committed to the airship for the task of reconnaissance over the North Sea. But as a result of two airship disasters in 1913, it had only one Zeppelin actually in operation at the outbreak of war.

As well as airships, the Military Aviation Service was equipped with a mixed collection of 246 aircraft comprising single and two-seater Type A monoplanes like the Rumpler and Etrich Taube, and Type B biplanes of which the Albatros, Aviatik and LVG were the most common.

These were all tractor types, since Germany did not then possess any pusher planes, and none of them was armed. In fact, the development of faster aircraft had been restricted in case speed should interfere with careful observation. The Service was completely subservient to the Army with its squadrons disposed between Army HQ and Army Corps.

Within two months of the outbreak of war, however, some of the Type Bs were equipped as bombers and formed into a bomber force known as the *Fliegerkorps des Obersten Heeresleitung* (Air Corps of GHQ) comprising thirty-six aircraft divided into

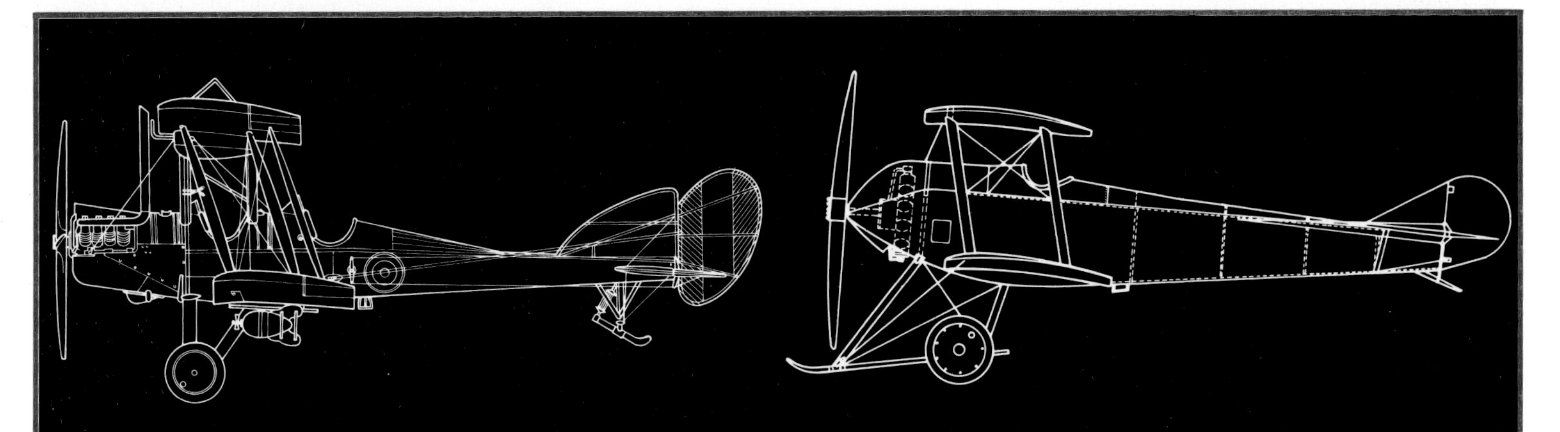

SOPWITH TABLOID

Gross weight: 1,120 lb **Span:** 25 ft 6 in **Length:** 20 ft 4 in **Engine:** 80 hp Gnôme **Armament:** 1 Lewis **Crew:** 1 **Speed:** 92 mph **Ceiling:** NA **Range:** $3\frac{1}{2}$ hrs **Bomb load:** 20–40 lb

The fastest biplane in the world when it first appeared in 1913. Capable of climbing to 1,200 ft in one minute

BE 12

Gross weight: 2,352 lb **Span:** 37 ft **Length:** 27 ft 3 in **Engine:** 150 hp RAF 4a **Armament:** 1–2 Lewis machine-guns **Crew:** 1 **Speed:** 102 mph at ground level **Ceiling:** 12,500 ft **Range:** NA **Bomb load:** 2×20 lb

A more powerful version of the BE 2c, introduced in an attempt to combat the menace of the Fokker monoplane in 1916

AVRO 504

Gross weight: 1,574 lb **Span**: 36 ft **Length**: 29 ft 5 in **Engine**: 80 hp Gnôme **Armament**: Optional Lewis **Crew**: 2 **Speed**: 62 mph at 6,500 ft **Ceiling**: 13,000 ft **Range**: 4½ hrs **Bomb load**: 4×20 lb

Britain's first effective light day bomber, notable for RNAS raids on Zeppelin sheds in Germany. Also used for bombing airships in flight

CAPRONI Ca 32

Gross weight: 7,280 lb **Span**: 72 ft 10 in **Length**: 35 ft 9 in **Engine**: 3×100 hp Fiat A10 **Armament**: 2 machine-guns **Crew**: 3–4 **Speed**: 72 mph at ground level **Ceiling**: NA **Range**: 340 miles **Bomb load**: 200 lb

The first production version of the Caproni to enter service with the Italian Army Air Force, in August 1915, and the basis of Italy's strategic bomber arm. An excellent plane to handle with greater range than most aircraft of that time

two wings which were given the code-name 'carrier-pigeon units'. This force was led by Major Wilhelm Siegert, a pilot himself and an aviation enthusiast, who was to play a vital part in the development of the German Army Air Service.

The air units of all the nations mentioned came under the control of the army, the navy, or both. Britain was late in the field and it was not until 1911 that the Air Battalion of the Royal Engineers was formed, comprising a miscellany of planes, small airships, man-lifting kites and balloons. A year later the Royal Flying Corps was formed as a joint service with naval and military wings. Although the objective of military aviation in Britain was limited to reconnaissance over land and water, the RFC had one great advantage: it was a single organisation and not split up into army and navy groups as in most other countries. However, six weeks before war broke out, when Britain had 113 aircraft operational, the Admiralty decided to form its own Royal Naval Air Service. This became largely responsible for the defence of Britain, especially against the threatened Zeppelin raids. The RFC was relegated to the status of a corps attached to the army; in August 1914, the four RFC squadrons operational at the time were sent to France to join the British Expeditionary Force.

British equipment

As far as equipment was concerned, a major difference in policy marked Britain's two services. The War Office had decided in 1911 that it would be more economical to build its own planes. Accordingly, it established the Army (later Royal) Aircraft Factory at Farnborough, employing Geoffrey de Havilland as chief designer and test pilot. The research effort at Farnborough concentrated on producing an aeroplane of inherent stability which would fly straight and level with little effort required on the part of the pilot so that he could devote most of his attention to observation. This was achieved with the BE2, which was given military trials in 1912. It was the first of a series of two-seater tractor biplanes, which reached its peak with the BE2c version. Well over 1,000 of this model were delivered during the first years of the war, making it the RFC's standard observation machine. However, very few were available at the outbreak of war and the War Office had to continue buying French aircraft to make up the deficiency. The result was that the RFC squadrons consisted of a mixed bag of Farman pusher biplanes, Blériot and Morane-Saulnier monoplanes alongside a few BE2s and BE8 'Bloaters'. This last, named from its fish-like appearance, in the early days was used as one of the RFC's first bombers.

The Royal Navy, on the other hand, had preferred to buy the products of the embryonic British aircraft industry and thus supported the development of some of the best aircraft used during the war. In addition to some French types, the RNAS was equipped with the single-seat Sopwith Tabloid, Bristol Scout, and Martinsyde SI, the two-seater Avro 504 – the first British bomber – and seaplanes like the two-seater Short Folder and the single-seat Sopwith Schneider. It was with a Folder, in July 1914, that the RNAS began to drop torpedoes, although the first torpedo launch from a plane had been made by the Italians several months earlier.

Most of the 224 aircraft in service with the Russian Army at the outbreak of war were of French and German design, built under licence in Russia, and as the war progressed, further aircraft were imported from France, Britain and the United States. Only in one field did the Russians lead the way with planes of their own design, and that was with the heavy bomber. The *Grand* biplane, designed by Igor Sikorsky (who was later to achieve fame as the pioneer of helicopters) was built in 1913. This was the world's first four-engined aeroplane, intended to carry passengers in great comfort. From it, Sikorsky developed a production series, the Il'ya Muromets, but with the threatened outbreak of hostilities ten of these were purchased by the Russian Army for military trials.

After experiments with various types of armament and bomb racks it was found that the huge planes with their roomy cabins had too low a speed and limited an altitude for offensive purposes. Accordingly, Sikorsky designed a lighter version, the Il'ya Muromets Type V, and deliveries of these began early in 1915 to the special 'Squadron of Flying Ships' formed the previous December. This was both the first specialised bomber to be built and also the first to be powered by four engines – initially British Sunbeams of 150 hp each. The name Il'ya Muromets became a class name for a variety of wartime types, some of them mounting machine-guns. These could fire from the sides of the fuselage through doors and windows, upwards from a crow's-nest position in the centre of the top wing, downwards from a platform under the fuselage and rearwards from an installation in the extreme tail, thus anticipating the heavily armed large bombers of the Second World War.

Over seventy of these remarkable aircraft were produced, and in some 400 raids over East Prussia only one was lost in air combat. The need for long-range and consequently big aircraft was obvious in a country as large as Russia, but the success of the Il'ya Muromets was also responsible for the Russians' preference for the heavy bomber as a weapon, which has lasted to the present day.

Source of supply

The needs of the other combatant nations were supplied primarily by the major powers, the Belgian Army for instance being equipped with French planes, while the even smaller Turkish air units used German types, most of them passed on after they had become out-dated on the Western Front. The more extensive squadrons of Austria-Hungary were equipped at the start with a variety of Etrich Taube monoplanes and Lohner arrow-wing (*Pfeil*) biplanes, together with Albatros B Is which had been designed in Germany by Ernst Heinkel and were made under licence in Austria by the Phoenix company.

Throughout the war Austria continued to rely on aircraft supplied by Germany or built under licence, but in its own right Austria was an important supplier of engines, especially the Austro-Daimler and the Hiero, on which Dr Ferdinand Porsche worked. Since engines were of such vital importance in aircraft design, it is worth considering their development before describing the first use of bombers in the First World War.

EARLY BOMBER DESIGN

WIRE AND PLYWOOD

By August 1914 the designers of aircraft engines had already established the main families that were to last until the general introduction of the gas turbine more than thirty years later. Many of the earliest engines were based on those used in motor-cars and thus had cylinders cooled by water jackets and disposed in rows, driving on a multi-throw crankshaft. But there was one outstanding engine, the Gnôme rotary, invented by Laurent Séguin in France in 1907, that established a totally new radial configuration.

New techniques

Unlike almost every other petrol engine of the time, the Gnôme was machined from high-tensile steel. This was costly even in mass-production, but it established a trend of fine precision engineering which gradually eliminated the crop of engines put together from cruder pieces of steel, cast iron, brass and copper. The spinning cylinders were easy to cool by the slipstream but introduced problems of carburisation and mixture distribution which were only partly overcome by the development of the *Monosoupape* Gnôme, with only one valve in each piston serving for both inlet and exhaust. Though the original 50 hp engine was developed to give 80, 150, and finally, in two-row form, over 200 hp, it was obsolescent by 1916. So too was the only other important family of engines with radially disposed cylinders in the First World War. These were the Swiss/British/French Canton-Unné or Salmson engines – static radials with fixed liquid-cooled cylinders and propellers mounted on the rotating crankshaft. They gave good service, especially in the Voisin pusher biplanes and the Short bomber seaplanes, but the experimental French SM I bomber of 1916 could hardly expect to be successful as its Salmson engine, arranged sideways in the fuselage, drove two propellers on the wing struts with long shafts and bevel gears.

By 1916 almost all the engines pouring off the assembly lines in ever increasing numbers were of the in-line or Vee type. A few had air-cooled cylinders (the cooling scoop of the British RE8 reconnaissance biplane could be seen a mile away) but the vast majority had water cooling, even though this was clumsy, heavy and vulnerable. Practically every aircraft on the side of the Central Powers used a six-in-line water-cooled engine, the most common makes being Mercedes, Maybach (based on an early airship engine) and Austro-Daimler. The French developed advanced and powerful models of Renault and Hispano-Suiza engines, first used in the Letord series and the Spad S XI respectively. And the winning Mercedes Grand Prix racing car of 1914 served as a starting point for the British Rolls Royce aero engines. By 1917 Rolls Royce had produced versions of the Vee-12 Eagle giving 360–375 hp, with outstanding efficiency and reliability, for the giant Handley Pages and Vickers Vimy bombers.

Though by this time the air-cooled radial was suddenly coming into favour, the powerful and efficient Vee-12 was dominant at the end of the war. This was also the arrangement adopted in the United States for the Liberty engine, created in a matter of days by a committee of engineers (mainly from automobile companies) and swiftly pushed through a troublesome development into production on an unprecedented scale. The Liberty, ultimately rated at well over 400 hp, served the US Army for fifteen years, beginning with the DH4, built under licence in America.

The greatest scope for variation in design lay in choosing the location of the radiator made necessary by the water-cooled engine. One of the simplest and least vulnerable schemes was the frontal car-type arrangement with the radiator forming a bluff face immediately behind the propeller as in the Handley Pages and DH9a (or, in the case of a pusher, such as the Gotha, at the front of the nacelle). Other bombers had radiators in a box flush with the top wing (LVG and Halberstadt); inclined on each side of the engine cowl (Voisin and Bréguet); disposed vertically on the struts above the engine (Caproni Ca 40); arranged vertically up the sides of the fuselage and then slanting in to meet above the engine (Armstrong Whitworth FK8); or in a box in front of the upper centre-section (Lloyds and Lohners). Many bombers of the Central Powers such as Aviatiks and DFWs had Hazlet radiators, looking just like those used for domestic heating, fixed on the side of the fuselage in sections so that they could be shortened in cold weather and enlarged in summer.

Steel reinforcement

A major factor in design was the materials available at any given time. Early aircraft made use of obvious proven materials, the preferred choice being carefully selected hardwood. For example the widely used Rumpler C-1 had ash for the top (compression) booms of the wing spars and spruce for the lower (tension) booms. Ribs were generally built up from pieces of hardwood and plywood, glued and pinned. Only at major joints and places bearing especially heavy loads were metals used – the most common material being steel. On the other hand, a large number of aircraft were built up from thin-walled steel tube,

GOTHA GV

Gross weight: 8,745 lb **Span**: 77 ft 9 in **Length**: 40 ft 7 in **Engine**: 2×260 hp Mercedes D IVa **Armament**: 3–4 machine-guns **Crew**: 3 **Speed**: 87 mph at ground level **Ceiling**: 21,320 ft **Range**: 520 miles **Bomb load**: 1,300 lb

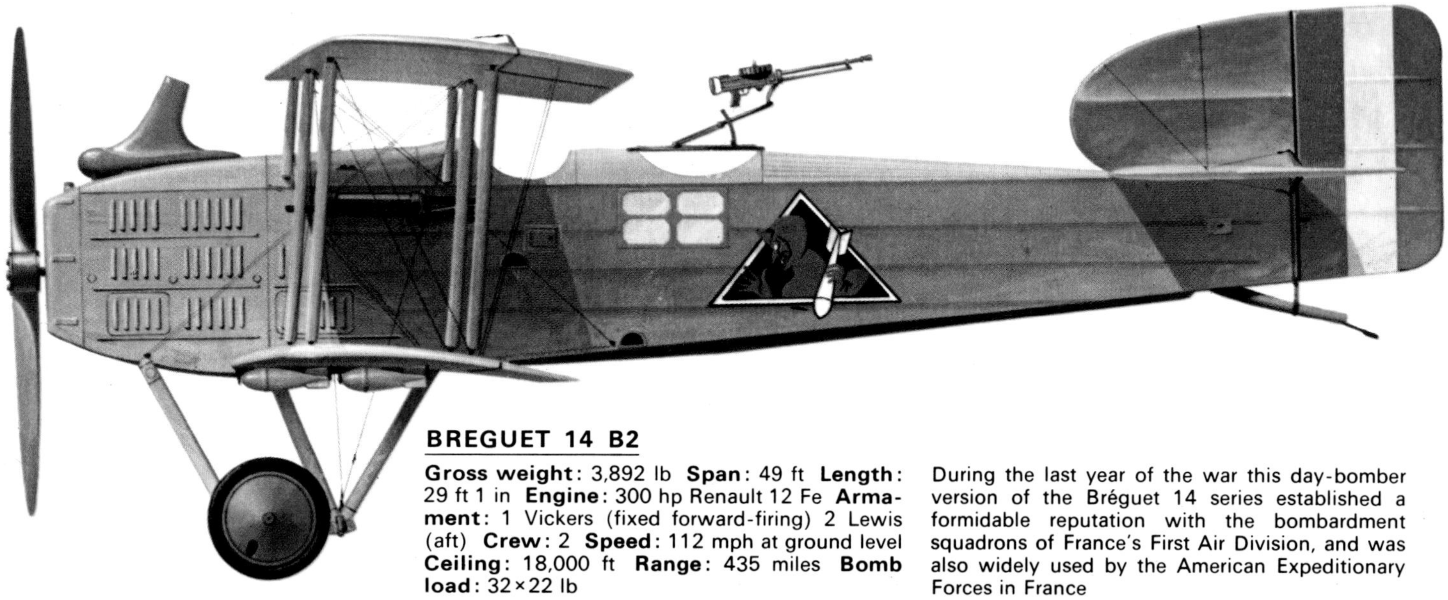

BREGUET 14 B2

Gross weight: 3,892 lb **Span**: 49 ft **Length**: 29 ft 1 in **Engine**: 300 hp Renault 12 Fe **Armament**: 1 Vickers (fixed forward-firing) 2 Lewis (aft) **Crew**: 2 **Speed**: 112 mph at ground level **Ceiling**: 18,000 ft **Range**: 435 miles **Bomb load**: 32×22 lb

During the last year of the war this day-bomber version of the Bréguet 14 series established a formidable reputation with the bombardment squadrons of France's First Air Division, and was also widely used by the American Expeditionary Forces in France

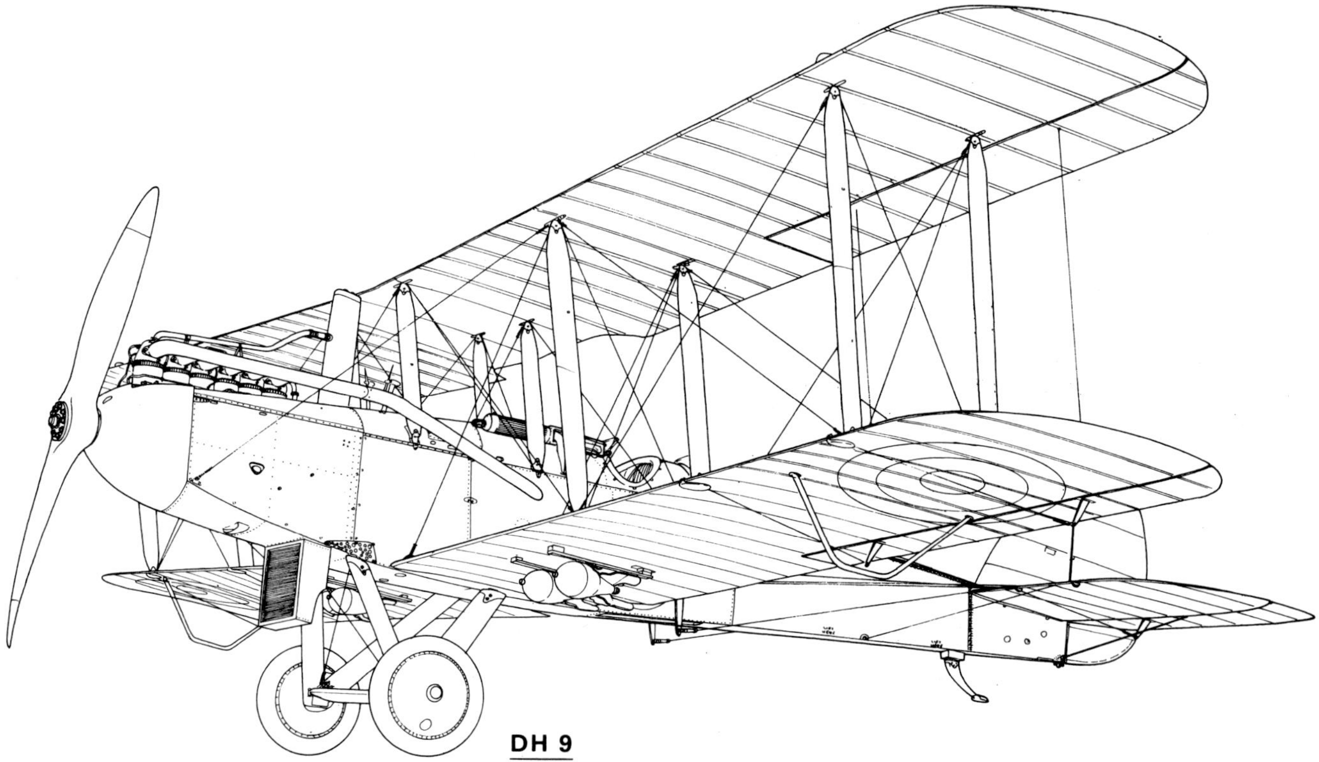

DH 9

Gross weight: 3,669 lb **Span**: 42 ft 5 in **Length**: 30 ft 6 in **Engine**: 230 hp BHP **Armament**: 1 Vickers; 1–2 Lewis machine-guns **Crew**: 2 **Speed**: 118 mph at 10,000 ft **Ceiling**: 17,500 ft **Range**: NA **Bombs**: 2×230 lb or 4×100 lb

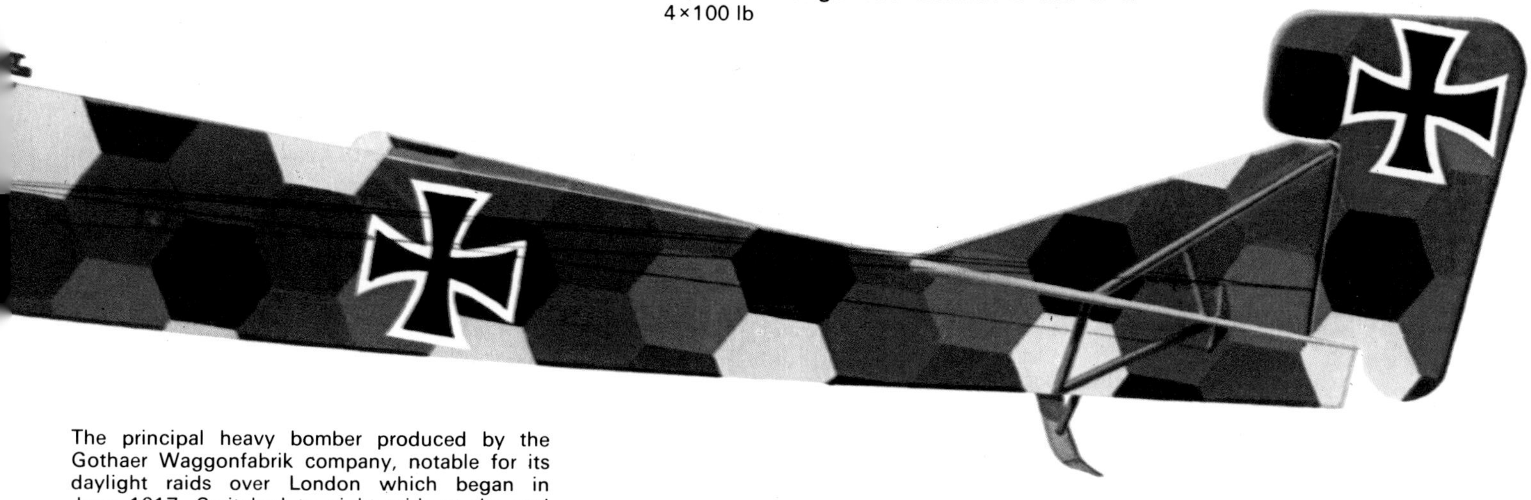

The principal heavy bomber produced by the Gothaer Waggonfabrik company, notable for its daylight raids over London which began in June 1917. Switched to night raids at the end of that year, when British fighters were introduced with the speed and operational altitude necessary for successful interception

Lamblin radiators on the DH 9

Flight International

either welded, or held by bolted or riveted joints. This was simple and quick to make and the weight factor was competitive. Even wooden aircraft often had steel-tube tails. Covering was invariably of doped fabric, though often the front fuselage was skinned in plywood. Undercarriage and wing struts were nearly always of steel tube, sometimes with light wood fairings to change the round tube to a streamline form. Wheels were thin steel rims held by multiple wire spokes, often faired by a disc of fabric. Very often there was no trailing-edge member in the wing except for a single wire, which was bent by the tension of the doped fabric to give a scalloped outline.

Such were the difficulties of making a strong, rigid biplane cellule (wing assembly) that the Paul Schmitt bombers had no fewer than twelve structural bays, with six pairs of interplane struts on each side of the fuselage. On such machines, streamlined rigging wire was a great advantage, especially the British Rafwire with a cross-section like that of a raindrop. Some of the fastest bombers, the Ansaldo SVA family for example, had no bracing wires at all. The Voisin bombers, though of primitive design and low performance, were of all-steel construction and could be left out in any weather in the certainty that they would not deteriorate or warp.

Deliberate warping of the wings was the common way of providing lateral control in 1914, but by 1915 nearly all new bombers had ailerons, often on all wings. Another change was that, whereas many 1914 bombers had rudders and elevators only, by 1915 it was usual to hinge these surfaces to fixed fins and tailplanes. Wheel brakes were never fitted but some aircraft, especially German ones, had a claw arrangement which would plough a furrow across the airfield to bring the machine more quickly to rest.

In November 1916 Bréguet produced the Type Br 14 in which extensive use was made of aluminium. This light metal was used for most of the wing structure and undercarriage, and even in sheet form for the fuselage decking around the cockpits. Though use was still made of wood, steel and fabric, aluminium helped to keep many thousands of Br 14 bombers in worldwide use until after 1930. In 1917, German Professor Hugo Junkers produced his J-1 in which almost the whole airframe was duralumin (aluminium/copper alloy), the unbraced wings and tail having a robust skin of corrugated dural.

Design errors

In the earliest bombers the first objective was to design a machine that would fly at all, because many failed to achieve even that. Next came reliability, while such considerations as flight performance and bomb load were to some degree bonuses. Aircraft design at that time was anything but an exact science. It was not uncommon for a design team to follow a winner with a distinctly inferior machine. For example, the early Caproni Ca 30 bombers were followed late in 1917 by the giant triplane Ca 40 family. These, though robust and well engineered, had such a 'built-in headwind' that they were easy meat for defending scouts and AA artillery in the daytime and had to be used at night. This made bombing even more random than before. These impressive-looking aircraft illustrated the fact that adding more power did not necessarily give better performance. In contrast the small Italian SVA series, with only 220 hp, carried a useful bomb load and were possibly the fastest machines used in the First World War.

Before 1920, aircraft design was very much a matter of opinion, often vehemently expressed yet backed by the slenderest of evidence. Some designers contended that the structural integrity of the triplane more than made up for its other shortcomings; most favoured the biplane, and a very small number (none was a designer of large bombers) considered the monoplane inherently superior. In the same way there was no evidence to suggest that four 100 hp engines might be superior to two 200 hp, beyond the obvious fact that, first, the aircraft would fly better with one engine failed, and second, the chances of engine failure were twice as great.

With most multi-engined bombers it was possible for a courageous crew member to reach a faulty engine in flight and attempt to rectify the trouble. In some designs, notably the German Siemens-Schuckert R-types, the engines were installed in the fuselage purposely to render the whole propulsion system and cooling radiators readily accessible during a mission. The usual fate of such designs was a short period on operations, followed by a much longer period as a trainer in an environment where poor performance was less likely to prove lethal.

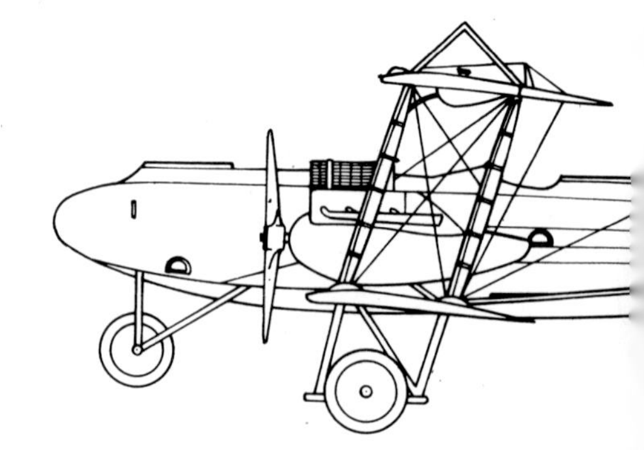

ARMSTRONG WHITWORTH FK 8

Gross weight: 2,447 lb **Span**: 43 ft 6 in **Length**: 30 ft 11 in **Engine**: 160 hp Beardmore **Armament**: 1 Vickers (fixed); 1 Lewis **Crew**: 2 **Speed**: 98 mph ground level **Ceiling**: 13,000 ft **Range**: 3 hrs **Bomb load**: 160 lb

HALBERSTADT CL II

Gross weight: 2,493 lb **Span**: 35 ft 4 in **Length**: 24 ft **Engine**: 160 hp Mercedes **Armament**: 1–2 Spandau; 1 Parabellum machine-gun **Crew**: 2 **Speed**: 103 mph at 16,000 ft **Ceiling**: 16,700 ft **Range**: 3 hrs **Bomb load**: 5×22 lb

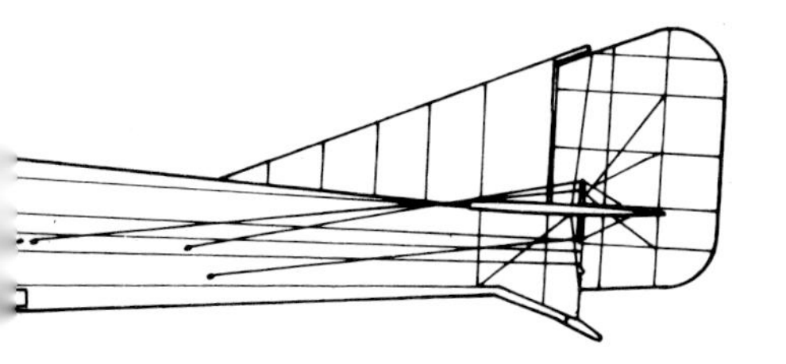

LETORD 4

Gross weight: 4,818 lb **Span**: 58 ft **Length**: 37 ft 1 in **Engine**: 2×160 hp Lorraine-Dietrich **Armament**: 3–4 machine guns **Crew**: 2–3 **Speed**: 82 mph at 6,500 ft **Ceiling**: 14,000 ft **Range**: 3 hrs **Bomb load**: 300 lb

RE 8

Gross weight: 2,869 lb **Span**: 42 ft 7 in **Length**: 27 ft 10 in **Engine**: 150 hp RAF 4a **Armament**: 2–3 machine-guns **Crew**: 2 **Speed**: 98 mph at 6,500 ft **Ceiling**: 11,000 ft **Range**: NA **Bomb load**: 260 lb

THE MENACE OF THE ZEPPELINS

The advantages of airships as bombers were enormous in the early days of the war. Almost as fast as the planes then in existence, their range and bomb-load were far superior. But their days were numbered: more effective defences and better fighters made their vulnerability painfully clear. By the end of their short career, however, the Zeppelins had firmly established the concept of strategic bombing

German airships were the first craft to be used for bombing in the First World War. Only two days after Germany's invasion of Belgium, the Zeppelin Z 6 was sent to attack Liège. It was damaged by gunfire from the ground however, and was wrecked during a forced landing near Cologne. Before the month of August was out, two more Zeppelins had been shot down while on their first operational missions. One of them was captured by the French. It was at such an early stage of the war that the Germans learned the bitter lesson of just how vulnerable were the mighty Zeppelins on which they had pinned such faith.

Their basic mistake had been to direct them over strongly defended battle areas during the hours of daylight when they made such large, slow-moving targets. Nevertheless the disasters shattered the enthusiasm of the German High Command for the airship as a weapon. Although a small number of army airships were later used on bombing raids over Britain, it was the German Naval Air Service which exploited the Zeppelin to its fullest extent, not only in strategic raids over Britain, but even more so in the reconnaissance over the North Sea which was its main task. Much of the success of the German navy against Allied shipping was due to the observation maintained by airship patrols, which during the course of the war, made 971 scouting flights over the North Sea, and 220 over the Baltic.

Meanwhile, the army learned to limit tactical Zeppelin raids over the front line to the hours of darkness, thus anticipating the dark-painted night bomber.

The first attack

Without the more sophisticated bombing devices developed later, bombs dropped at night were even more inaccurate than those dropped by day. So the Military Aviation Service turned its main attention to aircraft which were beginning to show they had uses other than mere reconnaissance. As early as 13 August 1914 a Taube flown by Lt Franz von Hiddeson dropped two light bombs on the outskirts of Paris. Urgent orders were put through for some of the large bomber aircraft which German designers had on their drawing boards but which had previously aroused little interest. At the same time a special bomber force of existing aeroplanes, unsuitable though they were, was set up under GHQ command.

In taking over the main responsibility for Zeppelin bombing raids on Britain, the German Naval Air Service pioneered some of the techniques used later by aircraft. In the same way, their efforts led to the development of anti-aircraft defences which stood Britain in good stead at the end of 1916 when the first German heavy bombers came into service. It was early in the January of 1915 that the Kaiser sanctioned airship raids on Britain but limited them to military establishments such as shipyards and arsenals. However, since the raids were made at night and the airships often drifted far off course, the commanders had little idea where their bombs might fall. Many fell on undefended villages in East Anglia, particularly after the black-out became widespread, making it even more difficult to differentiate between military and civilian targets.

The first airship raid took place on the night of 19 January 1915 when two Zeppelins dropped bombs on Kings Lynn, Yarmouth, and several villages in the area. The bombs themselves were not large, mostly 110-lb high explosives and 6½-lb incendiaries with a limited destructive capability. Less than half-a-dozen people were killed, but this was the first time that a civilian population had ever been subjected to systematic bombing, and the terror and sense of outrage that it produced was out of all proportion to the weight of bombs dropped.

Reprisals were called for, leading eventually to raids on Berlin by British bombers. Meanwhile, the Zeppelin raids continued: in twenty raids during 1915, thirty-seven tons of bombs killed 181 people and injured 455. So there seemed little point in pretending *not* to bomb London when the airship crews had little idea where their bombs were falling anyway. In fact the capital was bombed by mistake on 31 May, when seven civilians were killed and thirty-five injured. Two months later, the Kaiser lifted his ban on bombing London, and raids on that city, as well as others such as Liverpool and the Tyneside area, began in earnest.

The Zeppelin crews, though, didn't have everything their own way. They had to contend with storms and gales that often

forced them to crash land, usually with fatal results. This was the fate, only one month later, of the two airships which had made the January raid. And the organisation of the British defences improved as time went on. To begin with, the Royal Navy was responsible for the defence of London and the major cities while the Army took care of ports and military installations. Guns such as 3 and 4-in quick firers and 1-pounder pom poms were converted for anti-aircraft use and even machine-guns were placed on high-angle mountings and fitted to motorcars for mobility. Searchlights were introduced, manned first by special constables.

Counter measures

Until the crews gained experience, there were many false alarms when illuminated clouds were mistaken for Zeppelins. Nevertheless, just as the bombing brought a new terror not exactly justified by the damage to property and loss of life actually caused, so the airship crews learned what it was like to be in a huge, slow-moving target, flying at no more than 6,000 feet, held in the beam of a searchlight and being fired at from the ground. Such was the fear this aroused that when five Zeppelins tried to raid London in August, only one got within thirty miles and the returning crews told dramatic stories of searchlights and anti-aircraft fire which did not actually exist. They bombed the wrong targets and the firing was only from rifles.

The new series of giant Zeppelins which came into service in 1916 were able to fly as high as 12,300 ft, and a novel device was introduced to reduce their chance of being caught in searchlight beams. While the airship cruised safely above the clouds, a streamlined car with an observer inside was lowered nearly 3,000 feet on a steel cable so that the observer could direct the bombing by telephone. In the spring and summer of that year, the Zeppelin raids reached their peak, with a dozen or more craft taking part in a single attack. But the height at which they flew, although making it easier to elude the defences, imposed even greater strains on the crews who were often airborne for twenty-four hours or more at temperatures of 30° below zero in winter. And the ground defences were also improving. In February the Army took over the entire responsibility for home defences and several months later, the RFC's BE2c aircraft were fitted with fixed forward-firing machine-guns for the first time, following the 1915 invention by the French and Germans of interrupter gear which enabled these guns to be synchronised to fire through the propellers. It was this invention that turned the early reconnaissance aircraft into lethal fighters.

Aircraft had brought down Zeppelins before but by the unorthodox method of flying above and dropping bombs on them. The first to be destroyed in this way – and the first to be destroyed in aerial combat – was brought down on 7 June 1915 by Flt Sub-Lt R. A. J. Warneford, of the RNAS, flying a French Morane Parasol Type L. He set fire to the airship LZ 37 over Ghent by dropping six 20-lb bombs on it and was awarded the Victoria Cross. But by mid-1916, the British aircraft were armed with machine-guns which could not only be aimed more accurately but could fire incendiary bullets. These, along with phosphor shells from anti-aircraft guns spelled doom for the hydrogen-filled airships.

The first victory by a defending fighter at night came on 2 September 1916 when Lt William Leefe Robinson of 39 Squadron RFC shot down one of twelve naval and four military airships which had set out to raid London. Flames from the burning Schutte-Lanz airship SL 11 could be seen fifty miles away. Robinson too, was awarded the Victoria Cross for his success, which marked the beginning of the end of the airship menace.

The new class of airship which was coming into service could fly at 18,000 ft in an attempt to avoid the fighters, but at that height the crew suffered even more severely from the cold and had to use oxygen, while the craft themselves were subject to greater hazards from treacherous wind changes. When eleven airships set out to bomb London at the beginning of October, they became so scattered that only one person was killed in the city, while one of the Zeppelins was lost with its entire crew – shot down by a BE2c over Potters Bar. In the last raid of 1916, eight weeks later, two out of ten Zeppelins were lost. The total number of raids during the year was twenty-three, during which 125 tons of bombs were dropped, killing 293 people and wounding 691.

End of the airship

The Germans were reluctant to admit defeat but the short day of the airship as a bomber was over. Only eleven more raids were made against England, seven in 1917 and four in 1918. The last was on 5 August 1918 when five Zeppelins launched a surprise attack which resulted in the loss of their latest and best airship, the L 70, together with *Fregattenkapitan* Peter Strasser, the officer who had led the naval airship force so courageously since the very beginning of the war. It was not an end to bombing, of course, as towards the end of 1916 aircraft were beginning to take over that role with growing effectiveness. But the Zeppelins had played their part, albeit at a tremendous cost. Of the eighty-eight airships built during the war (seventy-two for the German navy), over sixty were lost; thirty-four due to accidents and forced landings caused by bad weather and the remainder shot down by Allied aircraft and ground fire. In fifty-one raids on Britain they dropped 5,806 bombs (a total of 196½ tons), killing 557 people, injuring a further 1,358, and causing an estimated £1½ million damage. This was not too highly significant in itself, considering the thousands who were dying in the trenches in France every day, but the raids were of considerable military value as they hampered war production and diverted men and equipment from more vital theatres of war.

It is estimated that the airship and aircraft raids together reduced the total munitions output by one sixth. And by the end of 1916, the British home-based air defences included twelve RFC squadrons and a large force of anti-aircraft guns and searchlights, requiring 12,000 men.

The airship raids were the first ever attempt to defeat a country by the bombing of military and civilian targets in the homeland rather than attacks on military targets in the battle zone – strategic and psychological bombing as distinct from tactical bombing. Its success gave rise to a whole new school of military thought which was put into effect with far greater destruction during the Second World War. Much of the initial success was due to the fact that bombing was an unknown factor before the First War and its effect on an unprepared civilian population was therefore considerably greater.

The wreckage of Zeppelin *L 10* in the shallows off Cuxhaven. Returning from a scouting flight on 3 September 1915, she was struck by lightning and fell in flames, killing all on board

Imperial War Museum

HEAVIER BOMBS, BETTER GUNS

Early aeroplane bombing raids were limited to the battle-zone and its vicinity. The German Zeppelins had the range to attack more distant targets, but the first strategic raid by plane was carried out by the British – not by the RFC but by the navy

One of the great advantages which the Zeppelin of 1914 had over the aeroplane was, of course, its range – more than 2,000 miles at a time when most planes were hard pressed to fly 150 miles without having to land to refuel. It was range that made it possible for the Germans to pioneer the bombing of an enemy's homeland and in particular his capital city. Military leaders believed that the capture of an enemy's capital city somehow marked his defeat. London was chosen by the Germans because it could be reached by flying across the North Sea and thus avoiding the battle zones of the Western Front, whereas Paris could only be reached by battling through the Allied air patrols over France. Only two airship raids were made on the French capital throughout the war and one of two Zeppelins making one attempt was destroyed. But apart from the need to avoid the Western Front, range gave a wide choice in the selection of targets. In fact, airship range was always greater than that of aircraft. In 1918, the Germans were even able to contemplate raids on New York with their newest Zeppelins which had a range of 7,500 miles. Strasser, head of the German Naval Air Service, was planning such a raid when he was killed with the destruction of the L 70.

Meanwhile, during the early stages of the war when planes were first used for bombing, their missions generally had to be confined to the battle-zone or targets in the near vicinity. The French Voisin and Farman bombers were particularly effective in tactical missions against military targets, proving themselves to be virtually an extension of artillery, for which the French had been enthusiasts since the days of Napoleon. The earliest French bombs were actually converted Canton-Unné 90-mm and 155-mm artillery shells with the addition of fins and impact fuses. The French might well have undertaken the first strategic aeroplane bombing raid of the war – a mass attack on the Kaiser's personal headquarters at Mézières in September 1914 – but for some reason the planned raid was cancelled.

The German 'carrier-pigeon' bomber units were also used during the first months of the war, although to a lesser extent because of the emphasis placed on airships. They might have been used for strategic raids as early as February 1915, when plans were made for them to bomb England. An experimental night bombing raid was carried out on Dunkirk at the end of January, but before the raid itself could be carried out, the force was transferred to the Eastern Front where it gave considerable assistance at the battle of Gorlice-Tarnow in March. As it was, the first ever strategic raid by a plane was carried out by the British – not by the RFC, as might have been expected, but by the RNAS.

'Samson's boys'

In August 1914, while the four RFC squadrons were sent to France to operate under army command from a base at Maubeuge, an RNAS squadron under Cdr Samson was despatched to Ostend to assist an attempted naval diversion by a brigade of marines.

Among the assorted aircraft were two Sopwith Tabloids, tiny single-seat tractor biplanes, which before the war had been a favourite sporting machine. The diversion was planned by Winston Churchill, then First Sea Lord, but it did not materialise and within three days the marines were

FRIEDRICHSHAVEN G III

Gross weight: 8,700 lb **Span**: 78 ft **Length**: 42 ft 2 in **Engine**: 2×260 hp Mercedes D IVa **Armament**: 4×7·92-mm machine guns **Crew**: 3 **Speed**: 88 mph at 3,280 ft **Ceiling**: 14,800 ft **Range**: 5 hrs **Bomb load**: 2,200 lb

The main production model of the Friedrichshaven G series which, together with the Gotha bombers, formed the mainstay of the German heavy bomber units during the last two years of the war

HANDLEY PAGE 0/100

Gross weight: 14,000 lb **Span**: 100 ft **Length**: 62 ft 10 in **Engine**: 2×250 hp Rolls Royce Eagle **Armament**: 4–5 machine guns **Crew**: 4 **Speed**: 95 mph at ground level **Ceiling**: 7,000 ft **Range**: 6 hrs **Bomb load**: 2,000 lb

The world's first effective heavy night bomber – the biggest British warplane of the war

recalled. Samson's squadron was supposed to go with them, returning to one of the RNAS air stations that had been established along the east coast as part of Britain's defences. But this did not suit the fiery Commander who had pioneered flight from ships at sea. Using Channel fog as an excuse he landed his squadron at Dunkirk and enlisted the aid of the British Consul for him to stay on to support the French. Churchill agreed to the establishment of a naval air base on the French coast to help protect Britain from airship raids, and so 'Samson's boys' became a permanent feature at Dunkirk.

The RNAS squadron was intended to carry out reconnaissance and engage any Zeppelins or enemy aircraft sighted. But Samson preferred more vigorous action and decided to attack the Zeppelins at their actual bases. The first British air raid into German territory took place on 22 September 1914 but no damage was caused. Meanwhile, several of the aircraft had been sent to Antwerp to help in the battle to prevent the German Army reaching the sea. British forces were forced to withdraw on 7 October and a day later the last RNAS aeroplanes to leave the Belgian city were the two Sopwith Tabloids, flown by Squadron Commander Spenser Grey and Flt-Lt R. L. G. Marix.

Before returning to Dunkirk they were ordered by Samson to attack the Zeppelin sheds at Cologne and Düsseldorf. Spenser Grey was prevented by mist from seeing his target and dropped bombs on Cologne's railway station instead. But Marix was more successful and from 600 ft his 20-lb Hale high explosive bombs fell on the Zeppelin shed at Düsseldorf which exploded into flames, completely destroying the brand-new Zeppelin Z 9 inside. This was the first-ever strategic bombing raid, since it was designed to cripple the enemy's war effort by striking at a military target behind the front line rather than in the battle zone. A few weeks later, three Avro 504 biplanes made a similar raid on the Friedrichshafen Zeppelin works on Lake Constance, a mission requiring a flight of about 250 miles over hostile territory, from a take-off point at Belfort on the French-Swiss border. The Avros attacked by flying to within ten feet of the lake's surface – probably the first low-level bombing strike in history – destroying one Zeppelin under construction, as well as the gasworks used for filling the airships.

Heavier bombers

The success of these attacks led the Air Department of the Admiralty to issue a specification for a much larger twin-engined bomber able to carry much heavier bombs than the 20-pounders which were in general use at that time, and the biggest that most planes could carry. This resulted in the first of the famous Handley Page series of bombers, the 0/100.

At the same time, the Germans were developing large R-class bombers such as the Friedrichshafen and Gotha types. These also made their appearance in 1916, the latter being one of the finest bombers of the war. The French were slower in building heavy twin-engined bombers and it was not until 1917 that the first of the Letord series, designed by Colonel Dorand of the French Service Technique, came into operation. The Russians of course already possessed a number of Il'ya Muromets, but these were hampered by maintenance problems and

HANDLEY PAGE 0/400

Gross weight: 14,022 lb **Span**: 100 ft **Length**: 62 ft 10 in **Engine**: 2×250 hp Rolls Royce Eagle **Armament**: 5× ·303 machine guns **Crew**: 4–5 **Speed**: 97 mph at ground level **Ceiling**: 8,000 ft **Range**: 4 hrs **Bomb load**: 2,000 lb

Improved version of the Handley Page 0/100 heavy night bomber, widely used by the British during 1917 and 1918 for raids on Germany

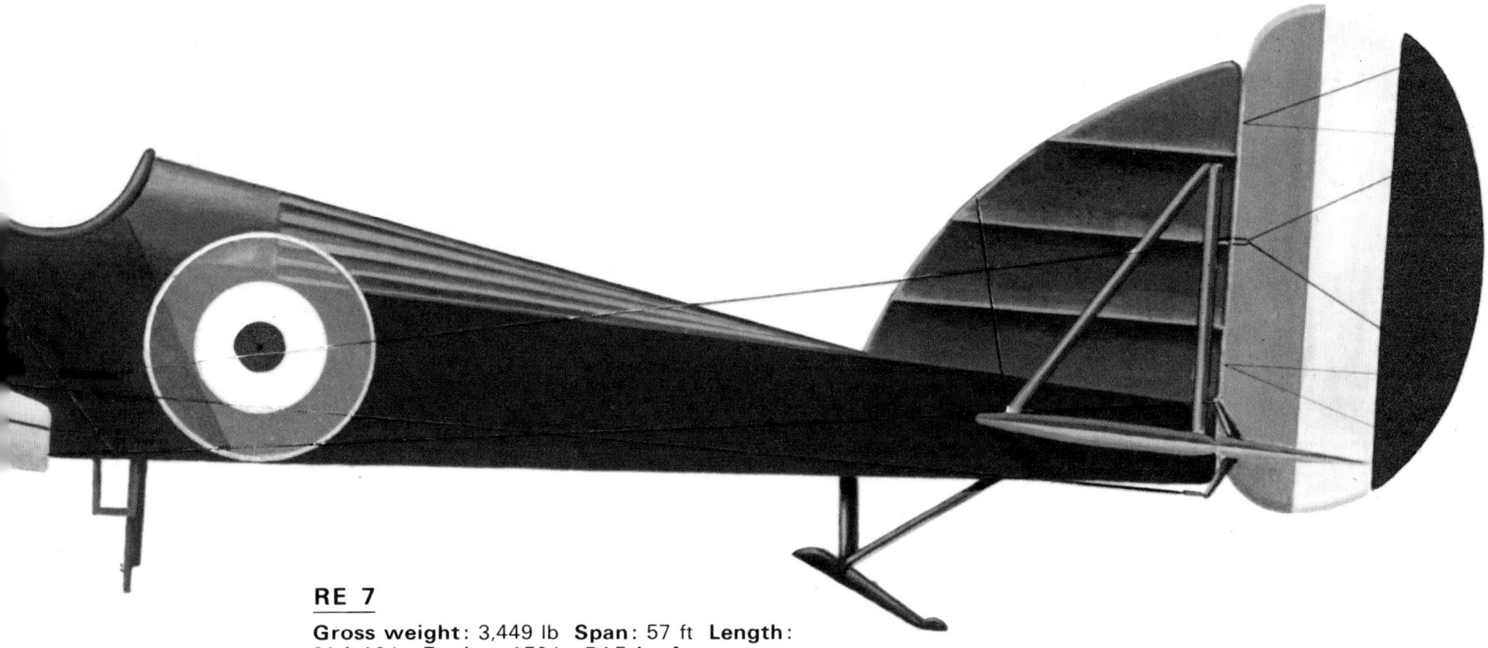

RE 7

Gross weight: 3,449 lb **Span**: 57 ft **Length**: 31 ft 10 in **Engine**: 150 hp RAF 4a **Armament**: 1 machine gun and small arms **Crew**: 2–3 **Speed**: 85 mph at ground level **Ceiling**: 6,500 ft **Range**: NA **Bomb load**: 336 lb

Introduced into service with the RFC early in 1916 and notable for its great weight-lifting capacity, in relation to its size

later operations were affected by the Russian revolution. The Italians, who only joined the war in May 1915, were also well advanced in the development of the heavy bomber, and the Caproni Ca 32 was in service by the end of the same year. It was evident that 1916 would see the introduction of specialised bombers in the air services of all the major combatant powers.

In the meantime, however, they had to use the planes already in existence. From early in 1915, the Allies increased their raids, while the French, in retaliation for attacks on Paris, began to include targets in Germany itself. Much of the French strategic bombing effort was, in fact, based on a doctrine of retaliation. On 26 May, for instance, following a German poison-gas attack the previous month, Commandant Göys led three squadrons of Voisin bombers on a raid against the poison-gas factories near Mannheim, a flight of five hours. Considerable damage was achieved and only one Voisin failed to return. Unfortunately this was the one piloted by Göys, who had been forced to land in Germany because of engine trouble. He was taken prisoner but eventually escaped and found his way back to France.

By June the French had begun to penetrate as far as Karlsruhe. Much of the early success of these bombing missions was due to the fact that there was virtually no opposition from German aircraft. This meant that raids could be carried out in daytime and at relatively low altitudes, so that even by the primitive method of dropping bombs over the side of the cockpit, a surprising degree of accuracy could be achieved. The British and French crews had a healthy respect for the Germans' improvised anti-aircraft guns. Many of these had been hastily converted from other uses: the 3·7-cm *maschinen flak*, for example, which could fire three shots a second with an accuracy up to 9,000 ft, was originally used by the navy on torpedo-boats. But there was little to fear from German aircraft, whose only armament was the small arms carried by the crews.

Even with such relatively ineffective weapons, the Allied pusher aircraft had an advantage over the German tractor types for their gunners had a much less restricted field of fire. This was even more marked when, in late 1914, the French began to arm their Voisin bombers with machine-guns carried by the gunner/observer seated in front of the pilot. These would have been more effective still had they not been the heavy Hotchkiss 8-mm type, which hampered the plane's performance and were difficult to operate in the air. Nevertheless they were more than a match for the German aircraft and during the early period of 1915, French bombers were virtually unmolested as they raided German targets.

Wider fire power

Meanwhile, a better and lighter air-cooled machine-gun had been designed by Col Isaac Newton Lewis of the US Army, and experiments in its use were made as early as August 1914 by individual pilots such as Lt L. A. Strange of No. 5 Squadron RFC. Simple mountings were devised to enable the observer of a two-seater – or even the pilot of a single-seater – to fire over the side of the cockpit. This meant that an enemy plane had to be approached in a crab-like manner to make it a suitable target, but many victories were obtained in this way, and aerial fighting became commonplace. An even more successful method in the case of single-seaters was to mount a machine-gun above the centre section of the top wing, so that it could be fired forwards above the propeller arc by means of a cable attached to the trigger.

This period of German docility, which gave the Allies supremacy in the air, came to an end in the spring of 1915 when the more powerful C-class planes of Rumpler, Albatros and Aviatik design came into service. These were armed with a Parabellum machine-gun, fired by the observer, who now sat behind the pilot so that he had a wider field of fire. It was now the turn of the slower pusher aeroplanes to suffer since they were blind from behind. The French followed the German example, but inexplicably, the British retained the old seating arrangement and the standard Farnborough-designed BE types of the RFC began to suffer disastrous losses. With the Germans fighting back, the Allied bombers no longer always got through.

An even greater blow to the Allies came in the summer of 1915 when the German single-seat Fokker monoplane (*Eindekker*) appeared. It was armed with a machine-gun placed directly in front of the pilot, and synchronised to fire between the blades of the revolving propeller. The aircraft itself could now be aimed at a target, making it much more effective than the free-swinging weapon that the observers on two-seater aircraft had to use. In spite of the lead that might have been achieved by the French, who had been the first to fit deflectors to propeller blades, and similar ideas that had been put forward and rejected in Britain, Allied fighter aircraft were not fitted with gun synchronising gear until 1916. The winter of 1915–1916 saw the Fokker achieving such supremacy in the skies above the Western Front that British pilots were angrily labelled 'Fokker fodder'.

Increasingly, the Allied bomber squadrons had to call on the faster and better armed single-seat scouts to provide fighter escorts, which severely restricted their range. To give themselves better protection the French bomber units developed the idea of formation flying, first realised by the remarkable Capitaine Happe of *Escadrille* MF29 and later adopted by the British, while more and more raids had to be carried out at night, reducing the effectiveness of the bombing. By the autumn of 1915 it was apparent to the military leaders of all the combatant powers that air power was an important new element in warfare. Reconnaissance was still its most useful function, especially in view of the growing use of photography. But it was equally important to deny the enemy similar facilities for reconnaissance, and this involved not only fighters to patrol the battle zone, but also bombers to raid the enemy's airfields and bomb his planes on the ground.

The fighters had advanced considerably with the development of fast and manoeuvrable single-seat aircraft armed with machine-guns. But the bombers, by and large, were still the general purpose types which had been in existence when the war began. It was now necessary to design bombers especially adapted to the task, with the defensive armament to take on fighters. From this point onwards, the story of air warfare became a continual struggle, both in the air and on the drawing board, between bomber and fighter aircraft.

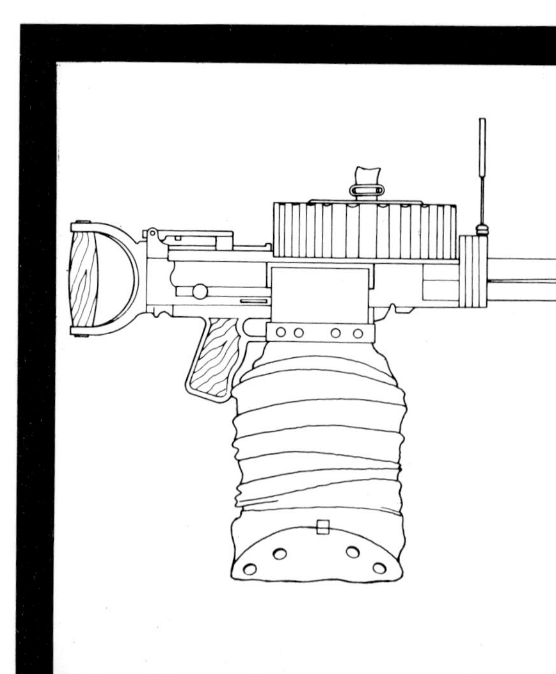

LEWIS ·303-in MACHINE-GUN

Invented by Col Isaac Newton Lewis of the US Army and adopted early in the war as their standard light machine gun by both the British Army and the RFC – and later by the French and Belgian forces. Gas-operated and fed at first by 47-round revolving drums – later by 97-round drums. For aerial use, a cartridge-case deflector and receptacle was provided to prevent ejected cartridges damaging the aeroplane, and electric heaters prevented freezing-up at height. Rate of fire was increased by 1918 to 850 rounds per minute

PARABELLUM 7.92-mm MACHINE-GUN

Weight: 22 lb **Cyclic rate:** 700 rpm

The most widely-used observers' machine gun in German aircraft from early 1915 until the end of the war. A lightweight form of Maxim with a firing rate of 700 rounds per minute, and a water-jacket slotted for air cooling in later models

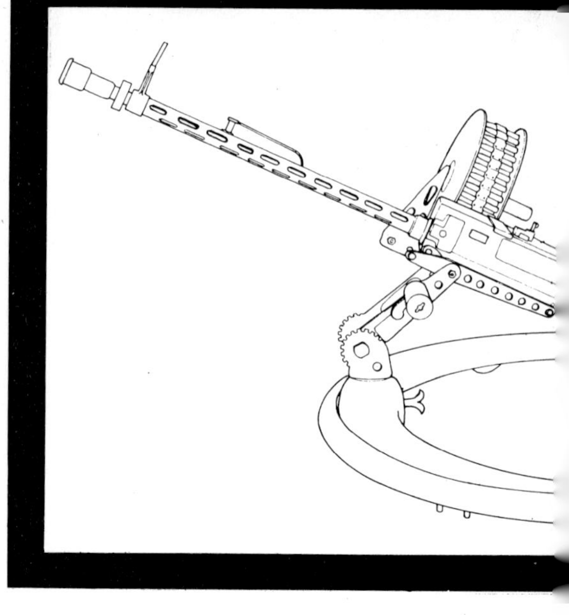

VILLA PEROSA 9-mm MACHINE-GUN

Weight: 8 lb approx. **Length**: 35·5 in **Calibre**: 9 mm **Magazine**: RD.S **Muzzle velocity**: 1,250 fps **Cyclic rate**: 900 rpm

Double-barrelled machine-gun invented by Major B. A. Revelli, primarily for use in Italian aircraft, but not really suitable because of the lack of striking power of its pistol-type ammunition. This was in spite of an extremely high rate of fire – 1,500 rounds per minute from each barrel, firing separately or simultaneously

British 3·6-in QF self-propelled anti-aircraft gun (left), developed during 1917–18. A very promising weapon but the war ended before it saw service

HOTCHKISS 8-mm MACHINE-GUN

This gas-operated air-cooled machine gun, fed by a belt wound round a drum and holding 25 rounds, was the most commonly-used type in French aircraft until 1915/16. It was replaced by the Lewis

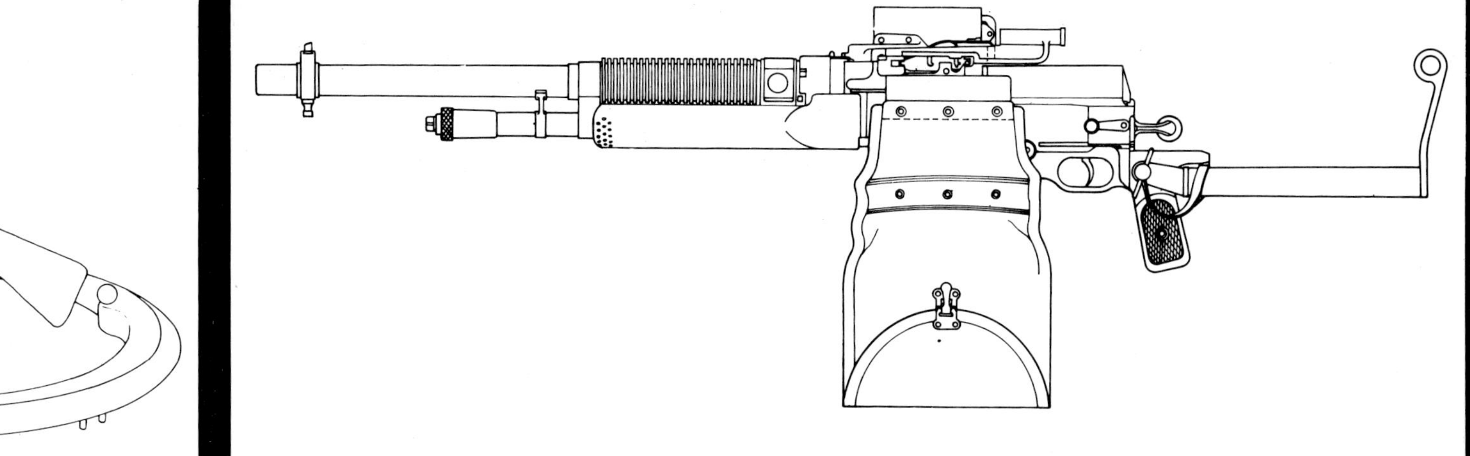

HANDLEY PAGE V 1500

Gross weight: 24,700 lb **Span**: 126 ft **Length**: 62 ft **Engine**: 4×375 hp Rolls Royce Eagle VIII **Armament**: 4 Lewis machine-guns **Crew**: 4–5 **Speed**: 90 mph at 6,500 ft **Ceiling**: 11,000 ft **Range**: 6 hrs **Bomb load**: 7,500 lb

Built secretly in Belfast towards the end of the war for the purpose of carrying a large bomb-load from British bases to Berlin. It was the biggest aeroplane to be built in Britain up to that time but it appeared too late for operational service

THE BOMBER SPREADS ITS WINGS

The first bombers were little more than general purpose aircraft adapted to carry indifferent bomb-loads. But in order to carry out the growing number of strategic raids against effective fighter opposition, armament, speed, range and ceiling all had to be increased. The first country to develop large, multi-engined bombers was Russia, but by 1916 most of the major powers were working on their own 'heavies'

The first multi-engined heavy bombers to be used in the war were the Russian Il'ya Muromets with which the Squadron of Flying Ships of the Russian Imperial Air Service was equipped at the end of 1914. Operations started in February 1915 with raids on towns and military targets in East Prussia, well inside the Muromets' combat range of about 300 miles. Among the successful attacks was the destruction of the German seaplane base on Angern Lake and the virtual obliteration of the HQ of the German Commander-in-Chief, General von Bulow, at Shavli in Lithuania.

These bombers were tough enough to take considerable punishment and still keep flying, helped by specially designed fire-proof fuel tanks and some metal-plate protection under the pilot's cabin. The heavy armament they carried, normally three machine-guns, with up to seven on some models, was usually more than a match for the German fighters of the period. The Muromets were also equipped with excellent bomb-sights which gave them an average of 75 per cent successful hits on target. If it had not been for constant maintenance problems and difficulties in obtaining engines and spare parts, the Russian bombing offensive would have been even more effective. As it was, the morale of the German aircrews fell to a very low ebb when it seemed that nothing could prevent the Muromets getting through. It was in an effort to inspire morale that Oswald Boelcke, the German fighter ace who had become a national hero after scoring eighteen victories in France, was sent on a tour of the Eastern Front in the spring of 1916. But not until 12 September of that year was the first and only Muromets brought down in air combat – and only after it had shot down three of its opponents and damaged a fourth.

Enclosed cockpits

The first Muromets type to enter operational service was the IM-B, which carried a crew of four – pilot, co-pilot, bombing officer and air mechanic – in completely enclosed accommodation with glazed window panels in the nose and fuselage sides. Its bomb load was 1,120 lb and three machine-guns were mounted in the fuselage sides for shooting at ground targets. It was powered by two 200 hp and two 135 hp Salmson radial engines. The next and most widely used type was the IM-V which had a smaller wing span and 150 hp Sunbeam liquid-cooled engines, originally bought from England and later made under licence. The bomb load was increased by 600 lb.

As a result of the introduction of armed fighters by the Germans, the defensive armament of the later types, the IM-G1, G2 and G3, was increased to include machine-guns mounted on the upper wing section, under the fuselage, and in the nose and tail, for which the crew was increased to seven: two pilots, one navigator, one mechanic and three gunners. The wing chord was also increased and the 2,000 lb bomb load was stored internally and the bombs dropped either vertically or horizontally.

Largest of the Muromets was the IM-YeA, with a wing span of 113 ft $2\frac{1}{4}$ in and a gross weight of 15,432 lb, but it was not put into production. A few of the slightly smaller IM-YeI were built, armed with seven machine-guns and powered by four 220 hp Renault engines. Although the Muromets crews were the élite of the Russian Air Service, the plane itself was not easy to fly and considerable training was required before crews could be sent to the Front. About half of the eighty IMs built were used for training purposes. Most of the machines were destroyed by their crews after the Revolution and the German invasion to prevent them falling into enemy hands, but a few remained to inaugurate passenger services in Russia after the Civil War.

CAPRONI Ca 5

Gross weight: 11,700 lb **Span**: 77 ft **Length**: 41 ft 4 in **Engine**: 3×300 hp Fiat **Armament**: 2 machine-guns **Crew**: 3 **Speed**: 95 mph at ground level **Ceiling**: 15,000 ft **Range**: 4 hrs **Bomb load**: 1,188 lb

With the Ca 5 series in 1917, Caproni returned to a biplane configuration after the Ca 4 triplane. Widely used as a day and night bomber in 1918

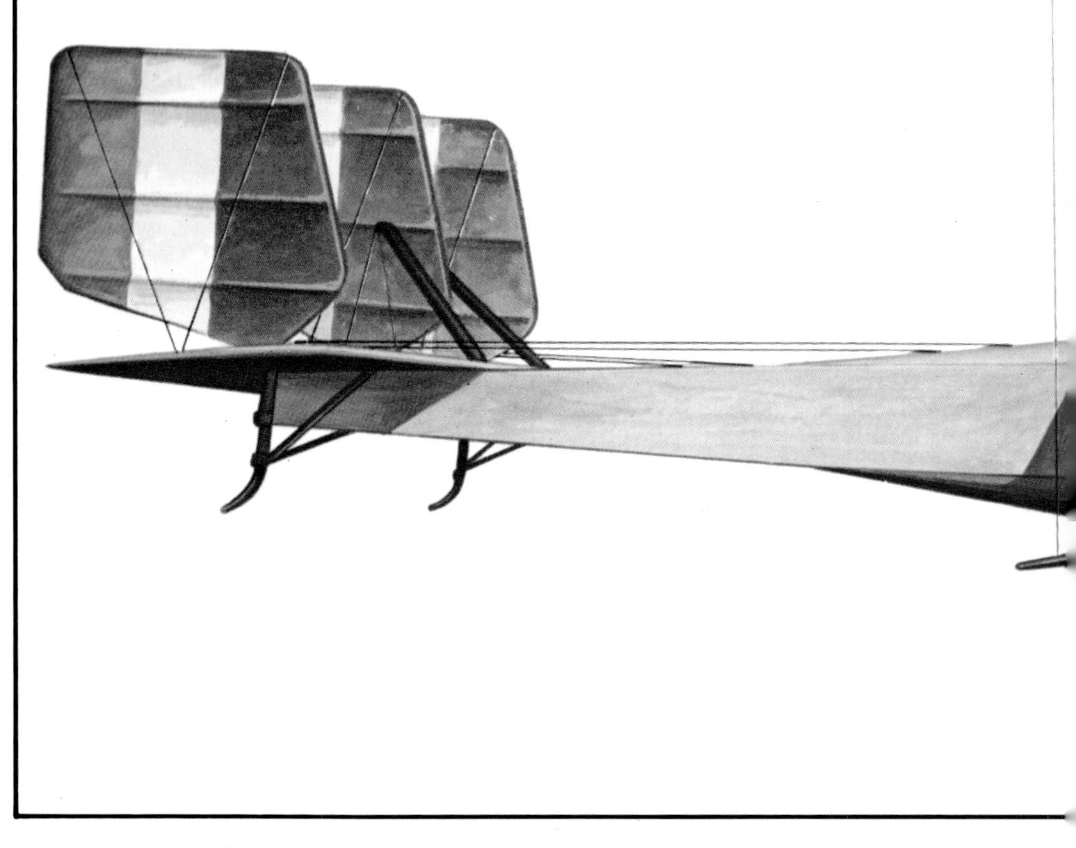

The next country to introduce large bombers into service was Italy, following its declaration of war against Austria-Hungary on 24 May 1915. These were the Caproni series, based on the original pre-war design of the Ca 31, but modified considerably as the war progressed. The first to enter operational service, in August 1915, was the Ca 32 biplane, powered by three 100 hp Fiat liquid-cooled engines. Its range of 340 miles enabled it to be used for strategic bombing attacks, but as the Austrian fighters improved in performance, the Ca 32 later had to be relegated to night bombing.

Meanwhile the most widely used type, the Ca 33, came into service towards the end of 1916 with a higher maximum speed of 94 mph. The two pilots sat side-by-side in the centre fuselage, a gunner operated a Revelli machine-gun from the nose position, and a fourth crew member in the rear cockpit operated up to three similar guns, fixed to fire in different directions.

The Ca 3 series, as they were designated, were all biplanes but with the next (Ca 4) series, starting with the Ca 40, a triplane design was used with huge 100 ft wings. The main production model was the Ca 42, powered by three 270 hp Fiat, Isotta-Fraschini or American Liberty engines. It was a sturdy and reliable plane with a combat range of seven hours, and could carry a bomb load of 3,910 lb, made up of small bombs mounted externally under the bottom plane. But its size and relatively low speed made it an easy target for enemy fighters, and it was reserved for night-bombing operations. For the next (Ca 5) generation Caproni returned to a biplane layout and these were beginning to replace the Ca 3 series when the war ended.

Semi-rigid airships and smaller bombers were also used by the Italians throughout the war but by far the greatest bombing effort was made by the Capronis. The first raids, beginning at the end of August 1915, were against military targets to the rear of the Austrian armies, such as railways, supply depots, troop concentrations and

especially airfields. Tactical operations remained the prime objective of the Italian Air Service until the end of the war but early in 1916, mainly at the instigation of Gabriele d'Annunzio, long-range strategic raids were undertaken.

Daylight attacks

The Capronis did not have the range to reach Vienna, 260 miles from their main base at Pordenone, but targets were available some 100 miles away across the Adriatic, such as the Austro-Hungarian naval base at Pola and the industrial city and seaport of Trieste. Daylight attacks were made on these and other strategic targets, at first by Capronis flying in formation but later escorted by Italian-built Nieuports. One of the biggest raids was made on 2 October 1917 by nearly 150 Capronis and eleven flying-boats on the naval base at Pola. As a result of the Caporetto disaster later in the month, however, when the Pordenone base was captured by the Austrians after the Italian retreat, strategic bombing became too much of a luxury and for the rest of the war the Caproni squadrons concentrated on tactical operations, mainly against Austrian airfields. A number of American pilots were attached to Caproni units to gain experience in bombing operations.

Just as the first British efforts at bombing were pioneered by the RNAS, so the first British heavy bomber was developed by the Admiralty for use by the navy's Air Arm. Following the success of the RNAS raids on Zeppelin sheds towards the end of 1914, the Air Department of the Admiralty was convinced of the value of air bombardment and laid plans for the creation of a strategic bombing force that could operate at long range from bases in France and England. There were, of course, no planes then available for such a purpose and engines were too scarce in 1914 and 1915 for a twin-engined layout to be attempted. As an interim measure a single-engined bomber was ordered from Sopwith, resulting in the introduction of the 1½ Strutter, while the Short company developed a single-engined landplane from their successful Short 184 seaplane. In the meantime, Captain (later Rear Admiral) Murray Sueter, Director of the Air Department, issued a specification for a large twin-engined aircraft capable of extended patrols over the sea.

The challenge appealed to Sir Frederick Handley Page who set about designing such a bomber, powered by two 120 hp Beardmore engines. So impressed was Murray Sueter with the design that he asked Handley Page to improve on it in order to produce a 'bloody paralyser' of an aeroplane. The result was the Handley Page 0/100 biplane, one of the most famous bombers of the war, which went into service in November 1916. It was intended to have two 150 hp Sunbeam engines but as construction progressed so did work by Rolls Royce on two engines which were to become the renowned Eagle and Falcon. Both were water-cooled twelve-cylinder Vee types, the Eagle being the largest. This was chosen for the 0/100, its horsepower de-rated from 300 to 250 to increase reliability. They were enclosed in armoured nacelles, each with a separate armoured fuel tank. Unusual features included the facility for folding the huge 100-foot wings, so that the aircraft could be stored in canvas field hangars, and a biplane tail unit.

The crew of three sat in a cabin which was originally intended to be enclosed with bullet-proof glass and armour plate, but in the production models, the enclosure and much of the armour plate was removed. The maximum bomb load was 2,000 lb, consisting either of a single 1,650-lb bomb or eight 250-lb, sixteen 112-lb, or three 520 or 550-lb bombs. Defensive armament consisted of one or two Lewis guns on a ring-mounting in the nose cockpit, one or two Lewis guns in the upper rear cockpit, and a single Lewis gun mounted to fire rearward and downward through a hole in the fuselage floor just behind the wings.

More stability

While work on the Handley Page 0/100 continued, in the spring of 1916 the RNAS went ahead with the formation of two strategic bombing wings at Luxeuil in Belgium and Dunkirk in France, in preparation for the Sopwith 1½ Strutter and the Short Bomber which had been ordered the previous year. By that time it was apparent that bombers would have to fight their way past defending fighters, in particular the Fokker *Eindekker*. Coincidentally the British had at last developed interrupter gear to enable the fixture of fixed forward-firing machine-guns, either Lewis or the more successful belt-fed Vickers which was later generally adopted.

This gear, originally designed by Lt-Cdr V. V. Dibovsky of the Russian Imperial Navy, and developed by Warrant Officer F. W. Scarff of the Admiralty Air Department (who had also been responsible for designing one of the best ring-mountings of the war for use by observer/gunners) was first installed in the RFCs single-seat Bristol Scout. But the first two-seater to use this synchronised gun was the 1½ Strutter, in addition to the usual free-mounted Lewis gun in the rear cockpit. The Strutter had been designed as a bomber, capable of carrying a 130 lb bomb load with the emphasis laid on stability rather than manoeuvrability. However, its armament made it an excellent fighter as well, especially when German pilots attacked from the front to avoid the observer's gun, only to be met by a deadly hail of fire from the pilot's synchronised Vickers.

With the Battle of the Somme about to begin the RFC was desperately short of fighter aircraft, and after appealing to the RNAS for help, the Admiralty handed over a large number of Strutters for army use, thus delaying its own plans for a strategic bombing offensive against Germany.

The other plane which had been ordered

VICKERS VIMY IV

Gross weight: 12,500 lb **Span**: 67 ft 2 in **Length**: 43 ft 6 in **Engine**: 2×360 hp Rolls Royce Eagle VIII **Armament**: 6 Lewis machine-guns **Crew**: 5–6 **Speed**: 103 mph at ground level **Ceiling**: 7,000 ft **Range**: 985 miles **Bomb load**: 2,476 lb

Initiated in 1917 as a heavy bomber to take part in Britain's plan for the strategic bombing of Germany, but it arrived too late to see operational service before the Armistice. After the war, the Vimy distinguished itself for long-distance flights, including the first non-stop crossing of the Atlantic by Captain John Alcock and Arthur Whitten Brown on 14/15 June 1919

was the Short Bomber, powered by a 250 hp Rolls Royce engine and with a maximum bomb load of 920 lb, twice that of the Caudron G4 which the RNAS also used at that time. With the introduction of the Short Bomber in the autumn of 1916, together with the Caudrons and a few Strutters, the RNAS began a bombing offensive against military and industrial targets in Germany and on German naval forces at Ostend and Zeebrugge, although not on the scale that had been planned.

The Short Bomber had a range of over 400 miles, which enabled it to raid targets far behind the front line, but its maximum speed was only 77 mph and it was inadequately armed, with only a single Lewis gun on top of the centre-section. Even to reach that the observer had to climb out of his cockpit and stand up on the fuselage. In company with the Caudron bombers, the Short had to be relegated to night bombing.

With the arrival of the Handley Page 0/100 in November 1916 however, the RNAS was able to increase its operations. The first two bombers were delivered to the 5th Wing at Dunkirk; a third landed by accident behind the enemy lines and was studied in great detail by the Germans. The first raids by the 0/100 were carried out in daylight, and it proved to be a formidable bomber, able to carry three times the load of the Short Bomber and six times that of the DH 4 day-bomber which had also just been brought into service. In the meantime the capability of fighter aircraft had also advanced, and when one of the valuable Handley Page bombers was brought down into the sea (admittedly after sinking an enemy destroyer), the type was used only for night bombing. Raids were directed mainly against U-boat bases, railway centres and airfields, while four aircraft were brought back to England for anti-submarine patrols over the North Sea. One machine made a remarkable flight from England to the island of Lemnos in the Aegean Sea, with stops in Paris, Rome and the Balkans. In June 1917 it bombed the Turkish capital of Constantinople, but on a second attempt two months later it came down into the sea with engine failure and the crew were taken prisoner, including the pilot, Flt-Lt J. Alcock (later one of the first two men to fly the Atlantic non-stop).

New fuel system

In the spring of 1917 the Germans began a systematic campaign to bomb London and other targets in England, using large bomber aircraft far more frightening than the Zeppelins. In retaliation, the British War Cabinet decided to launch a strategic bombing offensive against German cities and industrial targets. The task was given to Major General Hugh Trenchard, then commanding the RFC in France. In October 1917 he formed the 41st Wing at Ochey from where it was possible to reach German towns in the Saar, and such cities as Karlsruhe, Mainz, Koblenz, Cologne, Frankfurt and Stuttgart. In addition to the RFC day-bombers (FE 2bs and DH 4s), the Wing included a RNAS squadron of Handley Page 0/100s for night bombing. These were more effective than the day-bombers and led to the development of an improved version, the 0/400, which became the most widely used of the Handley Page types; some 400 were delivered before the end of the war, compared with less than fifty of the 0/100.

One of the features of the 0/400 was a completely redesigned fuel system, in which the fuel tanks were moved from the engine nacelles to a position above the bomb-bay, thus enabling the nacelles to be considerably shortened. The crew consisted of a pilot who sat in the main cockpit, a bomb-aimer who doubled as front gunner and observer from a cockpit in the extreme nose of the fuselage, and one or two rear gunners who occupied a cockpit in the mid-section just behind the wings. The bombs were suspended nose-upwards in separate honeycomb cells in the bomb-bay, each covered by a door which was pushed open by the weight of the falling bomb and closed by a spring. The bombs were released by cables from the nose cockpit where a bomb sight was mounted externally. One or two Lewis guns were mounted in both nose and rear cockpits; in the latter position, one gun was fired sideways or backwards from a raised platform while the other, when carried, could be fired downwards and backwards through a trapdoor in the floor.

Although starting the war with very

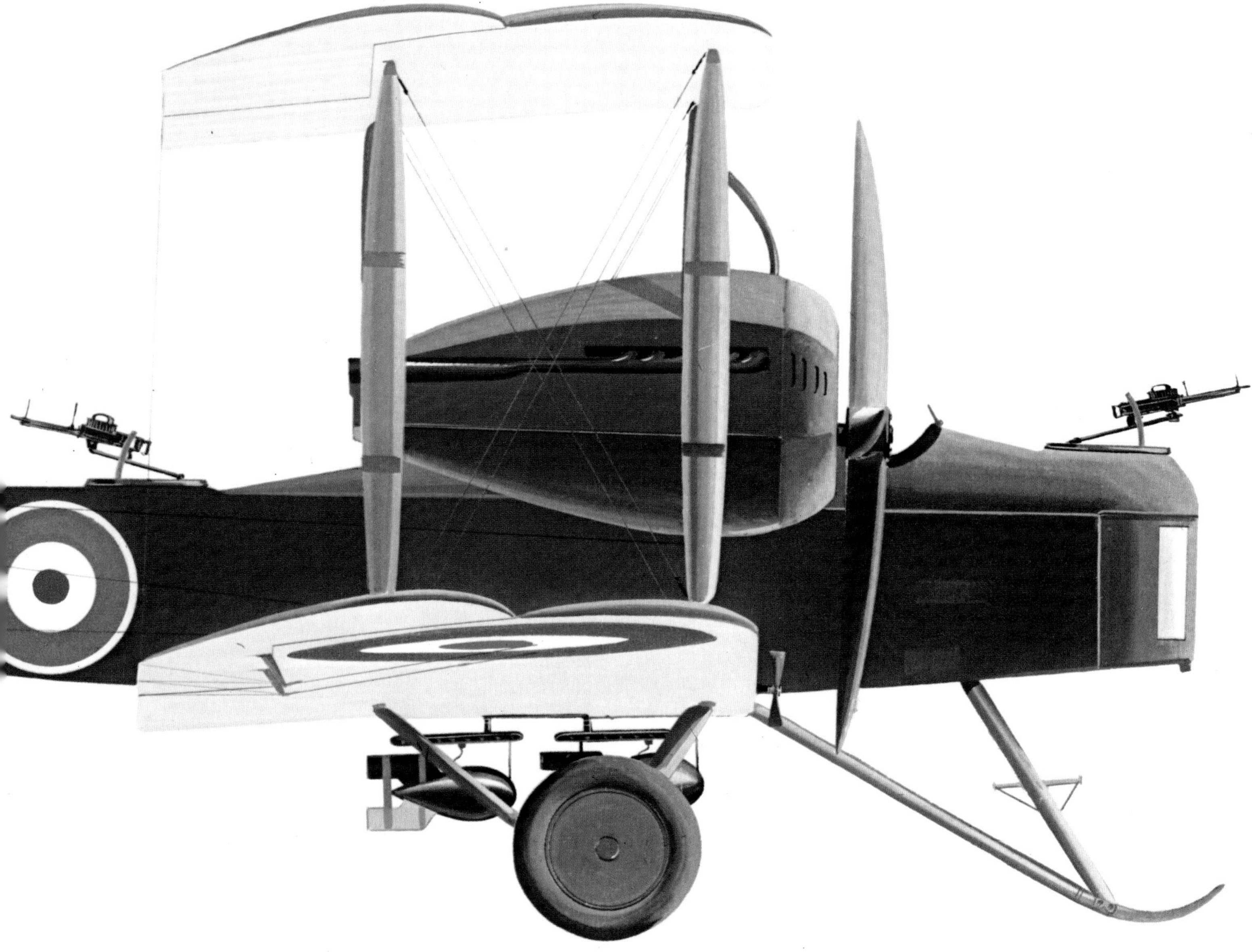

different functions, the RNAS and RFC had come to co-operate with each other for many operations, including Trenchard's strategic bombing wing which was later re-designated the VIII Brigade. During the last two years of the war there was a complete reorganisation of British military aircraft development in which the army followed the navy's policy of leaving aircraft design and manufacture to private industry. The Royal Aircraft Factory at Farnborough (which, in spite of some failures, produced in the SE 5a one of the best Allied fighters of the war) was directed to concentrate solely on research.

On 1 April 1918 the RNAS and RFC were merged into one service, the Royal Air Force, with the prime intention of pooling resources for a sustained strategic bombing campaign against Germany. Under the command of General (later Marshal of the RAF, Viscount) Trenchard, who was directly responsible to the newly formed Air Ministry, the RAF was the world's first major independent air service. On 6 June the strategic bombing wing he had previously commanded became the famous Independent Force of the RAF.

The Handley Page night bombers contributed a large proportion of the 665 tons of bombs dropped by the Independent Force and its predecessors the 41st Wing and VIII Brigade. One daring attack made was on the Badische Anilin factory at Ludwigshafen during the night of 25 August when the two Handley Pages came down to 200 and 500 feet respectively to place their bombs with the greatest accuracy, in spite of the searchlights and heavy anti-aircraft fire. This was no mean hazard by that stage of the war, considering the great advances made in the development of anti-aircraft defences. In raids during a single night the following month, six of the large bombers were brought down by anti-aircraft fire while attacking Saarbrücken and Trier. The five night bombing squadrons which were in operation during the last months of the war suffered eighty-seven crew members killed or missing and 148 aircraft destroyed. In the latter stages, the bombers were often employed against tactical targets to support the Allied offensives, and 220 tons of the bombs dropped were on enemy airfields, destroying many aircraft. From September onwards the Handley Pages often employed 1,650-lb bombs; one dropped on Kaiserlautern wiped out an entire factory.

Great secrecy

In order to carry an even bigger bomb load of 7,500 lb from bases in Britain to Berlin, including a single 3,300-pounder, the Handley-Page V/1500 was built in great secrecy in Belfast. Six had been delivered by the time the Armistice was signed, although none were used operationally. Nevertheless the V/1500 marked a triumph for British aeronautical development, with 126-foot wings which could still be folded, four 375 hp Rolls Royce Eagle VIII engines and a tail gun position which could be reached by climbing along a cat-walk. With a combat range of 1,200 miles and a maximum speed of just under 100 mph, it showed how far the design of bomber aircraft had advanced since the days of the Avro 504 and symbolised the policy of long-range strategic bombing on which Trenchard set such importance. It was a policy which was continued after the war and culminated in the RAFs mighty Bomber Command striking force of the Second World War. Two other heavy bombers were also developed for use by the Independent Force but, like the V/1500, arrived too late to see operational service. These were the twin-engined three-seater DH 10 Amiens and Vickers Vimy. The Amiens operated as a mail carrier after the war while the Vimy achieved fame with a series of record long distance flights, including the first non-stop crossing of the Atlantic by Alcock and Brown and the first flight from Britain to Australia.

One of the myths of early aviation history was that the Handley Page 0/100 which had been captured after accidentally landing behind German lines in November 1916 was used as a model for Germany's own heavy bombers, the famous Gotha biplanes, which appeared shortly afterwards. This was certainly not true for even before the war German designers including Count von Zeppelin had drawn up plans for multi-engined aircraft. But the main effort was concentrated on building airships, and it was only with the realisation that lighter-than-air craft were too vulnerable that development was pushed ahead on heavy bombers.

Even earlier, however, the Germans had produced twin-engined aircraft which were used as bombers. Late in 1914 the Friedrichshafen company, though mainly concerned with the design and construction of naval seaplanes, built the GI bomber, a twin-engined pusher biplane with a biplane tail unit. This did not enter production, but it did lead to the G II, small numbers of which entered service in late 1916. Powered by two 200 hp Benz engines and able to carry a bomb-load of about 1,000 lb, it had two Parabellum machine-guns for defensive armament, one in the nose and the other in a dorsal position. A larger and more powerful development was the G III, with 260 hp six-cylinder water-cooled Mercedes engines, a monoplane tail unit, and the ability to carry over twice the bomb-load. This was the main production model of the Friedrichshafen G series which entered service in early 1917. It carried a crew of three in the central fuselage area and an interesting feature of its design was the steel-tube frame of the square-section fuselage, covered with wood at the nose and tail and fabric over the central part. Modifications to later models included a return to the biplane tail unit on the G IIIa and tractor propellers on the G IV.

The Friedrichshafen types were generally similar in design to the series of twin-engined bombers produced by the Gothaer company, and together they formed the mainstay of the German bomber units (*Bombengeschwadern*) from 1916 until the end of the war. The principle Gotha types were the G IV and G V and it was their ability to fly at a high altitude – over 20,000 feet – carrying a bomb-load of 1,000 lb in external racks that made them ideal for taking over long-range bombing duties from Zeppelin airships. Another asset was that in addition to the usual machine-gun in the front cockpit, they had a second machine-gun mounted behind the wings, which could fire not only upwards, but also downwards and rearwards beneath the tail, for defence against fighters attacking from behind and below.

Terrifying raids

Although the first aeroplane raid on London took place on 28 November 1916, when a single LVG CII dropped six 22-lb bombs near Victoria, it was the Gotha which introduced a new and terrifying form of warfare by a succession of day and night raids on the city from May 1917 to May 1918. The first attempt, by a formation of twenty-one bombers on 25 May 1917, ended when they had to turn back because of heavy cloud and dropped their bombs on towns in Kent instead, killing nearly one hundred civilians. There was an outcry from the British public who, congratulating themselves that the Zeppelin menace had been overcome, now had to face daylight raids with no warning of the enemy's approach.

Worse was to follow. On 13 June a formation of fourteen Gothas led by Hauptmann Brandenburg circled over London with contemptuous ease, in full view of people watching from below. They dropped nearly one hundred bombs, mostly in the region of Liverpool Street station, killing 162 people and wounding 438 – higher casualties than all the Zeppelin raids had caused, and more than any single bombing attack on Britain during the entire war. Although ninety-two fighter aircraft took off from various parts of England, the bombers were able to fly at an even greater altitude on the way home, lightened of their bombs, and had disappeared by the time the fighters could climb to that height. Not a single bomber was lost in the raid.

In spite of the serious situation in France, where every aircraft was needed, two squadrons of the latest fighters – SE5as and Sopwith Pups – had to be withdrawn to help protect London from bombing. It was this dissipation of the Allied war effort on the Western Front, together with the effect on morale at home, which was the greatest success of the Gotha raids. Gradually, with strengthened fighter units and a complete reorganisation of anti-aircraft gun defences, the British began to take a heavy toll of the Gotha bombers, and in September they were forced to turn to night bombing. By this time they were being supported by the R-class bombers, produced by several different companies, but generally known as Zeppelin Staaken 'Giants'. They were the

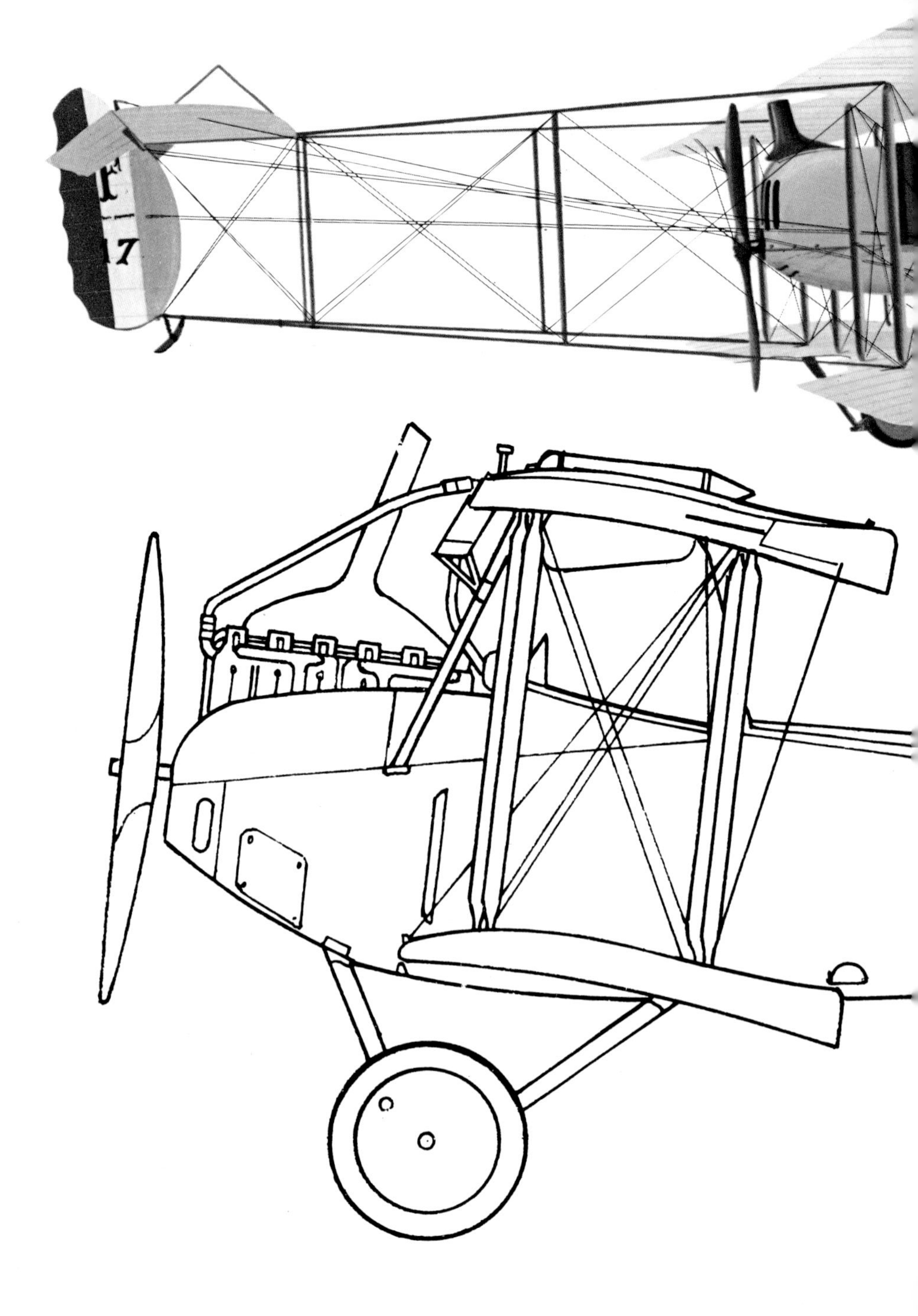

ZEPPELIN (STAAKEN) R VI

Gross weight: 25,265 lb **Span**: 138 ft 6 in **Length**: 72 ft 6 in **Engine**: 4×260 hp Mercedes D IVa **Armament**: 4 machine-guns **Crew**: 7 **Speed**: 81 mph at ground level **Ceiling**: 12,460 ft **Range**: 7–10 hrs **Bomb load**: 18×220 lb

The only one of the German R-type Giants to be produced in any quantity, employed on night raids over Britain and France in 1917 and 1918

BLACKBURN KANGAROO

Gross weight: 8,017 lb **Span**: 74 ft 10 in **Length**: 46 ft **Engine**: 2×250 hp Rolls Royce Falcon **Armament**: 2×·303 Lewis machine-guns **Crew**: 4 **Speed**: 100 mph at ground level **Ceiling**: 10,500 ft **Range**: 4 hrs **Bomb load**: 1,040 lb

A landplane development of the Blackburn G.P. seaplane of 1916, delivered to the RAF in 1918 and used mostly for anti-submarine patrols

FARMAN F60

Gross weight: 12,700 lb **Span**: 57 ft 8 in **Length**: 30 ft **Engine**: 2×190 hp Renault **Armament**: 1 Hotchkiss machine-gun **Crew**: 2 **Speed**: 96 mph at ground level **Ceiling**: 18,000 ft **Range**: 2½ hrs

The first of the French Goliath heavy night bombers which appeared towards the end of the war and afterwards, in its civil version, widely used in French commercial fleets until the late 1920s

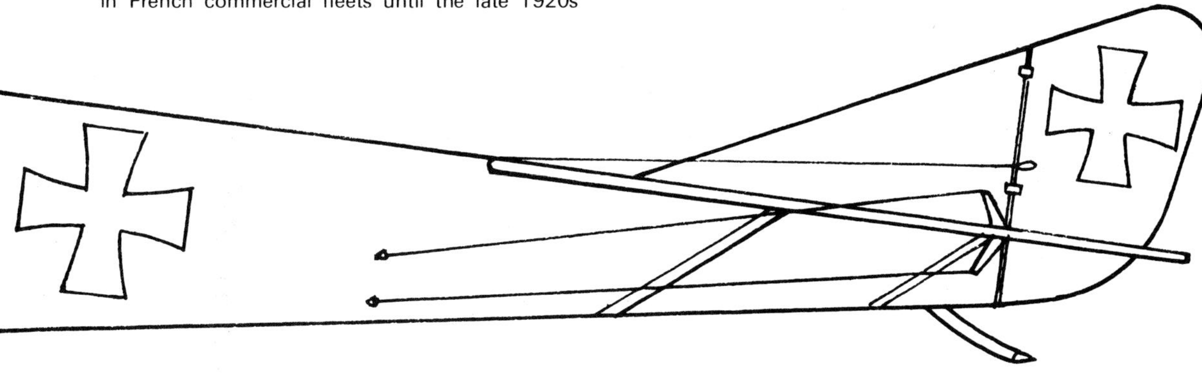

LVG CII

Gross weight: 3,091 lb Span: 42 ft 2 in **Length**: 26 ft 7 in **Engine**: 160 hp Mercedes D III **Armament**: 1 or 2×7·92-mm machine-guns **Crew**: 2 **Speed**: 81 mph at ground level **Ceiling**: 10,000 ft **Range**: 4 hrs **Bomb load**: 150 lb

A light bomber, as well as one of the newly-established C class of armed two-seater reconnaissance aircraft introduced by the Germans at the end of 1915, this plane is credited with the first daylight raid on London, which took place in November 1916

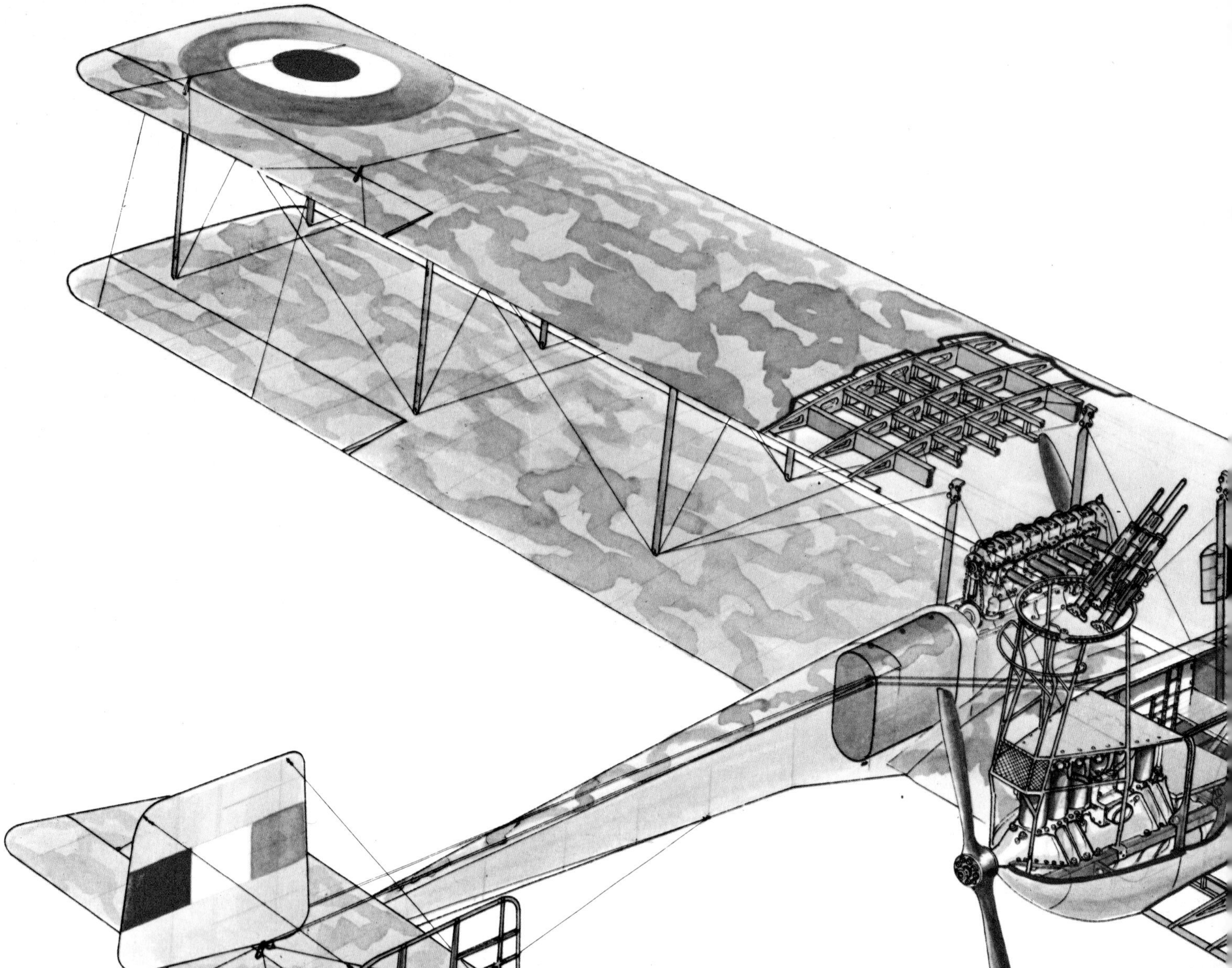

CAPRONI Ca 45

Gross weight: 11,460 lb **Span**: 76 ft 9 in **Length**: 41 ft 10 in **Engines**: 3×Isotta Fraschini 250 hp **Armament**: 4 machine guns **Crew**: 4 **Speed**: 93 mph **Ceiling**: 13,800 ft **Range**: 4 hrs **Bomb load**: 1,000 lb

The Ca 4 series were developed into seaplanes as well as torpedo bombers for shipping strikes. Caproni-design bombers were considered to be some of the most advanced of the First World War

Right: detail of Caproni cockpit construction: 600 hp Ca 5

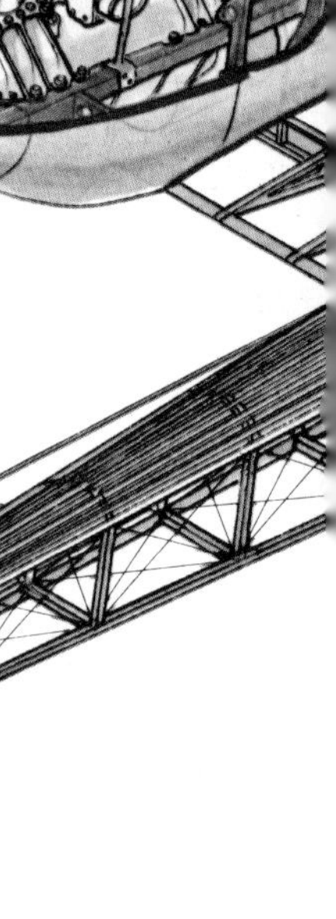

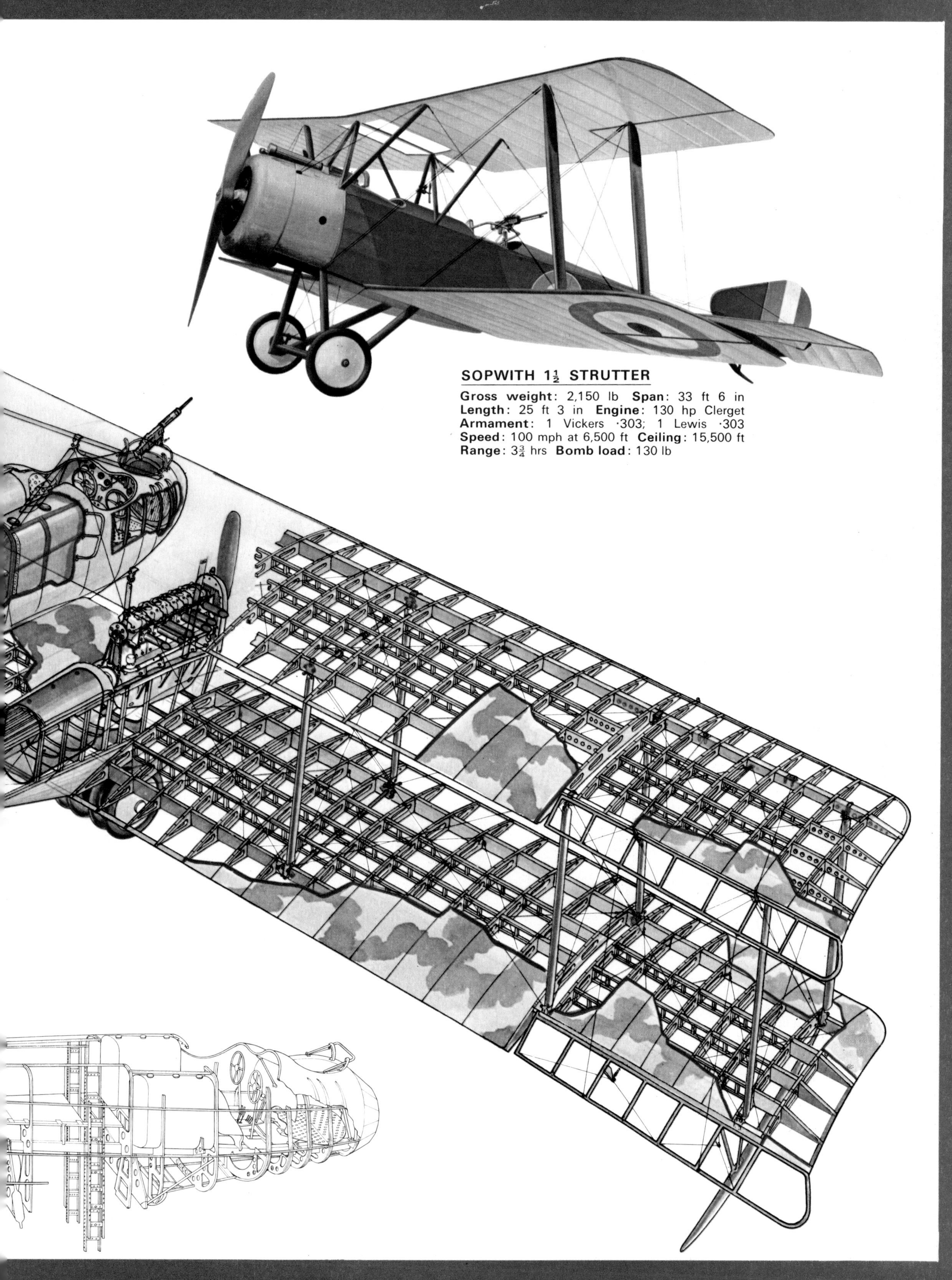

SOPWITH 1½ STRUTTER
Gross weight: 2,150 lb Span: 33 ft 6 in
Length: 25 ft 3 in Engine: 130 hp Clerget
Armament: 1 Vickers ·303; 1 Lewis ·303
Speed: 100 mph at 6,500 ft Ceiling: 15,500 ft
Range: 3¾ hrs Bomb load: 130 lb

biggest and in some respects the most remarkable aircraft of the war, and were produced only as single examples or in very small numbers.

The first of these leviathans to appear was the VGO I, with a wing span of over 138 ft, powered by three 240 hp Maybach engines, which flew for the first time in April 1915. The engine power was not sufficient for the huge, nine-ton aircraft and the later VGO III had six 160 hp Mercedes engines instead. Two of these were mounted in tandem in each of the port and starboard nacelles, driving pusher propellers, with the other pair side-by-side in the nose of the fuselage driving a single tractor propeller. After various modifications the R VI appeared in mid-1917 (the 'R' designation standing for *Riesenflugzeug* – giant aeroplane). This was the only type to be produced in any quantity.

The nose-mounted engines were abandoned and instead, four Maybach or Mercedes 260 hp engines were mounted in tandem pairs between the wings, driving tractor and pusher propellers. The nose cockpit was fitted with a machine-gun and the release mechanism for the eighteen 220-lb bombs carried internally. Two guns were located in a dorsal position and another two ventrally. The main cockpit was enclosed and the usual crew was seven. So great was the weight (nearly twelve tons fully loaded) that the undercarriage consisted of no less than eighteen wheels, two of which were under the nose.

In July 1917 the giant R-class bombers were first flown operationally on the Eastern Front, and gained some successes in attacks on railways and military installations. Between August and February the following year they were transferred to the Western Front and used initially for night raids on Britain, usually escorted by Gothas. In eleven such raids, during which single 2,200-lb bombs (the largest used in the war) were occasionally dropped, not one Giant was lost in action. The Gothas were less fortunate however, mainly because pilots of such improved fighters as the Sopwith Camel had learned to fly and intercept at night. After a raid on the night of 19 May 1918, when seven Gothas out of forty-three aircraft sent to attack London and Dover were shot down by fighters and ground fire, the German High Command ordered a stop to the bombing of Britain.

In fifty-two raids on Britain, one more than were carried out by airships, German aircraft achieved a statistically better result, killing 857 people and injuring a further 2,058. Just under £1,500,000 worth of damage was caused for the expenditure of only 2,772 bombs totalling about 196 tons.

Although the loss of life and amount of damage caused was hardly significant compared with what was happening in France, the psychological effect was considerable. This, however, operated to the detriment of Germany, for the anger aroused was directly responsible for retaliatory raids by the British, and was one of the factors which led to the merger of the RNAS and RFC to form the RAF.

The Giants continued to make bombing raids over Paris until those too were stopped. Thereafter they were used singly for tactical attacks on military targets a few miles behind the Allied lines, but it was a serious mishandling of machines that had been developed for long-range strategic bombing. They were too slow and made too big a target to operate successfully in the battle zone, and casualties were very heavy.

A better aircraft for tactical purposes was the other main type of twin-engined bomber built by the Germans, the AEG series.

This was a development of the K I three-seat general purpose biplane of 1915, later re-designated the G I when the Germans decided on the classification *Grossflugzeug* (big aeroplane) for all such types, irrespective of manufacturer. This model was used mainly on the Eastern Front during 1915 and, like the G II which followed, was only built in small numbers. The G III which began to appear in December 1915 carried a 660-lb bomb load and two machine-guns for defence. The major production model however was the G IV which came into service towards the end of 1916, powered by two 260 hp Mercedes engines driving four-blade opposite-rotating propellers. Neither its bomb load of 770 lb, nor its range – about 350 miles against the Gotha's 550 – could compare with those of the Gotha and other big bombers, but its speed of over 100 mph made it very suitable for attacking short-

A.E.G. G IV

Gross weight: 7,986 lb **Span**: 60 ft 2 in **Length**: 32 ft 4 in **Engine**: 2×260 hp Mercedes D IVa **Armament**: 3 machine-guns **Crew**: 4 **Speed**: 103 mph at ground level **Ceiling**: 13,100 ft **Range**: 4–5 hrs **Bomb load**: 770 lb

LINKE HOFFMAN R1

Gross weight: 19,845 lb **Span**: 105 ft $\frac{1}{2}$ in **Length**: 51 ft $\frac{1}{2}$ in **Engine**: 4×260 hp Mercedes (internal); 2 propellers **Armament**: 5×7·92-mm machine-guns **Crew**: 6 **Speed**: 87 mph **Ceiling**: 12,200 ft **Range**: 4 hrs **Bomb load**: proposed 2,000 lb

Experimental machine covered with transparent cellon to make it 'invisible' in the air

range tactical targets and for photographic reconnaissance. A larger version, the G V, with a biplane tail unit and a bomb load of 1,320-lb was beginning to appear at the end of the war.

Although the French made a number of spectacular day and night bombing raids in the early months of the war, mainly through the efforts of enthusiasts like Laurens, Happe and Göys, the French High Command was not very impressed with the results.

Towards the end of 1915 the bomber groups which had been built up under the command of Commandant de Göys were split up and the aircraft dispersed among various army commanders. In fact, the French showed little interest in any long-range strategic bombing during the war, largely due to Marshal Foch's obsessive desire to win the war through ground attack alone. The Independent Force of the RAF was originally intended to include French bomber squadrons but these never materialised. Consequently, France was much slower than the other major powers in developing large twin-engined specialised bombers.

The first to appear, in mid-1917, was the Letord 3, one of a series of three-seat aircraft designed for reconnaissance, fighter and night bombing roles by Colonel Dorand of the French Service Technique, and built in relatively small numbers in the last two years of the war. The Letord 3 had the characteristic back-staggered wings of other types in the series, and was powered by two 200 hp Hispano engines. A better version was the Letord 5 which was of sesquiplane configuration (the lower wing being half the size of the upper) with 220 hp Lorraine engines giving a speed of nearly 100 mph. It could carry a bomb load of 440 lb and two machine-guns. The Letord 7 which appeared in 1918 had the same wing arrangement as the Letord 3 only larger, and was notable for the cannon mounted in the nose of the fuselage in place of a machine-gun. Only the Letord 9, with a wing span of 85 feet and two 400 hp Liberty engines, began to match the Handley Page bombers, and that only flew in prototype before the war ended.

The only big French bomber to see any service during the last months of the war was the two-seat Farman F50, powered by two 265 hp Lorraine engines mounted on the lower wing on either side of the fuselage and resembling the general lines of the Gotha. Eight 165-lb bombs could be carried under the fuselage between the legs of the undercarriage, and the bomb aimer/gunner sat in the nose of the fuselage, in front of the pilot's cockpit. Only two Voisin units were re-equipped with F50s at the time of the Armistice, while a few were flown by the American Expeditionary Forces in France. The prototype of a larger bomber, the excellent Farman F60 Goliath, first flew in 1918 and, although too late for the war, it later became the standard French night bomber. Another type which was too late to see war service was the Caudron C23 powered by two 260 hp Salmson engines. In fact, a smaller Caudron twin-engined aeroplane, the G4, had been used for bombing since the spring of 1915, but it was too slow and poorly armed for daylight raids. Even in night bombing it suffered many casualties, and it was withdrawn the following year to be used mostly for training.

In general, all the big bombers that were built and brought into operation during the last two years of the war – the Capronis, Handley Pages, Gothas and Zeppelin-Staakens – were quickly transferred from day to night bombing as the capabilities of fighter aircraft improved and ground anti-aircraft defences became better organised. Such big aircraft, which after the war were to be of vital importance in the development of passenger airliners, were too expensive and in too short supply to be risked in hazardous daytime operations. Even at night they sometimes suffered heavy casualties – for instance, over one-third of the Handley Pages of the Independent Force were lost.

Night bombing inevitably was much less accurate than day operations but there were some targets, especially military installations, which required a high degree of accuracy if any success was to be achieved. There was an obvious need for smaller and faster bombers which could elude – or battle their way through – fighter opposition by day. These proved to be some of the best aircraft types produced during the war.

1915-16: THE FIGHTER COMES OF AGE

Early 1915 saw important innovations in the techniques of air warfare. Inspired by a French attempt, Fokker invented for the Germans an interrupter gear which permitted a machine gun to fire forward through the airscrew, and at the same time the French originated organised air fighting. *Below:* The charred remains of an Albatros and its pilot. *Right:* Allied fighters such as this Nieuport were still handicapped by inadequate armament

ECP Armées

Imperial War Museum

On April 18, 1915, an event which was to have extreme importance in the history of aerial fighting took place. A well-placed rifle bullet fired by a rifleman named Schlenstedt, defending Courtrai railway station, fractured the petrol pipe on a Morane-Saulnier monoplane in which the well-known French pilot Roland Garros (who had been the first to cross the Mediterranean by air, from Bizerta to St Raphael) was attacking the line. Garros landed, but before he could set fire to his machine it was captured by the Germans. The secret was then out: Garros, who had destroyed several German aircraft in the previous few weeks, was found to have a machine gun able to fire forwards through the airscrew.

The propeller, which was armoured with steel deflectors to avoid damage from the aircraft's own bullets, was shown to the Dutchman, Anthony Herman Gerard Fokker, whose M 5 monoplane was then undergoing service trials, and within 48 hours Fokker was claiming to have invented an interrupter gear to prevent bullets hitting the screw. But then Fokker's brilliance as a demonstration pilot was equalled only by his unscrupulousness and his flair for public relations. The irony in the situation lies in the fact that Fokker's new monoplane, which went into service as the E1 (*Eindekker*—monoplane), had been designed only after Fokker had acquired and analysed a Morane. Furthermore, Saulnier of Morane-Saulnier had himself invented and tried an interrupter gear but had discarded it because of the unreliable performance of service ammunition. He saw steel deflector plates as an improvement, and he may have been right in the early war years. 'Bad rounds' continued to bedevil machines with interrupter and synchronising gears on both sides throughout the war. This, rather than official stupidity, could possibly be the reason why the notion of using the airscrew to fire a gun had not been adopted before, though it is unlikely. Several patents existed besides that of Franz Schneider, the Swiss aeronautical engineer working first for the French Nieuport and later for the German LVG companies, whose device not only closely resembled Fokker's new 'invention' but had already been flown operationally in an LVG E VI monoplane which, according to one account, was shot down by rifle fire from the Morane two-seater of the French Sergeant Gilbert in December 1914. It is more likely, however, that it crashed as a result of structural failure. Drawings of the gear had also been published in *Scientific American*.

The 'Fokker Scourge'

If, however, the Fokker monoplane and its gun were not new, they were certainly *ben trovato*. They came at a time when the German air service was being remodelled and liberally dosed with 'offensive spirit' by a new *Chef des Feldflugwesens* (Chief of Field Operations), following a period of dreadful docility during which French Voisin and Farman bombers had raided the Fatherland unmolested, inflicting damage which had inspired notices on Rhineland walls saying *'Gott strafe England—und unsere Flieger!'* (God smite England—and our own airmen!) The outcry which followed the 'Fokker Scourge', so richly dramatised in the House of Commons during 1915/16, therefore had its German counterpart many months before. In the face of unarmed two-seater Type B reconnaissance biplanes and a German air service then forming part of an amorphous, largely 'chairborne' transport command, the machine gun carrying Voisins of the *1er Groupe de Bombardement* (GB 1) had had things all their own way. It is arguable therefore that the seminal aircraft of 1915 was not a Fokker monoplane at all, but Gabriel Voisin's *type treize-cinquante* (13·50 metre) which could not only bomb but shoot down defenceless *B-Flugzeuge*. The reason the Fokker caused such a stir when Immelmann scored his first victory on August 1, 1915, is very simple: the Germans had begun to shoot back.

Meanwhile at home, Major Siegert was appointed second in command to the new *Feldflugchef*, a very able 48-year-old staff officer of wide experience named Major Hermann von der Lieth-Thomsen. Thomsen's cry was: 'We've got the men, now give us machines!' The *Inspektion der Fliegertruppen, Idflieg* for short, was gingered up, industry organised and communications between Berlin and all fronts streamlined in every way. The German and Austrian motor car industries, drawing upon prewar racing experience, had already doubled the horse power of their 1914 designs, the specification of which had called for 80-100 hp. Mark II engines had been giving 120 hp reliably, and the Mark IIIs were now emerging, mainly in overhead-valve water-cooled six-cylinder-in line form, offering 150, 160 or even a claimed 180 hp, to power a new generation of greatly improved airframes.

The A-class monoplanes were already dead, and the B-class of unarmed two-seater biplanes was ripe for replacement by the *C-Flugzeuge* which would not only have more power and consequently a greater speed, higher ceiling and better climb, but in most cases the tremendous advantage of a 'sting in the tail', namely a defensive Parabellum MG14 light machine gun developed by DWM, makers of the famous infantry Luger automatic pistol. This armament had been under development since November 1914, and the C-class began to emerge, complete with an effective gun-ring for the observer's cockpit: the Rumpler C I (160 hp Mercedes D III), Albatros C I (160 hp Mercedes D III or 150 hp Benz Bz III) and Aviatik C I (Mercedes D III). The most important of these, perhaps, was the Albatros, for it was while flying aircraft of this type that Oswald Boelcke began to evolve the first techniques of air fighting. The Aviatik was less satisfactory, for in it the observer was still encaged beneath the centre section, as in the obsolete B-class machines, and virtually unable to use his gun. The 'standard' British observation machine of the period, designed at the Royal Aircraft Factory, Farnborough, and produced by innumerable sub-contractors, never lost its archaic 'B-class' layout: a BE2c pilot sat in the rear seat, while his observer struggled helplessly in the front seat, hedged about by wings, fuselage, wires and struts.

Ullstein

Above: The German **Fokker E III** monoplane, which wrought havoc among the Allied air forces almost entirely because of its interrupter-geared armament. *Engine:* Oberursel UI 9-cylinder rotary, 100 hp. *Armament:* one or two LMG .08 machine guns synchronised to fire through propeller. *Speed:* 87 mph at ground level. *Climb rate:* 700 feet per minute. *Span:* 31 feet 2¾ inches. *Length:* 23 feet 7½ inches *Opposite page:* Austrian troops on the Eastern Front man a primitive, entrenched anti-aircraft machine gun position

At first, however, BE pilots quite held their own, even against the Fokker E III. One such 'joyous scrap' is documented from both sides. On December 29 Lieutenant Sholto Douglas (later Marshal of the RAF Lord Douglas of Kirtleside) made a reconnaissance to Cambrai and St Quentin escorted by another BE of No 8 Squadron. Near Cambrai, says Douglas's report: 'We were set upon by six Huns. Glen, my escort, was shot down, followed by two of the Huns. I was then set upon by the remainder. Child, my observer, downed one Hun. We fought the remaining three for half an hour. Petrol began to get low and engine sump was hit. So, relying on the stability of the BE 2c as against the Fokker, I came down in steep spiral to 10 feet above the ground.' This fight is described from the German side as well, for one of the Fokkers was flown by Lieutenant Oswald Boelcke, who in one of his letters home describes Douglas as 'a tough fellow who defended himself stoutly'. Boelcke forced the BE down from 6,500 feet to 3,000 feet when, he says, it should have been an easy matter to shoot the Englishman down because he had mortally wounded his observer, but Boelcke had been in two previous fights and now ran out of ammunition. The two continued to circle round one another but neither could do the other any harm. 'Finally Immelmann came to the rescue and the fight began all over again. We managed to force him down to 300 feet and waited for him to land.' Fortunately Immelmann's gun jammed, as machine guns of all makes did at that time, and Douglas was able to land just behind the French lines.

There is more about this encounter in Lord Douglas's book *Years of Combat*, published in 1963. He comments on his lucky escape, and explains that Child, his observer, was not in fact killed. 'Oswald Boelcke was led into believing that he had killed my observer because Child, who was facing backwards and firing over my head, became so physically sick through the violence of the way in which I was having to toss our aircraft about that he finally fell over and threw up all over me.' So much for the story that BE 2cs were too inherently stable to be thrown about. It should be noted, too, that in this fight Lieutenant Child shot down one of the Fokkers and Douglas records that Glen, his escort, had shot down another a few days before.

In the early days of the Fokker menace there was controversy amongst BE pilots as to the best thing to do. Some, including Douglas, advised turning in under the Fokker as it dived to attack, thus getting out of the way, others, of whom Glen was one, believed in holding a steady course to provide one's observer with a steady gun-platform. It is interesting to note that the RFC (and especially the Third Wing) were sending at least one escort with each reconnaissance aircraft, while Boelcke and Immelmann were still stalking on their own, not as a pair. Tactics were still highly personal. The usual Fokker method was to attack in a dive; it is uncertain whether the famous 'Immelmann turn', in which the pilot pulls up into the first half of a loop to gain height then stall turns to face his adversary again, was Immelmann's own invention or that of the Bristol Scout pilot Gordon Bell during a brush with an *Eindekker*. It was certainly effective. So was a ploy used by the peacetime actor and Gun Bus pilot Robert Loraine of No 5 Squadron, obeying his CO's injunction to be 'more aggressive'. 'I had asked Lubbock (the observer) to hold his fire until I gave him the order, for I meant to engage at the closest possible quarters. As we drew near to the German, approaching each other nose to nose, I pretended to outclimb him. He opened fire at about 400 yards, and I stood my machine almost on its tail to lure him on. As he came, I quickly dived, passing just below him with about five feet between my upper plane and his wheels, firing from both guns meanwhile, continuous fire with the enemy pilot as target.' The Albatros fell 20 yards behind the British front-line trenches; Loraine, having over-revved his engine in a dive, force-landed neatly in a ploughed field. At this time the Gun Bus was employed on *ad hoc* tactical duties, for example, to drive away aircraft interfering with wire-cutting near Ypres. After Loraine had fitted experimentally a 110-hp Le Rhône engine and coarse-pitch propeller in place of the 80-hp Monosoupape Gnôme, the Vickers was found to be 4 mph faster than a BE 2c. Individual aircraft varied enormously, a fact which must be borne in mind when assessing published figures for speed and climb. For example, Loraine tested a BE 2c, taking one hour to reach 6,300 feet and one hour 30 minutes to reach 8,200 feet. With a similar engine in the same airframe he reached 8,700 feet in an hour.

First fighter units

As has been seen, however, before there could be a 'Fokker Scourge' there had to be a Morane and a Garros. Morane-Saulnier monoplanes had been used for racing before the war, when their clean monoplane lines and rounded fuselage cross-section made them highly competitive, despite the drag of cabane, bracing and the external wires by which the wings were warped.

Late in 1914, J. B. McCudden had used a rifle while flying as observer with Captain Conran of No 3 Squadron RFC on private offensive patrols; in January he reported that the squadron had received two Lewis machine guns for its Moranes, and the latter were being fitted with 'machine gun racks'. Similar offensive patrols were flown in Sopwith Tabloid, Martinsyde Scout, Bristol Scout and other fast single-seaters by picked pilots in the RNAS and RFC. A 'scout' or two was attached to each squadron, rather as riding-schools kept a hunter for the use of star pupils. It is surprising indeed that the term 'hunter' was not coined by the British, for the French already spoke of *avions de chasse*, and it was they who really originated organised air fighting.

Escadrilles de chasse were formed, one for each army. Their duties were to protect Allied reconnaissance machines and to escort bombers. With such practitioners as Garros, Vedrines and Pégoud flying Moranes the results could not be in doubt. Three famous escadrilles flying Moranes were MS 3, under *Commandant* Brocard, MS 23, under *Commandant* de Vergette, and MS 12, whose commander, *Commandant* Tricornot de Rose, did much to evolve the tactics of aerial combat. Passengers were given *mitrailleuses* for offence and defence and single-seater planes were often armed with a fixed machine gun to fire through an armoured propeller.

The world's first fighter aircraft

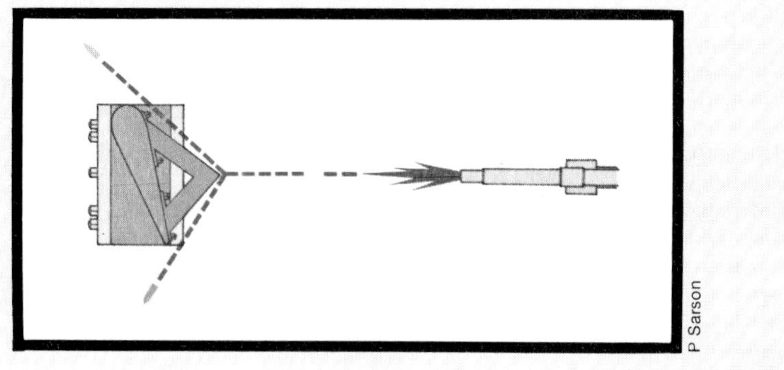
P Sarson

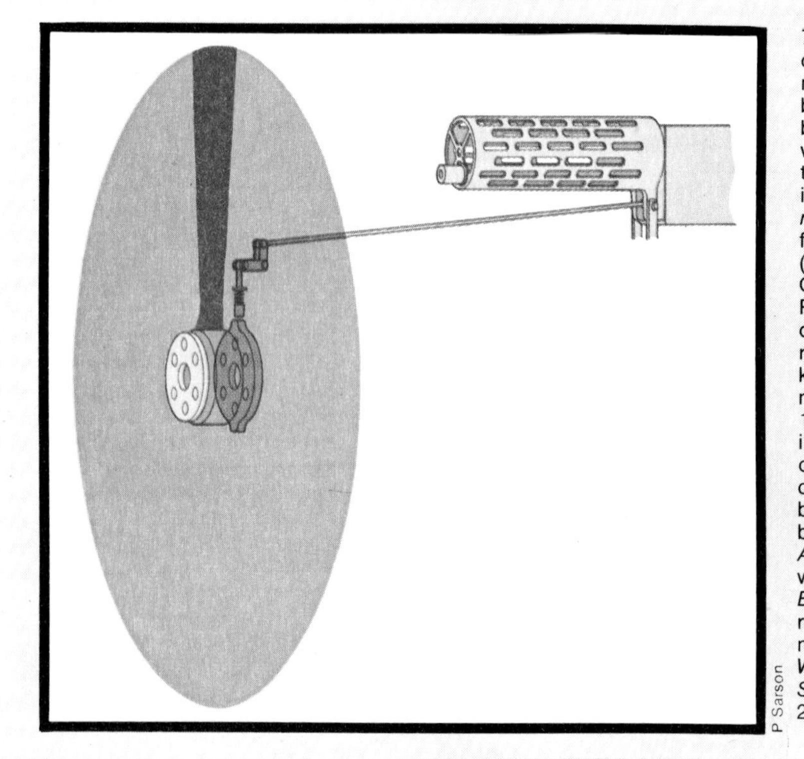
P Sarson

Top left: The Morane-Saulnier deflector gear. Its object was not to interrupt the stream of bullets from the machine gun, but to deflect those few which would otherwise have struck the propeller rather than passing between its blades. *Top: right:* A **Morane-Saulnier N** fitted with the deflector gear. (Contrary to popular belief, Garros was flying a Type L Parasol when he was shot down.) *Engine:* 80 hp Gnôme rotary. *Armament:* One Hotchkiss machine gun. *Speed:* 102 mph at 6,500 feet. *Ceiling:* 13,000 feet. *Length:* 21 feet 11¾ inches. *Left:* The Fokker synchroniser gear. In this gear, the cam aligned with the propeller blade stops the gun firing when blade is in front of the muzzle. *Above:* The **Fokker E 1**, fitted with the interrupter gear. *Engine:* 80 hp Oberursel UO rotary. *Armament:* LMG .08 machine gun. *Speed:* 80 mph. *Weight loaded:* 1,239 pounds. *Span:* 29 feet 3 inches. *Length:* 22 feet 1¾ inches.

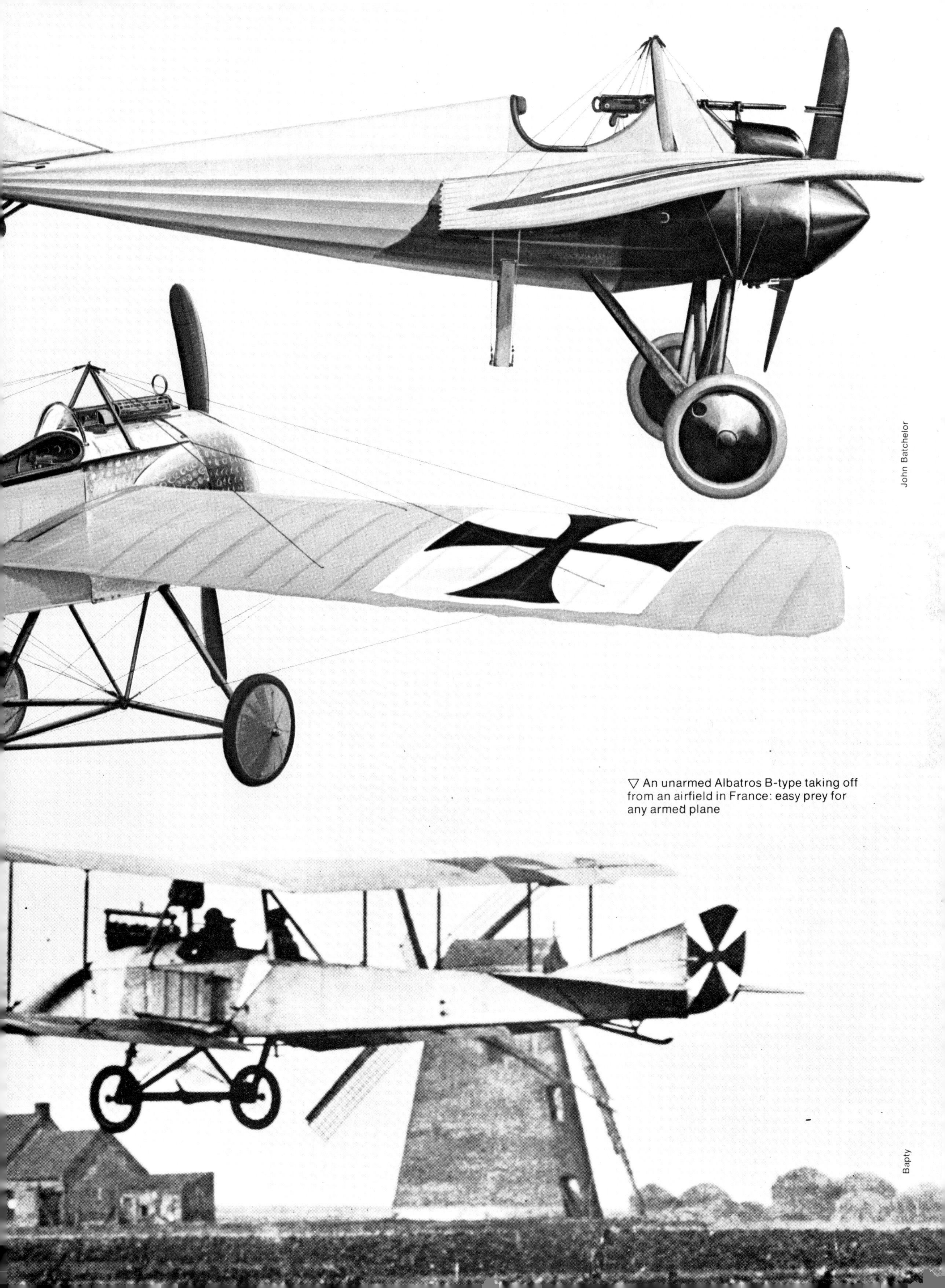

John Batchelor

▽ An unarmed Albatros B-type taking off from an airfield in France: easy prey for any armed plane

Bapty

Roger Viollet

Without a good interrupter gear, efficient armament could only be mounted at the expense of aerodynamic efficiency. This French Farman F40 used a pusher engine and a boom-mounted tailplane

Hardened steel deflector plates impaired the efficiency of the airscrew, but the tactical surprise of bullets coming from an apparently impossible direction brought many victims. Many types of Morane were used, with mid-wing, shoulder wing or a wing mounted above the fuselage, the last-named being known, for obvious reasons, as a 'parasol'. British Morane pilots included Flight-Sub-Lieutenant Warneford, VC, RNAS who brought down a Zeppelin while flying a Morane (he also flew a single-seater with deflectors), and Captain L. A. Strange, whose inventions included an offset Lewis gun-mounting for the pilot.

Garros force-landed his Morane on April 18 but his colleagues continued to score while the Fokker E I was incubating, using not only the single-seater 'Bullet', as the British called the Type N Morane, but also the L-type Parasol two-seater, which Brocard, Guynemer and others often flew solo on offensive patrols.

It may be wondered, in view of the chanciness of using a deflector propeller, and the non-availability of interrupter gears, why somebody did not bring out a fighter with a pusher engine. The answer is that several people had thought of it, and several effective pusher fighters eventually came into service. Two excellent two-seater pushers were in fact flying before the outbreak of war. Vickers exhibited a biplane, the 'Gun-bus', in 1913, and laid down a batch of 50 on their own initiative. Unfortunately the Wolseley engine chosen proved a failure, and the *Monosoupape* Gnôme rotary was not yet available. A rather similar machine with an even more dilatory history was the Royal Aircraft Factory's Farman Experimental (later called Fighting Experimental) FE2b.

The FE2b was easy to arm and made a useful fighting aeroplane. Orders were placed for it on the outbreak of war, but the six-cylinder Green engine chosen proved too heavy and the Beardmore, developed from a prewar Austro-Daimler, took some time to arrive. Two excellent single-seater pusher scouts were also on the stocks well before Immelmann first scored on August 1. The DH2, designed by Captain Geoffrey de Havilland, had undergone flight trials by July 1915 and the FE8, a Farnborough design by J. Kenworthy, had been started at the Factory in May. Contrary to aviation folklore neither of these aircraft was called into being by the Fokker; they were probably seen as an improvement on the Morane. All the same, the central feature which made the Morane and Fokker so effective was not appreciated at the time. The first DH2 had a Lewis gun on a moveable mounting controlled by the pilot. It was not realised that success lay in aiming the aircraft as a whole. This fact renders all the more remarkable the feat brought off by Major Lanoe G. Hawker, of No 6 Squadron RFC on July 25, just six days after another great pilot, Guynemer, had drawn first blood. That evening Hawker brought off a treble. He drove down one German C-class two-seater; another he forced down with a damaged engine; and the third he shot down in flames. All three were armed with machine guns: Hawker's Bristol Scout had one hand-loaded cavalry carbine on the starboard side firing obliquely forward to miss the propeller. He was awarded the VC.

An oblique mounting of this sort, adopted, also for the Strange Lewis gun for BE2c pilots was indeed one solution. Another, adopted on Strange's own Martinsyde scout was a Lewis on the centre section inclined upwards so as to miss the propeller. A quadrant mounting for such a gun was devised by Sergeant Foster of No 11 Squadron RFC. The oddest resolution of the tractor/pusher controversy was adopted by the Royal Aircraft Factory for its experimental BE9, which was basically a BE2c with the engine moved back and a nacelle for the observer rigged forward of the airscrew. Similar arrangements were adopted on the Spad A2.

Between them the Vickers Gun Bus, the FE 2b, and the DH 2 regained the mastery of the air. The Fokker Scourge may be said to have lasted six months. It was exceedingly tough while it lasted, especially to under-trained and inexperienced crews, who now formed a large proportion of the RFC. As Maurice Baring, Trenchard's ADC, wrote at the end of October, the RFC 'had been so used to doing what it wanted without serious opposition that not enough attention was paid to this menace, and the monoplane, in the hands of a pilot like Immelmann, was a serious, and for us a disastrous factor. But the point is that our work never stopped in spite of this. The work of the armies was done, Fokker Scourge or no Fokker Scourge'.

The original Fokker E I, 80-hp monoplane, underwent several changes. With clipped wings and 100-hp Oberursel it was known as the E II; redesigned with 31′ 2¾″ wings this became the most famous *Eindekker* of all, the Fokker E III. A captured 80-hp Le Rhône engine (which had mechanically operated valves, not atmospheric inlet valves like the Oberursel) performed better. Experiments were made with the 160-hp two-row Le Rhône radial from a special French Morane, and by November 1915 a prototype E IV was flying with a two-row 160-hp Oberursel. Armament and synchronising gears also progressed. The classic dive-and-shoot approach required concentrated fire for very short periods. Boelcke asked for and got a twin-Spandau installation. Immelmann asked for three, with the big Le Rhône to carry the extra load. He also had his guns tilted upward at an angle of 15 degrees. Boelcke said they should be aligned in the direction of flight. He reported that the 160-hp E IV was outclimbed by the Nieuport and that performance at height was unsatisfactory. Also, he said the engine quickly lost tune, and that fast turns in the E IV could only be made by blipping the engine off. He recommended the development of a new fighter, preferably a biplane.

Ironically, the worst point of the Fokker was the very feature that had brought it fame. The mechanical synchronising gear linkages gave perpetual trouble, and instances of pilots shooting away their own airscrews were very frequent. It happened to Boelcke, and it is recorded that Anthony Fokker himself put 16 shots through his own propeller. This happened to Immelmann twice, and a third such accident may have occasioned his death during a fight with an FE 2b of No 25 Squadron on June 18, 1916. The British naturally claimed a victory, for a bogey was laid. Immelmann's score at this time stood at 15, Boelcke's at 18. The latter's remarks on his colleague's death are convincing. 'Immelmann met his death by the most stupid accident,' he wrote home. 'The newspaper stories about an airfight are nonsense. Part of his propeller flew off, and the broken flying-wires, whirling round, ripped the fuselage apart.' There will always be argument, but at least the 'stupid accident' was not uncommon.

With the exception of the Nieuport Scout, with Lewis gun on the upper plane fired by Bowden cable, the most effective anti-Fokker aircraft were always the pushers, their rear-mounted engine and propeller allowing a clear cone of fire in a forward direction. The work started by the slow but effective Vickers FB 5 Gun Bus was carried on by the FE 2b. The single-seater DH 2 was also a pusher, and it was pushers which largely put an end to the Scourge. Meanwhile Allied types of interrupter-gear had been developed, and contrary to rumour they were not copied from the Germans. The first German example was captured on April 8, 1916; the first British aeroplane armed with synchronising mechanism to arrive in France was a Bristol Scout which landed exactly two weeks before. Operationally, however, only the Sopwith 1½ Strutters of No 70 Squadron and two squadrons of the unsatisfactory BE 12 received synchronised machine guns in time for the Battle of the Somme.

In 1915 engines were too scarce and too unreliable for the Allies to attempt a twin-motor layout, which would have provided high performance together with fore-and-aft shooting for pilot and observer. The Germans, however, evolved an effective three-seater *Kampfflugzeug* (bomber/escort aircraft) early in 1915 mainly for the Eastern Front. Designed to use a pair of the obsolete Mercedes D I 100 hp engines, the AEG GI *grossfleugzeug* had a span of 16 meters (52 feet 6 inches). It could carry its load at a maximum speed of 125 kph (78 mph), and thanks to the overhead-valve water-cooled engines in which the German industry specialised, possessed a useful ceiling.

From the start of the war until January 1915, Austro-Hungarian squadrons were not uniformly equipped, having a selection of Etrich *Taube* monoplanes and Lohner *Pfeil* arrow-wing biplanes with various in-line and rotary engines, together with Albatros BIs made under licence by Phönix. These aeroplanes were designed by Ernst Heinkel, who was to have a great influence on Austrian design. Just before the war, the Trieste magnate, Camillo Castiglione, had bought up the *Brandenburgischen Flugzeugwerke* at Brandenburg/Havel and the *Hanseatische Flugzeugwerke,* afterwards known as Hansa-Brandenburg, and Heinkel became chief engineer. Austria's most important contributions, however, were the Austro-Daimler and Hieronymus (Hiero) engines, on which Dr Ferdinand Porsche worked.

When Italy declared war on May 24, 1915, the Austrian air forces found the Alps somewhat hampering. The Italian air forces were at a high state of readiness, but were very under-equipped and lacking

Popperfoto

Anthony Fokker, the brilliant Dutchman who contributed so much to German aviation

in modern aircraft. Italy had also five airships. A French naval squadron went to Venice to assist, and the U-boat *U11* was damaged on July 1 by *Enseigne* de Vaisseau Roulier. Attempts to bomb the Austrian arsenals at Trieste and Pola were frustrated by the Italian aircraft's insufficient performance and the prevailing Austrian *C-Flugzeuge*.

Equipment for 'side-show' operations was seldom of the best, as the British found in East Africa. A German commerce-raider, the cruiser *Königsberg* had taken refuge in the Rufiji River in October

An RNAS Voisin LA on Imbros. This type was more than a match for any aircraft the Turks had

Imperial War Museum

The 'Fokker Scourge'

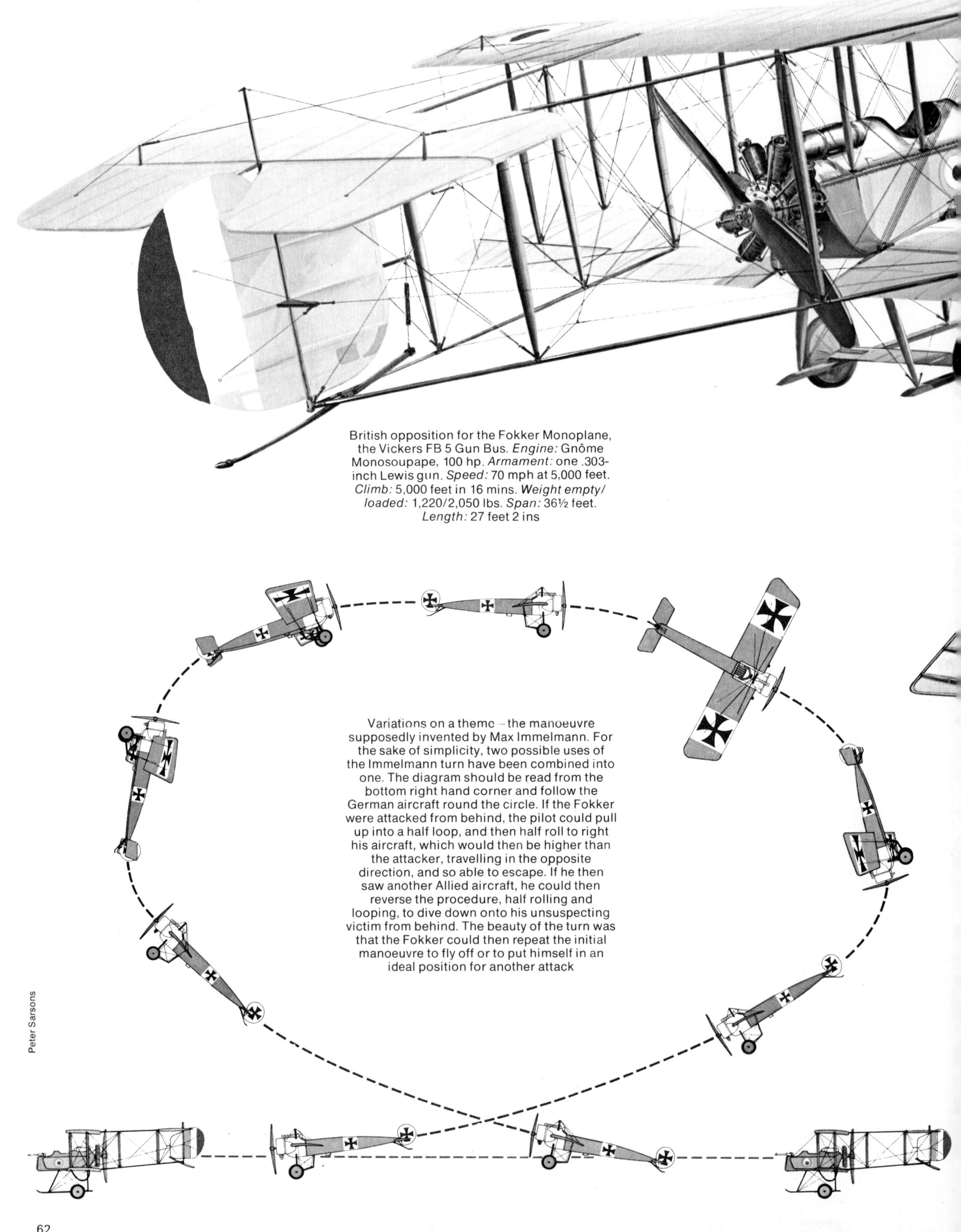

British opposition for the Fokker Monoplane, the Vickers FB 5 Gun Bus. *Engine:* Gnôme Monosoupape, 100 hp. *Armament:* one .303-inch Lewis gun. *Speed:* 70 mph at 5,000 feet. *Climb:* 5,000 feet in 16 mins. *Weight empty/ loaded:* 1,220/2,050 lbs. *Span:* 36½ feet. *Length:* 27 feet 2 ins

Variations on a theme – the manoeuvre supposedly invented by Max Immelmann. For the sake of simplicity, two possible uses of the Immelmann turn have been combined into one. The diagram should be read from the bottom right hand corner and follow the German aircraft round the circle. If the Fokker were attacked from behind, the pilot could pull up into a half loop, and then half roll to right his aircraft, which would then be higher than the attacker, travelling in the opposite direction, and so able to escape. If he then saw another Allied aircraft, he could then reverse the procedure, half rolling and looping, to dive down onto his unsuspecting victim from behind. The beauty of the turn was that the Fokker could then repeat the initial manoeuvre to fly off or to put himself in an ideal position for another attack

Peter Sarsons

The winter of 1915/1916 was the time of the 'Fokker Scourge' – when a mediocre, prewar, underpowered aircraft, the Fokker Monoplane, dominated the skies over the Western Front solely because it was armed with a machine gun synchronised to fire between the blades of a revolving propeller. A very small number of machines were fitted with two guns, but the loss of performance made this hardly worth while. **1.** Oberursel U 1 100 hp rotary engine. **2.** Wooden propeller. **3.** Forward fuel tank. **4.** 'Bungee' rubber cord undercarriage suspension bar. **5.** Primer pump. **6.** Main undercarriage structure, anchorage point for the main flying wires. **7.** Wire-spoked wheels. **8.** Built up ribs. **9.** Main spars. **10.** Leather torsion strips. **11.** Rear of undercarriage structure, carrying the pulleys for the wing warping wires. **12.** Wicker-work pilot's seat. **13.** Fuselage bracing wires. **14.** Wooden fin and elevätor, with no fixed surfaces. **15.** Tail skid, sprung with 'bungee' rubber. **16.** Welded steel tube fuselage structure. **17.** Doped linen covering. **18.** Rear fuel tank. **19.** Pylon for the landing wires. **20.** 7.92-mm LMG 08/15 synchronised machine gun

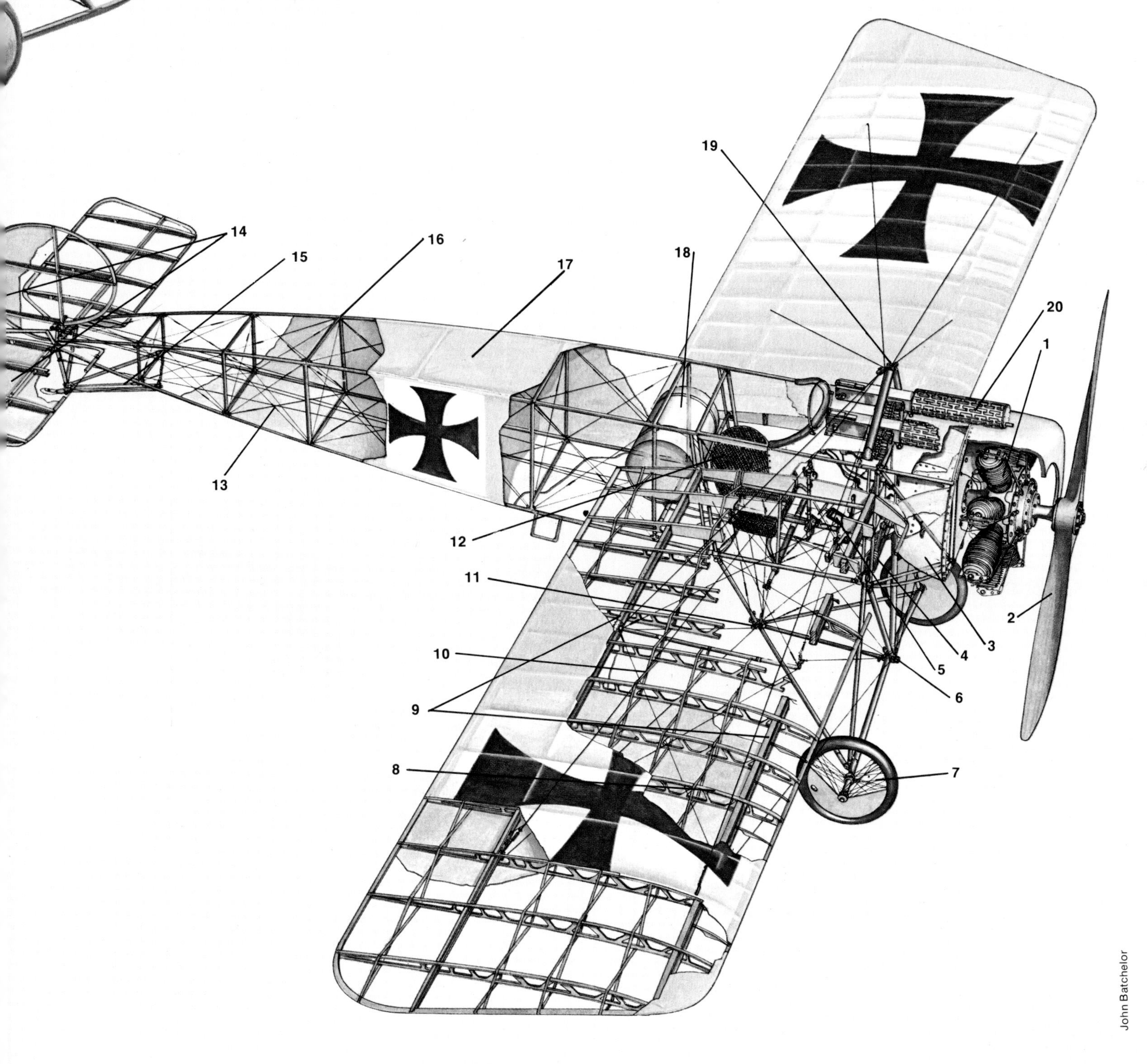

Julian Allen

'The knights of the sky' – new heroes for the sensation seeking masses at home – and some of the weapons which they used

Left and right: A French pilot (based on a picture of Lieutenant Nungesser), and a German pilot (right). The choice of flying clothing was conditioned by the time of year and the altitude at which the pilot expected to fly. In winter or at height the cold is intense, and privately purchased fur-lined clothing was warmer. *Below:* Aircraft armament. **1.** The old style – an unsynchronised Hotchkiss on a Deperdussin, aerodynamically appalling and also inefficient. **2.** The British .303-inch Lewis gun, sometimes seen without the casing around the barrel and gas cylinder. **3.** The German standard flexible gun for rear defence, the 7.92-mm Parabellum, a lighter version of the 'Spandau' and usually seen with a fretted water jacket. **4.** The Austrian Schwarzlose 8-mm machine gun. When adapted for aircraft use the gun was not very successful as its range was short and its rate of fire low. **5.** The standard British fixed gun, the .303-inch Vickers, also used by the French. **6.** A German 7.92-mm LMG 08/15 twin machine gun mounting. (These guns are known popularly as Spandaus after their place of manufacture.) This gun was the standard fixed armament on German aircraft, twin mountings starting in the middle of 1916

Julian Allen

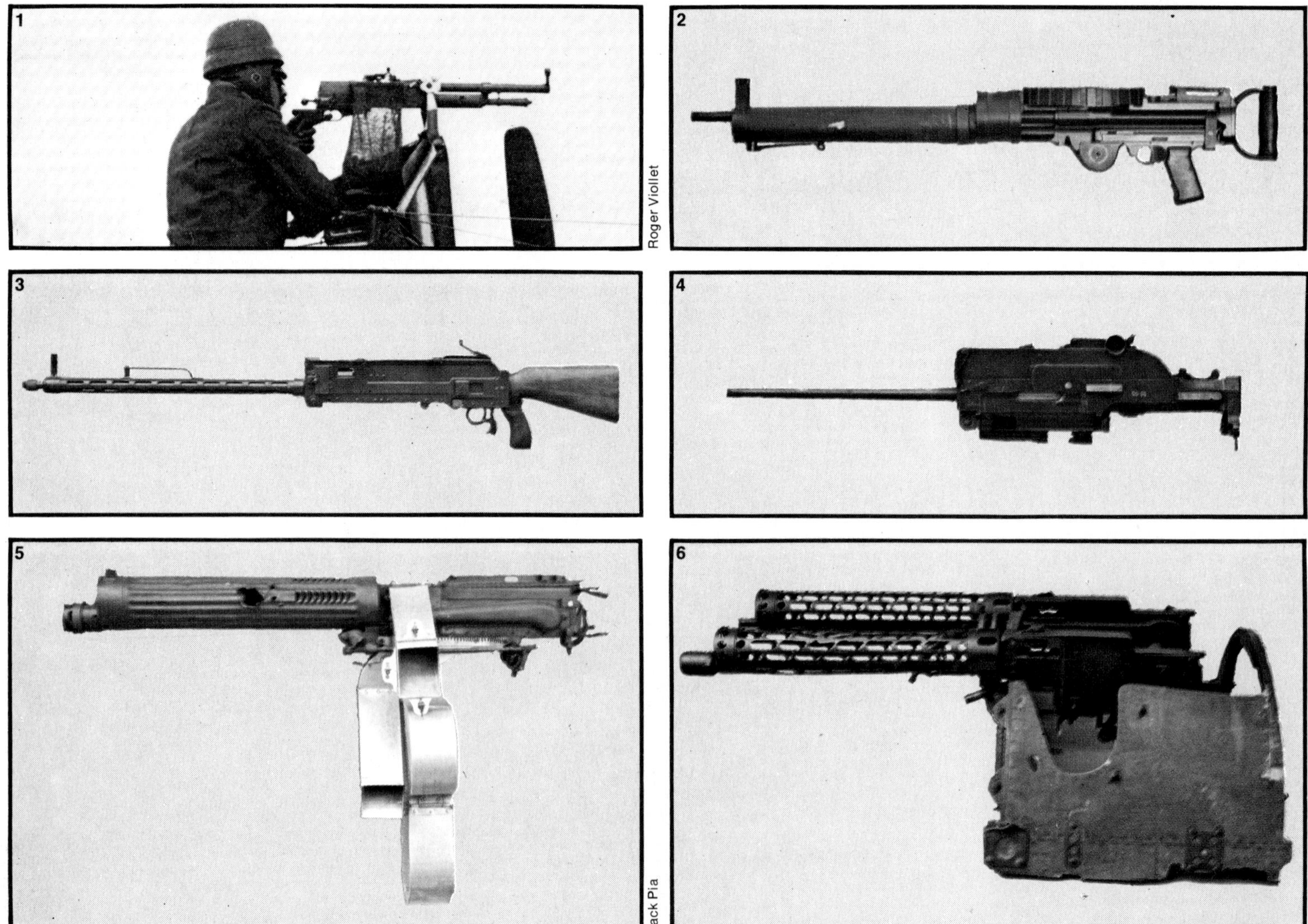

Roger Viollet

Jack Pia

Jack Pia

1914. Unsuccessful operations by Short Folder seaplanes, a Curtiss flying-boat and two Sopwith 807 seaplanes located and photographed but could not destroy the raider. Two Henri Farmans and two Caudron G IIIs arrived in June, and on the 11th of that month, shellfire directed by a Farman and a Caudron put an end to the *Königsberg*.

Following a nomadic existence during the retreat and occupation of so much of their country, the Belgians reorganised their air service early in 1915. In April the *Aviation Militaire* took up quarters at Coxyde and Houthem. Five *escadrilles* of Voisin, Henri Farman and Maurice Farman pusher biplanes were formed to support the Belgian divisions in the field.

When General Ludendorff was a mere colonel in October 1910 he took the opportunity of going up in an aeroplane with *Hauptmann* de le Roi and expressed himself 'delighted'. Ludendorff's appreciation of the possibilities of aerial reconnaissance received confirmation on both Fronts. In August 1914, *Feldfliegerabteilungen Nos 14, 15, 16, 17* and *29*, together with four *Festungsfliegerabteilungen* (fortress defence flights) went to the Eastern Front. Aerial reconnaissance certainly paid dividends: news of Russian troop movements brought back by *Leutnant* Canter and his observer, *Leutnant* Mertens, proved of vital importance for the Battle of Tannenberg. Landing where they could, and proceeding to General von François's headquarters by cycle, cart and commandeered motor car, they made possible a great German victory. As Hindenburg himself remarks in his memoirs, *'Ohne Flieger, kein Tannenberg'*: 'Without airmen there would have been no Tannenberg.'

Among the junior officers on this front was the cavalry subaltern Manfred von Richthofen, lately transferred to the air service, having decided that cavalry warfare was no occupation for an officer of the *1st Regiment (Emperor Alexander III) Uhlans*. Richthofen was posted to the East as an observer in June 1915. He had not applied for training as a pilot, being convinced the war would be over too soon, and took part during June, July and August in the Central Powers' advance from Gorlice to Brest Litovsk. His Albatros B I was brought down by infantry machine gun fire, but was able to land on ground which had just been taken from the Russians, a matter of yards only.

The Russian air services, through faulty organisation and widely stretched communications, made no great showing. Technically, however, they had much of interest to contribute, apart from French aeroplanes made under licence, the most advanced being some Sikorsky Ilya Mourometz four-engined bombers produced by the Russo-Baltic Wagon Works. An Anatra two-seater copy of the Voisin was fairly successful, but structurally weak, and Russo-Baltic produced the armoured RBVZ S17 and S20. In the armaments field they did even better. A Sikorsky S16 (80 hp Renault, later 100 hp Gnôme) was fitted with a machine gun synchronising interrupter gear invented by Lieutenant Poplavko, whose experiments with Maxim guns had been proceeding since 1913, while news of another Russian interrupter gear was brought to London late in 1914 by Lieutenant-Commander V. V. Dybovski of the Imperial Russian Navy, who, with Engineer Smyslov, was its co-inventor. Later, Dybovski was to co-operate fruitfully on such matters with Warrant-Officer Scarff, RNAS.

Staatsbibliothek/Berlin

The value of aerial reconnaissance. This photograph clearly shows the front line situation as French infantry advance across captured trenches during the Battle of the Somme on July 1, 1916

Until January 1916 air warfare was a very personal matter, not only in the dropping of messages over the lines, but in the picturesqueness of individual incidents: Guynemer, one Sunday morning after shooting down a German over Compiègne, where he lived, spotted his father coming out of church, landed beside the road and asked Papa to 'please find my Boche'. Another time, when the non-commissioned Guynemer landed beside an artillery battery, having shot down a German in flames, the battery commander fired a salvo in his honour and, stripping the gold braid from his own cap, presented it to the victorious pilot bidding him 'wear it when you, too, are promoted captain'.

However, aerial fighting was becoming ever more organised. During the French Champagne offensive of October, the Germans wisely decided to group their single-seaters, forming small *Kampfeinsitzerkommando* or Single-seater Detachments. Immelmann remained at Douai but Boelcke left for an advanced landing ground near Rethel to fly what became known as 'barrage patrols' against French fighter, corps and reconnaissance aircraft. He returned to Douai in December and continued, almost alone amongst German pilots, to patrol behind the Allied lines where Fokker pilots were not encouraged to venture owing to the secrecy of the synchronising gear and the unreliability of the engine.

The concept of barrage patrols was more fully worked out at Verdun, where the great German offensive was launched along a nine-mile front on February 21, 1916. Here too, Boelcke fought his own private war, *'alles ganz auf eigene Faust'*. Bored with escorting observation machines, he obtained permission to leave the rest of the KEK and establish a private landing-ground beside the Meuse, only seven miles from the front with one other pilot, an NCO and 15 men, after discharging himself from hospital to shoot down a Voisin which bothered the neighbourhood. Here was the true 'offensive spirit' so dear to Trenchard and the RFC.

At first the idea of barrage patrols worked well. The aim was to drive the French air force out of the sky, and every available aircraft was concentrated above the lines, except for those giving close support to the infantry, forerunners of the contact patrol machines employed on the Somme. The French, in their slow Farmans, Caudrons and Voisins were quickly downcast, but the defensive thinking of the

On the Eastern Front, during the Battle of Tannenberg in 1914, German infantry inspect the wreckage of a Russian reconnaissance plane shot down in the ruins of Neidenburg

Südd Verlag

John Batchelor

German High Command soon proved a costly mistake. Not only did the barrage fail to keep out all intruders, but the concentration of so many pilots on this task meant that vital jobs were left undone.

Most important of all, reconnaissance machines did not fly where they should. Had they done so, the High Command would have learned that the Verdun citadel was largely dependent upon one road for its supplies, a road used by some 8,000 lorries a day. Had they known this and bombed the convoys, Verdun might have proved a rout for the French. Instead, the French underwent a change of heart. Pétain took over and demanded from his fliers offensive tactics. Hurriedly moved in from other sectors the *escadrilles de chasse* were regrouped under *Commandant* de Rose, *Chef d'Aviation* of the Second Army. Among them came Brocard and the rest of his Storks, brought from the Sixth Army in Champagne. They found no lack of targets. The nimble Nieuport single-seater 'sesquiplanes' (for the lower plane was almost too small to count) found new German fighters against them, including the Halberstadt D I biplane (100-hp Mercedes), Pfalz monoplanes (which were almost indistinguishable from Fokkers) and later marks of the Fokker itself, which was now feeling its age. The extremely 'clean' LFG Roland C III had a useful turn of speed (103 mph), far higher than the other current German two-seaters such as the Rumpler CI (95 mph) and the LVG C II, whose maximum was 81 mph.

The Storks suffered severely, Guynemer was shot down, wounded in the face and arm; Brocard, his CO, wounded, Lieutenant Deullen wounded, Lieutenant Peretti killed. But the French had regained the offensive, 'and to foster this spirit *Commandant* de Rose took a leaf from the German book and instituted the 'ace' system, announcing the score as follows: Chaput 7, Nungesser 6 and a balloon, Navarre 4, Lenoir 4, Auger and Pelletier d'Oisy 3, and several pilots with two apiece. Guynemer's tally was five.

Meanwhile in the British sector flying hours mounted fast. In July 1915 the hours flown were 2,100, in August 2,674. In September, with the opening of the Battle of Loos they leapt to 4,740. New squadrons were continually being formed, trained—after a fashion—and flown to France. By

Left: France's premier fighter, the Nieuport 11 *Bébé*. *Engine:* Le Rhône rotary, 80 hp. *Max speed:* 97 mph at sea level. *Ceiling:* 15,000 feet. *Endurance:* 2½ hours. *Armament:* one .303-inch Lewis gun. *Weights empty/loaded:* 774/1,058 pounds. *Span:* 24 feet 9 inches. *Length:* 19 feet 0⅓ inches. *Below:* German-designed but used only by the Austrians — the Hansa Brandenburg C I

Bibliothek für Zeitgeschichte

the end of June, 1916 there were 27 operational squadrons with BEF, flying 421 aeroplanes, together with 216 aeroplanes at aircraft depots, and four kite balloon squadrons now handled by the RFC. The RNAS Dunkirk were also most active, not only against shipping, docks, submarines and Zeppelins, but also on bombing raids, working closely with the French, with whom they shared the aerodrome at St Pol, Dunkirk. They had also obtained some Nieuport fighters.

From the RFC communiqués it is clear that 'Offensive Spirit' was never lacking: nothing could be more 'offensive' than the action of the BE 2c of No 2 Squadron which, 'on artillery registration', climbed to engage an LVG 4,000 feet above although armed only with a rifle. By late December, however, BEs were better armed, and to make up for it the Germans had learned to make multiple attacks. Fokkers were numerous and aggressive, often attacking three at a time. Casualties were numerous amongst the inexperienced new crews until, profiting from Third Wing lessons, HQ RFC issued an order on January 14 that every reconnaissance aircraft must be accompanied by at least three other machines, in the closest possible formation. At the same time the growth of the RFC made necessary the adoption of larger units than the Wing, and Brigades were established, each comprising a Corps Wing and an Army Wing, one brigade being assigned to each army. The Army Wings took over most of the long-range and high-performance aircraft, and the policy of arming each squadron with a single type of aircraft became standard as supplies improved. Single-seater and two-seater fighter machines were no longer scattered throughout the service. The first homogeneous fighter squadron, No 11, had arrived in France on July 25, 1915, armed with Vickers Gun Bus two-seaters. The first single-seater Fighter Squadron to go into action reached France on February 7, 1916, No 24, under Major L. G. Hawker, VC. No 29 followed on March 25 and No 32 on May 28. These neat little pusher biplanes were fitted either with 100-hp Gnôme Monosoupape or 110-hp Le Rhône. Once their habits were understood they proved popular in the RFC, and highly unpopular with Fokker pilots, who had now met their match.

Higher and faster, but there were still many defects in the designs of some of the aircraft

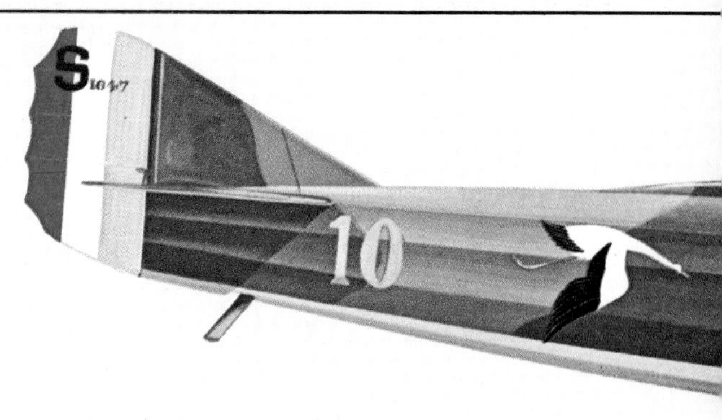

Right: The French **Spad VII** fighter, which entered service in September 1916, was one of the war's most outstanding aircraft. It was flown by the air forces of nearly every Allied power. **Advantages:** Excellent speed, extreme strength and the adaptability to accept more powerful engines. **Disadvantages:** One machine gun only, reduced agility and a radiator in the upper wing centre section (its water might scald the pilot if it were punctured). *Engine:* Hispano-Suiza 8 A, 180 hp. *Armament:* one .303-inch Vickers gun. *Weight empty/loaded:* 1,100/1,550 pounds. *Span:* 25 feet 8 inches. *Length:* 20 feet $3\frac{1}{2}$ inches. *Height:* 7 feet

The Gnôme Monosoupape rotary, 80 hp model
Advantages: Good power-to-weight and size-to-power ratios and relative mechanical simplicity. **Disadvantages:** Fine tolerances required in maintenance, tendency to shed cylinders and no proper throttle (the only way of controlling the engine was by cutting the ignition to a number of cylinders). Unlike more conventional engines, the rotary had a stationary crankshaft, around which rotated the cylinders and crankcase, with the propeller bolted to their front. The crankshaft itself **(1)** is bolted to the aeroplane's structure. Into the crankshaft are led three inlets (only two are visible) **(2)** for air, fuel and lubricant (castor oil, which does not mix with petrol). All three are taken to the crankcase **(3)**, where the fuel and air are mixed and vaporised. The mixture is admitted to the cylinder through apertures in the sides of the piston and the base of the cylinder (**4** and **5**), which can only happen when the piston **(6)** is at the very bottom of its stroke. The mixture is compressed as the piston rises again and is detonated by the spark plug, which is fired by the magneto **(7)** when the cylinder is in the right place. This forces the engine round, and as it does, the chamber is cleared through the outlet valve **(8)** opened by a pushrod **(9)** operated from a cam **(10)** on the longitudinal axis of the engine

Below: The British **RE 8** artillery spotter and reconnaissance machine. The type was introduced late in 1916 and remained in service in large numbers until the armistice despite its many shortcomings. **Advantages:** None. **Disadvantages:** The type was too stable, had weak upper wing extensions, was prone to spinning, and sometimes developed a dangerous 'air cushion' when landing. The engine was also unreliable when first introduced. *Engine:* RAF 4a, 150 hp. *Speed:* 103 mph at 5,000 feet. *Armament:* one .303-inch Vickers and one .303-inch Lewis gun plus up to 224 pounds of bombs. *Ceiling:* 13,500 feet. *Endurance:* 4¼ hours. *Weight empty/loaded:* 1,803/2,869 lbs. *Span:* 42 ft 7 in. *Length:* 27 ft 10½ in.

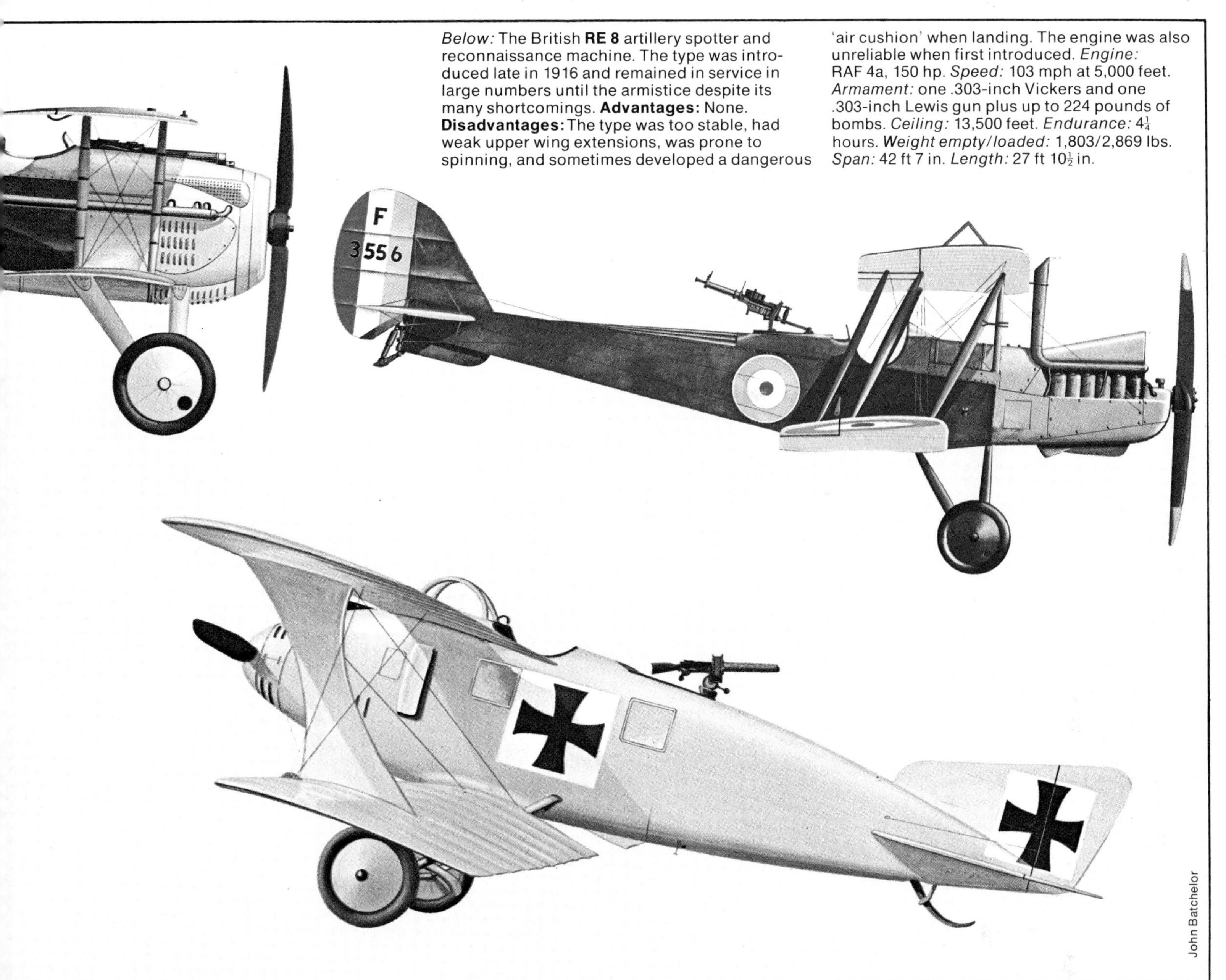

John Batchelor

Above: The German **LFG Roland C II** escort and reconnaissance machine. e type was marked by the very great care ken to ensure aerodynamic cleanliness. his care was reflected in the machine's od turn of speed. **Advantages:** A strong nd capacious fuselage and an excellent iew, particularly upwards as there was o wing above the crew to obstruct their view as in most biplanes. The view downward was also good as a result of the careful arrangement of the wing root cut-outs and the wings' stagger. **isadvantages:** The wings were too thin and tended to distort in service, with the result that climb and ceiling were affected adversely. *Engine:* Mercedes D III, 160 hp. *Armament:* one 7.92-mm Spandau for the pilot and one 7.92-mm arabellum for the observer. *Speed:* 103 mph at sea level. *Climb:* 12 minutes to 6,560 feet. *Ceiling:* 13,100 feet. *Endurance:* 4 to 5 hours. *Weight npty/loaded:* 1,681/2,825 pounds. *Span:* 33 feet 9½ inches. *Length:* 25 feet 3¼ inches. *Right:* The development of reconnaissance aircraft from 1914 to 916 (BE 2a to Albatros C VII) and comparative fighter performance at the end of 1916. Note that although every other aspect of performance has improved, climb rate has stayed at the 1914 level. In the fighter performance part of the chart, note that very little divides the types in speed and ceiling, but that the difference in climb rate is marked.

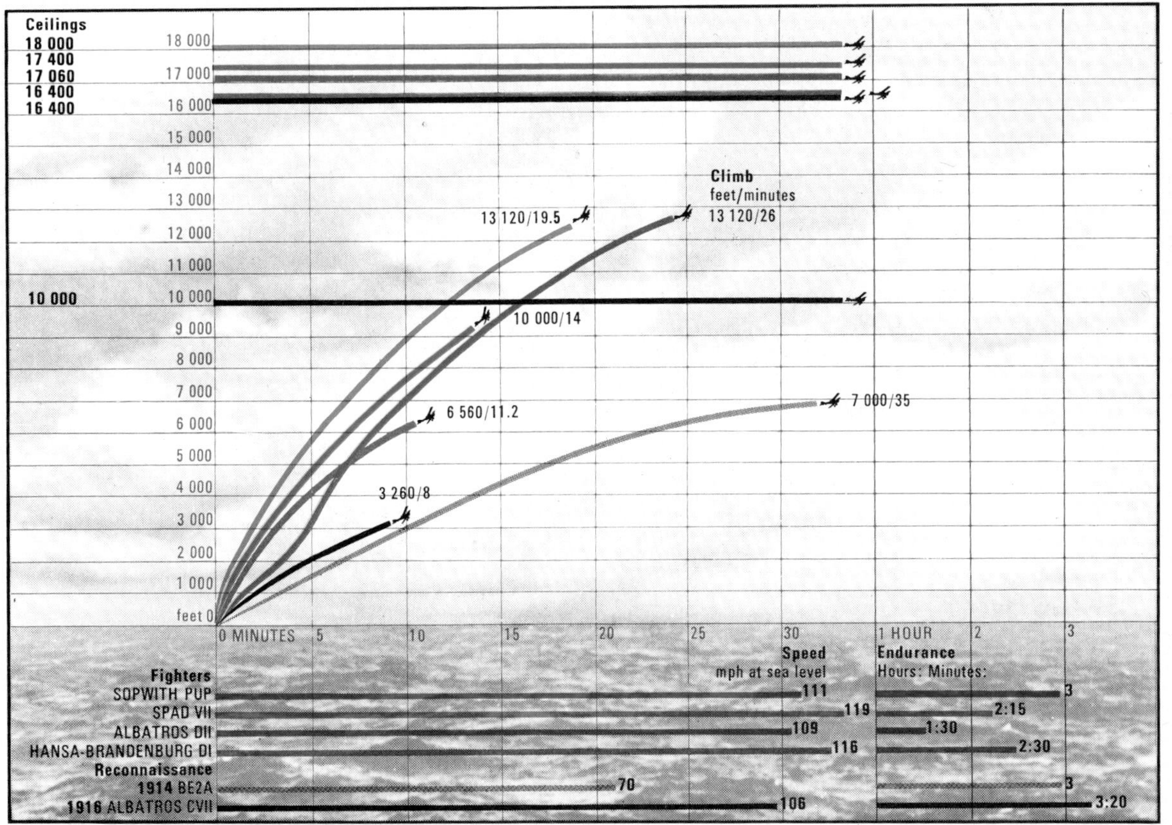

Bibliotheque Nationale, Paris

Top: A typical cockpit. The pilot had less in the way of struts and wires to contend with compared with earlier types, but he now has a gun butt just in front of his face. This would damage his face in any crash. *Above:* 'The end of a German aeroplane over Arras' by Bertram Sandy

CAMEL SCRAP

Recollections of a Fighter Pilot

On September 10 I led five Camels of 'A' Flight on the north offensive patrol, which covered an area to the north of Ypres. We had not been long over the lines, and were flying at 14,000 feet, when I saw below us over Houthulst Forest a formation of enemy planes, made up of two DFW two-seaters protected by five Albatros Scouts. I had previously arranged that, in the event of encountering escorted aeroplanes, I should attack with one Camel, while the deputy leader and the other Camels were to remain above to protect our tails from attack. On my left was a new pilot, 2nd-Lieutenant R. J. Brownell, MM, a Tasmanian, who is now in the Royal Australian Air Force. I had told him that, until he got used to flying over the lines and rapidly spotting enemy craft as distinct from friendly, he must keep right alongside my 'plane and do whatever I did, maintaining formation station in all attitudes. Lieutenants Crossland, Moody and Smith made up the remainder of the formation.

The enemy 'planes were flying south about 1,000 feet below and ahead of us well east of their lines, and probably climbing to gain height before crossing the trench-lines upon reconnaissance. I swung our formation round above them from the north-easterly course we followed and dived for the two-seaters. Brownell came down in station. He had seen nothing. He simply knew that I had dived and that he had to keep position. The remaining three Camels maintained their height.

Down I rushed through the crisp, cold air, watching my Hun through the sights, holding my control stick with both hands, thumbs resting on the double gun-triggers within the spade-shaped stick-top. The observer in my opponents' bus saw me and I saw him swing his gun to bear. I saw the double flash of his shots even as he grew to personality in my sights and I pressed the fateful triggers. At the very first burst he crumpled up and fell backwards into the cockpit. My streams of lead poured into the fuselage of the 'plane around the pilot's cockpit and the DFW tipped up and over sideways and fell tumbling down.

I looked round for Brownell and saw him close beside me on my level. Following me down in the dive without knowing why we dived, he suddenly found himself squarely on the tail of the second DFW. He pressed his triggers instinctively in a long burst. The Hun's tail rose upward. A curl of smoke came from his fuselage and he fell headlong, plunging like a flaming comet.

Above us the three Camels kept the five Albatros Scouts engaged, and, after seeing the two-seaters go down, Smith dived on the tail of one of the scouts and shot 100 rounds into it, until it fell out of control.

Next day, in misty weather, with a patrol of seven, I saw a concentration of enemy planes, some 21 strong, flying below us east of Langemarck. There were three of the new Fokker triplanes, while the remainder were Albatros Scouts. They greatly outnumbered our strength. I could not determine whether they had observed us or not, but in any case I decided to attack. I dived on one of the triplanes, closed right in and as my burst went home I saw him falling down below his own formation. I knew that the Hun formation was so strong that it would be but to court disaster to follow him down. As I pulled forward from among the Huns for breathing space to review the situation I saw that one of my formation who had followed me had done just the thing I knew was wrong.

Engrossed on the shooting of an Albatros he had passed right through the Hun level.

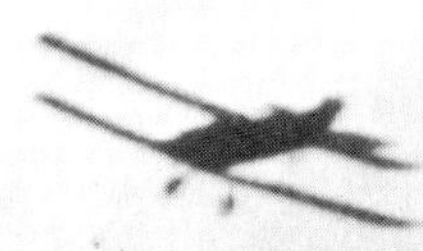

Instantly a Fokker pounced upon his tail. A burst of bullets caused the Camel pilot to look round and swerve away from the Albatros he followed. I saw the triplane close in upon the Camel's tail and I dived instantly upon it. As I dived I fired a short burst, before my sights were centred, because I knew that most Huns answered to the warning of bullets flying near. This fellow, however, was of a different breed. He looked round at me and, as I saw his begoggled face above his shoulder, he swerved slightly to one side, then followed on the Camel's tail.

I think the Camel pilot was wounded by the triplane's very first burst, because he did not use the Camel to manoeuvre as he might.

I increased speed and pulled closer to the triplane. Then I heard the splatter of Hun bullets rattling round my own ears. Glancing upward I saw two Albatros Scouts coming down upon me, but above them was another little Camel treating them the same.

I was almost dead upon the triplane's tail when the pilot looked around again. The range was so close that I could almost read the man's expression. I gave him another burst and saw the stream of tracer miss his head by inches as he swerved outward from my line of sight. The Camel was below him falling steeply in a gentle curve. When my burst ceased the German pilot looked again ahead.

Damn him! I thought. I'll get him next time. Each time I had fired a trifle earlier than I might have done, in the desire to shake him off the Camel's tail. And all the time we fell downward, losing height, fighting earthward from 14,000 feet along a pathway inclined at 60 degrees, rushing through the misty air towards the ground behind the German lines. From behind me came another burst of flying bullets.

Out of the corner of my eye I saw a solitary RE 8 heading towards us. I followed the swerving triplane and got squarely on his tail. Before I could fire he got out of my sights once more. Again I registered on him, dead. I pressed the triggers and saw my bullets flying home. His head did not look round this time. His angle of dive suddenly steepened. I increased my own to vertical, barely 20 feet behind him. Suddenly the RE 8 flashed in front of me between the German and my bus. I saw the wide-open mouth of the horror-struck observer. The wings passed across my vision as the pilot vainly strove to turn away.

For a fleeting instant of time I looked into the face of the observer and the cockpit in which he stood. He thought that I would hit him head on and wipe him from existence, torn to fragments with the whirring engine and propeller that I carried. So did I. For a fragment of time I hung in space, mentally, already dead. The observer and I saw each other as souls already hurled into the eternal cosmos.

There was but one thing to do.

'My God,' I breathed in prayer, even as I did it. I yanked the Camel's stick hard into my stomach and flashed between the two-seater's wings and tailplane as my gallant little Camel answered to the pull. By a miracle we missed collision, by a miracle my Camel held together. I flat spun upside down on top of a loop and fell out sideways. I had lost height so rapidly in my downward rush from 14,000 feet that the pressure in my fuel-tank had not had time to stabilise to meet the higher atmospheric pressure, and my engine ceased to run. Not certain of the cause I tried her on the gravity tank and she picked up. I turned west and scanned the sky. High overhead I saw 'planes pass between the mist and sky like goldfish in a bowl held up against a curtained window. Around me and on my level there was nothing to be seen, no aeroplanes, enemy or friendly, except the RE 8 fast disappearing westward in the mist, westward towards the lines. The triplane and the Camel both had vanished. The ground below was free from shell-holes, but indistinct on account of mist. I climbed upward as I travelled west and found some Camels of the squadron. Our patrol time was finished, and we returned to our aerodrome in formation. And as I went I cursed the damn-fool pilot of the British RE 8.

[*Reprinted from* Into the Blue *by Norman Macmillan, published by Duckworth.*]

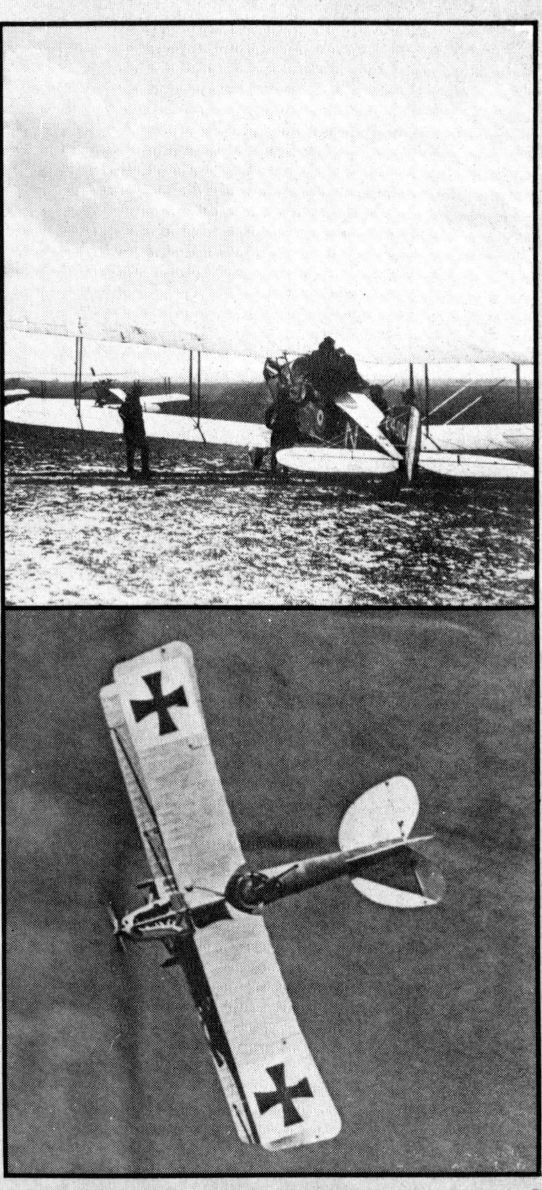

Top: The ground crew wait as the pilot and observer make their final preparations for a reconnaissance flight in their Bristol Fighter on a wintry day. *Above:* A fine air-to-air photograph of an Albatros C III 2-seater. Note the excellent field of fire for the observer

Above: The **Sopwith F I Camel**, the First World War's most successful fighter, with 1,294 aircraft downed to its credit. It owed much of its success to its phenomenal aerobatic capabilities, which were the result of its compact design, powerful controls and the fact that all the large weights were concentrated on or near the centre of gravity – in the first seven feet of the fuselage. The considerable torque of the rotary engine on the small frame was a vital factor in the Camel's lightning fast turn to the right, but it also meant that it was impossible to fly the Camel 'hands off'. Because of this difficulty, the type got an undeserved reputation as a killer, but all that was needed was great care, especially at take off and landing. The Camel was the first British fighter to have twin Vickers guns. **1.** Upper wing cutout for visibility. **2.** Ring sight. **3.** Vickers gun. **4.** Ammunition tank. **5.** Wooden propeller. **6.** Aluminium cowling. **7.** Rotary engine. **8.** Oil tank. **9.** Wing rib. **10.** Aileron control wire. **11.** Compression rib. **12** and **13.** Wing bracing wires. **14.** Main spars. **15.** Aileron operating horn. **16.** Aileron connecting wire. **17.** Bungee-sprung wheel. **18.** Rudder bar. **19.** Wicker seat. **20.** Fuel tank. **21.** Control column. **22.** Wire-braced wooden fuselage. **23.** Tailplane structure. **24.** Iron-shod skid. **25.** Fin and rudder. **26.** Bungee skid spring. **27.** Throttle and mixture controls. **28.** Instrument panel. **29.** Flying wire. **30.** Landing wire. **31.** Incidence bracing wires. *Engine:* Clerget (130-hp), Le Rhône (110-hp) or Bentley 1 (150-hp) rotaries. *Armament:* two Vickers guns. *Speed:* 122 mph at sea level. *Climb:* 16 minutes 50 seconds to 15,000 feet. *Ceiling:* 24,000 feet. *Endurance:* 2½ hours. *Weight empty/loaded:* 889/1,422 lbs. *Span:* 28 feet. *Length:* 18 feet 8 inches. Performance figures are as with the Le Rhône engine

Above: The **Fokker D VII**, Germany's best fighter of the war, designed by the little-known Reinhold Platz, who also designed the Dr I. Originally a welder, Platz began designing with little or no training. He possessed an enormous flair for designing strong but light structures (the fuselage was of metal tube) and had a superb intuitive eye for line. The D VII was noted for its great strength, good manoeuvrability and excellent performance at altitude. It had the remarkable ability of being able to hang on its propeller and fire upwards. The aircraft illustrated is that of Georg von Hantelman of *Jasta 15* of *Jagdgeschwader II*. *Engine:* Mercedes D III or BMW III inlines, 160- or 185-hp. *Armament:* two fixed Spandau machine guns. *Speed:* 116½ mph at 3,280 feet. *Climb:* 16,400 feet in 31½ minutes (Mercedes) or 16 minutes (BMW). *Ceiling:* 22,900 feet. *Endurance:* 1½ hours. *Weight empty/loaded:* 1,540/1,870 lbs. *Span:* 29 feet 3½ inches. *Length:* 22 feet 11⅝ inches. *Below:* 'The Blind Spot' by N. G. Arnold—A Camel closes up in the blind spot under a Hannoveraner's tailplane

John Batchelor

RAF Staff College

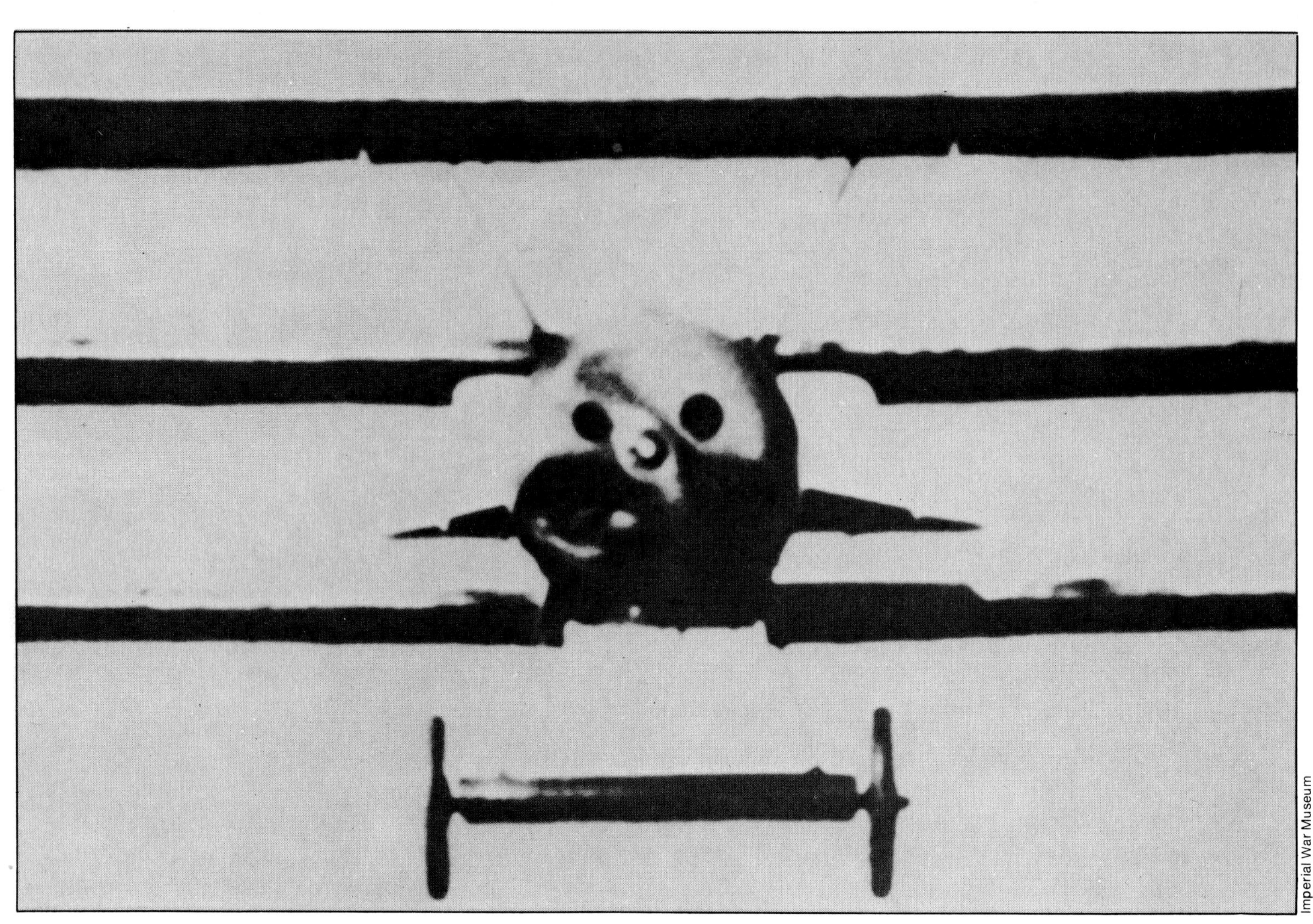

Imperial War Museum

There was a good deal of activity along the fronts, and it was rumoured that a big offensive was being prepared on the other side. Every day we saw long rows of captive balloons, which, against the summer sky, looked like a string of over-sized sausages. These balloons annoyed us and we decided that something would have to be done about them.

So one morning I started out early, at a time when I should have the sun at my back as I made my dive at the enemy balloon. I flew very high, higher, I think, than I had ever flown before. The altimeter showed 15,000 feet, the air was thin, and it was very cold.

The world below me looked like a huge aquarium. Above Lierval, where Reinhold had fallen, I sighted a hostile machine. From a distance it looked like a minute water beetle.

Then, from the west, a small object rapidly approached. Small and black at first, it quickly grew in size and I soon recognised it as a Spad, an enemy fighter on the lookout for trouble-seekers like myself. I braced myself in my cockpit, for I knew that there was going to be a fight.

We met at the same altitude. As the sun caught it, I saw the other man's machine was painted light brown. Soon we were circling round each other playing for an opening. Below we probably looked like two great birds of prey indulging in springtime frolics, but we knew that it was a game of death. The first man to get behind the other's back was the winner. In the single-seater fighters you could only shoot forward, and if your opponent got on your tail you were lost.

At the time of which he was writing, Ernst Udet was a novice, but he went on to be Germany's second greatest ace, with 62 victories. *Above:* The master – Richthofen and his Dr I

Sometimes we passed so near to each other that I could see every detail of my opponent's face – that is, all that was visible of it below his helmet. On the machine's side there was a Stork and two words painted in white. The fifth time that he flew past me – so close that I could feel the draught from his propeller – I managed to spell out a word, *V-i-e-u-x*. And *Vieux Charles* was Guynemer's insignia.

And, indeed, there could only have been one Frenchman who handled a machine with the skill that he showed. He was a man, who like all the really dangerous beasts of prey, always hunted alone. Guynemer it was who made a practice of diving at his victims from out of the sun, destroying them in a few seconds. In this way he had shot down my friend Puz. He had some 30 victories to his credit and I knew that I was in for the fight of my life.

I threw a half loop, with the object of getting at him from above but immediately he grasped my purpose, and half rolled out of the way. I tried another manoeuvre but again Guynemer forestalled me, and the jockeying for position continued.

Once, as I was coming out of a turn, he had advantage of me for a few seconds, and a regular hailstorm of bullets rattled against the wings of my 'plane.

I tried every trick I knew – turns, loops, rolls, sideslips – but he followed each movement with a lightning speed and gradually I began to realise that he was more than a match for me. Not only had he a better machine, but the man in it was a superior duellist. But I had to fight on, or turn away. To turn away would be fatal.

I went into a steep turn, and for a moment I had him at the end of my sights. I pressed the trigger . . . there was no response . . . my gun had jammed!

Holding the stick in my left hand, I hammered at the gun with my right. My efforts were unavailing.

For a moment I had considered the possibilities of escaping by diving away from him. But with such an opponent that would have been inviting disaster. In a few seconds he would have been on my tail, and could have shot me down with the utmost ease.

We still flew in circles round each other. It was a wonderful flying experience – if one could forget that one's life was at stake. I have never had to deal with a more

Imperial War Museum

The age of chivalry ended with the Red Baron, a ruthless hunter who, as a morbid hobby, used his victims' serial numbers as wallpaper

skilful opponent, and for a while I completely forgot that he was Guynemer, my enemy. It seemed to me, rather, that I was having some practice over the aerodrome with an old friend. This feeling, however, did not last for very long. For eight minutes we had been flying round each other in circles, and they were the longest eight minutes that I have ever experienced.

Suddenly Guynemer looped, and flew on his back over my head. That moment I relinquished hold of the stick, and hammered with both hands at the machine gun. It was a primitive remedy but it sometimes worked.

Guynemer had observed my actions and now knew that I was his helpless victim.

He again passed close over my head, flying almost on his back. And then, to my great surprise, he raised his arm and waved to me. Immediately afterwards he dived away towards the west.

I flew back home, stupefied.

There are some people who believe that Guynemer himself had a machine gun stoppage at the same time. Others claim that he feared that I, in desperation, might ram him in the air. I do not believe any of them. Rather do I believe that Guynemer gave proof that even in modern warfare there is something left of the knightly chivalry of bygone days. And, accordingly, I lay this belated wreath on Guynemer's unknown grave.

I reported for duty to the new squadron at ten o'clock one day, and at 12 o'clock on the same I made my first flight with *Jagdstaffel 11*. In addition, *Staffeln 4, 6* and *10* belonged to the squadron. Richthofen himself led *No 11 Flight*. I was made a member of it because he liked to have all new-comers where he could keep an eye on them.

There were five of us. The *Rittmeister* took the lead, then came Just and Gussmann, then Scholz and myself brought up the rear. It was the first time that I had piloted a Fokker Triplane.

We flew at an altitude of about 1,500 feet, setting a westerly course. Above the ruins of Albert we saw, just below the clouds, an RE 8, a British artillery co-operation machine that was evidently spotting for the guns. Although he was somewhat higher than ourselves, he apparently did not observe our approach, and continued to fly in circles.

I exchanged a quick glance with Scholz, who nodded. I left the flight, and went in to challenge the Briton.

I attacked from the front and opened fire at such close quarters that his engine was positively riddled with bullets. He at once crumpled up and the burning wreckage fell close to Albert.

A minute later I had rejoined the flight and continued with them towards the west. Scholz signalled his pleasure by waving to me. And Richthofen, who seemed to have eyes everywhere, also turned his head, and nodded to let me know that he had witnessed the incident.

Below, to our right, we saw the Roman road. The trees were still bare, and the columns of troops marching along the road looked as though they were moving behind iron bars. They were proceeding towards the west, English troops who had been beaten back by our offensive.

Flying low over the tops of the trees were several Sopwith Camels. These British single-seaters had the task of protecting the Roman road, which was one of the main arteries of their communications' system.

I had no time for further observations, for Richthofen set the nose of his red Fokker towards the ground and dived, with the rest of us following close on his tail. The Sopwiths scattered like chicks from a hawk, but one of them was too late – the one in the *Rittmeister's* sights.

It happened so quickly that one could hardly call it an aerial fight. For a moment I thought that the *Rittmeister* would ram him, so short was the space that separated them. I estimated it at 30 feet at the most. Suddenly the nose of the Sopwith tilted downwards and a cloud of white smoke shot from the exhaust. The ill-fated machine crashed into a field close to the road and burst into flames.

Richthofen, instead of changing direction as we expected, continued to dive until he was close above the Roman road. Tearing along at a height of about 30 feet from the ground, he peppered the marching troops with his two guns. We followed close behind him and copied his example.

The troops below us seemed to have been lamed with horror and apart from the few men who took cover in the ditch at the roadside, hardly anyone returned our fire. On reaching the end of the road the *Rittmeister* turned and again fired at the column. We could now observe the effect of our first assault: bolting horses and stranded guns blocked the road, bringing the column to a complete standstill.

[*Reprinted from* Ace of the Black Cross *by Ernst Udet, published by Newnes.*]

THE FIGHTERS MEET THEIR MATCH

Although large-scale strategic raids have always been the most dramatic form of bombing, it is debatable whether they have proved as valuable as local tactical raids in support of ground troops or against specific military objectives. This was certainly the case in 1914–18, and it was the small fast planes used in the latter role that made the most significant contribution

Bombing did not make a very great contribution to the First War and reconnaissance remained the most important use of aircraft. In spite of great technological advances, neither the bombers themselves, nor the bombs they carried were sufficiently powerful, or available in large enough numbers, to determine the outcome of any particular battle. Some of the bombing attacks were indeed spectacular, but it was the psychological fear they caused that created the spectre of terror bombing in the years after the war. This was reinforced by air force leaders who were to claim more for the power of strategic bombing than they could actually fulfil when the time came. But during the First World War, the most important contribution of both fighters and bombers was to control the air space over the battle zones by destroying the enemy's aircraft in the air and on the ground. Complete control could never be achieved, of course, and the balance swung to and fro depending on the quality and number of aircraft possessed by one side at any particular time.

In later wars, such as Germany's attack on Poland in 1939 and Israel's pre-emptive strike against the Arabs in the six-day war of 1967, complete control of air space was a decisive factor, but only in relation to the effort of ground forces and the strategic aims of the war. The much greater air superiority enjoyed by the Americans in Vietnam failed to achieve a decisive result because of the vagueness of the strategic aims. As the history of bombing has proved time and time again, attacks on military targets, especially airfields, are perhaps the most useful contribution that bombers can make in an overall war effort. The Luftwaffe's failure to maintain such attacks during the Battle of Britain, because the temptation to bomb civilian targets was too irresistible, altered the course of the Second World War. As the Germans, the British and – in another war – the Americans discovered, bombing civilians diverted an effort which might more usefully have been directed elsewhere. Not only did it fail to produce the expected psychological results, but it invariably strengthened a country's morale.

Shorter landing

During the First World War, therefore, in spite of the dramatic raids of heavy night bombers and their subsequent effect on the thinking of air force planners, it was the smaller and faster bombers, used for tactical raids in the battle areas, that made the most significant contribution. Some remarkable and highly successful aircraft were produced for that purpose. Although the British, through the efforts of the RNAS, were the first to carry out strategic raids, it was the French who employed bombing most widely during the early part of the war. The Voisin was the most predominant type of bomber aircraft at that time and it continued in service in various forms right up to the end of the war. It was very sturdy, due to the extensive use of steel in its construction, and was able to operate from small, rough fields, making for a short landing run. It was the first aircraft to be equipped with wheel brakes. But the early advantage of the pusher type of aeroplane was lost as soon as machine-guns were mounted in the rear cockpits of the faster tractor-driven types, and even more so with the development of fixed, forward-firing machine-guns.

The pusher was inevitably slower because of the drag created by the booms which carried the tail, the three-bay wing structure, and the complicated system of bracing struts and wires associated with such a configuration. By the autumn of 1915, the Voisin and the other pushers, with maximum speeds of little more than 70 mph, had to be relegated to night bombing. The resulting decrease in their effectiveness was largely responsible for the lack of interest shown by the French at this time in strategic bombing.

The first of a new family of Voisins, the Voisin VIII, with longer wings and distinctive streamlined fuel tanks mounted between them, appeared early in 1917. It was powered by a converted lorry engine, the 220 hp in-line Peugeot 8a, which gave it a speed of over 80 mph and a bomb load of 400 lb. Another feature was the replacement of the normal machine-gun with a 37-mm Hotchkiss quick-firing cannon. But the engine did not prove reliable, and the speed was still too low for it to be used for anything other than night bombing.

The Voisin X which appeared at the front early in 1918 had a much better performance and range, able to deliver 660 lb of bombs against a target 150 miles distant and return, but it too had to be confined to night bombing, for which purpose it was painted entirely in black.

Another pusher type of bomber which remained in service until the end of the war was the Bréguet-Michelin. This should have appeared in 1915, when its performance, superior to that of the Voisin, would have made it a useful day-bomber. In a competition with one of the early tractor biplanes produced by Paul Schmitt, the Bréguet-Michelin won hands down and promised to meet the specification for a powerful aeroplane capable of destroying enemy munition factories. But delays were caused by the initial failure of the 220 hp Renault engine, and by the time it appeared on the Western Front, in 1916, the development of fast fighter interceptors meant that it, too, had to be confined to night bombing. Meanwhile, Paul Schmitt had overcome his early difficulties and much was expected of the PS 7 single-engined tractor type. Again, how-

MARTINSYDE G 100 'ELEPHANT'

Gross weight: 2,458 lb **Span**: 38 ft **Length**: 26 ft 6 in **Engine**: 120 hp Beardmore **Armament**: 2 Lewis machine-guns **Crew**: 1 **Speed**: 108 mph at ground level **Ceiling**: 16,000 ft **Range**: 4½ hrs **Bomb load**: 1×230 lb or 4×65 lb

Based on a design for a long-range fighting scout, the Martinsyde 'Elephant' was introduced in 1915 as a bomber because of its ability to carry one of the large British bombs then being developed. It served in the interim before the specially designed bombers became available and was particularly effective in low-level attacks

ever, delays in production held back deliveries until 1917, and although it was used as a day-bomber, it was by then virtually obsolete.

The most successful of the single-engined French bombers, the Bréguet 14, was a remarkable aircraft in its own right, remaining in general service until 1930. It was a tractor type which first flew in November 1916 and was brought into service late in 1917. With a maximum speed of 112 mph at sea level, a service ceiling of 18,000 feet, a range of 435 miles and capable of carrying thirty-two 22-lb bombs, it at last provided the French with a first class day-bomber which could take on fighters on something approaching equal terms. It was built largely of light alloy and was powered by a 300 hp Renault engine which enabled it to climb to 16,500 feet in 39 minutes.

Of the seventeen versions produced, three were used as bombers – the B2 two-seater day-bomber, the BN2 two-seater night-bomber, and the B1 single-seater bomber. The Bréguet 14 enabled the French bombardment squadrons to resume daylight operations on a scale never before possible, and under the command of such men as Vuillemin and de Göys, the bomber crews took over from the fighter pilots as the élite of the French aviation groups. From early 1918 until the end of the war, the Bréguet formations of the First Air Division made daily raids on German military targets. A striking example of the power of mass-bombing was given on 4 June 1918, when a concentration of German troops in a ravine near the forest of Villers-Cotterets was virtually obliterated.

Also in June 1918, the first day-bomber squadron of the American Expeditionary Forces, the 96th Aero, commenced operations with Bréguet 14 B2s supplied three months earlier. The rest of the US bombing units, which flew day-bombers only, were equipped with American-built DH 4s with Liberty engines, one of the most successful British planes of the war. In August 1918 all the American air squadrons at the front were grouped into the Air Service of the First Army, under the command of General W. Mitchell. In 150 American bombing raids before the end of the war, about 140 tons of bombs were dropped.

Early in 1915 the German C-class of two-seater tractor biplanes began to enter service with engines giving up to 180 hp, double that of the unarmed B-class machines. The new types were notable for the Parabellum machine-gun mounted in the rear cockpit giving them a 'sting in the tail', and which, for a period, turned the tables against the Allies. The British BE2c observation machine suffered particularly heavy casualties, because it retained the original layout with the pilot in the rear seat, leaving the observer/gunner hemmed in by wings, wires and struts. During the following year a number of the German C-class planes were developed as light bombers and formed into bombing groups (*kampfgeschwader*), but because of the shortage of aircraft they couldn't often be spared for strategic bombing. A raid on the night of 20 July 1916 showed what might have been achieved, when four machines bombed a British ammunition dump near St. Omer, destroying over twenty sheds and some 8,000 tons of ammunition.

Staff re-organisation

The Battle of the Somme in the summer of 1916 left the Germans even more desperately short of aircraft. Most of them were required to protect and escort the vital reconnaissance machines, leaving none to spare for bombing sorties. The aviation units at this time were divided among the various army groups with little co-ordination between them and this also detracted from their operations. Accordingly, in October 1916, all the units were combined under one command, directly responsible to Army GHQ. General von Hoeppner was appointed commander of the new German Army Air Service with Major Thomsen as his chief of staff. The only aviation force not controlled by this new organisation was the Naval Air Service which continued to come under navy command. While the heavy multi-engined bombers began night bombing raids on both the Eastern and Western fronts, von Hoeppner built up C-class units for daylight sorties against military targets on the Western Front. In November 1917 the designation of the bombing groups was again changed to *Bombengeschwader*.

First of the C-class bombers to enter service was the Aviatik C III, with a maximum speed of 100 mph, a combat range of about 250 miles, and the ability to carry a bomb load of some 200 lb. The Albatros types used were the CIII, CVII and CX, the latter appearing in 1917 with a 260 hp Mercedes engine. All these were notable for their rounded tail units which had a 'fishtail' appearance. From the Rumpler firm came the CI and CIa, both of which were capable of carrying up to 220 lb of small bombs. The LVG C II, first appearing at the end of 1915, was credited with making the first daylight raid on London in November of the following year. During 1917, a CL category of plane was brought into service as a small, lightweight two-seater to undertake fighter escort duties. Two of these types, however, found additional employment in a ground-attack role in support of the infantry, when four or five 22-lb bombs could be dropped and enemy trenches machine-gunned. The Halberstadt CL II made its mark in attacking British troops during the Battle of Cambrai in November 1917. The other type, the Hannover CL IIIa, was unique among single-

SALMSON II

Gross weight: 2,798 lb **Span**: 38 ft 7 in **Length**: 27 ft 11 in **Engine**: 260 hp Salmson **Armament**: 2–3 machine-guns **Crew**: 2 **Speed**: 116 mph at 6,500 ft **Ceiling**: 20,500 ft **Range**: 3 hrs **Bomb load**: 200 lb

engined aircraft of the period for its biplane tail unit. It was so small and compact in design that Allied pilots often mistook it for a single-seater until, coming up to attack from behind in order to avoid the pilot's forward-firing gun, they were met with an unexpected hail of fire from the observer's machine-gun.

As well as the Caproni heavy bombers, the Italians also produced one of the fastest light bombers of the war, the Ansaldo SVA 5, in the summer of 1917. This single-seater biplane, powered by a 220 hp SPA in-line engine and with twin synchronised Vickers machine-guns mounted on top of the cowling, was originally intended to be a fighter. Although its maximum speed of 136 mph compared favourably with most fighters of the time, its lack of manoeuvrability made it unsuitable for fighting duties. However, it possessed two attributes which made it an excellent day-bomber; a range of over 600 miles, equal to that of the German Giants and almost double that of the Capronis, and the ability to carry a 200-lb bomb load. The SVA 5 entered service as a bomber in February 1918 and quickly established a reputation for itself, enabling the Italians for the first time to carry out long-range strategic raids on cities as far away as Innsbruck, Zagreb, Ljubljana and Friederichshafen. A two-seater version, the SVA9, was brought into service during the last months of the war, and one of these machines, with Gabrielle d'Annunzio as observer, led six SVA 5s on a 625-mile round journey from San Pelagio to Vienna to drop leaflets on the Austrian capital.

Many different types of British aircraft brought into service in the early days of the war were used as bombers, even those originally intended as fighters such as the FE2b two-seat pusher biplane produced by the Royal Aircraft Factory. Although not fitted with interrupter gear, the FE2b achieved considerable success as a fighter, with its two Lewis machine-guns and unobstructed view forward. One of its successes was claimed to be the shooting down of the German Fokker ace, Max Immelmann.

During daylight fighter-reconnaissance missions, eight 20-lb bombs could be carried, and a few aircraft of the type, fitted with Vickers one-pounder pom-pom guns, were found to be ideal for attacking trains. This kind of low-level ground-attack was primarily a British idea and was to lead later to the development of strike aircraft specifically designed for that purpose. By the end of 1916, however, the FE2b had been outclassed by the new Albatros and Halberstadt single-seat fighters and was used mainly for night bombing when up to three 112-pounders were carried.

British fighters continued to carry small bomb loads until the end of the war, primarily for ground-attack duties in support of the infantry. The two-seat Bristol Fighter, one of the best general purpose aircraft of the war, could carry up to twelve 20-lb bombs in racks under the bottom wing, and even the fast and highly manoeuvrable SE 5a and Sopwith Camel single-seat fighters could carry four 20-lb bombs. It was as a result of this experience that an experimental version of the Camel was built early in 1918 as an armoured trench fighter, fitted with two downward-firing machine-guns in addition to the one firing forwards, and with a sheet of armoured plate to protect the pilot from ground fire. The first British aircraft to be built specifically for this purpose was the heavily armour-plated Sopwith Salamander which could carry a remarkably heavy bomb load of nearly 650 lb in addition to its two machine-guns. It was built in some numbers but did not see active service before the war ended.

Meanwhile by 1915, the concept of bombing had been accepted, and plans put in hand for multi-engined heavy bombers.

DH 10 AMIENS Mk III

Gross weight: 9,000 lb. **Span**: 65 ft 6 in **Length**: 39 ft 7 in **Engine**: 2×400 hp Liberty **Armament**: 4 Lewis machine-guns **Crew**: 3 **Speed**: 116 mph at 6,500 ft **Ceiling**: 16,500 ft **Range**: 5 hrs **Bomb load**: 900 lb

One of several promising bombers being developed for the RAF, which arrived too late to see operational service before the end of the war. Later used for long-distance air mail services

DH 4

Gross weight: 3,312 lb **Span**: 42 ft 5 in **Length**: 30 ft 8 in **Engine**: 250 hp Rolls Royce Eagle **Armament**: 1×·303 Vickers; 1×·303 Lewis **Crew**: 2 **Speed**: 117 mph at 6,500 ft **Ceiling**: 16,000 ft **Range**: 3½ hrs **Bomb load**: 4×112 lb

But there was also a need for fast day-bombers which could drop larger bombs than the four 20-pounders carried by most of the adapted fighters. The first answer was the Martinsyde G 102 Elephant which appeared late in 1915, so named because it was a relatively large aeroplane for a single-seater, and designed to have an endurance of 5½ hours. It could carry loads of up to a single 336-lb bomb. While it had a high speed for the time of 104 mph, it was not very manoeuvrable, its ceiling was limited to 16,000 feet and it was used most successfully as a low-level bomber. Another type which could carry the 336-lb bomb was the Farnborough-designed RE7 which came into service early in 1916. This was originally intended as a two or three-seater reconnaissance machine, and the crew were normally armed only with rifles and pistols. The observer in the front cockpit had a very restricted field of fire, surrounded as he was by bracing struts and wires. The RE7 had a short-lived career, due to the development of fast and better-armed German fighters, but for a while its great weight-lifting capacity made it a useful bomber.

Early in 1917, there appeared in service with the RFC on the Western Front one of the best combat aircraft of the war and certainly the most outstanding day-bomber. This was the DH 4, designed by Geoffrey de Havilland and produced by the Aircraft Manufacturing Company (Airco). It was a straightforward two-seater tractor biplane, but unlike many aircraft coming into service at that time, part of whose construction was of metal, the DH 4 was built almost entirely of wood. It was fabric-covered, except for the front half of the fuselage, which was covered with plywood, and this improved both its appearance and its strength. There was more than the usual distance between the two cockpits, giving the pilot an excellent view for bombing, while the observer/gunner was far enough back to have a wide field of fire for his Lewis machine-gun. The only drawback was the difficulty in communication between the two crew members during combat. A speaking tube connecting the cockpits on some machines was of little use in view of the noise of the engines and slipstream, and most crews worked out a satisfactory system of hand signals. The pilot was provided with a Vickers machine-gun synchronised by the Constantinesco system. Later models had two forward-firing Vickers and some, built for the RNAS, had two Lewis guns on pillar mountings in the rear cockpit. The normal bomb load was two 230-lb or four 112-lb bombs, carried on racks under the fuselage and lower wings.

The prototype DH 4, first tested in the autumn of 1916, was powered by a 230 hp Beardmore-Halford-Pullinger engine, but this proved troublesome and was soon changed for the excellent 250 hp liquid-cooled Vee-twelve Eagle produced by Rolls-Royce. This gave it a remarkable speed of about 130 mph at 10,000 feet, and it could climb to this height in nine minutes. When the 375 hp Eagle was fitted later, the performance of the DH 4, both in speed (143 mph at sea level) and ceiling (22,000 ft), outclassed all but a very few of the opposing German fighters. In addition to the Western Front, it saw service in Italy, the Aegean, Macedonia and Palestine. It was the only British aircraft to be built in any number by the Americans, who produced nearly 5,000 with Liberty engines and twin forward-firing Marlin guns. Some 600 were in service with the American bomber units in France at the end of the war.

From the moment of its introduction, the DH 4 was successfully used by the RFC for daylight attacks on military targets, while the RNAS used the type mostly for anti-Zeppelin patrols – it was a DH 4 which shot down the Zeppelin L 70 in August 1918. But the real impetus given to British bomber production came after the Gotha raid on London in June 1917 when more damage was caused than during all the previous Zeppelin raids. It was decided to increase the strength of the RFC from 108 squadrons to 200, most of the new ones to be equipped with bombers to undertake a retaliatory strategic bombing campaign against German cities and industrial targets. Large numbers of the DH 4 were ordered, together with a new version, the DH 9, which had a longer range. This was basically similar to the DH 4, except that the pilot's cockpit was moved aft so that he could communicate more easily with his observer.

The DH 9 seemed to offer all the advantages of its predecessor and more, for it was expected to carry a heavier bomb load as well. But there were development problems with the BHP engine which had to be derated to 230 hp and further modified to facilitate production, at which point it was re-named the Siddeley Puma. The resulting loss of performance – the DH 9 could barely reach 13,000 feet with a full bomb and petrol load – rendered it considerably inferior to the older Rolls-Royce powered DH 4. By the time this was fully appreciated it was already being produced in large numbers and brought into service with the Independent Force. A marked improvement was achieved with the DH 9A, powered mostly by the 400 hp Liberty engine, although a few were fitted with the Rolls-Royce Eagle. This version could carry a maximum bomb load of 660 lb, and a normal load of two 230-lb bombs, at 17,000 feet without loss of height. It had a good enough performance to carry out daylight raids without escort, but unfortunately there were difficulties in obtaining the Liberty engine. Only four units had been re-equipped with 9As by the end of the war and they were only in active service for about two months.

The ill-fated DH 9 therefore had to bear the brunt of daytime operations with the Independent Force, with some pilots making as many as six sorties a day. Losses were high because of the reduced speed and ceiling, as well as the unreliability of the engines. During one raid against Mainz in July 1918, seven out of twelve DH 9s were shot down by German fighters and three had to turn back with engine failure. The day-bombers paid the highest price for the strategic bombing offensive against Germany; casualties among the four de Havilland squadrons were 25 killed, 178 missing and 58 wounded, with over 100 aircraft brought down over enemy territory and 201 wrecked in crashes on the Allied side of the lines.

This was a very different story from the early months of the war. It is fair to say that the bomber came of age during the First World War, proving all fears of its destructiveness to be well-founded. But defences against the bomber – fighters and anti-aircraft guns – had also developed. Some of the highest losses in men and aircraft were sustained by the bomber squadrons, especially those whose task it was to undertake precision bombing by day.

Light bombers on the production line of a French factory during 1918

Flight International

SHORT BOMBER

Gross weight: 6,800 lb **Span**: 85 ft **Length**: 45 ft **Engine**: 250 hp Rolls Royce Eagle **Armament**: 1 Lewis machine-gun **Crew**: 2 **Speed**: 77·5 mph **Ceiling**: 9,500 ft **Range**: 6 hrs **Bomb load**: 920 lb

A landplane development of the Short 184 seaplane, brought into service with the RNAS in 1916 to initiate the concept of strategic bombing behind the front line

BLOODY APRIL: SLAUGHTER IN THE SKY

The four months which culminated in 'Bloody April', 1917, taught one very important lesson: numerical superiority in the air cannot make up for technical inferiority. The preparations for the Battle of Arras and the battle itself came at a time when the Royal Flying Corps was suffering from a preponderance of obsolete aeroplanes, inadequate training for pilots and slow delivery of new types. The German air force, on the other hand, had recently been reorganised, new fighter aircraft were in production and, most important of all, morale, thanks largely to the inspiration of Oswald Boelcke, recently killed in an accident on the Somme, was higher than it had ever been. It is significant that when General Nivelle was discussing his proposed big push at a London conference in January, Sir Douglas Haig expressed the view that

Below: The **Sopwith 1½-Strutter.** Britain's first effective bomber/fighter-bomber had both backward and forward firing guns, air brakes and a variable incidence tailplane. *Engine:* Clerget rotary, 130 hp. *Armament:* one .303 Vickers and one .303-inch Lewis gun plus up to 224 lbs of bombs. *Speed:* 100 mph at 6,500 feet. *Endurance:* 4 hours

Below: The **AEG G III,** a slow and ponderous early German twin-engined fighter. *Engines:* Mercedes D IV, 220 hp, *Armament:* two 7.92-mm Parabellum machine guns plus up to 600 lbs of bombs. *Speed:* 99 mph at sea level. *Range:* 450 miles. *Ceiling:* 13,100 feet. *Span:* 60 feet 6 inches. *Length:* 30 feet 2¼ inches

the Royal Flying Corps would not be ready for an offensive by April 1. However, in February Allied strategy was neatly upset by the German High Command. Instead of waiting for the pincer movement which was to have nipped off the salient created by the Somme fighting, the German armies moved back to the Hindenburg Line defences they had been building throughout the winter. After much bad weather had hindered flying, a patrol of RFC Sopwith Pup single-seaters returned from offensive patrol to report large dumps burning and villages in flames: the salient was being evacuated and the country between the old and the new front lines laid waste in a 'scorched earth' policy. Complete plans for the German withdrawal were captured on March 14 and a British advance accordingly planned for March 17. For the first time since 1914 there would be something approaching open warfare as the British Fourth and Fifth Armies moved steadily forward for the next two weeks. There was little air opposition because on March 3 the Germans in their turn had captured General Nivelle's strategic plans for the great thrust on the Aisne and were massing their air forces to the north and south of the fighting around the Hindenburg Line, knowing that no important offensive could be launched from the now fluid British front line. The Aisne/Champagne sector was the affair of the French, and the main RFC concentration, supported by RNAS fighter squadrons, was on the Third Army front near Arras, and opposite the German fighter station at Douai, once the home of Immelmann and Boelcke, now HQ of Manfred von Richthofen's new *Jagdstaffel 11,* with V-

strutter Albatros D IIIs (160/175 hp in-line Mercedes D IIIa engine).

During the British advance to the Hindenburg Line, 'Contact Patrol' techniques learned on the Somme were put into effect, Aeroplanes co-operated closely with infantry and cavalry, carrying messages (dropped in message-bags), and sending out W/T 'zone calls', identifying tactical targets for the gunners and discovering (usually by drawing infantry fire) the German strongpoints. In practice aircraft were little needed, since opposition was slight and ground communications (cavalry and field telephone) reasonably effective. For long-distance reconnaissance of and behind the Hindenburg Line the army wings of the Fourth and Fifth Brigades, RFC, made some use of single-seater fighters – a return to the original idea of 'scouts'. Photographic maps were made by FE 2bs of No 22 Squadron escorted by No 54's Sopwith Pups.

The Battle of Arras began for the ground forces on Easter Monday, April 9, for the airmen five days before that. Their job was to clear the air of German machines so that corps aircraft of the First Army (holding a line roughly from the Béthune-La Bassée road south to the village of Angres, opposite Loos) and the Third Army (concentrated opposite Vimy Ridge and down to the Scarpe) could get on with their work of trench-mapping, artillery ranging and counterbattery work.

The German air force, well equipped with tractor single-seaters – Halberstadt and Albatros scouts, each armed with a pair of LMG 08/15 machine guns synchronised to fire through the propeller, in contrast with Allied machines' one gun, had profited by the lull between the Battle of the Somme and the Battle of Arras to train the hand-picked pilots of which the new *Jagdstaffeln* (fighter squadrons) were composed. A steady procession of sitting targets was provided by the BEs of the RFC on corps work when head-winds often reduced cruising speed to a snail's pace.

The RFC now learned the dangers of standardising and keeping in service an obsolete machine. A formation of six BE bombers, each virtually unarmed, required an escort of six FE 2b fighter-reconnaissance aircraft plus an 'umbrella' of six Sopwith Pups – an expensive way indeed of delivering six 112-pound bombs or a shower of 20-pound Cooper bombs from 6,000 feet with primitive bomb-sights. But Major-General Trenchard, commanding the RFC in France, and his French opposite number, *Commandant* du Peuty, in charge of the *Groupement de combat* on the Aisne, believed firmly that an offensive policy must be maintained whatever the cost. The aeroplane, they held, could not be used defensively because the sky was too vast. 'Victory in the air,' de Peuty announced in a note from GQG on April 9, 'must *precede* victory on land.' Again, 'Your task is to seek out, fight and destroy *l'aviation boche*.' The constant presence of Allied aircraft far behind the German lines not only worried the civilian population but pinned down quantities of fighters and AA gunners who could otherwise have been employed against 'corps aircraft' engaged in vital mapping, artillery spotting and counterbattery work above the trenches. Furthermore, reasoned Trenchard, if his airmen managed to retain the initiative when poorly equipped, there would be absolutely no holding them when equipment improved. Events were to prove him right.

April 1917 started early upon its 'Bloody' reputation. In the five days before the infantry attack, in a snow-storm, on April 9, 75 British aeroplanes were shot down with a loss of 105 crew (19 killed, 13 wounded and 73 missing). Wastage too was very high: 56 aeroplanes crashed and written off. Pilots were being posted to squadrons with as little as 10 hours solo to their credit and often with no experience whatever of the type they were to fly in combat. The average expectation of life for a British airman on the Western Front during the month of April 1917 was 23 days. The 25 squadrons, one third of which were single-seater units, lost 316 airmen killed in action from an establishment of 730 air-crew, a casualty rate of over 40% not counting those wounded, missing and grounded.

A magnificent exploit on the credit side, however, was a raid on Douai aerodrome by FE 2ds of 100 Squadron during the night of April 5/6. Two days later the FE 2ds made another raid on Douai, bombing the aerodrome and railway station twice. Meanwhile the squadron's two FE2bs, whose Vickers one-pounder pom-pom guns had arrived that day, attacked trains and other ground targets.

The worst piece of news reaching RFC HQ during the opening week concerned the Bristol Fighters, of which so much had been expected. Six F2As led by Captain W. Leefe Robinson, VC, of Zeppelin fame, had been 'jumped' by Manfred *Freiherr* von Richthofen and four of his *Staffel* in Albatros D III single-seaters from Douai. Richthofen shot down two, and two more fell to his comrades; the remaining two reached home, one badly damaged. From the wreckage the Germans could learn only that the unidentifiable engine was a V-12 of considerable power. The lesson drawn belatedly by the RFC was that the Bristol should be flown like a scout, using the synchronised Vickers as main armament, the observer's Lewis being a heaven-sent bonus to protect the tail. Flown thus, the Bristol was a most formidable fighting machine.

In the opening days of the Battle of Arras air fighting ran through the gamut of aerial tasks: unsuccessful attacks on kite balloons, artillery shoots to flatten German wire, photography, bombing and fighting. As infantry moved forward through unseasonable Easter snow, contact patrol aeroplanes, using Klaxon horn and Verey pistols, kept track of the advance. Zone calls were sent out to indicate special targets, and the gunners' response proved so prompt and accurate in counterbattery work that aircraft were able to turn upon infantry targets – the 'trench-strafing' which was to become a permanent and hazardous feature of squadron life. On the 10th, Nieuports of 60 Squadron went on tactical photographic reconnaissance, an unusual job for single-seaters. On the 11th Richthofen equalled Boelcke's score of 40 by shooting down a BE 2c of No 13 Squadron which lost a wing as it dived. Miraculously the crew escaped with bruises.

Unwilling to leave the front for a spell of celebration – and propaganda – leave, the *Jasta* commander insisted upon adding one more to his score. In fact he added two: on April 13, the first fine day of the battle, an RE 8 shortly after 0830 hours and an FE 2b at mid-morning. The former was one of six RE 8s, in which four were escorting the other two. All six were shot down, because the slow and cumbersome biplane was no match for a single-seater and by a series of misfortunes the OPs of three Spads, six FE 2ds and a flight of Bristol Fighters which were supposed to escort them past Douai failed to appear. Richthofen was allowed to remain at the front. British 'Offensive Patrols' met few HA (Hostile Aeroplanes), which were all joining in the battle, but RFC bombers were active all day, and that evening's mission against

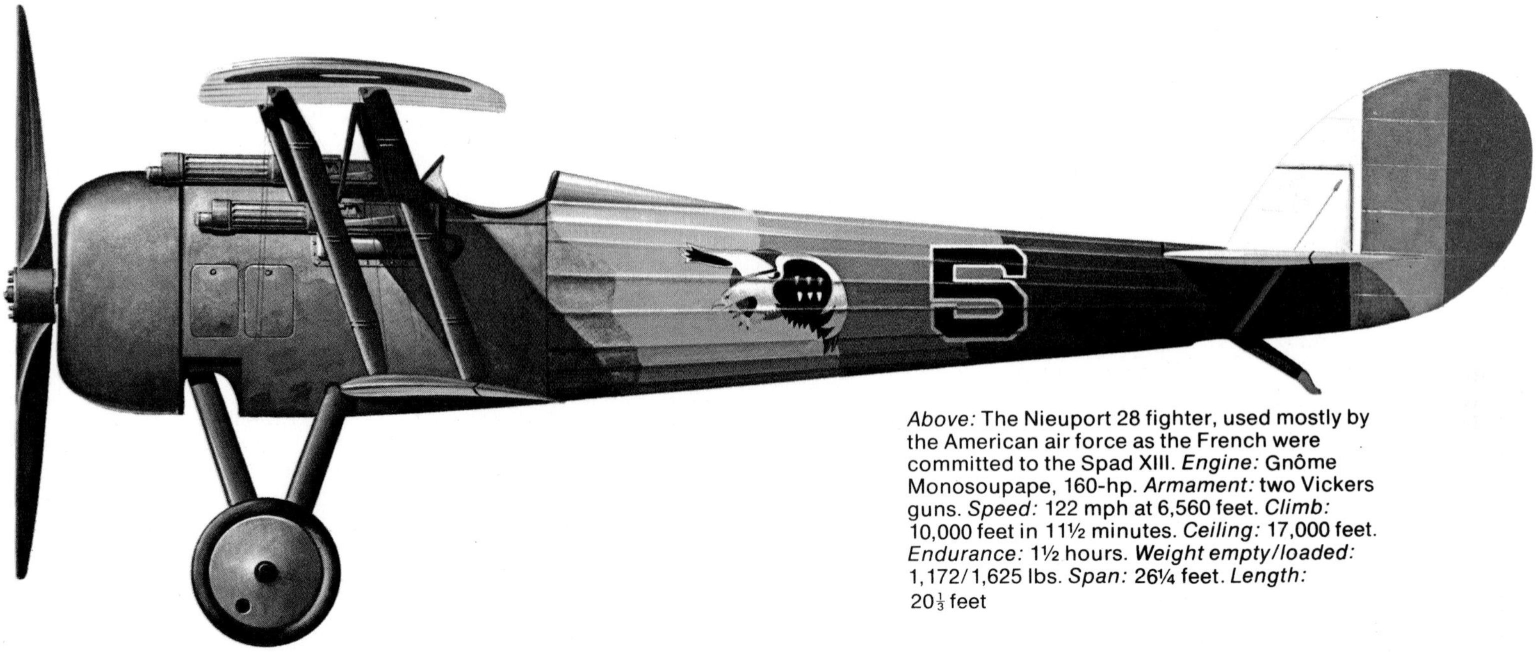

Above: The Nieuport 28 fighter, used mostly by the American air force as the French were committed to the Spad XIII. *Engine:* Gnôme Monosoupape, 160-hp. *Armament:* two Vickers guns. *Speed:* 122 mph at 6,560 feet. *Climb:* 10,000 feet in 11½ minutes. *Ceiling:* 17,000 feet. *Endurance:* 1½ hours. *Weight empty/loaded:* 1,172/1,625 lbs. *Span:* 26¼ feet. *Length:* 20⅓ feet

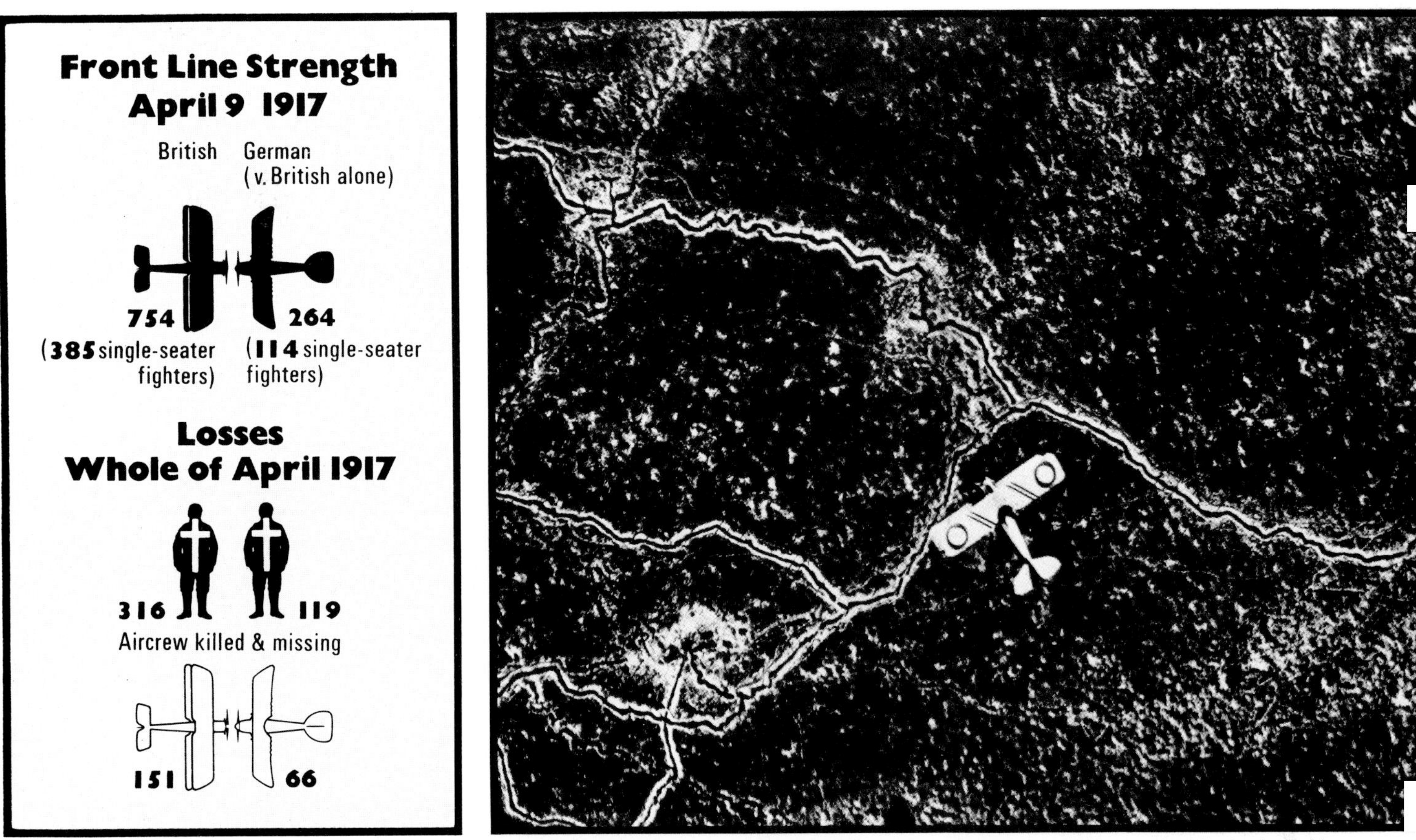

Bayer Hauptstaatsarchiv/Munich

Left: The credit and debit of 'Bloody April', in which the RFC suffered aircrew losses totalling 40%. *Right:* A Spad VII over the Hindenburg Line

Henin-Liétard railway station shows the scope and complication of such missions. Six 230-pound bombs and seven 112-pounders were dropped, the force comprising 12 Martinsyde G 102 'Elephants' escorted by five Spads and six Sopwith Pups, plus nine FE 2d pusher bombers with an escort of six Nieuports. Only one Martinsyde was lost, but on the way home the FE leader mistook a patrol of V-strutter Albatros for friendly Nieuports, and *Jasta 11* claimed three more victims.

It was a high time for the great individualists, the *as* (aces) as the French called them. The activities of the great fighter pilots are, of course, much discussed, but it may be noted here that Boelcke's record score of 40 was being challenged not only by his pupil, Richthofen, but also by the Frenchmen Georges Guynemer and René Fonck, and the young Englishman Alfred Ball. Guynemer and Ball, particularly, believed in hunting alone and attacking unseen from extremely close range, although they took part also in Flight and Squadron patrols.

Thanks largely to Boelcke, whose *Jagdstaffel* had practised full squadron take-offs and patrols as early as September 1916, much had been learned about fighter tactics. Acting at first in pairs as Boelcke and Immelmann had done in the Fokker *Eindekker* days, single-seater pilots had learned to operate in flights of three, or, preferably, four (two pairs), under a flight commander. After trying line-ahead, line abreast and echelon formations, both sides hit upon the Vee ('vic') and diamond, with the leader in front where his view was clear and his Verey light or 'wing waggling' signals could be seen. Pilots picked their own targets when the signal to attack was given, and reformed afterwards at a prearranged rendezvous. Four machines were regarded as the maximum for one leader to control, and when larger formations were used these were built up from several groups each under its own flight commander.

Into the battle the High Command of the *Luftstreitkräfte* moved reinforcements comprising two *Jagdstaffeln* (fighter squadrons), four *Abteilungen* of corps aircraft, and two *Schutzstaffeln* of armoured close-support biplanes with downward-firing guns, the new AEG J I two-seaters (200-hp Benz water-cooled six-cylinder engine). Their appearance coincided with the withdrawal of No 3 (Naval) Wing from Luxeuil, the base from which Sopwith 1½-Strutters had been engaged in strategic bombing of Germany. This enterprise, very much to the taste of RNAS pilots, was not relished politically by the French, who feared damage to the property of loyalists in Alsace-Lorraine and lived in dread of reprisals against French towns including Paris, which lay alarmingly close to the front.

The second phase of the Battle of Arras opened on April 16, when General Nivelle launched his widely publicised offensive on the Aisne. The fighters were commanded by *Commandant* du Peuty, the able ex-cavalryman whose 'offensive thinking' had early influenced Trenchard. Du Peuty was still under 40, a fact which did not endear him to certain senior officers. Under his command came *Groupes de combat* 11, 12 and 14, plus three *escadrilles* of Nieuport and Caudron machines – on paper four *groupes,* or 200 aeroplanes. In fact he had 131 machines on April 16, and only 153 by April 21, his maximum, to which could be added 30 machines from the Paris defences. Staff arrangements were woefully, and it seems almost wilfully, muddled. Pilots were sent to Le Bourget on ferry duty who should have been in action, and the front of the *Groupe des Armées de Réserve* was divided geographically, not according to commands. The staff had also decreed, on April 1, that each army must file its expected air requirements by 2000 hours the previous day.

German supremacy

There were to be six standing patrols along the whole front, three for each sector comprising:

- two patrols (one offensive, one defensive) at 6,000-8,000 feet (corps aircraft height); and
- one high patrol.

There was no zone call system, and often fighter *escadrilles* were not warned of local attacks or changes of plan.

German fighter supremacy was such that on April 13 it was requested that zero hour for the offensive on the 16th should be advanced to first light, as German dawn patrols would otherwise discover all. German fighters did, in fact, harry the front line during the attack, driving away French artillery and contact patrols. There was a continual cry for close, that is defensive, fighter support, notably from General Mangin, and in fact during the Verdun attack low patrols did operate at 2,000-3,000 feet between 0500 and 0615 hours to drive off marauding HA and to attack balloons. Bad weather limited du Peuty's long-range offensive patrols ('fortunately', said his detractors), and when these did go out, in patrols of six, 'never less than five', the Germans avoided combat, thus giving unconscious support to du Peuty's opponents on the French staff, who were quick to speak of 'wasting petrol', 'shadow-boxing' and the like. Theirs was to be the last word. *Commandant* du Peuty eventually resigned, and despite his cavalry background joined an infantry unit in the trenches, where he was killed.

In machines, too, France was weak. The Spad S VII (150-hp Hispano-Suiza) was a good fighter, as witness the scores of Guynemer and other aces, but the Voisins and Farmans were

Two of the best general purpose and reconnaissance aircraft to operate over the Western Front. *Top:* The French Salmson **2A 2**. The two most notable features of this machine were the absence of any fixed fin or tailplane and the provision of a water-cooled radial engine. 3,200 of the type were built. *Engine:* Salmson-Canton-Unné radial, 260 hp. *Armament:* one fixed Vickers gun and two flexible Lewis guns. *Speed:* 115 mph at 6,560 feet. *Ceiling:* 20,500 feet. *Endurance:* 3 hours. *Weight empty/loaded:* 1,676/2,954 lbs. *Span:* 38 feet 8½ inches. *Length:* 27 feet 10⅜ inches. *Crew:* 2. *Above:* The German **LVG C VI**, a development of the CV, which had been hampered by inferior handling characteristics and visibility. The C VI was much improved in these. *Engine:* Benz Bz IV inline, 200 hp. *Speed:* 106 mph at sea-level. *Climb:* 15 minutes to 9,840 feet. *Ceiling:* 21,350 feet. *Endurance:* 3½ hours. *Weight empty/loaded:* 2,046/3,058 lbs. *Span:* 42 feet 7¾ inches. *Length:* 24 feet 5¼ inches. *Crew:* 2. *Right:* The ill-fated **Bristol M 1C**, one of the best fighters produced in Great Britain during the First World War, but relegated to service in the Middle East. It was not mass-produced as it was claimed that its landing speed was too high at 49 mph. It seems more likely, however, that it was suffering from the War Office's prewar prejudice against and ban on monoplanes. It was very fast and manoeuvrable, and would have made a significant difference to the RFC during 'Bloody April'. *Engine:* Le Rhône rotary, 110 hp. *Armament:* one fixed Vickers gun. *Speed:* 130 mph at sea-level. *Climb:* 10 minutes 25 seconds to 10,000 feet. *Ceiling:* 20,000 feet. *Endurance:* 1¾ hours. *Weight empty/loaded:* 896/1,348 lbs. *Span:* 30 feet 9 inches. *Length:* 20 feet 5½ inches

Above: The Halberstadt **CL IV**, in Turkish markings. This, like the LVG C VI on the opposite page, was a development of an earlier type, in this instance the CL II. The improvements achieved with the CL IV lay in the field of handling, rather than absolute performance. This was achieved by repositioning the wing, shortening the fuselage and altering the size and shape of the tail surfaces extensively. After these modifications, the CL IV made an excellent escort and ground attack fighter in 1918. *Engine:* Mercedes D III, 160 hp. *Armament:* one or two fixed Spandau machine guns and one flexible Parabellum machine gun, plus anti-personnel grenades and four or five 22-lb. bombs. *Speed:* 103 mph at 16,400 feet. *Climb:* 32 minutes to 16,400 feet. *Ceiling:* 16,700 feet. *Endurance:* 3½ hours. *Weight empty/loaded:* 1,602/2,350 lbs. *Span:* 35 feet 2⅞ inches. *Length:* 21 feet 5½ inches. *Crew:* 2. Crew communications were especially good

John Batchelor

hopelessly outclassed. Only slightly better able to defend itself was the Caudron 4, a twin-engined three-seater (two 130-hp Hispano-Suizas) which lasted until replaced by the Letord I (two Hispano-Suiza V-8s). The *Aviation Militaire* also possessed for some reason the Paul Schmitt 7, an extraordinary biplane of great span, minimal performance and no fewer than 12 sets of interplane struts. The PS 7 (265-hp Renault) was unique in that the angle of incidence of the entire biplane cellule could be varied to give either maximum speed or maximum lift, but the drag was so great that neither speed nor lift was sufficient. The Paul Schmitt was armed with two machine guns and proved extremely unhandy in the air. Strangely, all documents relating to its adoption are missing from the French archives. The French also used Sopwith 1½-Strutters in two-seater and single-seat bomber form. Criticising it, with some justification, as more of a touring machine than a combat aeroplane, they applauded its *'exploits sportifs'* with the 240-pound bomb. French aviation, so brilliant during the early war years, was far from happy in spring 1917, despite the gallantry of individual airmen.

The new German tactics of ignoring offensive patrols the better to concentrate above the trenches were employed also on the Arras front, where the Germans, said General Trenchard, were 'undoubtedly slipping underneath our high patrols without being seen by them'. Even when a force of Bristol Fighters and RNAS Sopwith Triplanes trailed their coats above Douai itself *Jasta 11* failed to rise. Richthofen preferred to meet Nieuports in the air, which he did on April 16. Six Nieuports met four Albatros and four Nieuports went down.

Economical of aeroplanes, the Germans made few fighter sweeps behind the British lines, and because in their 1914 retreat they had prudently dug in on high ground affording a view over the plains, they had less need of aerial reconnaissance than had the RFC. Strangely, they made no sustained bombing attack on Calais, Boulogne and Dieppe, where disembarkation could have been severely hindered.

As the ground forces prepared for a new assault in the Arras sector to take some of the sting out of Nivelle's failure further south, bad weather kept most machines on the ground. The four days from the 16th to the 20th were virtually 'washed out'. On the 21st a preliminary bombardment flattened German wire and sorties were made against the balloons directing counterbattery fire. Two were shot down on the Third Army front and one on that of the Second Army. Three others were damaged but hauled down in time because the Germans had discovered a method far quicker than the winch: the cable was passed under a pulley and hitched to a lorry which then drove away, towing the balloon rapidly to the ground. The counter to this, invented by Major L. Tilney, CO of No 40 Squadron (Nieuports), was a hedge-hopping fighter attack at ground level. The Nieuport 17 sesquiplane was still the favourite mount of Captain Ball, the RFC's top-scoring pilot. He preferred it to his new SE 5, which was now operational after No 56 Squadron's CO had improved upon the Royal Aircraft Factory's design of the cockpit. W. A. Bishop, another future VC, also cherished his Nieuport 17 although clearly it was outperformed, and its single Lewis doubly outgunned, by the Albatros V-strutters it had inspired. A further four Nieuports were lost to *Jasta 11* pilots on April 21, but the RFC was past its bad time. The factory strikes at home which had halted production had now largely been settled and supplies of vital new aircraft were reaching the front. The SE 5 was in action, Sopwith Pups and Triplanes were more than a match for the German fighters, and the Sopwith Camel was on its way. Admittedly the SE was in trouble with its Hispano engine and with a new and secret gun-synchronising device for its Vickers but there was a Lewis on the centre-section and these teething troubles would soon be overcome.

Could the agility of the Triplane match the heavier armament of the Albatros?

The new synchronising gear had the great advantage that it could be fitted quickly to any type of engine. Invented by George Constantinesco, a Rumanian mining-engineer and developed by him with Major C. Colley, Royal Artillery, the device was known in the RFC as the CC gear, and must count as one of the simplest and most useful inventions of the war. It worked on the same principle as a modern car's hydraulic brakes, and may be described diagrammatically as a column of liquid in a pipe sealed by a plunger at each end. Pressure exerted at one end, by an engine cam, could not fail to reach the other and exert a similar and simultaneous pressure on, for example, the trigger of a gun. Tested on a BE 2c in August 1916, the design was adopted forthwith. The first squadron so equipped, No 55 (DH 4s), landed in France on March 6, 1917. Meanwhile obsolete machines like the BE 2c, FE 2b, 'Strutter' and the early marks of Spad continued to suffer, and occasionally to mistake Albatros for the friendly though outmoded Nieuport.

Left: Leutnant Werner Voss' Albatros D III fighter. The D III had double the armament of contemporary Allied fighters, but its wings were relatively weak and water from the centrally-placed radiator was likely to scald the pilot if it were punctured in combat. *Engine:* Mercedes D IIIa inline, 160/175 hp. *Armament:* two Spandau machine guns. *Speed:* 103 mph at sea level. *Climb:* 3.3 minutes to 3,280 feet. *Ceiling:* 18,050 feet. *Endurance:* 2 hours. *Weight empty/loaded:* 1,454/1,949 lbs. *Span:* 29 feet 8¼ inches. *Length:* 24 feet.

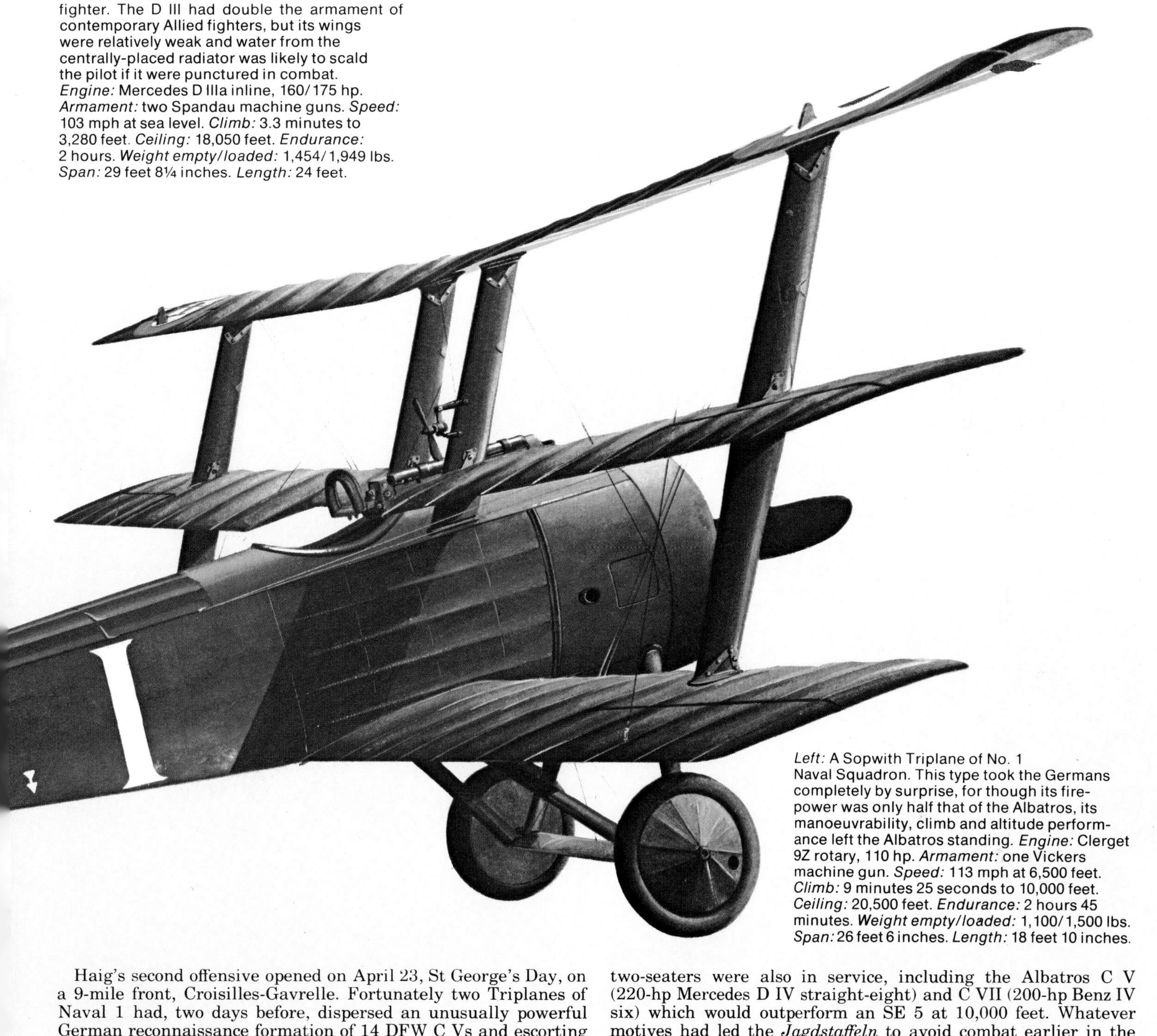

Left: A Sopwith Triplane of No. 1 Naval Squadron. This type took the Germans completely by surprise, for though its firepower was only half that of the Albatros, its manoeuvrability, climb and altitude performance left the Albatros standing. *Engine:* Clerget 9Z rotary, 110 hp. *Armament:* one Vickers machine gun. *Speed:* 113 mph at 6,500 feet. *Climb:* 9 minutes 25 seconds to 10,000 feet. *Ceiling:* 20,500 feet. *Endurance:* 2 hours 45 minutes. *Weight empty/loaded:* 1,100/1,500 lbs. *Span:* 26 feet 6 inches. *Length:* 18 feet 10 inches.

Haig's second offensive opened on April 23, St George's Day, on a 9-mile front, Croisilles-Gavrelle. Fortunately two Triplanes of Naval 1 had, two days before, dispersed an unusually powerful German reconnaissance formation of 14 DFW C Vs and escorting Albatros, disappointing them of vital information. Tiny, compact and with the masses of engine, pilot and tanks closely concentrated, the 'Tripehound' was immensely manoeuvrable and in its element at 16,000 feet, where this engagement took place.

Over the lines on St George's Day, German fighters from a variety of units harried the unfortunate corps aircraft as they wheeled in figures of eight spotting for the guns, while army squadrons gave what support they could. In an area bounded by Lens, Henin-Liétard, Bullecourt, Sains and the battle line itself 48 British scouts and Bristol Fighters plus 20 two-seater fighter-reconnaissance machines were on Offensive Patrol, while the number of famous names figuring in the day's engagements read like 'Who's Who': Ball, Bishop, Hermann Göring, Lothar von Richthofen (brother of Manfred) and of course Richthofen himself. That evening a bombing raid on Epinoy by six FEs of 18 Squadron escorted by five Pups was attacked by two formations of Albatros and Halberstadt fighters and there developed one of the first big 'dog-fights' of the war, as British Fighters, Triplanes and Nieuports hastened to join in a fight, which lasted for an hour. Later FE 2d night bombers of 100 Squadron overflew Douai to bomb Pont à Vendin station, also machine gunning troop trains whereby desperately needed German reinforcements arrived late and almost too tired to relieve their comrades in the trenches.

During daylight fighter opposition was intense. New German two-seaters were also in service, including the Albatros C V (220-hp Mercedes D IV straight-eight) and C VII (200-hp Benz IV six) which would outperform an SE 5 at 10,000 feet. Whatever motives had led the *Jagdstaffeln* to avoid combat earlier in the month, they were now deployed in full force and full of spirit. On the morning of April 29, picturesquely, the Richthofen brothers each shot down a Spad before entertaining their father, Major Albrecht *Freiherr* von Richthofen, to lunch in the mess. At 1600 hours Manfred destroyed an FE after a stiff fight over Inchy, while on yet another sortie the two brothers scored again, against a pair of BE 2ds. In a final combat of the day, when *Jasta 11* was involved with 11 Triplanes of Naval 8 and one Nieuport of 60 Squadron, Manfred secured his 52nd victim, but only after Captain F. L. Barwell's Nieuport, absurdly underpowered and underarmed in comparison with the Albatros, had defended itself magnificently for almost half an hour. Not all Manfred von Richthofen's victims were easy ones, though it must be pointed out that although without so many defenceless BEs and antiquated pushers in the sky his score would undoubtedly have been smaller.

The Red Baron

Quantity production of factory-designed BE 2, FE 2 and RE 8 biplanes made up to some extent for the Allies' lack of high ground. It was therefore essential for the Germans to shoot them down. With so many targets the German rate of scoring was high – four times (and on some sectors even five times) the RFC rate; but the RFC fighters were usually matched against fighters, either on offensive patrol or while driving the predatory Albatros from its

Right: German air force personnel gather round to inspect a captured Nieuport. *Below:* An Albatros C X reconnaissance machine, which joined the C VII in service in early 1917 and soon entirely supplanted it

Bayer Hauptstaatsarchiv/Munich

prey. Their antagonists, the *Jagdstaffeln* invented by Boelcke in 1916 and efficiently developed by Richthofen, had done well, thanks to good equipment, good training—and plentiful targets. There was also the *panache* that characterised the elder Richthofen. It was a master stroke to paint the aeroplanes of his squadron in brilliant colours—quite against German army regulations—while reserving the only almost totally red machine for himself, a return to the personal style of the mediaeval knight, with his crest and coat of arms. No better publicity device has ever been invented than the blood red aircraft of 'the Red Knight'.

Further to raise the rate of scoring it was now decided to increase the local striking power of the *Jagdstaffeln* by banding together four of them into a larger group. *Jasta 11* was combined with numbers *3, 4* and *33* into an independent fighter wing called *Jagdgruppe 1* which first went into action, rather clumsily, on April 30, the day on which *Rittmeister* Manfred von Richthofen went on leave to celebrate his 52 victories. Reorganised on his return, and now comprising *Jagdstaffeln* numbers *11, 10, 6* and *4*, this unit became the true 'Richthofen Circus', a private army of mobile trouble-shooters known after July as *Jagdgeschwader 1*.

'Bloody April' was over. The supply of new machines from England improved and new types came into service capable of outfighting the Albatros D III and Halberstadt scouts which had taken such toll during the worst month in the history of British air fighting overseas. French airmen too had taken a terrible beating during the ill-fated 'push' of General Nivelle, now fortunately superseded.

In the RFC casualties would have been lighter if those responsible for supply had been more flexible in outlook. It would have been perfectly possible to update the Royal Aircraft Factory's series of helpless BE two-seaters so that pilot and passenger changed places, giving the observer a clear field of fire. Frederick Koolhoven of Armstrong-Whitworth had refused to build BEs and the result was the FK 8, the 'Big Ack', a far more robust and effective machine. The lack of British engines, a result of blind trust in the French aviation industry, led to many casualties, for a rotary Le Rhône or Clerget of 110-hp or 130-hp, although marginally sufficient for a single-seater fighter, was woefully inadequate in two-seaters like the Sopwith 1½-Strutter. The Factory's air-cooled stationary engines, based on Renault designs, lacked smoothness, power and reliability, while the cooling scoops devised by Factory designers had a disastrous effect on the performance of BE and RE aeroplanes.

Technical inferiority must always mean a high casualty rate. Machines already proved obsolete against the Fokker monoplane in 1915 could not be expected to hold off an Albatros D III, and it is not surprising that some squadrons during Bloody April lost more aircrew than there were chairs in the Mess. Perhaps Trenchard's policy of 'offensive at all costs' was unduly robust for the machines under his command. But the Royal Flying Corps did all he required of it during both periods of German air supremacy, and the fact that RFC pilots never lost their offensive spirit was to prove decisive during the coming struggles with the 'Circus', and the tremendous ground-strafing days of 1918.

Bayer Hauptstaatsarchiv/Munich

THE EYES OF THE FLEETS

Opposite page, top: The **Franco-British Aviation Type H** flying boat. Despite its name, the FBA concern was almost entirely French, and built a series of excellent flying boats for the air services of the Allies, starting with the Type B in 1915 and culminating with the Type S in 1918. Illustrated is the first model to be powered with an inline engine, the Type H anti-submarine and coastal patrol flying boat. This model was built in great numbers (at least 982) in Italy, and had the distinction of being produced in larger quantities than any other such machine in the First World War. *Engine:* Hispano-Suiza inline, 150- or 170-hp, Lorraine inline, 160-hp or Isotta-Fraschini inline, 180-hp. *Armament:* one machine gun (Lewis or Revelli) and a small bomb load. *Crew:* 3. *Speed:* 90 mph at sea level. *Climb:* 3,280 feet in 8 minutes. *Ceiling:* 16,000 feet. *Range:* 373 miles. *Weight empty/loaded:* 2,170/3,218 lbs. *Span:* 46 feet 7 inches. *Length:* 33 feet 2 inches. *Centre:* The Italian **Macchi M 7** fighter flying boat of 1918. Only three had been delivered before the Armistice, but they would have been more than a match for the Austro-Hungarian fighters of the same configuration. *Engine:* Isotta-Fraschini V-6B, 250-hp. *Armament:* two Fiat machine guns. *Speed:* 130 mph at sea level. *Climb:* 16,400 feet in 22 minutes. *Ceiling:* 16,400 feet. *Range:* 522 miles. *Weight empty/loaded:* 1,710/2,381 lbs. *Span:* 32 feet 8 inches. *Length:* 26 feet 7 inches. *Bottom:* The **Porte-Felixstowe F 3,** one of Britain's best boats of the war, developed from a Curtiss design by Commander J. Porte RN. The design was for an anti-submarine and patrol bomber, and was built mainly in 1918. *Engines:* two Rolls-Royce Eagle VIII, 345-hp each. *Armament:* four Lewis guns and four 230-lb bombs. *Crew:* 4. *Speed:* 93 mph at 2,000 feet. *Climb:* 10,000 feet in 24 minutes 50 seconds. *Ceiling:* 12,500 feet. *Endurance:* up to 9½ hours. *Weight empty/loaded:* 7,958/13,281 lbs. *Span:* 102 feet. *Length:* 49 feet 2 inches. *This page, below:* The German **Hansa-Brandenburg FB** patrol flying boat. Only six were built for the German navy, though the type was used in some numbers by the Austro-Hungarian navy in the Adriatic between 1915 and the end of the war. *Engine:* Austro-Daimler inline, 165-hp. *Armament:* one Parabellum machine gun. *Crew:* 3. *Speed:* 87 mph at sea level. *Climb:* 3,280 feet in 8½ minutes. *Range:* 683 miles. *Weight empty/loaded:* 2,513/3,571 lbs. *Span:* 52½ feet. *Length:* 33¼ feet

A Sopwith Pup is swayed out of its hangar on an early aircraft carrier, another dimension in the use of aircraft on the seas

1918: THE GREAT LEAP FORWARD

Had the war continued into 1919 there would have doubtless been great advances in the technology of war, but none so much as in aeronautics. By 1918 the Germans and the Allies had made enormous strides in basic design, engine power and in structures and materials

Double page, top: The classic two-seater of the First World War, the Bristol F2B fighter. The photograph shows four F2B's of 22 Squadron taking off in France in June 1918. *This page, top:* The Vickers FB 27 Vimy bomber, destined for a great future in 1919. *Centre left:* The Pfalz D XII fighter. Though overshadowed by the remarkable Fokker D VII, the D XII was nevertheless an excellent machine. *Above:* The Junkers CL I ground attack fighter, whose advanced features included cantilever monoplane wings and a metal skin. The gunner had a good field of fire and the pilot two machine guns, compared with the more standard one of most such machines. *Left:* The ultimate in the Sopwith stable of rotary-engined fighters, the 7F I Snipe. *Opposite page, top left:* The Junkers D I fighter, of which the CL I was a scaled-up version. This was the world's first all-metal service warplane, and proved very nimble and strong. *Top right:* The Pfalz D XV was fast and scheduled for large production in 1919. Note the fuselage mounted between the wings and the lack of exterior wires. Centre left: The Nieuport 29C 1 fighter. It was very fast (143 mph at sea level) and the first Nieuport fighter to have a stationary engine. *Centre right:* The Siemens-Schuckert D VI experimental fighter, featuring a parasol wing and a jettisonable belly tank for its fuel. *Bottom:* The Martinsyde F 4 fighter, the fastest Allied fighter of the war at 145 mph

Imperial War Museum

1
S.V.A.
11779
5
2

Left: 'Panorama of the Western Front' by W. G. Wyllie. *Below:* 1918 aircraft. **1.** The Italian Savoia-Verduzio-Ansaldo 5 bomber and reconnaissance machine, of the 87° *Squadriglia (La Serenissima).* The SVA 5 had good climb and range, and an odd fuselage marked by a change from rectangular to triangular section aft of the cockpit. *Engine:* SPA 6A inline, 205-220 hp. *Armament:* two Vickers guns. *Speed:* 143 mph at sea level. *Climb:* 12 mins 50 secs to 13,120 feet. *Endurance:* 4 hours. *Weight empty/loaded:* 1,500/2,315 lbs. *Span:* 29 ft 10¼ ins. *Length:* 26 ft 7 ins. **2.** The French Spad S XIII, in the markings of a pilot of the US 94th (Hat in the Ring) Squadron. The S XIII was an improved version of the VII. *Engine:* Hispano-Suiza 8, 220-235 hp. *Armament:* two Vickers guns. *Speed:* 138 mph at 6,560 ft. *Climb:* 12 mins 10 secs to 13,124 ft. *Ceiling:* 21,800 ft. *Endurance:* 2 hours. *Weight empty/loaded:* 1,245/1,807 lbs. *Span:* 26 ft 6¾ ins. *Length:* 20 ft 4 ins. **3.** The German Albatros D Va, an up-engined version of the D III. The one illustrated was flown by *Leutnant* von Hippel of *Jasta 5. Engine:* Mercedes D IIIa, 170-185 hp. *Armament:* two 'Spandau' machine guns. *Speed:* 116 mph at 3,280 ft. *Climb:* 22.8 mins to 13,120 ft. *Ceiling:* 20,500 ft. *Endurance:* 2 hours. *Weight empty/loaded:* 1,511/2,061 lbs. *Span:* 29 ft 8¼ ins. *Length:* 24 ft 0⅝ ins. **4.** The French Nieuport 17, this machine being flown by Charles Nungesser. *Engine:* Le Rhône rotary, 110 hp. *Armament:* one Vickers gun. *Speed:* 107 mph at 6,500 ft. *Climb:* 9 mins to 10,000 ft. *Ceiling:* 17,500 ft. *Weight empty/loaded:* 825/1,232 lbs. *Span:* 26 ft. *Length:* 19 ft 7 ins

Royal R.A.F. Staff College

3

4

John Batchelor

Above: The **Bristol F2B** reconnaissance fighter. *Engine:* Rolls Royce Falcon III, 275 hp. *Armament:* one fixed Vickers and one or two free Lewis guns plus 12 20-lb bombs. *Speed:* 123 mph at 5,000 feet. *Climb:* 11 minutes 15 seconds to 10,000 feet. *Ceiling:* 21,500 feet. *Endurance:* 3 hours. *Weight empty/loaded:* 1,934/2,779 lbs. *Span:* 39 feet 3 inches. *Length:* 25 feet 10 inches

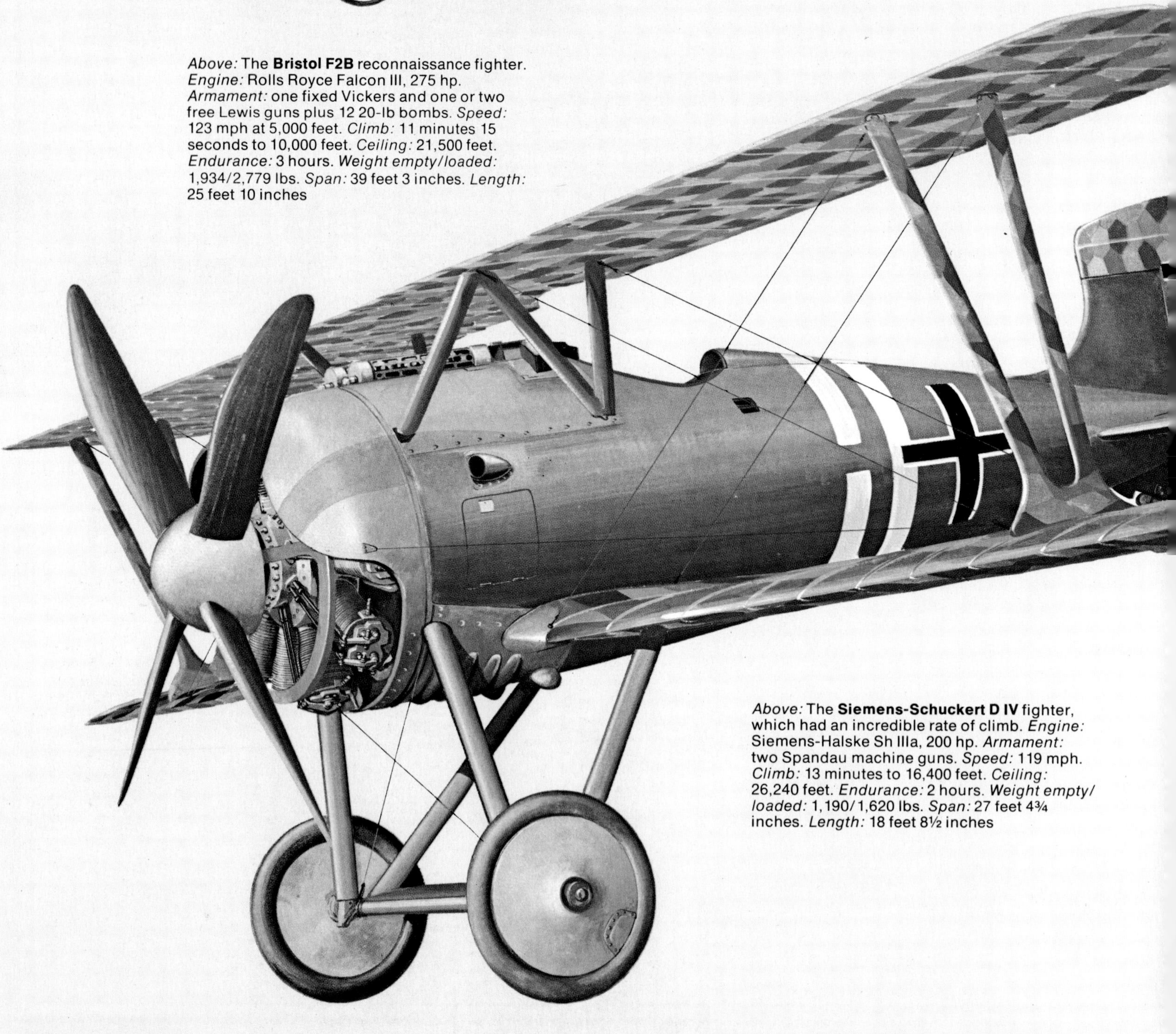

Above: The **Siemens-Schuckert D IV** fighter, which had an incredible rate of climb. *Engine:* Siemens-Halske Sh IIIa, 200 hp. *Armament:* two Spandau machine guns. *Speed:* 119 mph. *Climb:* 13 minutes to 16,400 feet. *Ceiling:* 26,240 feet. *Endurance:* 2 hours. *Weight empty/loaded:* 1,190/1,620 lbs. *Span:* 27 feet 4¾ inches. *Length:* 18 feet 8½ inches

The "Cat's Whiskers": the ultimate aircraft of WW1

Below: The **Fokker D VIII** fighter, possessed of good performance and quite outstanding manoeuvrability. *Engine:* Oberursel U II, 110 hp. *Armament:* two Spandau machine guns. *Speed:* 127½ mph at sea level. *Climb:* 10¾ minutes to 13,120 feet. *Ceiling:* 19,680 feet. *Endurance:* 1½ hours. *Weight empty/loaded:* 893/1,334 lbs. *Span:* 27 feet 4⅜ inches. *Length:* 19 feet 2¾ inches

Below: The German **Hannover CL IIIa** escort fighter and ground attack aircraft, introduced in 1918. *Engine:* Argus As III inline, 180 hp. *Armament:* one fixed Spandau and one free Parabellum machine gun. *Speed:* 103 mph at 16,400 feet. *Climb:* 5 minutes 18 seconds to 3,280 feet. *Ceiling:* 24,600 feet. *Endurance:* 3 hours. *Weight empty/loaded:* 1,577/2,378 lbs. *Span:* 38 feet 4¾ inches. *Length:* 24 feet 10½ in.

Above: The **Packard-Le Père LUSAC II** two-seater fighter that would have been the equivalent of the Bristol F2B had the war continued until 1919. Thirty were built and 3,495 cancelled. *Engine:* Liberty 12A, 400 hp. *Armament:* two fixed Marlin and two flexible Lewis guns. *Speed:* 132 mph at 2,000 feet. *Climb:* 9 minutes 48 seconds to 10,000 feet. *Ceiling:* 20,000 feet. *Range:* 320 miles. *Weight empty/loaded:* 2,466/3,746 lbs. *Span:* 41 feet 7 inches. *Length:* 25 feet 6 inches

Photo: An RFC pilot prepares for take-off in an RE 8 artillery observation aircraft

Below: The **Thomas-Morse S-4C** advanced fighter trainer designed in 1917 as a combat plane, but shown in practice to be underpowered by its US-built rotary engines. *Engine:* Le Rhône rotary, 80 hp. *Speed:* 95 mph at sea level. *Climb:* 22 minutes to 10,000 feet. *Ceiling:* 15,000 feet. *Weight empty/loaded:* 964/1,374 lbs. *Span:* 26 feet 6 inches. *Length:* 19 feet 10 inches

Imperial War Museum

BETWEEN THE WARS

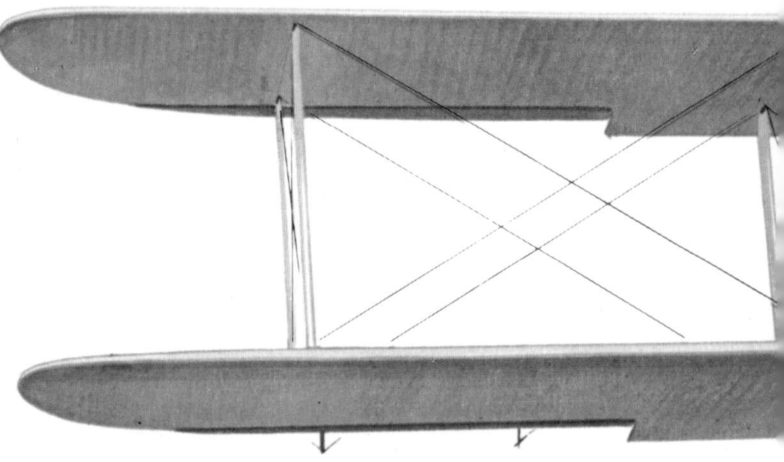

In the post-war years, de-militarisation and financial stringency put many obstacles in the way of the bomber's development. Private designs proliferated, but in the absence of any official policy, progress was haphazard and unco-ordinated. Some remarkable aircraft were produced nonetheless, and all the bombers used operationally during the Second World War were being developed by the mid-1930s

In many ways the most advanced plane of the First World War was the Junkers D 1 which embodied many of the features that were to become generally accepted in the 1930s. It was a cantilever monoplane with an all-metal airframe covered with thin sheet iron, resulting in such a strong structure that no struts or bracing wires were required to support the wings. Although the D1 was first flown in 1916, only a few were built during the war because of production problems. Under wartime conditions, aircraft were needed in such large numbers – France produced some 60,000, Britain 53,000, Germany 48,000, Italy 20,000 and the USA 12,000 – that preference often had to be given to simplicity of construction over ingenuity of design.

The large number of aircraft produced meant that there was a considerable surplus when the war ended, except in Germany. This ultimately turned out to Germany's advantage, since she had to build up a new air force from scratch, without the encumbrance of older types of aircraft. Meanwhile, a number of the large Allied bombers such as the DH 10 Amiens and the Il'ya Muromets, were used to pioneer civil transportation, opening up passenger, freight and mail routes around the world. Expenditure on military aircraft was severely cut back after the 'war to end wars', and it was not long before aircraft specifically designed as civil airliners had taken a technical lead over the bomber types from which they were originally developed.

Almost all the bombers used during the Second World War were the result of a technological revolution which took place in the early 1930s. This was led by the development of airliners in the USA and saw the increasing use of all-metal cantilever monoplanes with stressed alloy skins, retractable undercarriages, flaps, constant-speed propellers with variable pitch, and with radios among more efficient navigational aids. But for most of the period between the wars however, the biplane had remained the predominant type, and the first bombers to be produced after the First World War continued to be constructed mainly of wood.

In Britain, for instance, the twin-engined Vickers Virginia, the main RAF heavy night bomber from 1924 to 1937, was of conventional wood and fabric construction, as was the Martin MB-2, in service from 1919 to 1927. This, the first American-designed bomber, was intended to improve on the performance of the Handley Page 0/400 then being built under licence in the USA. A similar French type was the Farman F 60 series, which appeared in the closing stages of the First World War, and remained in service until 1928, while a civil version developed from the Goliath was used with considerable success by French commercial fleets during the same period. In Italy, the large multi-engined Caproni bombers were replaced by the single-engined Caproni Ca 73 series, notable for their unusual inverted sesquiplane arrangement. Another single-engined bomber of conventional wood and fabric construction was the de Havilland R1, a Soviet version of the remarkable DH 9A – the first Russian aircraft to be mass-produced – which served from 1923 to 1935.

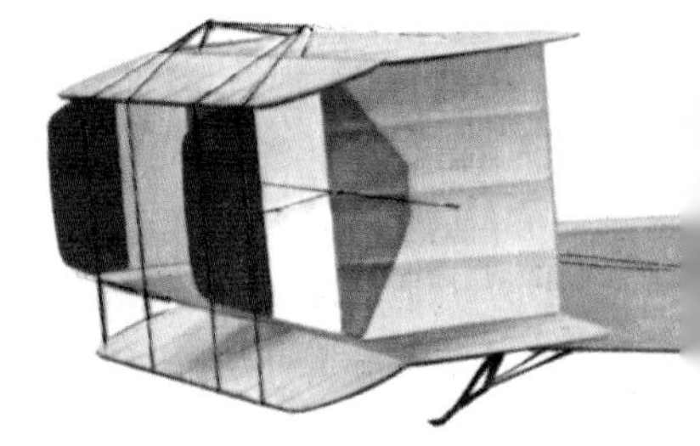

Limited service

The gradual change from wood to metal construction for military aircraft took place almost universally in the mid-1920s. Although the Avro Aldershot, one of the first new bombers to be designed for the RAF after the First World War, had only a single engine, it was intended as a heavy night bomber and could in fact carry a bomb load of 2,000 lb, equal to that of most twin-engined types of the period. But the Air Staff decided against the idea of single-engined heavy bombers and the Aldershot saw only limited service.

A similar policy decision was taken in the USA where the Huff-Daland bomber (the name was later changed to Keystone), brought into service to replace the Martin MB-2 in 1927, was changed from a single

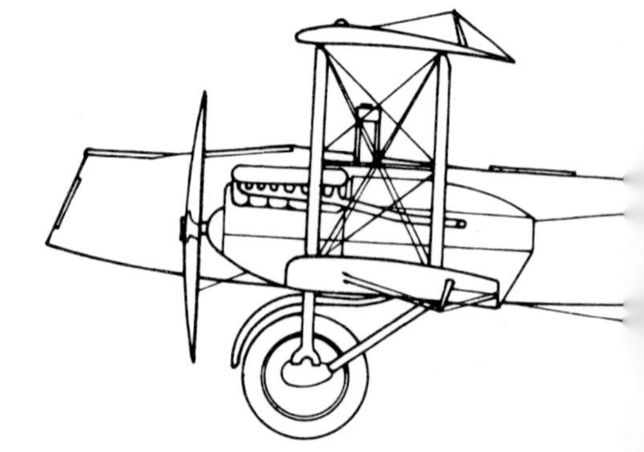

AVRO ALDERSHOT

Gross weight: 10,950 lb **Span**: 68 ft **Length**: 45 ft **Engine**: 650 hp Rolls Royce Condor III **Armament**: 1 Lewis machine-gun **Crew**: 3 **Speed**: 110 mph at ground level **Ceiling**: 11,500 ft **Range**: 652 miles **Bomb load**: 2,000 lb

Entered RAF service in 1924 with a bomb-load equal to that of many twin-engined bombers

VICKERS VIRGINIA

Gross weight: 12,467 lb **Span**: 86 ft 6 in **Length**: 50 ft 7 in **Engine**: 2×450 hp Napier Lion **Armament**: 2–4×·303 machine-guns **Crew**: 4 **Speed**: 104 mph at ground level **Ceiling**: 15,530 ft **Range**: 985 miles **Bomb load**: 3,000 lb

The main heavy night bomber in service with the RAF from 1924 to 1937

MARTIN MB-2

Gross weight: 12,064 lb **Span**: 74 ft 2 in **Length**: 42 ft 8 in **Engine**: 2×420 hp Liberty **Armament**: 5×0·3-in machine-guns **Crew**: 4 **Speed**: 99 mph at ground level **Ceiling**: 8,500 ft **Range**: 558 miles **Bomb load**: 2,000 lb

Deisnged by Glenn L. Martin, one of America's leading air pioneers, the MB-2 formed the bulk of the US Army's bomber force in the early 1920s

KEYSTONE B-4A

Gross weight: 13,209 lb **Span**: 74 ft 8 in **Length**: 48 ft 10 in **Engine**: 2×575 hp R-1860-7 **Armament**: 3×0·3 machine-guns **Crew**: 5 **Speed**: 121 mph at ground level **Ceiling**: 14,000 ft **Range**: 855 miles **Bomb load**: 2,500 lb

One of the final production series, for which orders were placed in 1931, of the long line of Huff-Daland/Keystone bombers

A postcard of the period showing the Curtiss Army biplane winning the Schneider Trophy in 1925. This was the last occasion on which a biplane won the trophy. The engine was similar to that adapted by Richard Fairey for use in the Fairey Fox, the fastest bomber of its day (see below)

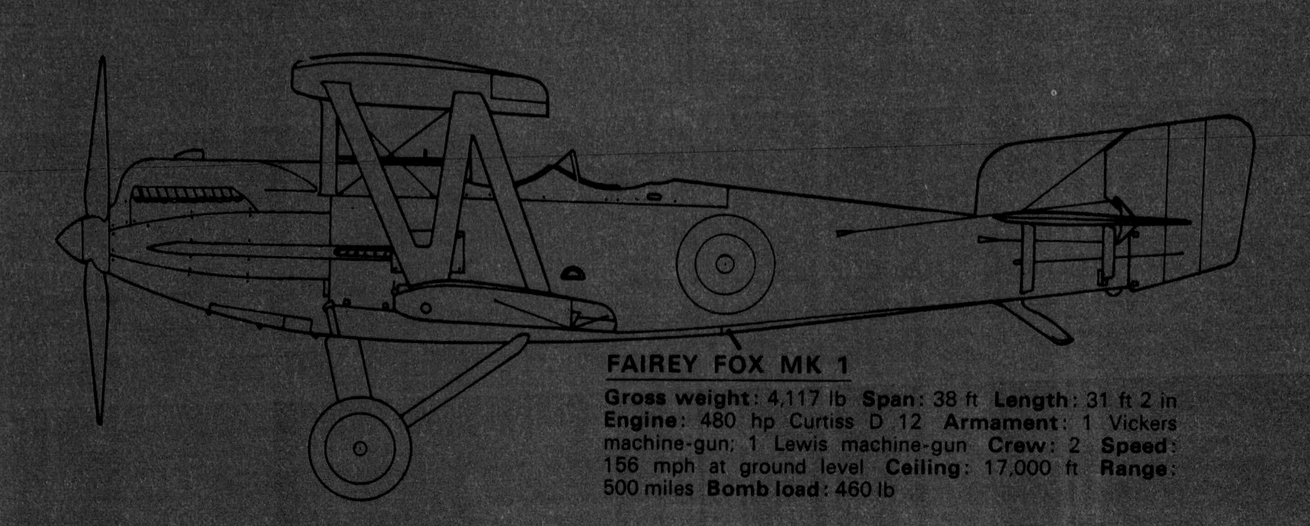

FAIREY FOX MK 1

Gross weight: 4,117 lb **Span**: 38 ft **Length**: 31 ft 2 in **Engine**: 480 hp Curtiss D 12 **Armament**: 1 Vickers machine-gun; 1 Lewis machine-gun **Crew**: 2 **Speed**: 156 mph at ground level **Ceiling**: 17,000 ft **Range**: 500 miles **Bomb load**: 460 lb

FAIREY FAWN (above)

Gross weight: 5,834 lb **Span**: 49 ft 11 in **Length**: 32 ft 1 in **Engine**: 470 hp Napier Lion II **Armament**: 1 Vickers machine-gun; 1 Lewis machine-gun **Crew**: 2 **Speed**: 114 mph **Ceiling**: 13,850 ft **Range**: 650 miles **Bomb load**: 460 lb

MITSUBISHI B2M (right)

Gross weight: 7,937 lb **Span**: 49 ft 11 in **Length**: 33 ft 8 in **Engine**: 600 hp Mitsubishi-built Hispano-Suiza **Armament**: 2×7·7-mm machine-guns **Crew**: 3 **Speed**: 132 mph **Ceiling**: 14,300 ft **Range**: 1,100 miles **Bomb load**: 1×1,764 lb Torpedo

Built for the Japanese Navy Air Force to a British Blackburn design, and in service from 1932 to 1937

SOPWITH SALAMANDER

Gross weight: 2,512 lb **Span**: 31 ft 3 in **Length**: 19 ft 6 in **Engine**: 230 hp B.R. **Armament**: 2×·303 Vickers machine-guns **Crew**: 1 **Speed**: 125 mph at 500 ft **Ceiling**: 13,000 ft **Range**: 3 hrs **Bomb load**: NA

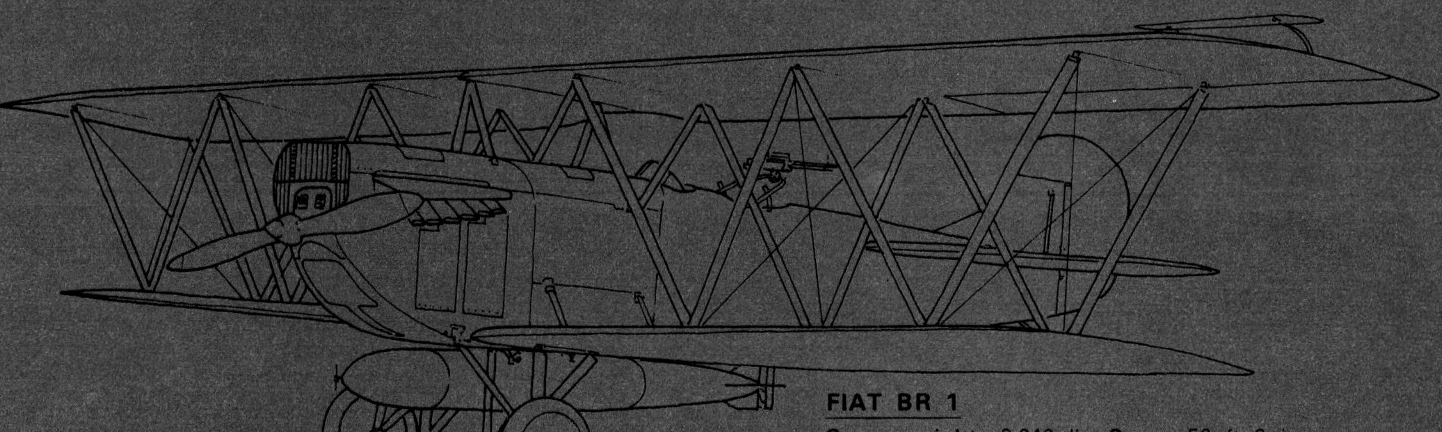

FIAT BR 1

Gross weight: 8,640 lb **Span**: 56 ft 9 in **Length**: 34 ft 4 in **Engine**: 700 hp Fiat A-14 **Armament**: 1 Fiat machine-gun **Crew**: 2 **Speed**: 153 mph **Ceiling**: 18,000 ft **Range**: 404 miles **Bomb load**: 1,000 lb

First of the BR (*Bombardamento Rosatelli*) series produced in the early 1920s for the Italian Air Force

engine to a twin-engined type. One reason was safety, in that a multi-engined plane could keep flying even with one engine out of action; another was that by placing the engines on or between the wings, the nose was left clear, giving the gunner and/or bomb aimer a better field of vision.

There was still a need for light two-seater day-bombers powered by a single engine, although such a classification became obsolete in the 1930s, when many day-bombers were built with two engines. The first new day-bomber to be received by the RAF after the war was the Fairey Fawn, a wood and fabric biplane, in service from 1923 to 1926, whose performance was actually inferior to the wartime DH 9A. This was replaced by the Hawker Horsley which remained in service until 1934. The Horsley, of mixed wood and metal construction, had an excellent load-carrying ability – either 600 lb of bombs or a single 2,150-lb torpedo in the torpedo-carrier version – and was almost as manoeuvrable as the fighters of those days.

But undoubtedly the best of the light bombers of wood construction was the Fairey Fox. Part of the reason for the poor performance of the Fairey Fawn had been the stringent official specifications to which it had been built. Richard Fairey decided to build a much faster bomber as a private venture in the hope of obtaining a production order. In the early 1920s he had seen an American Curtiss seaplane win the Schneider Trophy at a speed of over 177 mph and he was so impressed that he obtained the right to use certain features of its design, particularly the slim Curtiss D 12 in-line engine which he built under licence as the Fairey Felix. The Fairey Fox, which appeared in 1926, was one of the most beautiful biplanes ever built and not only the fastest bomber of its day, with a speed of 156 mph, but faster and more manoeuvrable than most fighters. In fact, only one RAF squadron was equipped with this outstanding aircraft, and in the event, production models were powered by the Rolls-Royce F Kestrel. But it established a line of bombers which saw much use in Belgium, where both Kestrel and Hispano-Suiza engines were installed.

Japan's first

The first light bomber to be built in Japan for the Japanese Army Air Force was the Mitsubishi 2MB1, introduced in 1927, while two years later the Kawasaki Type 88 reconnaissance biplane was adapted to perform light bombing duties.

The transition in bomber design from wood to metal, though still fabric-covered to begin with, took place in the mid-1920s, with the final change to all-metal stressed-skin airframes beginning by the early 1930s. Before describing the introduction of these types, however, consideration has to be given to the other vital aspect of design, namely engine development.

In 1917 it had been decreed that the dominant British engine should be the ABC Dragonfly radial, a nine-cylinder air-cooled unit of modern design which was supposed to give over 400 hp. Had the war continued, this would have led to a crisis in British aviation, because by the time it was realised that it was a complete technical failure the Dragonfly was being produced on a large scale. It was not until after 1920 that the fine Rolls-Royce Eagle was backed up by two other outstanding engines, the Napier Lion and Bristol Jupiter.

The Lion, designed by Rowledge, had three banks each containing four water-cooled cylinders, the so-called 'W' or broad-arrow arrangement. It was rigid and refined, and though used at 450 hp in bombers such as the Handley Page Hyderabad (the last twin-engined bomber of wooden construction to be used by the RAF except for the Mosquito of the Second World War), it gave 1,320 hp in racing form. Roy Fedden's Jupiter, fitted originally in place of the Eagle in the Vickers Vimy, was the world-dominant engine of the 1920s, and was built under licence in no less than sixteen countries. Starting in 1918 as a 375–400 hp nine-cylinder radial, it grew to more than 500 hp and was then developed into the Pegasus, rated at more than 1,000 hp by 1938. Its history was one of strenuous effort to improve a basically sound mechanical design whilst introducing geared drive, supercharging, and better forms of low-drag aircraft installation.

Britain's prejudice

The Jupiter/Pegasus family took full advantage of the fact that there is always a great difference in temperature between an air-cooled cylinder head and the slipstream, whereas in the hottest countries there is less difference between the temperature of the air and the water passing through a radiator. Conversely, in the coldest climates, a water-cooled engine could freeze. Thus many British bombers designed for water-cooled engines were sold in very hot or very cold countries with air-cooled radials instead. But in Britain there was a prejudice in favour of the liquid-cooled engine, partly because of its success when used in Schneider Trophy racing. The belief grew that the supposedly 'streamlined' vee-12, exemplified by the 450–640 hp Rolls-Royce Kestrel and later by the 1,000 hp Merlin, was more efficient than the bluff-looking radial. No such belief was harboured in the USA, even though there was no lack of American in-line engines.

The vee-12 Hispano family, of 600–1,200 hp, was made in vast numbers, not only in France and other European countries but also in the Soviet Union where it was practically the standard engine for the most powerful military aircraft until after 1941. France's Lorraine Dietrich and Italy's Fiat and Isotta-Fraschini engines served to underline the European reliance on liquid-cooled vee types. In Germany the new *Luftwaffe* was born around the BMW VI (used in the prototypes of such bombers as the Dornier Do 17 and Heinkel He 111), some radials, and the unique opposed-piston diesel two-stroke, developed painstakingly by Junkers in the mistaken belief that it would give greater efficiency and longer range.

In the USA, in spite of extreme federal parsimony, the Curtiss D 12 was developed into the 575 hp Conqueror by 1926 and powered bombers well into the 1930s. Packard had a share of the business with a series of big vee-12 engines, some of which gave no less than 800 hp. But the Huff-Daland bomber, fitted with these big engines, was replaced by a model equipped with twin 400 hp Liberty engines, mounted upside down to raise the thrust axes to the correct levels. Increasingly, the air-cooled radial became dominant in the USA, especially after the emergence of the superb 425 hp Wasp, made by the newly-formed Pratt & Whitney company, late in 1925.

By 1930 nearly all American bombers were powered by various single-row and twin-row radials built by Pratt & Whitney and the Wright company. By 1937 the major engines of the future were seen to be the P & W R-1830 (radial, 1,830 cubic inches capacity) Twin Wasp, giving 1,000 hp, and the similarly powered Wright R-1820 Cyclone which, unlike the 14-cylinder Twin Wasp, had a single row of nine big cylinders. In 1937 the Cyclone entered combat service in the Boeing B-17 Fortress, the first really successful heavy bomber, and the Douglas B-18 derived from the DC 3. All the big American radials had one inlet and one exhaust valve in each cylinder head. They had geared drives and General Electric was nearing final success in its 20-year effort to perfect a turbo-supercharger spun by the white-hot exhaust gas. This was to prove of vital importance in the Second World War.

Meanwhile, Fedden's team at Bristol was looking keenly at the American radials which in turn owed so much to their own Jupiter engine. Fedden was daunted by the mechanical complexity of trying to devise valve gear for a two-row radial engine with four valves in each head. He had long used two inlet and two exhaust valves, giving better 'breathing' than the American engines, and was reluctant to halve the number. At the same time, though his Mercury (used in the Blenheim) and Pegasus engines were by 1930 showing great promise for a wide range of future aircraft, he wanted to look much further ahead. After extensive experiments with several schemes, he made the bold decision to try to develop a successful sleeve-valve engine. This type had been used in various forms since the turn of the century, but had never been completely successful. It nearly eluded his own team too, and vast effort and expense was needed. The problem lay not so much in perfecting the engine, but in making the engine a standard production type with interchangeable sleeves, instead of a hand-built engine

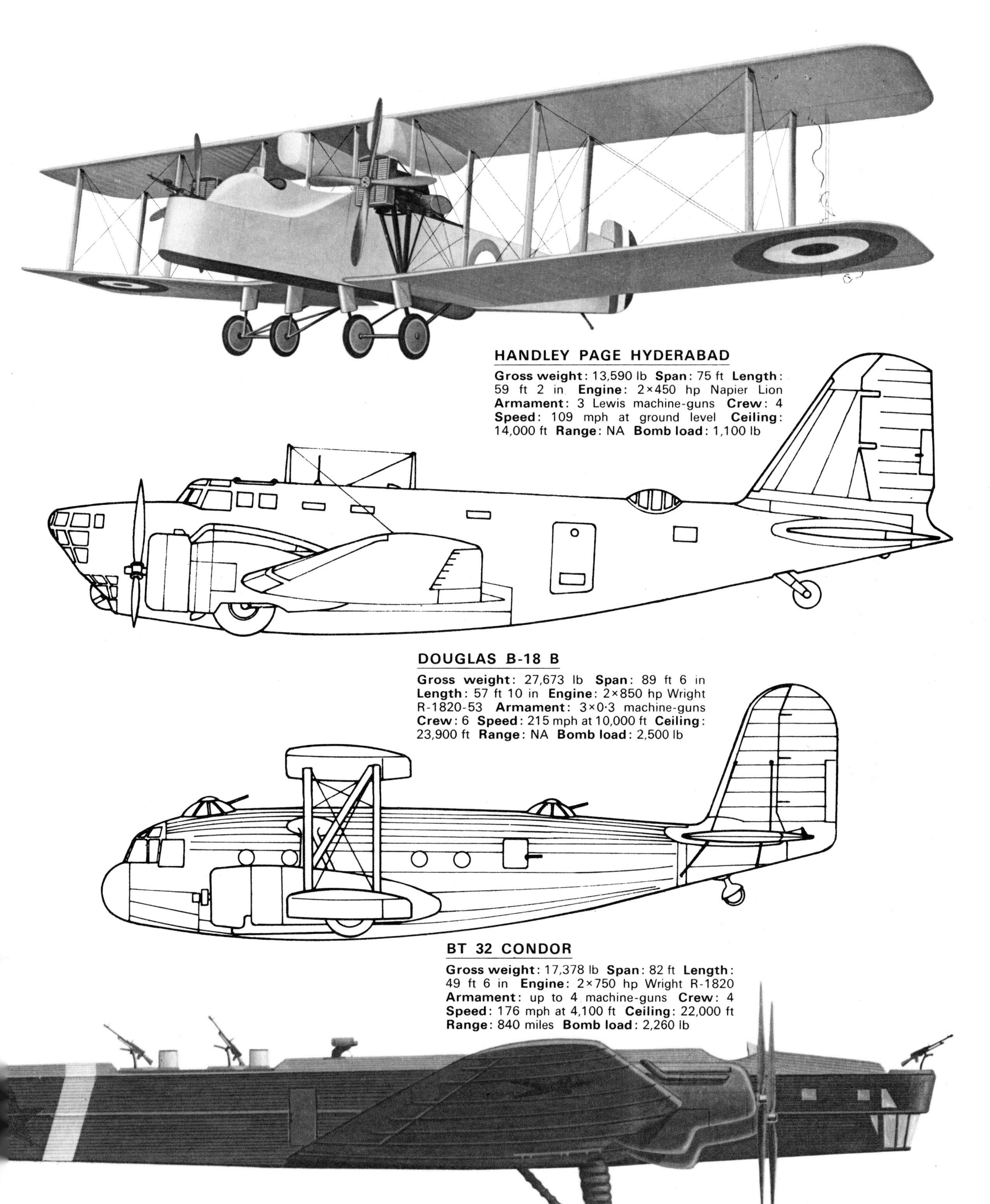

HANDLEY PAGE HYDERABAD

Gross weight: 13,590 lb **Span**: 75 ft **Length**: 59 ft 2 in **Engine**: 2×450 hp Napier Lion **Armament**: 3 Lewis machine-guns **Crew**: 4 **Speed**: 109 mph at ground level **Ceiling**: 14,000 ft **Range**: NA **Bomb load**: 1,100 lb

DOUGLAS B-18 B

Gross weight: 27,673 lb **Span**: 89 ft 6 in **Length**: 57 ft 10 in **Engine**: 2×850 hp Wright R-1820-53 **Armament**: 3×0·3 machine-guns **Crew**: 6 **Speed**: 215 mph at 10,000 ft **Ceiling**: 23,900 ft **Range**: NA **Bomb load**: 2,500 lb

BT 32 CONDOR

Gross weight: 17,378 lb **Span**: 82 ft **Length**: 49 ft 6 in **Engine**: 2×750 hp Wright R-1820 **Armament**: up to 4 machine-guns **Crew**: 4 **Speed**: 176 mph at 4,100 ft **Ceiling**: 22,000 ft **Range**: 840 miles **Bomb load**: 2,260 lb

TUPOLEV TB-3 (ANT-6)

Gross weight: 38,360 lb **Span**: 132 ft 10 in **Length**: 81 ft **Engine**: 4×750 hp M-17 **Armament**: 5×twin 7·62-mm machine-guns **Crew**: 6 **Speed**: 134 mph at ground level **Ceiling**: 12,500 ft **Range**: 1,350 miles **Bomb load**: 4,850 lb

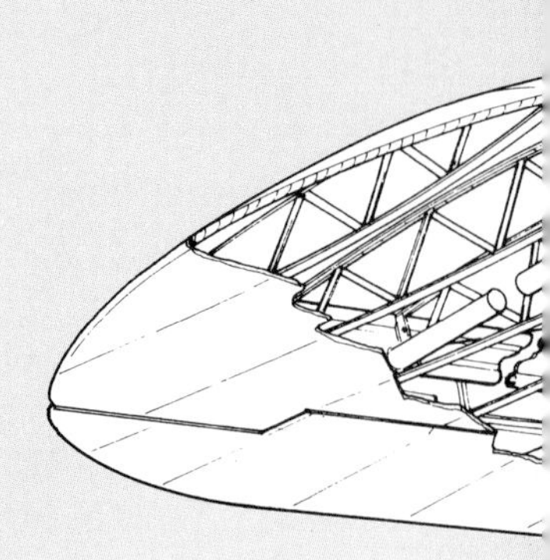

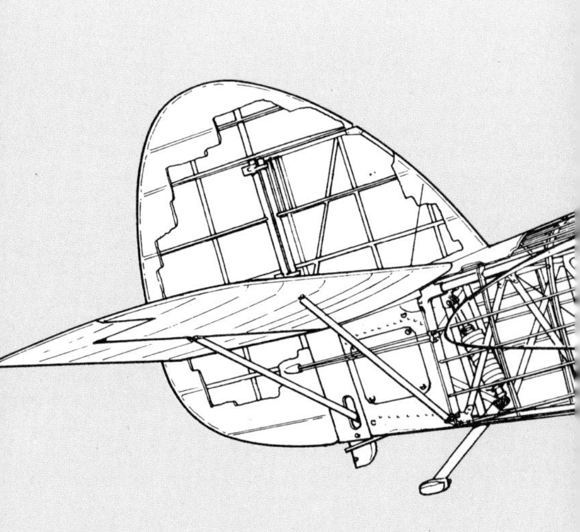

HAWKER HART (above right)

Gross weight: 4,554 lb **Span**: 37 ft 3 in **Length**: 29 ft 4 in **Engine**: 525 hp Rolls Royce Kestrel **Armament**: 1 Vickers machine-gun; 1 Lewis machine-gun **Crew**: 2 **Speed**: 184 mph at 5,000 ft **Ceiling**: 21,350 ft **Range**: 470 miles **Bomb load**: 520 lb

Section drawing of the RAF's standard light day bomber from 1930 to 1939. Its performance was better than most contemporary single-seater fighters. Used especially for colonial policing duties, for which many variants were produced

Above: armourers working on Browning and Lewis guns, aligning the gun sights

Centre: aligning gun sight

Left: apprentices receiving instruction on bomb preparation

Flight International

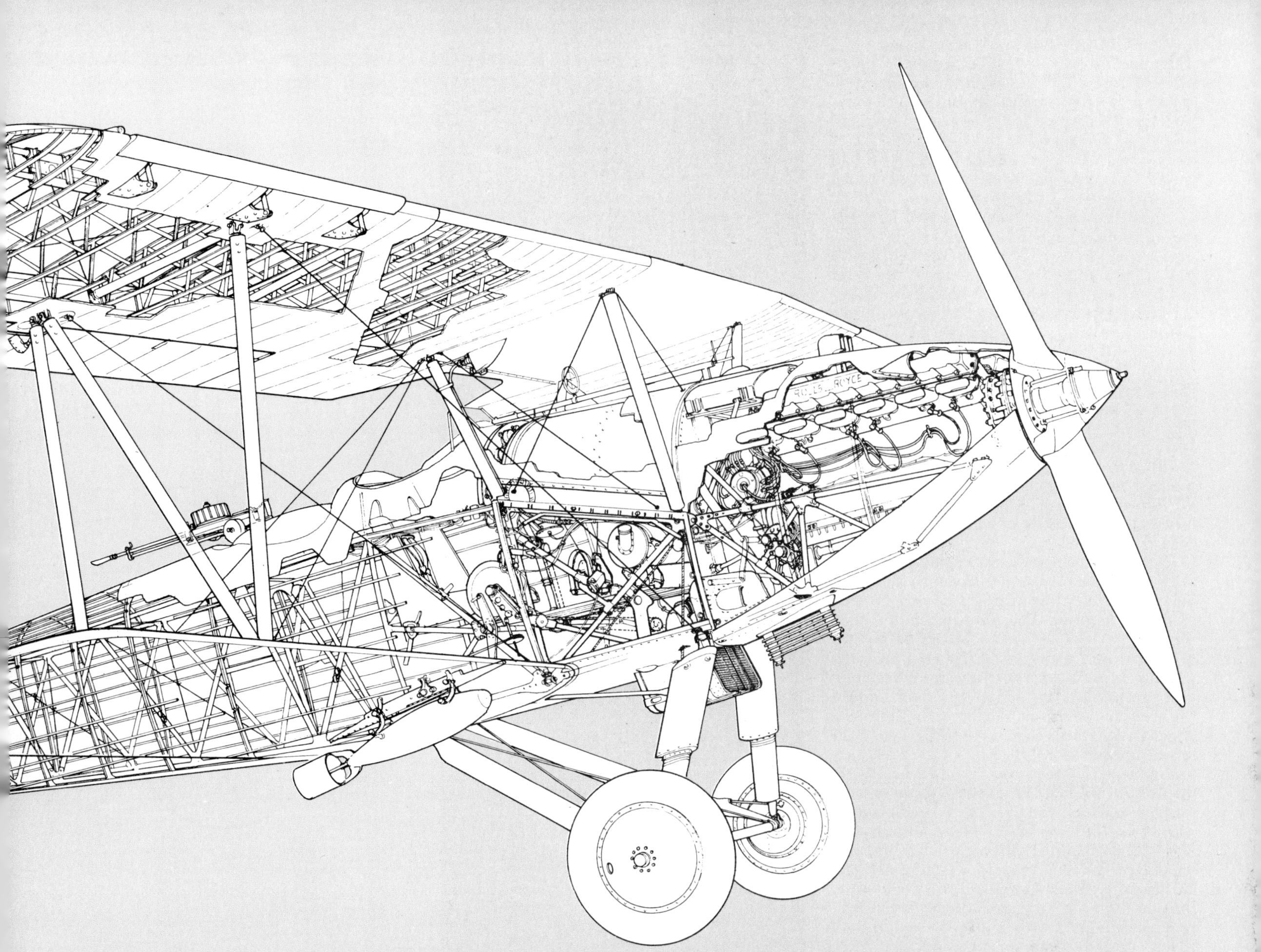

with each set of sleeves individually matched to its own set of cylinders and pistons.

In most of the aircraft-building countries, there were numerous companies making aero engines. Their efforts to make a living resulted in a profusion of engine types, when it would probably have been more cost/effective to have concentrated on one or two designs in each broad power class. In the first half of the 1930s British bomber design would not have been notably handicapped if the Bristol Pegasus had been specified universally and all other engines in the 500–900 hp range had been cancelled. But no such decision was taken, and a diverse profusion of engines resulted, despite the fact that until 1935, when Hitler's announcement revealed the *Luftwaffe* to be among the foremost of the world's air forces, most governments cut bomber procurement to a minimum.

The atmosphere of economy largely explains why the big bomber with three, four, or even more engines, common in 1916–18, was almost non-existent in 1919–1938. Only in the latter year was a production order placed for an American four-engined bomber (the first B-17 Fortresses), and the RAF four-engined 'heavies' did not come into use until more than two years after the war began. The only nation to use fleets of four-engined bombers was the Soviet Union, whose Tupolev TB-3 monoplane came into service in 1931. This massive aircraft, powered by four Hispano-Suiza vee-12 engines, had a greater loaded weight than any contemporary landplane. Experiments were even conducted into carrying two parasite fighters on the wings. The TB-3 and its derivatives were sufficiently reliable to play a major role in early Russian polar exploration in the era before the Second World War.

More metal structures

It was the use of metal in place of wood that gave large aircraft sufficient strength to enable them to be constructed in monoplane form. In France, the metal preferred by most designers was light alloy duralumin. This was used in the construction of the twin-engined Liore and Olivier LeO 12, first exhibited at the Salon de l'Aeronautique in 1924 and later taken into squadron service on an experimental basis. Few machines of the type were actually built but a widely used development was the three-seat LeO 20, also built of duralumin, which equipped many French night bomber squadrons from 1927–1937, rivalling the Farman F 160 to 168 series. One of the most successful metal biplanes however was the single-engined Bréguet 19 two-seat light bomber which remained in service from 1925 for some fifteen years. It was also used by many foreign air forces, and built under licence in Belgium, Greece, Japan, Spain and Yugoslavia.

Another single-engined biplane of light alloy construction, which appeared in 1928 was the Amiot 122 BP3, the latter designation showing it to be a bomber-escort three-seater. The Amiot 122 had the handling characteristics of a light single-engined aircraft with the load-carrying ability of larger twin-engined types, and remained in service in various forms until 1935. Two other excellent single-engined biplane light bombers were the Czech Aero A11 and the Dutch Fokker CV-C, both introduced into service in 1923. The CV-C, one of the best combat aircraft ever designed by Anthony Fokker, had a welded steel-tube fuselage and wooden wings, and remained operational until the late 1930s.

The first British heavy bomber of metal construction was the Handley Page Hinaidi, a 1929 development of the Handley Page Hyderabad. The Hinaidi was replaced in 1933 by the Handley Page Heyford whose outstanding feature was the attachment of the fuselage to the upper instead of the lower wing. It also had a rotatable ventral turret which could be drawn up into the fuselage when not in use, its cylindrical shape quickly giving rise to the nickname 'dustbin'. These Handley Page twin-engined biplanes were built of a steel-tube structure with internal wire bracing. Another metal twin-engined biplane which came into service in 1928 was the Boulton Paul Sidestrand, but instead of being a night bomber, it was sufficiently fast and manoeuvrable to be used for daytime duties and was designated as the RAF's first medium bomber. It was replaced in 1934 by an improved version, the Boulton Paul Overstrand, which could carry a heavier bomb-load and was the first British bomber to have a power-operated enclosed gun turret in the nose. Apart from these two, British day-bombers were all single-engined two-seaters until the arrival of monoplanes in the late 1930s.

The usual metal in the early composite or metal-framed bombers was high-tensile steel, and there was a considerable reluctance on the part of designers to use light alloys. The steel was used both as tube and as strip, often welded at the joints. When aluminium alloys were brought in there was a great difference of opinion as to how they should best be employed. Sydney Camm, at the Hawker company, devised a patented form of 'bulb flange' in the shape of a tube assembled from sections of strip rolled to particular profiles. These flanges were then riveted to aluminium-alloy sheets to serve as spar booms – the strong top and bottom of the wing spars – in the way that later aircraft used booms of much thicker angle and T-sections.

Camm's fuselages were typical in having either circular-section tube with the sides flattened at the joints or else square-section tube throughout. The flat sides could then fit snugly against heavy bolted or riveted plates which were added to reinforce the main joints. Ways were also found of making strong streamlined struts from hollow light-alloy sections, though high-tensile steel wires were invariably still needed for bracing and for 'rigging' the structure (adjusting the tensions in different wires to obtain exactly the desired shapes, wing angles and tail incidence). It was because this new form of metal construction was easy to maintain in operational conditions that Hawker won a competition in the late 1920s when the Air Ministry decided to have a high-performance all-metal aircraft.

The Hawker Hart remained the standard RAF light day-bomber from 1930 to 1937, with a speed of 175 mph and a better all-round performance than most single-seat fighters of the period. The last RAF biplane bomber was the Hawker Hind. This type was in service from 1935 to 1938 as an interim replacement for the Hart, until the monoplane Fairey Battles and Bristol Blenheims began to enter service in RAF Bomber Command in 1937.

In Japan, the last biplane bomber to be produced for the Japanese Army Air Force was the Kawasaki Ki-3, a single-engined two-seater which entered service in 1933 as the Type 93 light bomber. By then, however, advances were being made in the production of bombers in monoplane form.

The big question

It was during the 1920s and 1930s that aircraft design became something of an exact science, though questions remained which caused endless arguments: should a bomber have air-cooled radial or liquid-cooled vee engines? Should it be a fabric-covered biplane or a fabric-covered monoplane – or, boldest of all, an all-metal stressed-skin monoplane? Fabric was used as the covering for the RAF's first twin-engined cantilever monoplane, the low-wing Fairey Hendon which entered service in 1936, and the Caproni Ca 101 and Ca 111 high-wing monoplanes, used extensively during the Italian campaign in Ethiopia. Some, such as the Handley Page Harrow and the Dornier Do 11, 13 and 23 bombers,

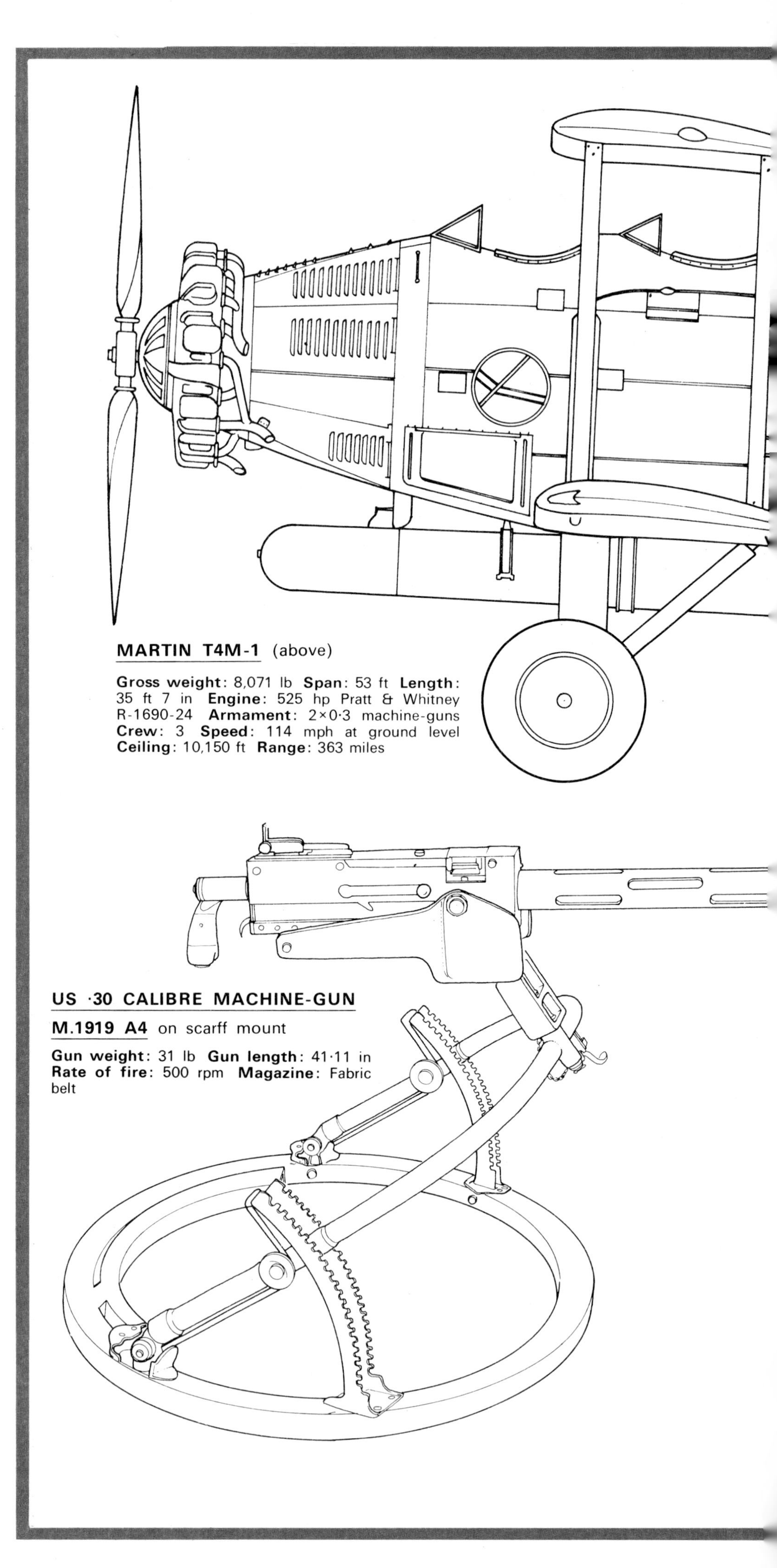

MARTIN T4M-1 (above)

Gross weight: 8,071 lb **Span**: 53 ft **Length**: 35 ft 7 in **Engine**: 525 hp Pratt & Whitney R-1690-24 **Armament**: 2×0·3 machine-guns **Crew**: 3 **Speed**: 114 mph at ground level **Ceiling**: 10,150 ft **Range**: 363 miles

US ·30 CALIBRE MACHINE-GUN M.1919 A4 on scarff mount

Gun weight: 31 lb **Gun length**: 41·11 in **Rate of fire**: 500 rpm **Magazine**: Fabric belt

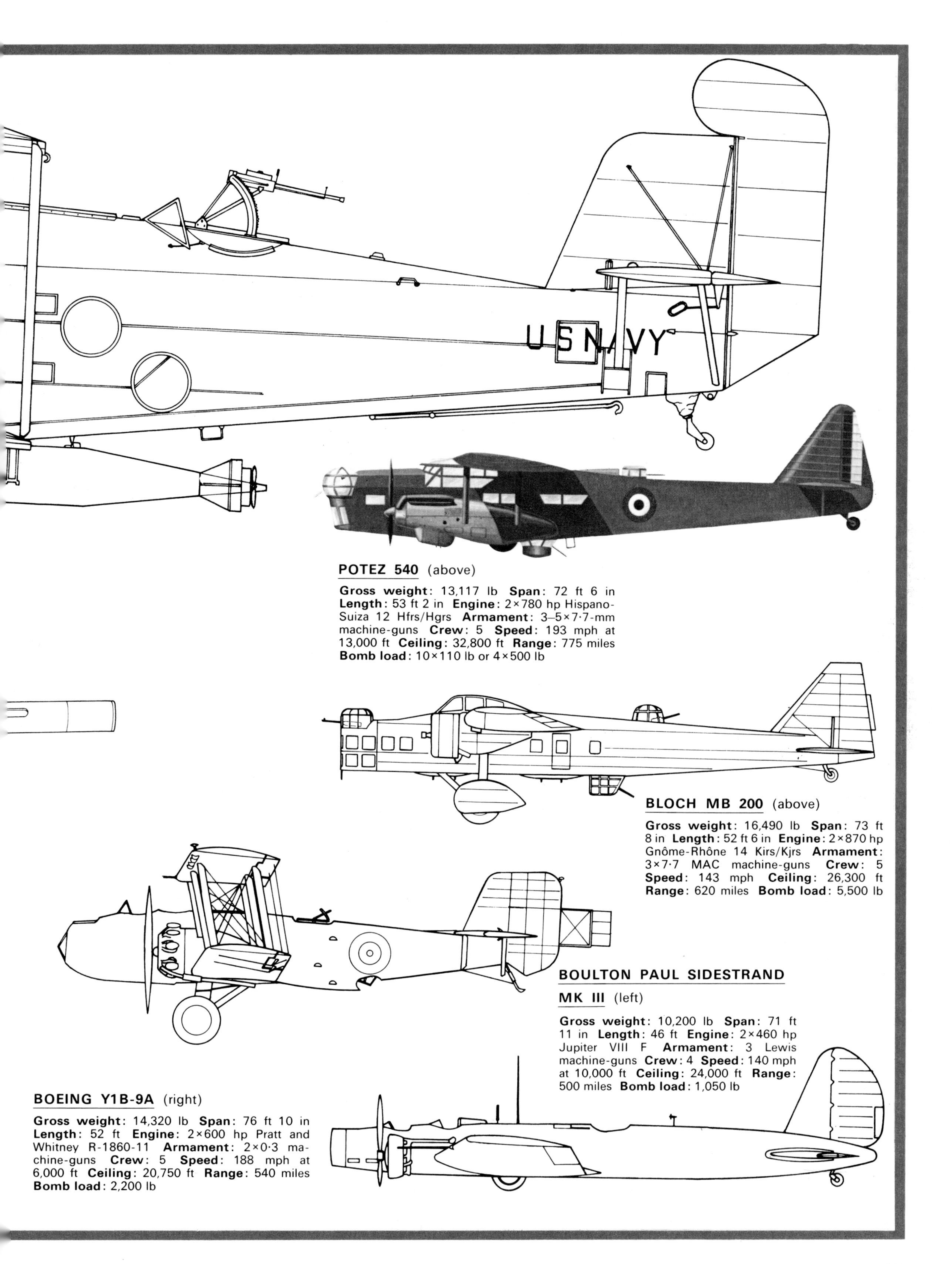

POTEZ 540 (above)

Gross weight: 13,117 lb **Span**: 72 ft 6 in **Length**: 53 ft 2 in **Engine**: 2×780 hp Hispano-Suiza 12 Hfrs/Hgrs **Armament**: 3–5×7·7-mm machine-guns **Crew**: 5 **Speed**: 193 mph at 13,000 ft **Ceiling**: 32,800 ft **Range**: 775 miles **Bomb load**: 10×110 lb or 4×500 lb

BLOCH MB 200 (above)

Gross weight: 16,490 lb **Span**: 73 ft 8 in **Length**: 52 ft 6 in **Engine**: 2×870 hp Gnôme-Rhône 14 Kirs/Kjrs **Armament**: 3×7·7 MAC machine-guns **Crew**: 5 **Speed**: 143 mph **Ceiling**: 26,300 ft **Range**: 620 miles **Bomb load**: 5,500 lb

BOULTON PAUL SIDESTRAND MK III (left)

Gross weight: 10,200 lb **Span**: 71 ft 11 in **Length**: 46 ft **Engine**: 2×460 hp Jupiter VIII F **Armament**: 3 Lewis machine-guns **Crew**: 4 **Speed**: 140 mph at 10,000 ft **Ceiling**: 24,000 ft **Range**: 500 miles **Bomb load**: 1,050 lb

BOEING Y1B-9A (right)

Gross weight: 14,320 lb **Span**: 76 ft 10 in **Length**: 52 ft **Engine**: 2×600 hp Pratt and Whitney R-1860-11 **Armament**: 2×0·3 machine-guns **Crew**: 5 **Speed**: 188 mph at 6,000 ft **Ceiling**: 20,750 ft **Range**: 540 miles **Bomb load**: 2,200 lb

HANDLEY PAGE HEYFORD

Gross weight: 16,750 lb **Span**: 75 ft **Length**: 58 ft **Engine**: 2×600 hp Rolls Royce Kestrel **Armament**: 3×·303 Lewis machine-guns **Crew**: 5 **Speed**: 142 mph at 13,000 ft **Ceiling**: 21,000 ft **Range**: 920 miles **Bomb load**: 3,500 lb

The most unusual feature of this heavy night bomber, which remained in front-line service with the RAF from 1933 to 1939, was the attachment of the fuselage to the upper wing instead of the lower, as in conventional practice

HAWKER HIND (above)

Gross weight: 5,298 lb **Span**: 37 ft 3 in **Length**: 29 ft 7 in **Engine**: 640 hp Rolls Royce Kestrel V **Armament**: 1 Vickers machine-gun; 1 Lewis machine-gun **Crew**: 2 **Speed**: 186 mph at 15,000 ft **Ceiling**: 26,450 ft **Range**: 430 miles **Bomb load**: 510 lb

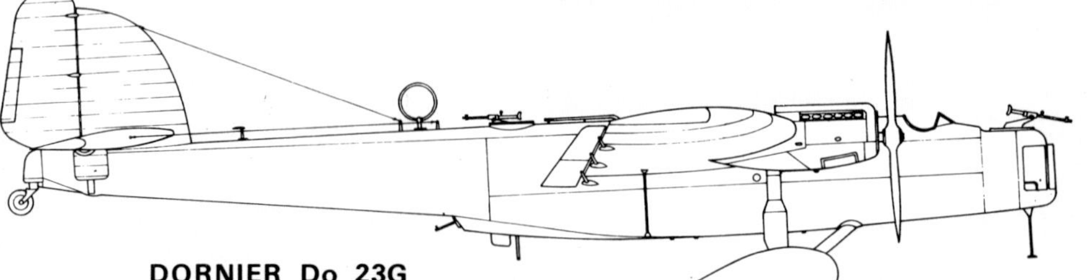

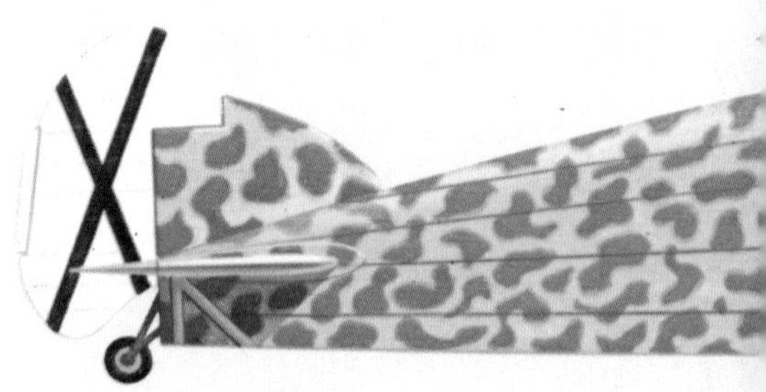

DORNIER Do 23G

Gross weight: 20,282 lb **Span**: 84 ft **Length**: 61 ft 8 in **Engine**: 2×550 hp BMW VIU **Armament**: 3×7·9-mm machine-guns 15 **Crew**: 4 **Speed**: 161 mph at 4,000 ft **Ceiling**: 13,780 ft **Range**: 839 miles **Bomb load**: 2,200 lb

Based on the Do F mail and freight transport of the late 1920s, the Do 23 was the first medium bomber to serve in the newly-formed *Luftwaffe* in the mid-1930s

AERO A 11

Gross weight: 3,265 lb **Span**: 42 ft **Length**: 26 ft 11 in **Engine**: 240 hp Walter W-IV **Armament**: 1×7·7-mm machine-gun **Crew**: 2 **Speed**: 134 mph at 8,200 ft **Ceiling**: 23,622 ft **Range**: 466 miles **Bomb load**: 110 lb

The standard light bomber used by the Czechoslovakian Air Force during the 1920s, produced in many variants – including the first Czech floatplane

HAWKER HORSLEY

Gross weight: 7,800 lb **Span**: 56 ft 9 in **Length**: 38 ft 2 in **Engine**: 670 hp Rolls Royce Condor IIIA **Armament**: 1 Vickers machine-gun; 1 Lewis machine-gun **Crew**: 2 **Speed**: 126 mph **Ceiling**: 14,000 ft **Range**: 10 hrs **Bomb load**: 1,500 lb

This plane replaced the Fairey Fawn (see page 51) in RAF service in 1927 and remained the standard British day bomber until 1934

CAPRONI Ca 101

Gross weight: 10,968 lb **Span**: 64 ft 7 in **Length**: 47 ft 2 in **Engine**: 3×240 hp Alfa Romeo D 2 **Armament**: 3×7·7-mm machine-guns **Crew**: 5 **Speed**: 103 mph at 3,500 ft **Ceiling**: 20,000 ft **Range**: 1,240 miles **Bomb load**: 1,102 lb

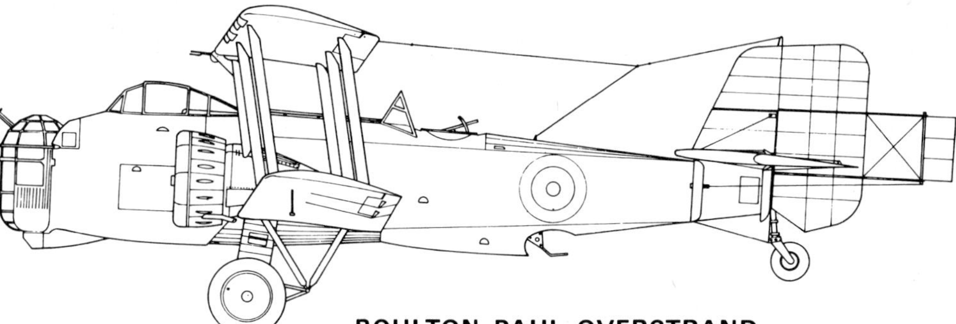

BOULTON PAUL OVERSTRAND

Gross weight: 12,000 lb **Span**: 72 ft **Length**: 46 ft **Engine**: 2×580 hp Bristol Pegasus 2M3 **Armament**: 3 Lewis machine-guns **Crew**: 5 **Speed**: 153 mph at 6,500 ft **Ceiling**: 22,500 ft **Range**: 545 miles **Bomb load**: 1,600 lb

developed from the Do F mail and freight transport, at a time when the *Luftwaffe* was being secretly built up under the guise of civil aircraft, used a mixture of fabric and metal covering for different parts of the fuselage and wings. But structurally, military aircraft were conservative and all-metal stressed-skin airframes were rare until well after 1935.

This was surprising because, during the First World War, Junkers and other designers had shown that light-alloy skin could be used to bear part of the structural loads. A major advance was made in 1920 when at the London Aero Show, Oswald Short displayed the Silver Streak biplane which had a monocoque metal-covered fuselage, not only stronger and lighter than wood but easy to mass-produce.

The first Russian-designed metal bomber – the two-seat single-engined Tupolev R-3 biplane brought into service in 1926 – was also covered with corrugated Kolchug aluminium sheeting. This alloy was named after the Russian town where it was originally produced and claimed to be stronger than normal duralumin. A similar all-metal construction and covering was used in the Tupolev TB-1 twin-engined cantilever low-wing monoplane which was brought into service the following year. The TB-1 was a very large machine with an especially thick wing, capable of carrying a crew of six and a maximum bomb-load of 6,600 lb, and set the pattern for Soviet bomber design until the end of the 1930s.

'Iron Annie'

Germany had a long tradition of metal built and covered aircraft, and in 1926 the German designer Rohrbach perfected a complete system for making stressed-skin monoplanes with no bracing anywhere. Most German 'civil' aircraft of the middle and late 1920s were designed with military uses in mind, and such types as the three-engined Junkers Ju 52 'Iron Annie', which made its operational debut during the Spanish Civil War, served as interim bombers until the arrival of aircraft developed from airliners and specifically designed for bombing.

Some of the earliest mass-produced stressed-skin machines were the ugly, unstreamlined bombers of the French Armée de l'Air, such as the Amiot 143 multi-purpose battleplane and the Farman F 222, both twin engined high-wing monoplanes. Stressed-skin construction did not appear to do much either for the Bristol Bombay and Armstrong Whitworth Whitley, the two earliest large RAF aircraft of this type, though it was essential for faster machines like the Bristol Blenheim and Fairey Battle.

It was the USA in the early 1930s that led the switch to modern monoplane design. Stressed-skin construction made possible the rapid development of fast cantilever monoplane civil transports, notably the Boeing 247, Douglas DC-2 and Lockheed Electra, and stimulated the use of this form of construction for combat aircraft. The first of the new bomber designs was the twin-engined Boeing YB-9 low-wing monoplane in 1931, which incorporated such advanced features as semi-retractable undercarriage and variable-pitch propellers. Although not built in quantity and used only on a trial basis by the US Army Air Corps, the YB-9 offered, without any reduction of bomb-load, a dramatic improvement over the Keystone biplane bombers which were its predecessors.

An even greater advance was made with the Martin B-10, brought into service in 1934, with a fully-retractable undercarriage and enclosed cockpit. Its maximum speed of 212 mph at 6,500 ft made it faster than most fighters, and it was the first American monoplane bomber to be built in quantity. At the end of the 1930s, the MB-10 was being replaced by the Douglas B-18, developed from the DC-2 civil transport. Although an excellent aircraft, this was overshadowed by the four-engined Boeing B-17 Flying Fortress, produced from the Boeing 299 prototype of 1934.

Several of the American machines, especially the Northrop and Douglas types, had multi-spar wings with the advantage, not fully appreciated at the time, of being able to log large numbers of flying hours without suffering from any form of fatigue. Even if any structural member happened to crack, there were always alternative load-paths to bear the stresses.

It was partly in a search for a safer and

JUNKERS Ju 52

Gross weight: 24,200 lb **Span**: 95 ft 10 in **Length**: 62 ft **Engine**: 3×830 hp BMW 132T **Armament**: 2×7·92-mm machine-guns 15; 1×13-mm machine-gun; **Crew**: 4 **Speed**: 165 mph at 3,000 ft **Ceiling**: 16,600 ft **Range**: 800 miles **Bomb load**: 3,300 lb or 10–15 paratroops

Although this, the famous 'Iron Annie' of the *Luftwaffe* made its operational debut as a bomber during the Spanish Civil War, it became better known as a military transport plane in the Second World War. It saw service in every major German invasion campaign. It is shown here in its Second World War colours

DOUGLAS YB-7 (below)

Gross weight: 11,177 lb **Span**: 65 ft 3 in **Length**: 46 ft 7 in **Engine**: 2×675 hp Curtiss V-1570-27 **Armament**: 2×0·3 machine-guns **Crew**: 4 **Speed**: 182 mph at ground level **Ceiling**: 20,400 ft **Range**: 411 miles **Bomb load**: 1,200 lb

Prototype of the Douglas B-7 which was the US Army's first monoplane bomber in 1930

more efficient form of metal construction that Barnes Wallis devised his 'geodetic' system in the early 1930s. Wallis had been chief designer of the Vickers airship R 100 of 1929, and he developed its structure into a completely new form of metal basketwork, assembled from large numbers of standard metal sections. Riveted together by small tabs and connectors, they formed a complete wing or fuselage. All the members had the shape of intersecting curves and each carried either tension or compression but no bending.

The first geodetic aircraft, the private venture single-engined Vickers Wellesley which ultimately went into service in 1937, showed its great efficiency compared with the rival types built to the official G 4/31 specification. Its high-aspect ratio wing helped the Wellesley set the world distance record in 1938, by which time Vickers were in production with the geodetic Wellington. One of the big advantages of geodetic construction was that battle damage could easily be repaired by cutting out and replacing the small pieces of basketwork. A feature of this type of structure was that the skin should be unstressed, so that all the geodetic machines had fabric covering.

Most of the bombers used operationally during the Second Worlds War were being developed in the mid-1930s. Meanwhile, several modern all-metal cantilever monoplane types entered service towards the end of the 1930s but had been largely replaced by the time war broke out. One was the Bloch 200 which met a French specification for a five-seat night bomber in 1932. Unfortunately its top speed of 143 mph was some 30 mph slower than expected and by the time of the German offensive none of this type was in squadron service. The Bloch 210 was an improved version, with a speed of 186 mph at 13,000 feet, and saw operational service with the Republican forces during the Spanish Civil War. It was during that war of course that the Germans took the opportunity of testing their new aircraft in combat conditions, discovering for instance that the performance of the early Ju 86s was inadequate against contemporary fighter opposition.

Another war in which bombers were given their first important test in combat was the Sino-Japanese war which broke out in 1937. Two single-engined monoplane bombers had by that time been brought into service with the Japanese Army Air Force, the Kawasaki Ki-32 and the Mitsubishi Ki-30 which had a combat range of over 1,000 miles. Together with the twin-engined heavy bombers, the Mitsubishi G3M built for the Japanese Navy Air Force and the Mitsubishi Ki-21 built for the Army, the Japanese launched a succession of strategic attacks against Chinese airfields and virtually destroyed the Chinese Air Force. However, they were unable to undertake strategic bombing on the same scale against the Soviet Union in 1939 because of the existence of large numbers of Russian fighters.

The new generation

The disarmament policy of most of the Allied powers prevented the construction of aircraft to meet such policies as strategic bombing, until after 1935 when the threat of war spurred rearmament programmes. Design was dominated by the immediate needs of the customer. The wars of the 1920s were mostly colonial skirmishes in which European colonial powers needed little more than light single-engined bombers for their policing operations – hence the emphasis, especially in Britain, on building fighter-bombers. It was partly the success of bombing operations against ill-armed tribesmen that gave rise to exaggerated claims for the importance of strategic bombing.

The Second World War was to see the introduction of a completely new generation of bomber aircraft, flying at three times the speed of their First World War counterparts and delivering bombs ten times more powerful than the largest used in 1918, while the development of radar added a new dimension to aerial warfare. But the actual ways in which bombers were used differed little from the first war, except that they were on a vastly greater scale. The difference in the Second World War was that air power had become of such vital importance that without at least some degree of balance in the control of air space, battles would be lost and entire countries fall to an enemy who had mastery of the skies.

MITSUBISHI Ki-2I

Gross weight: 10,031 lb **Span**: 65 ft 6 in **Length**: 41 ft 4 in **Engine**: 2×570 hp Nakajima **Armament**: 2×7·7-mm machine-guns **Crew**: 5 **Speed**: 158 mph at 9,500 ft **Ceiling**: 22,890 ft **Range**: 560 miles **Bomb load**: 660 lb

AMIOT 143 (left)

Gross weight: 19,568 lb **Span**: 80 ft 2 in **Length**: 58 ft 11 in **Engine**: 2×870 hp Gnôme-Rhône **Armament**: 4×7·5-mm MAC machine-guns **Crew**: 5 **Speed**: 190 mph at 13,000 ft **Ceiling**: 21,200 ft **Range**: 800 miles **Bomb load**: 1,984 lb

MARTIN B-10

Gross weight: 14,600 lb **Span**: 70 ft 6 in **Length**: 44 ft 9 in **Engine**: 2×775 hp Wright R-1820-25 **Armament**: 5×·303 Browning machine-guns **Crew**: 4 **Speed**: 213 mph at 10,000 ft **Ceiling**: 24,200 ft **Range**: 1,240 miles **Bomb load**: 2,260 lb

DH 9A

Gross weight: 4,645 lb **Span**: 45 ft 11 in **Length**: 30 ft 3 in **Engine**: 400 hp Liberty **Armament**: 1 Vickers machine-gun; 2 Lewis machine-guns **Crew**: 2 **Speed**: 116 mph at 10,000 ft **Ceiling**: 17,000 ft **Range**: 3 hrs **Bomb load**: 660 lb

CURTISS B-2 CONDOR

Gross weight: 16,516 lb **Span**: 90 ft **Length**: 47 ft 6 in **Engine**: 2×600 hp Curtiss 1570 Conqueror **Armament**: 6 Lewis machine-guns **Crew**: 6 **Speed**: 132 mph at ground level **Ceiling**: 17,000 ft **Range**: 780 miles **Bomb load**: 4,000 lb

Although losing a USAAC bomber contract to Keystone in 1928 – the Curtiss B-2 was too large for most existing hangars – its performance was so good that a limited quantity was produced

FARMAN 222 BN 5 (below)

Gross weight: 41,220 lb **Span**: 118 ft 1½ in **Length**: 70 ft 4½ in **Engine**: 4×860 hp Gnôme-Rhône **Armament**: 3×7·62-mm machine-guns **Crew**: 6–7 **Speed**: 202 mph at 13,000 ft **Ceiling**: 27,885 ft **Range**: 932 miles **Bomb load**: 9,259 lb

One of the aircraft intended to form the mainstay of France's heavy bomber force in the late 1930s, but relatively few had been delivered by the time of the outbreak of the Second World War

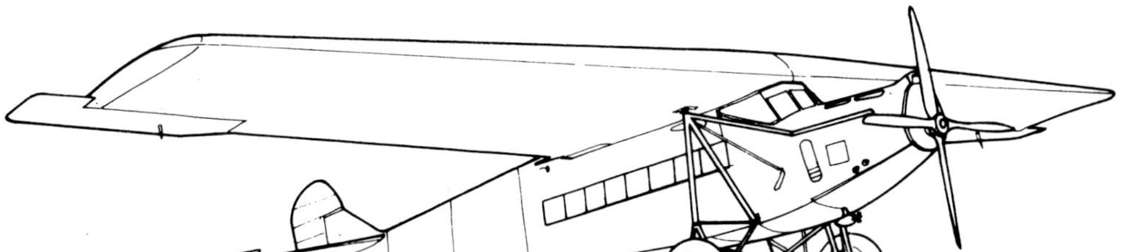

FOKKER F VIIA-3m/M

Gross weight: 9,000 lb **Span**: 63 ft 4 in **Length**: 47 ft 10 in **Engine**: 2×200 hp Armstrong Siddeley Lynx **Armament**: 2×7·62-mm machine-guns **Crew**: 4 **Speed**: 115 mph **Ceiling**: 15,500 ft **Range**: 634 miles **Bomb load**: 2,200 lb

The DH9 day-bomber of 1917 was a failure because of its underpowered and unreliable BHP engine, but when the American Liberty engine became available, the improved DH 9A proved itself to be one of the most outstanding aircraft in RAF service from August 1918 to 1931. The 'Nine-ack' as it was known was also put into production in the USA and USSR.

JUNKERS Ju 52/3M

Gross weight: 24,320 lb **Span**: 95 ft 10 in **Length**: 62 ft **Engine**: 3×830 hp BMW 132T **Armament**: 1×13-mm machine-gun; 2×7·9-mm machine-guns 15 **Crew**: 4 **Speed**: 189 mph **Ceiling**: 18,000 ft **Range**: 930 miles **Bomb load**: 3,306 lb

AIR POWER 1939

After the Armistice in November 1918 the greatly expanded armed forces of the Allies were hastily and clumsily demobilized. Improvised war organizations were dismantled, and the watchwords of the British government were economy and retrenchment. The war had been won, there was no visible threat to Allied security, and Great Britain and France were swept by a wave of anti-war feeling, largely induced by the terrible casualties and intolerable conditions of trench warfare.

In 1925 the League of Nations had set up a Preparatory Commission to explore the ground for a general disarmament conference. Progress in this field is never rapid, and for many years the commission was involved in interminable difficulties and arguments. Eventually a Disarmament Conference was convened in Geneva in 1932, at which proposals for outlawing air bombardment and drastically limiting the loaded weight of military aircraft were discussed. Hoping for success in these negotiations, the British government declined to authorize the design and construction of any effective bomber aircraft. In addition, it had introduced in 1924 what became known as the 'Ten-year Rule', which postulated that there would be no major war for ten years. Unfortunately each successive year was deemed to be the starting point of this tranquil epoch, and so the period always remained at ten years.

The Disarmament Conference finally broke up in May 1934 without achieving any result whatsoever. But meanwhile Hitler had come to power in Germany, and was clearly bent on a massive programme of rearmament. In 1933 the British government at last permitted the issue of Air Staff requirements for a high-performance multi-gun fighter, which in due course produced the Hurricane and Spitfire. It is often asserted that these two aircraft, and especially the Spitfire, were forced on a reluctant Air Ministry by a far-sighted aircraft industry and its capable designers. There is not a word of truth in this. Both aircraft were designed, ordered, and built to Air Ministry specifications.

Even after the collapse of the Disarmament Conference in 1934 the British government was reluctant to rearm. Alone among nations the British seem to think that if they rearm it will bring about an arms race. The result of this curious delusion is that they usually start when the other competitors are half-way round the course. The bomber force was therefore given a very low priority, but development of the fighters was allowed to proceed, though without any undue haste.

In 1935 two British ministers, Mr Anthony Eden and Sir John Simon, visited Germany. They reported that Hitler's rearmament in the air had proceeded much farther and faster than the British government had believed possible. This was because the Germans had made a secret agreement to train the Soviet air force, which enabled them to keep in being a sizeable corps of expert pilots and technicians. The government was alarmed, and ordered quantity production of the Hurricanes and Spitfires before the prototype had even flown—the so-called 'ordering off the drawing-board'.

Gloster Gladiator II
Gross weight: 4,864 lb. *Span:* 32 ft 3 in. *Length:* 27 ft 5 in. *Engine:* 840 hp Bristol Mercury VIII. *Armament:* 4 x ·303 machine-guns. *Crew:* 1. *Speed:* 257 mph at 14,600 ft. *Ceiling:* 33,500 ft. *Range:* 444 miles. The RAF's last front-line biplane fighter, the Gladiator, fought in Norway and France where it inflicted casualties on far superior opponents. During the Battle of Britain only one squadron operated the type over the far north of the Home Islands, but the tough little fighter went on to win greater laurels in the Middle East and the Mediterranean

Lord Trenchard, chief of the Air Staff from 1919 to 1928, had always believed that in air defence the bomber was as important as the fighter. He maintained that the air war should be fought in the skies over the enemy's territory, and he therefore advocated a bomber force powerful enough to take the offensive, and attack an enemy's vital centres from the outset. He argued that this would rob an enemy of the initiative and throw his air force on to the defensive.

Eventually Trenchard's views were accepted by the British government, and in the air defence of Great Britain two-thirds of the squadrons were to be bombers and one-third fighters. But because it was thought that the bombers were offensive while the fighters were defensive in character, it was judged that the building up of fighter strength would not be liable to trigger off an arms race. The seventeen authorized fighter squadrons were in existence by 1930, but at that date no more than twelve of the thirty-five authorized bomber squadrons had been formed, most of them equipped with small short-range day bombers. In 1935 the alarm caused by German rearmament in the air occasioned a further shift of emphasis in favour of the fighters. A system of radio-location, later called radar, which would provide invaluable early warning and make it possible to track incoming raids, was pioneered by Robert Watson-Watt, and given all possible encouragement.

At the outbreak of war in September 1939 the odds against the RAF, in terms of modern aircraft, were about four to one. Although money had been poured out like water during the years since the Munich crisis, it had been too late to redress the balance. Only time—as much time as possible—could do that.

Supermarine Spitfire prototype
Developed from the Supermarine S6B racing seaplane which won the Schneider Trophy for Britain in 1931, the Spitfire was the most famous fighter of the Second World War. It was the only Allied fighter to remain in production throughout the war

Messerschmitt Bf 109 prototype
The Bf 109 prototype was built in 1935 around the 610 hp Junkers Jumo 210A engine. This was not available for the first flights, so a Rolls-Royce Kestrel V was temporarily installed. More 109s were produced than any other single seat fighter in aviation history – over 35,000 of various types

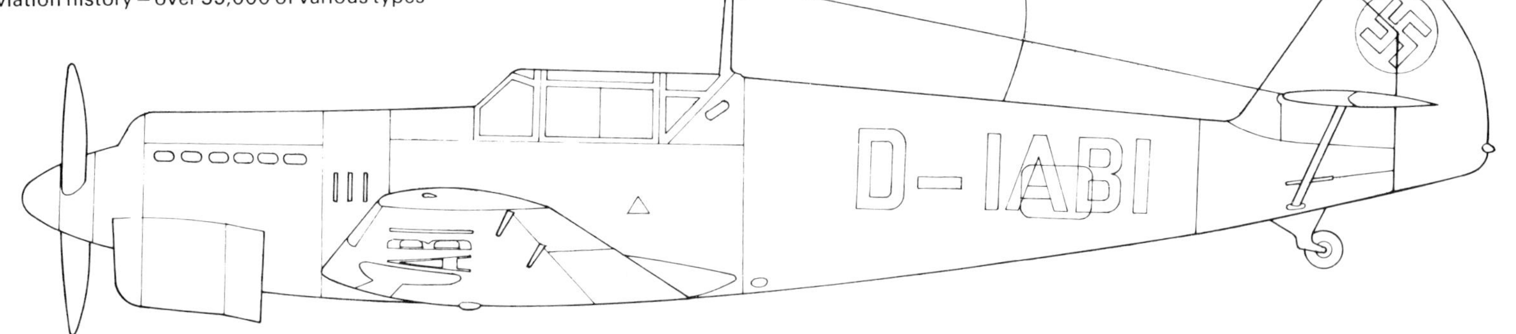

One key to Germany's quick victory over Poland and France was air power. Gaining command of the air by destroying enemy air forces on the ground, the angular Stuka dive-bombers ranged ahead of the Panzers, acting as flying artillery. But at Dunkirk their awesome reputation was tarnished by their failure to destroy the encircled BEF; and over Britain the terror weapon of 1939 was blunted by a modern and determined fighter defence. Once separated from its Messerschmitt escort, it was an easy prey for the Spitfires and Hurricanes of the Royal Air Force, and after a few weeks of serious losses the Stuka was largely withdrawn from operations over Britain.

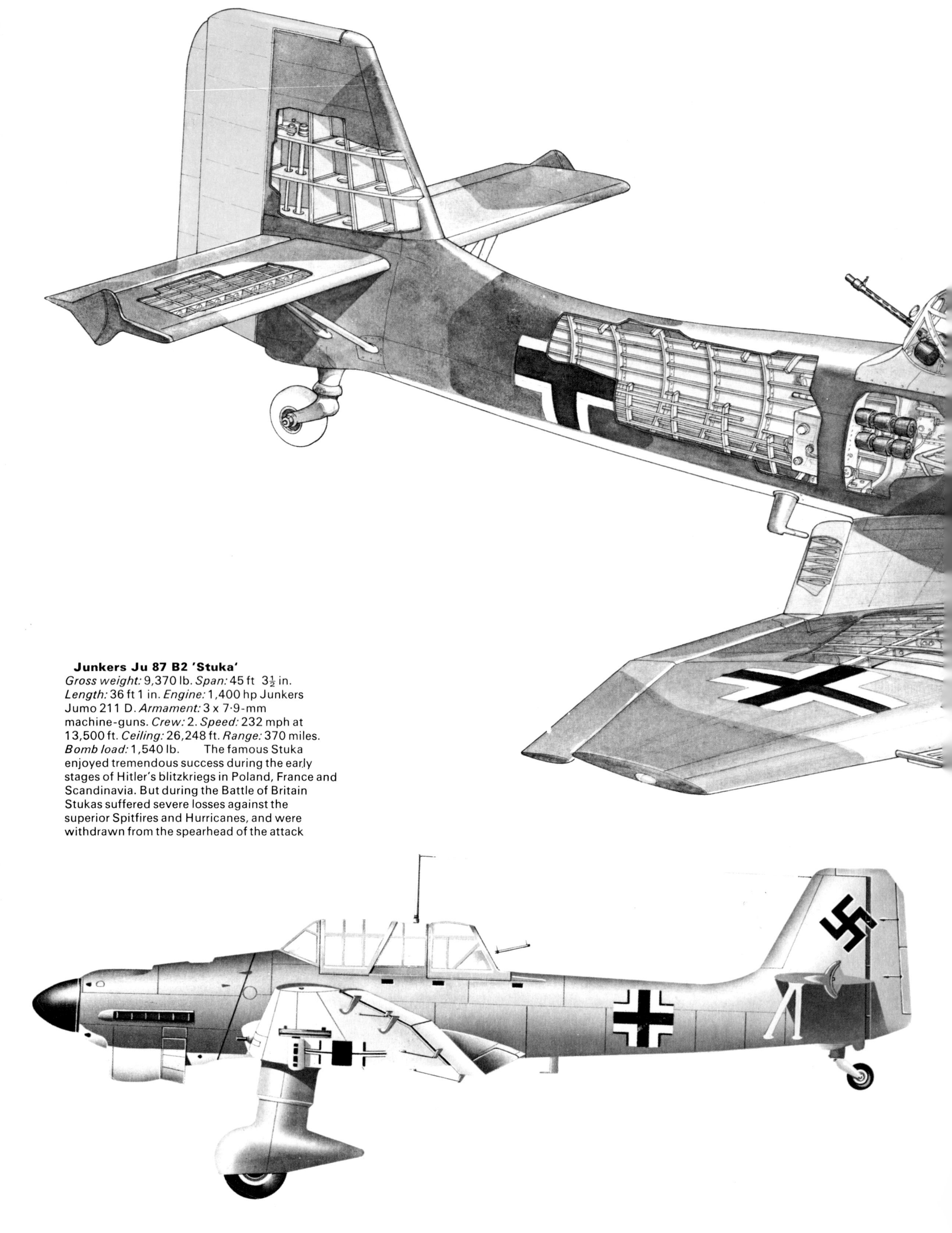

Junkers Ju 87 B2 'Stuka'
Gross weight: 9,370 lb. *Span:* 45 ft 3½ in. *Length:* 36 ft 1 in. *Engine:* 1,400 hp Junkers Jumo 211 D. *Armament:* 3 x 7·9-mm machine-guns. *Crew:* 2. *Speed:* 232 mph at 13,500 ft. *Ceiling:* 26,248 ft. *Range:* 370 miles. *Bomb load:* 1,540 lb. The famous Stuka enjoyed tremendous success during the early stages of Hitler's blitzkriegs in Poland, France and Scandinavia. But during the Battle of Britain Stukas suffered severe losses against the superior Spitfires and Hurricanes, and were withdrawn from the spearhead of the attack

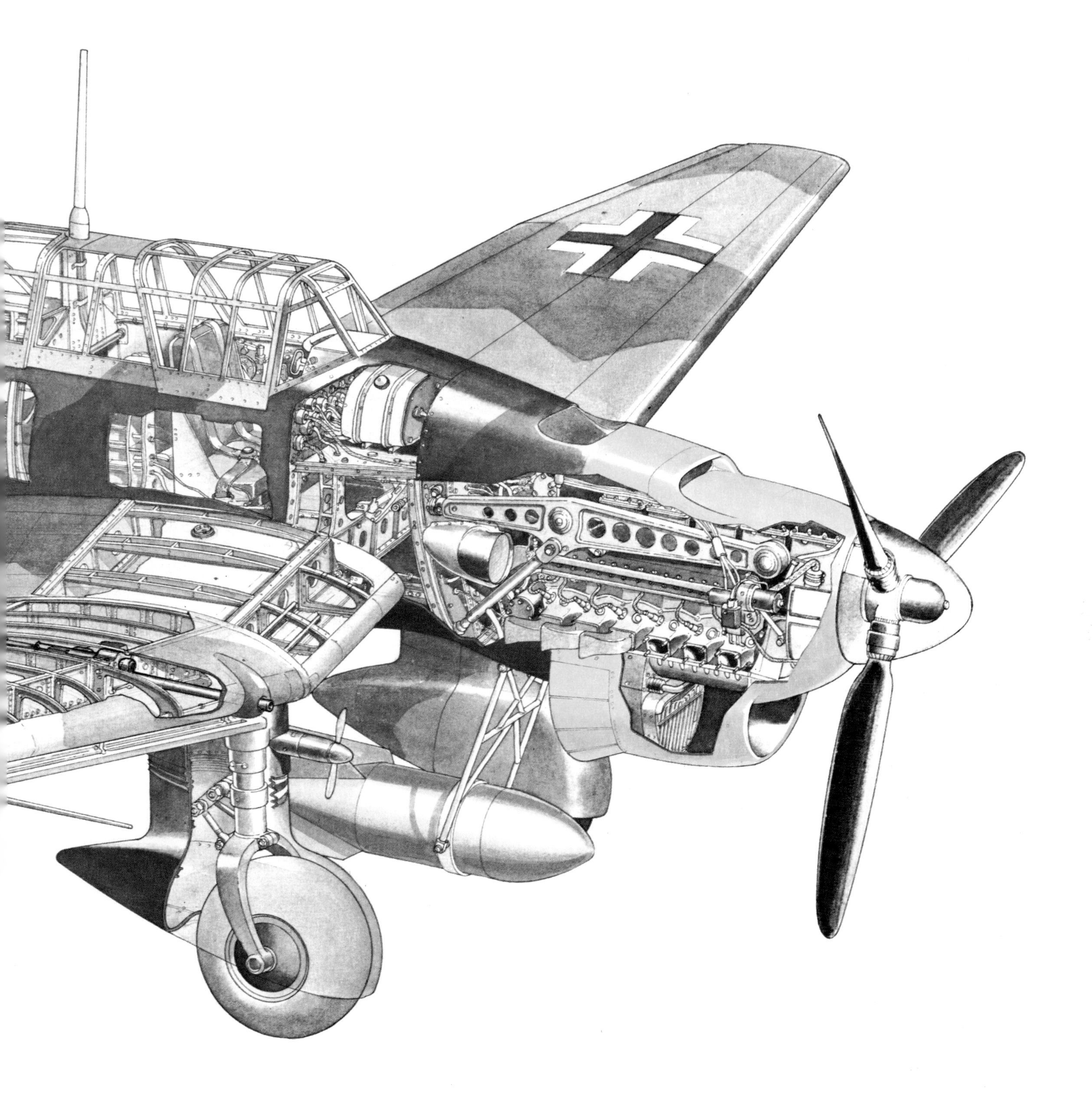

Heinkel He 111 B2
Gross weight: 22,046 lb. *Span:* 74 ft 2 in. *Length:* 57 ft 5 in. *Engine:* 2 x 950 hp DB 600. *Armament:* 3 x 7·9-mm machine-guns. *Crew:* 4. *Speed:* 186 mph at ground level. *Ceiling:* 22,966 ft. *Range:* 1,030 miles. *Bomb load:* 3,307 lb.
The B2 version of the He 111 served with the Condor Legion in the Spanish Civil War, outpacing all opposing fighters and carrying out unescorted raids at will. But the resulting over-confidence was shattered by opposition from Spitfires and Hurricanes in 1940 and the He 111 was soon relegated to night duties

German Fighter Pilot, 2nd Lieutenant

A German 2nd Lieutenant fighter pilot began training at an elementary flying training school which entailed gliding on Course 1, elementary flying on Course 2, and single-engine fighter training on Course 3. He then went on to advanced training and lastly to his operational training unit: altogether it took seven to eight months and 107 to 112 hours at the controls. He wore the national eagle emblem on his right and pilot's insigne on his lower left breast. On his visored cap, more rakish than others in the army, was the national rosette flanked by oak leaves and spreading wings surmounted by a flying eagle. Yellow piping and a large 'W' decorated his epaulettes; his collar patch was an eagle and oak leaves on a yellow background. He wore jackboots, grey-blue wool-rayon breeches, jacket with patch pockets, grey shirt, black tie and a Sam Browne belt with eagle-emblem buckle. His flying suit had zippered slash pockets and his flying boots were lined. He had passed a rigid physical examination and was eligible for pilot training after the age of 18. Under normal conditions, *Luftwaffe* pilots enjoyed better food than the rest of the army and the pay was higher

Junkers Ju 87 B2 'Stuka' Cockpit

1 Visual dive indicator
2 Gun sight
3 Artificial horizon
4 Compass repeater
5 Speedometer
6 Boost pressure
7 Altimeter
8 Rev counter
9 Flap indicator
10 Intercom connection
11 Crash pad
12 Manual engine pump
13 Engine priming pump
14 Electrics panel (radio)
15 Oil cooler flap control
16 Rudder bar pedal
17 Target view window
18 Control column
19 Target view window flap control
20 Fuel metering hand priming pump
21 Throttle
22 Starter switch
23 Main electrics switch
24 Coolant temperature
25 Fuel contents
26 Oil temperature
27 Oil contents
28 Compass
29 Oil pressure gauge
30 Clock
31 Dive pre-set indicator
32 Fuel pressure gauge
33 Radio altimeter
34 Rate of climb indicator
35 Water cooler flap indicator

AUF ZU
ZIEHEN

Messerschmitt Bf 109 E-3
Gross weight: 5,875 lb. *Span:* 28 ft 4½ in. *Length:* 32 ft 4½ in. *Engine:* 1,054 hp DB 601A. *Armament:* 4 x 7·9-mm machine-guns. *Crew:* 1. *Speed:* 348 mph at 14,560 ft. *Ceiling:* 34,450 ft. *Range:* 410 miles. This plane fought with *Jagdgeschwader* 26; it later crashed in Kent

Dewoitine 520
Gross weight: 5,909 lb. *Span:* 33 ft 5 in. *Length:* 27 ft. *Engine:* 930 hp Hispano-Suiza 12Y 45. *Armament:* 4 x 7·65-mm machine-guns; 1 x 20-mm cannon. *Crew:* 1. *Speed:* 329 mph at 18,000 ft. *Ceiling:* 33,000 ft. *Range:* 550 miles. This plane fought with 'Joan of Arc' squadron

VICTORS AND VANQUISHED IN THE BATTLE OF FRANCE

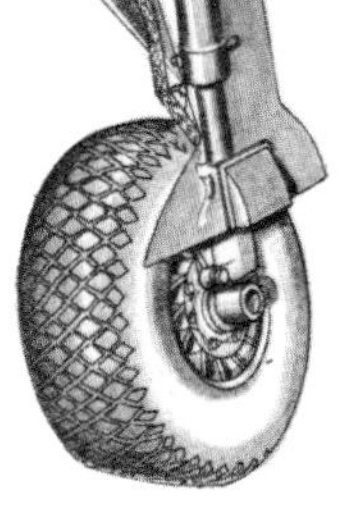

Morane-Saulnier 406
Span: 35 ft 1 in. *Length:* 26 ft 10 in. *Engine:* 850 hp Hispano-Suiza 12Y-31. *Armament:* 1 Hispano 9 cannon; 2 or 4 machine-guns. *Crew:* 1. *Speed:* 305 mph at 16,500 ft. *Ceiling:* 32,300 ft. The most famous French fighter of the war, over 1,000 were built. The prototype was the first French aircraft to exceed 250 mph in level flight, in 1935

R.A.F. Fighter Command
Command Headquarters
Group Headquarters
Sector station
Fighter base
Low-level radar station
High-level radar station
Towns bombed
German bases
Fighter
Twin-engined Me 110
Bomber
St (Stuka) Dive-bomber
0 50 100
Miles
LUFTFLOTTE 5
from Norway and Denmark
Glasgow
NORTHUMBER-LAND
Newcastle
Sunderland
FIGHTER COMMAND GROUP 13
Middlesbrough
Belfast
YORKSHIRE
Driffield
Hull
NORTH SEA
Liverpool
Manchester
Mersey-side
Sheffield
Nottingham
FIGHTER COMMAND GROUP 12
Range of Low-level Radar
Range of High-level Radar
Norwich
Birmingham
Coventry
Amsterdam
NETHERLANDS
Rotterdam
Ipswich
Martlesham
Debden
London
North Weald
Stanmore
Northolt
Uxbridge
Hornchurch
Rochford
Swansea
Cardiff
FIGHTER COMMAND GROUP 11
Croydon
Rochester
Eastchurch
Bristol
Biggin Hill
Kenley
Manston
Canterbury
Andover
Middle Wallop
West Malling
Detling
Worthy Down
Hawkinge
Lympne
FIGHTER COMMAND GROUP 10
Southampton
Portsmouth
Tangmere
Calais
Antwerp
Ghent
Exeter
Portland
Ventnor
St
Lille
BELGIUM
LUFTFLOTTE 2
Plymouth
ENGLISH CHANNEL
Amiens
Cherbourg
Le Havre
Paris
LUFTFLOTTE 3
FRANCE
Rennes
A. W. Gatrell & Co Ltd

THE BATTLE OF BRITAIN

From the very outset of the war a great German air assault had been expected in Britain. It was for fear of this that mothers and children had been evacuated from the big cities, the blackout enforced, gas masks and Anderson shelters distributed, thousands of beds held vacant in the hospitals. But no 'knock-out blow' from the air, or indeed any kind of blow at all—other than minelaying and raids on Scottish naval bases and east coast convoys—had disturbed the uncanny peace of the British Isles during the autumn and winter of 1939-40.

This quiet remained unbroken even when, in the spring of 1940, the war in the west came abruptly to the boil. Strange as it seemed at the time, there were in fact good reasons for Britain's unexpected immunity. Britain herself had not launched a strategic bombing offensive against Germany during the 'Phoney War' for fear of retaliation while the Allies were still the weaker side in the air. Germany had not launched any such offensive against Britain because she did not think she could achieve decisive results from German bases and because the Luftwaffe was largely cast for the role of support.

This self-imposed restriction lasted until the German army entered the smoking ruins of Dunkirk. Within less than 48 hours, on the night of June 5/6, the Luftwaffe began to show a more lively interest in the British homeland. Some 30 German bombers—far more than on any previous occasion—crossed the east coast to attack airfields and other objectives; and the following night similar forces repeated the experiment. Then came a lull while the German armies in France struck southwards, again supported by the Luftwaffe. It lasted until the French sought an armistice, whereupon within a few hours German aircraft resumed night operations over Britain. From then on until the opening of their full daylight air offensive in August, the Germans repeatedly dispatched bombers—70 of them on the busiest night—against widely separated targets in England. Their intention was to give their crews experience in night operations and the use of radio navigational aids, to reconnoitre, and to maintain pressure inexpensively (their usual losses were one or two aircraft each night) until captured airfields in France and the Low Countries could be made ready for operations of a more intensive kind.

Meanwhile there was always the chance—or so it seemed to Hitler—that such operations might not be necessary. The Führer accordingly put out 'peace-feelers', at the same time encouraging preparations for the next stage of hostilities. This next stage, the invasion or occupation of Britain, was not one to which the Germans had already devoted long thought. The speed and completeness of the German victory in France had taken even the optimistic Hitler by surprise; and though his armed forces had given some casual attention in the autumn of 1939 to the general problems of invading Britain, it was not until German troops actually reached the Channel coast on May 20, 1940, that the project really came to life. From then on the German navy, anxious not to be caught out by Hitler, began serious planning; but the German army showed comparable interest only after the total defeat of France. On July 2 Hitler formally directed his services to proceed with this invasion planning, though on a purely provisional basis. On July 19 came his public peace offer; on the 22nd, its rejection.

The Luftwaffe was able to use the entire coastline of occupied Europe: the British resources were to be strained to their furthest limits ◁

If the Germans were to take advantage of the 'invasion season' in the Channel that year, their three services would now have to formulate and agree plans with extraordinary speed. This difficulty struck the German naval and military chiefs more forcibly than it did Hitler, who declared to his paladins that only the rapid elimination of Britain would enable him to complete his life's work by turning against Russia. On July 31 he accordingly disregarded the fast-waning enthusiasm of the German navy and army and ordered that an attempt must be made to prepare the invasion operation, to which the code-name *'Seelöwe'* ('Sea Lion') was given, for September 15. The following day, August 1, he issued a directive concerning the only part of the venture on which all three German services were thus far agreed. It was for the preliminary stage, which must consist of the subjugation of the RAF. 'The German air force is to overcome the British air force with all means at its disposal, and as soon as possible.' With these words, Hitler finally decreed the Battle of Britain.

600 RAF sorties a day

While the plans for Sea Lion and the preliminary air battle were taking shape, the Luftwaffe was not of course idle. From its captured airfields it continued to harass Britain by night, and from July 10 onwards it waged increasing war by day against British shipping in the Channel. The German bombers were usually detected by the British radar stations, but since the attacks were delivered at the periphery of the British defensive system they set the Fighter Command a difficult problem. In such circumstances it was highly creditable to the command that the British fighters inflicted more casualties than they themselves suffered: between July 10 and August 10, as we now know, the Germans lost 217 aircraft, Fighter Command 96. On the other hand the German attacks, though sinking only a modest tonnage of British shipping, imposed a severe strain on Fighter Command, which was compelled to fly some 600 sorties a day at extended range at a time when it was trying to build up resources for the greater trials clearly soon to come. As Air Chief Marshal Sir Hugh Dowding, Air Officer C-in-C of the Fighter Command, pointed out to the Air Ministry and the Admiralty, if constant air protection was to be given to all British shipping in home waters, the entire British fighter force could be kept fully employed on that task alone.

These German attacks on shipping, however, were only a prelude to the air battle which the Luftwaffe had now to induce. The prerequisite of Sea Lion was that the Germans should gain air supremacy over the Channel and southern Britain. Only if the RAF were put out of business could the Germans hope to cross, land, and maintain communications without an unacceptable rate of casualties; for the destruction of the RAF would not only obviate British bombing attacks, but would also enable the Luftwaffe to deal, uninterrupted from the air, with the Royal Navy. And beyond this there was always the hope, ever present in the minds of Hitler and his service chiefs alike, that the Luftwaffe's success alone might be so great as to bring Britain to submission, or very near it. In that case, an invasion about which neither the German navy nor army was really happy could become something much more to their liking—a virtually unresisted occupation.

As the moment drew near for the Luftwaffe's great assault, the forces arrayed stood as follows. On the German side there were three *Luftflotten,* or air fleets. The main ones were Luftflotte II, under Field-Marshal Kesselring, in northern Germany, Holland, Belgium, and in north-eastern France; and Luftflotte III, under Field-Marshal Sperrle, in northern and western France. By day, these two air fleets threatened the entire southern half of England, up to and including the Midlands; and by night they could range still farther afield. In addition, to disperse the British defences and to threaten Scotland and north-eastern England there was also a smaller force, Luftflotte V, under General Stumpff, based in Denmark and Norway. Between them, the three air fleets on August 10 comprised over 3,000 aircraft, of which about three-quarters were normally serviceable at any one time. Roughly 1,100 of the 3,000 were fighters—for the most part Messerschmitt 109E's, virtually the equal of the opposing Spitfires of that date, but handicapped in a protective role by their limited range.

To escort bombers to the more distant targets, including those to be reached across the North Sea from Norway, there were some 300 Messerschmitt 110s; but these twin-engined fighters, though sturdy, could not compare in manoeuvrability with the single-engined Spitfire or Hurricane. The remaining 1,900 German aircraft were almost entirely bombers, mainly the well-tried if slow Heinkel 111, the slim, pencil-like Dornier 17, and the fast and more recent Junkers 88, but including also about 400 Junkers 87s—the Stukas, or dive-bombers. These had established a legendary reputation on the battlefields of Poland and France, but their range was very short and they had yet to face powerful opposition.

On the British side, the situation was a great deal better than it had been a few weeks earlier. On June 4, following the heavy losses of Hurricanes in France, Fighter Command had been able to muster

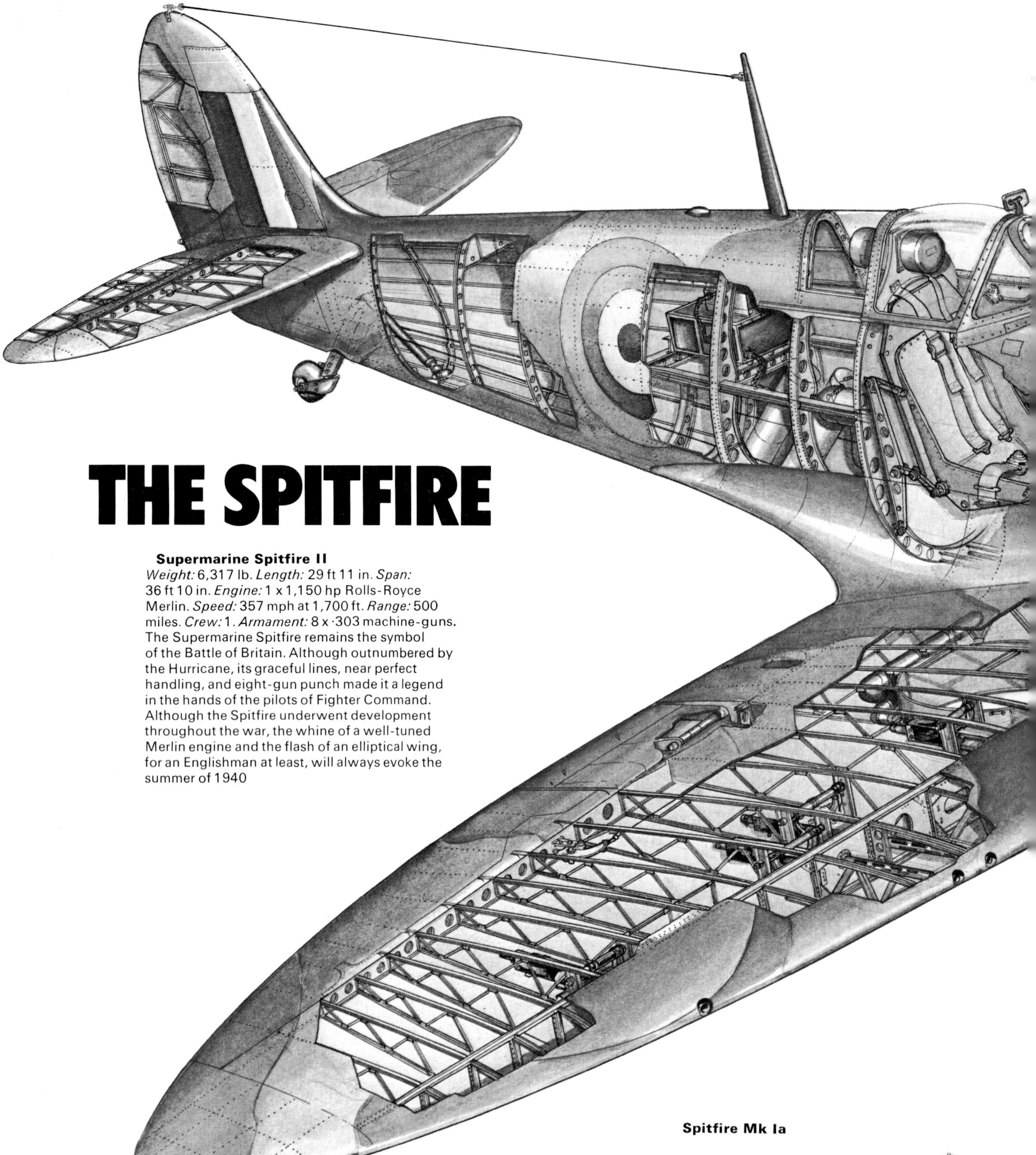

THE SPITFIRE

Supermarine Spitfire II
Weight: 6,317 lb. *Length:* 29 ft 11 in. *Span:* 36 ft 10 in. *Engine:* 1 x 1,150 hp Rolls-Royce Merlin. *Speed:* 357 mph at 1,700 ft. *Range:* 500 miles. *Crew:* 1. *Armament:* 8 x ·303 machine-guns. The Supermarine Spitfire remains the symbol of the Battle of Britain. Although outnumbered by the Hurricane, its graceful lines, near perfect handling, and eight-gun punch made it a legend in the hands of the pilots of Fighter Command. Although the Spitfire underwent development throughout the war, the whine of a well-tuned Merlin engine and the flash of an elliptical wing, for an Englishman at least, will always evoke the summer of 1940

Spitfire Mk Ia

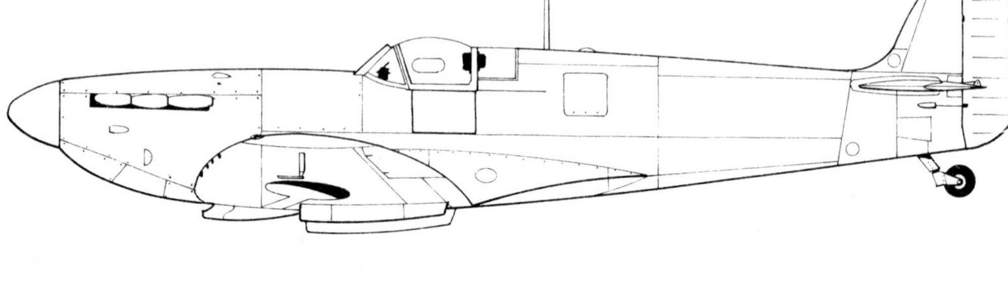

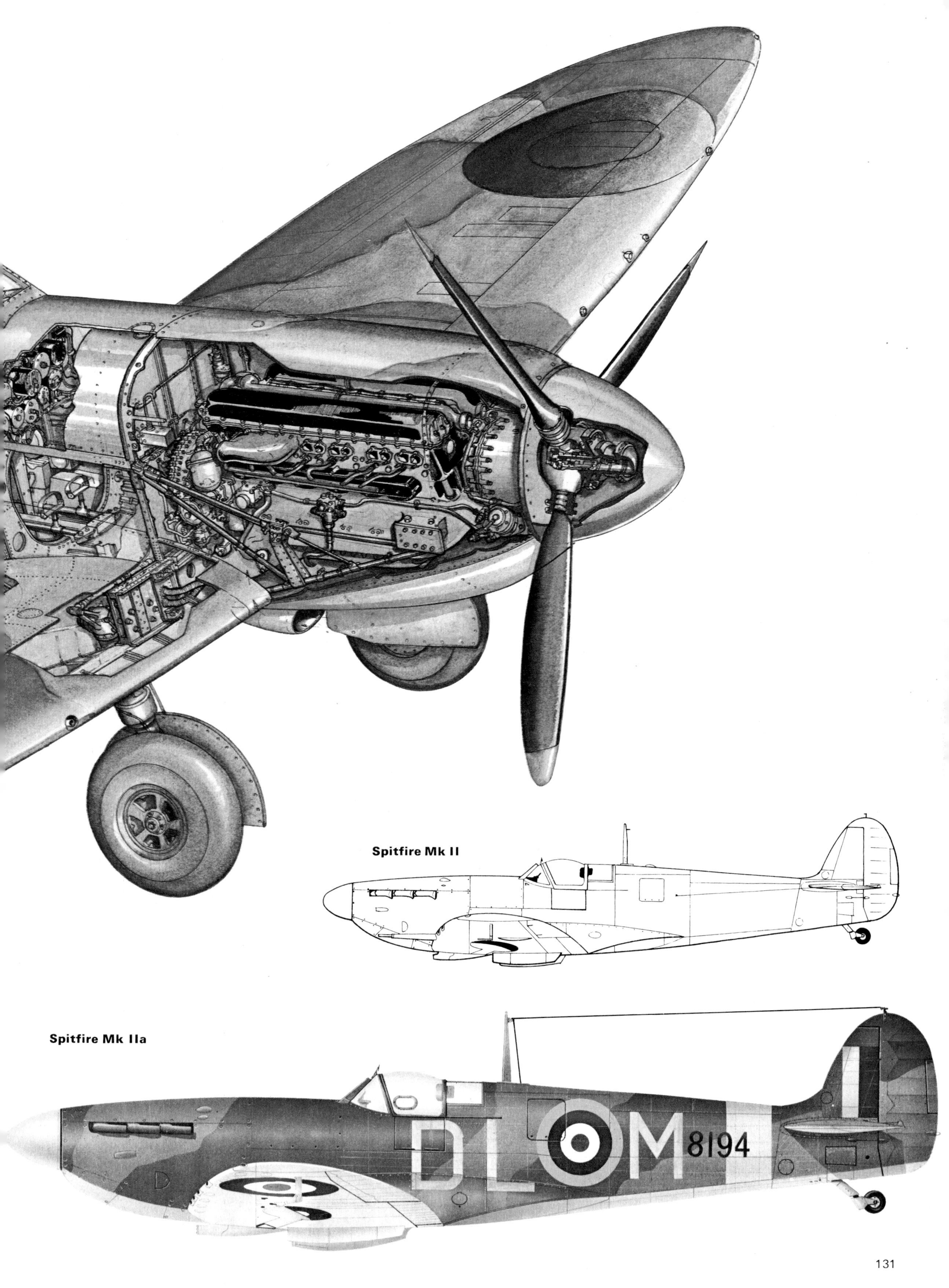

Spitfire Mk II
Spitfire Mk IIa
DL
M
8194

Boulton Paul Defiant Mk I
Span: 39 ft 4 in. *Length:* 35 ft 4 in. *Engine:* 1,030 hp Rolls-Royce Merlin III. *Armament:* 4 x ·303 in. machine-guns in power-operated turret. *Speed:* 303 mph at 16,500 ft. *Ceiling:* 30,350 ft. A modernised version of the two-seat patrol fighter concept of 1918, the Defiant was an easy target for German single-seaters

RAF Fighter Pilot, Pilot Officer
A Pilot Officer, lowest commissioned rank in the RAF, began training as an Aircraftsman II at an initial training school and first flew on his two-month elementary course, soloing after about seven hours' instruction on a Tiger Moth. After another four months, on Proctors, he qualified for his wings and commission, then went to an operational training unit to fly fighters with experienced instructors. Altogether he would have spent over a year in training and up to 200 hours in the air as well as 'blind flying' time in a Link trainer. His minimum age was 18, maximum 35; average height was 5 ft 8½ in. He had passed a written entrance examination, a physical examination, and a colour blindness test. He wore either a serge woollen blue-grey uniform or a four patch-pocket barathea with blue shirt, black tie and black shoes. His rank insigne was a 'half-narrow' blue and grey ring around both sleeves; his wings were white-drab silk with a crown over the RAF monogram and brown silk laurel wreath. He was paid 11 shillings a day, plus £25 a year flying pay and dependents' allowance

ROYAL AIR FORCE: BATTLE AGAINST TIME

Cockpit of a Spitfire Mk II
Pilot's eye-view of the Spitfire's business end. With an eight-gun armament, constant speed propeller, retracting undercarriage, and 1,175 horsepower engine, a complex array of controls had to be shoehorned into a small space. The bucket seat took the pilot's parachute

UP
UP
DOWN
AIR
MPH
ARTIFICIAL HORIZON
CLIMB
DESCENT
DIRECTION INDICATOR
L
R
R.P.M.
BOOST
OIL
TEMP
RAD
TEMP
GALLONS FUEL
ON
FUEL
OFF

only 446 modern single-engined fighters – Spitfires and Hurricanes – with another 36 ready in the Aircraft Storage Units (ASUs) as replacements. But on August 11, on the eve of the main air battle, Fighter Command had 704 of these aircraft in the squadrons and 289 in the ASUs. Its fighting strength had been virtually doubled during those ten critical weeks since Dunkirk, thanks to the fruition of earlier Air Ministry plans and the tremendous efforts of the aircraft industry under the stimulus of the newly appointed Minister of Aircraft Production, Lord Beaverbrook.

Strengthening the shield

During those same ten weeks the British air defence system, built up against an enemy operating from Germany and possibly the Low Countries, had also been extended, thanks to schemes already worked out and in progress, to deal with forces operating from France and Norway. To the existing groups within Fighter Command – No. 11 Group, guarding the south-east, No. 12 Group, guarding the east and Midlands, and No. 13 Group, guarding the north-east up to the Forth – had been added another: No. 10 Group, guarding the south-west. The intermittent defences of the north-west, including Northern Ireland, had been thickened, as had those of Scotland.

This was not only a matter of providing more fighter aircraft and the pilots to fly them. It was also a matter of extending the main coastal radar chain, adding special radar stations to detect low-flying aircraft, extending Observer Corps posts for inland tracking over the south-western counties and western Wales, adapting more airfields for fighter operations, installing guns, searchlights, balloon barrages. All this was the concomitant, on the air defence side, of the gun-posts and the pill-boxes, the barbed wire and the dragon's teeth, that the inhabitant of southern England, enrolled perhaps in the newly formed Local Defence Volunteers and on watch at dawn and dusk for the arrival of German paratroops, saw springing up before his eyes along his familiar coasts and downlands.

The island's air defences had grown stronger and more extensive, but many grave deficiencies remained. Of the 120 fighter squadrons which the Director of Home Operations at the Air Ministry considered desirable in the new situation created by the German conquests, Dowding had less than 60 – and eight of these flew Blenheims or Defiants, no match for the Me-109s. Of the 4,000 anti-aircraft guns deemed necessary even before the German conquests, Anti-Aircraft Command still had less than 2,000. The early warning and inland tracking systems were still incomplete in the west and over parts of Scotland. There was a shortage of fighter pilots: new planes could be produced quicker than new skilled men to fly them. But whatever the deficiencies of the air defence system by day, they were as nothing compared with its alarming weaknesses by night, when ordinary fighters were useful only in the brightest moonlight, and when the men of the Observer Corps had to rely on ineffective acoustical detectors instead of their clear eyesight and a pair of binoculars.

Britain, however, had assets not yet mentioned. Among others, there was RAF Coastal Command, prepared both to carry out reconnaissance and to help in offensive operations; and there was RAF Bomber Command. Most of the latter's aircraft could operate safely only by night, and by night it was by no means certain that they could find and hit the more distant targets. The daylight bombers – about 100 Blenheims – were capable of much greater accuracy; but they needed fighter support, which could be supplied only at short range (assuming the Hurricanes or Spitfires could be spared). Against targets near at hand – airfields, ports, and shipping just across the Channel – the British bombing force was capable of playing a vital part. Against distant objectives, its effectiveness at that date was more problematical.

In sum, the opposing forces, disregarding reconnaissance aircraft and units still stationed in Germany, consisted of about 1,900 bombers assisted by 1,100 fighters on the German side, and of about 700 fighters assisted to a limited extent by 350 bombers on the British side. The Germans had the advantage not only of numbers but of the tactical initiative – of the fact that they could strike anywhere within their range – while the British defences could react only to the German moves.

The British air defence system, however, though incomplete, was the most technically advanced in the world. The early warning supplied by the radar stations (which in the south-east could pick up enemy formations before they crossed the French coast), the inland tracking by the Observer Corps, the control of the British fighters from the ground in the light of this information and the continuous reporting of the fighters' own position – all this, designed to obviate the need for wasteful standing patrols, meant that the British fighters could be used with economy and could take off with a good chance of making interception.

One other factor, too, helped the British: the Luftwaffe's offensive against Britain was largely an improvised one; and Luftwaffe C-in-C Göring, though an able man, was also a vainglorious boaster who in technical proficiency was not in the same class as the opposing commander. The single-minded Dowding, in charge of Fighter Command since its formation in 1936 – the man whose obduracy had preserved Britain's fighter resources against the clamour to squander them in France – knew his job. Göring, as much politician as airman, scarcely knew his; while theoretically controlling and co-ordinating the entire offensive, in practice he was incapable of more than occasional acts of intervention. On the next level of command, Kesselring, in charge of the main attacking force – Luftflotte II – was for all his successes in Poland and France a novice in the forthcoming type of operation; while Air Vice-Marshal Keith Park, commanding the main defending force – Group 11 – had earlier been Dowding's right-hand man at Headquarters, Fighter Command. Unlike their opposite numbers, the two principal British commanders had lived with their problem for years. Their skill, experience, and devotion, like those of their pilots, offset some of the British inferiority in numbers.

Operation Eagle

By August 10 the three Luftflotten stood ready to launch the major assault – Operation Eagle *('Adler')* – which would drive the RAF from the skies of southern Britain. Four days, in the opinion of the German Air Staff, would see the shattering of the fighter defences south of the line London-Gloucester, four weeks the elimination of the entire RAF. Allowing for the ten days' notice required by the German navy for minelaying and other final preparations before the actual D-Day, the date of the invasion could thus be set for mid-September.

August 11 was a very cloudy day, and the Germans confined their activity to bombing Portland and some east coast shipping. On the following day came what seemed to the British to be the beginning of the main attack: five or six major raids and many minor ones, involving several hundred aircraft, including escorted Ju-87s, struck at airfields and radar stations along the south coast and at shipping in the Thames Estuary. Of the six radar stations they attacked, the raiders damaged five but knocked out only one – that at Ventnor on the Isle of Wight. It could not be replaced until August 23 – a sharp blow. Among the airfields, they hit Lympne, a forward landing ground, and Manston and Hawkinge, two important fighter stations in Kent, but all were back in action within 24 hours. Fighters from No. 11 Group challenged all the major raids, and frustrated completely one aimed at Manston. In the course of the fighting the Germans lost 31 aircraft, the British 22.

According to the German records, the next day, August 13, was Eagle Day itself – the opening of the Eagle offensive proper. The attack went off at half-cock in the morning, when a message postponing operations till later in the day failed to get through to some of the German squadrons. In the afternoon the main assault developed with a two-pronged thrust, Luftflotte II attacking over Kent and the Thames Estuary, while Luftflotte III, challenged by No. 10 Group, attacked over Hampshire, Dorset, and Wiltshire. The raiders hit three airfields severely – Eastchurch, Detling, and Andover – but none of these belonged to Fighter Command; their attacks on fighter stations such as Rochford were beaten off.

In the whole day's operations – which witnessed 1,485 German sorties and ended with a successful night attack on a Spitfire factory at Castle Bromwich, near Birmingham – the Germans lost 45 aircraft, Fighter Command only 13 (with six of the British pilots saved). This was a poor sort of Eagle Day for the Germans, but they were nevertheless well satisfied with their progress. They calculated that between August 8 and 14, in addition to successful attacks on some 30 airfields and aircraft factories, they had destroyed more than 300 British fighters in combat. In fact, they had destroyed less than 100.

After lesser activity on August 14 – a matter of some 500 German sorties, directed mainly against railways near the coast and against RAF stations – the Luftwaffe on August 15 attempted the great blow with which it had hoped to open the battle some days earlier. In clear skies the Germans sent over during the day no less than seven major raids, using all three Luftflotten in a series of co-ordinated attacks on widely separated areas. The first clash came at about 1130 hours, when some 40 escorted Ju-87s of Luftflotte II struck at Lympne and Hawkinge airfields in Kent. Then, about 1230 hours some 65 He-111s escorted by 35 Me-110s of Luftflotte V, operating from Stavanger in Norway, headed in to the Northumberland coast in an attempt to bomb airfields in the north-east. These formations were barely retiring when at 1315 hours another force of Luftflotte V, consisting of about 50 unescorted Ju-88s operating from Aalborg in Denmark, approached the Yorkshire coast on a similar mission. Little more than an hour later at 1430 hours, and once more at 1500, Luftflotte II struck again, on the first occasion north of the Thames Estuary against Martlesham airfield and on the second against Hawkinge and Eastchurch airfields and aircraft factories at Rochester.

Next it was the turn of Luftflotte III: at 1720 hours some 80 bombers, heavily escorted, came in to the south coast at Portland, bombed the harbour, and then attacked airfields at Middle Wallop and Worthy Down. Finally, at 1830 hours, 60 or 70 aircraft of Luftflotte II again penetrated over Kent, hitting West Malling airfields and the airfield and aircraft factories at Croydon. To round off the day's work, another 60 or 70 bombers made sporadic attacks during the hours of darkness.

All this German effort was fiercely challenged. Though the bombing had its successes, notably at Middle Wallop, Martlesham, and Driffield (Yorkshire) airfields and at Croydon, in no case did the British fighters allow the raiders to operate unmolested, and in many cases the primary objectives escaped unscathed. Especially significant was the fighting in the north-east, where No. 13 Group, involved for the first time in the battle, intercepted the formations from Norway well out to sea, and with the help of the anti-aircraft guns on Tyne and Tees destroyed eight He-111s and seven Me-110s, with no British losses. A little farther south, too, No. 12 Group and the local guns, tackling the formations from Denmark, brought down eight of the enemy with no loss on the British side. The Germans thus failed in their main hope – that Dowding, in his anxiety to protect the vital and heavily threatened south-east, would have left the north almost undefended. Instead, they discovered, to their cost, that their attacks across the North Sea were met before they reached the British coast, and that the Me-110s in a long-range escorting role were useless against Spitfires and Hurricanes. The lesson was sufficiently expensive to convince the Germans not to launch any further daylight attacks from this area.

The fighting on August 15 was the most extensive in the whole Battle of Britain. With 520 bomber and 1,270 fighter sorties, and attacks stretching from Northumberland to Dorset, the German effort was at its maximum. But so too was the German loss – 75 aircraft as against 34 British fighters. This did not prevent an effort of almost equal magnitude on the following day, when the Germans sent across some 1,700 sorties, attacked a number of airfields (with particular success at Tangmere), and lost 45 aircraft in the process. With Fighter Command losing 21, the balance remained in the British favour.

The Luftwaffe switches strategy

The four days of intensive attack calculated to clear the skies of southern England were now over, and the Germans took stock. In the opinion of their Intelligence, Fighter Command, if not exhausted, was down to its last 300 aircraft. This appreciation was very wide of the mark, for Dowding still had nearly twice that number of Hurricanes and Spitfires in the front line, in addition to another 120 or so Blenheims, Defiants, and Gladiators. However, it encouraged the Germans to believe that another day or two of major effort might see the end of British opposition. On August 18 the Luftwaffe accordingly struck again in full force, chiefly against airfields in Kent, Surrey, and Sussex; but in doing so they lost 71 aircraft while the British lost no more than 27. Clearly Fighter Command was still unsubdued. After a few days of minor activity owing to bad weather, the Germans therefore made their first great change of plan.

Up till then, the main German objectives had been airfields fairly near to the coast; after August 12 they had given up intensive attacks on radar stations – fortunately for Fighter Command – because they found them difficult to destroy. The airfields and other coastal targets they had continued to attack, partly to deny the airfields to the British during the proposed invasion period, but still more to force Fighter Command to join battle in their defence. The German theory was that by such attacks they might, without severe losses to themselves, inflict heavy losses on the RAF – for raids on coastal targets or those not far inland did not involve prolonged exposure to the British defences – while at the same time the Me-109s would be free from worries on the score of endurance and accordingly able to give maximum protection to the German bombers. Such was the German strategy when the battle began. It had not disposed of Fighter Command, so it was now changed in favour of attacks farther inland.

The first phase of the battle was thus over. So far, Fighter Command had more than held its own: 363 German aircraft had been destroyed between August 8 and 18, as against 181 British fighters lost in the air and another 30 on the ground. The period had also seen what proved to be the last daylight attack by Luftflotte V, and the last attempt by Luftflotte II to make regular use of its Ju-87s – both notable successes for the British defences.

At the same time, however, there was one aspect of the struggle which gave Dowding and the Air Ministry acute anxiety. During the same ten days, when Fighter Command had lost 211 Spitfires and Hurricanes, the number of replacements forthcoming from the aircraft industry had fallen short of this total by at least 40. In the same period, Fighter Command had lost 154 experienced fighter pilots: but the output of the training schools had been only 63 – and those less skilled than the men they replaced. Fighter Command, while inflicting nearly twice as many casualties as it was suffering, was thus in fact being weakened – though not, as yet, at anything like the speed desired by the enemy.

It was to increase the rate of destruction of the British fighter force – which unchanged would have left Fighter Command still in existence in mid-September – that the Germans now switched to targets farther inland. They reckoned that by making their prime objective the fighter airfields, and in particular the sector airfields of No. 11 Group from which the British fighters in the south-east were controlled, they would not only strike at the heart of the British defences, but would also compel Fighter Command to meet their challenge with all its remaining forces. In the resulting air battles, they hoped to achieve a rate of attrition that would knock out Fighter Command within their scheduled time: though they also knew that in penetrating farther inland they were likely to suffer greater losses themselves. To guard against this, and to destroy as many Hurricanes and Spitfires as possible, they decided to send over a still higher proportion of fighters with their bombers.

The sector stations of No. 11 Group stood in a ring guarding London. To the south-west, in a forward position near Chichester, lay Tangmere. Nearer the capital and south of it there were Kenley in Surrey and Biggin Hill in Kent, both on the North Downs. Close to London in the east lay Hornchurch, near the factories of Dagenham; and round to the north-east was North Weald, in metropolitan Essex. Farther out there was Debden, near Saffron Walden. The ring was completed to the west by Northolt, on the road to Uxbridge, where No. 11 Group itself had its headquarters – which in turn was only a few minutes' drive from that of Fighter Command at Stanmore. All the sector stations normally controlled three fighter squadrons, based either on the sector station itself or on satellite airfields.

Strikes at the source

The Germans had already severely damaged two of the sector stations – Kenley and Biggin Hill – on August 18. Now, on August 24, they struck hard at North Weald and Hornchurch. On August 26 they attempted to bomb Biggin Hill, Kenley, North Weald, and Hornchurch, were beaten off, but got through to Debden. On August 30 they hit Biggin Hill twice, doing great damage and killing 39 persons. The following day – the most expensive of the whole battle for Fighter Command, with 39 aircraft lost – they wrought great damage at Debden, Biggin Hill, and Hornchurch.

On September 1 Biggin Hill suffered its sixth raid in three days, only to be bombed again less than 24 hours later; and on September 3 the attack once more fell on North Weald. On the 5th the main raids again headed towards Biggin Hill and North Weald, only to be repelled, while on the 4th and 6th the attacks extended also to the Vickers and Hawker factories near Weybridge. The Hawker factory, which produced more than half the total output of Hurricanes, was a particularly vital target. Its selection showed that the Germans, perplexed by the continued resilience of Fighter Command, were also trying to cut off the British fighter supply at its source.

Between August 24 and September 6 the Germans made no less than 33 major raids, of which more than two-thirds were mainly against the sector and other stations of Fighter Command. This assault imposed on the command a still greater strain than the preceding one, against targets in the coastal belt. The fighting was more difficult for the British pilots, in that the proportion of German fighters to bombers became so high, and sections of the fighter escort so close; and over the whole fortnight a daily average of something like 1,000 German aircraft, of which 250 to 400 were bombers, operated over England. Twice, on August 30 and 31, the number of intruders was nearer 1,500.

In the course of the combats and the ensuing night operations the British defences destroyed 380 German aircraft, as against a Fighter Command loss of 286: but many other British fighters were seriously damaged, and no less than 103 fighter pilots were killed and 128 wounded out of a fighting strength of not much more than 1,000. In addition six of the seven sector stations of No. 11 Group sustained heavy damage: and though none was yet out of action, Biggin Hill could control only one squadron instead of its normal three.

So Fighter Command was being steadily worn down. The wastage, both of fighters

Messerschmitt Bf 109 E-4
Gross Weight: 5,530 lb. *Span:* 32 ft $4\frac{1}{2}$ in. *Length:* 28 ft. 8 in. *Engine:* 1,150 hp DB 601A. *Armament:* 2 x 7·92-mm machine-guns; 2 x 20-mm cannon. *Speed:* 357 mph at 12,300 ft. *Ceiling:* 36,000 ft. *Range:* 412 miles. This was the aircraft of Adjutant of J.G.3 'Udet' Franz von Werra, which crashed in Kent on 5 September 1940. Von Werra was the only German officer to escape his captors and return to Germany during the Second World War

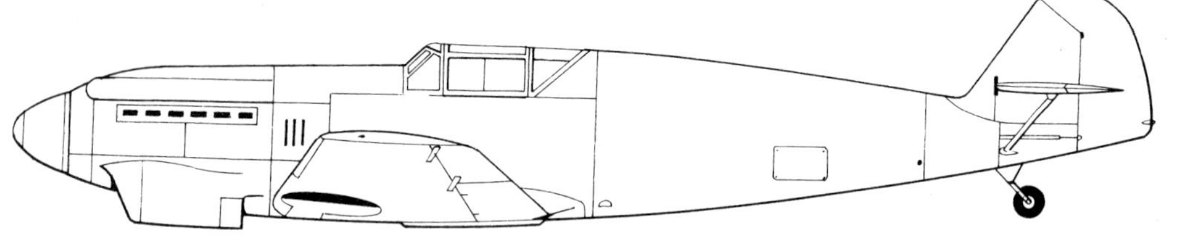

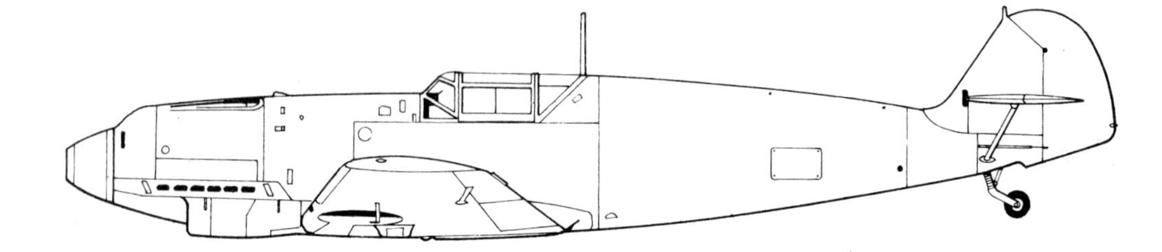

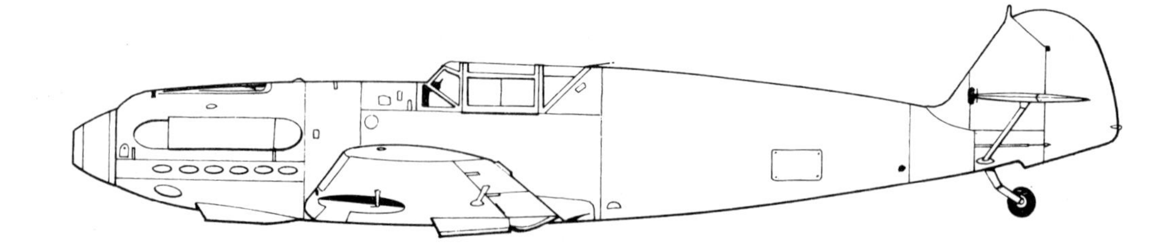

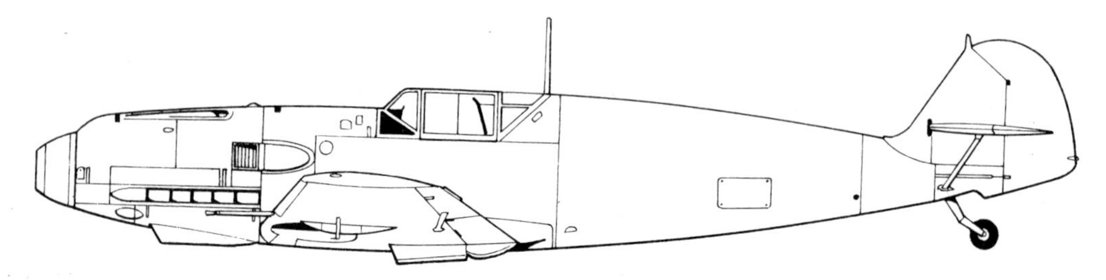

MESSERSCHMITT Bf 109

Bf 109 V-1 (top)
Prototype of the Bf 109 which first flew in September 1935, powered by a 695 hp Rolls-Royce Kestrel V engine because of the shortage of Jumo 210 units

Bf 109 B-1 (second)
Span: 32 ft 4½ in. *Length:* 28 ft. 6½ in. *Engine:* 635 hp Jumo 210D. *Armament:* 1 x 20-mm cannon; 2 x 7·9-mm machine-guns. *Speed:* 292 mph at 13,100 ft. *Ceiling:* 26,575 ft. One of the fighter types which equipped the Condor Legion during the Spanish Civil War

Bf 109 D-1 (third)
Powered by the 960 hp DB 600 engine which gave an increased speed of 323 mph

Bf 109 E-3 (bottom)
Span: 32 ft 4¼ in. *Length:* 28 ft 3¾ in. *Engine:* 1,100 hp DB 601A. *Armament:* 3 x 20-mm cannon; 2 x 7·92-mm machine-guns. *Speed:* 354 mph at 12,300 ft. *Ceiling:* 36,000 ft. Known throughout the Luftwaffe as 'Emil', this was the principal fighter type used during the Battle of Britain

and of pilots, was far exceeding the output. In one sense the command was winning the battle; in another—if the Germans could maintain the pressure long enough—it was losing it.

The Germans, however, were not intending to fight a prolonged battle. They, too, could not afford heavy losses indefinitely—as may be seen from their decision after August 18 to hold back most of the vulnerable Ju-87s for the actual invasion, from their caution in employing Me-110s, and from their increasingly closer and more numerous fighter escort. Their attack, as we have seen, was meant to be a brief one, geared to Operation Sea Lion; and for Sea Lion they were now running short of time. This Hitler recognised at the end of August when he agreed that D-Day, provisionally set for September 15, should be postponed to September 21. For this date to be kept the German navy had to receive the executive order by September 11: and Göring's Luftwaffe had thus to administer the *coup de grâce* to the British fighter forces within the next few days. The attack on sector stations and other inland targets might be doing well, but in itself it was not proving decisive. On September 7 the Germans accordingly switched to another target, farther inland than most of the sector stations and, as they believed, still more vital—London.

Target London

The German decision to attack London was inspired by three beliefs. In the first place, operations against London could be expected to bring about still greater air battles and so—the Germans hoped—still higher wastage in Fighter Command. It was for this reason that Kesselring, though not Sperrle, strongly supported the change of plan. Second, an assault on the capital, if reinforced by attacks during the night against other main cities as well, might paralyse the British machinery of government in the final period before the invasion, or even terrorise the British people into submission. Third, an attack on the British capital would be, as the Germans saw it, an act of retribution. On the night of August 24/25, during the course of the Luftwaffe's usual scattered night operations, some badly aimed or jettisoned bombs had fallen on central London—the first of the war. Churchill and the War Cabinet had immediately ordered retaliation against Berlin; and during the following nights RAF bombers had found and hit the German capital—an occurrence which Göring had assured Hitler could never happen. The enraged Führer promptly vowed revenge and with Göring's eager concurrence unleashed the Luftwaffe against its supreme target.

On the night of September 4 German bombers laid flares over London; on the following two nights small numbers of aircraft dropped bombs on Rotherhithe and other places near the docks. These were the warming-up operations.

In the late afternoon of September 7 some 300 German bombers escorted by 600 fighters crossed the Kent and Sussex coasts or penetrated the Thames Estuary in a series of huge waves. A few bombed the oil installations at Thameshaven, still burning from earlier attacks; the rest, instead of bombing the sector stations, which the British fighters were alert to guard, held on until they reached the outskirts of the capital itself. Though nearly all the British squadrons ordered up eventually made contact, most of the raiders were able to put down their high explosive and incendiaries before they were molested. The attacks fell in full force on London's dockland east of the City. Huge fires sprang up among the dockside warehouses, especially at Silvertown, and these the Germans used as beacons to light their way to further attacks during the ensuing hours of darkness. That night, when 250 German bombers ranged over the capital in a prolonged assault from dusk to dawn, millions of Londoners had their first experience of what they imagined was Blitzkrieg, and what they were soon to call 'The Blitz'.

The climax of the battle was now approaching. Göring took personal charge of operations, and the bombers from Norway and Denmark joined Kesselring's forces for what were meant to be the final and deciding blows. Meanwhile, however, the German invasion preparations had not gone unobserved: since August 31 Spitfires and Hudsons of RAF Coastal Command had been returning with an impressive photographic record of the growing number of barges and other invasion craft in the ports and estuaries across the Channel. On August 31 in Ostend, for instance, there were 18 barges; by September 6 there were 205.

As the concentrations increased, Bomber Command began to attack them, using at first its daylight Blenheims. By September 6 the enemy preparations were sufficiently obvious for the British authorities to order Invasion Alert 2: 'Attack probable within three days.' The following day, when the German bombers turned against London, it seemed that the hour of supreme trial might be at hand. Alert 2 then gave place

Hawker Hurricane Mk I
Span: 40 ft. *Length:* 31 ft 5 in. *Gross weight:* 6,447 lb. *Engine:* 1,030 hp Rolls Royce Merlin II. *Armament:* 8 x ·303 machine-guns. *Speed:* 324 mph at 17,500 ft. *Ceiling:* 34,200 ft.
The Hurricane was developed in 1934 from the Hawker Fury and is best known for its part in the Battle of Britain when it shot down more enemy aircraft than all other air and ground defences combined. The aircraft illustrated was flown by the British ace Squadron Leader Stanford Tuck, whose machine bore 25 victory swastikas beneath the cockpit

to Alert 1: 'Invasion imminent, and probable within twelve hours.'

That night, as the German bombs began to crash down on London, the code-word 'Cromwell' went out to the Southern and Eastern Commands of Britain's Home Forces, bringing them to immediate readiness. In the prevailing excitement a few commanders of Home Guard units rang church bells to call out their men, so spreading the impression that German paratroops had actually landed. Meanwhile, forces of the Royal Navy waited at immediate notice, and the Hampdens of Bomber Command – 'heavy' bombers of the time – joined Blenheims, Hudsons, and Battles in intensified attacks on French and Belgian ports.

It was with the British fully alert to what the next few hours or days might bring that the Luftwaffe now strove to repeat the hammer blows of September 7. On September 8 bad weather limited their daylight activity; but at night Luftflotte III was able to send 200 bombers against London in a lengthy procession lasting more than nine hours. The zone of attack now extended from dockland to the capital as a whole, with special attention to railways and power stations, and by the morning every railway line running south of London was for a brief time unserviceable.

On the next day, September 9, clouds again restricted activity in the morning, only for a further assault to develop in the late afternoon. More than 200 bombers with full escort headed for London; but such was the promptness and vigour of the interception that less than half reached even the outskirts of the capital, and the bombs fell widely over the south-eastern counties. No. 12 Group's Duxford wing of four squadrons, led by the legless pilot Squadron Leader Douglas Bader, enjoyed a notable success. All told, the British pilots shot down 28 German aircraft for the loss of 19 of their own.

Very different once more was the story at night. Again nearly 200 aircraft bombed the capital in attacks lasting over eight hours; this time some 400 Londoners were killed and 1,400 injured – all with negligible loss to the Luftwaffe.

Hitler again shifts D-Day

September 10 was a day of cloud, rain, and light German activity – though at night there was the usual raid on London, while other German bombers attacked South Wales and Merseyside. The next afternoon, while the Germans tried to jam some of the British radar stations, Luftflotte III attacked Southampton, and Luftflotte II sent three big raids against London. Many of the bombers got through to the City and the docks; and the balance of losses – 25 German ones, against 29 by Fighter Command – for once tilted against the British. On their return, some German pilots reported that British fighter opposition was diminishing. But though the Luftwaffe still hoped to complete its task, the date was now September 11, and Fighter Command was still in existence. With the German navy requiring ten days' notice before D-Day, an invasion on September 21 thus became impossible. Accordingly Hitler now gave the Luftwaffe three more days' grace, till September 14, in the hope that a decision could then be taken to invade on September 24.

As it happened, September 12 and 13 were days of poor visibility, unsuitable for major attacks. Even the nightly efforts against London – which was now enjoying the heartening noise of greatly reinforced gun defences – were on a reduced scale. When September 14 came, Hitler could only postpone the decision for a further three days, till September 17. This set the provisional D-Day for September 27 – about the last date on which the tides would be favourable until October 8. The Führer's order was contrary to the advice of his naval chiefs, who urged indefinite postponement – a tactful term for abandonment. Their worries had been sharply increased by the mounting intensity of the RAF's attacks on the invasion barges, large numbers of which had been destroyed the previous evening.

The Luftwaffe now strove to clinch the issue in the short time still at its disposal. Despite unfavourable weather, on the afternoon of September 14 several raids struck at London. Some of the German pilots reported ineffective opposition, and Fighter Command lost as many aircraft as the enemy. The night proved fine, but on this occasion no more than 50 German bombers droned their way towards London. The Luftwaffe was husbanding its efforts for the morrow.

Sunday September 15 was a day of mingled cloud and sunshine. By 11 am the British radar detected mass formations building up over the Pas-de-Calais region. Half an hour later the raiders, stepped up from 15,000 to 26,000 feet, were crossing the coast in waves bent for London. Park's fighters met them before Canterbury, and in successive groups – two, three, then four squadrons – challenged them all the way to the capital, over which No. 12 Group's Duxford wing, now five squadrons strong, joined the conflict. In the face of such opposition, the raiders dropped their bombs

Fiat C.R. 42 Falco (Falcon)
Span: 31 ft 10 in. *Length:* 27 ft 1 in. *Engine:* 840 hp Fiat A.74 air-cooled radial. *Armament:* 1 x 12·7-mm. 1 x 7·7-mm machine-guns later increased to 4 x 12·7-mm. *Speed:* 267 mph at 17,450 ft. *Ceiling:* 34,500 ft. C.R.42s formed the fighter component of Mussolini's token Corpo Aereo Italiano based in Belgium for raids on eastern England

inaccurately or jettisoned them, mainly over south London.

Two hours later a further mass attack developed. Again British radar picked it up well in advance: and again – since they had had time to refuel and rearm – Park's fighters challenged the intruders all the way to, and over, the capital. Once more the Germans jettisoned their bombs or aimed them badly, this time mainly over east London, and, as before, further British formations harassed the raiders on their way back. Meanwhile a smaller German force attacked Portland. Later in the day other raiders – some 20 Me-110s carrying bombs – tried to bomb the Supermarine aircraft works near Southampton, only to meet spirited and effective opposition from local guns. When darkness fell, 180 German bombers continued the damaging but basically ineffectual night assault on London, while others attacked Bristol, Cardiff, Liverpool, and Manchester.

So closed a day on which Göring had hoped to give the death-blow to Fighter Command. In all, the Germans had sent over about 230 bombers and 700 fighters in the daylight raids. Their bombing had been scattered and ineffective, and they had lost the greatest number of aircraft in a single day since August 15 – no less than 60. Fighter Command had lost 26, from which the pilots of 13 had been saved.

This further German defeat on September 15 – combined with the attacks of British bombers against barge concentrations – settled the issue. When September 17 came, Hitler had no alternative but to postpone Sea Lion indefinitely. A few days later, he agreed to the dispersal of the invasion craft in order to avoid attack from the air. The invasion threat was over.

Göring orders more raids

Göring, however, was not yet prepared to admit failure: he still clung to the belief that given a short spell of good weather the Luftwaffe could crush Fighter Command and thereafter compel Britain to submit, even without invasion. Between September 17 and the end of the month his forces strove to attack London by day, whenever weather permitted, in addition to aircraft factories elsewhere. On only three days – September 18, 27, and 30 – was he able to mount a major assault on the capital, and on each occasion British fighters prevented intensive bombing and took a heavy toll of the raiders. The loss of 120 German aircraft during these three days (as against 60 by Fighter Command) was not one which afforded Göring much encouragement to continue.

Had the Luftwaffe's corpulent chief known them, he would not have derived any greater encouragement from the casualty figures during the whole three weeks his air force had been attacking London. Between September 7 and 30 Fighter Command had lost 242 aircraft, the Luftwaffe 433. Equally important, though Dowding was still gravely worried by the continuing loss of pilots (on September 7 his squadrons had only 16 each instead of their proper 26), his anxieties about aircraft were diminishing. From the time the Germans abandoned their attack on sector airfields in favour of an assault on London, the wastage of Hurricanes and Spitfires had been more than counterbalanced by the output of the factories.

The prize of victory had thus eluded Göring's grasp. On October 12 Hitler recognised this by formally postponing Sea Lion until the spring of 1941. In fact, this meant abandonment: Hitler's mind was now fixed on Russia. Until the German war machine could roll east, however, there was everything to be said, from the German point of view, for maintaining pressure on Britain, so long as it could be done inexpensively. During October the Luftwaffe, assisted by a few Italian aircraft, kept Fighter Command at stretch in daylight by sending over fighter and fighter-bombers, which did little damage but were difficult to intercept. At night the German bombers, operating with virtual impunity, continued to drop their loads on London.

The story of the 'Night Blitz' is one of civilian suffering and heroism, of widespread yet indecisive damage – and of slowly increasing success by the British defences. In the battle of wits against the intruders, perhaps the most vital developments were the discovery (and distortion) of the German navigational beams, the provision of dummy airfields and decoy fires, and the advances in radar which made possible accurate tracking overland.

Radar advances resulted in gun-laying radar that gave accurate readings of heights, and so permitted the engagement of the target 'unseen', and in ground-controlled interception (GCI) radar stations which brought night fighters close enough to the enemy for the fighters to use their own airborne radar (A1) for the final location and pursuit. It was only towards the end of the Blitz, however, that the GCI/A1 combination emerged as a real threat to the attackers, who began to lose three or four aircraft in every 100 sorties, instead of merely one.

Meanwhile, the Luftwaffe was able to lay waste the centres of a score or more of British cities. After the early raids in August, the weight of attack by night fell for a time almost entirely on London. Between September 7 and November 13 there was only one night on which London escaped bombing, and the number of German aircraft over the capital each night averaged 163. With the final postponement of Sea Lion, the attack then extended also to longer-term, strategic objectives – the industrial towns, and later mainly the ports, so linking up with the blockading actions of the German submarines.

On November 14 the devastation of Coventry marked the change of policy; thereafter Southampton, Birmingham, Liverpool, Bristol, Plymouth, Portsmouth, Cardiff, Swansea, Belfast, Glasgow, and many other towns felt the full fury of the Blitz. In the course of it all, until Luftflotte II moved east in May 1941 and the attacks died away, the Germans killed about 40,000 British civilians and injured another 46,000, and damaged more than 1,000,000 British homes, at a cost to themselves of some 600 aircraft. On the economic side, they seriously impeded British aircraft production for some months, but in other directions the damage they did was too diffuse to be significant.

Hitler's first setback

The 'Blitz' ceased not because of the increased success of the British defences, but because most of the German aircraft were needed elsewhere. Had Russia collapsed within the eight weeks of the German – and the British – estimate, they would doubtless have returned quickly enough, to clear the way for invasion or to attempt to pulverise Britain into submission. As it was, Russia held, and though the British people were subjected to further bombardments, they were not again called upon to face a serious threat of invasion.

Though the Night Blitz was inconclusive, the daylight Battle of Britain was thus one of the turning points of the war: it was the air fighting of August and September 1940, together with the existence of the Royal Navy and the English Channel, which first halted Hitler's career of conquest. The 1,000 or so pilots of Fighter Command who bore the brunt of that fighting – including the 400 or more who lost their lives – saved more than Britain by their exertions. By earning Britain a great breathing space in which the further progress of events was to bring her the mighty alliance of Russia and the United States, they made possible the final victory and the liberation of Europe from the Nazi terror.

IMPORTANT EVENTS OF 1940

August 1: Hitler decrees the Battle of Britain with the command: 'The German air force is to overcome the British air force with all means at its disposal, and as soon as possible.'

August 13: 'Eagle Day': the Luftwaffe launches its air offensive against Britain, with 1,485 sorties. The Germans lose 45 aircraft, the RAF 13.

August 15: In the most intense attack of the Battle of Britain, the Luftwaffe sends a total of 1,790 sorties over England. They lose 75 aircraft, while Britain loses 34.

August 17: The Germans establish an 'operational area' around Britain; in it, all ships are to be sunk without warning.

August 25: The RAF conducts its first raid on Berlin.

September 3: Britain cedes to the USA bases in the West Indies and elsewhere in exchange for 50 destroyers.

September 7: Some 300 German bombers, escorted by 600 fighters, penetrate the Thames Estuary and bomb London's dockland.

September 13: *Italy invades Egypt.*

September 15: The RAF claims to have shot down 183 German aircraft during daylight Luftwaffe raids on Britain – a figure subsequently found to have been greatly exaggerated.

September 17: Hitler postpones Operation Sea Lion 'until further notice'.

September 23/25: *British and Free French forces attempt to take Dakar.*

October 12: Operation Sea Lion is postponed until 1941.

A formation of the much-vaunted Me-110s; they had long range but rather poor manoeuvrability, and thus they suffered heavy losses in the battle ▷

Cockpit Armament Bf 110
1 Rheinmettal MG 15 machine-gun with 750 rounds. Rate of Fire : 1,100 rpm.

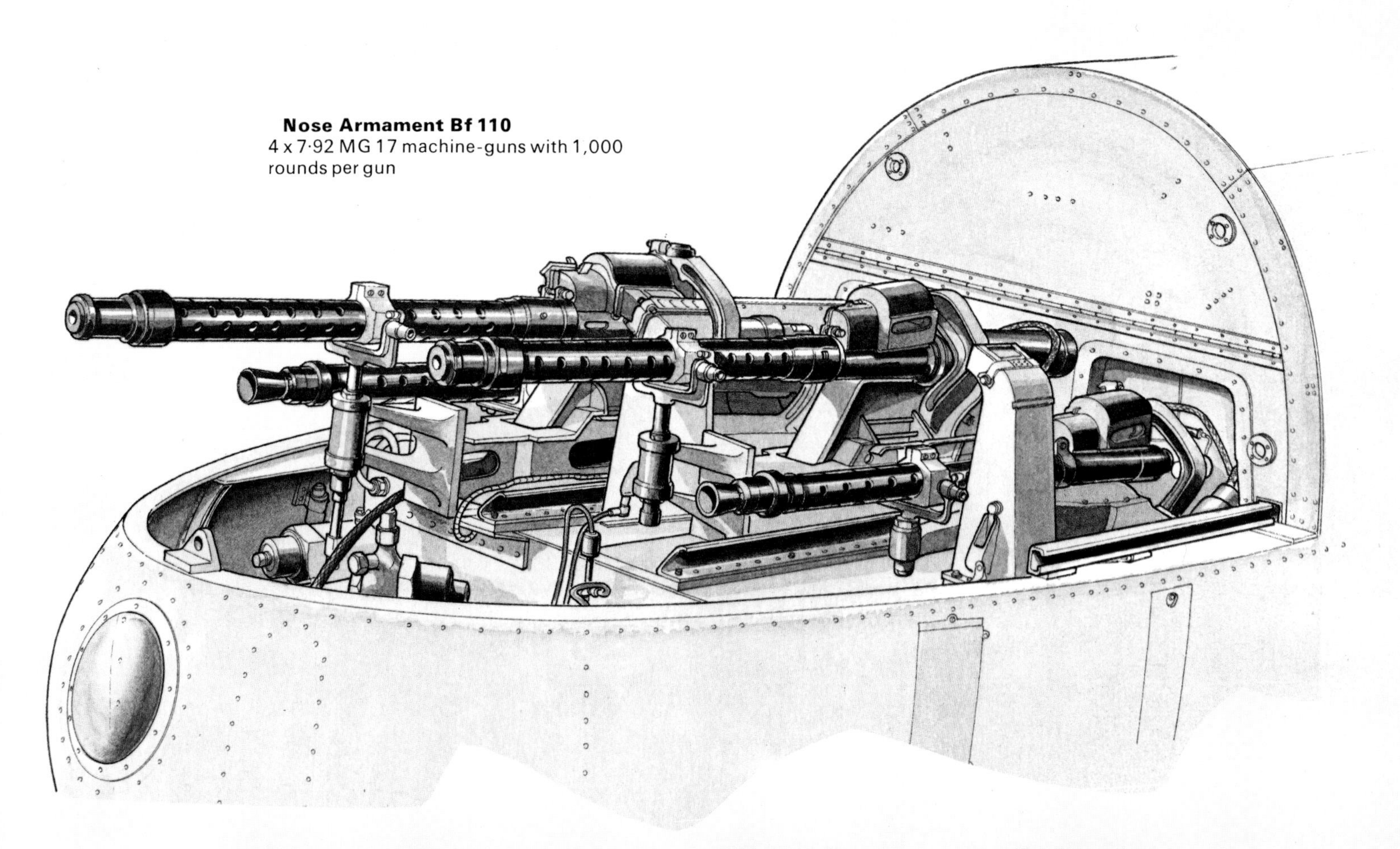

Nose Armament Bf 110
4 x 7·92 MG 17 machine-guns with 1,000 rounds per gun

MESSERSCHMITT Bf 110

Span: 53 ft $4\frac{3}{4}$ in. *Length:* 39 ft $8\frac{1}{2}$ in. *Armament:* 4 x 7·9-mm machine-guns; 2 x 20-mm MG FF cannon. *Engine:* 2 x 1,150 hp Daimler-Benz DB 601A. *Crew:* 2. *Speed:* 349 mph. *Range:* 530 miles.   The concept of the long-range super-fighter, heavily armed and able to smash through enemy fighter defence, was a major part of Göring's plan of attack. Unfortunately for the Luftwaffe the chosen instrument proved a complete failure. The big Messerschmitt packed a fearsome punch in its nose batteries of cannon and machine-guns but was too sluggish and unwieldly to take on RAF opposition. Indeed their very presence became a major defensive liability for the hard-pressed Bf 109E pilots

Junkers Ju 88A-1
Gross weight: 27,500 lb. *Span:* 59 ft 11 in. *Length:* 47 ft 1⅓ in. *Engine:* 2 x 1,200 hp Junkers Jumo 211. *Armament:* 3 x 7·92-mm machine-guns. *Crew:* 4. *Speed:* 286 mph at 18,000 ft. *Ceiling:* 30,150 ft. *Range:* 1,550 miles. *Bomb load:* 5,510 lb. The Ju 88, designed in 1936 as a fast bomber, became famous in the Second World War as an aircraft capable of taking on any role, serving as everything from dive-bomber to night fighter. During the Battle it showed its paces as bomber, reconnaissance and anti-shipping aircraft

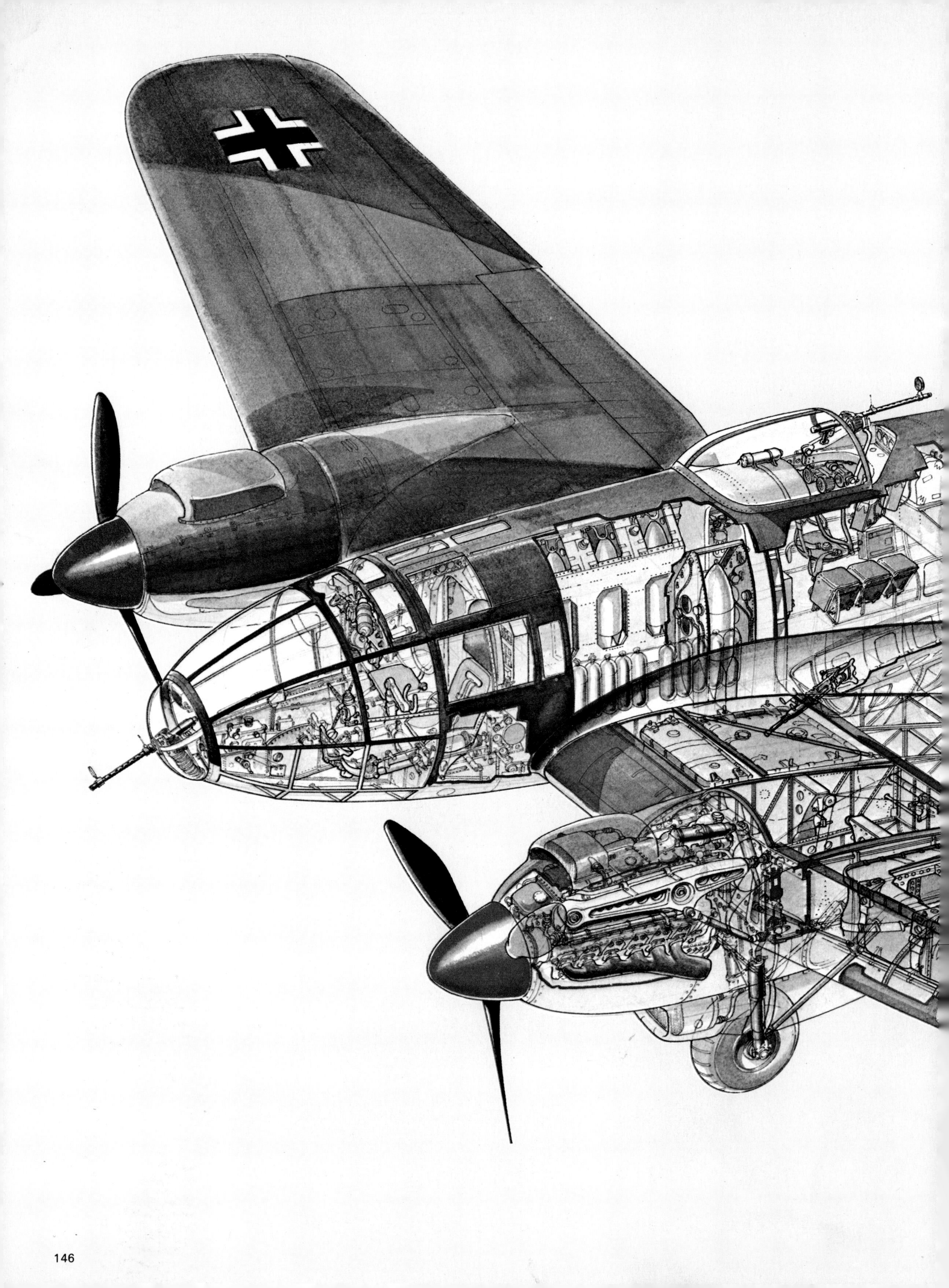

Heinkel He III H3
Weight: 19,130 lb. *Span:* 74 ft $1\frac{3}{4}$ in. *Length:* 53 ft $9\frac{1}{2}$ in. *Armament:* 5 x 7·92-mm machine-guns; 1 x 20-mm cannon. *Engine:* 2 x 1,200 hp Jumo D-1. *Crew:* 5/6. *Speed:* 258 mph. *Range:* 760 miles. The twin-engined Heinkels were the principal weapon in the German heavy bomber squadrons and had proved their tactical value in campaigns from Spain to the fall of France. As a strategic bomber however, attacking the industries and defences of Britain, the type proved lacking in offensive power and defensive armament

SWORDFISH TO SUPERFORTRESS

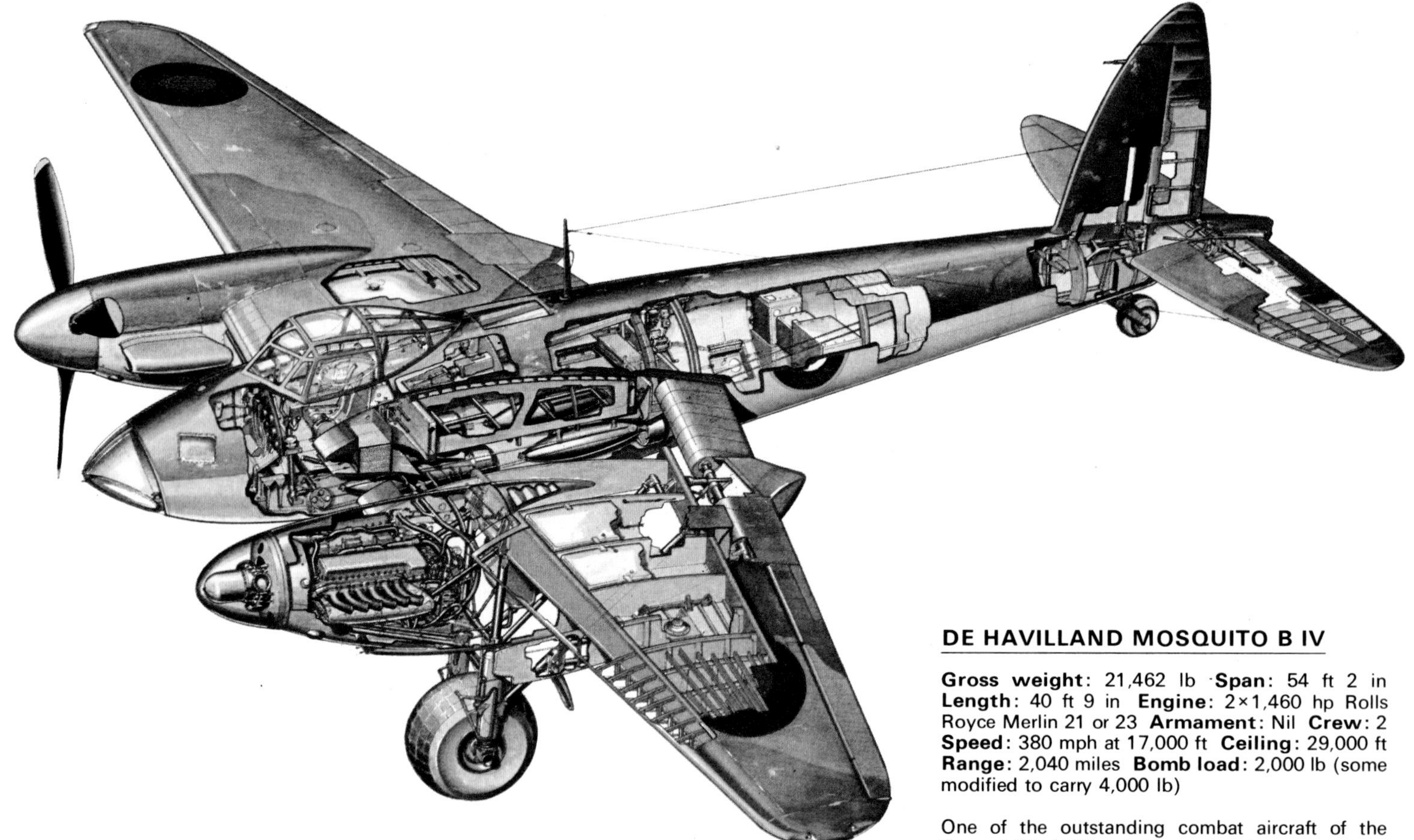

DE HAVILLAND MOSQUITO B IV

Gross weight: 21,462 lb **Span**: 54 ft 2 in **Length**: 40 ft 9 in **Engine**: 2×1,460 hp Rolls Royce Merlin 21 or 23 **Armament**: Nil **Crew**: 2 **Speed**: 380 mph at 17,000 ft **Ceiling**: 29,000 ft **Range**: 2,040 miles **Bomb load**: 2,000 lb (some modified to carry 4,000 lb)

One of the outstanding combat aircraft of the Second World War, built mostly of wood and too fast to be intercepted on bombing missions; guns were only carried on fighter variants. The B IV was the first bomber version to enter RAF service

The Second World War was delayed just long enough for almost all of the old aircraft with fabric-covered airframes of wood, mixed wood and metal or steel-tube, to have been withdrawn from service and replaced by modern types. The redoubtable Fairey Swordfish carrier-based torpedo-bomber was the only aircraft of the older type to serve throughout the war in the European theatre, its low performance being balanced by robust construction, ease of repair, good weight-lifting ability from small carrier decks and general utility except in the face of lethal defensive fire. Among other fabric-covered machines to survive were the Vickers Wellington and Warwick twin-engined bombers which remained in production until 1945.

But as a rule, bombers of the Second World War had light-alloy stressed-skin construction, built in cantilever monoplane form with monocoque fuselages. Undercarriages were made to retract into the wing, engine nacelles, or other compartments, at first by laborious winding of a hand-wheel and later by directing hydraulic power to a ram or electric power to a motor. The original hydraulic systems were crude and heavy, filled with oil at 1,000 lb/ sq in. Later aircraft had more complex systems operating at 2,500 lb/sq in and serving undercarriage retraction, wheel brakes, landing flaps, bomb doors and sometimes propeller pitch or gun-turret drive. American aircraft favoured all-electric systems, with as many as one hundred and eighty motors to drive various items of equipment.

More powerful flaps

With wing loadings rising from around 10 lb/sq ft, typical in 1930, to 40/65 lb/sq ft, the wings needed powerful flaps to increase lift at take-off (when they were depressed to about ten degrees) and at landing (depressed to the maximum of perhaps forty-five degrees to give both extra lift and extra drag). The Armstrong Whitworth Whitley, designed as a troop carrier around 1932, was redesigned as a bomber in 1934. The original design had no wing flaps and the wing was accordingly set at a large angle of incidence. The flapped Whitley always flew in a characteristic nose-down attitude, and would probably have been faster with the wing made thinner and set at a shallower angle.

Junkers devised a 'double wing' type of flap comprising a completely separate auxiliary surface hinged well behind the main wing trailing edge. This was fitted to the Ju 86 and Ju 87, but the far more effective Ju 88 had powerful conventional slotted flaps. Both the Ju 87 and Ju 88 had special dive-brakes hinged under the wings and extended broadside-on to the airflow to permit very steep attacks (almost ninety degrees) without reaching excessive speeds.

In the USA, Lockheed used the advanced Fowler flap, still in evidence today. This extended backwards on wheeled carriages running on fixed tracks to give extra area on take-off. When fully extended, the tracks pulled the carriages sharply down to give very high drag as well. This was a useful feature of the Lockheed Hudson and Ventura, designed specifically for British requirements, which would otherwise have been difficult to land. Even with full flap, the Martin B-26 Marauder was not easy to land, and this hastened the development of the modern type of aircraft which is driven on to the runway at high speed and stopped with powerful brakes.

Special mention should be made of the four-engined Consolidated B-24 Liberator, possibly the first of the modern bombers. This was based on the Davis wing, a design of very high aspect ratio giving great efficiency and capable of heavy loading to well over 60 lb/sq ft. Such a wing was a radically new innovation when the Liberator first flew, as the Model 32, in 1939. It was only possible because of its advanced stressed-skin structure, which allowed a large quantity of fuel to be carried inside the slender wing as well as the main units of the landing gear and the Fowler flaps. Compared with British bombers such as the Avro Lancaster, which had thin skin and heavy highly-stressed spar booms, the wing of the Liberator was uniformly loaded throughout with slimmer spars and thicker skin, reinforced by many long stringers.

There was little that was unconventional about the structures of most of the main Second World War bombers. Nearly all had stressed-skin airframes, with quite thin skin, held by flush riveting and with large, high-tensile steel pins securing the fork fittings where wings joined the fuselage or where outer wings joined the centre section. Compared with earlier aircraft the smooth, regular skin made performance higher and more precisely predictable, and the time-consuming task of airframe rigging receded into the background. Yet occasionally, there were still maverick aircraft which did not conform to the general pattern. Either they consistently flew slower than the others, or suffered from disconcerting and sometimes dangerous flight characteristics – or they proved themselves to be among the most successful aircraft of the war.

In the latter category, apart from the geodetic Vickers bombers, an outstanding example was the de Havilland Mosquito. This cantilever mid-wing monoplane, initiated as a private venture in 1938 and nearly cancelled before it first flew in November 1940, ultimately became one of the most versatile combat aircraft of the war. It was planned purely as a high-speed unarmed bomber fast enough to avoid interception, and for various reasons, including the metal shortage, it was built of wood. The de Havilland company had devised a method of making the main sections from a sandwich

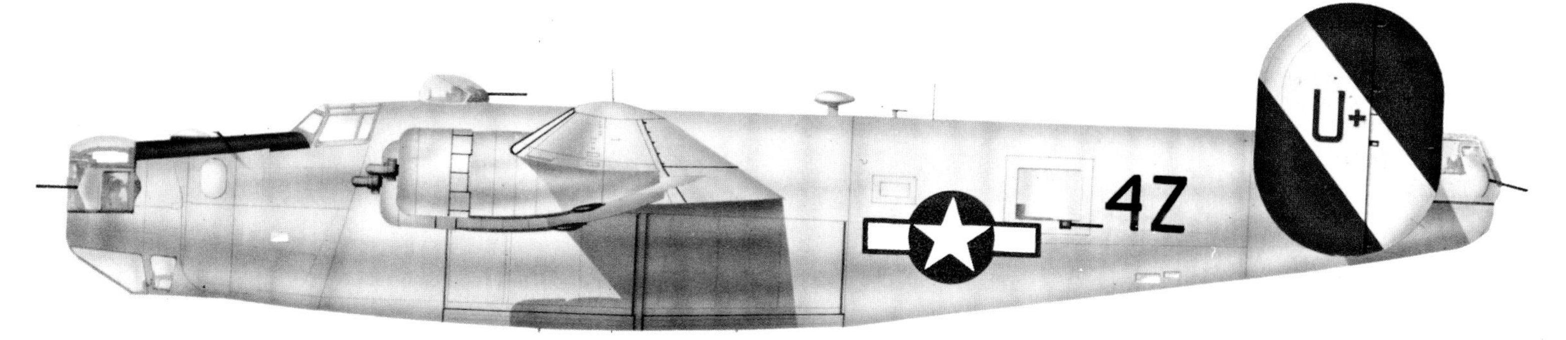

CONSOLIDATED B-24 LIBERATOR

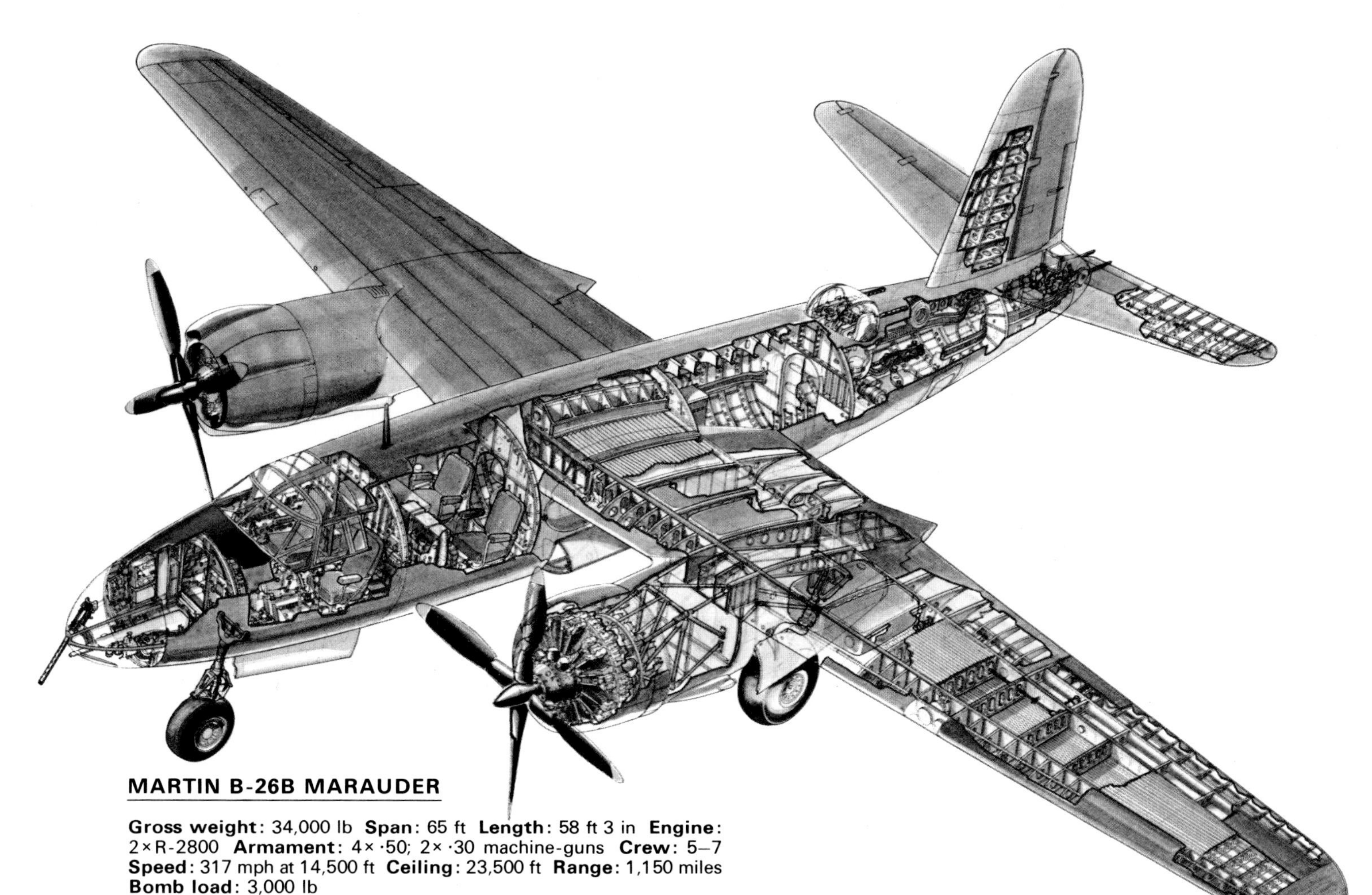

MARTIN B-26B MARAUDER

Gross weight: 34,000 lb **Span**: 65 ft **Length**: 58 ft 3 in **Engine**: 2×R-2800 **Armament**: 4× ·50; 2× ·30 machine-guns **Crew**: 5–7 **Speed**: 317 mph at 14,500 ft **Ceiling**: 23,500 ft **Range**: 1,150 miles **Bomb load**: 3,000 lb

An improved version of the B-26A, with a longer nose wheel unit and increased armament, which entered service in May 1943

of hardwood ply veneers with a thick core of light balsa wood, which gave a robust, rigid and smooth-surfaced airframe. Light alloy and steel fittings were used at the main stress areas and joints, and fabric formed a top skin over the entire airframe, including the control surfaces which were generally of light alloy.

Since a wooden structural member has a larger section than a metal one, the Mosquito had an outstanding ability to absorb battle damage. Shell splinters and bullets which would have severed a metal structure merely left a hole in the wooden one. This ability, combined with its speed of over 400 mph, made Mosquito losses towards the end of the war by far the lowest of any RAF bomber – only one per 2,000 sorties. As wood structures are inherently heavier than metal, the efficiency and weight-lifting power of the Mosquito was remarkable, and it was the only light bomber capable of carrying a 4,000 lb block-buster bomb. It was particularly effective against pin-point targets, but its manoeuvrability and performance at altitudes of up to 40,000 ft also made it an outstanding night fighter.

Apart from the Fi 103 Flying Bomb, produced by the Germans towards the end of the war with a predictably simple structure assembled from welded steel sheet, the only other bomber to make a major break with tradition and still be put into large-scale production was the Boeing B-29 Superfortress, brought into operation in 1943. Planned as the ultimate strategic bomber that could be created with the technology of 1940, it brought together every available new advance that appeared worthwhile. The great range (3,250 miles) and payload (16,000 lb of bombs) demanded led to an unprecedented size and weight, and this in turn led to the use of light-alloy sheet several times thicker (up to 0·188 in) than anything used in such machines as the Heinkel He 111 or Lancaster.

Absolute precision

This at once precluded the kind of workshop practice that had been common since the start of stressed-skin construction. No longer could sections of skin be filed to fit, or ill-fitting rivets be put into re-drilled holes. Each hole had to be a precision job, in exactly the correct place to mate with the underlying structure, and countersunk to take a large rivet or screw fitting flush with the surface. It was no longer sufficient merely to bend the skins around the wings or fuselage as they were riveted on. They had to be formed in three dimensions by large press-tools. Though far stronger and more robust than any earlier airframes, the B-29 wing structure did have the drawback of being difficult to repair without special equipment.

The B-29 also marked a great increase in complexity. For example, it had five electrically-driven gun-turrets, four of them remotely controlled from sighting stations, with an override system to give a gunner control of all four turrets if he should have a good target. A further notable advance was that the crew were accommodated in a pressure cabin, linked by a pressurised tunnel to the smaller pressurised compartment of the two rear-fuselage gunners and the pressurised tail turret. All in all, the B-29 was a tremendous stride forward towards the even more complicated jet bombers of today.

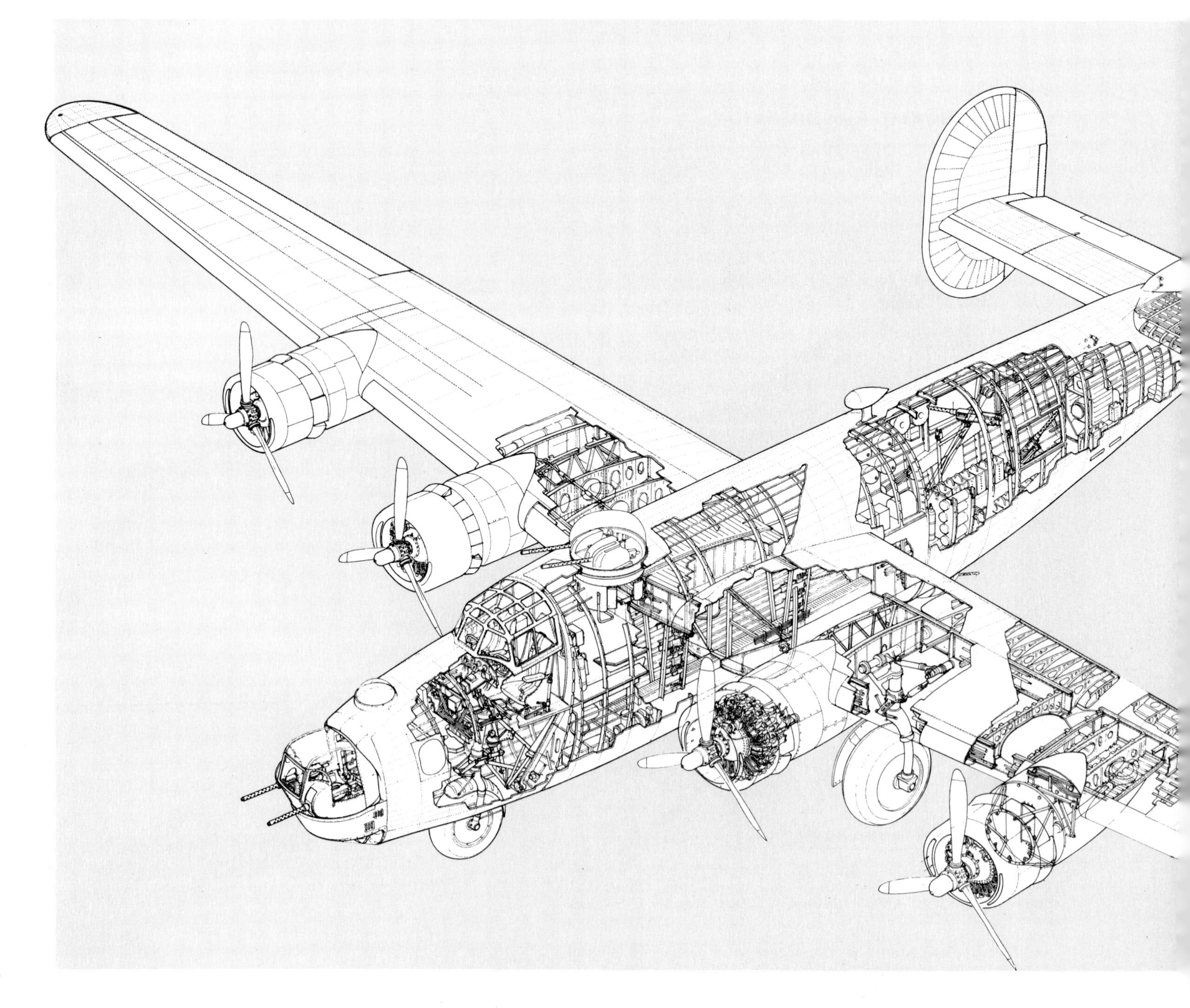

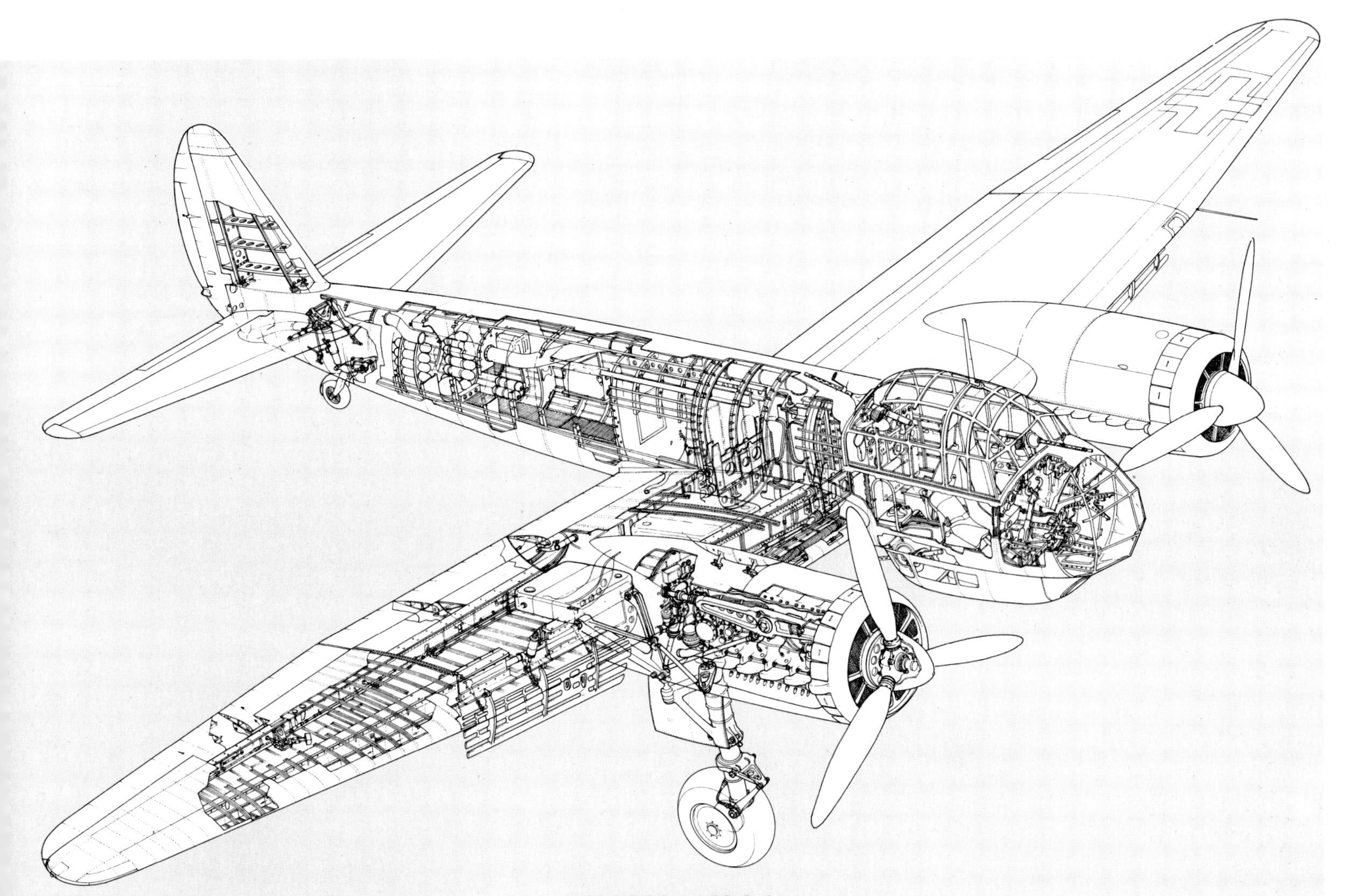

JUNKERS Ju 88 A-1

Gross weight: 27,500 lb **Span**: 59 ft 11 in **Length**: 47 ft 1⅓ in **Engine**: 2×1200 hp Junkers Jumo 211 **Armament**: 3×7·92-mm MG 15 machine-guns **Crew**: 4 **Speed**: 286 mph at 18,000 ft **Ceiling**: 30,150 ft **Range**: 1,550 miles **Bomb load**: 5,510 lb

Probably the most versatile aircraft of the war, more Ju 88s were built between 1939 and 1945 – over 15,000 in all, of which 9,000 were bombers – than all other German bombers combined. It was the subject of more modifications than any other combat aircraft of the war, as shown by the types illustrated overleaf

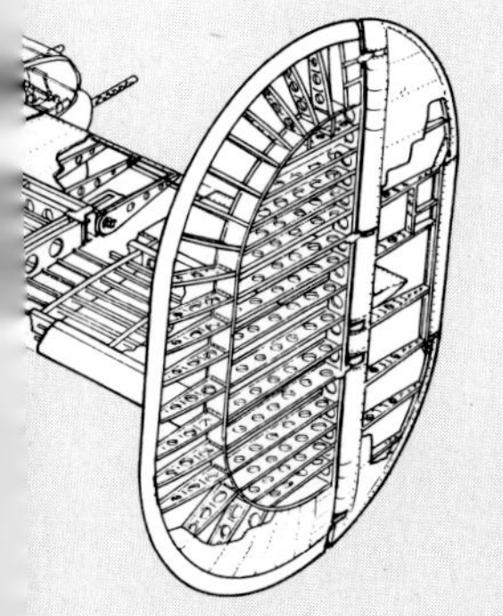

CONSOLIDATED B-24 LIBERATOR

Gross weight: 64,500 lb **Span**: 110 ft **Length**: 67 ft 2 in **Engine**: 4×Pratt & Whitney R-1830-65 **Armament**: 10×·50 Browning machine-guns **Crew**: 9 **Speed**: 300 mph at 25,000 ft **Ceiling**: 28,000 ft **Range**: 2,100 miles **Bomb load**: 12,800 lb

One of the best-known American aircraft of the Second World War, the Liberator served with distinction in many different roles. It was of particular value to RAF Coastal Command in covering that part of the Atlantic formerly out of range of land-based bombers

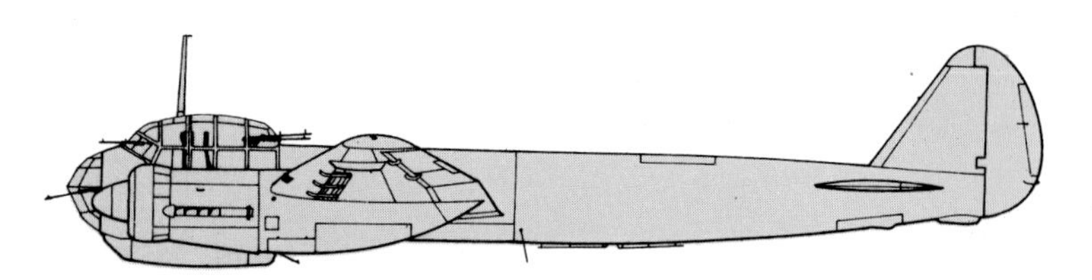

JUNKERS Ju 88 A-5

The A-5 was similar to the A-1, which made its debut in September 1939, but had its wing-span increased to 65 ft 10½ in, and a larger bomb load (6,614 lb) which reduced its maximum speed to 273 mph

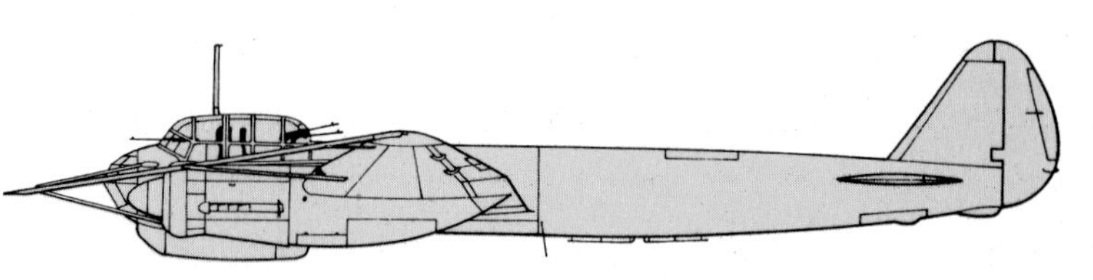

JUNKERS Ju 88 A-6

Generally similar to the A-5, the A-6 carried as standard a balloon-cable fender and destroying gear. This was so unwieldy, however, that it was soon withdrawn from service

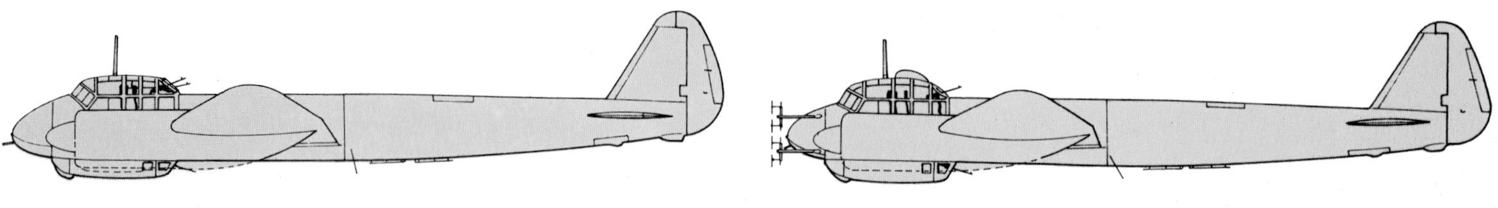

JUNKERS Ju 88 C-4

JUNKERS Ju 88 C-6b

The C-series were all primarily fighters, developed parallel with the A-series of bombers

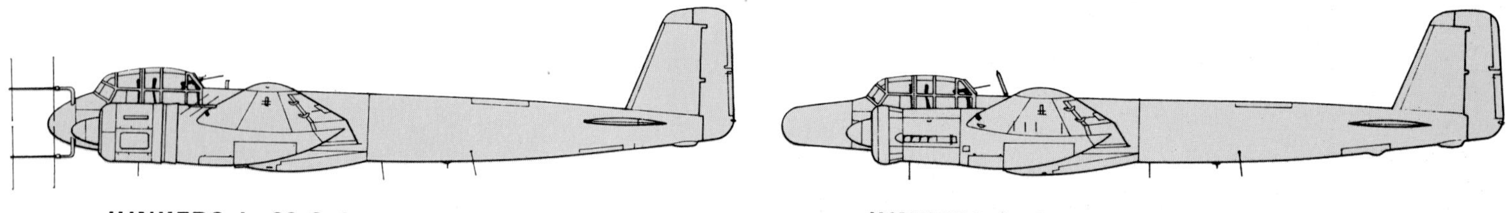

JUNKERS Ju 88 G-4

JUNKERS Ju 88 G-7c

The G-series of Ju 88s were specialised night-fighters

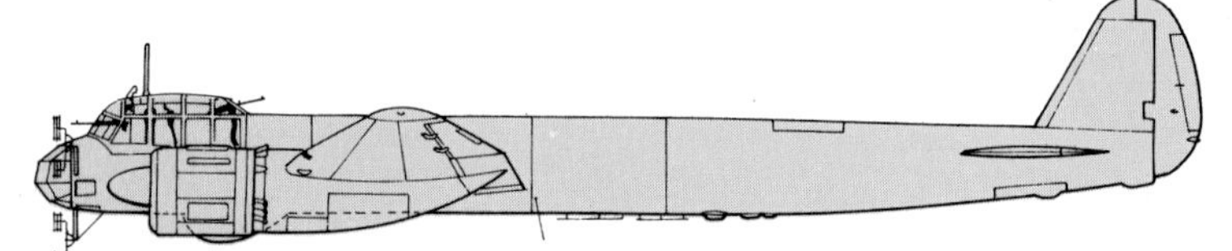

JUNKERS Ju 88 H-1

The H-1, characterised by an elongated fuselage to house extra fuel tanks, was a long-range photo reconnaissance aircraft

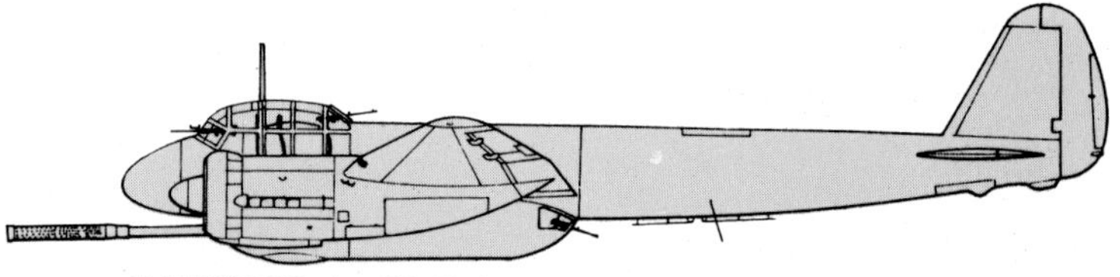

JUNKERS Ju 88 P-1

The P-1 was an anti-tank ground attack machine, used mainly on the Russian front and armed with a single forward-firing 75-mm BK 7·5 long-barrel cannon, in addition to rearward-firing twin MG 81 machine-guns fitted in a gun fairing which could be jettisoned if necessary

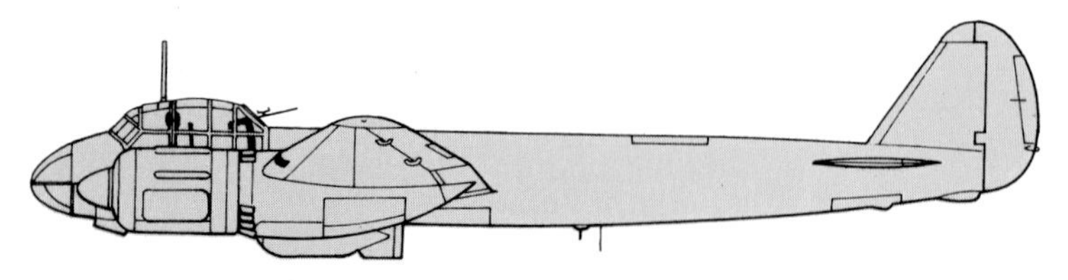

JUNKERS Ju 88 S-1

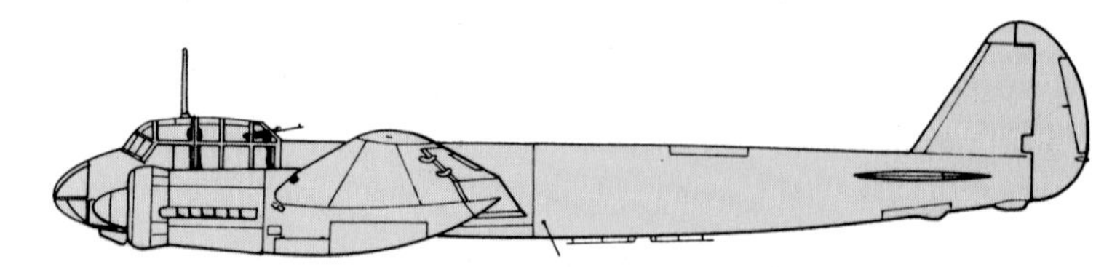

JUNKERS Ju 88 S-3

By 1943 the A-series were too slow for unescorted daylight operations, so development went ahead on the S-series, in which the bomb-load was reduced to 1,760 lb, and the upper nose guns and ventral gondola removed in order to increase speed. The glazed nose reverted to a shape similar to the early prototypes. The S-1 was the initial production model of the series, with 1,700 hp BMW 801G engines with GM-1 power boost, and only one rearward-firing 13-mm MG 131. The S-3 was powered by 1,750 hp Jumo 213E-1 engines

THE STING IN THE TAIL

RHEINMETTAL M15

7·92-mm MACHINE-GUN

Weight: 15 lb 12 oz **Length:** 42½ in **Calibre:** 7·92-mm
Magazine: saddle type of 75 rds **Rate of fire:** 1100 rpm

The atmosphere of extreme financial stringency that surrounded armaments in most countries during the 1920s tended to restrict the pace of development and efforts were concentrated on making the best and most economical use of available equipment. This was invariably similar to that used in the First World War, if not actually ex-wartime stock. Thus the dominant aircraft guns in the RAF were the manually trained Lewis and the fixed Vickers, while the Marlin remained the chief American gun, despite the fact that both the rifle-calibre Browning and the 20-mm Hispano had completed their initial development before November 1918 and were available for use.

In the inter-war period, the Scarff ring, usually carrying single or twin Lewis guns, was almost universal for RAF bomber defence and was widely used elsewhere. Much heavier guns were carried in some aircraft, but only in a somewhat ineffectual and experimental way. For example, several British machines such as the Vickers and Westland COW-armed designs, the Bristol Bagshot and the Westland Westbury, had fitted the big 37-mm (1·46-in) Coventry Ordnance Works cannon dating from 1918. Later, in 1934, the Blackburn Perth three-engined flying-boat, then the RAF's biggest and heaviest aircraft, went into service with one of these guns in the bows, in addition to three Lewis guns on the usual Scarff rings at bows, amidships and stern. The 1½ lb shells could have been dangerous to surfaced submarines, but there is no record that they were regarded as useful defence weapons.

Brief trials were also conducted in the USA, France and the Soviet Union with 20-mm and 37-mm guns on large aircraft, but with inconclusive results.

A far more important trend was the realization that, as aircraft speeds were rising steadily from the 100 mph maximum of the typical bomber of the mid-1920s to at least twice that speed, some form of shelter would be needed by the gunners. Indeed, there was evidence that the aerodynamic drag of the guns, when firing to either side, would become so great as to make manual aiming impossible. The answer appeared to be some form of power-driven turret, such as had long been used on warships; the main difficulties were weight and the provisions of drive power.

Windshields to turrets

The first companies to produce workable turrets were Martin in the USA, with a nose turret for the Type 130 B-10 bomber mounting a 0·30-in Browning gun, and Boulton Paul in Britain with a pneumatic-motor traversed nose turret for the Overstrand, fitted with a Lewis. Turrets were also produced in France by 1934, but these were at first manually operated and served merely as windshields. The Amiot 143 for instance used un-powered turrets for the Lewis gun in the nose and for two similar guns in the ventral position amidships; together with another gun in the rear cabin section under the wing, the Amiot 143 could defend itself against attack from any direction, foreshadowing the B-17 Flying Fortress. Later, the French MAC 1934 rifle-calibre gun supplemented and then replaced the Lewis.

Crude turrets also appeared on small numbers of Italian and Russian heavy bombers and on such flying-boats as the Short Sunderland, Consolidated PB2Y Coronado, Martin PBM Mariner, Blohm und Voss 138, Kawanishi H6K and H8K, and several Russian Beriev designs. There were many instances in the Second World War of flying-boats fending off repeated attacks by fighters. A Sunderland, attacked by six Ju 88s, shot down one and crippled a second; another Sunderland shot down three Ju 88s out of eight – simply because of fire-power. Large aircraft were no longer defended merely by three Lewis guns on Scarff rings but by multiple belt-fed guns accurately trained by power-driven turrets.

By 1935, it was widely accepted that to have any hope of survival in enemy airspace, a large bomber would have to have power-driven gun-turrets. The turret was no longer a mere windshield but a precision aiming device, complete with a sighting system and operator controls so that the gunner could train his guns effortlessly and accurately, even with a 200-knot slipstream or when being pulled in a tight turn. By the start of the Second World War, there were almost twenty companies making power-driven bomber defence turrets. Every large bomber in production in either Britain or the USA had at least one turret.

But in most other countries, the power-driven turret was ignored, or accorded low priority. Germany clung to the belief that bombers could be adequately defended by two or four hand-held machine-guns, and similar thinking persisted in Italy, Japan and the Soviet Union. In France, however, every conceivable kind of bomber defence was tried – including catapults lobbing aerial mines timed to explode close to attacking fighters. Several French bombers had powered turrets, in some cases mounting 20-mm cannon, such as the extremely graceful twin-engined LeO 451, an excellent aircraft but which appeared too late to be of value to the French during the Second World War; a number were later used as transports by the *Luftwaffe*. The earlier Farman 223, first produced in 1937, had

20-mm guns in electrically-powered dorsal and ventral turrets which, in a hectic month of combat in June 1940, proved to be very effective even at long ranges, although handicapped by the fact that the gunners had only lately seen the equipment for the first time.

A typical example of how the turret evolved during the period before the war was the case of the Vickers Wellington. The prototype B 9/32, flown in June 1936, had transparent domes in the nose and tail which in production aircraft were expected to carry a single Lewis gun fired by hand through a slot, sealed on each side of the gun by a sliding wind-shield. By 1937, the Mark I production machine had power-driven turrets of a rudimentary kind. Each mounted twin belt-fed Browning guns which were elevated and traversed hydraulically by a Frazer-Nash system, while firing through an aperture in a broad flexible belt, arranged to slide freely in runners between the fixed upper (transparent) and lower parts of the installation. By 1939 the Mark 1A had gone into production with powered turrets of modern design, each with twin Brownings, and the Mark III of 1941 mounted the four-gun rear turret introduced to the RAF with the Whitley Mark IV and the production Sunderland of 1938.

This rapid advance in bomber armament had been made despite the fact that in the mid-1930s, the RAF had no modern gun of any kind, nor any under development. The position had been rectified in July 1935 by the conclusion of a licence agreement with the Colt Automatic Weapon Corporation for the conversion of their Browning machine-gun to take British 0·303-in rimmed ammunition and for the manufacture of the resulting gun in Britain. Later, in 1939, a licence was obtained for the 20-mm (0·787-in) Hispano cannon which went into large-scale production at the British MARC factory at Grantham and the BSA plant at Sparkbrook, though the first deliveries of this much bigger gun, in July 1940, were all for fighters.

With very few exceptions, such as the French bombers, the only defence of large combat aircraft in 1939 comprised rifle-calibre guns fired either by hand and trained manually or, in the case of British heavy bombers, aimed by a power-driven turret. It was to be a matter of profound importance that the *Luftwaffe*, misled by the ease with which the He 111 and Do 17 operated over Spain in 1937–39, standardised bomber-defence armament with three or four hand-held MG-15 machine-guns. Although this 7·92-mm gun was a good modern design, it was fed by hand-loaded magazines and in any case lacked the punch needed to deter the fighters the German bombers were soon to meet over England.

Except for the special case of the de Havilland Mosquito, which was able to rely on its remarkable flight performance, British bombers of the Second World War relied for their defence mainly on power-driven turrets equipped with rifle-calibre Browning guns. Operational experience resulted in a gradual shift of the main weight of firepower towards the rear. For example, the Handley Page Halifax began life in November 1940 with a two-gun nose turret, two-gun dorsal turret and four-gun tail turret, but from 1943 onwards the standard armament was merely a single hand-operated gun in the nose and four-gun dorsal and tail turrets.

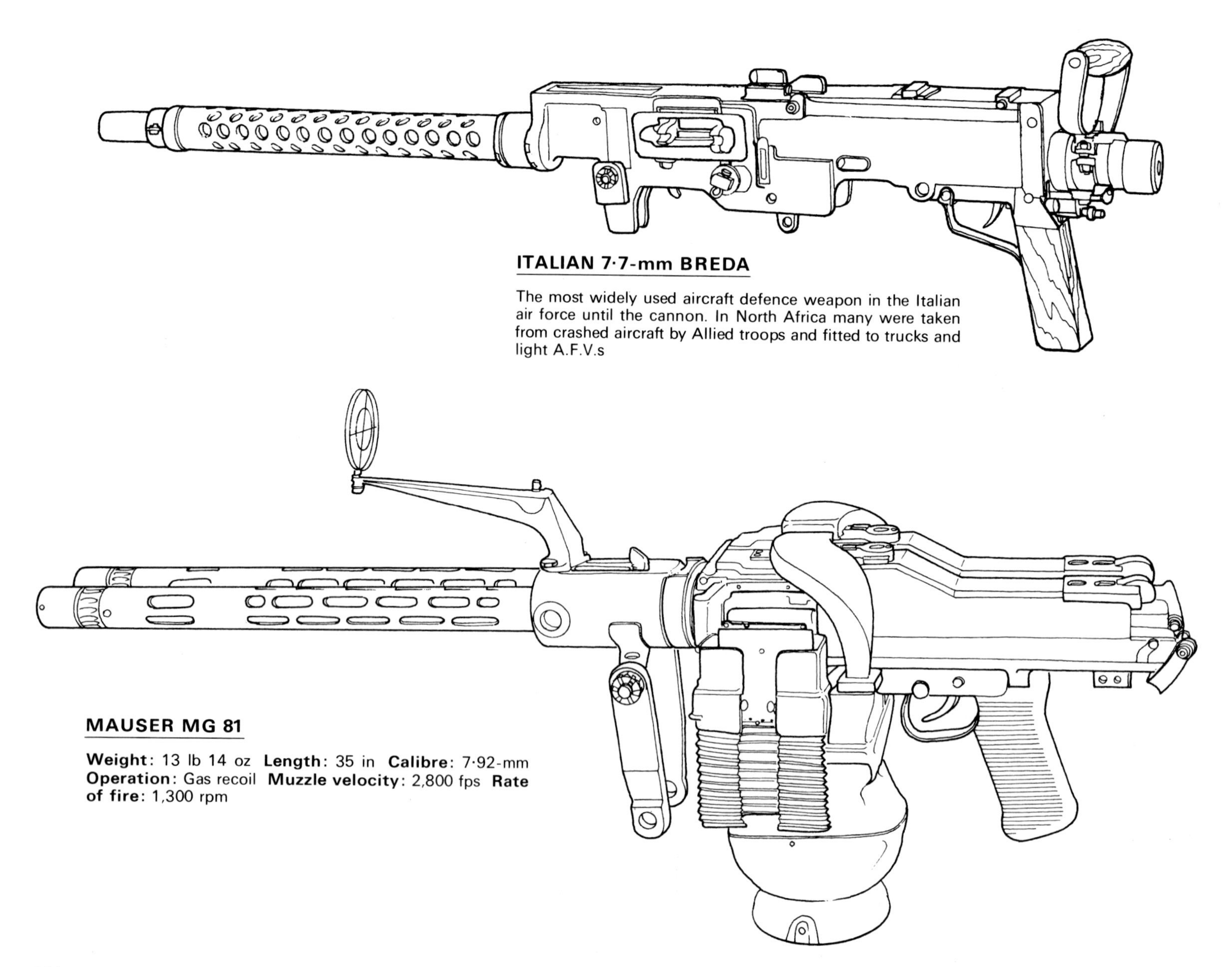

ITALIAN 7·7-mm BREDA

The most widely used aircraft defence weapon in the Italian air force until the cannon. In North Africa many were taken from crashed aircraft by Allied troops and fitted to trucks and light A.F.V.s

MAUSER MG 81

Weight: 13 lb 14 oz **Length**: 35 in **Calibre**: 7·92-mm **Operation**: Gas recoil **Muzzle velocity**: 2,800 fps **Rate of fire**: 1,300 rpm

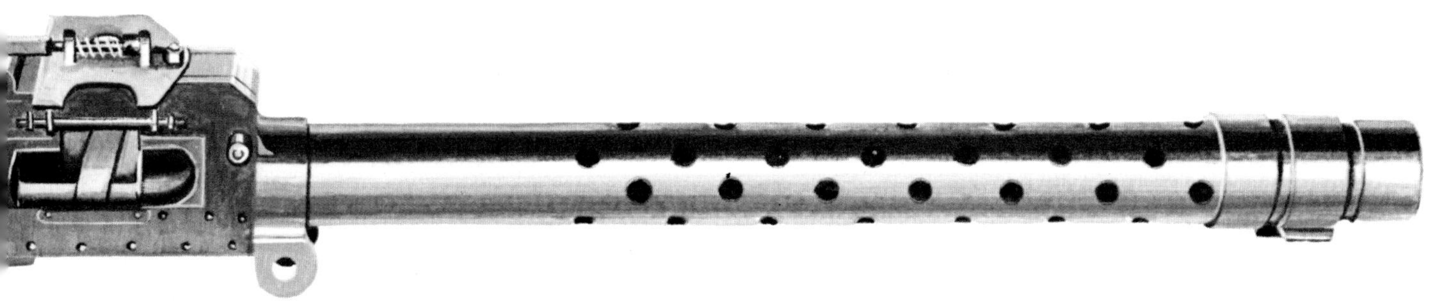

JAPANESE 7·7-mm TYPE 89 AIRCRAFT GUN

Calibre: 7·7-mm **Magazine**: belt feed **Muzzle velocity**: 2,070 fps **Rate of fire**: 550 rpm

Together with the Lancaster, the Halifax formed the backbone of RAF Bomber Command's night attacks on Occupied Europe between 1941 and 1945, and in both aircraft the turrets could fire for extended periods. In 1939, the typical ammunition capacity of a turret was 500 rounds per gun, but for the last two years of the war British heavy bombers frequently carried 8,000 rounds, weighing almost 800 lb, stored in long boxes in the rear fuselage. There was no powered feed system, each Browning merely pulling its long belt by tension from the gun itself. The gunner, seated in the turret behind local small areas of armour-plate, had a reflector sight and either a joystick or handlebar-type controls for elevation and traverse. Flash eliminators prevented the gunner from losing his night-adapted vision when he fired at attacking fighters.

Straight and level

Although the penalty in weight and drag of these turrets was considerable, there was never any doubt they were effective even though the gunner often had to fire just as the aircraft entered a violent evasive manoeuvre. In sharp contrast, the policy of the day-bombers of the US Army Air Force (which became the US Air Force in 1946) was to maintain straight and level flight in formation and to defend themselves against fighter attack by massed firepower. By 1941, American bombers had abandoned most rifle-calibre guns in favour of the Browning 0·5-in (12·7-mm), used in both hand-held and turret mountings. By 1943 the heavies of the US 8th Air Force, which daily penetrated German airspace, were in greater need of defensive armament than bombers had ever been. Though each aircraft mounted ten or eleven 0·5-in guns, eight of them in four powered turrets, the opposition was so intense that losses were very severe. Increasingly, the enemy fighters devised methods of attack that reduced their exposure to the bombers' fire, eventually standing-off and firing at long range with 30-mm cannon, rockets and, ultimately, guided missiles. Though the American bombers carried more than 2,000 lb of armour, and the crews wore new flak jackets which protected the torso by overlapping squares of manganese steel, the slow day-bomber was sorely pressed.

German bombers even earlier had shown themselves to be anything but invincible, particularly during the Battle of Britain. Their design was such that all that could be done, short of an extensive redesign for which the German aircraft industry was not equipped, was a succession of modifications. During the Battle of Britain, the Ju 88 was urgently modified until, in its A-4 version, the original three MG-15 machine-guns had

TWIN ·303 LEWIS A.A. MOUNTING

A typical British A.A. mount used against low flying aircraft. This pair of Lewis machine-guns could send up a total fire-power of 1,150 rpm

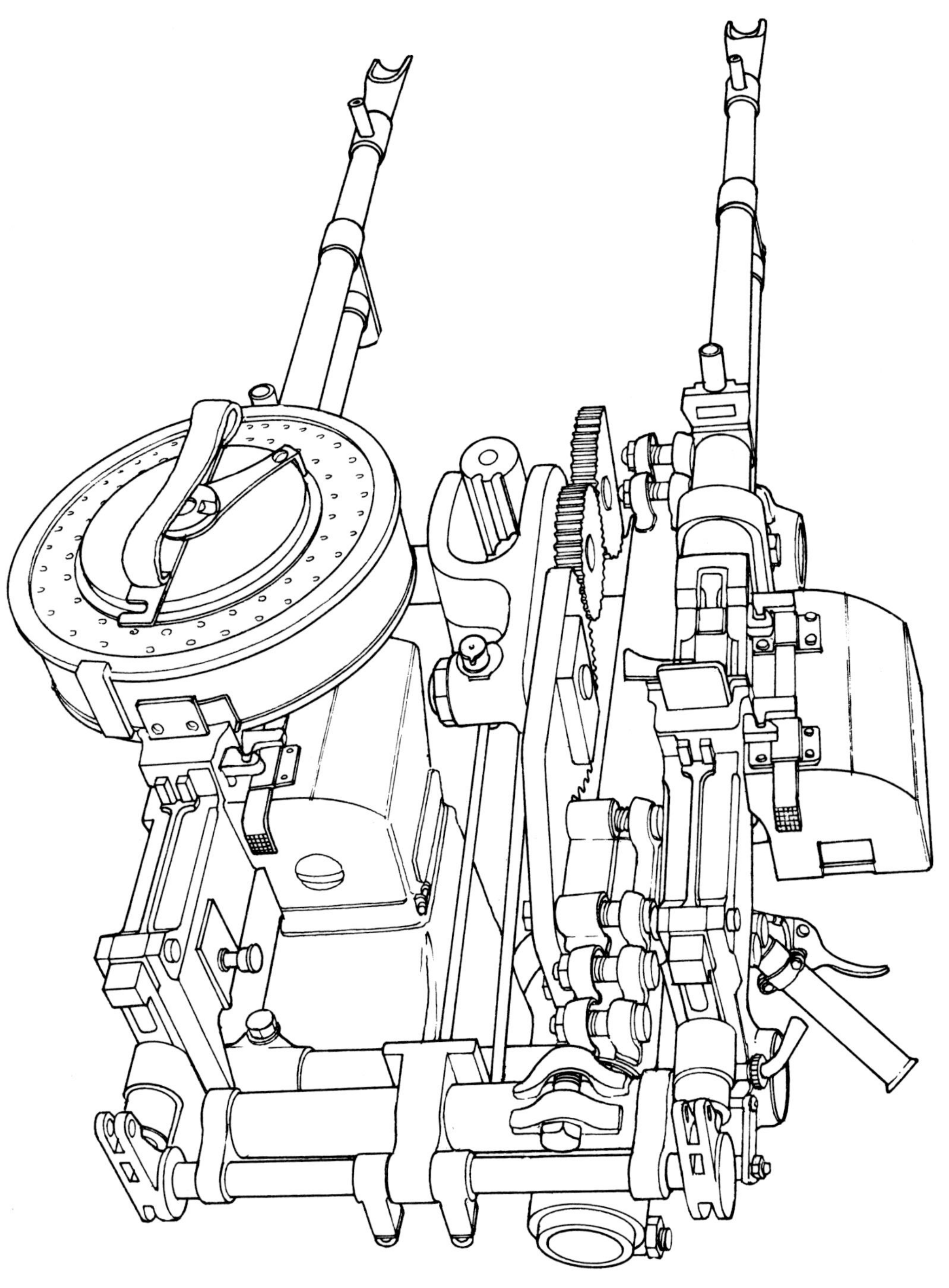

B-17D 'FLYING FORTRESS'

Gross weight: 50,000 lb **Span**: 103 ft 9 in **Length**: 67 ft 11 in **Engine**: 4×Wright Cyclone R-1820 **Armament**: 6× ·50; 1× ·30 machine-guns **Crew**: 9 **Speed**: 323 mph at 25,000 ft **Ceiling**: 37,000 ft **Range**: 2,100 miles **Bomb load**: 10,500 lb

Spearhead of the USAAF's daylight raids on Occupied Europe. The D model carried less armament than later versions, one of which – the B-40 fighter – carried up to 30 machine-guns and cannon in an unsuccessful attempt to provide an escort for B-17 formations

B-17E 'FLYING FORTRESS'

Gross weight: 53,000 lb **Span**: 103 ft 9 in **Length**: 73 ft 10 in **Engine**: 4×Wright R-1920-65 **Armament**: 15 machine-guns **Crew**: 9 **Speed**: 317 mph at 25,000 ft **Ceiling**: 36,600 ft **Range**: 3,300 miles **Bomb load**: 4,000 lb

This version of the famous B-17 was the first to live up to the name 'Flying Fortress', with the addition of tail, ventral and front upper gun turrets, the last power-operated

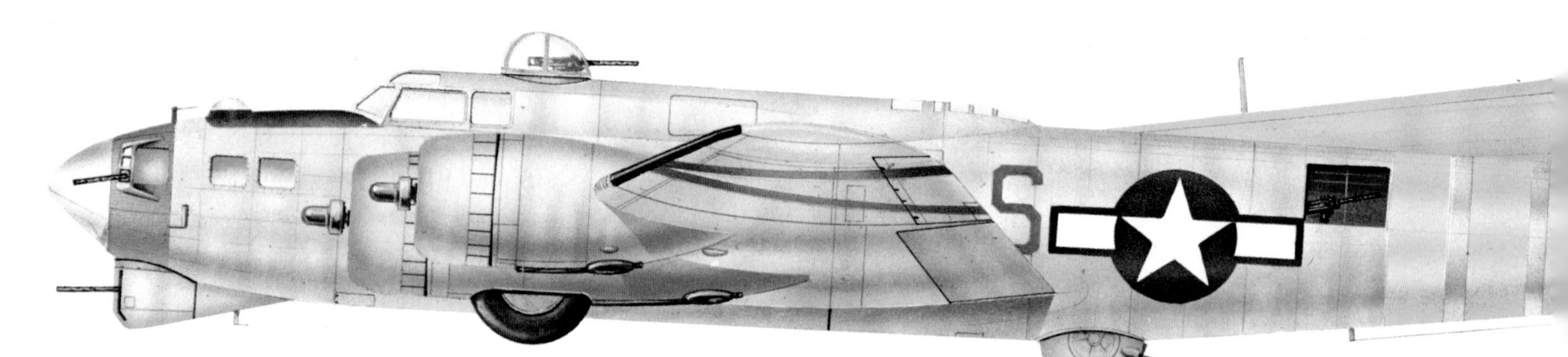

B-17G 'FLYING FORTRESS'

Gross weight: 65,500 lb **Span**: 103 ft 9 in **Length**: 74 ft 4 in **Engine**: 4×Wright Cyclone R-1820 **Armament**: 11 machine-guns **Crew**: 10 **Speed**: 287 mph at 25,000 ft **Ceiling**: 35,600 ft **Range**: 2,000 miles **Bomb load**: 6,000 lb

Among other modifications, the G model of the B-17 introduced a two-gun 'chin' turret to help repel attacking fighters

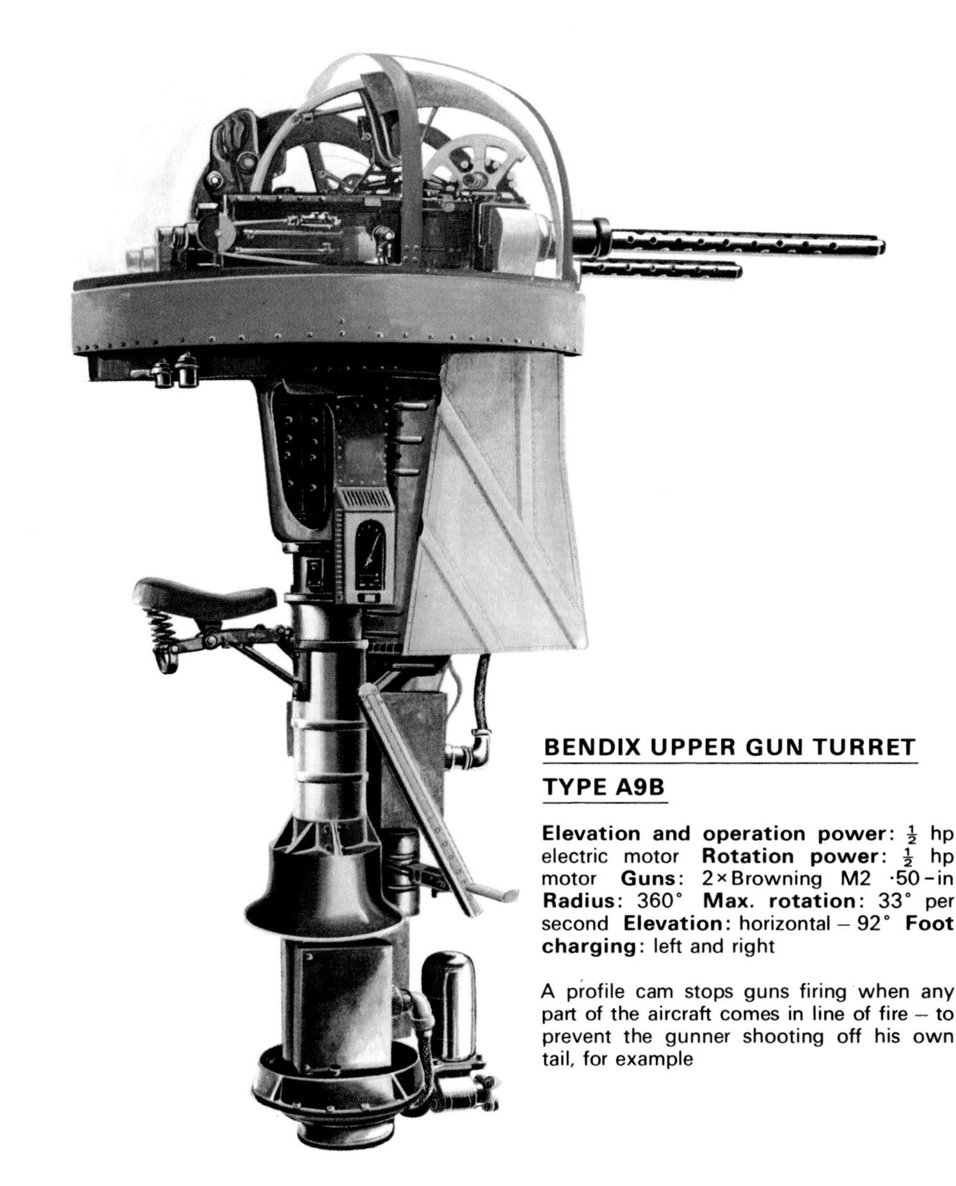

BENDIX UPPER GUN TURRET

TYPE A9B

Elevation and operation power: $\frac{1}{2}$ hp electric motor **Rotation power**: $\frac{1}{2}$ hp motor **Guns**: 2×Browning M2 ·50-in **Radius**: 360° **Max. rotation**: 33° per second **Elevation**: horizontal – 92° **Foot charging**: left and right

A profile cam stops guns firing when any part of the aircraft comes in line of fire – to prevent the gunner shooting off his own tail, for example

been augmented by two to three additional MG-15s, a 13-mm MG-131 cannon and usually one or two fixed MG-81 machine-guns. In many aircraft the upper rear gunner had to manage four separate hand-held MG-15s projecting at different angles on ball-and-socket mountings. Turrets were rare, although MG-131 guns in electrically-powered turrets were fitted to the Do 217 E-2 and many other Do 217 sub-types, and various Fw 200 C Condors had turrets with either the MG-131 or the far more powerful MG-151/15, a high-velocity 15-mm weapon.

But German armament was at best a botch-up born of urgent necessity. Late models of the Do 217 had four fixed rearward-firing MG-81s in the extreme tail and some had a pair of these fixed in the rear of each engine nacelle, all eight guns being 'sighted' and fired by the pilot – using nothing more accurate than a rear-view periscopic sight.

The one area in which the Germans did considerable pioneering work was in remotely controlled 'barbettes' (unmanned gun positions). These were lighter than the conventional form of turret and offered less drag. Moreover, in theory at any rate, it was possible for a gunner at a single sighting station to control several barbettes and bring many heavy-calibre guns to bear on a single target. The first aircraft to be equipped with this type of armament was the Messerschmitt Me 210 two-seater night fighter, with a 13-mm MG-131 on each side of the rear fuselage, aimed by the navigator in the rear cockpit. A refined version of the same scheme was used on the much more numerous Me 410. The He 177 heavy bomber usually had a 13-mm MG-131 barbette on the upper forward fuselage and all the candidates for the new Bomber-B specification – the Do 317, Fw 191 and Ju 288 – would have had three to five remotely controlled cannon barbettes offering very great firepower and low drag. But the war ended before these could be put into production.

The armament of Italian, Japanese and Russian bombers was less advanced and chiefly consisted of 7·7-mm, 12·7-mm or 20-mm guns in individual hand-held mountings. However, the Japanese did use a crude form of electrically-driven 20-mm turret on the Mitsubishi Ki-67 and G4M2 bombers, produced respectively for the Army Air Force and Navy Air Force, while the Soviet Union adopted a manned unpowered turret in the rear of both inner engine nacelles on the big four-engined Petlyakov Pe-8.

The greatest and most advanced form of firepower was used in the American heavy bombers. The Douglas A-26 Invader of 1944 was fitted with remotely-controlled upper and lower twin 0·5-in turrets and usually had very heavy fixed nose armament fired by the pilot, who could also use the upper turret when it was locked facing forward. But the biggest advance of the whole war was seen in the Boeing B-29 Superfortress strategic bomber which, though fully pressurised, had five sighting stations and five powered turrets (four of them remotely controlled) with ten or twelve 0·5-in and one 20-mm guns, giving it a remarkable concentration of firepower.

THE RADAR WAR

Bristol Beaufighter night-fighter and anti-shipping strike aircraft. Armament: four 20-mm cannon, six ·303-inch machine-guns; one 2,127-lb torpedo OR one 1,650-lb torpedo and two 250-lb bombs OR eight rocket projectiles. Max speed: 320 mph. Range: 1,480 miles

John Batchelor

1. Before the advent of electronic aids, both sides had to use a technique of dead reckoning combined with visual fixes on known landmarks en route to the target. Here British bombers use a coastal pinpoint on their way to Germany

2. One early German bombing aid was based on two overlapping 'Lorenz' radio beams, aligned on the target, which transmitted 'dots' on one side of the course and 'dashes' on the other. When on course, it emitted a steady note

German *X - device* **(3)** and British 'Oboe' **(4)** fixed the position of an aircraft by matching two separate radio or radar transmitters. Both systems signalled the moment for bomb release when precisely over the target

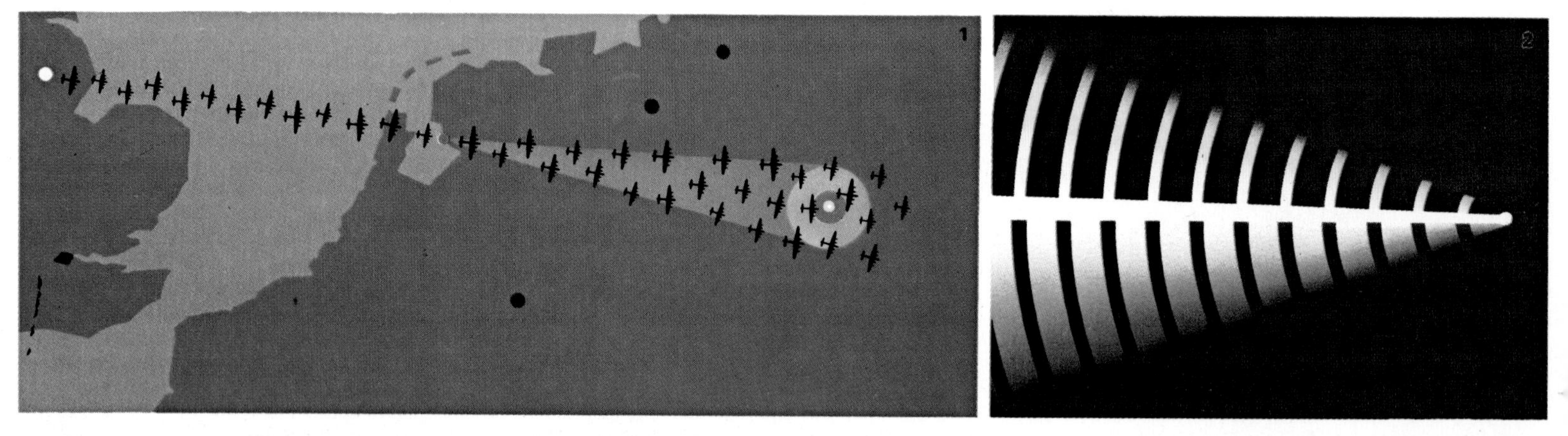

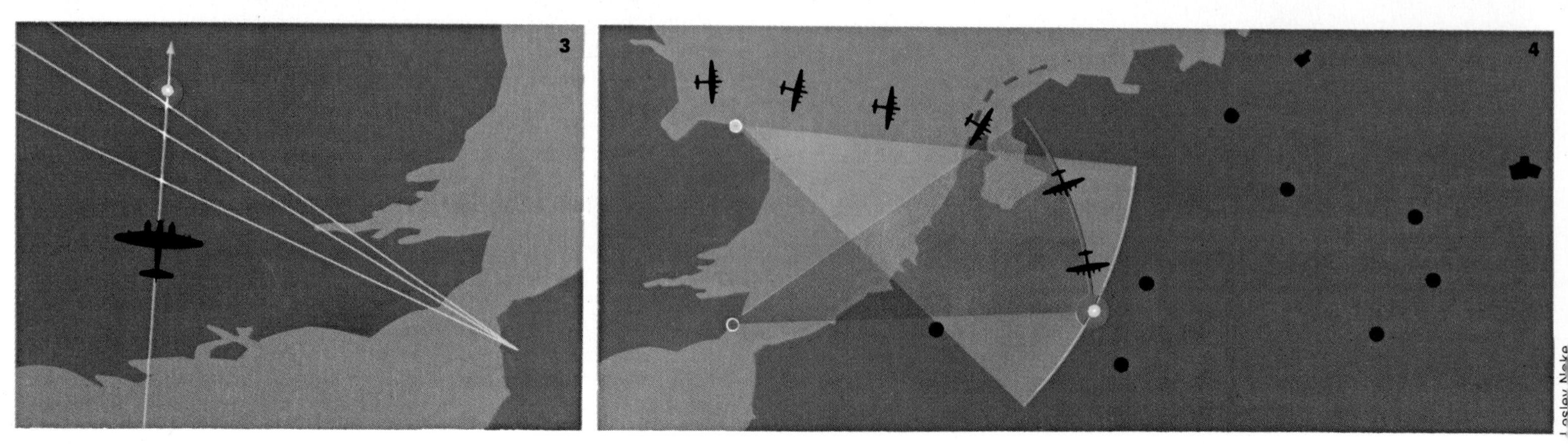

Lesley Noke

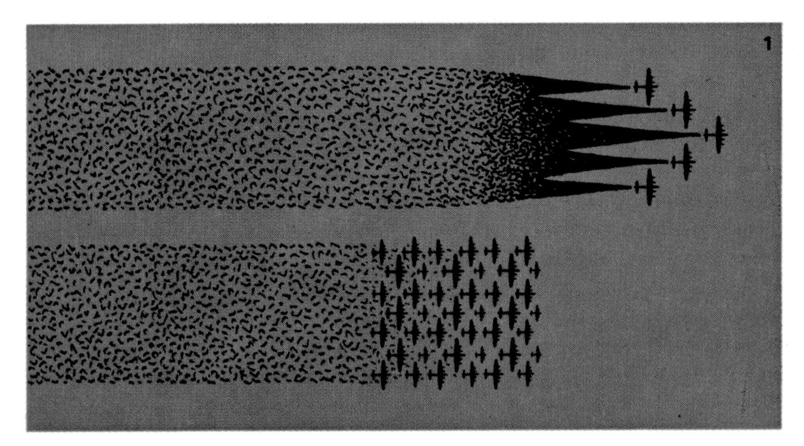

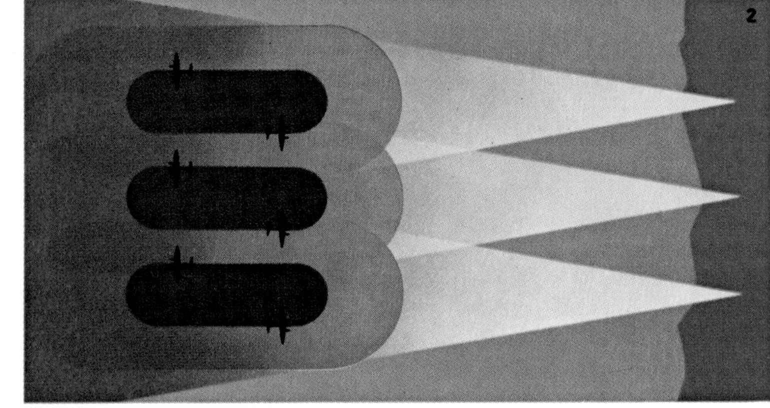

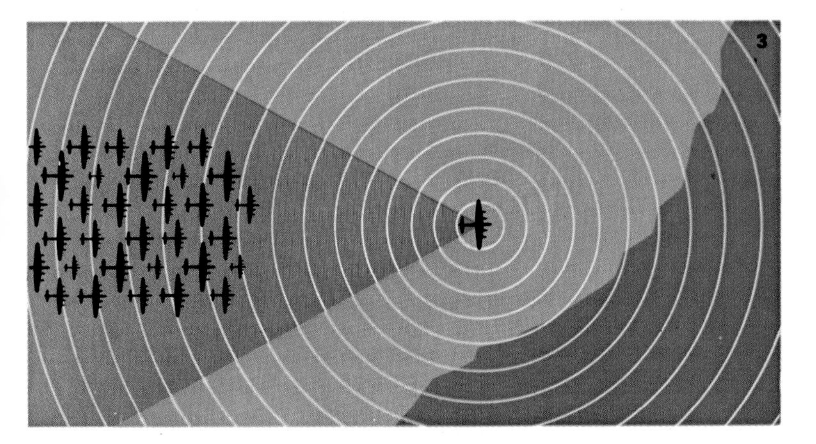

1. 'Window' was lengths of tinfoil corresponding to the wavelengths of German radar, which, when dropped, produced a vast number of echoes which blotted out other echoes. One small group of aircraft released a large amount of foil, while the main bomber force dropped it more slowly, thus producing two identical but confusing plots on German screens. **2.** Pairs of British aircraft, circling and radiating jamming signals with their 'Mandrel' devices, formed a barrier which the German radar could not penetrate and the British bombers could fly in undetected. **3.** 'Jostle' was the biggest radio transmitter to be taken into the air at the time; one aircraft carrying it could transmit a warbling, raucous note in all directions, on the same wavelength as the German fighter control. And 'Piperack', a rearward-facing device, shielded bombers in the cone behind the jamming aircraft. **4.** On March 20-21, 1945, an RAF raid on Hemmingstedt went in without jamming, while the raid on Bohlen was screened by a decoy raid to the south, two bomber streams over the target, the use of 'Window' on feints towards Kassel and Halle, and a 'Mandrel' screen just behind the front line as a shield against the Luftwaffe's night-fighters.

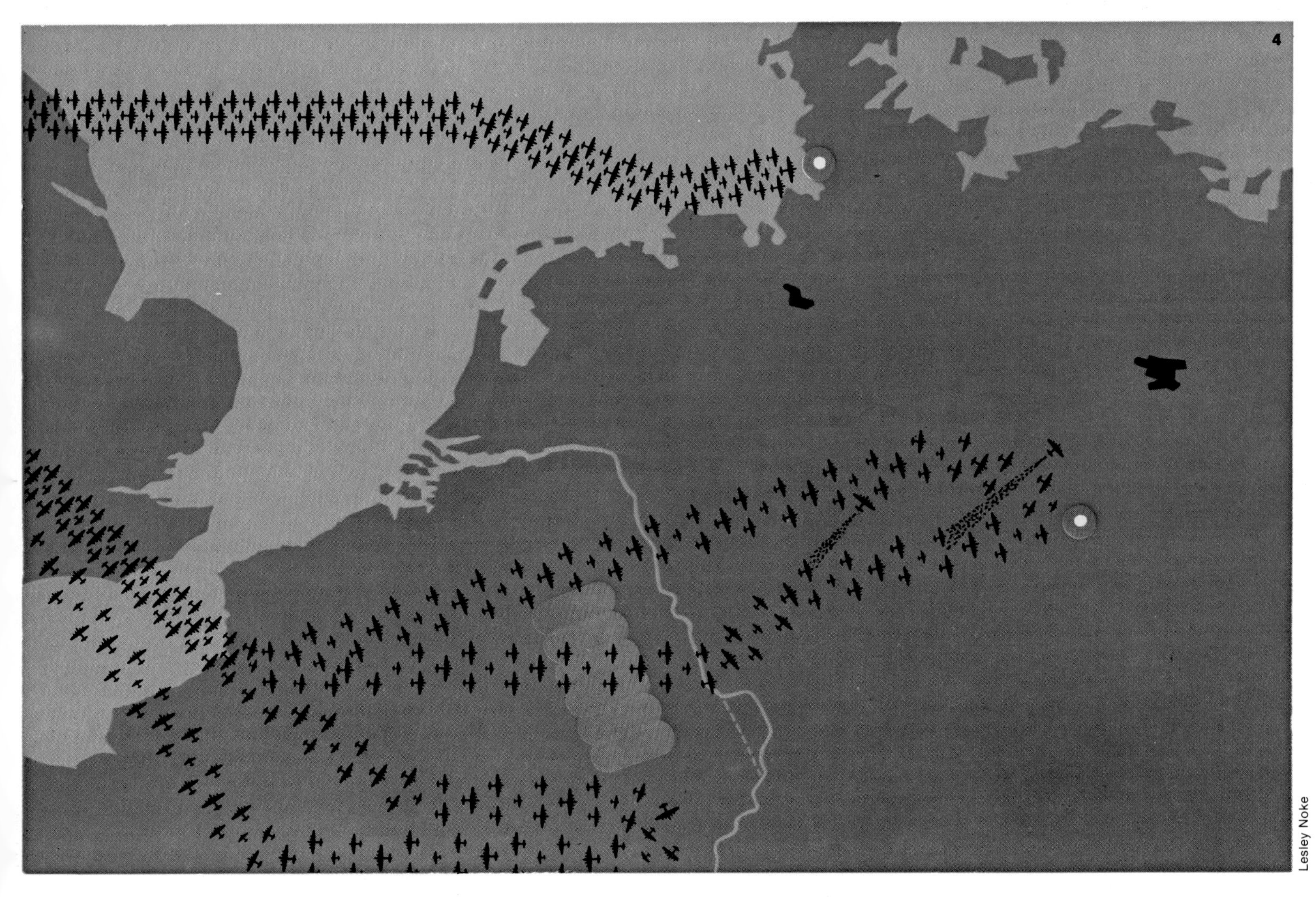

Lesley Noke

Seldom can an art of war have been so swiftly and dramatically evolved: bombing operations which had begun as inaccurate raids by a few score of aircraft developed with the aid of radar into mighty sledgehammer blows involving hundreds of heavy bombers, highly accurate and deadly destructive. And it was the myriad collection of electronic black boxes aboard each bomber – outwitting those guiding the enemy defences – which made this whole revolution possible

Air power dominated the Second World War. The aircraft became the major instrument of offence and defence in the air, and was a vitally important weapon in support of ground forces, in maritime warfare, in reconnaissance, and in transport. Again and again events proved that the side with superiority in the air enjoyed a considerable, often decisive, advantage over its opponent.

The air weapon, however, is peculiarly susceptible to small technical disparities, and both sides recognised this. During the six years of war the pace of aeronautical development was staggering. The maximum speed of fighters rose from 360 mph to 540 mph, that of bombers from 290 mph to 460 mph; range and altitude performance improved by similar measures. But such advances in aircraft performance would have counted for little if the fighters and bombers had not been able to find their targets or, having found them, lacked the power to destroy them.

During the 1930s scientists both in Britain and in Germany had realised that the newly discovered radio and radar techniques could be used to assist bombers to find their targets in bad weather or in darkness. In Britain such ideas had to remain 'on ice', for the limited development effort available at that time had logically to be concentrated on the vitally needed home radar defensive chain. But in Germany, where no such priority was accorded to the defence, two separate radio aids to bombing emerged.

Both German systems employed the so-called 'Lorenz' beam, which comprised two adjacent radio beams that overlapped slightly. In one beam Morse dots were transmitted, and in the other Morse dashes. The signals interlocked, so that where the two radio beams overlapped a steady note was received (see diagram).

The simpler of the German radio navigational methods was called *Knickebein* – 'the bent leg' – and employed two of the Lorenz beams. One held the bomber on a course which took it right up to the target, while the second Lorenz beam crossed the first at the bomb release point (see diagram). The system was moderately accurate. Using it a good crew had a 50% chance of placing the bombs inside a circle 1 mile in diameter at a range of 180 miles from the beam transmitter. At greater ranges the accuracy was lower. The great virtue of the *Knickebein* system was its simplicity, and the device could be used by the mass of the German bomber crews.

For more precise bombing the Germans had developed a rather more complex method which also employed Lorenz beams – the X-device. The X-device (see diagram) used four beams, each of which was radiated on a different frequency. One, the approach beam, pointed straight at the target. The other three beams crossed the approach beam at precise intervals just short of the target. The bomber crews would fly up the approach beam towards their objective and the first of the cross beams, which they passed 50 kilometres (31 miles) from the target, served as a warning that the target was getting close. When 20 kilometres (12 miles) from the release point the aircraft flew through a second cross beam. As it did so the navigator pressed a button to start one hand of a special clock, not unlike a stop-watch, but with two hands which rotated independently. Five kilometres (3 miles) from the release point the aircraft passed the third and final cross beam, and the navigator again pressed the button on his special clock: the hand which had been moving now stopped, and the other hand started rotating to catch it up. When the two hands coincided, a pair of electrical contacts closed, and the bombs were *automatically* released.

All in all the X-device was a frighteningly sophisticated method, considering that it was ready in 1938, before the war had even begun. The combination of the clock and the Lorenz beams provided accurate data on the bomber's speed over the ground, one of the most important facts to be known for precision bombing once the aircraft had been routed accurately over the target. With the X-device a good crew could place its bombs within a circle 120 yards in diameter when 70 miles from the beam stations, a circle which increased to 400 yards in diameter when the aircraft was 180 miles from the stations. Because of its complexity the X-device could be used only by specially trained crews. As a result its use was confined to one precision bombing unit, *Kampfgruppe* ('Wing') 100.

The British answer

By the middle of 1941 work on the RAF's first radar navigational aid was well advanced and the set – called GEE – was already nearing the service trials stage. The GEE system employed three ground transmitters, each one situated about 100 miles from the other two. These transmitters acted in unison and radiated a complex train of pulses in a set order. In the aircraft the navigator was provided with a special radar receiver, which enabled him to measure the time difference between the reception of the various signal pulses. By referring these differences to a special GEE map, the navigator was able to determine his position to within 6 miles when 400 miles from the most distant transmitter; at shorter ranges the accuracy was much better. In effect, the GEE transmitters laid an invisible radio grid across the continent of Europe; by listening to the character of the transmissions, the GEE operator could determine on which 'lines' of the grid his aircraft lay. Obviously this was a great improvement on *Knickebein,* for with the German device an accurate positional fix was possible only at the point at which

two Lorenz beams crossed. The proportion of successful sorties—that is, those on which the crews released their bombs within 3 miles of the aiming point—rose from 23 to 33% of the whole. It was a worthwhile improvement, but hardly spectacular.

GEE proved to be as easy for the Germans to jam as *Knickebein* had been for the British, and by August 1942 the device was nearing the end of its usefulness to crews flying over enemy territory. This was the birth of the H2S radar device. The rotating aerial system was modified to tilt the radar beam downwards, and the returning echoes were displayed on a cathode-ray tube in such a way that the sweeping radar trace sketched out a passable representation of the surrounding countryside, just like a map. The modified radar underwent its first trial towards the end of 1941. Soon after the takeoff Dr O'Kane, the radar set's operator, observed a large bright spot on his screen—the city of Southampton. The absence of echo signals from the sea threw the coastline into sharp relief, and O'Kane had little difficulty in following the position of his aircraft.

From the start it was clear that H2S could go a long way towards solving Bomber Command's target finding problem. The new set was independent of beacons, and so its range was in effect limited only by the range of the carrying aircraft itself. The new device was ordered into production at the very highest priority.

But even the extremely advanced H2S did not bring a sudden end to the target finding problems. The set produced problems of its own, not the least of which was the need for skilful operation if the device was to give its best. As the Luftwaffe had learned in 1940 and 1941, it was an excellent scheme to have the main bombing force aircraft release their loads on marker fires started at the target by picked crews using special equipment—provided the fires were started in the right place. But if the markers went wide, the majority of the bombs would fall wide as well. Indeed, it speaks highly for those men concerned with the introduction of the device that such incidents did not happen more often. Gradually, as the air- and ground-crewmen became more familiar with H2S, the device brought about a marked improvement in the accuracy of attacks.

A wonder device named 'Oboe'

While the effective operating range of H2S was virtually unlimited, the second device which had been readied for service during 1942 had only a limited range. But to compensate for this its accuracy was very good indeed. The new device, 'Oboe', made use of the fact that a radar set can measure the range of an object to within very fine limits, and that this accuracy does not diminish with distance. Two radar-type transmitters were used, one at Dover and the other near Cromer, which sent out a stream of pulses to the aircraft. The pulses triggered off a special airborne transmitter, which replied with pulses of its own. By measuring the distance between the first transmitter and the aircraft in the normal radar way, it was possible to direct the pilot by means of radioed instructions to fly along a circular path to the target, centring on the transmitter at Dover. The second transmitter station at Cromer also transmitted and received signals from a second repeater-transmitter in the aircraft. In this way the ground operators there were able to track the aircraft in range as it moved along the circular path controlled by the Dover transmitter. When the Cromer station observed the aircraft to be at the computed bomb-release point, it radioed a 'bomb release' signal.

Oboe gave bombing accuracies of the order of 200 yards. Its maximum range, determined by the curvature of the earth and the height of the aircraft, was 270 miles from the further ground station if the aircraft flew at 28,000 feet. This took in most of the Ruhr with ease, though it meant that few other targets in Germany could be attacked using beacons in England. After the recapture of France ground beacons were set up there, and during the latter stages of the war almost every important target in Germany could be attacked using Oboe guidance. A further limitation of the method was that each pair of ground transmitters could control only one aircraft at a time. Since a bombing run took about ten minutes, this limited the number of aircraft that could be controlled to six per hour per pair of transmitters. This factor limited the use of Oboe to the Pathfinder Force, where it was fitted in high-flying Mosquito aircraft.

BRISTOL BLENHEIM Mk IV

Gross weight: 12,500 lb **Span:** 56 ft 4 in **Length:** 42 ft 9 in **Engine:** 2×920 hp Mercury XV **Armament:** 5×·303 machine-guns **Crew:** 3 **Speed:** 266 mph at 11,800 ft **Ceiling:** 22,000 ft **Range:** 1,450 miles **Bomb load:** 1,320 lb

Primarily intended as a light bomber, the Blenheim served throughout the war in many roles for the RAF and was the first night-fighter to use airborne interception radar

EYES IN THE SKY

Even during the First World War, aircraft had been used to take photographs of the enemy's lines. And although prewar developments were left largely to private initiative, it was quickly accepted at the outbreak of war that aerial reconnaissance had a vital part to play

When the Second World War began, photo-reconnaissance was not, of course, a new technique. It was used in the First World War, when (despite initial fears that it was 'unsporting' to take pictures of the enemy's rear lines) many important pictures were taken, and indeed by the end of that war photo-reconnaissance was well established as a necessary adjunct of strategic planning. Not only that; later it was being used widely for mapping previously unexplored territories. By the time that a second war was becoming increasingly likely – certainly by 1938 – there was a good deal of effort on all sides to revive and improve the techniques of photo-reconnaissance; and by the outbreak of war the opposing factions were all, in their different ways, prepared for action in this field.

In Germany the Luftwaffe's programme of expansion went hand in hand with improved photographic techniques. The Germans had developed long-focus lenses and, by perfecting fine-grain developing techniques, they were able to take high-quality photographs of unprecedented accuracy. These photographs were examined with lenses giving a magnification of several diameters, and calculations of height were done by simple trigonometry from length of shadow and other related factors. After the war, when the British unearthed large stores of photographs near the German town of Bad Reichenhall, they admitted, with much surprise, that the detail was excellent. Stacked neatly in large crates, hidden in a barn, these photographs gave a good indication of the intelligent use of photographic technology which the Germans had evolved. Photographs of bombing targets in England, of troop movements at the front – both were equally impressive.

The Luftwaffe records in detail were never seen, however. Most of them were stored away in the crypts of the Lady's Chapel in Dresden. This was indeed a beautiful church, and so the Germans felt that the security offered was great. But in the bombing of Dresden on February 13 and 14, 1945, the film library was ignited by incendiaries dropped by Allied planes. The fire raged throughout the following night, and so intense was the heat that the sandstone pillars were cracked asunder and the entire dome of the church fell in, destroying the Luftwaffe's records.

The French were the first among the Allies to use aerial photography in the war. The effort was not very seriously undertaken, but the *Deuxième Bureau* was, before the beginning of the war, already collecting pictures taken from passenger aircraft during normal scheduled flights. The results were useful and interesting, though not of course as technically competent as would be achieved by a full-scale effort in photo-reconnaissance. There was, however, one important lesson that the experience taught us all: secrecy. There was no difficulty at all in obtaining pictures from a civilian aircraft shortly before the outbreak of hostilities, and so it was quickly realised by the British that the effort would have to be secret to succeed. Not a word was said outside official circles; and although there was every reason to suppose that the British were carrying out photo-reconnaissance (to do so in some form was, after all, perfectly obvious) the Germans were never aware of the extent of the coverage – nor, more important, the skill of the technicians who interpreted the photographs.

Startling British results

Interpretation was one sphere where the British experts were well ahead of the Germans and, unknown to the enemy, they were obtaining more and more information about German installations. The reason for this was basically simple. The German and French pictures were merely vertical views of the ground (highly detailed views, in the German case); interpretation was done by visual inspection and measurement; and the results were plotted accordingly. The British system, however, relied on the use of stereoscopy – three-dimensional examination which could reveal far more detail than a mathematically-interpreted two-dimensional cover could ever hope to show. The results were startling.

The British photo-reconnaissance effort began, in fact, before the war, and the story is worth recording. It centres on an Australian, Sidney Cotton, who had a lucrative aerial-survey business. Cotton, on a strictly unofficial basis, set up the first photo-reconnaissance outfit with the complete blessing of the Chief of Air Staff. He was provided with a Lockheed 12A, a small airliner with a ceiling and range that were ideal for the purpose, and three cameras, carefully concealed, were mounted to scan the strip of ground beneath the aircraft as it flew. The aperture through which they scanned the ground beneath was closed by a sliding hatch so that, from the ground, it was in this state quite impossible to know that there was anything odd about the aircraft at all. To finish the job, the plane was painted a pale, greenish blue colour – just the shade one might expect to be chosen by an extrovert Australian joy-rider. But of course, it was also exactly the colour to make the plane as inconspicuous as possible when in flight.

As a cover the Australian set up a company called 'Aeronautical Research and Sales Ltd' of St James's Square, London; the business was stated to include the marketing of colour film (which indeed it did) and it involved much travelling around the European business network – including frequent trips over German factories and large industrial cities. And during the trips, the Lockheed was busily collecting thousands of exposures of the ground it covered.

On one occasion it is told that Cotton flew to Germany during a Nazi rally, and while waiting for his colour-film agent to arrive from Berlin, he agreed to take some inquisitive German officers for a flight. They were impressed by the large aircraft that he used, and were most agreeable to the suggestion that they should fly along the Rhine. This the pilot was glad to do and, with the cameras collecting information silently as they went, he took them for a round tour of many military installations, flying everywhere at only a few thousand feet. The results, needless to say, were invaluable.

Each time he made the trip to Germany, Cotton would vary the route and so broaden the aerial cover obtained, and this continued until August 1939. Suddenly, Cotton was grounded in Berlin. At first he was worried, but then found that all civilian aircraft had been stopped from flying. The implications were clear, and when he was eventually allowed to fly out, just a week before Hitler invaded Poland, he was given a route that he must follow – and if he left it by as much as a mile, he would be shot out of the sky.

It was with much trepidation that Cotton made his last flight as an unofficial aerial spy. But within a few months, this time within the official fold of the RAF, he was back at work, with 'Shortie' Longbottom, the RAF pioneer aerial photographer. Two Spitfires were obtained and fitted with cameras in each wing and, by November 1939, good quality photographs were being taken from over 30,000 feet. They showed many leading centres of German activities with graphic clarity, despite the formidable height at which they were taken. Yet there were drawbacks still: the vapour trail which the plane produced was often clearly visible from the ground and – more important – it was well-nigh impossible to find a way of gleaning enough information from the results to be really useful.

It was at this point that, once again, free enterprise raised its head. This time it was in the form of Michael Spender, who had done more work than most in the interpretation of aerial photographs taken for survey purposes. Spender used a large stereoscope which enabled the contour of the ground to be not simply revealed but magnified many times. It showed that a tiny dot, for example, might in reality be a flat disc or a tall tower . . . it was an invaluable technique. Alongside the viewing plane on which the photographs were mounted was a hinged pointer which drew out special selected points, indicated by the expert examiner on a separate sheet of paper. From

An aerial photograph taken during a raid on Biggin Hill airfield, with German markings indicating bomb bursts and presumed installations

1. Bomb explosions
2. Hangars
3. Assembly shops
4. Store houses
5. Repair shops & store houses
6. Workshop
7. Briefing hall
8. Barrack huts
9. Power station
10. Administration block
11. Dispersed aircraft

Sado-Opera Mundi

Imperial War Museum

△ At Peenemünde in June 1944 RAF reconnaissance reveals **(A)** light flak positions, **(B)** two V-2 rockets, and **(C)** rocket transport wagons

Imperial War Museum

△ In September 1944, after heavy bombing, subsequent reconnaissance shows the damage; the flak guns have been moved

▽ Barbed-wire defences, built by the Germans to prevent a repetition of the Bruneval raid, only highlight the positions

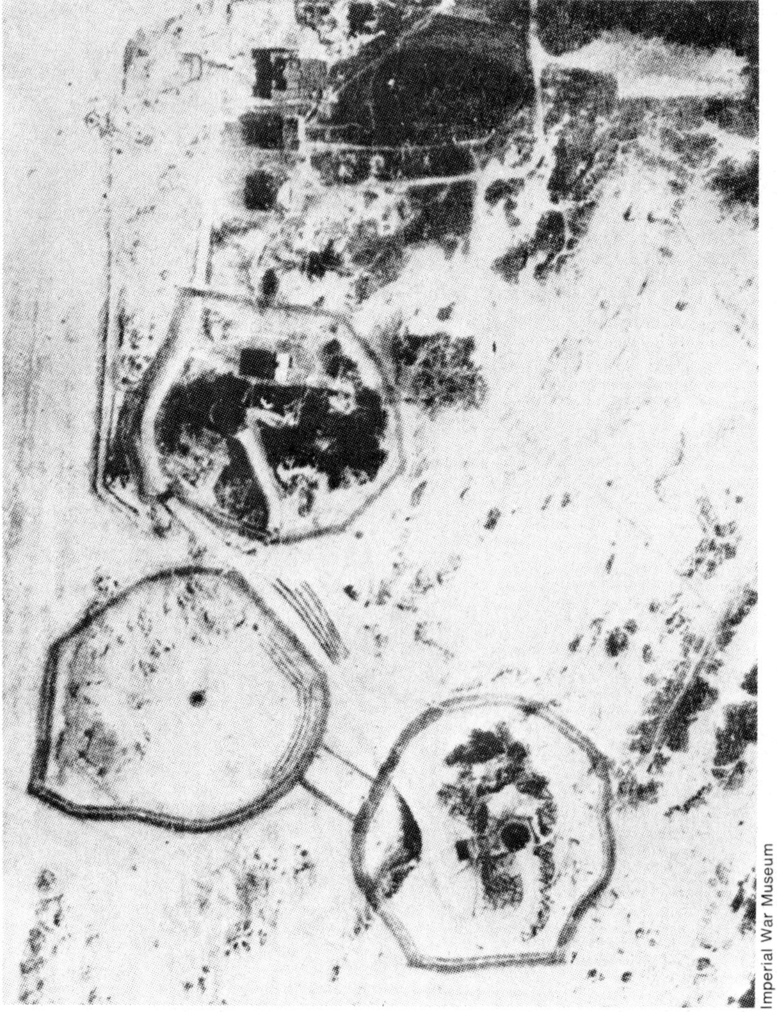

Imperial War Museum

▽ A German picture of Liverpool. Superimposed are targets for attack (in rectangles) and damage inflicted (in circles)

Sado-Opera Mundi

such details as size, location, and many other parameters of the objects on the photographs could be accurately measured.

Early in 1940, as the Allied group responsible for air photography took shape, they moved to a base some 40 miles east of Paris. And it was here that the British and French photo-reconnaissance experts put their heads together for the first time. The French had relied on large-scale, detailed photographs and at first were sceptical about the British efforts, taken from such great heights. But of course the stereoscopy technique, which was by then becoming routine, showed how much more detail was possible. A Colonel Lespair was in charge of the French group, and he is said to have produced a chart which he told Cotton to take to London whenever he felt the need for some evidence to advocate his case for improved equipment or conditions. The gist of the chart was a set of statistics: Bomber Command had photographed, it was said, 2,500 square miles for the loss of 40 aircraft; the French had covered 6,000 square miles for the loss of 60 – but Cotton and Longbottom with the Photographic Unit, using one Spitfire, which remained intact, had covered 5,000 square miles without loss!

This approach worked. When Cotton returned to England to ask for the expansion of his organisation, the agreement was forthcoming – despite the jealousy of Bomber Command, which continued to take its own reconnaissance and 'result of attack' pictures.

An incautious press release

Within a few weeks this situation began to change. Bomber Command had been unable to photograph properly several areas in Germany, all important to future strategy. Cotton sent one of his new Spitfires to the area, and the photographs were taken without a hitch; indeed, when German fighters did materialise the pilot simply opened the throttle and sped homewards, leaving the Messerschmitts behind him – proof, if any were needed, of the importance of the Spitfire's greater speed in photo-reconnaissance. Distinguished Flying Crosses were awarded to some of these pilots at the time – and an incautious press release sent to the aircraft magazines nearly wrecked the secrecy of the results. It spoke of 'a new method of aerial photography' and mentioned 'overlapping photographs' – but fortunately the Germans did not appreciate the significance of this statement.

By now the value of the technique was clear to all concerned, and not only did the Photographic Development Unit take over the detailed air-photography for the RAF, but also for the army. However by June 1940 the Germans were getting close; and, after several moves to areas of France that were further out of range of the advancing German tide, the unit was eventually forced to return to England and to Heston, the base where it had all started.

At about the same time, in the former offices of the Aircraft Operating Company, the first British training school for photo-interpreters was set up – and then Cotton was relieved of his post by an Air Ministry decision. It was felt, said the official notification, that photo-reconnaissance had passed the experimental stage and so should become a unit of the RAF, rather than a separate entity. Commander Geoffrey Tuttle was put in charge, the name of the unit was changed to Photographic Reconnaissance Unit – PRU for short – and so the machinery was ready for the more serious developments in the later stages of the war. It was this unit, incidentally, which supplied the details of 'Operation Sea Lion', when nearly 2,000 Axis ships were massed along the European coast facing the shores of England, and ready for invasion . . . but the Battle of Britain changed the course of the war, and the threat was averted for the time being.

Expansion continued; new departments were founded and the headquarters moved from Wembley to Danesfield, a large country house at RAF Medmenham. It was then that the Americans – who had at the time no photo-interpreters at all – sent trainees for instruction and, by 1942, the USA was also taking and interpreting photographs by stereoscopy. The fact that the Germans were using radar was spotted at this time, too, by the discovery of a dish-shaped direction aerial at Bruneval. Subsequently the installation was attacked, and the RAF planes also began the defensive practice of dropping aluminium foil from their normal flight positions to confuse and 'dazzle' the enemy radar detectors. 'Window' was a successful ruse, and saved a great many lives during the war.

An epic of aerial detection

By mid-1942 photo-reconnaissance was an established part of the Allied war effort – and it was in the middle of May in that year that one of the greatest epics of aerial detection began. A Spitfire on another mission – it was flying along the Baltic coast – happened to pass over a relatively small river-mouth island. The pilot, Flight-Lieutenant Steventon, noticed with interest a large number of buildings, obviously in active use and apparently surrounded by much new building work. Nearby were several rounded constructions, which the interpreters noted before moving on to the more serious work in hand – these pictures were, after all 'extras' to the sortie, and were not really interesting enough to spend too much time on. The island itself was seen to lie on the mouth of the Peene river; and the developments were taking place on Peenemünde – home of the V-rockets.

Previously the so-called 'Oslo Report' had suggested that Peenemünde was the site of important rocket developments, and scattered Intelligence had tended to confirm it. But even so (and notwithstanding the singular nature of the Peenemünde constructions that were photographed) the idea was taken no further. Yet, as we have seen, even by this time the rocket establishment was well under way. In February 1943 a note was sent to the RAF Medmenham headquarters; rocket development had been reported, it said; could the interpreters keep a look out for a rocket projector of any kind?

When Dr R. V. Jones, a senior Intelligence official, was informed of these first few shreds of information he insisted that the news should be kept secret – even within official circles – until confirmed or finally disproved. The War Office was not so sure, however, and called in two scientists, Professor C. D. Ellis and Dr A. D. Crow. After much negotiation and discussion, it was decided to call in an independent investigator to examine the facts impartially. His appointment was, as it turned out, somewhat controversial, since many of the experts involved were not convinced that he had the seniority, the experience, or indeed the years to be competent. The man concerned was Duncan Sandys.

Sandys was then 35, and Joint Parliamentary Secretary to the Ministry of Supply; and, despite what the critics said, he was clearly in an excellent position to infuse a note of greater urgency into the investigation. However, the opposition continued; Sandys had been invalided out of service after a car crash in Wales during his earlier Z-battery days; he had married Diana Churchill shortly afterwards, and so had become the Prime Minister's son-in-law. The critics probably felt that the situation smacked of nepotism, but though the marriage may well have helped the Prime Minister and Mr Sandys to get to know each other better, there can be little doubt that he was, in fact, right for the job.

After seeing the coverage of Intelligence photographs that had been ordered, it was Duncan Sandys who, in April 1943, asked for a more detailed coverage of the Peenemünde area – though even he, at the time, had no notion of just how important the move would prove to be. As a result, Flight-Lieutenant Kenny of RAF Medmenham found himself looking at the Peenemünde photographs again. Alongside the buildings on the island he noted an elongated structure which he could only interpret as sludgeways for dredging operations. Everyone else in his section agreed. In reality the objects were rather more sinister – these were the first V-1 launching ramps ever to be seen by English eyes. Indeed, a few days later a photograph revealed the vapour cloud of a rocket test, and even the rocket itself was visible.

In May several 'cylindrical objects' were photographed. Yet, despite the attention being devoted by British experts to the possibility of German rocket attack, and the general knowledge of what, roughly, a rocket would have to look like, still no definite diagnosis was forthcoming. In the following month more pictures were taken, and once again the interpreters were looking at the German rockets ready for firing. (One of them was actually shown by Flight-Lieutenant Kenny to the Prime Minister during an official visit to Medmenham!) It was in July that Dr Jones observed that, unless he was very much mistaken, there appeared to be large rockets in some of the photographs. As a result the interpreters eventually conceded that giant 'torpedoes' might be the explanation after all.

Decisive factor

One obvious answer was near at hand. Within weeks there were heavy raids on Peenemünde, and with the recognition of the nature of the threat it was possible to keep a more constructive watch on German progress. As V-1 and V-2 installations were spotted, they were bombed; and there can be no doubt that the aerial photographs – which by the end of the war would be able to show the presence of people from a height of over 30,000 feet – were a leading factor in the British onslaught against the German secret weapon establishments.

Certainly it is true to say that the lessons learned during the war years have been taken to heart since. Many of the technical developments have since been applied by the new generation of rocketeers – the space explorers, and the satellite-based Intelligence investigators – that mark the endeavour of the modern world.

A Japanese dive-bomber swoops on USS Hornet *while a torpedo plane circles, Battle of Santa Cruz*

DIVE-BOMBERS

'WHEN WE SAY DIVE WE MEAN STRAIGHT DOWN'

Scout-bomber/strike-reconnaissance attack aircraft are better known as dive-bombers, dive-bombing being their most spectacular and devastating form of attack. Though tried in limited form by the Royal Flying Corps during 1918, the first true dive-bombing was carried out by the US Marines in 1919 in Haiti and later in Nicaragua in 1928, using Curtiss Helldivers, when the lives of their comrades on the ground would have been endangered by any less precise bombing method.

As early as 1927 the US Navy began to practise dive-bombing with all types of aircraft except the VPB patrol bombers and VTB torpedo bombers, using such machines as the Curtiss BFC and BF2C (redesignated Hawk III and Hawk IV). These were developments of the Hawk I and II export Hawks and the US Navy's F11 C-2 fighters. During his many visits to the US, Ernst Udet was intrigued by this form of bombing, which was then being demonstrated at air shows by Maj Al Williams, USMC Ret, and others. Using his Gulfhawk I, a Curtiss F6C owned by the Gulf Oil Company, Williams was a regular performer and crowd-pleaser as he roared straight down to deposit a bag of flour or a dummy bomb on a target in front of the grandstand with almost unerring accuracy.

Udet was sufficiently impressed to persuade his old First World War chum, Hermann Göring, to purchase two of the export Hawks for demonstration and testing back in Germany. These two aircraft, with manufacturer numbers 80 and 81, were delivered during the first two weeks of October 1933 and cost the then high price of $11,500 each. When Udet took delivery, he promptly christened them Iris and Ilse and set out to convince the budding Luftwaffe that this was the way of the future. Unfortunately one of the Hawks crashed in 1934 and the other was relegated to the Berlin Museum after having been flown extensively in demonstrations and outlived its usefulness. At the end of the Second World War this remaining Curtiss Hawk ended up in the Air Museum at Krakow, Poland.

The tactic of dive-bombing was continuously practised by the US Navy, to a lesser extent by the Fleet Air Arm and, presumably, by the Imperial Japanese Navy. The nature and size of ships make them very elusive targets, especially when they take evasive action, and there is little possible benefit from near misses by bombs dropped in salvo. Unless it is a very near miss, causing hull damage by concussion, conventional salvo bombing could waste a lot of bombs with little or no effect on the target. With a dodging and turning ship, the difficulty of getting a direct hit is increased many times.

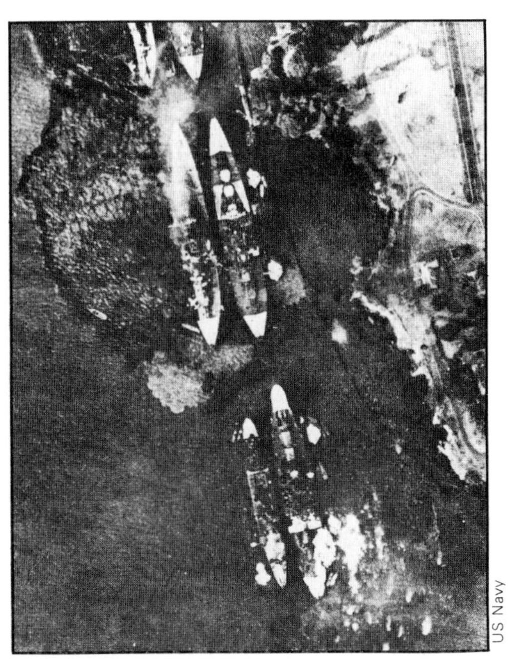

US Navy

'Battleship Row', Pearl Harbor, 7 December 1941 Bomb-aimer's view of stricken US Pacific Fleet

Single-engined aircraft normally used by the Navy do not carry many bombs, so it is necessary to use bombs of sufficient size to do meaningful damage and to place those bombs with great accuracy. Payloads rarely exceed 1½ tons, making it normal practice to use smaller bombs in quantity only against land or harbour targets. This does not mean that level bombing is not used in battle, for the sheer magnitude of bombs raining down on a fleet of ships or a landing zone from whatever source lends substantial assistance to the attacking force as a destructive and distractive element. There is also a strong possibility of a hit or near miss silencing a ship's anti-aircraft guns.

Dive-bombing, on the other hand, is a reasonably accurate delivery method in which the plane is lined up with the target so precisely that it is almost like sighting down the barrel of a gun. Evasive action is still possible, but the pilot can correct for this with small movements of the controls of his aircraft until the instant of release, which can be at a very low altitude, depending on the skill, daring and physical tolerance of the pilot.

Dive-bombers try to approach a target at high speed taking advantage of any cloud cover and, when possible, diving out of the sun in order to increase the problems for the defending anti-aircraft gunners. While speed is an asset in getting to the target, and away from it after the bomb is released, it is a disadvantage to build up too much speed in the dive. To do so increases the difficulty in aiming, as well as the stress on a plane and crew during the pull-out. Aerodynamically clean, the dive-bomber would build up a tremendous speed if not retarded by some means. It is therefore necessary to fit these aircraft with speed-retarding dive brakes. These enable the pilot to adjust his dive speed to be fast enough to press home the attack and still slow enough to pick up the target and make a good recovery.

Confusing the Gunners

The ideal is a true vertical dive which enables the pilot to confuse the ship's gunners by giving him a choice of any angle for recovery. Simply by rolling the plane while in the vertical position, the pilot can avoid giving away his intended direction of recovery and thus confuse the gunners who would normally try to 'lead' him like a clay pigeon during his recovery trajectory, when the plane is most vulnerable. The pull-out rate and altitude is determined more by what the pilot can stand, physically, than by what the plane can take.

Dive-bomber pilots are quick to point out that 'when we say dive, we mean straight down'. However, it did not always work out that way in practice, for the pull-out often caused the pilot to black out due to blood being driven from the pilot's head by centrifugal force (referred to as 'Gs'). Medical scientists and technicians combined forces to develop anti-G suits to retard the flow of blood from the pilot's head by exerting pressure on arterial pressure points and the stomach area, reducing, or at least delaying, the normal tendency to black out.

Contrary to general belief, a pilot does not just line up a target, particularly a moving target, in his sights and hold this position. He continues to fly the plane, adjusting for wind, target movement and, most probably, bursts of flak. During the dive he must avoid skidding or the bomb will be deflected away from the aiming point. Finally, the pull-out point must be determined and this varies with the pilot's personal tolerance for the centrifugal force and the type of bomb, since he wants to be levelled out and well on his way before the bomb bursts.

Among the advantages of dive-bombing is the fact that anti-aircraft fire never has succeeded in stopping a dive-bombing attack, and it is far more accurate than other systems. Ideally, an attack should be a coordinated effort between the dive-bombers to disable the target ship and torpedo bombers to come in for the kill. As one wag put it, 'If you want to let in air, you use bombs, and if you want to let in water you use torpedoes'.

The spectacular aspect is well known but the second, and equally important, function of this type of aircraft is scouting for an enemy force. The strike-reconnaissance/scout-bomber must have the range to carry out this mission as well – and sometimes both missions must be combined. Such was the case when Lt-Cdr C Wade McClusky set out to find the large Japanese fleet which was headed for Midway Island.

The fleet had been reported by a US Army B-17 to be headed toward the island, but numbers and types of ships were missing from the brief radio transmission. McClusky led an air group of 33 Douglas SBDs of VB 6 and VS 6 off the *Enterprise* in search of the enemy force. Unknown to McClusky, the Japanese Fleet had turned and was steaming north-east instead of toward the island. Not finding them in the expected position, he continued to search until he made contact and began the attack that was to become the Battle of Midway. A few minutes later a second group, VS 3 and VS 5 from the *Yorktown*, led by Lt-Cdr Max Leslie, joined the battle. In the ensuing action, the Japanese lost four carriers, the *Kaga*, *Akagi*, *Hiryu* and *Soryu*. This decisive victory was accomplished at a cost of 32 casualties and the loss of all but six of the 41 torpedo bombers from VT 8 and VT 6.

At the outbreak of the Second World War the aircraft considered to be in this combat grouping were the British Blackburn Skua, the Japanese Aichi D3A Val and the US Douglas SBD Dauntless. As the war progressed, lessons learned in the various engagements were incorporated in the aircraft under development. Among the planes of this second grouping were the Nakajima B6N1/2 Jill and the Aichi B7A1 Grace, the Curtiss SB2C and the Fairey Barracuda (discussed under the heading of torpedo bomber/attack aircraft). The Barracuda, as noted, was designed or adapted to do virtually everything and ended up doing none of its tasks exceptionally well.

One of the least known aircraft of the war was the Blackburn Skua. This lack of recognition would be strange except that at the time the Skua was making its mark in history, censorship was the order of day. The Skua was not produced in any great quantities so it was not seen sitting around every airstrip as were Moths and Cubs. In fact records show that only 165 were manufactured. But among its accomplishments it is credited with the destruction of the first German plane by a British aircraft during the war. The event took place on 25 September 1939, when a Skua shot down one of three Dornier Do 18 flying boats which were shadowing British fleet units off the coast of Norway.

State of the art

The Skua, like the Aichi Val and the Douglas SBD, represented the state of the art of the late 1930s, each reaching fleet operation status in 1937–39 and all scheduled for replacement just prior to the outbreak of war. HMS *Ark Royal* received six Skuas in November 1938, just in time for the opening action of the war. Operationally, the Skua played a very active role in the early days of the war, not because of great faith in dive-bombing on the part of the Royal Navy who favoured the torpedo as a weapon, but because in many instances it was the only aircraft available.

Blackburn Skua
The Royal Navy's first operational monoplane was conceived as a dual purpose fighter and dive-bomber, and saw combat in Norway, over Dunkirk and Dakar
Span: 46 ft 2 in *Length:* 35 ft 7 in *Engine:* Bristol Perseus XII, 890 hp *Armament:* 4 Browning mg; 1 Lewis mg *Max Speed:* 225 mph at 6500 ft *Ceiling:* 19,100 ft *Range:* 760 miles *Bombload:* 1 × 500-lb bomb

For example, in early April 1940 when the Germans launched their attack on Norway and Denmark, the cruisers *Köln* and *Königsberg* along with a gunnery training ship, *Bremse*, were to attack the port of Bergen. The shore-based batteries damaged the *Königsberg* sufficiently to cause her to tie up to a breakwater at Bergen. This news was transmitted to the Royal Navy who dispatched the only aircraft available, the Skua. Two squadrons, 803 and 800, totalling 16 Skuas, loaded with 500-lb bombs and enough fuel for a 600-mile round trip, managed to struggle off the airfield at Hatston in the Orkneys on 10 April 1940. Diving out of the sun, the traditional attack position for dive-bombers, the pilots of the Skuas managed to score at least three direct hits, plus numerous near misses which caused the *Königsberg* to disappear in a sheet of flames and debris. The cost to the Royal Navy was three damaged Skuas and one lost.

During the evacuation of Dunkirk in June 1940, all available aircraft were pressed into service to provide air cover. Skuas from 801 and 806 Squadrons took their place along with other aircraft types to provide much needed cover for the beleaguered British Expeditionary Force. After Dunkirk, the Skuas saw action in the Mediterranean, where 800 and 803 Squadrons, on board the *Ark Royal*, attacked units of the French Fleet, dive-bombing and putting out of action the new 35,000-ton battleship *Richelieu*.

There followed several engagements aiding convoys en route to the besieged island of Malta. Finally, in 1941, the Skuas were replaced by Fairey Fulmars for operational flying, but continued in service as trainers and for target towing. The rapid pace of aircraft development with the beginning of the war proved too fast for the sturdy Skua which had been designed in 1934 and first flown in 1937.

The Skua was an all-metal, single-engine monoplane. The fuselage, in compliance with specifications 0.27/34, was designed to be waterproof. It was divided into three watertight compartments to provide flotation should a ditching at sea be necessary. This was a valuable foresight as a number did ditch.

Production aircraft were fitted with the Bristol Perseus XII sleeve-valve engine – a unique engine, substituted for the Bristol Mercury which was required to outfit the Bristol Blenheim.

Blackburn Roc
The tactical concept of the Roc – bringing its four-gun turret to bear in broadside attacks on enemy aircraft – proved a failure and the type saw little combat, ending its days as a target tug
Span: 46 ft *Length:* 35 ft 7 in *Engine:* Bristol Perseus XII, 890 hp *Armament:* 4 × ·303 Browning mg *Max Speed:* 223 mph at 10,000 ft *Ceiling:* 18,000 ft *Range:* 810 miles

The Skua was the first all-metal monoplane to reach operational status with the Fleet Air Arm and was the first British aircraft designed specifically for dive-bombing. One surprising detail in view of its slow speed (225 mph max) was its alternative role of fighter and the location of the fuel tanks in the fuselage between the front and rear cockpits. A similar tank location in the De Havilland DH-4 of the First World War earned for it the unenviable name of 'Flying Coffin', but this was before self-sealing fuel tanks were developed.

The rugged but awkward angled landing gear and tail hook, plus the folding wing panels, completed the Skua's fitting-out for carrier service. Range was 760 miles; endurance was 4.5 hours at cruising speed of 145–165 mph.

Its armament was modest. Typical of that found in aircraft at the beginning of the war, it consisted of four forward-firing ·303 cal Browning machine-guns mounted in the wings and a single ·303 cal Lewis gun in a flexible mount in the rear cockpit. Ordnance consisted of one 500-lb bomb carried externally on a fork mount to ensure clearance of the propeller and up to eight 30-lb bombs on external wing racks. The latter were used primarily for practice since the only bombs of any value in this weight class were anti-personnel fragmentation bombs.

The Aichi D3A 'Val', built in 1937, was by far the most important of the Japanese dive-bombers and was considered obsolete by the time it was used so effectively at Pearl Harbor. Although the Yokosuka D4YI Suisei (Comet), code named by the Allies 'Judy', was in the development stage, it was not to see service until February 1944 off Truk Island, so the Val really had the war to itself in the dive-bomber class. It was the first all-metal dive-bomber built by the Japanese and was based on engineering knowledge obtained from the Heinkel He 118 which had been purchased by the Japanese for study purposes.

Slow and vulnerable

The Val was not too popular because of its relatively slow top speed of 232 mph and was also quite vulnerable in spite of the agility characteristic of Japanese aircraft of that period. Like its contemporaries it carried a single 550-lb bomb externally. For shorter ranges this load was supplemented by two smaller bombs fitted to wing racks, each of about 130 lb.

The devastation of Pearl Harbor was largely due to the Val. Following that historic attack the Val's next appearance was in the Indian Ocean in April 1942 where, for the second time, the Japanese convinced an anxious world that sea power was at the mercy of air power, particularly if the ships did not have adequate defensive air power of their own. It was an expensive lesson in ships and men, for the British carrier *Hermes* and the cruisers *Cornwall* and *Dorsetshire* all were sunk.

Following the major battles of Midway and Coral Sea, where the Japanese lost the major part of their trained and experienced

The American battleship USS Arizona *reduced to a blazing hulk by Japanese dive and torpedo bombers*

US Navy

aircrews, the accuracy of their bombing fell to 10% hits in contrast to the 80% and 82% hit ratio that prevailed when they attacked the British ships in the Indian Ocean. The Japanese never managed to replace the experienced pilots lost in these battles.

Failure of the Yokosuka D4Y Judy to meet the operational requirements resulted in a continuation of production of the Val in an improved model, the Aichi D3A2, fitted with a more powerful engine, the Kinsei 54, and additional fuel capacity to increase the operating range.

Imperial War Museum

'Vals' in formation. They were the first Japanese type to bomb US targets

From China to Leyte Gulf

In addition to the Pearl Harbor attack and the fateful battles of the Coral Sea and Midway, the Val was present in the earlier operations in China, at Wake Island, Darwin, Eastern Solomons, Santa Cruz, Philippine Sea (known as the 'Marianas Turkey Shoot') and finally the Battle of Leyte Gulf. By this time, Japan no longer had a carrier force and all navy aircraft, regardless of their intended use, were forced to operate from land bases. From this point onward, attacks by the Japanese consisted mostly of Kamikaze attacks. For this, the remaining Vals were converted to single seat configuration.

The Val was a single engine, low-wing monoplane whose fixed landing gear had streamlined covering over the legs and pants over the wheels. The fixed landing gear was one of the most obvious identification characteristics and contributed to lack of speed but was considered an asset when the plane was in its bombing dive. To facilitate stowage aboard carriers, the wing tips could be folded at a point six feet inboard from the tips. Like other aircraft of this period, its armament was not highly regarded. It carried two 7·7-mm guns firing forward and a single 7·7-mm gun mounted in the rear cockpit for defensive purposes and for strafing the decks of enemy ships as the bomb run was completed.

A total of 1294 Vals were produced between 1937 and 1944, 478 of which were the earlier model 11s (D3A1), powered by the 1075 hp Mitsubishi Kinsei 43 radial air-cooled engine. The second variant, the Model 22, powered by the Mitsubishi Kinsei 54, a twin-row 14 cylinder engine, boosted the power to 1200 hp and increased the speed to 266 mph. A total of 816 of the Model 22s (D3A2s) were built between 1942 and 1944.

Aichi D3A2 'Val'
This rugged carrier-borne dive-bomber was in the forefront of the attacks on Pearl Harbor and on the Royal Navy in the Indian Ocean, and sank more Allied fighting ships than any other Axis aircraft type
Span: 47 ft 2 in *Length:* 33 ft 5 in
Engine: Mitsubishi Kinsei 54, 1100 hp at 20,000 ft *Armament:* 3×7·7-mm mg *Max speed:* 267 mph at 9845 ft *Ceiling:* 34,450 ft *Range:* 840 miles *Bombload:* 1×550-lb plus 2×132-lb bombs

John Batchelor

A flight of US Navy Dauntless dive-bombers heads for the Japanese base at Palau in the western Pacific

DOUGLAS SBD DAUNTLESS

The SBD dive-bomber, approaching obsolescence by 1941, was one of the most important instruments in the American victories and still outperformed its successor, the Helldiver at Coral Sea, Midway, and the Philippine Sea
Span: 41 ft 6 in *Length:* 33 ft *Engine:* Wright Cyclone, 950 hp *Max speed:* 255 mph at 14,000 ft *Ceiling:* 25,200 ft *Range:* 773 miles *Armament:* 2 × ·5-in mg *Bombload:* 1 × 500-lb bomb

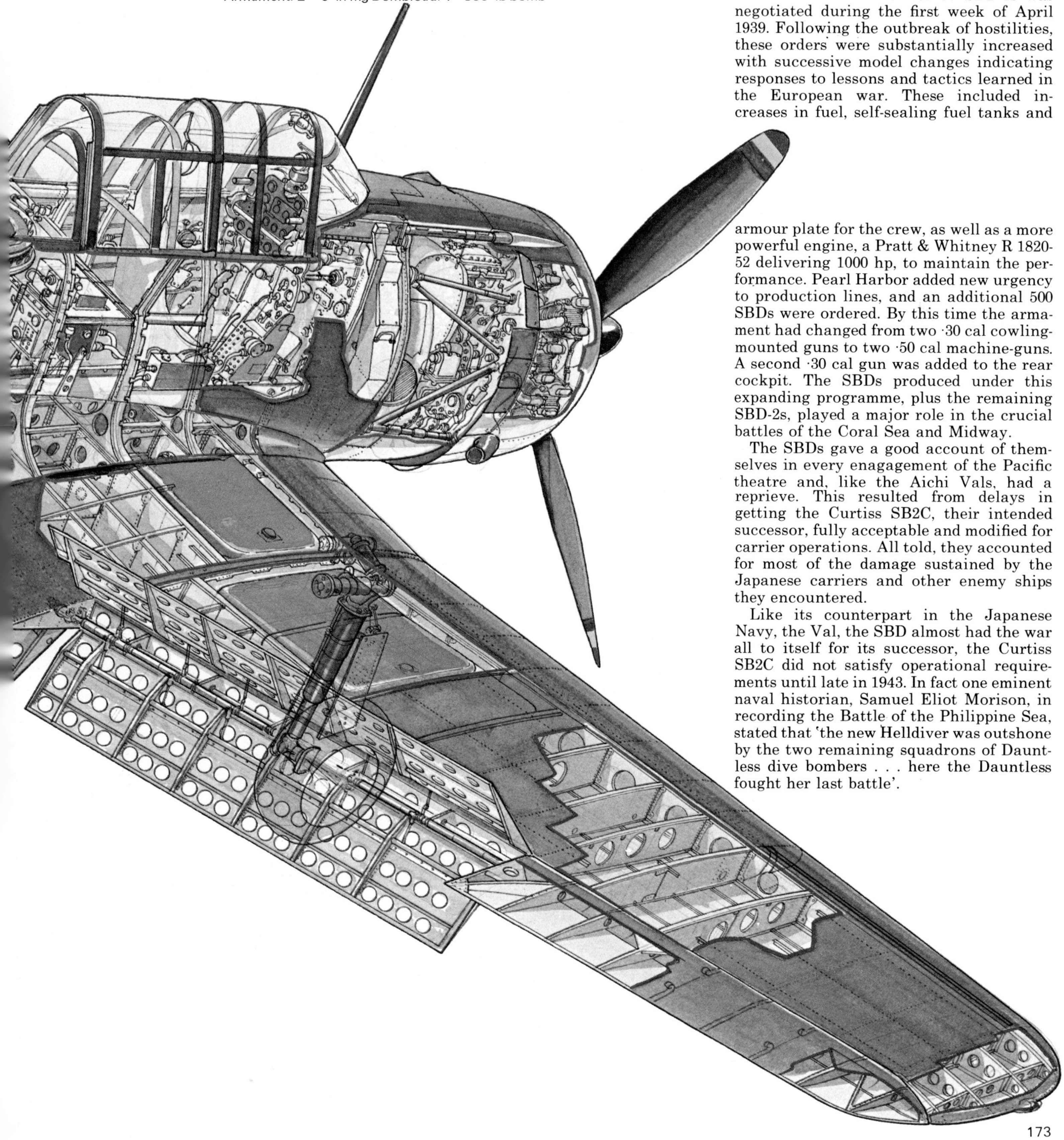

Designed in 1938 and accepted by the US Navy in February 1939, practically on the eve of war, the Douglas SBD Dauntless nevertheless represented pre-war technology. Fortunately, its design was quite adaptable, within limits, to changes dictated by combat experience. Above all it was a compact, rugged machine that could take a lot of punishment at the hands of both friend and foe. Friends were likely to expect too much from it in load carrying and handling and an enemy target or aircraft could be expected to throw everything at it.

The SBD had only barely passed its teething period when war broke out. The first planes were accepted in February 1939 and the first contract for 57 SBD-1s was negotiated during the first week of April 1939. Following the outbreak of hostilities, these orders were substantially increased with successive model changes indicating responses to lessons and tactics learned in the European war. These included increases in fuel, self-sealing fuel tanks and armour plate for the crew, as well as a more powerful engine, a Pratt & Whitney R 1820-52 delivering 1000 hp, to maintain the performance. Pearl Harbor added new urgency to production lines, and an additional 500 SBDs were ordered. By this time the armament had changed from two ·30 cal cowling-mounted guns to two ·50 cal machine-guns. A second ·30 cal gun was added to the rear cockpit. The SBDs produced under this expanding programme, plus the remaining SBD-2s, played a major role in the crucial battles of the Coral Sea and Midway.

The SBDs gave a good account of themselves in every enagagement of the Pacific theatre and, like the Aichi Vals, had a reprieve. This resulted from delays in getting the Curtiss SB2C, their intended successor, fully acceptable and modified for carrier operations. All told, they accounted for most of the damage sustained by the Japanese carriers and other enemy ships they encountered.

Like its counterpart in the Japanese Navy, the Val, the SBD almost had the war all to itself for its successor, the Curtiss SB2C did not satisfy operational requirements until late in 1943. In fact one eminent naval historian, Samuel Eliot Morison, in recording the Battle of the Philippine Sea, stated that 'the new Helldiver was outshone by the two remaining squadrons of Dauntless dive bombers . . . here the Dauntless fought her last battle'.

Aichi B7A Ryusei (Shooting Star) 'Grace'
Exceptionally large for a Japanese carrier aircraft, the B7A was designed for a new class of ships. The loss of the Imperial Navy's carriers saw the big attack bomber operating only fitfully from land bases
Span: 47 ft 3 in *Length:* 37 ft 8 in
Engine: Nakajima Homare 23, 1670 hp at 7875 ft
Armament: 2×20-mm cannon; 1×7·92-mm mg
Max speed: 352 mph at 21,490 ft *Ceiling:* 36,910 ft *Range:* 1151 miles *Bombload:* 1764-lb torpedo or 1800 lb bombs

Armament of the SBD-5 (the most numerous variant of the type) consisted of two ·50 cal guns mounted in the top deck of the cowl and a brace of ·30 cal flexible-mounted guns in the rear cockpit for the radio-operator.

Ordnance could consist of a variety of loads including (published specifications to the contrary) a 1600-lb bomb on the centre rack plus two 100-lb bombs on wing mounts, all externally mounted. In a scouting configuration, drop-tanks could be attached to the wing mounts for greater endurance.

In the final version of the SBD-6, the engine was the 1350 hp Pratt & Whitney R-1820-66 and the published weights were 6554 lb empty and 10,882 lb at gross take-off weight. Unlike most of its contemporaries, the SBDs did not have folding wings to improve their shipboard stowage ability. Instead they had the same basic wing construction as their parent, the Northrop XBT-2 (XSBD-1), the Northrop Gamma and the ubiquitous DC-3 Dakota. The similarities of design are more than incidental.

Designed to replace the Douglas SBD, the Curtiss SB2C Helldiver was long overdue in combat. A succession of problems and modification programmes delayed the first squadron delivery of SB2C-1s until December 1942, a full year after Pearl Harbor. The original contract for the XSB2C-1 had been negotiated and signed in May 1939. Between these two dates a seemingly endless series of problems conspired to delay production. Difficulty with stability and control tests, cooling problems and loss of test aircraft kept engineers and test pilots busy for many months trying to resolve the problems as they occurred. In addition to design problems there was the question of engineering the plane for production by the thousand. Parts that normally would have been handmade out of a number of small components now were redesigned for mass production, often resulting in single unit forgings to economise on both man-hours and weight.

Weight reduction was an ever-present

Curtiss SB2C Helldiver
Designed to fit the standard US carrier deck-elevator, the Helldiver suffered constant stability problems but it won honours in the USN's last dive-bomber action at Leyte Gulf, and in the attacks on the Japanese super-battleships *Yamato* and *Musashi*
Span: 49 ft 9 in *Length:* 36 ft 8 in
Engine: Wright R-2600-8, 1700 hp *Max speed:* 294 mph *Ceiling:* 23,000 ft *Range:* 695 miles

albatross around the necks of the SB2C engineers. The SB2C was designed to carry bombs 50% heavier than those carried by the SBD it was to replace, and this added weight was to be carried in an internal bomb-bay. This was difficult to accomplish for two reasons. Firstly, increasing loads were being hung on the SBD in response to combat necessity and bombs 50% heavier were also larger, making it difficult to carry them internally. Secondly, external racks, while increasing the frontal drag, also permitted a wider variety of sizes and configurations.

By the time the problem areas were determined and the appropriate corrections made by modifications, the war was well under way. Most of the really big and decisive battles were over by 11 November 1943 when Squadron VB 17 from the *Bunker Hill* equipped with SB2Cs attacked the harbour at Rabaul. From this date until the end of hostilities the Helldiver was the standard dive-bomber, USN, replacing the SBD in all remaining major actions of the war.

Only a small number of SB2Cs were ordered by Allied forces. The Royal Australian Air Force ordered 150 A-25As, a land-based Army version, but took delivery of only ten, since by this late date there was no longer a requirement for land-based dive-bombers. Twenty-six SBW-1Bs were delivered to the Royal Navy from Canadian Car & Foundry Production. Like the Helldiver, which carried on a traditional Curtiss name, the A-25As were also to carry a traditional name of 'Shrike'.

The 'Beast', as it was called by its crew, was not particularly well liked, although it established a good record before the end of the war. It could carry up to 2000 lb of bombs in the bomb-bay and was tested to carry a Mk 13 torpedo though this was never used during the service life of the aircraft. In a similar vein the SB2C-2 was tested with floats with the idea of using it for close support of expeditionary landings. This configuration was never to see combat use. Depending on the dash number, the SB2Cs were armed with either four ·50 cal machine-guns or two 20-mm cannons plus two ·30 cal machine-guns in a flexible mount for the rear seat gunner.

Cancellation recommended

Directional stability was to plague the design during all its operational life. The short fuselage required to fit two aircraft on to each of the 40 ft × 48 ft elevators contributed to this. To improve the directional stability, the engine was moved forward one foot and compensating area added to the fin and rudder. On shake-down carrier qualification tests aboard the *Yorktown*, the SB2Cs had many problems, including structural failure, collapsed tail wheels and missed hook contact. Based on this experience, the ship's commander, Capt J J Clark recommended cancellation of the entire contract. This was in June 1942, only six months after Pearl Harbor when all the emphasis was on planes to win the war.

This was hardly the climate to start over again with a new design. As a result all parties pressed on, throwing good money after bad to make it work in spite of all its deficiencies. Under any other circumstances Captain Clark's recommendation would have spelled the end of this plane. The production lines turned out 600 SB2Cs before all the bugs were under control. The 601st plane was the first to be delivered without a stop-over at one of the modification centres.

With the Pacific war nearly over and most of the Japanese carriers destroyed or damaged beyond repair there was really little left for the Helldivers to do. The one exception was the Battle of the Philippine Sea, where the SB2Cs gave a good account of themselves. They were to be the last dive-bombers of the Second World War.

After undergoing additional modifications to make them suitable for different tasks, the SB2Cs and their derivatives the A25s, were phased out of service and most of them scrapped.

Of limited importance during the Second World War, but built to requirements and from lessons learned in combat, the Aichi B7A1 *Ryusei* (Shooting Star) 'Grace' did not establish any record of action from carriers although it was designed as a follow-on to the Nakajima B6N2 Jill and the D4Y Judy. Only 105 of these aircraft plus nine prototypes were completed before the end of hostilities and after the destruction of the Japanese carrier fleet.

The Grace was the first Japanese aircraft to be designed for internal stowage of a 1760-lb torpedo. In addition, it could carry a second torpedo externally. It was distinctive in design, having an inverted gull-shaped wing for the same reason as the Vought F4U Corsair, namely the need to shorten and therefore reduce weight of the retractable landing gear. It also featured coordinated droop ailerons (10°) which provided additional drag and lift when the flaps were lowered.

An 1825-hp Nakajima 'Homare' 12 engine made the Grace substantially faster than its predecessors with 356 mph being achieved during tests. Unfortunately, the engine was not fully developed, needed time-consuming maintenance and lacked reliability.

Among the dive-bomber category the Junkers Ju 87 is not generally known as a carrier-based type though as a dive-bomber it is probably better known than any other plane. The fact that it was considered and even stressed and fitted with catapult and arrester hook escapes any but the most intense researcher.

At the beginning of the war Germany had under construction an aircraft carrier, the *Graf Zeppelin*, which was abandoned early in the war. The principal dive-bomber, the Ju 87C or Stuka as it was best known, was to have been the dive-bomber assigned to this ship. The Ju 87C was a special modification of the Ju 87B-1 and was fitted with jettisonable landing gear in anticipation of the probability of a ditched landing. This

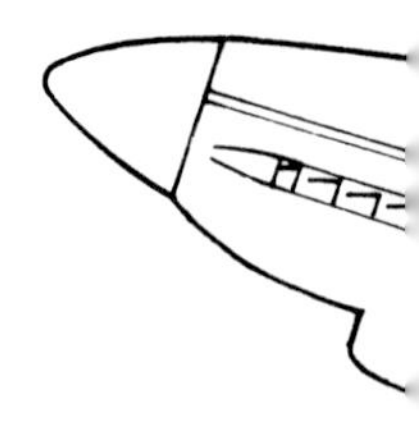

Yokosuka D4Y2 Suisei (Comet) 'Judy'
The fastest carrier-borne dive-bomber of the Second World War, the 'Judys' were very susceptible to battle damage and took a savage mauling in the 'Marianas Turkey Shoot'
Span: 37 ft 8 in *Length:* 33 ft 6 in
Engine: Aichi Atsuta AE1P, 1340 hp at 5580 ft
Armament: 2×7·7-mm mg; 1×13-mm mg
Max Speed: 360 mph at 17,225 ft
Ceiling: 35,105 ft *Range:* 909 miles
Bombload: 1234 lb

Towards the end of the war, many types of Japanese

modification feature, to the best of our knowledge, was not used by Germany's ally Japan in the design of the Aichi D3A Val.

Only a few were produced and these were converted back to the Ju 87B-1 configuration when the carrier plans were abandoned.

The last of the carrier-based attack bombers or dive-bombers built by the Japanese was the Yokosuka D4Y1 *Suisei* (Comet), Allied code name 'Judy', which first entered service in its scout-reconnaissance role during the Battle of Midway. It was produced in a variety of models and in surprisingly large numbers – 2038 – which exceeded the production of Curtiss SB2Cs, even though Japan was under direct attack during the latter days of the war and disruption was certain to prevail during this time.

The Judy was interesting in a number of respects, one of which was the use of the liquid-cooled Aichi AE1A Atsuta 12 engine which produced 1200 hp. Most carrier-based aircraft, with the notable exception of the D4Y1 and D4Y2 Judy and the British Fairey Barracuda and Fulmar used air-cooled engines. Even the later versions of the Judy, D4Y3 and D4Y4, used air-cooled radial engines, the Mitsubishi Kinsei Model 62.

In each of these exceptions to the existing tradition, the resulting aircraft was very attractive. The Aichi Atsuta 12 was a version of the German Daimler-Benz engine built under licence. Poor reliability prompted the Aichi engineers to suggest changing the engine to the 1560-hp Mitsubishi Kinsei 62, an air-cooled radial. This modification was designated D4Y3. Of the 2038 D4Ys produced, at least 822 were powered by radial air-cooled engines.

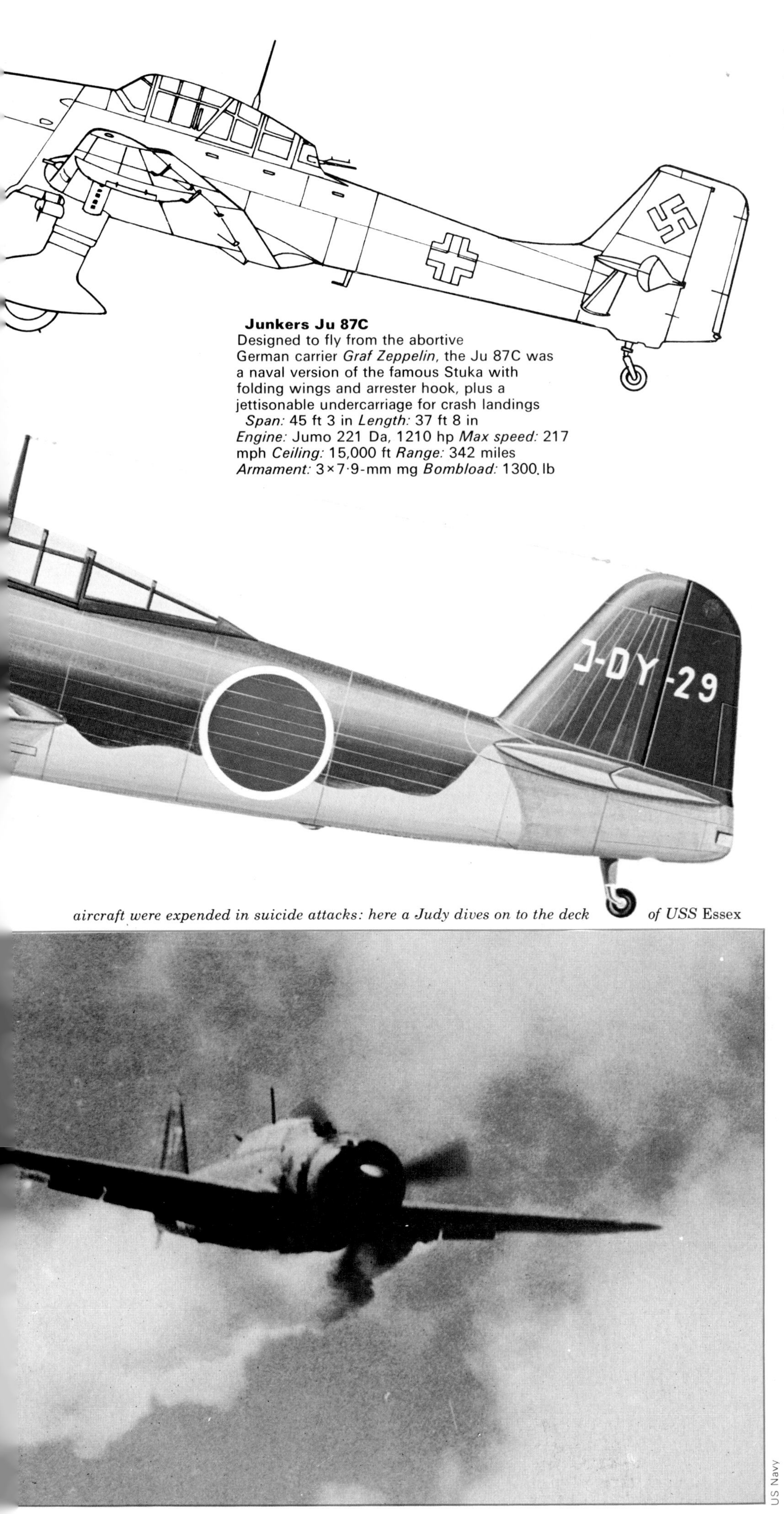

Junkers Ju 87C
Designed to fly from the abortive German carrier *Graf Zeppelin*, the Ju 87C was a naval version of the famous Stuka with folding wings and arrester hook, plus a jettisonable undercarriage for crash landings
Span: 45 ft 3 in *Length:* 37 ft 8 in *Engine:* Jumo 221 Da, 1210 hp *Max speed:* 217 mph *Ceiling:* 15,000 ft *Range:* 342 miles *Armament:* 3×7·9-mm mg *Bombload:* 1300 lb

aircraft were expended in suicide attacks: here a Judy dives on to the deck of USS Essex

US Navy

Reconnaissance only

Like all naval carrier aircraft, the Judy was of a multi-purpose design, for dive-bombing/attack, night-fighter and finally as special attack (Kamikaze) aircraft. Until March 1943 the Judy experienced wing flutter when tested as a dive-bomber. As a result they were restricted to their reconnaissance configuration when they made their combat debut, flying from the aircraft carrier *Soryu* during the Battle of Midway. The D4Y2, powered by the 1400-hp Aichi Atsuta 32, had the airframe strengthened, making it serviceable in its intended principal role of dive-bomber. Unfortunately, time was running out for the Japanese fleet, much of which had slipped beneath the Pacific waters. During the period when the type was being strengthened, those produced were in action as reconnaissance aircraft flying from all the carriers remaining in action.

The night-fighter conversion was an interesting but relatively ineffective modification designed to attack B-29s which were then making regular runs over Japan. In this conversion a 20-mm cannon was fitted in the fuselage to fire upward at a 30° angle. Interesting as it was this was not an effective weapon since the plane itself had very poor performance. It had a 50 to 80 mph speed advantage over its predecessor, the D3A Val, and the contemporary SB2C. However, the latter carried at least twice the load of the D4Y and had almost twice the range.

Due to the pressure of the American forces moving steadily toward the Japanese homeland, desperate measures were adopted. The Kamikaze groups used specially designed aircraft, as well as modified production aircraft. Like the remaining Vals, the Judy was also used for this duty.

Pearl Harbor:

Imperial War Museum

THE ATTACK

Oahu, Hawaii, December 7, 1941

The Pearl Harbor air-strike was an act of ruthless, machine-like destruction: never before had air power virtually wiped out an enemy fleet in one action. True, the Japanese victory was not quite complete: two American aircraft-carriers of the Pacific Fleet escaped to play a vital role in the months ahead. But the main Japanese triumph was unalterable: after Pearl Harbor there could be no immediate American challenge to the Japanese battle fleet

In the original Japanese war plan, the complex multi-pronged southward drive by expeditionary forces to capture Thailand, Malaya, the Philippines, and the Dutch East Indies was to be covered by the whole Imperial Navy. The United States Pacific Fleet, envisaged as hurrying towards the Philippine Sea to the rescue, was to be harried by air and submarine attacks launched from the Marshall and Caroline Islands, before being brought to action by the superior Japanese Main Fleet.

Early in 1941, however, critical eyes had been brought to bear on this plan by the C-in-C of the Japanese Fleet, Admiral Isoroku Yamamoto. Unlike the military faction led by General Tojo, Yamamoto saw clearly that—though the well-prepared Japanese war machine would be able to carry all before it in the initial stages of such a plan—the immense industrial potential of the United States must eventually bring it to a halt. When that time came, a negotiated, compromise peace would be possible only if Japan had so firmly established herself in her newly-won empire in south-east Asia that eviction would be an insuperable task for the Western Allies. For this, time was needed. Yamamoto wished to gain this time by eliminating the US Pacific Fleet.

An early convert to the decisive role of carrier-borne air power in naval warfare, he had the perfect weapon to his hand in the shape of the six fleet carriers equipped with the most advanced naval aircraft in the world. Rear-Admiral Takijiro Onishi, Chief-of-Staff of the shore-based XI Air Fleet, was instructed to examine the possibility of a carrier-borne air attack on Pearl Harbor. Onishi recruited the best-known hero of such operations in the China War, Commander Minoru Genda. By May 1941, working in great secrecy, Genda had completed a study which promised success—provided that all six fleet aircraft-carriers were committed and complete secrecy imposed.

Put before the Chief of the Naval General Staff, Admiral Nagano, the plan was turned down on the grounds that the aircraft-carriers were required for the southwards drive, and that an operation depending absolutely on surprise at the end of an ocean passage of 3,400 miles was too much of a gamble. Nevertheless, confident that Nagano's objections would be overcome in time, Yamamoto gave orders for a special training programme to be begun by his carrier air squadrons, concentrating on torpedo, dive-bombing, and high-level bombing attacks on targets in enclosed stretches of water such as Kagoshima Bay in southern Kyushu. Except for a handful of staff officers engaged with Genda in preparing the detailed plan, the object of these practices was revealed to no one.

Technicians at the main naval base of Yokosuka were given the task of adapting airborne torpedoes so that they could be dropped from a greater height than normal and still enter the water in a horizontal attitude, thus avoiding diving deeply at the beginning of their run. The need for such a

Japan's Naval Strike Aircraft

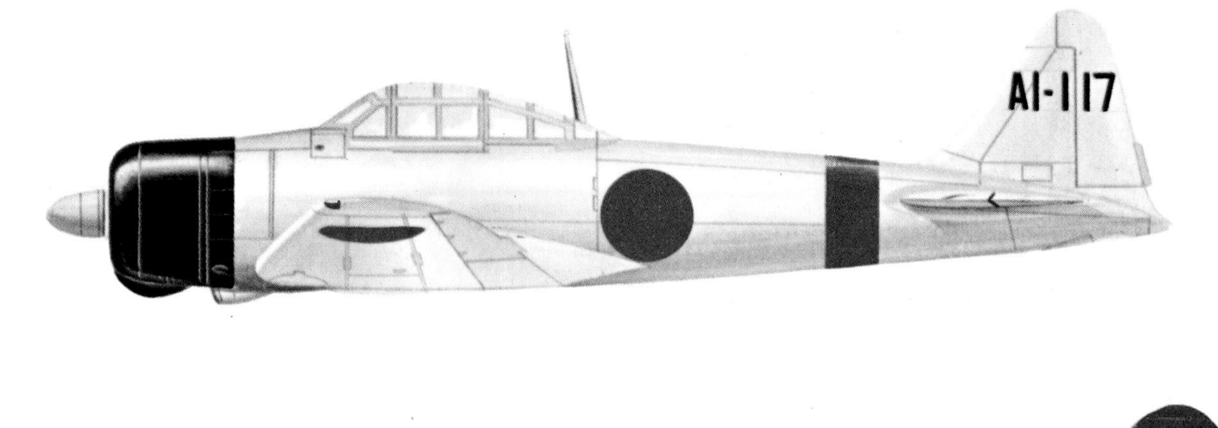

Mitsubishi A6M2 Zero-sen *(Zeke)* The Zero outclassed every Allied fighter in the Pacific in December 1941. Light and manoeuvrable, it had a high fire-power, and could also act in a fighter/bomber role. **Max speed:** 351 mph. **Max range:** 975 miles. **Armament:** two 20-mm cannon, and two 7·7-mm machine-guns

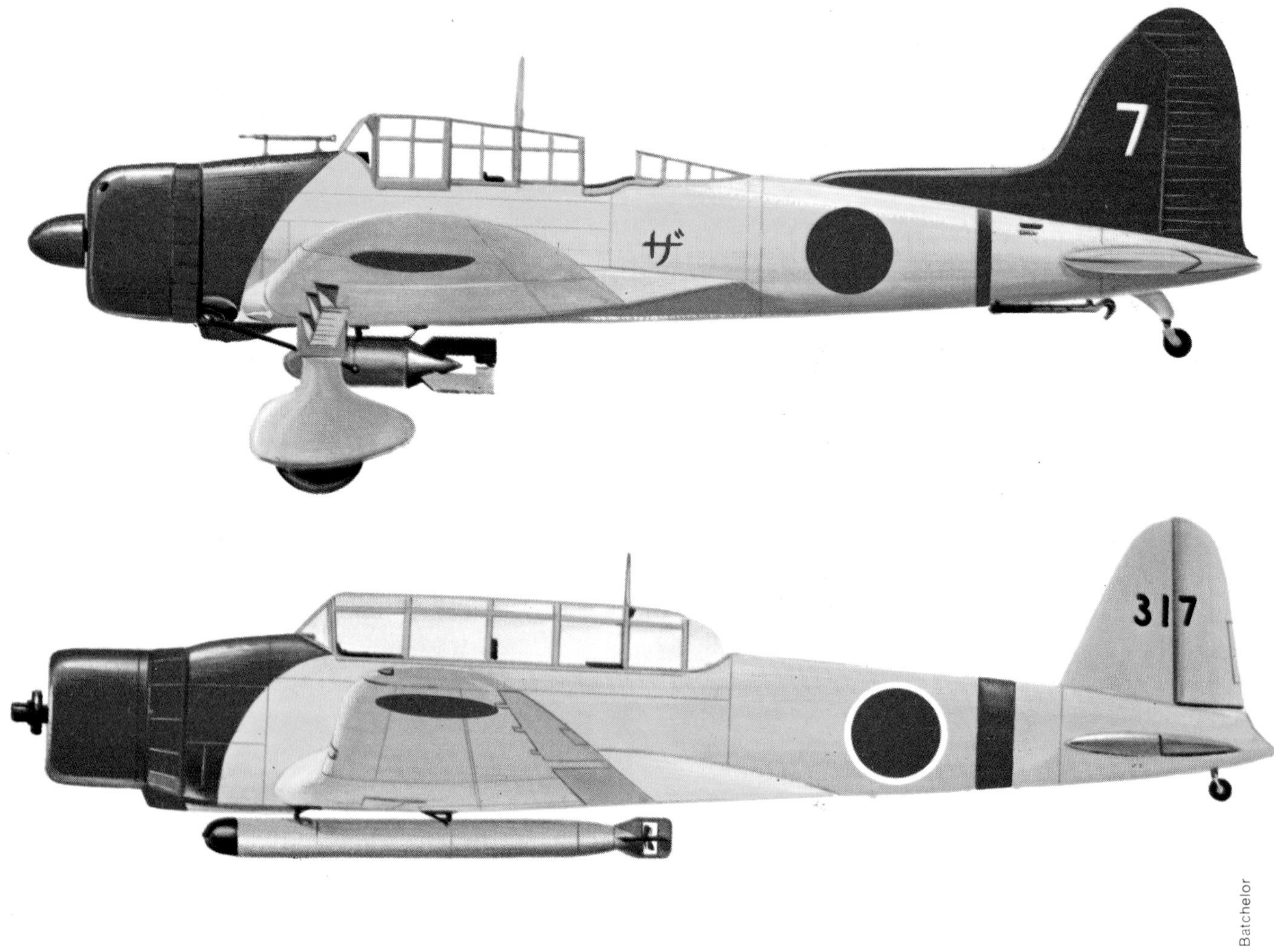

Aichi D3A2 *(Val)* The *Val* carried home the Japanese dive-bombing attacks at Pearl Harbor. It had been designed in imitation of the pre-war German dive-bombers, and was Japan's first low-wing, all-metal monoplane dive-bomber. **Max speed:** 266 mph. **Max range:** 970 mi. **Bomb load:** 816 lb.

Nakajima B5N2 *(Kate)* At the time of Pearl Harbor, the *Kate* was Japan's principal torpedo-bomber, and could also serve as a level bomber. **Max speed:** 235 mph. **Max range:** 1,400 miles. **Weapon load:** one 1,764-lb torpedo

John Batchelor

refinement was not revealed; but by September, torpedoes fitted with special fins which would enable them to be effectively launched in the narrow, shallow waters of Pearl Harbor had been successfully tested and production was being feverishly pressed ahead to meet a deadline in mid-November.

The withdrawal of the Japanese aircraft-carriers to home waters resulted in a cessation of radio messages intercepted by the radio traffic analysis units in Hawaii and Manila. The Japanese carrier-force was for a time 'lost' to the American trackers. These correctly assessed the reason and in due course the aircraft-carriers came on the air again; but the accuracy of this appraisal was to lead to a similar and, this time, faulty assumption later.

The Konoye Cabinet fell on October 16, the new Prime Minister being the aggressive General Tojo. Alarm signals, announcing a 'grave situation' went out from Washington to Admiral Kimmel and General Short – heads of the navy and the army commands in Hawaii. But now these reports were tempered by the continuing Washington belief that an attack on Russia's maritime provinces was the most probable Japanese move. The fact that the Japanese navy had, as long ago as July, finally won the long argument with the army with regard to war plans, and that the southward drive had been agreed upon, had escaped the US Intelligence organisations.

So far as General Short was concerned, this appreciation greatly reduced the probability of any attack on US territory. He was more concerned with the presence of a large local Japanese population in Hawaii and the need to take precautions against sabotage and subversion.

The possibility of an air attack if and when war should break out had been perfunctorily considered, and occasional drills on a peace-time footing had been concerted with the navy. They had not been very impressive. A few primitive, mobile radar sets had been arriving since August and had been set up at various points round the coast of Oahu. They suffered many teething troubles and breakdowns. Communications between them and a temporary control centre, and between the control centre and the various commands, was by means of the public telephone system. Operators both of the radar sets and at the control centre were to a large degree untrained or inexperienced; the various units were manned only for a few hours each day, principally for training purposes.

Nevertheless, progress towards efficiency seemed adequate to the general who had informed Admiral Kimmel as long ago as August that the aircraft warning system was 'rapidly nearing completion'.

To the navy, however, both in Washington and Hawaii, the new situation seemed more fraught with threatening possibilities. Although a Japanese attack on Russia was considered the most likely, an attack on the United States or Great Britain was by no means ruled out, and the Pacific Fleet was ordered to take 'due precautions including

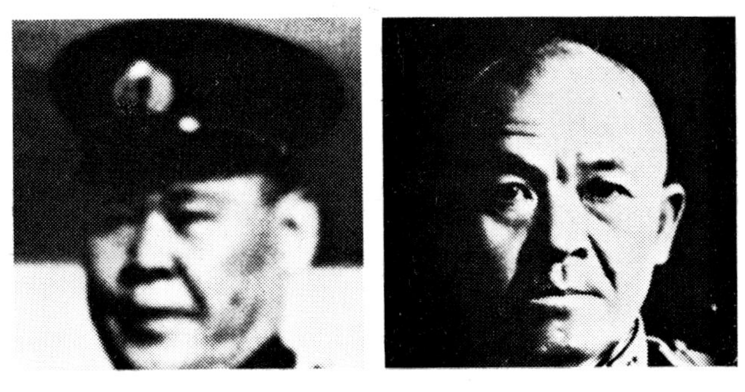

◁ Admiral Kimmel, US Navy commander at Pearl Harbor (far left). General Short, the US Army commander there

▷ Admiral Nagano, Chief of the Japanese Naval General Staff (left). Admiral Nagumo, commander of the Japanese carrier force

such preparatory deployments as will not disclose strategic intention nor constitute provocative actions against Japan'.

In case of hostile action by Japan against US merchant shipping, all vessels in the western Pacific were ordered to make for friendly ports. Instructed to 'take all practical precautions' for the safety of airfields at Wake and Midway (the air staging posts on the route to the Philippines), Kimmel dispatched reinforcements of marines, stores, and ammunition to both islands and stationed additional patrol planes there. Extra precautions were also taken against surprise submarine attack in the exercise areas.

The idea of an air attack on Pearl Harbor or its defences appears to have crossed nobody's mind.

Objective: Pearl Harbor

At about this time, aboard the Japanese aircraft-carrier *Akagi,* flagship of Vice-Admiral Chuichi Nagumo, commanding the Fast Carrier Striking Force, a scale model of Pearl Harbor was unveiled under the eyes of the assembled officer pilots of the air groups and of Yamamoto himself. Now, under seal of secrecy, Yamamoto gave them the electrifying news of their intended objective. Training was thereafter resumed at an even fiercer intensity and with added enthusiasm. On November 1 the C-in-C issued the basic operation order, naming Sunday, December 7 (Hawaiian time) as the day of destiny. Two days later Admiral Nagano was at last won over to give his consent.

Between November 10/18, singly or in pairs, the ships of Nagumo's striking force – six aircraft-carriers, two battleships, three cruisers, nine destroyers, and eight oil tankers – slipped away from their anchorages and, by devious routes, steered for a secret rendezvous in the desolate Tankan Bay on Etorofu, the largest of the Kurile Islands far to the north. Strict radio silence was imposed on all from the moment of sailing while the remainder of the fleet at Kure in the Inland Sea kept up a flow of radio messages for the benefit of American radio intelligence.

At about this time, too, and with the same secrecy, 16 submarines of the 'Advanced Expeditionary Force' left harbour and headed eastwards across the wide Pacific. Five of them carried two-man, midget submarines charged with the task of penetrating Pearl Harbor simultaneously with the air attack. The remainder, besides scouting for the carrier force, were expected to find opportunities for attacking any American ships that escaped seawards.

Signs of some impending major Japanese operation were not lacking in Hawaii or Washington. On November 1 the radio traffic analysis unit had reported that all call-signs of Japanese naval units had been changed. In itself, this was not of outstanding significance: change of call-signs from time to time was a normal procedure. But a second change only a month later, on December 1, could only be an indication of preparations for active operations.

In the interval the radio traffic analysis organisation had managed to re-identify a certain number of units, but had lost all contact with the Japanese aircraft-carriers. Relying upon previous correct assumptions on similar occasions, they decided that the latter were in home waters of the Inland Sea.

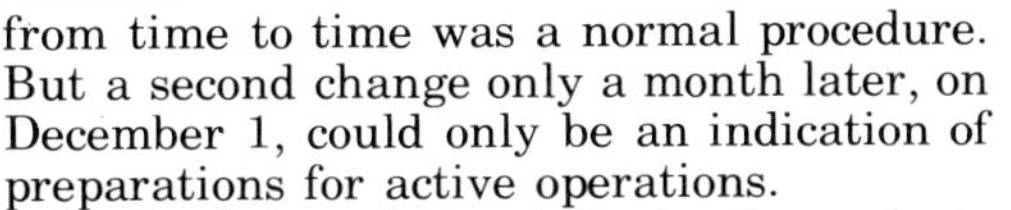

From the other source of radio intelligence, the 'Purple' diplomatic code, information of a different sort was obtained, information which, if examined alongside the results of traffic analysis, must have been seen to be of the most sinister import. From November 5 onwards, message after message to the Japanese envoys in Washington warned them that the 25th was a deadline for a successful outcome of their negotiations. On the 22nd, Tokyo extended the deadline to the 29th after which, they said, 'things will automatically begin to happen'. Meanwhile, each side conveyed to the other its final terms for a settlement, the Japanese on the 20th, the Americans on the 26th: neither set of terms was conceivably acceptable by both sides and only deadlock was achieved.

So, by the last week of November, negotiations had finally broken down. War was now clearly imminent; but as the Americans were bound to avoid being the first to open fire, or even to take any provocative action, choice of time and place lay in the hands of the Japanese. Intelligence sources, the deciphering system in particular, had to be relied upon to give advance warning. A steady flow of intelligence had, indeed, been reaching the American government and service chiefs, which clearly indicated preliminary Japanese moves for some southwards expedition.

On November 24 American naval commanders abroad were warned that a 'surprise aggressive move in any direction including attack on Philippines and Guam is a possibility'. Three days later a signal from the Chief of Naval Operations opened with the ominous phrase: 'This dispatch is to be considered a war warning,' and went on to list the possible Japanese objectives as 'either the Philippines, Thai or Kra Peninsula or possibly Borneo.' The Hawaiian Islands or even Wake and Midway were not mentioned.

The day before this signal was sent, from the cold windswept waters of Tankan Bay the anchors of Admiral Nagumo's ships had been weighed to rise, streaming mud and water, and thud home in the hawse pipes. A flurry of white foam round the ships' sterns as their screws pointed them to the harbour entrance and then, one by one, they had gathered way and vanished into the stormy northern sea to head due east along the 43rd Parallel, clear of all regular shipping routes.

Aboard the unlovely, flat-topped aircraft-carriers an atmosphere of excitement prevailed. A few hours earlier all but the privileged few already 'informed' had heard, for the first time, the mission on which they were bound – to strike a devastating surprise blow on the sea power of the nation which stood between Japan and the glorious destiny mapped out by her leaders. A feeling of joyful anticipation could be sensed everywhere, except perhaps on the admiral's bridge of the flagship *Akagi,* where Nagumo contemplated the risks of an operation to which he had only hesitantly agreed under the persuasions of his aviation staff officers and his Commander-in-Chief, Admiral Yamamoto.

An unsuspecting target

Some 3,000 miles away to the south-east lay Pearl Harbor, bathed in its perennial sunshine, all unaware of the approaching blow. The only visible results of the war warning signal was a certain amount of movement of army trucks and soldiers as General Short's troops took up their stations for 'Alert No. 1' – precautions against sabotage by the local Japanese population. In naval units, where a minor degree of alert with a proportion of anti-aircraft guns manned had been in force for some time, no additional precautions were taken. The aircraft-carriers *Enterprise* and *Lexington* had been dispatched to carry Marine fighter planes to Wake and Midway. The remainder of the fleet stayed at sea during the week, returning for leave to Pearl Harbor on weekends.

During the first few days of December, the deciphering system revealed that Japanese diplomatic and consular posts had been ordered to destroy most of their codes and ciphers and all confidential documents.

Though this was an added indication that war was imminent, it did not point at Pearl Harbor as a possible Japanese objective. A series of intercepted reports from the Japanese consul at Honolulu on the berthing of ships of the Pacific Fleet might have done so had it not been that similar reports from consuls elsewhere were also being regularly transmitted. The loss of contact with the carriers by radio traffic analysis was another important straw in the wind – but, as mentioned before, this was misinterpreted to indicate that they were lying peacefully in home waters. No long-range reconnaissance flights were ordered, nor was any alteration made in the fleet training programme which would bring the fleet into harbour at the weekend for rest and recreation.

But the overriding reason for discounting any likelihood of an attack on Pearl Harbor was the clear evidence of a huge amphibious operation in the south getting under way. Japanese troop convoys heading into the Gulf of Siam had been sighted and reported by British and American air reconnaissance planes during December 6, and American opinion simply could not conceive that the Japanese had the capacity—or the imaginative boldness—to mount a simultaneous operation elsewhere involving their carrier force.

Far away to the north-west of Hawaii, the Japanese carrier force had advanced unseen, its concealment assisted by foul weather, storms, and fogs which, however, added to the anxiety of Nagumo, who had to have a spell of fine weather in which to replenish from his tankers. Then, on December 1, came the awaited confirmatory signal for the operation—*Niitaka Yama Nobore* ('Climb Mount Niitaka')—announcing that the die had finally been cast. At last, on the 2nd, the weather moderated, the warships' oil tanks were refilled, and the following evening the force turned south-east, heading for a position 500 miles due north of Pearl Harbor, which it was planned to reach on the evening of the 6th. Now the final decision to make the attack lay with Nagumo, a decision which would depend on last-minute messages from the Japanese agent in Honolulu as to the presence of the US Pacific Fleet.

Meanwhile, messages in the 'Purple' code, indicating Japanese rejection of the American ultimatum of November 6, were being intercepted and deciphered. The main message was a long-winded presentation of the Japanese case transmitted in 14 parts, only the last of which contained anything new—a formal breaking-off of negotiations. This was in American hands by 0300 hours Washington time on the morning of December 7.

At about the same time (the evening of the 6th by Hawaiian time), emotional ceremonies of dedication were taking place aboard the aircraft-carriers of Nagumo's force. All hands had been piped to assemble on the flight decks, patriotic speeches were made; to the masthead of the *Akagi* rose a historic signal flag used by Admiral Togo before the Battle of Tsushima 36 years earlier; and when the excited ships' companies finally dispersed, the force swung round on to a southerly course and at high speed steered for the flying-off position arranged for dawn on the morrow.

While the ships raced on into the night, another vital message in the 'Purple' code was being read, deciphered, and translated at the Bainbridge Island radio station, Washington. It instructed the Japanese ambassador to submit the message breaking off negotiations to the US Secretary of State at precisely 1300 hours, December 7 (Washington time). Translated by 0600 hours, it was not until 0915 that this reached Admiral Stark, Chief of Naval Operations, and another 35 minutes passed before it was seen by the Secretary of State. It was pointed out to both that 1300 hours would be about sunrise at Honolulu. Yet a further 70 minutes of inactivity passed before General Marshall, Chief of the US General Staff, saw the message on return from his regular morning ride. He at once proposed to Stark that a joint special war alert should be sent out. When Stark disagreed, Marshall drafted

▽Zeros on the flight-deck of one of Nagumo's carriers. (Bottom) A Japanese *Kate* torpedo-bomber prepares for take-off

US Navy

US Navy

his own message to army commanders, concluding: 'Just what significance the hour set may have, we do not know, but be on the alert accordingly.' It was handed in for enciphering and dispatch at 1200 hours. But long before it reached Pearl Harbor, the crump of bursting bombs and torpedo warheads had made it superfluous.

At that moment (0630 hours Hawaiian time) the first wave of Nagumo's striking aircraft had already been launched – 50 bombers, each armed with one 1,760-pound armour-piercing bomb, 70 more each carrying a torpedo, 51 dive-bombers each loaded with one 550-pound bomb, and 43 Zero fighters to provide escort and to deliver ground-strafing attacks.

It had not been without doubts and hesitation that Nagumo had given the final order – for the agent's report on ships in Pearl Harbor had made no mention of the US aircraft-carriers *Lexington* and *Enterprise* which, in fact, were away on their missions to Wake and Midway. The lure of the eight imposing battleships of the Pacific Fleet and their numerous attendant cruisers and destroyers, however, had been sufficient to harden his decision.

Off Pearl Harbor, indeed, the first acts of war were already taking place. The US minesweeper *Condor*, carrying out a routine sweep, signalled the destroyer *Ward*, on night patrol, that a periscope had been sighted, but no alarm was passed to the harbour control station. After the *Ward* had searched fruitlessly for more than two hours, the periscope was again sighted and marked by smoke bomb from a seaplane, and the destroyer then gained contact with a midget submarine and sank it with depth-charges and gunfire at 0645 hours. A message reporting the encounter reached the Port Admiral at 0712 hours, and, after some delay, was passed to Admiral Kimmel.

At 0750 hours, as Kimmel was hurrying to his office, an explosion on Ford Island, the Naval Air Station, in the middle of the harbour, gave the first startling indication that Pearl Harbor was under air attack.

Since 0615 hours the first wave of Japanese aircraft had been winging their way southwards led by Commander Mitsuo Fuchida, the air group commander, in the leading high-level bomber. A pair of trainee radar operators at the mobile station at Opana, practising with the equipment beyond the normal closing-down hour of 0700 hours, saw them appear on the screen at a range of 137 miles and plotted their approach just as a matter of interest: they were told by the information centre, to which they reported, that the contact could be disregarded as it was probably a flight of Fortresses due to arrive that morning from the mainland.

Fuchida led his swarm of aircraft down the western coast of Oahu, watched with idle curiosity by the many service and civilian families living along the shore, who took them for the air groups returning from the *Lexington* and *Enterprise*. By 0750 hours Fuchida could see across the central plain of the island to Pearl Harbor, its waters glint-

▽The US destroyer *Shaw* vanishes as its magazines explode. (Right) A *Val* dive-bomber, just after releasing its bomb US Navy

AMERICA'S AIR ARM

When the war in the Pacific opened, the American and Allied air forces were tactically and numerically inferior. Their standard fighter aircraft (F-2A Buffalo and the P-40) were totally outclassed by the Japanese Zero. The B-17 Flying Fortress bomber proved a formidable weapon, but for all its toughness and hitting power its value was jeopardised by the lack of Allied fighter protection—and this only time could remedy

◁ **Lockheed P-38 Lightning**
Known to the Germans as the *Gabelschwanzteufel* ('Two-tailed devil'), the Lightning first saw service in the Mediterranean theatre in late 1942, during Operation Torch. *Max speed:* 414 mph. *Max range:* 450 miles. *Armament:* one 20-mm cannon, four ·50-inch machine-guns; various combinations of bombs and rockets

Curtiss P-40 was the first mass-produced US monoplane fighter, and constituted more than half the US fighter strength at the beginning of the war. It was supplied to the RAF, where it was known as the Tomahawk. **Max speed:** 357 mph. **Max range:** 1,400 miles. **Armament:** two ·30, two ·50 machine-guns ▽

Brewster F-2A Buffalo was the US Navy's first monoplane fighter. Official vacillation resulted in its near obsolescence by the beginning of the Pacific war. **Max speed:** 321 mph. **Max range:** 965 miles. **Armament:** four ·50 machine-guns △

Boeing B-17 Flying Fortress served with the US Army Air Force throughout the war, also serving with the RAF. Japanese pilots respected its bristling armament. **Max Speed:** 300 mph. **Range:** 1,850 miles. **Armament:** up to 13 ·50 machine-guns; up to 8,000 lb of bombs

△ North American P-51B Mustang
The Mustang was to the US air force what the Spitfire was to the RAF – but the American fighter had a far greater versatility: it served as long-range fighter, as fighter-bomber, dive-bomber, for close support, and for photo reconnaissance. *Max speed:* 441 mph. *Max range:* 1,300 miles. *Armament:* four wing-mounted ·50-inch machine-guns; two 500-lb bombs (or extra fuel tanks)

▽▽ Bell P-39 Airacobra
The Airacobra was no match for the new fighter designs; but nevertheless it served in large numbers in Russia and with the Free French air forces. *Max speed:* 360 mph. *Max range:* 1,100 miles. *Armament:* one 37-mm, two ·50-inch machine-guns in nose; four ·30-inch machine-guns in wings

▽ Republic P-47 Thunderbolt
One of the most welcome surprises to the Allied fighter pilots was the ability of the bulky Thunderbolt (nearly twice as heavy as the Spitfire) to 'mix it' in combat with the more graceful Axis designs. *Max speed:* 426 mph. *Max range:* (clean) 637 miles. *Armament:* six or eight wing-mounted ·50-inch machine-guns; one 500-lb bomb

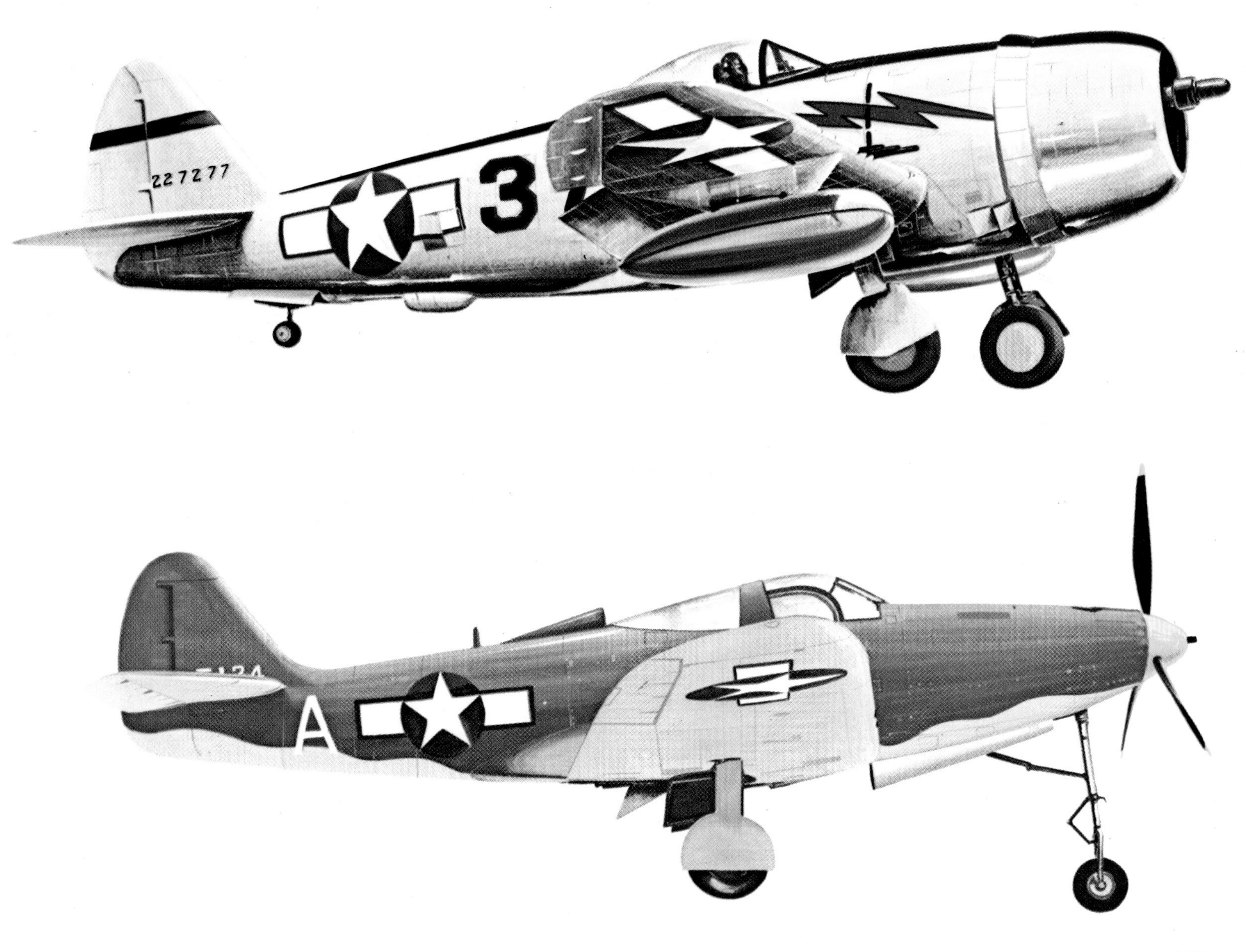

ing in the early sunshine of a peaceful Sunday morning, and through binoculars he was able to count the seven capital ships moored two by two in 'Battleship Row' on the eastern side of Ford Island (see map).

Surprise was complete: he gave the order to attack.

From endlessly repeated practice and meticulous study of maps and models of Oahu and Pearl Harbor, every Japanese pilot knew exactly what he had to do. While the squadrons of dive-bombers split up into sections which were to swoop simultaneously on the several army, navy, and marine airfields, the high-level bombers settled on to their pre-arranged approach course, bomb aimers adjusting their sights, and the torpedo-bombers began the long downward slant to their torpedo launching positions abreast the battleships. A few minutes before 0800 hours, to the scream of vertically plummeting planes, bombs began to burst among the aircraft drawn up, wing-tip to wing-tip in parade-ground perfection on the various airfields. Simultaneously the duty watch aboard the ships in 'Battleship Row', preparing for the eight o'clock ceremony of hoisting the colours, saw the torpedo-bombers dip low to launch their torpedoes and watched, horror-stricken, the thin pencil line of the tracks heading for their helpless, immobile hulls. Not an American gun had yet opened fire. Not an American fighter plane had taken off.

The absolute surprise achieved by the attack on the airfields, where the bursting of bombs was followed by the tearing chatter of cannon-fire from diving Zero fighters, eliminated any possibility of an effective fighter defence. In the harbour, five of the battleships—*West Virginia, Arizona, Nevada, Oklahoma,* and *California*—were rent open by torpedo hits in the first few minutes; only the *Maryland* and *Tennessee,* occupying inside berths, and the flagship *Pennsylvania* which was in dry dock, escaped torpedo damage. Other ships torpedoed were the old target battleship *Utah,*

US Navy

△Ford Island and 'Battleship Row' under Japanese attack; note explosions on far side of Ford Island, and Japanese aircraft

△Wrecked navy seaplanes after a raid: the Japanese disposed of any American challenge to their command of the air over Oahu

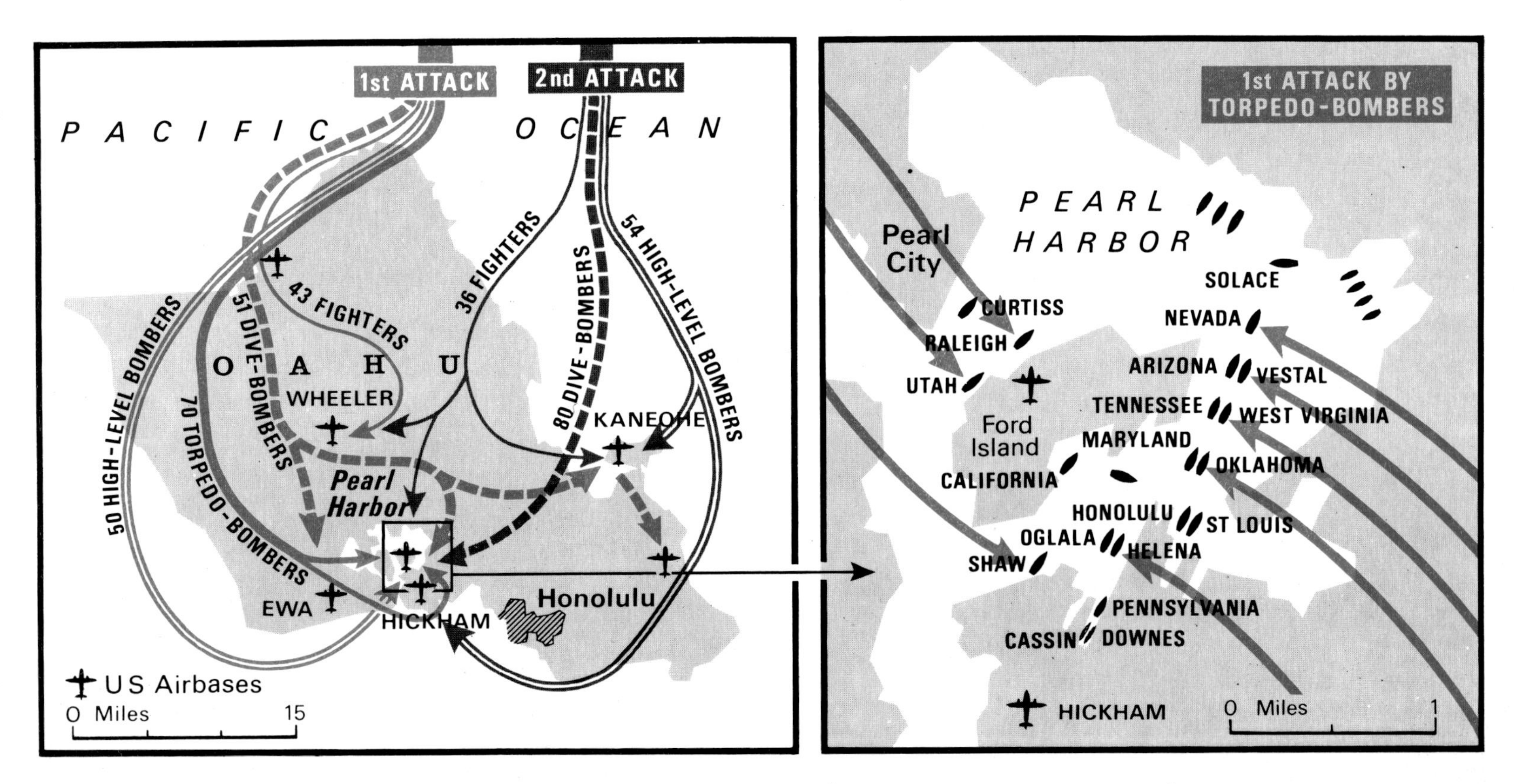

and the light cruisers *Raleigh* and *Helena*.

Nevertheless, although to the shudder and shock of underwater explosions was soon added the rising whine of dive-bombers and the shriek and shattering detonation of bombs from them and from the high-flying bombers, the American crews, for the most part, went into action with speed and efficiency, shooting down several of their attackers. Damage-control parties worked manfully to minimise the consequences of flooded compartments, counter-flooding to keep the foundering ships on an even keel, restoring electric and water power and communications, fighting the fires. One battleship, *Nevada,* even succeeded in getting under way and heading for the harbour entrance.

Meanwhile, however, high up above the smoke and confusion, hardly able at first to credit the total absence of any fighter opposition, and little inconvenienced by the sparse gunfire directed at them, Fuchida's high-level bombers were picking out their targets and aiming with cool precision. An armour-piercing bomb sliced through the five inches of armour of a turret in the *Tennessee* to burst inside it; another plunged down through the several decks to explode in the forward magazine of the *Arizona,* which blew up. Both the *Maryland* and the *California* were hit with devastating effect.

When a lull occurred at 0825 hours, as the first wave of Japanese aircraft retired, almost every US aircraft at the air bases was damaged or destroyed, the *West Virginia* was sinking and on fire, the *Arizona* had settled on the bottom with more than a thousand of her crew fatally trapped below. The *Oklahoma* had capsized and settled on the bottom with her keel above water; the *Tennessee,* with a turret destroyed by an armour-piercing bomb, was badly on fire; and the *California* had received damage that was eventually to sink her, in spite of all efforts of her crew. Elsewhere, all that was visible of the *Utah* was her upturned keel. The *Raleigh,* deep in the water from flooding and counter-flooding, was being kept upright only by her mooring wires.

While all this had been taking place, at least one Japanese midget submarine—besides that sunk by the *Ward*—had succeeded in penetrating the harbour, passing through the gate in the boom defences which had been carelessly left open after the entry of two minesweepers at 0458 hours. During a lull in the air attacks this submarine was sighted just as it was firing a torpedo at the seaplane tender *Curtiss*. The torpedo missed and exploded harmlessly against the shore, as did a second one. The submarine was attacked by the destroyer *Monaghan* and sunk by depth charges. Of the other three midgets launched from their parent submarines, two were lost without trace; the third, after running on a reef and being fired at by the destroyer *Helm,* was finally beached and her crew taken prisoner. The parent submarines and the 11 other large boats of the Advanced Expeditionary Force achieved nothing.

The second wave of Japanese aircraft—54 bombers, 80 dive-bombers, and 36 fighters, led by Lieutenant Commander Shimazaki of the aircraft-carrier *Zuikaku*—had taken off an hour after the first wave. They were met by a more effective defence and thus achieved much less. In the breathing space between the two attacks, ammunition supply for the US anti-aircraft guns had been replenished, gun crews reorganised, and reinforced; and a number of the Japanese dive-bombers were shot down. Nevertheless they succeeded in damaging the *Pennsylvania,* wrecking two destroyers which were sharing the dry-dock with her, blowing up another destroyer in the floating dock, and forcing the *Nevada*—feeling her way towards the harbour entrance through the billowing clouds of black smoke from burning ships—to beach herself. Meanwhile the high-level bombers were able to make undisturbed practice and wreak further damage on the already shattered ships.

At 1000 hours it was suddenly all over. The rumble of retreating aircraft engines died away leaving a strange silence except for the crackle of burning ships, the hissing of water hoses and the desperate shouts of men fighting the fires. For the loss of only nine fighters, 15 dive-bombers, and five torpedo-bombers out of the 384 planes engaged, the Japanese navy had succeeded in putting out of action the entire battleship force of the US Pacific Fleet.

To the anxious Nagumo the success seemed so miraculously complete, and the price paid so small, that when Fuchida and other air squadron commanders urged him to mount a second attack, he felt it would be tempting fate to comply. Against their advice, he gave orders for his force to steer away to the north-west to rendezvous with his replenishment aircraft-carriers, and thence set a course for Japan.

This was a bad mistake—but Nagumo, who was no airman, was not alone at that time in a lack of appreciation of the fact that the massive gun armaments of majestic battleships were no longer the most effective means of exercising sea power. In the vast spaces of the Pacific, only the aircraft-carrier had the long arms with which to feel for and strike at an enemy fleet—and a rich reward would have awaited a second sortie by his exultant airmen. Not only was the *Enterprise* approaching Pearl Harbor from her mission to Wake, and could hardly have survived a massed aerial attack, but the repair facilities of Pearl Harbor and the huge oil-tank farm, its tanks brimming with fuel, still lay intact and now virtually defenceless. Without them the naval base would have been useless for many months to come, forcing what remained of the US Pacific Fleet to retire to its nearest base on the American west coast, out of range of the coming area of operations in the south-east Pacific.

Thus Yamamoto's daring and well-planned attack failed to reap the fullest possible harvest—though undoubtedly the blow it delivered to the United States navy was heavy indeed. But it had one effect even more decisive than that on sea power, for it brought the American people, united, into the war.

Perhaps only such a shock as that delivered at Pearl Harbor could have achieved such a result.

Grumman F4F Wildcat
Grumman's first monoplane fighter for the US Navy, this tubby, highly manoeuvrable fighter put up heroic resistance to the Japanese onslaught of 1941 and early 1942, and was rushed into British service as the 'Martlet I'
Span: 38 ft *Length:* 28 ft 9 in *Engine:* Pratt & Whitney R-1830-76 Twin Wasp, 1200 hp at take-off *Max speed:* 330 mph at 21,100 ft *Ceiling:* 37,500 ft *Range:* 845 miles at cruising speed *Armament:* 4×·5-in mg

FIGHTERS

BOMBER ESCORT OR CARRIER PROTECTOR?

Designed to maintain local mastery of the air, the fighter and the fighter pilot must both be a rather special combination. In the Second World War the lesson was learned once again that any air force must have a high proportion of fighters. This was soon apparent when aircraft carrier commanders found it necessary to hold in readiness a substantial number of their fighter complement to protect their own ships from enemy attacks. It was necessary to maintain a Combat Air Patrol (CAP) constantly ready to divert or destroy attacking enemy aircraft. The problem was how many to keep in orbit in the vicinity of the carrier or its task force when at the same time the torpedo planes and the dive-bombers needed air support during their attacks.

It was often necessary to keep the majority of the fighters close at hand to protect the carriers. When this happened, the small number that could accompany the torpedo planes and/or the dive-bombers were usually totally inadequate and often resulted in a high loss rate to the attack planes. Conversely, should the planes be assigned to accompany the dive-bombers and torpedo planes then the carrier with its critically important landing deck was left in a vulnerable situation. To accommodate both these requirements, the percentage of fighters in relation to other types of aircraft rose from roughly 18% to 60% of the aircraft complement of the carrier.

Another factor which made these aircraft ratios necessary was the increasing use of fighters in an attack role, loaded with ordnance almost beyond belief. In these cases, the fighters operated in the role of fighter-bombers delivering bombs, rockets and/or napalm on the first attack wave, and reverting to their fighter role after dropping their ordnance stores. It was partially because of the multitude of attack functions taken over by the fighters that scout-bombers became less and less necessary as the war progressed.

In fighter aircraft superior speed, while an important consideration, is not adequate in itself, nor is rate of climb the whole answer. Manoeuvrability by itself is also meaningless, but to combine the three in a machine superior to those of an opponent is the goal of the aircraft designer.

In the case of naval aircraft, additional requirements are imposed by their operation at sea and often far from friendly land bases. Among these requirements is adequate endurance and the strength to withstand launching and retrieval. Prior to the Second World War, two-seater fighters were purchased, and well into the early part of the war such planes as the Fairey Fulmar were operated – not because of any outstanding superiority but because of a lack of anything better. They were adequate when attacking slow bombers or reconnaissance aircraft but were at a grave disadvantage when opposed by single-seat fighters. The additional crew member and the accommodations for him penalised the plane's action. The most successful and most numerous naval fighters of the Second World War were single-seat planes.

Japan, among the major naval powers, had the best shipboard fighters when the war began. The French were woefully inadequate, as were the British, and the US was only slightly better off. The European nations had almost totally neglected sea-based airpower for a variety of reasons. The US was still suffering from short rations and shortsightedness, a hangover from the depression years.

The Mitsubishi A6M2 was the outstanding fighter aircraft in the opening days of the Pacific war and came as a considerable surprise to most military authorities. The intensive security maintained by the Japanese largely accounted for this surprise. The A6M2, better known as the Zero or Zeke because of the designation of the aircraft as the Navy type '0' carrier fighter, was much maligned in the US as being a copy of one or more well known US aircraft. The Zero nevertheless gave a good account of itself and its pilots.

The US Grumman F4Fs were able to hold their own although the Zero had an advantage in most categories. By being able to absorb a lot of battle damage and still carry on, the F4F's four ·50 cal machine-guns were capable of tearing up the light structure and unprotected fuel tanks of the Zeros. High on the list of design criteria for the Japanese naval fighters was high manoeuvrability and high speed. To obtain these, it was necessary to compromise by using a light structure and by elimination of frills such as self-sealing fuel tanks and armour plate protection for the pilot and vital parts of the aircraft. They were, in fact, the correct choice for the war 'game-plan' of the Japanese commanders for a fast-moving war of short duration. Their misfortune was in not destroying the *Lexington* and *Enterprise* at Pearl Harbor.

New generation

The well-trained and heroic pilots of the US Navy, flying the rugged Wildcats and other carrier aircraft, held on and turned the tables when the new generation of planes was ready for combat operations. US planes like the Grumman F6F Hellcat were designed with the specific purpose of attaining air superiority over the Zero. The Japanese, on the other hand, did not have access to industrial resources to match those of the US, which was able to maintain production lines of F4Fs and SBDs while at the same time design and build the second generation aircraft.

The Japanese, in the meantime, were hard pressed to accomplish the same results although in retrospect one can only admire their determination, the variety of aircraft types and numbers produced during the war. The Zero, along with the Zeke and other variations, was the principal Japanese carrier fighter from the beginning to the end of the war.

In the European theatre the British Navy paid a high price for peacetime lethargy or perhaps for the honest ignorance of fiscal and military officialdom. When the war clouds were growing in intensity, the Fleet Air Arm, which attained an independent status in May 1939, was still using the Gloster Sea Gladiator, a conversion of the RAF's last biplane fighter.

The success of the Hurricane and Spitfire prompted the Royal Navy to request a monoplane fighter. This resulted in the Fairey Fulmar, a two-seater which was to become the Navy's first all-metal monoplane fighter. The Blackburn Skua, previously mentioned, was to have been an all-purpose machine supposedly capable of operating as a fighter as well as a dive-bomber, but as a fighter it was badly outclassed.

With this situation Britain, hardpressed on many fronts, built Fairey Fireflys and adopted the Grumman Martlet I, basically the F4F with the single row Wright R-1820 instead of the more normal twin row Pratt & Whitney R-1830. These Martlets were originally ordered by the French and were diverted to the Fleet Air Arm after the French capitulation in June 1940. They were well tested and coming off production lines at a rate to satisfy US and British requirements.

Holding the line

The plane that held the line and kept the Imperial Japanese Navy busy during the early stages of the war was the Grumman F4F, a comparatively small single-engine, mid-wing monoplane. A pugnacious looking machine in the air, it was almost ugly on the deck, propped up on its narrow tread retractable landing gear. In the early models, the gear was manually retracted by thirty turns of a crank at the pilot's right hand. This feature was never particularly liked by pilots for more often than not it resulted in a porpoising flight path just after lift-off. In any event it was better than that of the Polikarpov I-15, the little Russian biplane fighter used by the Republicans in Spain. In the I-15, each landing gear leg had to be cranked up independently by hand, resulting in a roll, or partial roll, first one way and then another.

The F4Fs, christened 'Wildcats', were just coming into carrier service when war broke out. The fall of France in June 1940 resulted in increased orders for the Wildcat which, up to this point, was going through the normal peacetime development progression of service trials leading to full acceptance by the Navy. The original design competition was announced in 1935 to replace the Grumman F3F-1 biplane then in

USS Hornet, *the carrier that launched Doolittle's raid on Tokyo and was later sunk off Guadalcanal*

US Navy

service. The competition was won by the Brewster F2A Buffalo but the US Navy gave Grumman a contract for a new prototype, designated XF4F-3. This turned out to be a very fortunate occurrence because, in service, the Buffalo showed a distressing weakness of the landing gear.

However, the Buffalo could easily outmanoeuvre the Wildcat in simulated combat but, on returning to the carrier, the odds were in favour of an unserviceable plane – not because of combat damage but because of landing damage. The F4F on the other hand was rugged and reliable in all situations but was lacking in climb and manoeuvrability when compared with its antagonist, the Japanese Zero. It more than made up for these deficiencies in its firepower of four (and later six) wing-mounted ·50 cal machine-guns, self-sealing fuel tanks and armour for pilot protection. The merit of these features was clearly demonstrated by the nearly seven to one combat-kill ratio over its opponents, many of them Japanese Zeros.

One design feature which caused problems and resulted in one fatal crash was inflation, in the air, of the specified flotation air bags. Elimination of these and the mechanism for hydraulically folding the wings provided space in the wings and weight reduction which made it possible to add another pair of guns and ammunition to bring the armament up to six ·50 cal machine-guns. This battery of guns proved to be the answer to any other deficiencies the Wildcat might have had, for when the pilot got on a target there was little doubt about the outcome.

Having quickly learned of the manoeuvrability and climb characteristics of the Zero, the US Navy pilots concentrated on head-on or diving attacks. In the head-on attack the Wildcat had the advantage of the high velocity ·50 cal guns, while the Japanese 7·7-mm machine-guns barely scratched the Wildcat and their slow-firing, low-velocity 20-mm cannon were quite inaccurate. The diving attack used the strength of the Wildcat, while its ability to manoeuvre even at high speed was another plus factor since the Zero was found to have problems with aileron control at the higher speeds encountered in dives. The F4F was never redlined for terminal dive speeds which is testimony to its durability.

The Wildcat was considered to be a transitional fighter by the US Navy, intended to hold on until a second generation could be produced. Whatever the intent, it is recorded fact that the F4F was present and gave a good account of itself and its pilots in most of the major engagements in the Pacific and in the Atlantic as well.

The F4F was present at Pearl Harbor, where 11 Wildcats were caught on the ground and nine destroyed. As the war progressed the Japanese pushed on with their attacks on Wake Island. This was one of the most heroic defensive battles, and one which was to spur the American war production efforts, bringing the Wildcat to the attention of the American public. With seven of the newly arrived Wildcats destroyed during the first Japanese attack, the remaining aircraft, never more than three in the air at the same time, succeeded in destroying a twin-engine Japanese bomber and at least one Zero in air combat. In addition, Capt Henry T Elrod, USMC,

Fairey Fulmar I
The Royal Navy's first 8-gun fighter, the Fulmar kept the two-seater layout for a navigator/observer and was outmatched by its land-based contemporaries and their naval derivatives
Span: 46 ft 5 in *Length:* 40 ft 3 in
Engine: Rolls-Royce Merlin VIII, 1080 hp
Max speed: 280 mph *Ceiling:* 26,000 ft
Range: 800 miles *Armament:* 8 × ·303-in mg

Blackburn Firebrand TF 5
Conceived as early as 1939, the Firebrand torpedo-fighter was dogged by development difficulties, and became operational in 1945, too late to see action
Span: 51 ft 3½ in *Length:* 38 ft 9 in
Engine: Bristol Centaurus IX, 2520 hp
Armament: 4 × 20-mm cannon *Max speed:* 340 mph at 13,000 ft *Ceiling:* 28,500 ft *Range:* 740 miles *Bombload:* 1 × 1850-lb torpedo or 2 × 1000-lb bombs

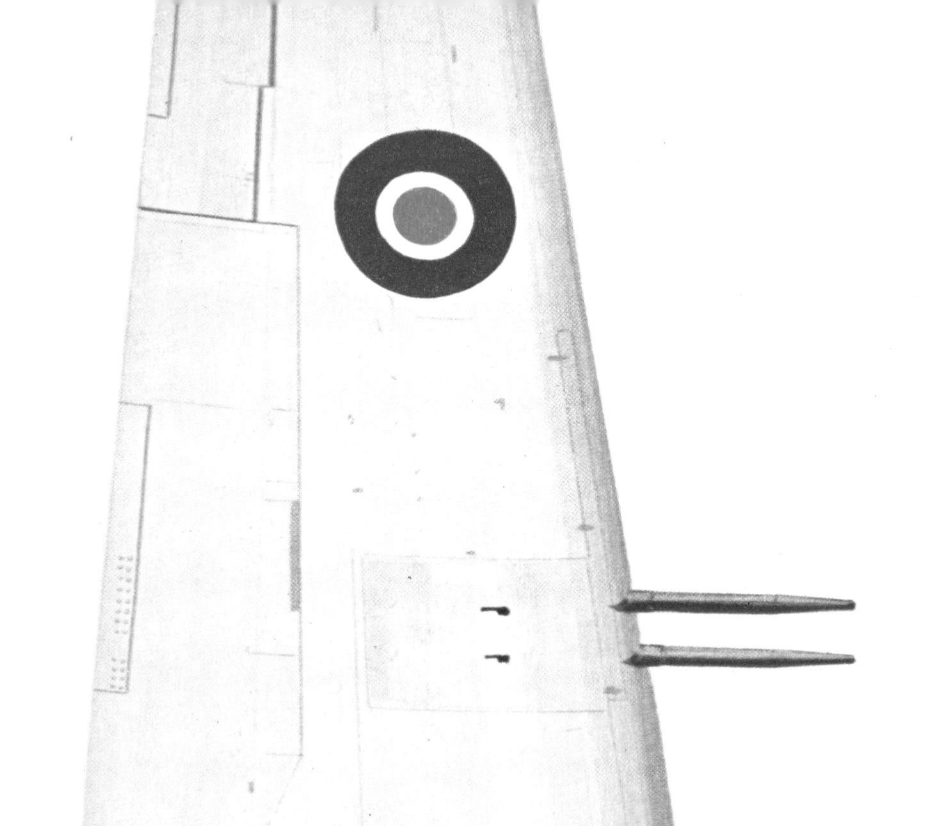

bombed and sank a Japanese destroyer before the defenders were overrun.

One of the first American heroes of the war was Lt Edward H 'Butch' O'Hare. On 20 February 1942 he and his squadron were flying Wildcats from the *Lexington* when they encountered a large force of Mitsubishi G4M1 Bettys returning to their base after a raid. In the ensuing battle, O'Hare shot down five enemy aircraft and damaged a sixth. He became one of the first US aces of the war and received the Medal of Honor.

The first of the folding-wing variants was the F4F-4 the prototype of which had a hydraulic folding system which was abandoned. The geometry of the characteristic Grumman wing-folding system was such that the wings were rotated some 90° about a central axis and folded back flush alongside the fuselage. This made the folding comparatively easy and, at the same time, reduced the overall height and volume of the Wildcat for stowage aboard ship. The F4F-4 made its debut at the Battle of Midway.

The Wildcat in any of its variations was a rugged machine and could not be considered inspiringly handsome by even its most avid admirer, but it could and did do the job it was designed to do. It was a chunky little mid-wing monoplane with a narrow-tread retractable landing gear, the mechanics and geometry of which had been well tested in earlier Grumman designs and dated back in concept to such planes as the Loening amphibians of 1927.

Pre-war design

Like so many of its contemporaries, the F4F's design dated back to the mid 1930s, its successor, the Grumman F6F, being the first plane to be designed from lessons and techniques learned during the war. Skill and adaptability on the part of the pilots, many of whom became aces flying Wildcats, made up for the plane's deficiencies.

Modifications were made along the way to adapt to changing conditions. The original four guns were increased to six, the solid wing of the F4F-3 became folding wings in the F4F-4 and FM-1, propellers were changed along with power plants, and the single-stage Pratt and Whitney engine was improved with the addition of two-stage, two-speed superchargers. In the FM-2, produced by General Motors, the guns were again reduced in number to four and the plane reduced in weight to improve its operation from the Jeep Carriers.

Developed at a time when procurement of aircraft for British air services came within the jurisdiction of the RAF, the Fairey Fulmar was hurriedly designed to fill a gap, since none of the existing aircraft then in RAF service could readily be adapted to the requirements visualised for the new armoured carriers.

Some allowances should be made for the shortcomings of the Fulmar when compared with other fighters, for it was designed to a different set of conditions as reflected in the specifications. The RAF had reserved for itself and its aircraft the task of defending ships while they were in range of land-based enemy aircraft. With these segments accounted for, if not tested in practice, the Royal Navy's fighter requirements were reduced to that of accompanying torpedo and strike/dive-bomber aircraft and driving off any reconnaissance aircraft. To meet these requirements, the Fulmar was designed to incorporate two seats, the rear one for an observer/navigator/telegrapher. Note that the term 'gunner' is conspicuous by its absence, as the rear seat occupant was already burdened with three jobs. In any case a good number of observers would have willingly taken on the gunnery duty as well if the designers had only had the foresight to include one or more guns for the rear seat. Thus it was that the observer was 'along for the ride' when the combat situation was at its worst. The pilot could not count on enemy fighters to avoid a direct stern attack.

With its several shortcomings, including lack of armour protection for the pilot, the Fulmar did give a good account of itself during the opening days of the war in the European theatre, accounting for 112 enemy aircraft shot down and 80 more damaged, which was about one third of the total Royal Navy victories.

Liquid-cooled engine

The Admiralty's preference for an air-cooled engine was not incorporated in the design, making the Fulmar one of the few aircraft designed for carrier operation that used liquid-cooled engines. As designs for the Fairey Barracuda were firmed up, it was proposed and accepted to use the same engine, the Rolls-Royce Merlin 30 in both the Barracuda and the Fulmar II. This was intended to reduce the maintenance parts problem, although no great performance gains resulted from the change.

In armament the Fulmar was equal to the Hawker Hurricane, having eight wing-mounted ·303 cal machine-guns which were impressive in number, but not in range. With the development of radar, the spacious rear cockpit made the Fulmar a logical plane for the Fleet Air Arm to use as a night fighter where its lack of speed would be less detrimental. In addition, the range of the Fulmar would allow it to remain airborne for five hours or more when fitted with auxiliary fuel tanks.

In combat service, the 15 Fulmars of 806 Squadron did provide air superiority for the Fleet operating in the eastern Mediterranean until they were overcome by Luftwaffe aircraft in early January 1941. In most of

Mitsubishi A5M4 'Claude'
This single-seat carrier fighter had fought over China and given Japanese Navy fighter pilots combat experience. Although obsolescent by 1941, the last 'Claudes' (the Allied code-name) were expended as Kamikaze suicide aircraft
Span: 36 ft 1 in *Length:* 24 ft 10 in *Engine:* Nakajima Kotobuti 41, 785 hp at 9485 ft *Armament:* 2×7·7-mm mg *Max speed:* 252 mph at 6890 ft *Ceiling:* 32,150 ft *Range:* 746 miles

Mitsubishi A6M5 Reisen (Zero Fighter) 'Zeke'
Universally known as the 'Zero', the potency of the A6M fleet fighter gave the Allies a shock during the Japanese onslaught of 1941 and 1942, but the A6M5, the final production version, was outclassed by the new generation of US carrier fighters from 1943
Span: 36 ft 1 in *Length:* 29 ft 11 in *Engine:* Nakajima Sakae NK1F, 1100 hp at 9350 ft *Armament:* 2×7·7-mm mg; 2×20-mm cannon *Max speed:* 351 mph at 19,685 ft *Ceiling:* 38,520 ft *Range:* 1194 miles

the actions in which the Fulmars participated they accounted for more enemy planes down than they lost themselves. Considering relative performance, these results are quite remarkable and a tribute to the crews. Only one specimen is known to survive: NI 854, in the Fleet Air Arm Museum, RNAS Yeovilton, Somerset.

Rude awakening

Until the surprise attack on Pearl Harbor, the Mitsubishi A6M2 'Zero' was comparatively unknown even to the organisation most likely to encounter it, the US Navy. Although it had been reported by Gen Claire Chennault in 1940 after his 'Flying Tigers' had encountered a number of them over China, little effort was made to determine the capability of this new fighter. Even if an attempt had been made to learn more, it is quite unlikely that any results would have been forthcoming, for the Japanese were the most security conscious of nations at that time.

As a result of the lack of knowledge of the Zero, the Allies of the Pacific theatre, particularly the US, suffered a rude awakening by the attack at Pearl Harbor and the seeming invincibility of the onrushing Japanese war machine as it pushed steadily down the Asian Coast and through the islands of the western Pacific. Following these surprises, intelligence teams and engineering and military analysts groped for an explanation of this successful design. It was reputed to be a copy of the best features of the Vought V-143, the Hughes Racer and, possibly, one or two other aircraft for good measure.

The fact was that this, like any other plane of that date, was 'a copy of all that preceded it' according to the designer, Jiro Horikoshi, who had been assigned to lead the Mitsubishi design team. It was in fact an example of the state of the art when the Zero was designed. It could not be attributed to any one or more designs as a copy. Like the bee, the design team sampled many designs, taking the best and blending them to achieve the results required.

With the outbreak of hostilities between Japan and China in July 1937, the performance requirements increased as a result of combat experience. Specifications had

Associated Press

The slightly damaged USS Maryland *against a backdrop of smoke after the Pearl Harbor attack*

increased to such a degree that a Nakajima design team elected to concentrate on other projects, pulling out of the competition and leaving the project and problems with the Mitsubishi team. They succeeded to a remarkable degree and produced a plane that will be remembered along with the First World War Spad and Fokker D VII.

It was a classic and exceptionally fine compromise, as all aircraft designs must be. The design started with a compromise choice of engine, the 875 hp Mitsubishi Suisei 13 engine, although the designer favoured the larger, more powerful but heavier Mitsubishi Kinsei 40 engine. It wasn't until much later – too late – in the war that the Kinsei was to be adopted. Contrary to general belief, the lack of protective armour for the pilot was not an oversight, or a result of disregard for the crew, but a hard compromise choice dictated by the performance characteristics considered to be essential. The gamble almost paid dividends, for the Japanese had things pretty much their way at first and for several months until the Zero's weaknesses were found and exploited by the US pilots.

The Zero's first flight

The first prototype, the A6M1, made its first flight on 1 April 1939. Storm clouds were gathering in Europe and the US Exclusion Act of 1924 was still a very sore point with the Japanese, not so much because of its results but because it implied that Japan was less than a major international power.

The aircraft was officially designated Navy type 0 carrier fighter on 31 July 1940, and shot down its first enemy aircraft on 13 September 1940 when 13 planes flying over China surprised and downed 27 Polikarpov I-15s and I-16s without suffering any losses themselves. At this time General Claire Chennault, who was then reorganising the Chinese Air Force, advised his colleagues in the US of this new fighter, but his warning was either ignored or forgotten.

The high point of the A6M2's service was the Pearl Harbor attack of 7 December 1941 and the invasion of Wake Island soon after. There followed a succession of victories as the Japanese pushed further south, eventually attacking Port Darwin, Australia, on 15 February 1942, destroying eight Australian aircraft in air combat and an additional 15 on the ground – again without losses to themselves. Following this, the Japanese fleet under Admiral Nagumo headed for the Indian Ocean where they sank the British fleet units consisting of HMS *Dorsetshire,* HMS *Cornwall* and the carrier HMS *Hermes*.

The Japanese were now riding high on wings of victory, but at the same time the

Mitsubishi A6M2 Zero
Jiro Horikoshi's brilliant fighter design first saw action in September 1940 when A6M2s destroyed 99 Chinese aircraft for the loss of 2 Zeros. The A6M2 was the model in service during the 1941–42 period of runaway Japanese victories
Span: 39 ft 4 in *Length:* 29 ft 9 in
Engine: Nakajima NK1F Sakae 12,950 hp at 13,780 ft *Max speed:* 331 mph at 16,000 ft
Ceiling: 32,810 ft *Range:* 1160 miles
Armament: 2×20-mm cannon; 2×7·7-mm mg

USS *Yorktown listing heavily after a savage battering during the Battle of Midway. But her Dauntlesses had smashed two Japanese carriers*

US was marshalling its military strength and heading for the Battle of the Coral Sea on 7/8 May 1942, the first battle ever to be fought entirely by aircraft with the surface ships out of sight of each other. It was at this point of the war that the tide began to turn. The Grumman F4Fs held the line and each carrier force had one carrier seriously damaged, and the Japanese lost the light carrier *Shoho*.

Shortly afterwards, on 3/4 June 1942, the Battle of Midway was underway. Again, the Zero extracted a heavy price, but this time the victims were mostly the TBDs which, through an error in timing, were left unprotected during their run. In turn, the Japanese paid an extremely heavy price with the loss of most of their carrier force and their complement of aircraft and crew was sadly depleted as well. These carrier losses included the *Kaga, Akagi* and *Soryu*, and the *Hiryu* which was set afire, but not before her aircraft crippled the *Yorktown*.

In connection with this battle, a diversionary attack was made on the Aleutians during which one Zero was forced to land due to fuel loss. Though wrecked on landing in a bog and killing the pilot, this Zero was to play an important role. Salvaged and restored to flying condition, it was thoroughly tested at Anacostia and North Island Naval Air Stations, and its strong and weak points documented. With this final bit of technical intelligence, the US aircraft industry was able to finalise the design of aircraft then in production, notably the Grumman F6F Hellcat and the Vought F4U Corsair. The Hellcat was, in fact, the first fighter designed specifically to gain mastery over the Zero. Despite the fact that the Zero had been improved, it was no match for a plane built right from the start to conquer it.

With the Japanese carrier fleet no longer a threat, the remaining Zeros were forced to operate from land bases, where they distinguished themselves and their crews by having their endurance and that of their pilots developed to a degree that amazed everyone. During the first year of the war a Japanese force consisting of less than 200 Zeros leapfrogged its way through the Philippines and down the coast of Asia, concentrating on the defeat of a hodgepodge of obsolescent aircraft such as Brewster F2A Buffaloes, Curtiss CW-21Bs, Hawk 75s, P-40s and Hawker Hurricanes.

A Japanese Zero assembled from parts of five Zeros shot down in the battle for Buna airstrip. Information about the Zero's performance was vital to Allied pilots in their fight against it

US Air Force

The Zero was built in a number of variants and model improvements including the A6M2, Zero (Zeke), A6M2-N (float fighter 'Rufe'), A6M2-K (two-seat trainer), A6M3 'Hamp' (Models 22 & 23) and A6M5 Zeke 52 which itself had a number of variations.

By mid 1943, the Zero and the Hamp had been surpassed by most Allied fighters yet they were always potent adversaries when flown by an experienced pilot. The Grumman F6F in particular and the Vought F4U were to provide air superiority over the Zeros.

Inevitable end

In one last desperate role, the A6M2s were used as Kamikaze weapons. Equipped with one 500-lb bomb, the Zeke was used in the much described spectacular attacks on US ships. While the A6M2 Kamikaze accounted for a high percentage of the attacks and actual hits, the effort was not worth the price, for the US attacks had reached a crescendo of such proportions and determination that, at best, the Kamikaze could only hope to delay the inevitable.

The Vought F4U Corsair was unique in several respects, one of the war's most versatile aircraft, an excellent fighter and a dive-bomber/attack plane. It was capable of lugging and delivering external ordnance loads up to a total of 4000 lb. It was this dual capability that reduced the requirement for additional dive-bombers and other specialised aircraft such as the Curtiss SB2Cs.

The Corsair was the first fighter to be powered by a 2000 hp engine, and in later configurations such as the Goodyear-built F2G was powered by the 3500 hp Pratt & Whitney R-4360 engine. To use this high power at high altitudes it was necessary to install a large, slow-turning propeller. To provide ground clearance for this propeller and still keep the landing gear short and rugged for arrested landings was a problem which was solved by the unusual bent wing configuration. The resulting wing position made unnecessary the extensive filleting usually required to smooth out the air flow at the juncture of the wing and fuselage. The short landing gear also served as a dive brake, with the added advantage of retracting backward into the wing.

This configuration improved pilot visibility on the approach and final leg of landing and when landing, the stall occurred in the trough of the gull close to the fuselage.

Imperial War Museum

Chance-Vought F4U-7 Corsair
Earning a legendary reputation during the Second World War, the ungainly Corsair was still fighting over Indo-China in 1954 flown by pilots of the French Navy Air Force
Span: 40 ft 11 in *Length:* 30 ft 8 in *Engine:* Pratt & Whitney R-2800-18W Double Wasp, 2000 hp at 1500 ft *Max speed:* 415 mph at 19,500 ft *Ceiling:* 34,500 ft *Range:* 1562 miles *Armament:* 4×·5-in mg *Bombload:* 2×1000-lb bombs

The added advantage of this wing design was that the folding point of the wing was also located at the low point of the trough, making it possible to maintain the low clearance for the hydraulically actuated folding system to be operated in the confined spaces aboard carriers. Because of less headroom aboard British carriers, the wing tips of Corsairs assigned to the Royal Navy were shortened by removal of eight inches from each wing tip resulting in a squared off wing tip and a slightly higher stalling speed – but little else was changed.

The structure of the F4U was simplified by using large single panels whenever possible and fabricating these by arc welding whenever practical. One unusual feature was the rather generous use of fabric in a plane of this late date.

Veterans of the Second World War will readily recall the distinctive sounds of aircraft which caused instinctive reactions among ground crews and particularly anti-aircraft gunners and troops in the front lines. The engine exhaust, propeller or cooling system produced distinctive sounds which inspired fear or exhilaration. In the case of the Corsair, the whistling sound generated by the wing root air intakes was so pronounced that enemy troops referred to it as 'Whistling Death', for it extracted a high price in air combat and an even greater one among the ground troops in its role as an attack plane, bombing, launching rockets and strafing.

Because of its rather unconventional appearance it was also known by US and Allied personnel as the 'Bent-wing Bird'. With the exception of the Stuka and the Grace, there was no other Second World War aircraft with this unusual wing configuration.

The Corsair had a prolonged adolescence. While it was designed for carrier operation, a variety of idiosyncrasies, including a bounce when landing aboard carriers, kept it from its intended role until 1944, although the first 22 F4Us had been proclaimed combat-ready as early as December 1942. In spite of its early rejection from carrier qualification it was operated by Marine and Navy squadrons VMF 124 and VF 17 from land bases, establishing a victory/loss ratio of better than 11 to 1.

The first action in which Corsairs took part was to escort Consolidated PB4Y-1, single-finned Navy Liberators, all the way

Fleet Air Arm Corsair II fighters in echelon formation. The type provided cover for the Tirpitz *raids*

National Maritime Museum

to Bougainville, a task which had been impossible for the Grumman F4Fs. The new pilots got a thorough baptism of fire the next day when, together with an array of Liberators, P-40s and P-38s, they were attacked by 50 Zeros with a loss of two each of Liberators and P-40s and four P-38s. From this inauspicious beginning the tables turned, for the Corsairs completed their war service with the destruction of 2140 enemy aircraft in air combat against a loss of only 189.

In addition to daytime combat, the F4U was successfully adapted to night fighter duties by the use of a radar antenna pod mounted near the tip of the starboard wing. The night fighter group operated on a fire alarm basis, moving about the combat zone as the need arose.

In spite of its weight, the Corsair was more than a match for any aircraft that the Japanese had available and in simulated combat tests it proved superior to any other plane in the US service at that time. Of the 9418 Corsairs produced, Vought produced 4669 with the two subcontractors, Goodyear and Brewster, producing 4014 and 735 respectively. In service they were assigned to 19 Marine squadrons, a total of 6255 planes, and 19 squadrons of the Royal Navy (1977), many of which had the modified wing tips. In addition to the above services, the Royal New Zealand Air Force acquired 425 during the war.

After the end of hostilities a number were allocated to various South American countries and to the air forces of a number of smaller nations, where they served well. Fortunately, a number of Corsairs of various modifications are still retained in museums around the world.

The Japanese name of Reppu (Violent Wind) was given to the Mitsubishi A7M1 in advance of its actual testing, which accounts for the misnomer. It was in fact a great disappointment in speed and climbing

Side View of FG-1D Corsair
Goodyear-built FG-1D (the classification changed with a different maker) of 2nd Marine Air Division

Mitsubishi A7M2 Reppu (Hurricane) 'Sam'
Conceived as a replacement for the A6M Zero, with armour plate and self-sealing fuel tanks, the Reppu's production was strangled by earthquakes and B-29 raids and none saw action
Span: 45 ft 11 in *Length:* 36 ft 1 in
Engine: Mitsubishi MK9A, 1800 hp at 19,685 ft
Armament: 2×13·2-mm mg; 2×20-mm cannon
Max speed: 390 mph at 21,665 ft *Ceiling:* 35,760 ft *Range:* 2·5 hr cruising plus 30 min combat

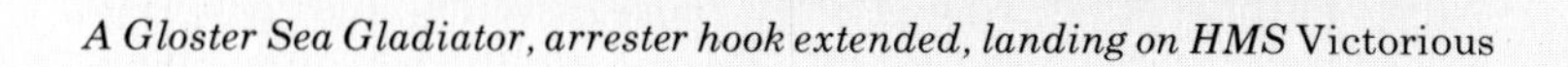

Imperial War Museum

A Gloster Sea Gladiator, arrester hook extended, landing on HMS Victorious

Gloster Sea Gladiator
The last biplane fighter to serve with the Royal Navy, the Gladiator was navalised by addition of an arrester hook and dinghy stowage and fought over Norway and in the Mediterranean. Its role in the epic 1941 defence of Malta was largely an invention of British propaganda
Span: 32 ft 3 in *Length:* 27 ft 5 in *Engine:* Bristol Mercury VIIIA, 840 hp *Max speed:* 245 mph at 10,000 ft *Ceiling:* 32,000 ft *Range:* 425 miles *Armament:* 4 × ·303-in Browning mg

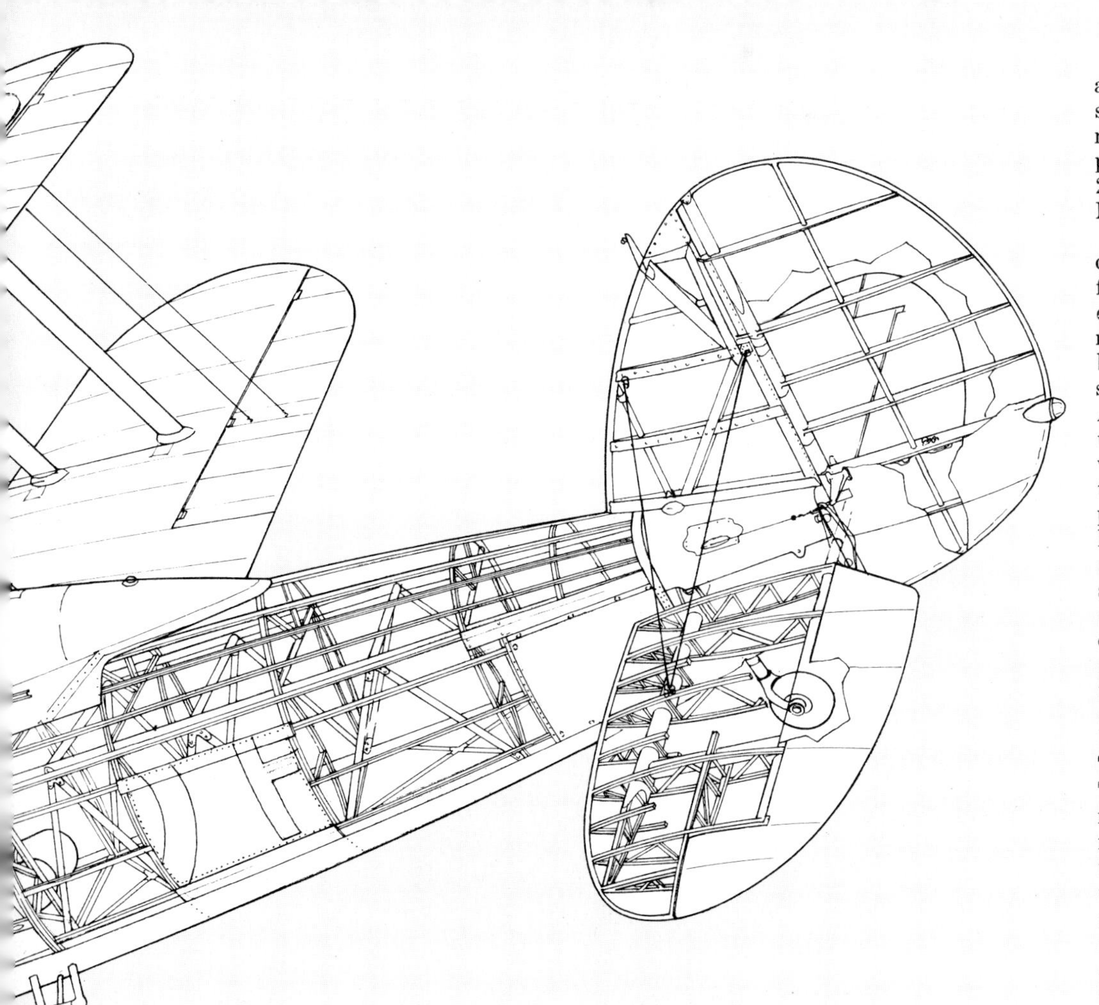

ability, both of which were intended to surpass the A6M Zero's capability. The main reason was the change in power plant from the Mitsubishi Mk 9A engine of 2100 hp to the more readily available Nakajima Homare of 1800 hp.

In addition the A7M1 was to have the qualities which the Zero lacked – greater firepower and armour – while retaining its desirable features, including carrier equipment. The resulting performance was so bad (347·5 mph max), that production was suspended in August 1944. A second model, A7M2, was completed in October, this time using the original engine. Maximum speed was 390 mph, 10 mph less than the specifications called for, but sufficient to result in a production order on an accelerated basis. In December 1944, the Nagoya industrial area where the A7M2s were under construction was hit by the double blow of an earthquake and intense B-29 raids, which disrupted production to the extent that only eight Reppus had been completed by the end of hostilities and none had reached operational status.

The last biplane fighter

The Gloster Sea Gladiator was a naval modification of the RAF's last biplane fighter. The outbreak of war in 1939 caught the Fleet Air Arm with these remnants of the biplane era. Though procurement thinking had changed to monoplanes, few if any were actually available. The Fairey Fulmars and Blackburn Skuas were rushed as an intermediate step into the monoplane era. The Sea Gladiator did not phase out in peacetime, however, for it did provide effective cover for the Fairey Swordfish during the Norwegian campaign. Fortunately, one of these may be retrieved from a Norwegian lake, which should have provided excellent preservation treatment in contrast to those forced down at sea.

By the latter part of 1940 all remaining Gladiators had been withdrawn in favour of the Skua. Its construction was aluminium, with surfaces and parts of the fuselage fabric covered.

Stubby and manoeuvrable in comparison with its contemporary Grumman F4F Wildcat/Martlet, the Brewster F2A Buffalo did see action in the defence of Crete and against the Japanese in the Dutch East Indies, as well as over Cairo, Rangoon, Burma and Singapore – and in the Battle of Midway where US Marine Squadron VMF 221 used 20 F2A Buffalos and 7 Grumman F4F-3s based on Midway itself. The loss of 13 Buffalos to the more manoeuvrable Zeros ended the career of the Buffalo.

Brewster F2A Buffalo
This diminutive, underpowered American fighter flew from British carriers as a stopgap measure during the defence of Crete in March 1941. Very few served with the US Navy
Span: 35 ft *Length:* 26 ft *Engine:* Wright Cyclone, 1200 hp *Max speed:* 313 mph at 13,500 ft *Ceiling:* 30,500 ft *Range:* 650 miles *Armament:* 2×·5-in mg

Fairey Firefly I

Combining the roles of fighter and long-range reconnaissance aircraft, and fitted with folding wings and full naval equipment, the Firefly was one of the most complex fighters of its day

Span: 44 ft 6 in *Length:* 37 ft 7 in
Engine: Rolls-Royce Griffon IIB, 1490 hp at 14,000 ft *Max speed:* 315 mph at 16,500 ft
Ceiling: 30,100 ft *Range:* 850 miles *Crew:* 2
Armament: 4×20-mm cannon *Bombload:* 2000 lb

Imperial War Museum

A formation of US Navy Grumman Hellcats, the type that replaced the Wildcat at war against the Zero

Grumman F6F Hellcat
Based on the Wildcat formula, but incorporating the lessons of combat experience, the Hellcat's speed and climb were excellent and it could outmatch the Zero in a dogfight
Span: 42 ft 10 in *Length:* 33 ft 6 in
Engine: Pratt & Whitney R-2800-10, 2000 hp at 1000 ft *Max speed:* 371 mph at 18,700 ft
Ceiling: 35,000 ft *Range:* 1495 miles
Armament: 6×·5-in mg plus 2×1000-lb bombs

The Buffalo had the unique distinction of winning the US Navy design competition against the Grumman F4F and still falling by the wayside. Production was not one of the Brewster Company's strong points, either with the Buffalo and Buccaneer/ Bermuda of their own design or when they were called upon as a second source for the Vought F4U/F3A.

The US Navy found the Buffalo particularly susceptible to deck landing damage due to a weakness in the landing gear. As a result, the Grumman Wildcat superseded the Buffalo to become the standard carrier fighter of both the US Navy and the Fleet Air Arm until the Vought F4U and Grumman F6F replaced them.

In comparative tests with the Hurricane I, the Buffalo was slightly more manoeuvrable but slower to accelerate in a dive. Though designed for carrier operation, when sold to the British it was found to be one foot too large in wing span and could not be accommodated on carrier elevators. Instead it was used in the Near East over Cairo, where the fine silt was less harmful to the air-cooled radial engine than it had been to other planes' close tolerance liquid-cooled engines.

Other features which prevented it from assignment to serious combat were lack of firepower (the Buffalo had two ·50 cal and two ·30 cal machine-guns) and of armour plate, which was neither thick enough nor large enough. These were its major failings, its other deficiencies being sufficient to relegate it to training missions or desperation defence requirements.

A two-seat fighter/reconnaissance aircraft, the Fairey Firefly was built to a requirement dating back to the mid-1920s and as a replacement for the stop-gap Fairey Fulmar, which served well if not spectacularly during the early part of the war.

The war was well under way in Europe and the US was recovering from the shock of Pearl Harbor, the complete tally of the disaster not yet fully appreciated, when the Firefly prototype was first flown on 22 December 1941. While resembling the Fulmar in general plan and profile – making it hard to differentiate between them at a distance – the Firefly was, aerodynamically, an improvement, while the substitution of the 1730 hp R-R Griffon II B and later the 1990 hp Griffon XII did much to improve the performance with an immediate 40 mph increase in top speed.

Along with the increased performance, the armament was changed from the eight ·303 cal guns of the Fulmar to the four 20-mm cannon of the Firefly. The wing plan form adopted was quite similar to that of the graceful, elliptical wings of the Supermarine Spitfire. Were it not for the generous expanse of clear glass aft of the wing, the Firefly might easily have been mistaken for the Spitfire. The Firefly got a comparatively late start, but by the end of 1946 over 950 Mk 1s and night fighter modifications had been built, over 800 of them by the Fairey plants. The remainder were built by General Aircraft Company.

The Firefly distinguished itself in action in the Far East as an attack plane launching rockets against important targets such as the oil refineries in Sumatra in January 1945, effectively knocking out the major source of petroleum products for Japanese ships and aircraft. Earlier attempts by British Engineers to destroy refinery storage tanks during the retreat from the Malay Peninsula resulted in amusing and embarrassing results when the high octane fuel refused to burn. The intensity of fumes snuffed out attempts to ignite it with any of the normal – and some far from normal – forms of incendiary materials.

Night fighter Firefly

One of the principal variants of the Firefly Mk 1 was that of night fighter. As in the case of the Fulmar, the spacious rear cockpit was quite adequate for the radar equipment; however, the early forms of radome successfully cluttered up the otherwise clean aerodynamics, resulting in lower speeds, and the weight of the early radar equipment altered the centre of gravity, making it necessary to move the engine 18 inches forward to compensate. This combination of pilot and radar operator is practically standard for current combat aircraft including fighters. The radar/ counter measures crew member in currently operational fighters is regarded as essential to the performance and safety of the aircraft. In the days of the Firefly, however, the second crew member was a definite obstacle to high performance in an aircraft when compared with the single-seat, single-engined contemporaries. Its top speed was 316 mph, only slightly greater than that of the Brewster Buffalo, whose every

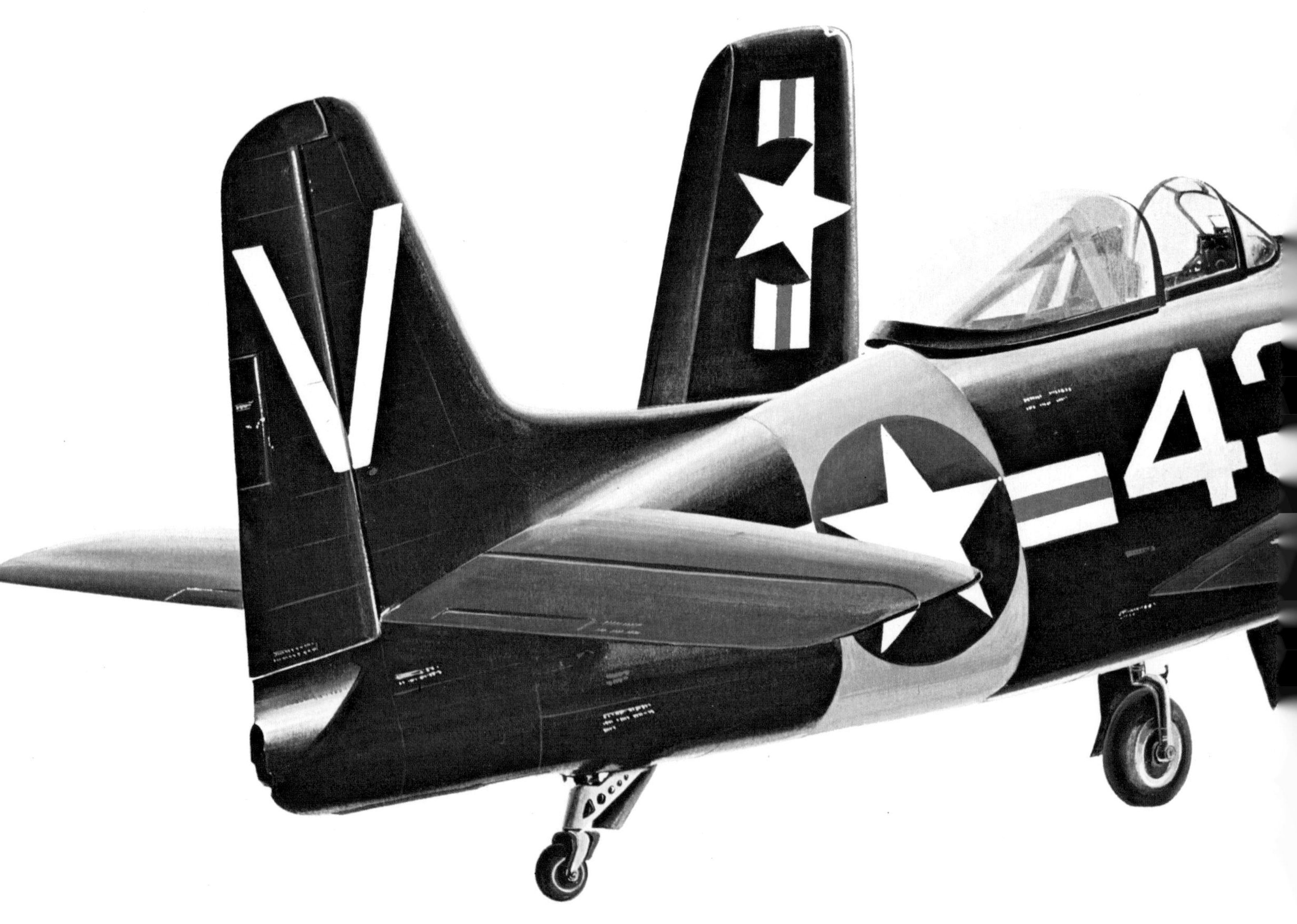

performance was surpassed rather quickly and early in the war.

During the preliminaries to the sinking of the German battleship *Tirpitz*, the Firefly was used to attack auxiliary ships and silence anti-aircraft gun emplacements in preparation for the battleship's destruction by RAF Lancasters.

The Grumman F6F Hellcat, successor to the F4F Wildcat/Martlet, was built in the Grumman tradition of robust, rugged structure with good flight control characteristics and, in this case, performance adequate to gain air superiority over the Japanese Zero.

During the first 16 months of the Pacific War, the Wildcat was on its own and did a remarkable job considering that normal terms of measurement would have shown it to be inferior to its enemy, the Zero. The brutish Hellcat was designed to remedy the situation with speed and climb ability superior to the Zero's. It was the first plane built after Pearl Harbor and incorporated the features demanded by Navy pilots allowing them to initiate or break off combat at their choosing.

Grumman F8F Bearcat
The Bearcat appeared too late to see combat, but had brought the Grumman fighter design precepts to perfection. Lighter than the Hellcat by 3000 lb, its superior performance was gained at the expense of firepower
Span: 35 ft 6 in *Length:* 28 ft *Engine:* Pratt & Whitney R-2800-22W Double Wasp, 2100 hp at take-off *Max speed:* 424 mph at 17,300 ft *Ceiling:* 33,700 ft *Range:* 955 miles *Armament:* 4×·5-in mg *Bombload:* 2000 lb or 4×5-in rockets

The results of tests on the Zero forced down in the Aleutians established the design parameters for the Hellcat which was then being designed. It was, in fact, designed to better the performance of the Zero as its primary mission. That reserves in structural strength were there also was important but almost of secondary importance at this time.

Like its sister-ship on the Grumman production lines, the TBF Avenger, the Hellcat was big and spacious inside and of simplified rugged structure to ensure ease of production and maintenance aboard carriers. Carrying this simplification further, the wings were folded manually with the locking pins operated hydraulically from the cockpit and made safe by manually controlled lock pins. For stowage aboard ship the wings were rotated about the front spar and then folded backward alongside the fuselage, leading-edge downward, like those of the Wildcat and the Avenger.

The landing gear rotated 90° as it retracted rearward, like that of the Curtiss P-40 and Vought F4U. Cover plates smoothed over the wheels and struts when fully retracted. When in the extended position, a cover plate at the upper end of the gear leg added to the drag produced by the gear. The six ·50 cal machine-guns were mounted in the panels just outboard of the line where the wings broke for folding.

The fuselage was a semimonocoque structure with rings and stringers, covered by stressed skin. Adequate armour plate was installed for pilot protection and a turnover structure was incorporated as well.

Performance had been improved, with the speed 60 mph faster than the F4Fs. Range was increased and the ammunition carried was 400 rounds per gun – nearly doubling the capacity of the F4F. Most important, the Hellcat could be flown and flown well by the inexperienced pilots who were then coming into combat theatres fresh from the training centres.

The first flight of the XF6F-3 took place in July 1942 and the first full squadron of Hellcats was delivered by December of the same year. The F4F and the TBF production was farmed out to General Motors where the designation was changed to FM-1 and TBM, but little else changed as production continued unabated. Fourteen months from design to production was a record of which Grumman could be proud and one that instilled pride in the workers for the esprit de corps of Grumman employees was the envy of the other wartime manufacturers, especially their neighbour, Brewster.

The first combat flown in F6Fs was a VF 5 flight, in support of the strike aircraft from Task Force 15, consisting of *Essex*, light carrier *Independence* and the second *Yorktown* in their attack on the Marcus Islands on 31 August 1943. Numerous encounters further endeared the Hellcat to its pilots and improved their skills for the big battles just over the horizon. The Battle of the Philippine Sea, 19-20 June 1944 (known as the 'Marianas Turkey Shoot'), was one of the most decisive battles of the war. On 19 June aircraft of Task Force 58 destroyed 402 enemy aircraft, and by 10 August carrier aircraft had sunk 110,000 tons of enemy ships and destroyed 1223 enemy aircraft.

Staggering losses

The date, 20 June, was memorable for other reasons. In a dusk battle at extreme range, Task Force 58 lost 104 aircraft out of 216 launched. Of the Hellcats six were lost in the vicinity of the Japanese fleet of Admiral Ozawa, while 17 splashed down with dry tanks on the way home. The divebombers (SB2C – Helldiver) and torpedo bombers (TBF – Avenger) lost 60% or more of their planes over the target or en route back to Task Force 58. This battle and the Battle of Leyte Gulf, 23-26 October, resulted in 1046 enemy aircraft destroyed during the month of October and another 770 during November. The staggering losses in planes and aircraft carriers, as well as other surface ships, spelled the end of the once powerful Japanese carrier aviation.

In all these battles the Hellcat played an important role in protecting the strike force and defending the massed US carrier force against the determined and suicidal attacks of the Japanese carrier pilots.

The Hellcat also found favour with the Fleet Air Arm and was used extensively in Atlantic operation, notably from HMS *Emperor*, which carried out anti-shipping attacks along the Norwegian coast and provided fighter cover during eight attacks on the German battleship *Tirpitz* from April to August of 1944. Most of the Fleet Air Arm action took place in the Pacific where the F6F-5 (Hellcat II) was the standard. All told, the Royal Navy used over 1260 Hellcats. It was designed to do a job well and, by any standard, it succeeded.

The Hawker Sea Hurricane ('Hurricat' or 'Catafighter') was used as a stopgap measure when the German submarine and long-range Focke Wulf Fw 200 Condor became a menace in early 1941. The age of the Hurricane design made it unwise to expend design and fabrication effort to develop folding wings. Therefore, the plane was used as it was by catapulting it off CAM (Catapult Armed Merchantmen) ships. Each flight ended in a ducking for the pilot and loss of the aircraft, which probably accounts for the fact that only one Hurricane I is known to exist of all those that fought in or during the Battle of Britain. This one remaining Hurricane is on exhibition in the Science Museum in London.

The only situation where plane and pilot were recovered was during training, in port, or possibly when the convoy of which the CAM ship was a part was within range of land. Otherwise the normal method was for the pilot to take to his parachute and Mae West life preserver, hopefully to be picked up by ships of the convoy after the danger of attack was passed.

In addition to the CAM operation, a number of Hurricane IBs were adapted to operate from carriers by reinforcing the airframe to permit catapulting, and addition of an arrester hook. A number of variants were introduced with the addition of four 20-mm cannon mounted in the universal wing and, with a change in engine to the Merlin XX, these became Hurricane IICs.

Fleet Air Arm pilots originally flew the Hurricats off the CAMs but later were relieved by RAF pilots who well remember the shock of the catapult launching.

Of the carrier-based Sea Hurricanes, some were assigned to the CAM escort carrier HMS *Avenger* on the Russian Convoy PQ 18 to Murmansk, after the previous Convoy, PQ 17, which was without air cover, was pounded continuously en route by German aircraft based in Norway and Finland. On this convoy, the Sea Hurricanes accounted for five German aircraft destroyed and 17 more damaged with a loss of one pilot and four Hurricanes. They were to give a good account of themselves for some time, taking part in the defence of Malta and escorting convoys as late as August 1942 and during the North African Torch landings on 8–11 November 1942. By this time replacement aircraft, Seafires and Grumman F6F Hellcats were being placed aboard the carriers. The remaining Sea Hurricanes were stripped of their sea-going gear and returned to land duties.

The Supermarine Seafire was a well-tried and proven design modified to naval operating standards. The rather unusual configuration of the Seafire III, when the wings were folded for storage aboard carriers, led to the nickname of 'Praying Mantis'. The tips were folded downwards at the wing tip joint at the outboard aileron gap; then the main panels, outboard of the coolant radiators, were folded upward to form an almost equilateral triangle. The main panels were unbolted by unscrewing locking bolts inside the wheel wells. The wings were supported in their folded position by telescoping tubes which were normally stored in lateral slots in the upper wing surface. Folding was accomplished by a three or four man crew and reduced the original span to 13 ft 4 in, which was 23 ft less than the unfolded span of 36 ft 10 in.

Earlier Seafires made do with the non-folding standard Spitfire wing as most of them were conversions of existing standard models. Seafires were used extensively, taking over from the Sea Hurricanes in 1941 after it was shown that fast, single-engined, single-place fighters were needed aboard carriers and in naval operations.

On the offensive

The first operational use of the Seafire was from HMS *Furious*, *Formidable* and *Argus* flying in support of Operation Torch, the Allied landings in North Africa on 8–11 November 1942. Then, on 10 July 1943 the Seafires took to the offensive again, flying from HMS *Furious* and *Indomitable* in support of the Allied landings in Sicily. During this campaign, which lasted until 18 August, Allied airmen lost 274 planes and accounted for 1691 enemy aircraft.

Operation Avalanche, the invasion of the Italian mainland, began on 2 September. Fleet Air Arm squadrons operating from the escort carriers *Attacker*, *Battler*, *Hunter*, *Stalker* and *Unicorn* provided the total air cover for the beachhead during the early stages of this engagement. For the landing troops, the low wind velocity experienced was a pleasure since sea sickness was minimised but the Seafire pilots operating from

A Seafire Mk XV touches down aboard the Pretoria Castle. *Note the sting-type arrester hook*

A Hawker Hurricane 1A being catapulted from a Catapult Armed Merchantman (CAM ship). The Hurricane provided valuable cover for Atlantic and Arctic convoys. Each mission meant the loss of the plane, but the Hurricane was becoming obsolescent, and was unsuitable for conversion to a proper carrier plane. Mk 1B specifications: Span: *40 ft* Length: *31 ft 5 in* Engine: *Rolls-Royce Merlin II, 1310 hp* Max Speed: *298 mph at 16,400 ft* Ceiling: *30,000 ft* Armament: *8 × ·303 mg*

the Jeep carriers soon realised that the maximum speed for the CVEs, about 17–18 mph, was not the best speed for the take-off and landing of the Seafire. During these hectic days amid low wind conditions a number of Seafires were damaged during deck operations, usually landings, when they came in too fast and tore the arrester hook from the aircraft.

The Seafires continued to serve well, flying top cover for the attacks on the *Tirpitz* and whenever their presence was needed, whether from shore or carrier base. The last action for the Seafires in the European theatre was in the Aegean Sea area during the latter part of 1944.

Meanwhile, in the Pacific theatre, the Seafires found themselves at a disadvantage, for ranges (or endurance) which had been quite acceptable in the European theatre were not adequate in the broad expanse of the Pacific. The normal two-hour endurance of the Seafire limited its usefulness as well as that of its carriers. The decision was made to retire the Seafires in favour of the F6F Hellcats and F4U Corsairs after nearly 1700 Seafires had been built or converted.

Although the Seafire was without a doubt the finest low-level fighter produced by the Allies, its range, firepower and ordnance capabilities did not match those of the later developed Hellcat and Corsair that had been designed from the outset for long endurance, heavy firepower and incredible ordnance capacity. These same features eventually made redundant such specially designed dive-bombers as the Curtiss SB2C.

Supermarine Seafire Mk III
A straightforward adaptation of the Spitfire, fitted with arrester hook and catapult spools, the Mk III had double-jointed folding wings (inset) to clear the low hangar ceilings typical of British aircraft carriers
Span: 36 ft 8 in *Length:* 30 ft *Engine:* Rolls-Royce Merlin 55, 1470 hp *Armament:* 4×·303-in mg; 4×20-mm cannon plus 1×500-lb or 2×250-lb bombs *Speed* 342 mph at 20,700 ft *Ceiling:* 37,500 ft *Range:* 508 miles

National Maritime Museum

THE DUEL OVER GERMANY

On July 28, 1943, horror struck the city of Hamburg: a savage RAF raid kindled the first 'firestorm' and more than 50,000 people died in the holocaust. The German fighter defences, which had previously been holding their own against the RAF attacks, had been thrown into chaos by the new 'Window' radar countermeasure and desperate solutions had to be found. Found they were – and within nine months the RAF itself faced disaster over Nuremburg

It was still light at 2155 hours on the evening of July 24, 1943, when the first of the 'Pathfinder' aircraft – Lancaster G-George of No. 7 Squadron – roared down the runway at Oakington airfield near Cambridge. Regular as clockwork, at half minute intervals, the remaining bombers at Oakington followed it into the air. Soon this scene was being repeated at more than a score of bomber airfields spread throughout East Anglia, Lincolnshire, and Yorkshire.

In the half light the bombers clawed for altitude, moving eastwards in an untidy mass like a swarm of bees. By midnight the force had assembled over the North Sea, a mighty phalanx of 791 aircraft – 347 Lancasters, 246 Halifaxes, 125 Stirlings, and 73 Wellingtons – sprawled out over an area 200 miles long and 20 miles wide. This airborne armada moved eastwards at 225 miles per hour – $3\frac{3}{4}$ miles per minute. And as the aircraft formed up, attentive German eyes followed their progress.

Shortly before 2300 hours, an early warning radar site near Ostend reported: 'Approximately 80 aircraft at Gustav Caesar 5, course east, altitude 23,000 feet.' At the headquarters of the Luftwaffe III Fighter Division, at Arnhem-Deelen in Holland, a small spot of light moved swiftly across the darkened situation map. It came to rest at position GC-5 on the German fighter grid, just to the north of Ipswich. Soon the spot of light was joined by others as more and more bombers appeared over the radar horizon. The attack was obviously going to be a big one. Where this time?

As yet the Germans could only speculate on the raiders' goal, whose mere name had dried the throat of many an experienced bomber crewman at the briefing earlier: Hamburg. Hamburg was well known to the men of the RAF. By the third week in July 1943, the port had been raided on 98 occasions. Her defences were formidable: she was ringed by no less than 54 heavy flak and 22 searchlight batteries, and six major night fighter airfields were within easy flying distance. Previous operations had, in consequence, cost the RAF heavily.

If it was the flak that caused damage and forced bomber crews to jink their aircraft, thus making accurate bombing difficult, it was the venomously efficient night fighters that were the real killers. Their tactics had been evolved by General Josef Kammhuber, the commander of the Luftwaffe night fighter force, and tested and improved during a hundred battles. His system, code-named 'Himmelbett' (four-poster bed), depended for its success on a lavishly equipped chain of ground radar stations. Each station had a maximum effective interception range of 30 miles, and to form a defensive barrier through which the raiders would have to pass, Kammhuber erected a line with Himmelbett stations at 20-mile intervals. This line extended down occupied Europe, shaped like a giant inverted sickle: the 'handle' ran through Denmark, from north to south, the 'blade' curved through northern Germany, Holland, Belgium, and eastern France to the Swiss frontier. Each station was equipped with one 'Freya' and two Giant 'Würzburg' radar sets.

At the approach of the raiders the fighters were scrambled, and told to orbit radio beacons positioned next to the radar stations. Once there, a short-range, narrow-beam Giant Würzburg radar would swing round and hold the fighter in its gaze. Meanwhile the long-range, wide-beam Freya radar directed the second Giant Würzburg on to the approaching bomber. With precise information relayed from the operators of the two Giant Würzburg sets, the German ground controller radioed his orders to the fighter pilot, to bring the latter on to the quarry's tail. In the rear of the cockpit the fighter's own radar operator would be watching the flickering tubes of his lightweight 'Lichtenstein' radar for the first glimpse of the enemy. Once in contact with the bomber the German crew would radio a brief 'Pauke' call. 'Pauke', literally 'beat the kettledrum', was the Luftwaffe equivalent to the RAF 'Tally Ho!': it meant the target was in sight, and about to be engaged. The fighter radar operator now passed his pilot a running commentary of instructions until the latter caught sight of the exhaust flames from the bomber's motors. The hunter closed on his victim, endeavouring to get into a firing position without being seen. Like that of the infantry sniper, the task of the night fighter crew – of either side – amounted to little short of cold-blooded murder. If it was possible to get to within 50 yards behind and astern of a still unsuspecting victim, a favourite German tactic was to pull the fighter up on to its tail, at the same time opening fire. The battery of cannon pumped out a stream of explosive shells, to rake the raider from stem to stern. All too often the first thing the hapless bomber crew knew of the attack was the shudder as their aircraft buckled under the impact of exploding shells. The German fighter crews were fighting to defend their homes and loved ones; they did so with the same determination that had characterised the RAF during the Battle of Britain.

By July 1943 the German defences were knocking down an average of more than five out of every 100 bombers attacking their homeland, and this rate was rising steadily. Three quarters of those lost fell to fighters, the rest to flak and accidents.

Clearly, it was vital to the continued success of the British bomber offensive that some means of neutralising the devastatingly efficient Himmelbett system should be found. Technically the answer was to be amazingly simple: little strips of aluminium foil. Known by the cover-name 'Window', the strips measured 30 centimetres long and 1·5 centimetres wide and came in bundles of 2,000, held together by an elastic band. When released from an aircraft, the bundle broke up, to form a 'cloud' of strips which gave a 'blip' on a radar screen the same size as that from the bomber itself. By releasing one such bundle per minute from each aircraft in a concentrated bomber stream, it was possible to saturate the area with 'blips', thus making radar-controlled interceptions impossible.

During 1942 British scientists had conducted a series of trials with the 'Window' strips, under the greatest secrecy. Quite independently, and under equal secrecy, their German counterparts had been doing exactly the same thing. In both countries the men reached the same conclusion: the new countermeasure was dynamite. If used properly it could wreck the radar-dependent air defences of either nation. Neither side had then felt that its bomber arm had a margin of strength over its opponent's sufficient to justify the risk of introducing such an innovation. But by the summer of 1943 the striking power of RAF Bomber Command had expanded out of all recognition, while the demands of the war of attrition on the Eastern Front had reduced the German bomber force to comparative impotence.

Germany's shield: and Britain's bizarre response

By 1943, the Germans had perfected a defence system against the British night attacks. **(1)** From a series of radar stations strung across northern Europe at 20-mile intervals a long-range, early-warning radar, 'Freya' (far right) would pick up the bomber (red beam). **(2)** As it closed, one short-range narrow-beam Giant 'Würzburg' set (right) would fix on to the bomber (blue beam), while another would fix on to the night fighter orbiting the station. This would then be guided to the bomber until **(3)** the fighter's 'Lichtenstein' radar (orange beam) had made contact with its quarry. **(4)** The British countermeasure 'Window' was extremely simple: on normal 'Würzburg' screens (A,B,C) bearing and elevation tubes (centre and right) showed the target on both sides of a base line. When the target was dead central on both screens, the radar was fixed on target. But by dropping clouds of aluminium foil strips the British could produce an effect (a,b,c) which made precise measurement impossible

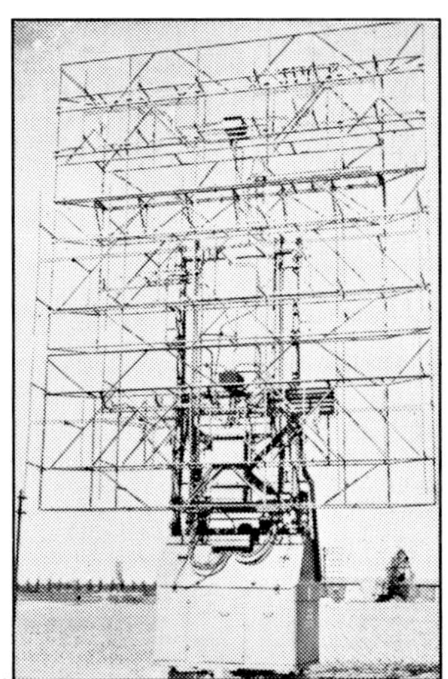

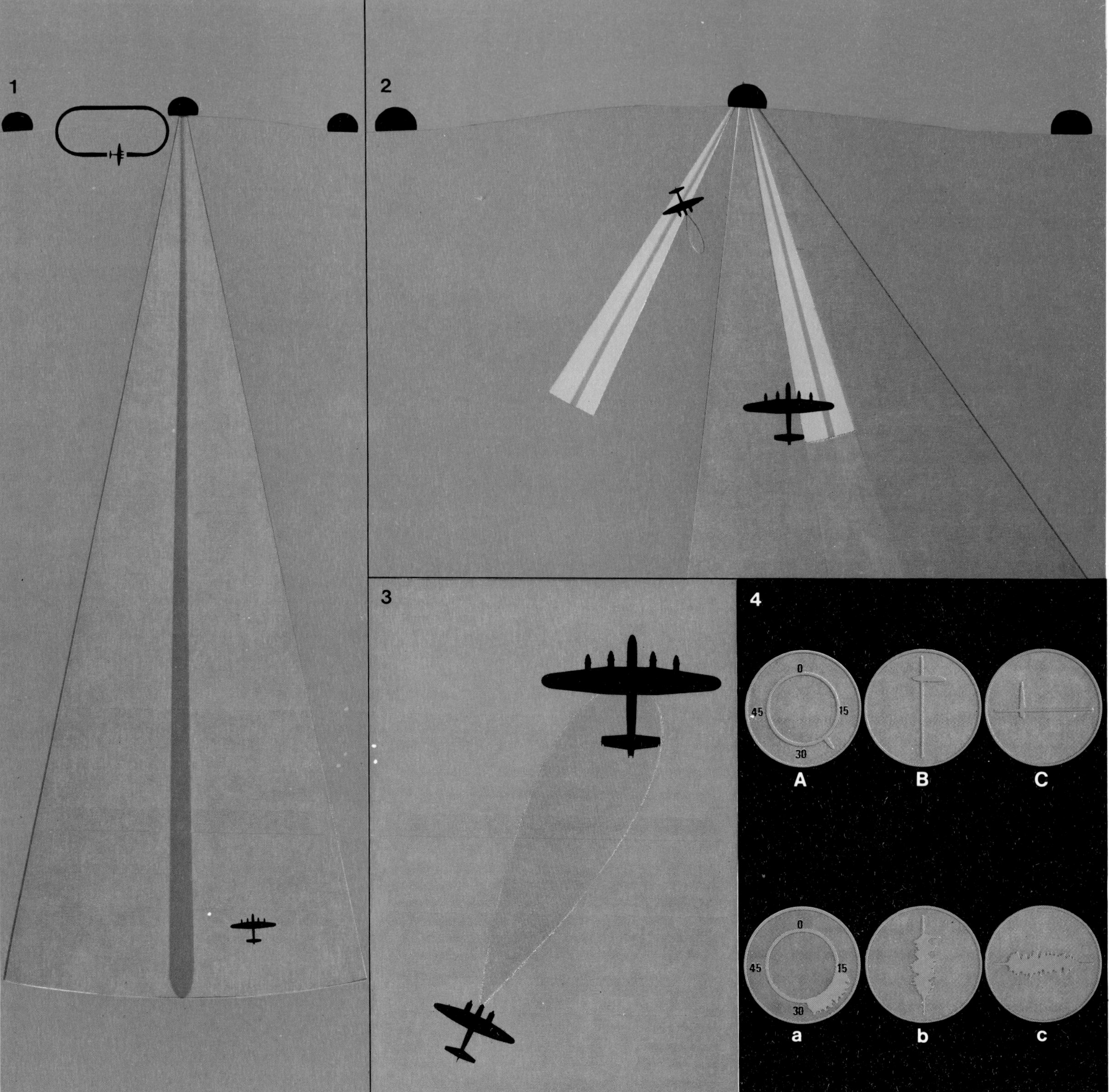

Chris Harrison

'FLAK MAY HAVE CRIPPLED MANY BRITISH BOMBERS—BUT THE VENOMOUSLY EFFICIENT NIGHT FIGHTERS WERE THE REAL KILLERS'

Messerschmitt Bf-110G: Although unsuccessful as a long-range fighter and fighter-bomber, the Me-110 was used widely and successfully as a night fighter. **Span:** 53 feet 4⅞ inches. **Length:** 41 feet 6¾ inches. **Speed:** 342 mph at 22,000 feet. **Ceiling:** 26,005 feet. **Range:** 1,305 miles. **Armament:** Two 30-mm and two 20-mm cannon, and two 7·9-mm MG. **Crew:** Three

Junkers Ju-88G6: This variant of the famous medium bomber was one of the most widely-used night fighters. It could carry 'Schräge Musik'—upward-firing cannon mounted in the central fuselage. **Span:** 65 feet 10½ inches. **Length:** 47 feet 1½ inches. **Speed:** 311 mph at 20,000 feet. **Ceiling:** 32,500 feet. **Range:** 1,950 miles. **Armament:** Three 20-mm cannon, three 7·9-mm MG, and two 20-mm Schräge Musik cannon. **Crew:** Three

The first use of 'Window'

On July 15, 1943 a meeting of the War Cabinet, presided over by Winston Churchill, finally permitted the use of the new counter-measure.

Now, at 0025 hours on the morning of July 25, 1943, as the leading bombers in the stream passed the island fortress of Heligoland on their way to Hamburg, the first 'Window' bundles were dropped into the black air beneath each bomber.

The first report of anything out of the ordinary came from radar station 'Hummer', on Heligoland itself. By 0040 hours the incoming bombers could be seen on the radar screens, together with the 'Window': since each cloud of foil remained effective for 15 minutes before the strips dispersed, the British force appeared to have a strength of 11,000 bombers! The Germans could not believe their eyes. The Hummer station reported back that it was 'disturbed by many apparent point-targets looking like aircraft, either stationary or slow moving. The picking-up of genuine aircraft is made extremely difficult. Once they have been picked up it is possible to follow them, but only with difficulty.' Station 'Auster', on the southern tip of Sylt, reported similar trouble. So, in turn, did the rest of the radar stations sited around Hamburg proper.

Circling over their appointed radio beacons, the German night fighter crews waited with growing impatience for instructions from their ground controllers.

But below them all was chaos.

Soon the ether was thick with confused appeals and exclamations: 'The enemy are reproducing themselves.' 'It is impossible—too many hostiles.' 'Wait a while. There are many more hostiles.' 'I cannot control you.' 'Try without your ground control.'

When the first wave of bombers—110 Lancasters from No. 1 and 5 Groups—arrived over Hamburg at 0103 hours their crews were struck by the air of unreality: instead of the precise control which had always been the case in the past, the searchlights now seemed to be groping blindly. Where beams did cross, others would quickly join them, and as many as 30 or 40 beams would build up to form a cone—on nothing.

The radar sets controlling the searchlights were now useless, as were those which controlled the guns. The gunners were forced to abandon predicted fire, and now they loosed off round after unaimed round ineffectively into the sky.

Saved from the accustomed harassments of fighters on the approaches to the target, and searchlights and shell bursts over it, the British crews now made their bombing runs on the almost defenceless Hamburg. The Pathfinders' radar-aimed yellow markers had fallen accurately round the aiming point, and had been followed almost immediately by reds from the Visual Marker Force.

The leaders of the Luftwaffe had never expected that they would be called upon to meet a concentrated bomber attack. But as the British and American air forces began the raids which were to develop into 'round the clock' attacks, the Germans were forced to improvise: a number of fighter-bombers and medium bombers were adapted to carry heavy gun armament plus the Lichtenstein radar, while development of specialised aircraft was accelerated

Dornier Do-217N: Another medium bomber which was developed for use as a night fighter. **Span:** 62 feet 4 inches. **Length:** 58 feet 9 inches. **Speed:** 320 mph at 18,700 feet. **Ceiling:** 31,170 feet. **Range:** 1,550 miles. **Armament:** Four 20-mm cannon, four 7·9-mm MG, one 13-mm MG in a remote-control dorsal turret, and one 13-mm MG in a dorsal turret. **Crew:** Three

John Batchelor

Heinkel He-219A Uhu (Owl): Although the prototype of this formidable specialised night fighter first flew in 1942 it never achieved widespread operation. Only 268 were built. **Span:** 60 feet $8\frac{1}{3}$ inches. **Length:** 50 feet $11\frac{3}{4}$ inches. **Speed:** 416 mph at 22,965 feet. **Ceiling:** 41,660 feet. **Range:** 960 miles. **Armament:** Two 30-mm and two 20-mm cannon, and two 30-mm Schräge Musik cannon

It was upon these, and the green markers dropped at intervals by 'Backers-up' of the Pathfinder force, that the first and succeeding waves of bombers aimed their loads: scores of the huge 8,000- and 4,000-pound 'blockbusters', thousands of the smaller 1,000-pound bombs, and a veritable rain of the nasty little 4-pound incendiaries. In general the crews far above the target were able to make out only the flashes as their high-explosive bombs burst, and a few shimmering fires started by the incendiaries. But at 0110 hours there was an explosion which lit up the sky for miles around.

After bombing, the RAF crews flew south for six minutes to get well clear of the target. Then the pilots swung their machines round on to a north-westerly heading parallel to the one that had brought them in. To the men now returning from battle there was no doubt that this new-fangled 'Window' stuff really did work. In fact Bomber Command lost only 12 aircraft (1·5%) out of the large attacking force. The new 'Window' tactic had clearly been a great success. Had the raid cost the 6% losses normal for a raid on Hamburg, the RAF would have lost about 50 bombers. So about 35 or more had been saved, by the dropping of 40 tons of 'Window' —92,000,000 strips of aluminium foil.

But Sir Arthur Harris had already warned that the 'Battle of Hamburg' was not going to be won in a single night: 'It was estimated that at least 10,000 tons of bombs will have to be dropped to complete the process of elimination. To achieve the maximum effect of air bombardment this city should be subjected to sustained attack.'

So it came about that RAF Bomber Command launched a further attack on Hamburg at 0057 hours on the morning of July 28. The 722 bombers involved flew across the city from north-west to south-east this time, and by 0112 hours crews running in to bomb saw beneath them a vast carpet of fire, covering almost the whole of the north-east quarter of the city. Into this inferno succeeding aircraft were dropping thousands of incendiary and high-explosive bombs.

During the whole of July, less than 1·7 inches of rain had fallen on the city, and the previous day had been very hot: the kindling was everywhere. Under the torrent of well-placed incendiary bombs the fires soon took hold. With the city's water supplies disrupted and the civil defence headquarters already blitzed in the previous raid, the blaze was able to rage unchecked.

The firestorm

In principle, a firestorm is horrifyingly simple, and from the comfort of an armchair is an interesting exercise in applied physics. A multitude of fires heat the air above them, and as the hot air rises more air rushes in to take its place; this inrushing air fans the

A running battle over Germany

After 'Window' had enabled the RAF to burn Hamburg almost undisturbed, the Germans introduced several new tactics. In 'Wild Boar' the night fighters waited over the target to intercept the bombers by visual sighting alone; for 'Tame Boar' radar guided the fighters into the areas where the 'Window' was thickest so that they could close with the bomber streams and then search for their targets independently. On March 30, 1944, 'Tame Boar' proved its value in a battle against bombers attacking Nuremburg *(below)*. The night was clear so that visual sighting was easy, while strong winds made the bomber streams lose cohesion. As the bombers came over Beacon 'Ida', the first fighters were zeroed in by the ground controllers *(right)*, and all along the route to Nuremburg new groups were being fed in, until more than 200 night fighters from all over Germany were engaged in the running battle. The British lost over 94 aircraft in that one raid

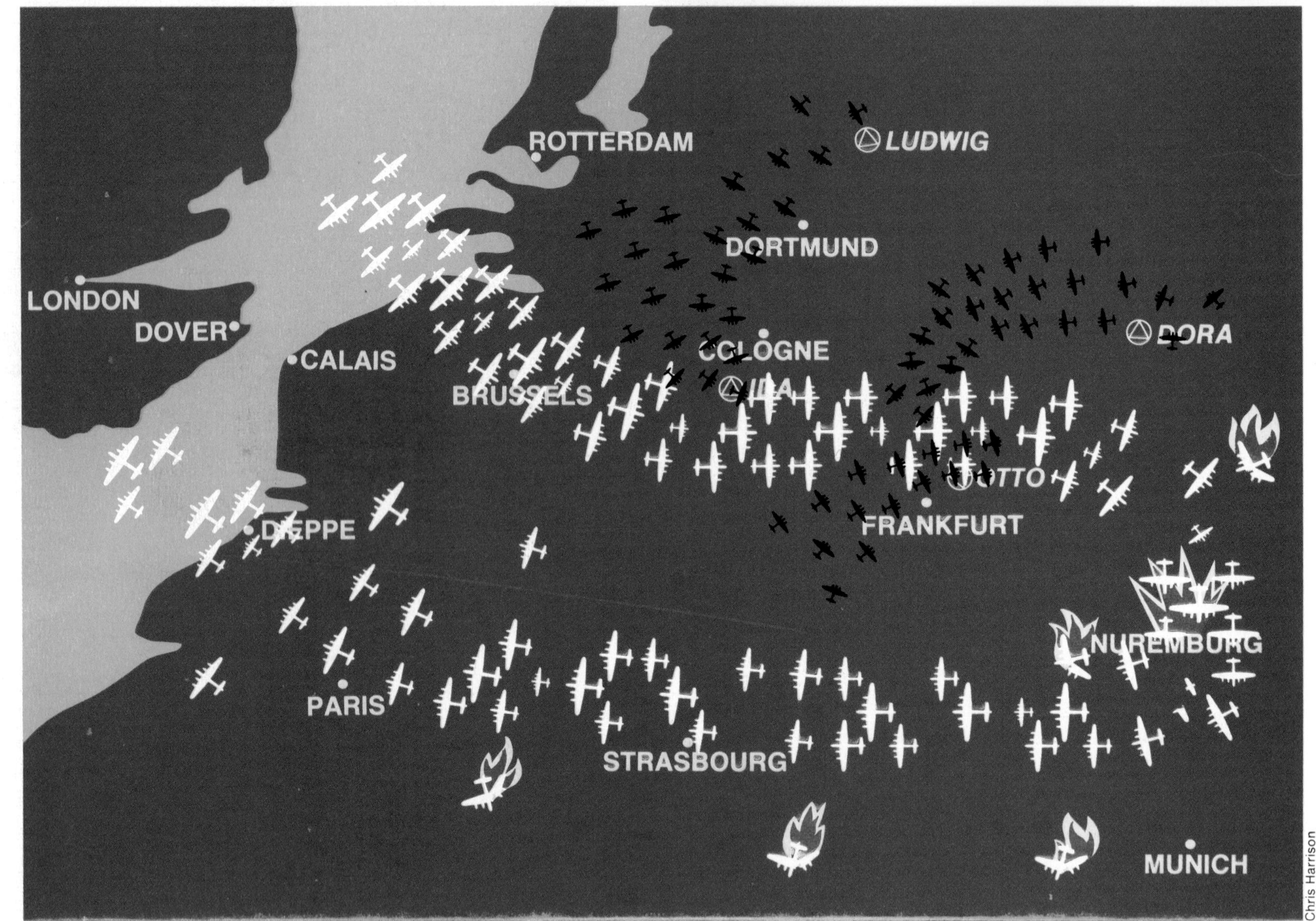

Chris Harrison

flames, before itself becoming heated and rising, and the process repeats itself continuously while the flames blaze hotter and hotter. This was what now happened in Hamburg. Soon, in places, the temperature exceeded 1,000° Centigrade, the mighty convection currents causing winds of up to 150 mph—twice hurricane force. As the air sucked in to the larger fires fanned the small ones, these too grew in size; quickly the fires linked with each other, until a built-up area 3½ miles long and 2½ miles wide was burning itself to death: 9 square miles of fire. It was a highly populated area that was going up in flames and Major-General Kehrl, the Hamburg civil defence chief, later reported:

The scenes of terror which took place in the firestorm area are indescribable. Children were torn away from their parents' hands by the force of the hurricane and whirled into the fire. People who thought they had escaped fell down, overcome by the devouring heat, and died in an instant. Refugees had to make their way over the dead and dying. The sick and the infirm had to be left behind by the rescuers as they themselves were in danger of burning . . .

On the following morning, July 29, Gauleiter Kaufmann appealed to all non-essential civilian personnel to leave Hamburg. They needed no second bidding. Between dawn and dusk nearly 1,000,000 civilians, many of them swathed in bandages, streamed out of the city limits.

Bomber Command visited Hamburg again on July 30, and yet again on August 2, to add to the earlier holocaust. The number of people killed has never been established, but informed sources put the total at about 50,000. As the number of British civilians killed in German attacks on Britain up to this time was some 51,000, in one week the slate had been wiped almost clean.

Following the Hamburg fiasco the German night fighter tactics underwent a sweeping reorganisation. The system of close ground control, which General Kammhuber had pioneered, was largely

Hamburg: a wave of terror

The first raid on Hamburg on the night of July 24/25 had caused widespread damage, but the city continued to function. 'At least 10,000 tons of bombs will have to be dropped to complete the process of elimination. To achieve the maximum effect of air bombardment this city should be subjected to sustained attack' announced Air Chief-Marshal Harris, and so the RAF visited Hamburg again on the night of July 28 *(below)*, and a new horror was added to the practice of aerial warfare. Colonel Adolf Galland describes the effect of the first firestorm on German morale: 'A wave of terror radiated from the suffering city and spread throughout Germany. Appalling details of the great fires were recounted, and their glow could be seen for days from a distance of 120 miles. A stream of haggard, terrified refugees flowed into the neighbouring provinces. In spite of the strictest reticence in the official communiqués, the Terror of Hamburg spread rapidly to the remotest villages of the Reich. Berlin was evacuated with signs of panic.' *Right:* Major Hajo Herrmann (centre, with Göring, left), one of the leading 'Wild Boar' pilots, personally led his fighters into action

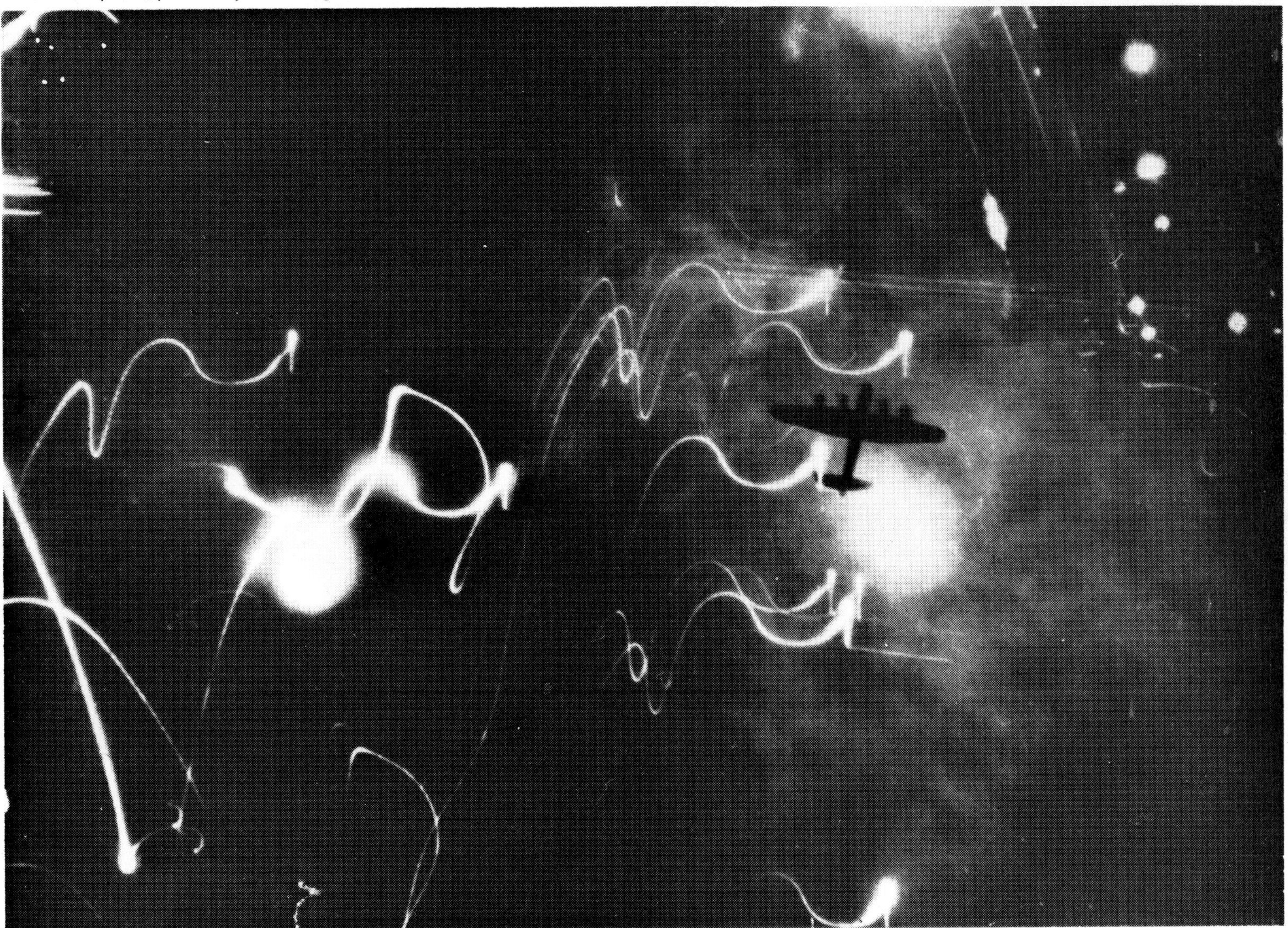

abandoned and in its place the Luftwaffe introduced two new night fighting methods: 'Wild Boar' *(Wilde Sau)* and 'Tame Boar' *(Zahme Sau)*. Kammhuber himself was quietly shunted out of his position as commander, and replaced by General Josef Schmid.

The Wild Boar tactic called for the concentration of night-fighting units over the target itself. There the massed searchlights, the vast conflagrations and the British Pathfinders' own marker fires lit up the sky for miles around, silhouetting the bombers for the German fighters. Thus the latter could now attack visually, and there was no need for the previously essential and comparatively expensive radar-equipped two-seater fighters. And significantly, for this same reason, Window could not degrade the system in any way. Under the command of Major Hajo Herrmann, the originator of the system, a number of specialist Wild Boar units were formed and equipped with single-seater Messerschmitt Me-109 and Focke-Wulf FW-190 day fighters.

The twin-seater radar-equipped specialist night fighters could also engage in Wild Boar-type tactics at the target, but to use their potential to the full, Colonel von Lossberg, a night fighting expert, devised the Tame Boar method. His idea was for the now jammed ground control stations to direct the fighters into the area where the Window concentration was densest, and once there the German pilots were to search visually for targets. When they were in the concentrated bomber stream, and aligned on the same heading, Lossberg hoped it would be possible to set up long running battles which would last the whole of the time the bombers were over occupied Europe.

Obviously, both the new German tactics demanded accurate and up-to-date information on the position of the bomber streams, but, while the radar network was dense and efficient enough for this purpose along the old Himmelbett line, elsewhere in Germany sets were comparatively few and far between. Luftwaffe signals

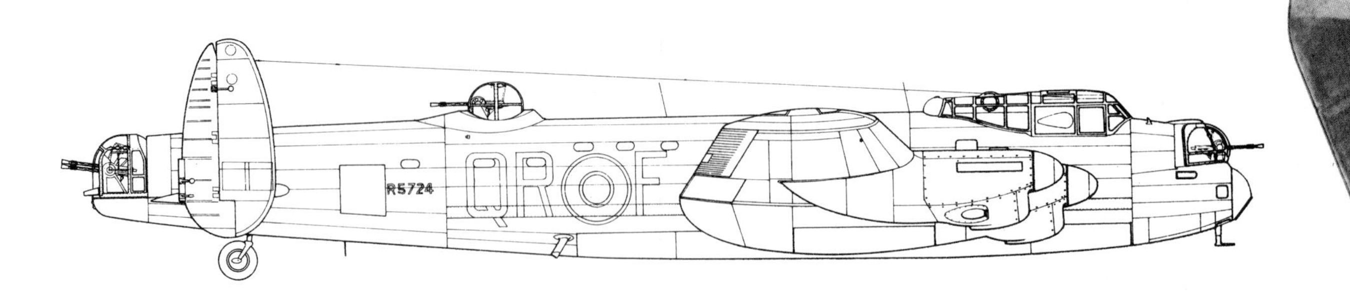

AVRO LANCASTER Mk I

Gross weight: 63,000 lb **Span**: 102 ft **Length**: 69 ft 6 in **Engine**: 4×1,280 hp Rolls Royce Merlin XX **Armament**: 10× ·303 Browning machine-guns **Crew**: 7 **Speed**: 280 mph at 18,500 ft **Ceiling**: 23,500 ft **Range**: 2,700 miles **Bomb load**: 14,000 lb

The most famous and successful heavy night bomber of the Second World War, the Lancaster first entered service with RAF Bomber Command in 1942

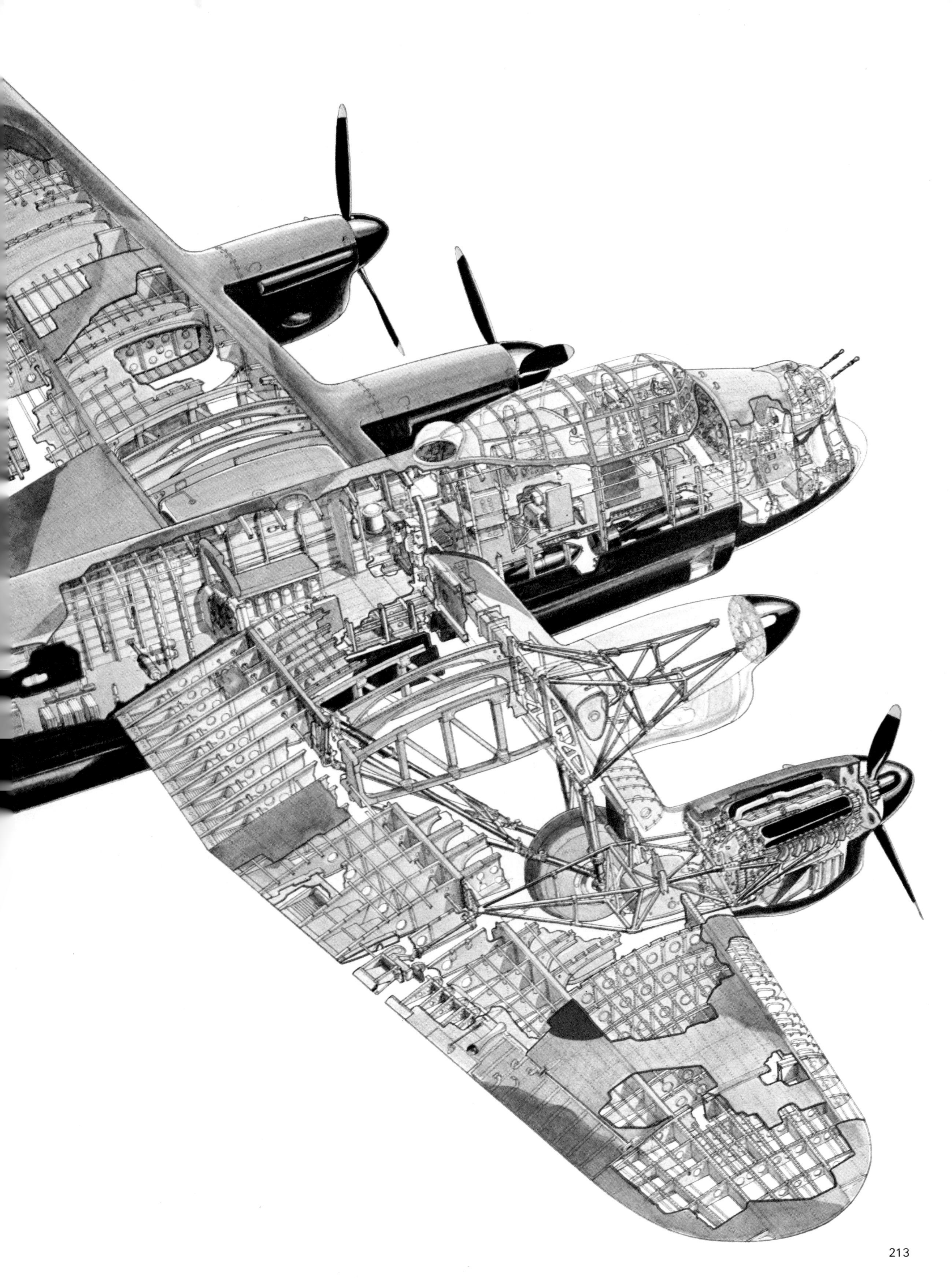

Bapty & Co Ltd

After the holocaust

When Hamburg's week of terror ended, more than 50,000 people had died *(left),* and 9 square miles in the centre of the city had been burned out. The most terrible description of the effect of the firestorm comes from this secret report, sent to the top leaders of Germany: 'Trees three feet thick were broken off or uprooted, human beings were thrown to the ground or flung alive into the flames by winds which exceeded a hundred and fifty miles an hour. The panic-stricken citizens did not know where to turn. Flames drove them from the shelters, but high-explosive bombs sent them scurrying back again. Once inside, they were suffocated by carbon-monoxide poisoning and their bodies reduced to ashes as though they had been placed in a crematorium, which was indeed what each shelter proved to be. The fortunate were those who jumped into the canals and water-ways and remained swimming or standing up to their necks in water for hours until the heat should die down.'

Below: Birth of the first firestorm: a photograph taken during the raid of July 28, showing the widespread fires shortly before they linked up

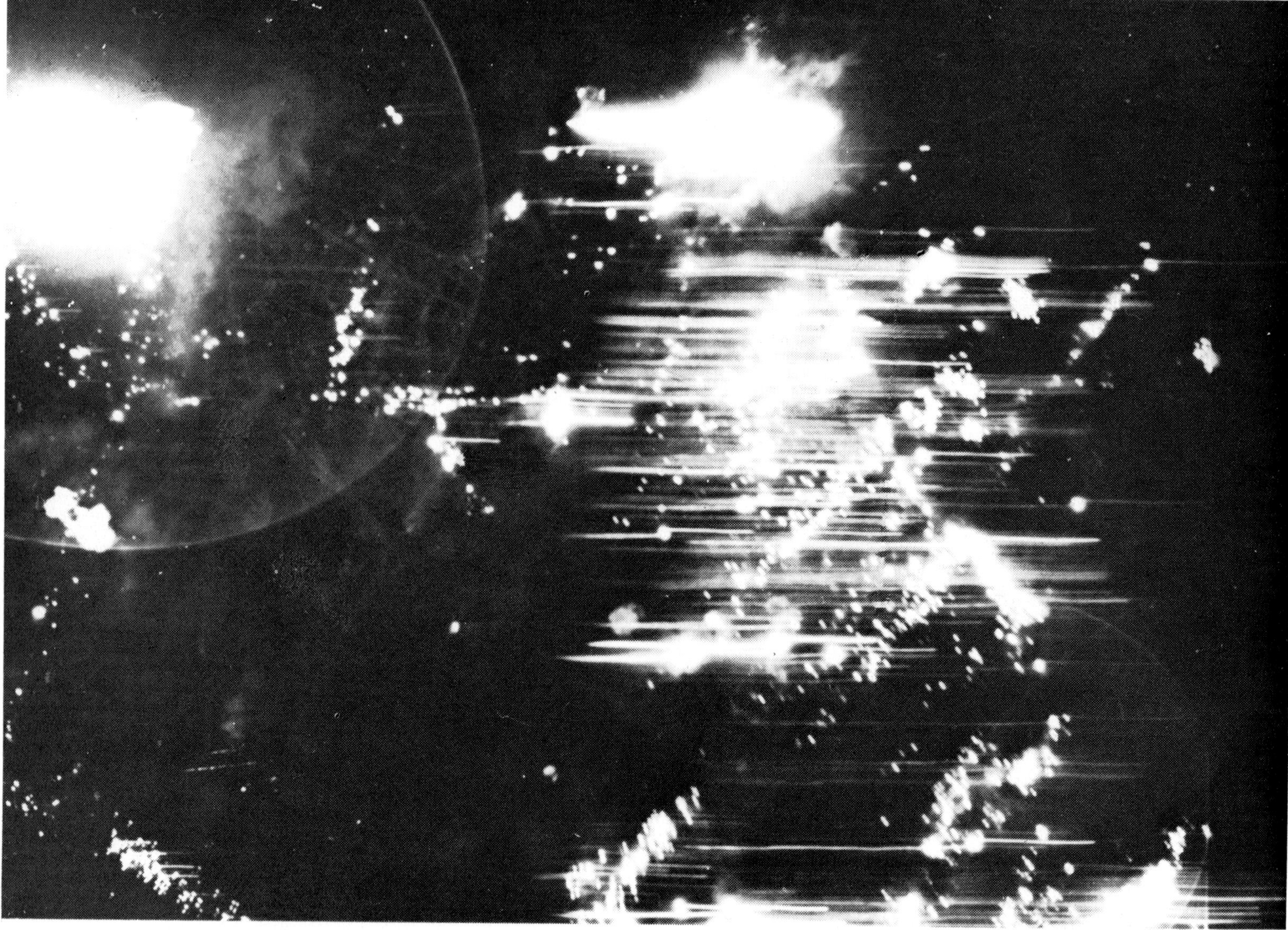

Imperial War Museum

personnel struggled to reposition radar sets in the new enlarged fighting area, but while they did so, some means had to be found of keeping tabs on the continually moving bomber streams. Fortunately for the Germans, the solution was presented by the raiders themselves.

To find their targets, the RAF Pathfinder crews used H2S—for those days an extremely advanced radar device which scanned the ground over which the aircraft flew. The German signals service exploited this factor by setting up a chain of 'Naxburg' and 'Korfu' ground direction-finding stations, which were able to follow precisely the sources of the distinctive H2S signals. Since the Pathfinders were invariably at the van of the bomber streams, this clever ploy meant that the raiding forces could be tracked with a high degree of accuracy almost from take-off to landing.

In the late summer of 1943, as the German fighter force gradually became more familiar with the new tactics, British losses started to rise again. Both the Wild Boar and Tame Boar methods relied heavily on a running commentary broadcast from powerful ground transmitters, which passed details of the position, height, course, and estimated strength of the bomber streams. As British Intelligence officers listened in to the broadcasts one thing became clear: if this information could be denied to the German pilots, the new tactics might be set to nought.

So, once again, it was necessary to step up the radio countermeasures offensive. This time the target was the German fighter control channels, which now became a cacophony of wails, shrieks, and groans. To this the Luftwaffe replied by transmitting orders simultaneously on a large number of separate frequencies, and introducing transmitters radiating even higher powers.

One interesting little piece of chicanery tried at this time rejoiced under the cover-name 'Corona'. If the German aircrews depended on orders radioed from the ground to find the bombers,

The bombing was costly in life to both sides. *Below:* A Liberator bursts into flames after being hit by flak. Over Schweinfurt the Americans lost 60 aircraft in one raid alone. And the RAF lost 95 aircraft (of 795) over Nuremberg in one night. *Bottom:* Bomb damage in Hannover. In one raid on October 19, 1943, 2½ square miles of this city were destroyed

US Air Force

would not false orders from a station in Britain lead them astray? The idea was first tried on the night of October 22, during a 569-aircraft attack on Kassel. The furious German fighter controller warned his crews not to be tricked by the enemy, and shouted 'In the name of General Schmid I *order* all aircraft to Kassel.' During the rumpus that followed the German swore into his microphone, at which the German-speaking 'ghost' controller in Britain remarked: 'Now the Englishman is swearing!' Beside himself with rage the German shouted back: 'It isn't the Englishman who is swearing, it's me!'

But in spite of this hilarious interlude, Bomber Command was to lose 42 aircraft (6·2%) of the force dispatched. The German orders went out on many frequencies, and for technical reasons it was impossible for the British to carry on separate arguments on each. After a few evenings the 'Corona' operators ceased trying to imitate the German controllers, and instead took to reading bits of Goethe, turgid pieces of German philosophy, and even playing records of Hitler's speeches on the German fighter control channels.

As the summer of 1943 turned to autumn, the first German night fighters arrived at the front fitted with a new radar device, code-named 'SN-2', in place of the Window-vulnerable 'Lichtenstein'. Because it worked on a much lower frequency than the earlier radar, SN-2 was able to see through the Window with little difficulty. The introduction of the new set, in combination with the Tame Boar tactics, was to have an important bearing on events during the winter to come.

On November 3, 1943, Air Chief-Marshal Sir Arthur Harris minuted to Churchill: 'We can wreck Berlin from end to end if the USAAF will come in on it. It may cost us 400-500 aircraft. It will cost Germany the war.'

This was the kind of promise that Churchill could not resist, and Harris was authorised to launch the 'Battle of Berlin'. The

American bomber force, however, was still licking its wounds following the attempt to push unescorted bomber formations through the German defences in daylight. It had suffered swingeing losses in the process, and could not now 'come in on it'. Harris decided to go it alone.

The first attack on the German capital of the new series was launched on November 18, 1943, and only nine of the 444 heavy bombers engaged failed to return. Bombers returned to Berlin three more times during November, and four times during the following month, and on each occasion losses were surprisingly low in view of the target's importance—possibly in consequence of the bad weather over Germany at the time.

This was an auspicious start, but as the new year opened Bomber Command's losses began to rise alarmingly. The first of a series of great and costly battles occurred on the night of January 21, when 55 bombers were lost out of 648 which set out for Magdeburg.

The bomber crews had fought back hard, but the German losses for the evening amounted to only seven aircraft—though one of the German fighters shot down that evening was a Junkers 88 piloted by the famous ace Major Prince zu Sayn Wittgenstein, the top-scorer with 83 'kills' to his credit. Wittgenstein's radar operator, Sergeant Ostheimer, later described how, after taking off at 2100 hours on a Tame Boar operation:

At about 2200 hours I picked up the first contact on my [SN-2] radar. I gave the pilot directions and a little later our target was seen: it was a Lancaster. We moved into position and opened fire, and the aircraft immediately caught fire in the left wing. It went down at a steep angle and started to spin. Between 2200 and 2205 hours the bomber crashed and went off with a violent explosion. I watched the crash.

Again we searched. At times I could see as many as six aircraft on my radar. After some further direction, the next target was in sight—another Lancaster. After the first burst from us there was a small fire, and the machine dropped back its left wing and went down in a vertical dive. Shortly afterwards I saw it crash. It was some time between 2210 and 2215 hours. When it crashed there were heavy detonations; most probably it was the bomb load.

After a short interval we again saw a Lancaster. After a long burst of fire the bomber caught fire and went down. I saw it crash some time between 2225 and 2230 hours. Immediately afterwards we saw yet another four-engined bomber: we were in the middle of the bomber stream. After one firing pass, this bomber went down in flames, at about 2240 hours. I saw the crash.

Such a personal score of four raiders in less than 40 minutes was by no means unique in the German night fighter force. Once within the tight mass of heavily laden bombers, the cannon-armed fighters were able to wreak havoc—and with the bitter memory of Hamburg still fresh in their minds, Wittgenstein and his colleagues fought like tigers.

Within a few minutes of the fourth 'kill' Ostheimer had directed the Prince into a firing position yet again, and the first burst set the bomber on fire. But then the fire went out—and as Wittgenstein moved in for a further attack, his own aircraft rocked under the impact of an accurate burst of machine-gun fire. Ostheimer managed to bail out and land safely, but the Prince was killed. Almost certainly the attack had come from one of the other bombers in the stream, thus avenging its fallen comrades.

As the new year progressed the German defences took an increasingly heavy toll of the attacking bomber force. On January 28, 43 bombers failed to return of 683 attacking Berlin, and the month that followed was even worse. On February 15, 42 were lost out of 891 attacking Berlin, and four days later the command lost 78 out of 823 attacking Leipzig; in March, 72 bombers out of 811 dispatched were lost during the Berlin attack on the 24th. Even a successful attack on Essen two days later, when only nine failed to return out of 705, was overshadowed by the appalling total cost.

During this period the German exploitation of the bombers' own radiations reached a high pitch of efficiency. That Sir Arthur Harris continued to send out H2S-equipped aircraft, even though he had a shrewd idea of the dangers involved, was not due to any pious belief that the Germans might fail to grasp their opportunity. In truth a fine balance had to be struck between, on the one hand, the effectiveness of the bombers in finding and destroying targets, and on the other hand the degree of risk involved in so doing. By removing H2S from its aircraft Bomber Command could undoubtedly have cut losses. But to have done so would have deprived the force of the only radar bombing aid that could be used over Berlin, and the striking power of the force would have been reduced considerably. If, as Harris sincerely believed, Bomber Command could repeat the Hamburg pattern on five or six important cities and thus bomb Germany out of the war, then the stakes were high enough to justify the greatest risks.

A measure of the success of the Allied bombing raids—the Krupp Arms Works in Essen lies in ruins

Bomber Command did not visit Germany again until March 30. This was to be Harris's final attempt to smash a major German city before the operational control of his force passed to General Eisenhower, in preparation for the forthcoming invasion of Europe. The target for the 781-aircraft force was Nuremberg.

Even before the leading aircraft had crossed the coast of Britain the ever-watchful German listening service had correctly deduced the direction of approach from the H2S bearings. As a result the Chief Operations Officer to the Luftwaffe III Fighter Division was able to order his crews to assembly over radio beacon 'Ida', in the path of the bomber stream, in good time.

Because of unexpectedly strong winds, the bomber stream began to lose cohesion very early on, and even before the first turning point the aircraft were advancing on a front 40 miles wide. And due to the night's unusual meteorological conditions, worse was to follow. Each minute, the petrol burned in one aero engine produced one gallon of water as steam; normally the steam dispersed, but in this very cold night it condensed and the long white condensation trails of vapour suspended in the sky, chased remorselessly behind each bomber as it crossed the Rhine moving eastwards. It was a clear night, and the glow from the half moon gave the vapour trails a phosphorescent quality.

The British radio-jamming barrage was as powerful as ever, and the German fighter corps diarist noted: 'Corps VHF [radios] jammed by bell sounds. R/T traffic hardly possible. Jamming of corps HF [Radios] by quotations from Hitler's speeches. Corps alternative frequency and divisional frequencies all strongly jammed . . .'

But as the mass of bombers passed almost exactly over the Ida beacon, where the fighters were already waiting, the jamming availed them little.

It was over Ida itself that the Luftwaffe III Fighter Division joined battle, and within minutes the horrified British crews were being treated to the spectacle of bomber after bomber going down in flames. This was the beginning of a running fight that was to last for 250 miles and, even as the first shots were being fired, other fighter divisions were converging on the bomber stream from all over Germany. The II, from northern Germany, joined via radio beacons Ludwig and Ida; the 1st from bases in the Berlin area, moved westwards on a collision course with the bombers, and joined the stream via beacon Dora; the VII Fighter Division, coming up from southern Germany, was fed in via radio beacon Otto. In all, 21 squadrons of night fighters, some 200 aircraft, went into action: it was an ideal night for the Tame Boar tactics, and they wrought fearful execution on the bomber force.

At the bombers' altitude there was a 50-mph tail-wind which took many of the bombers far to the east of their intended track, par-

The crucial equation: bombs dropped against German production

The ultimate justification for the Allied bomber offensive was that it struck directly at the German war machine and could thus cripple her forces at the front. The graphs below, taken from figures published in the British Official History, show the mounting total of bombs dropped, and the output of three key German industries

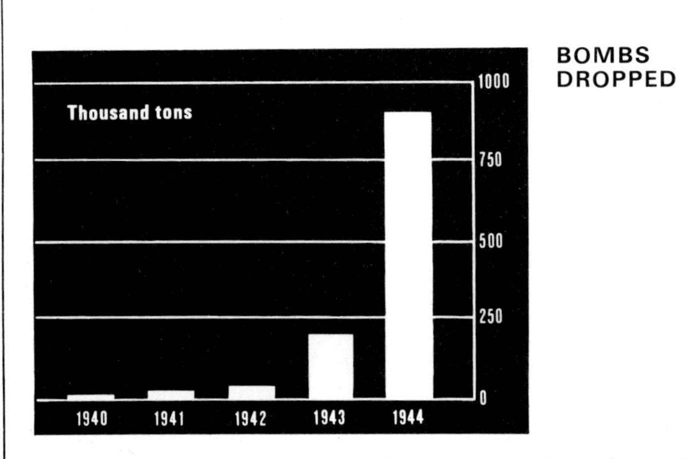

It was not until the war ended that the Allies were able to take stock of the effect of the vast weight of bombs which they had hurled at Germany, and realise that in almost all types of production German output had risen almost as swiftly and steadily as the weight of bombs. The massive rise of bombs dropped during 1944 reflects the achievement of a continuous day-and-night offensive co-ordinating the attacks of RAF Bomber Command and the USAAF

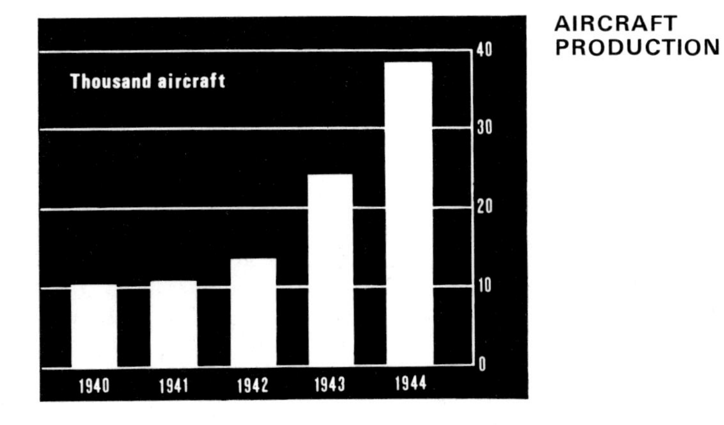

One way in which the attacking forces were to gain air supremacy over their targets was by smashing the air frame and aero engine factories of the defenders. This the Allies tried, but German countermeasures proved so successful – dispersing the large factories into small units scattered all over the country which were difficult to locate and attack – that their aircraft production rose steadily, and it was not until the Allies were able to introduce long-range escort fighters for their daylight raids that they were able to achieve a reasonable level of superiority

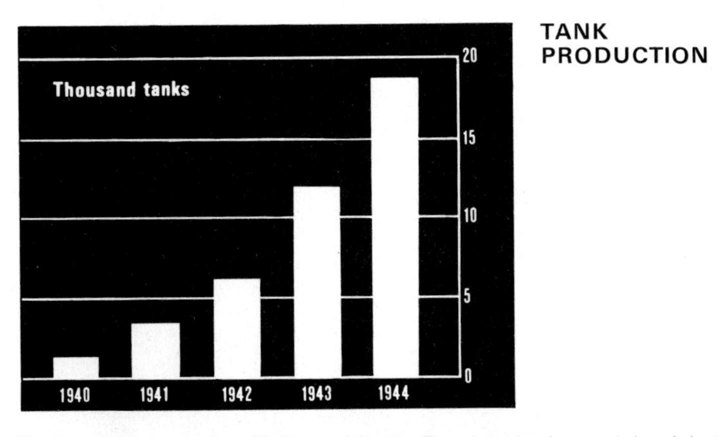

During the years before D-Day while the Russians had complained that they were bearing the whole brunt of the war, the British and American strategic bombing offensive had been the great symbol of what the Western Allies were doing to strike directly at Germany. But in tanks, as in aircraft, the German production totals continued to rise – although this is not to say that they would not have risen considerably faster had the bombing not taken place

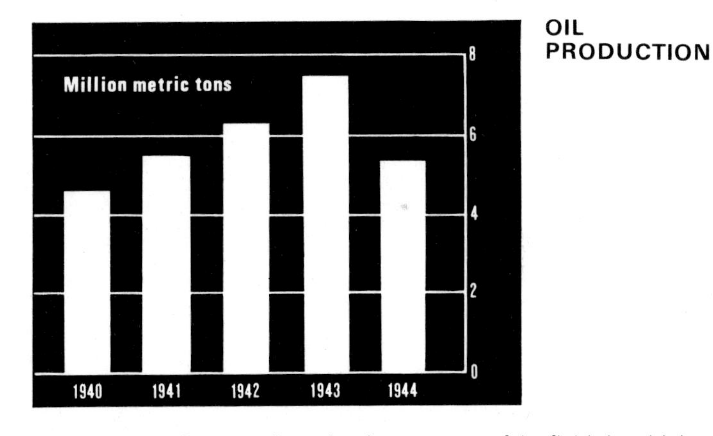

The assault on German oil production was one of the fields in which the Allied bomber offensive was shown to be conspicuously successful. The Germans had long realised the threat which hung over this most vital and vulnerable part of their economy, but, except for two raids on Ploesti, it was not until October 1943 that US bombers were unleashed in concentrated attacks on the plants in the Ploesti and South German areas. At first the damage to production was slight, but during the summer of 1944 German oil output collapsed and her forces were condemned to near immobility during their most vital battles

ticularly during the final south-eastern leg of the approach to the target. The Germans consequently had some difficulty in making out which target the bombers were making for, but if there was doubt where the British were going, there could be no doubting where they had been: the bombers' track from Ida on was clearly marked by the trail of wrecked aircraft burning on the ground. Not until 0152 hours, two minutes before the bombing was due to start, was Nuremburg first mentioned in the German 'running commentary'.

Because of the scattering effect of the strong winds, and the persistent harassing from the night fighters, the actual attack on Nuremburg was diffuse and ineffective. Indeed, so widely scattered was the bomber stream as it withdrew, that the German night fighters lost it almost completely and the surviving bombers were at least allowed to make their return flights virtually unmolested.

For Bomber Command the cost of the Nuremburg raid had been very high indeed: 94 Lancasters and Halifaxes failed to return, and thus Sir Arthur Harris's daring attempt to end the war by strategic bombing ended in failure. The failure came close to crippling Bomber Command: during the 35 major attacks between November 18, 1943, and March 31, 1944, it had lost 1,047 aircraft; a further 1,682 machines had limped back damaged – and although it had been hit hard, Germany was still very much in the war.

In the night skies on the routes to Berlin, Magdeburg, Leipzig, and Nuremburg the men of the German night fighter force had avenged their humiliation over Hamburg in the summer of 1943. Now, in the spring of 1944, they stood at the pinnacle of their success, blooded and confident in the new Tame Boar tactics.

The Key Raids against Germany

[Statistics compiled by the IWM.]

1940, May 15/16: RAF Raid on the Ruhr
Night precision raid on oil plants and marshalling yards. Of 99 planes involved, 1 lost. Amount of damage unknown but probably negligible. This raid opened strategic air offensive against Germany. (RAF had previously confined itself to raids on coastal targets and military communications, and to dropping leaflets.)

1940, December 16/17: RAF Raid on Mannheim
Night area raid on city centre. Of 134 planes involved, 3 lost. Only scattered damage inflicted: many bombs fell outside target area. First RAF 'area' raid. Lacking means to carry out effective precision attacks, Bomber Command bombed main industrial cities. Object was to disrupt German war production and break civilian morale.

1942, March 28/29: RAF Raid on Lübeck
Night area raid on town centre. Of 234 planes involved, 12 lost. Some 1,500 houses destroyed, much damage to factories. But production nearly normal one week later. First large-scale incendiary raid.

1942, April 17: RAF Raid on Augsburg
Daylight precision raid on MAN diesel engine factory. Of 12 Lancasters involved, 7 destroyed, 5 damaged (no fighter cover). Main assembly shop and other buildings damaged but production hardly affected. Raid showed that it was impractical for heavy bombers to make precision attacks in daylight, and reinforced RAF's faith in the night offensive.

1942, May 30/31: RAF Raid on Cologne
Night area raid on city centre. Of 1,046 planes involved, 40 destroyed, 116 damaged. Nearly half of city devastated, 474 people killed, over 40,000 homeless. But Cologne made a surprisingly rapid recovery. First of the 'Thousand Bomber' raids.

1942, August 17: 8th AF Raid on Rouen
Daylight precision raid on Sotteville marshalling yards. Of 12 B-17s involved, no losses. Some damage to rolling stock and rails but only temporary. US 8th AF's first attack. US firmly committed to daylight precision raids.

1943, March 5/6: RAF Raid on Essen
Night area raid on Krupp works. Of 442 planes involved, 14 destroyed, 38 damaged. Heavy damage to Krupps, 160 acres of Essen devastated. But British estimates exaggerated effect of raid on production. First use of 'Oboe' radar device helped to overcome industrial haze in the Ruhr area.

1943, May 16/17: RAF Dams Raid
Night precision raid on Möhne, Eder, and Sorpe dams. Of 19 Lancasters involved, 8 destroyed, 6 damaged. Möhne and Eder dams breached; Sorpe dam only damaged. Some 1,000 people drowned and severe flooding, but raid had no appreciable effect on German war economy. Landmark raid in development of precision bombing techniques.

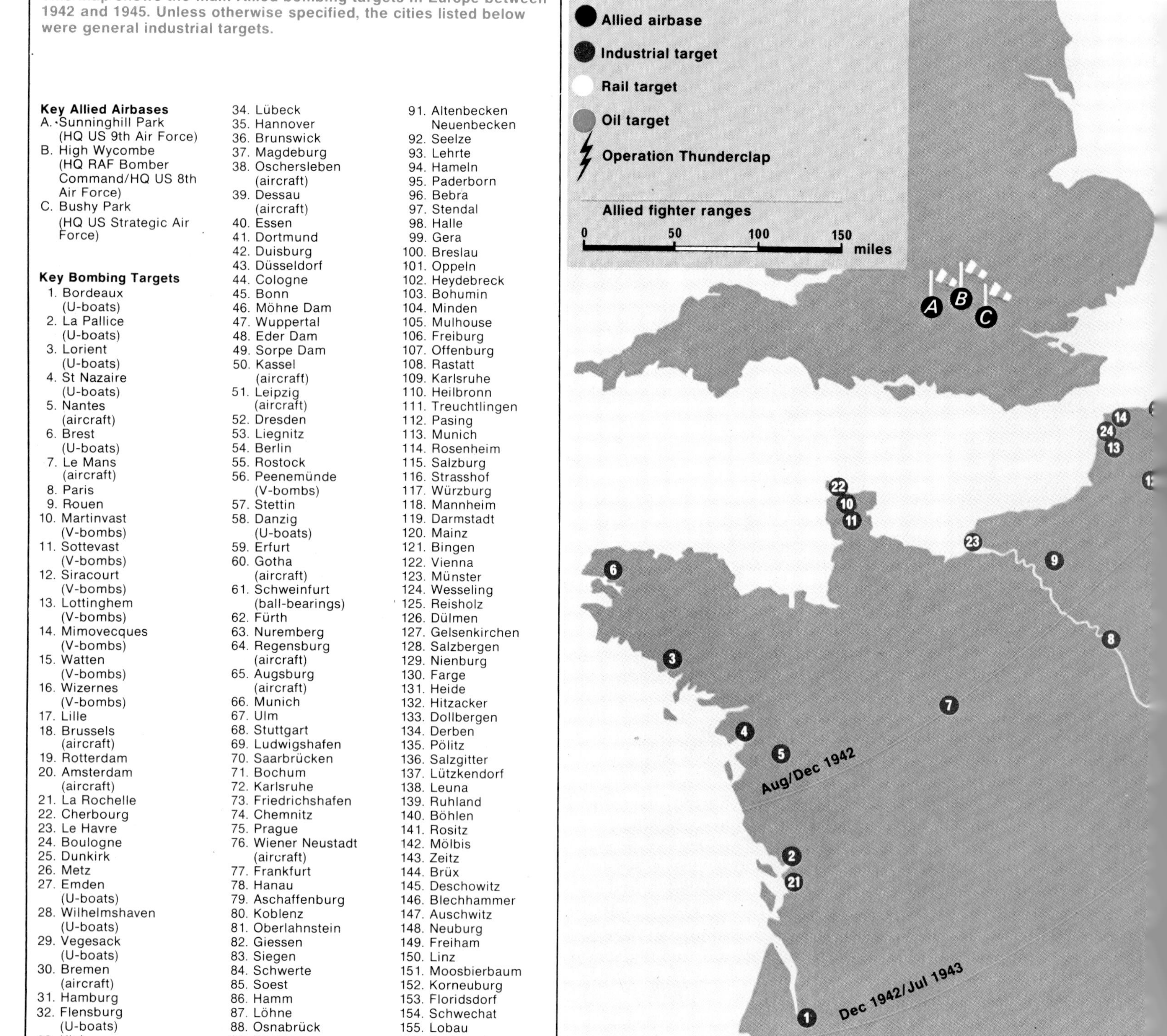

1943, July 24/25: RAF Raid on Hamburg
Night area raid on city centre. Of 791 planes involved, 12 destroyed, 31 damaged. Over 2,200 tons of bombs dropped. Widespread damage to residential areas. Fires still burning 24 hours after raid. Major success for Bomber Command. German radar confused by 'Window' – strips of tinfoil used for first time. This raid followed by mass attacks on nights of July 27, 29, August 2. Hamburg left in ruins. Over 42,000 people thought to have been killed.

1943, October 14: 8th AF Raid on Schweinfurt
Daylight precision raid on ball-bearing works. Of 291 planes involved, 60 destroyed, 138 damaged. Most damaging of the 16 Schweinfurt raids but caused only temporary setback in production. Germans reorganised ball-bearing industry before next attack 4 months later. Bombers escorted only part of way to target. Crippling losses caused by German fighters exploded theory of self-defending bomber formation, forced US to curtail daylight bombing offensive.

1943, November 18/19: RAF Raid on Berlin
Night area raid on city centre. Of 444 planes involved, 9 lost. Some 1,500 tons of bombs dropped. Damage unknown but probably considerable. First of 16 mass raids on Berlin, involving over 9,000 planes in all. These raids less effective and more costly than ones on Hamburg and the Ruhr, owing to distances, strength of defences, weather.

1944, March 8: 8th AF Raid on Berlin
Daylight precision raid on Erkner ball-bearing works. Of 590 planes involved, 37 lost. Heavy damage to works (75 direct hits). Production at standstill for some time. Third US raid on Berlin. Bombers escorted by large force of P-51s. Beginning of US daylight air command.

1944, March 30/31: RAF Raid on Nuremberg
Night area raid on city centre. Of 795 planes involved, 95 destroyed, 71 damaged. Some 2,500 tons of bombs dropped but raid too dispersed to cause serious damage. Heaviest defeat suffered by Bomber Command in war. Nuremberg was to RAF night raids what Schweinfurt was to US day raids. Both showed that without command of the air long-range bombing could not be kept up indefinitely. After Nuremberg RAF broke off mass raids on distant targets.

1944, September 23/24: RAF Canal Raid
Night precision raid on Dortmund-Ems Canal, inland waterway linking Ruhr with other industrial areas. Of 141 planes involved, 14 lost. 11 'Tallboy' bombs (12,000 lb each) dropped. Canal breached, 6-mile section drained.

1945, February 13/14: RAF Raid on Dresden
Night area raid on city centre. Of 805 planes involved, 8 lost. Immense damage to old town and inner suburbs: 1,600 acres devastated. Incendiaries kindled worst firestorm of war. Estimates of killed range from 35,000 to 135,000 (latter figure almost certainly too high). Most destructive – and most controversial – European raid of war. Dresden, whose strategic importance is questionable, was crowded with refugees and virtually undefended. Bombed again next morning by 400 planes of US 8th AF.

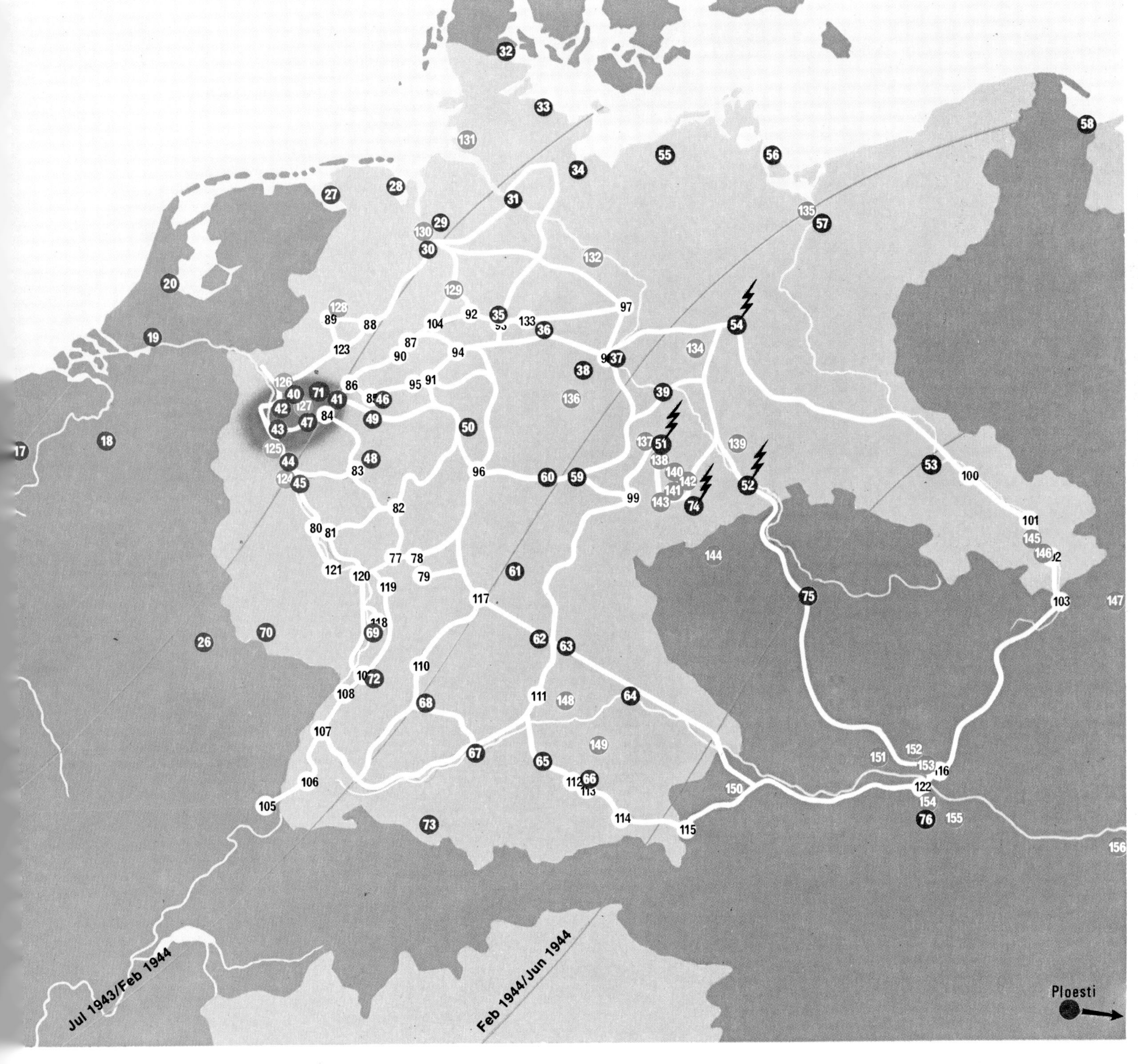

THE BOMBER OFFENSIVE

GETTING THROUGH TO THE TARGET

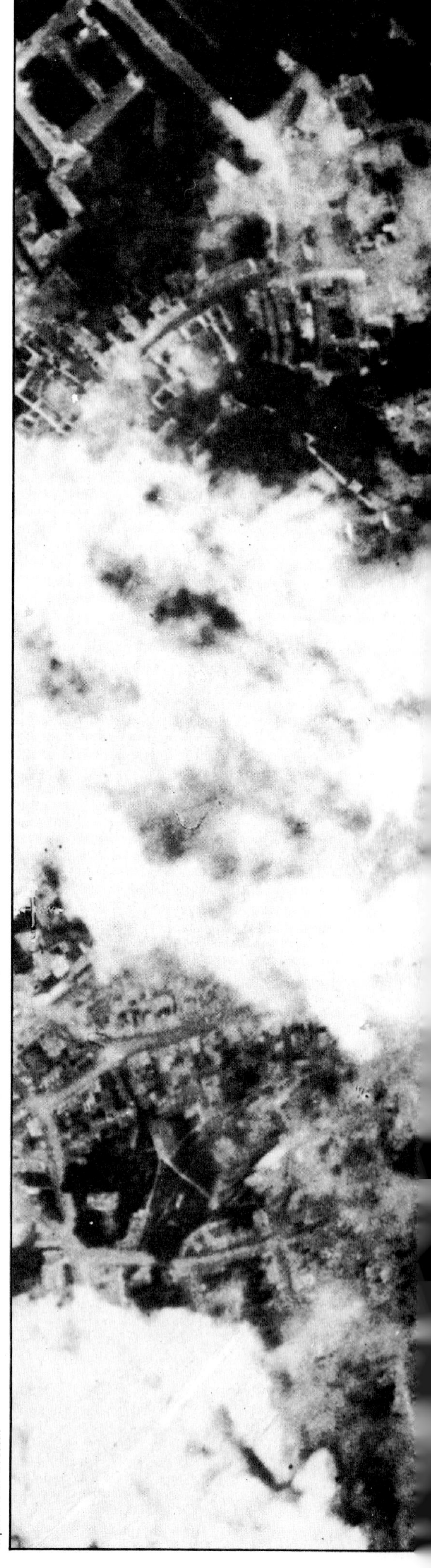

Bombing, both tactical and strategic, was a most important part of the Allied war effort. Radar, of course, played a vital part in this, and against the background of a continuous battle of wavelengths, bombs of all types and sizes were produced.

One of the most common misconceptions generally held about the Allied bombing offensive is that the Allied air forces were quite happy with small bombs until sometime in the middle of the war when they realised that heavier bombs were going to be needed, whereupon they went into a crash designing action. Like many other common beliefs, this isn't entirely true. The Royal Air Force were well alert to the need for heavy bombs and were busy with the designs of bombs up to two tons in weight well before the war broke out.

The principal trouble lay in the contemporary aircraft. In the pre-war days, it would seem, the aircraft designers set out firstly to make an aeroplane which flew at the speed and height required, and afterwards set about hanging a bombload on it. It was not until the experience of war showed the fallacy of this method that they reversed their priorities and began designing bombloads and then putting a suitable aeroplane around the outside of them. Once this system took over, it was possible to fit the enormous bombs in and actually carry them. While the Flying Fortress and some of its contemporaries could carry impressive weights of bombs, their construction made it necessary for the bombs to be small ones, and it was not until the advent of the British Lancaster, with its 33-ft long unobstructed bomb-bay, that really big bombs could be carried.

However, not all bombs have to be big ones, and some of the most effective bombs, and the ones of which little is known, were quite small. They were also highly specialised in their application, as, for example, the British 8-lb 'F' bomb. The letter 'F' seems to have had no special significance, since many of the British bombs were in a lettered series, but it is coincidence that this bomb was officially demanded for 'fouling' airfields. In other words, they were to be scattered by dozens across German military airfields in order to prevent aircraft from taking off or landing and involve the airfield staff in a massive clean-up operation before the field could be serviceable. These small bombs were fitted with an 'anti-disturbance and delay' fuze so that after landing on the ground they would lie there and detonate at random intervals up to six or seven hours after landing. This, of course, constituted a considerable hazard and it was necessary to

A 'Grand Slam' is hoisted from an RAF bomb dump. Such a colossal bomb (22,000 lb) could drill deep into the ground setting off 'earthquake' tremors to destroy the most massive of structures

Imperial War Museum

The radar war: Jamming and counter-jamming

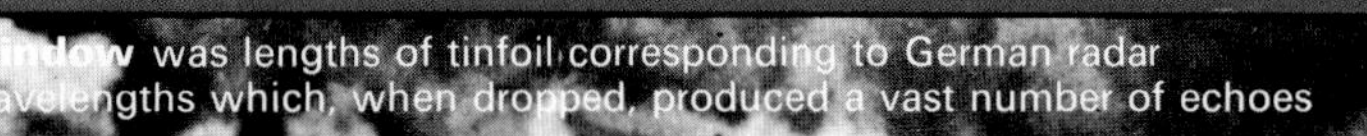

Window was lengths of tinfoil corresponding to German radar wavelengths which, when dropped, produced a vast number of echoes

Mandrel: pairs of circling aircraft radiating signals with jamming devices formed a barrier which German radar could not penetrate

Piperack was an enormous jamming transmitter carried in a lead aircraft, behind which Allied bomber streams could shelter in a radar-proof cone

Imperial War Museum

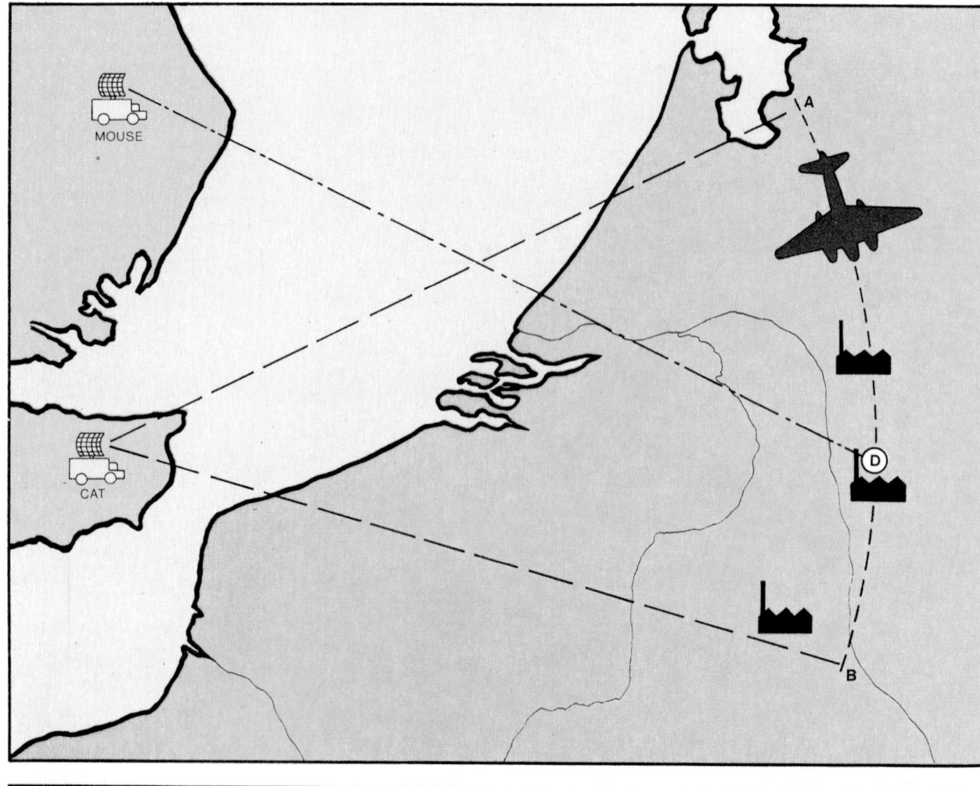

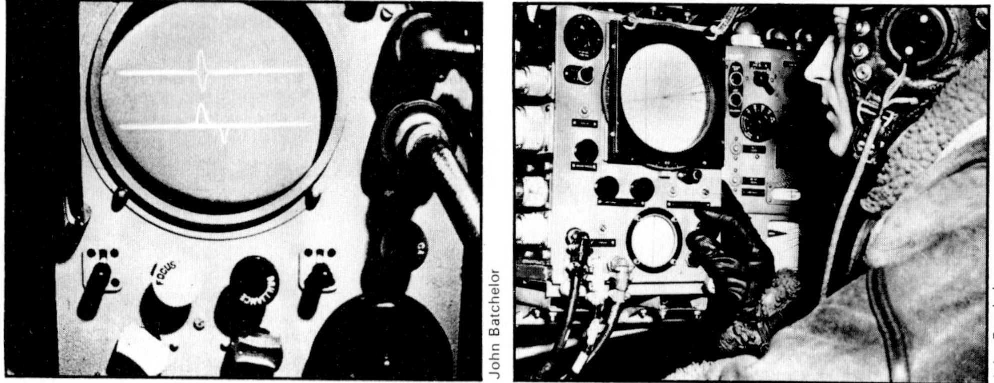

Oboe: Signals were transmitted from 'Cat' and 'Mouse', and returned by the aircraft, thus fixing its distance from the Cat. When it reached a pre-calculated distance from the Mouse it was over the target D. Oboe's range of 270 miles encompassed the Ruhr. *Above:* Oboe's twin 'blip' screen and navigator's position. A pair of transmitters controlled one aircraft, limiting its use to Pathfinder Mosquitos

get out on the field and clear them away. In order to confound this activity, the other half of the fuze, which became sensitive only after landing, reacted to any movement of the bomb. Any attempt to pick it up or sweep it away detonated the charge to the detriment of whoever was trying to shift it. Numbers of these bombs were also included in normal air raids on factories and other targets in order to make life difficult for the fire-fighting parties.

An interesting American development in the bomb field was the attempt to produce a 'Slow Burning Explosive', called SBX for short. Experience had shown that the sharp blast of a conventional high explosive bomb frequently had little effect on a building other than blowing in all the windows, while records of industrial and mining explosions showed that the slow, heaving effect of coal-dust and similar explosions seemed to have a better effect in wrecking buildings and work began on trying to adapt this principle to a weapon.

Bombs filled with coal-dust and flour, stone-dust and similar finely divided substances were developed, and controlled experiments in old buildings showed that the theory was quite correct: SBX – a comparatively small bomb completely obliterating a large building in slow motion – had a devastating effect. But the practical problems of controlling the operation so as to obtain the perfect proportions of dust and air eventually defeated the experimenters. Finally, of course, the development of the nuclear bomb removed any need for the SBX bomb.

In the large bomb field, most of the oddities came from Britain, the USA being solely interested in straightforward large bombs which would achieve their aim by blast effects alone. But in Britain was Barnes Wallis, a remarkable inventor who had some definite ideas on making bombs work in other ways. His most famous achievement was, of course, his cylindrical bomb used for the attack of the Möhne, Eder and Sorpe dams in Germany, but some of his other designs were probably more significant. His 22,000-lb 'Earthquake' or 'Grand Slam' bomb, for example, was a piercing bomb which went through the sound barrier on the way down, developing sufficient terminal velocity to plunge deep into the ground before detonating. Thus, when it went off, it sent shock waves through the earth to attack the foundations of nearby structures. Its most famous application was against the Bielefeld Viaduct, which carried a main railway line of vital importance to the German war economy. Several raids had been directed against this target, but it was a difficult article to hit and it had survived most of the war unscathed. A single Earthquake bomb dropped several yards away was sufficient to bring several arches of the viaduct crashing down, closing that particular line for the remainder of the war.

Six-ton smash

An earlier design of Wallis's, the 12,000-lb 'Tallboy', had similar characteristics and was widely used for interdiction bombing prior to the Allied invasion and for attacking rocket launching sites. One spectacular result was the attack by the Royal Air Force of a railway tunnel in France, through which trains carrying troop reinforcements were likely to be rushed to counter the invasion. A single Tallboy dropped on the hill above penetrated through the solid stone overlay, entered the tunnel and detonated, and brought the entire hill down on top of the line. This meant another rail link was permanently closed to the German Army.

The most formidable targets on the Continent to confront the RAF were the immensely strong submarine pens which the German Navy had built in the Channel Ports to protect their U-Boats. These were massive concrete structures inside which

Razon Bomb (Range and AZimuth ONly)
In a standard bombing approach, once the bomb aimer released his bombs that was it. By fitting a radio receiver, movable rudders, and a gyro-stabilizer to a standard 1000-lb GP Bomb, US designers came up with a formidable unpowered guided missile

the submarines could shelter while being repaired, serviced and restocked preparatory to a fresh sweep into the Atlantic. The roofs of these pens were initially some 3·5 metres thick, but they were generally added to with successive layers of concrete and brick until some of them reached 30 or 35 ft in thickness. Normal bombs simply landed on the roof, detonated, and did no damage at all, and it was not until the advent of the Tallboy and Grand Slam bombs that any impression was made.

But the full and final answer to the U-Boat

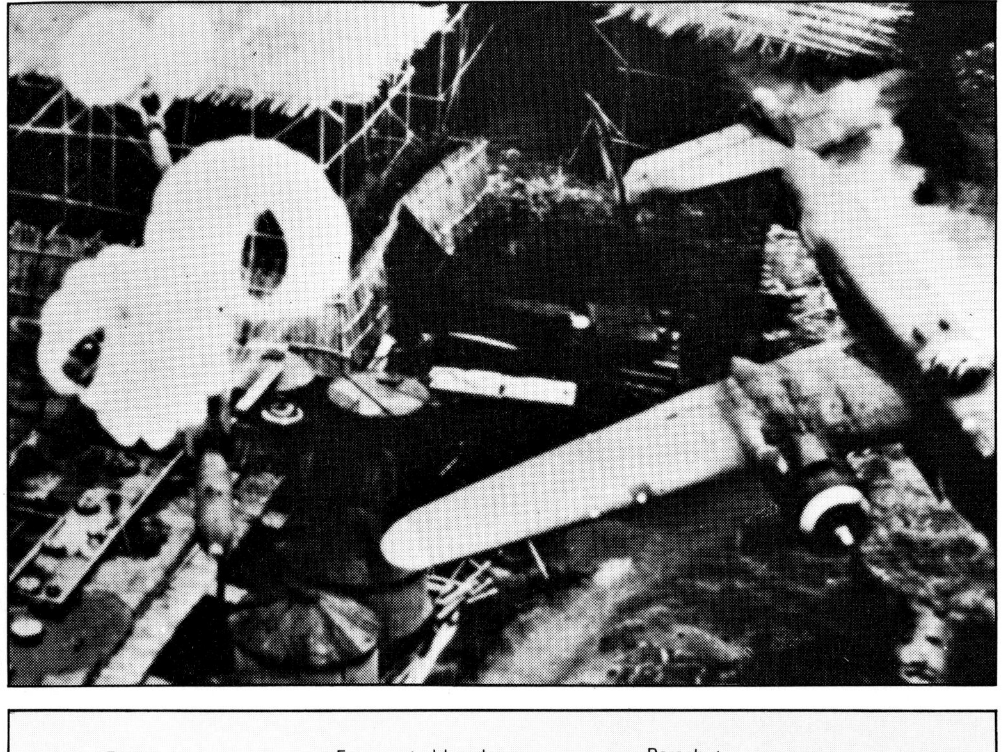

Sudd-Verlag

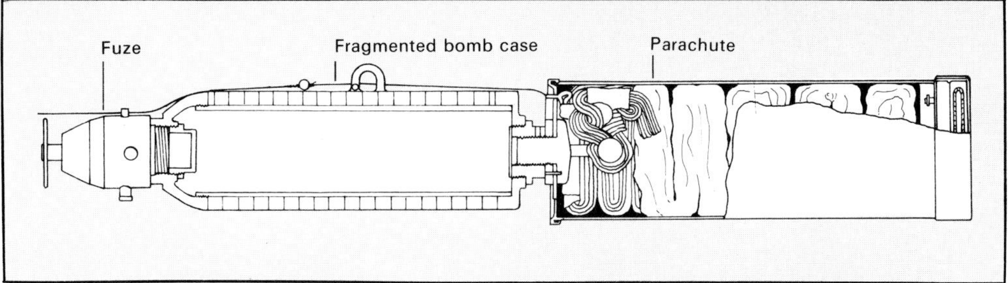

Parachute Fragmentation Bomb A small fragmentation bomb incorporating a parachute container: on being dropped from an aircraft, the parachute opened and the bomb floated down to explode in mid-air, showering shrapnel. *Top:* A B-25 Mitchell parachute bomb over a Japanese factory

pens turned out to be a bomb developed by, of all people, the Royal Navy. It may seem a little odd that the sailors were concerning themselves in what appeared to be Air Force business, and indeed the project ran into stiff opposition on no better grounds than that, but looked at from another direction it was quite logical. The Navy's business was to deal with the U-Boat, and if they could catch the U-Boat while it was unprepared in its pen, then this offered a considerable advantage in the battle. Hence their interest in aerial bombing of the pens.

The Navy's idea was born in September 1943 when Commander (later Captain) Terrel OBE, one of the staff of the Admiralty Miscellaneous Weapons Development Department, suggested using a rocket to drive a piercing bomb through the roof of the submarine pens so that the bomb could be detonated inside the pen. A design was drawn up for a 4500-pounder propelled by nineteen 3-in rocket motors. It was to be dropped from an aircraft at 20,000 ft and, after falling slowly, a barometric device would initiate an ignition system and fire the rockets 5000 ft above the ground. This would accelerate the bomb to a speed of 2400 ft per second to give it immense penetrative ability.

Indeed, it was this last portion of the flight which caused the greatest worries, since it meant that the bomb would pass through the sonic barrier, and at that stage of the war there was very little known about the performance of missiles at supersonic speed. The Barnes Wallis Tallboy and Earthquake bombs were also supersonic at the end of their drop, and had to be given canted fins to rotate them in order to overcome stability problems in the transsonic region, and the Air Force were not slow to point out the potential troubles ahead. But the Navy, very shrewdly, pointed out that they had been firing cannon shells at supersonic speeds since before the Air Force existed, and they were going to make their bomb the same shape as a cannon shell. The arguments were interminable and on a very high level indeed, but eventually the Admiralty were given authority to go on with their design, and in the spring of 1944 the first trial bombs were dropped. The design worked surprisingly well, and the Admiralty's faith in their design was vindicated. But now came problems in getting the necessary manufacturing capacity for the bombs, and it was not until February 1945 that the weapon was first used in action.

Due to its size the rocket bomb could only be carried beneath the wing of the American B-17 Flying Fortress, and the first attack with the bomb was mounted by the US 92nd Bombardment Group against the U-Boat pens at Ijmuiden in Holland. The bombers achieved direct hits on the difficult targets from 20,000 ft, and the bomb-aimers reported seeing flames and smoke coming out of the entrance to the pens, indicating that the bombs had, as planned, penetrated the concrete cover and detonated inside the pen, destroying the anchored U-Boats there. In the following month an attack was made on the heavily protected U-Boat assembly plant at Farge, on the Weser River 15 km north of Bremen. This was still uncompleted at the end of the war and was the hardest target of all, the roof being a solid prefabricated slab seven metres thick. Even this did not stop the rocket bombs. Unfortunately for the research scientists who were learning something new with each attack, the war ended without any further attacks with this weapon.

The rocket bomb turned out to be startlingly accurate, but the same could not be said for all bombs, since the mass-produced blast bombs were devoid of any sort of ballistic shaping and were little more than square-ended drums of explosive with fins on the end to give them some reasonable stability. Another factor militating against accuracy was the question of flying a bomber into a hail of anti-aircraft fire and expecting the bomb-aimer to keep cool, calm and collected while he aimed his bombs. As a result the Americans began to look at the prospect of developing bombs which could be released some distance away from the target and guided in their flight. The first to appear was 'Gargoyle', a winged bomb fitted with liquid-fuel rocket boosters. This had no guidance, but the rocket boost and wings gave it a degree of stability which allowed its flight to be accurately predicted. This went into production late in 1944 but was never used during the war.

More effective was the radar-guided bomb 'Bat'. Using rocket-boost, this had a range of 20 miles and could be controlled with remarkable accuracy. It was never used in the European Theatre but saw some striking successes in the Far East, where Japanese supply lines in Burma were cut by guiding the Bat on to river bridges. Among its achievements was the sinking of a Japanese warship in April 1945 at the maximum range of the bomb.

'Bat' Guided Bomb
The US 'SWOD Mk 9 "Bat" 1000-lb Bomb' was a radar guided air-to-surface missile with a 1000-lb warload. In April 1945 an air-launched Bat sank a Japanese destroyer 20 miles from its launch point, its maximum range

Armour piercing 10-ton bombs

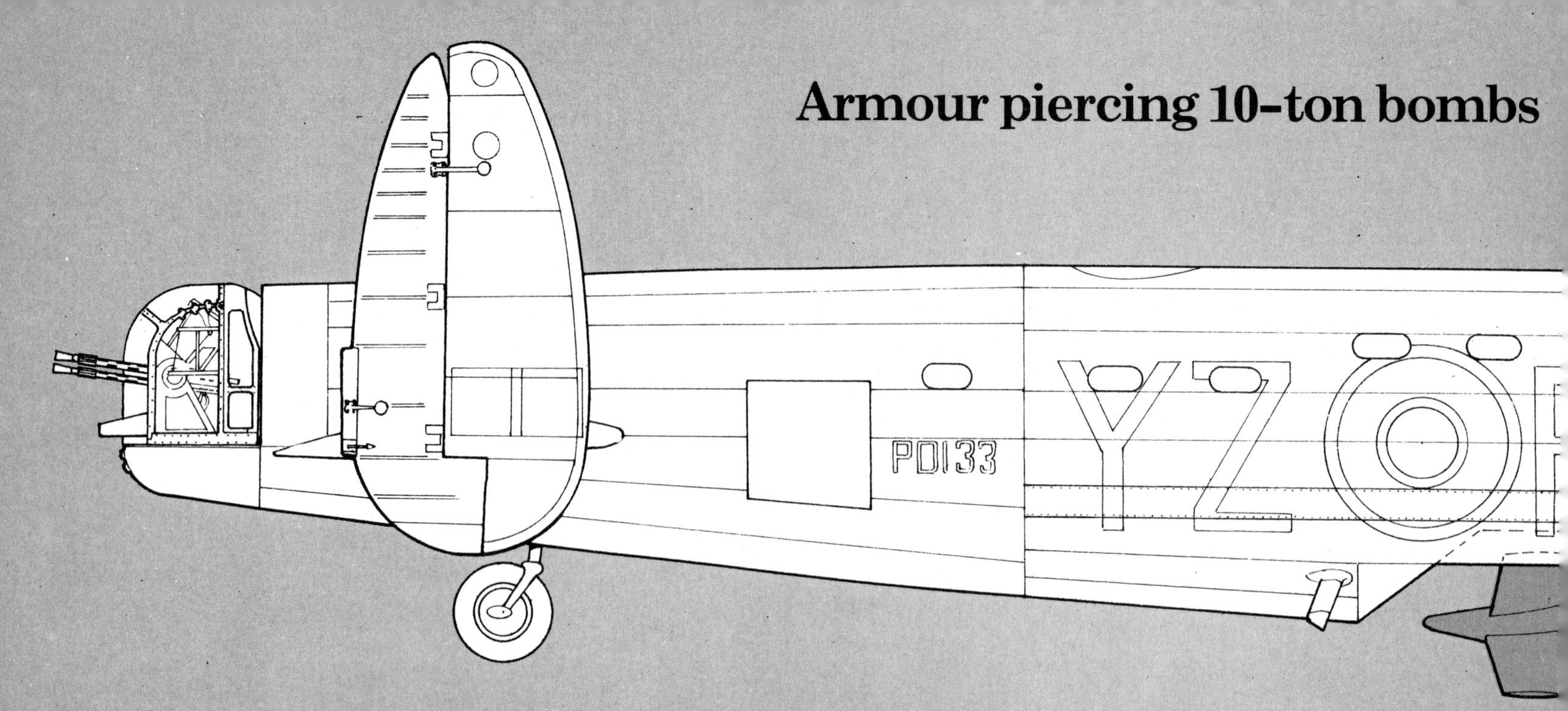

Imperial War Museum

Imperial War Museum

Primary target of the deep-penetration super-bomb offensive were the massive concrete U-Boat pens (above) stretching along the Atlantic Coast from Brest to Bergen. Barnes Wallis's bombs were both streamlined and armoured, capable of withstanding the shock of smashing into concrete at a velocity greater than the speed of sound to explode deep within the target. Left: What the 'Grand Slams' did to the U-Boat pens, 15 feet of reinforced ferro-concrete drilled straight through

falling at Mach 1: The way to crack the toughest nuts

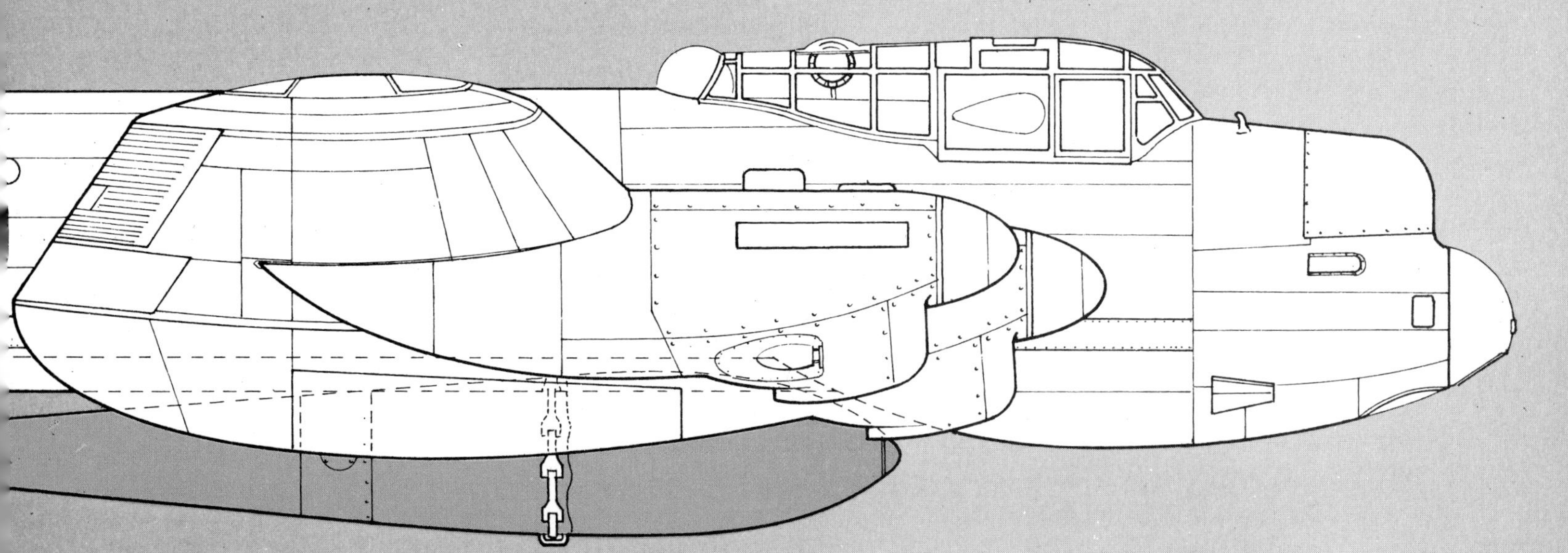

Avro Lancaster B Mk I Special ('Grand Slam')
A special version of the Lancaster to enable it to lift the 22,000-lb 'Earthquake' or 'Grand Slam' bomb
Span: 102 ft *Length:* 69 ft 6 in *Engine:* 4×1280 hp Rolls-Royce Merlin
Max speed: 280 mph *Armament:* 4 mg *Bombload:* 22,000 lb

Imperial War Museum

What 'Tallboys' did to the Tirpitz. *Thirty-two Lancasters bombed the battleship at its heavily guarded anchorage in Tromsöfiord (below). Two bombs penetrated its armour to explode deep inside the hull, capsizing the ship*

Winching a 'Tallboy' up to a Lancaster BIII. With its cavernous bomb-bay, the Lancaster could carry the 12,000-lb bomb to almost any part of Germany

Imperial War Museum

Lancaster Special B Mk III ('Dam Buster')
A Lancaster of the type that attacked the Ruhr Dams
Span: 102 ft *Length:* 69 ft 6 in *Engine:* 4 Packard Merlin 224 *Armament:* 6 mg *Speed:* 287 mph at 11,500 ft *Ceiling:* 24,500 ft *Range:* 1660 miles *Bombload:* 14,000 lb

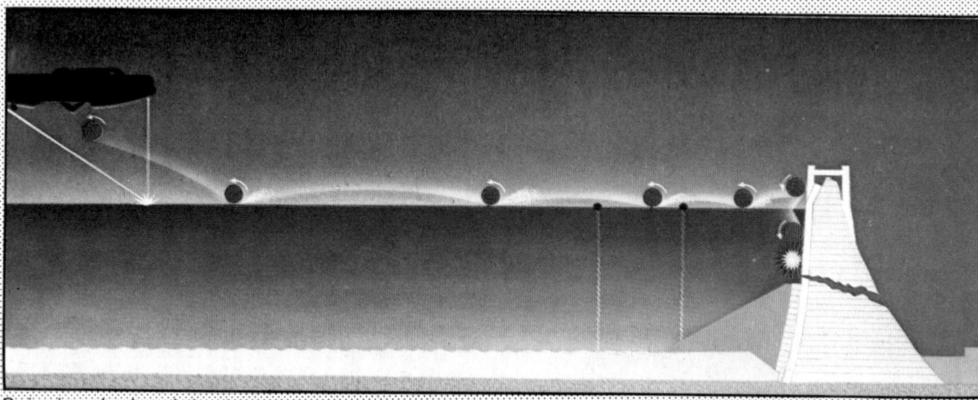

Spinning the bomb backwards made it hurdle the torpedo nets, press itself against the inner face of the dam and sink to explode at its base – as was essential. It was the 'earthquake' effect of the shock waves which did the damage. Dropping height was determined by the alignment of pre-fixed lights, while distance was computed by sighting the dam towers in a simple frame pre set from reconnaissance to give the exact distance

The Dam Busters: The story of the Bouncing Bomb

The target: Möhne Dam and its torpedo nets

Imperial War Museum

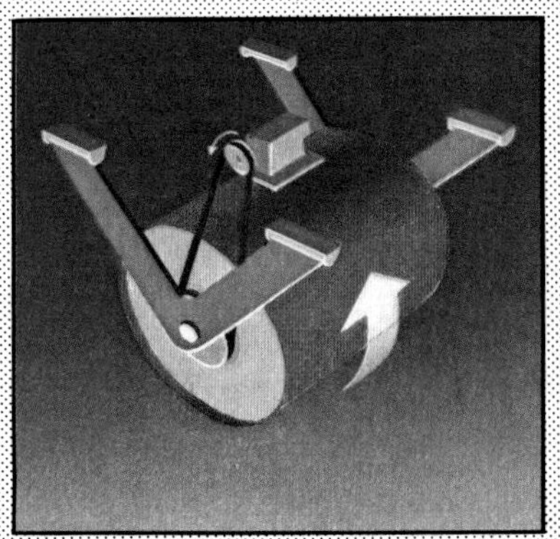

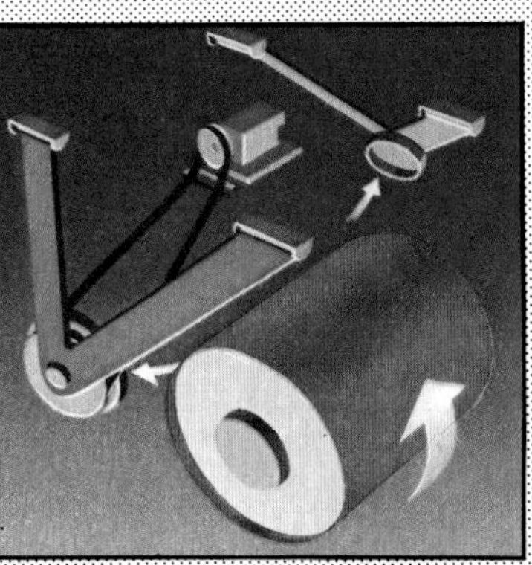

Ten minutes before attack, the cylindrical bomb was spun backwards at 500 rpm, and released by allowing the calipers to spring outwards

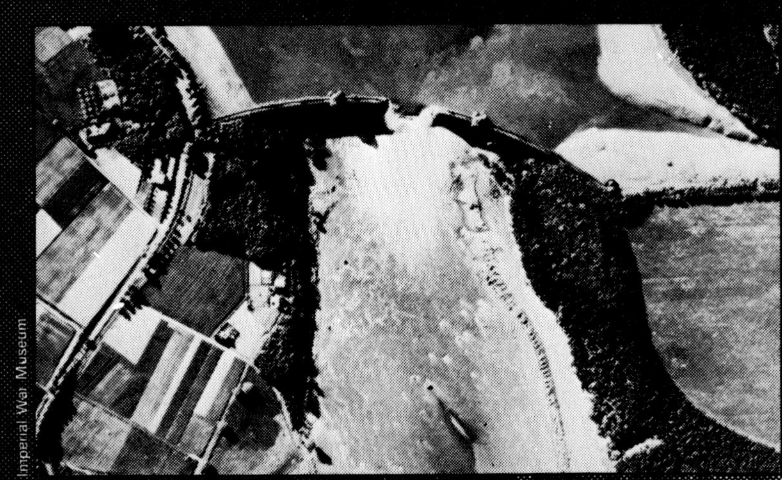

Imperial War Museum

The morning after the raid, with Möhne Lake rapidly emptying

Mosquito B IV with Highball
The high-speed Mosquito was the experimental test-bed for Barnes Wallis's shipping strike development of the bouncing bomb. Designed for use against the Japanese, the war ended before it became operational

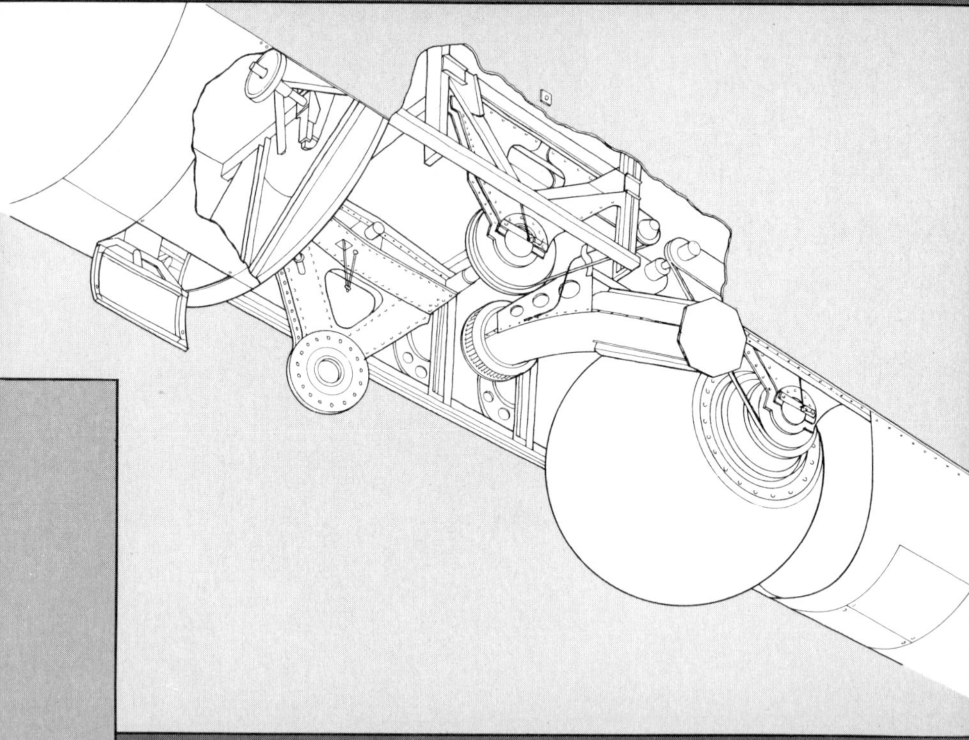

Twin Highball Skip Bomb
Highball was experimentally installed in tandem in a Mosquito B IV. A spherical case was devised with excellent 'bouncing' characteristics and strong enough to withstand impact with the water

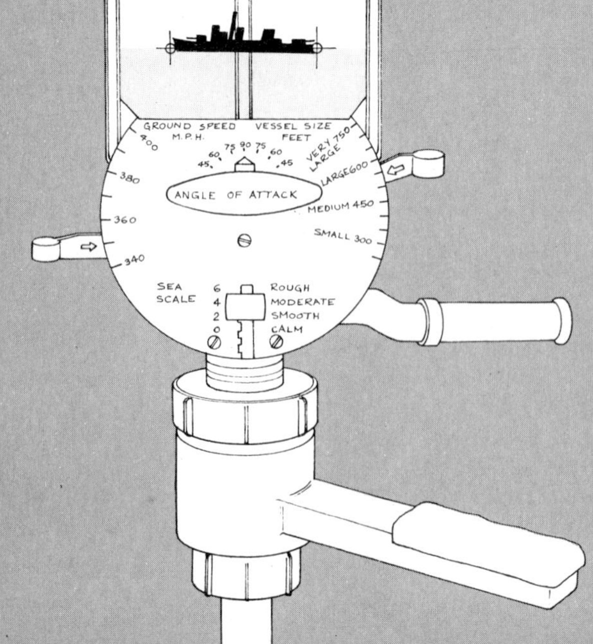

Highball Bomb Sight
All the relevant information on the attack – size and speed of target, angle of attack and condition of sea – was computed on the special bomb sight, which set the viewfinder and ensured that the bomb was aimed correctly

The Highball project: A potent new way of attacking a ship

Imperial War Museum

Barnes Wallis – designer of the R100, the geodetic Wellington, the Dambuster bomb, the 'Grand Slam' and 'Tallboy', and the experimental Highball bouncing bomb

Vickers Ltd

Vickers Ltd

Mosquito launches a Highball (left) at a pre-set height. The bomb bounces towards its surface target carrying a far greater warhead than any standard air-launched torpedo. These stills are taken from a film of a test launch

Rockets from an RAF Typhoon hurtle towards a barge on the Schelde estuary in Holland

Imperial War Museum

Hawker Typhoon
A relative failure as a fighter, equipped with rockets the Typhoon became a formidable ground attack aircraft, either as tactical flying artillery or attacking communications targets
Span: 41 ft 7 in *Length:* 31 ft 10 in *Engine:* Napier Sabre IIA, 2180 hp *Max speed:* 404 mph at 10,000 ft *Range:* 374 miles *Armament:* 4×20-mm cannon or 8×60-lb rockets

Ground attack aircraft: Fitting rockets to a fighter meant a new instrument of precision destruction

Beaufighter-launched rockets streak in to destroy the German headquarters on the Aegean island of Calino in 1944 after the first salvo had missed (left)

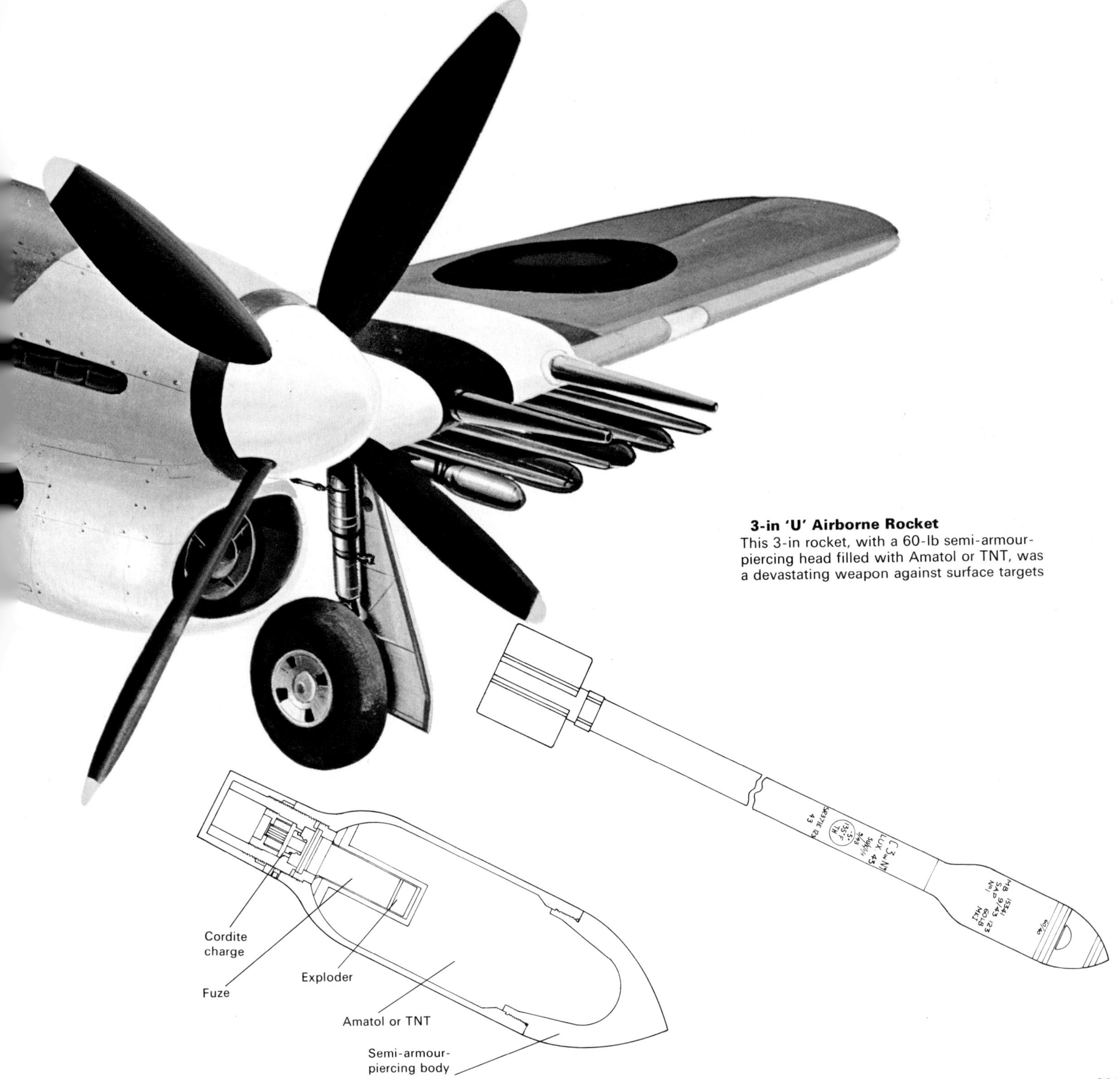

3-in 'U' Airborne Rocket
This 3-in rocket, with a 60-lb semi-armour-piercing head filled with Amatol or TNT, was a devastating weapon against surface targets

BUILD-UP FOR D-DAY

The importance of air power in particular relation to the success or failure of Overlord was fully realised in the summer of 1943. The combined bomber offensive, authorised at Casablanca in January, designed to destroy the enemy economy and to undermine the morale of the German people, had not, at first sight, brought satisfactory results. In July, General Morgan – now known as COSSAC – revealed his disquiet:

The most significant feature of the German Air Force in Western Europe is the steady increase in its fighter strength which, unless checked and reduced, may reach such formidable proportions as to render an amphibious assault out of the question. Above all, therefore, an overall reduction in the strength of the German fighter force between now and the time for surface assault is essential. . . . This condition, above all others, will dictate whether amphibious assault can or cannot be successfully launched on any given date.

A month earlier it had been noted on a higher level that unless the fighter strength of the enemy could be broken 'it may become literally impossible to carry out the destruction planned'. A new plan was drafted, Operation 'Pointblank', raising the reduction of the German fighter strength to the first priority while retaining the ultimate object of the bomber offensive.

These conclusions, with their notes of pessimism, were not shared by the bomber commanders, and were echoes of a new problem of immense significance. Air power, and particularly the bomber, had introduced a new dimension into warfare. Despite results, which were at best inconclusive, and the continued growth of enemy fighter strength, the commanders of the Allied strategic air forces had reached the conclusion that they controlled the decisive instrument; that they could achieve victory alone. General Spaatz, commanding the US Strategic Air Force Europe (USSAFE), believed simply that Overlord was unnecessary. Air Chief-Marshal Harris, his British opposite number, agreed with him. General Arnold, the representative of the US air arm on the Joint Chiefs-of-Staff, had reached a similar conclusion. None of these commanders 'objected' to Overlord, or resented its demands upon their forces. They believed simply that if they continued with their bombing strategy the demands would be met.

In the early days of 1943, the Americans had refused to profit by British experience and had sustained heavy losses in daylight raids, particularly over Stuttgart and Schweinfurt. By the end of the year these growing pains had been overcome, and the strategic air forces of the two nations were well integrated in an almost continuous all-round-the-clock bombing programme. The continued growth of the German fighter force, despite the priorities of Pointblank, was not necessarily a guide to its real strength, and the confidence of the bomber commanders remained unshaken. They 'knew' – they 'felt' – that they were winning, even if the statistics failed to prove it.

All this was highly unsatisfactory to the military commanders and planners, and Air Marshal Tedder wrote later: 'I could not help feeling a certain sympathy for my soldier and sailor colleagues in the earlier days who could not understand why, before their operations began, I could only say that I "thought" and "felt" the air situation would be all right . . .'

Clash over choice of targets

Even if the claims of the Air Marshals were not yet wholly true – and they would never be true while war held its historic meaning – the signs were sufficiently ominous. Nazi Germany was being dissected, and destroyed behind its armies. The vast concentrations of heavy industry in the Ruhr and Saar valleys, coal, oil, synthetic fuels, ball bearings, roads, railways, cities, and hamlets were all being steadily reduced to rubble at the whim of this man or that. The bomber chiefs were agreed on their mission, but not on their choices of targets. Oil, General Spaatz believed, was the essential upon which a modern nation at war must depend. Ball bearings, said another. Communications and morale, yet others.

These beliefs made the commanders of the strategic bomber forces careless of the tactical demands of armies. Strategically, they declared, the bomber is winning the war. To divert the bomber from its strategic mission was old fashioned and short-sighted. The German armies in the field, immensely powerful as they were, were nevertheless powerless to prevent the utter destruction of the homeland and people it was their rôle and purpose to defend.

Military thinkers, prominent among them Captain B. H. Liddell Hart, discerned the new pattern and portent of 'war' with which we now uneasily co-exist. Liddell Hart's warning that 'You cannot surrender to a bomber in the sky' went unheeded. Meanwhile, on the very highest levels there were forebodings of a very grave nature. Early in 1943, air photography and espionage, aided by the daring of Polish allies, had produced physical evidence of the enemy progress in the development and manufacture of rockets and pilotless aircraft capable of carrying warheads of high explosive distances of 150 miles plus. Such weapons might prove devastating in a high degree, and posed new problems of defence. In addition, the terrible secret of atomic progress engendered fears of enemy achievement in that field. The world had begun to fill with dark shadows, altering all accepted values, forewarning that the days of courage, ethics, morality, 'right or wrong', and those attributes of humanity known as 'virtues', were drawing to a close. The implications must undermine the faith in a just cause, in the virtues of steadfastness which, hitherto, had stimulated and sustained peoples to defend themselves successfully against odds.

Politics, and its age-old weapon of war, was giving way fast to blackmail, and its weapon of the 'push button'. The odds were new and had to be considered urgently in the context of survival in a fight to the finish against an enemy who, it could be predicted, would stop at nothing. Never was the calm light of reason more necessary to mankind; seldom has it been less in evidence.

The bomber commanders, confident in their power, accepted an urgent mission to add the destruction of rocket and 'flying bomb' sites and bases to their commitments, and on August 17 Air Chief-Marshal Harris opened the attack with 571 heavy bombers on the enemy rocket base at Peenemünde. Finally, bombed out of Peenemünde, the German rocket experts under General Dornberger moved into 'factories' deep in the Harz mountains, and continued their production on a reduced scale; while the 'ski-sites' for launching their pilotless aircraft grew in numbers, demanding constant vigilance and hammering from the air.

Attacking the V-weapons

The main burden of the attacks against rocket bases and ski-sites was borne by the tactical air forces. By the end of 1943, 93 sites for launching the pilotless aircraft known as the V-1, and to Air Intelligence as FZG-76, were pin-pointed within a 150-mile radius of London, and most of them in the Pas de Calais region. Nine thousand sorties were flown against these sites in the ensuing three months, and the enemy was forced to find alternative means of launching. Meanwhile the attacks by heavy bombers had severely hindered German development of the A-4, presently to be known as the V-2, and the major fear of the Overlord command was confined to the lesser, more recognisable – and defensible – danger of the V-1.

Despite successes it seemed that the Allies were faced with a grim race against time, even up to the end of March 1944. It was by then known that the enemy had improvised some form of modified launching site, very easily hidden from view. Many of these were suspected to exist in the Pas de Calais and the Cherbourg Peninsula, but the heavy and varied demands on the entire Allied air strength as Overlord approached its hour, made it difficult to press consistent attacks.

The army commanders were at no time inclined to underestimate the gravity of the threat, and in early December COSSAC had made an assessment. The immediate decision was to 'leave things as they were', but it was not until March 28 that Eisenhower, emerging from 'a sea of troubles', reported that the 'secret weapon' attack 'would not preclude the launching of the assault from the south coast ports as now planned, and that the probable incidence of casualties does not make it necessary to attempt to move the assault forces west of Southampton'.

The task would have been monumental. From the Wash southward and westward to the Severn Estuary, Britain was girdled with a belt 10 miles deep, a maze of assembly points, dumps, vehicle parks, camps, training grounds, embarkation 'hards', barbed wire, airfields, anti-aircraft and searchlight sites as well as all

Below: **Lancasters, workhorses of the British Bomber Command**

Allied air power, it had long been realised, would be the key to Overlord's success: only with the Luftwaffe neutralised could the men and landing vessels hope to reach the beaches of Normandy. Moreover, Germany's war potential had to be weakened and her supply lines to the future front destroyed. The task was enormous—and so were the arguments over how it was to be carried out

Imperial War Museum

'In the weeks before D-Day, German troops lay almost helpless under the Allied bombs'

The heavy bombers of the 8th Air Force and Bomber Command provided the punch to destroy the large targets, but much of the detailed work in the Transportation Plan—the destruction of smaller targets such as trains or vehicle convoys—was undertaken by the ubiquitous medium bombers and ground-attack aircraft of the tactical air forces under Air Chief-Marshal Leigh-Mallory

Martin B-26 Marauder: **At first known as the 'Widow maker' due to a large number of early accidents.** ***Span:*** **71 feet.** ***Length:*** **58 feet 3 inches.** ***Maximum speed:*** **282 mph at 15,000 feet.** ***Range:*** **1,150 miles at 214 mph.** ***Armament:*** **Up to 12 .50-inch MG, 4,000 lb of bombs.** ***Crew:*** **Up to seven**

North American B-25 Mitchell: **The most widely used US bomber of the war; some versions were adapted to carry a 75-mm cannon.** ***Span:*** **67 feet 6.7 inches.** ***Length:*** **52 feet 10 inches.** ***Maximum speed:*** **284 mph at 15,000 feet.** ***Range:*** **1,525 miles at 233 mph.** ***Armament:*** **Up to 14 .50-inch MG, up to 4,000 lb of bombs.** ***Crew:*** **Six**

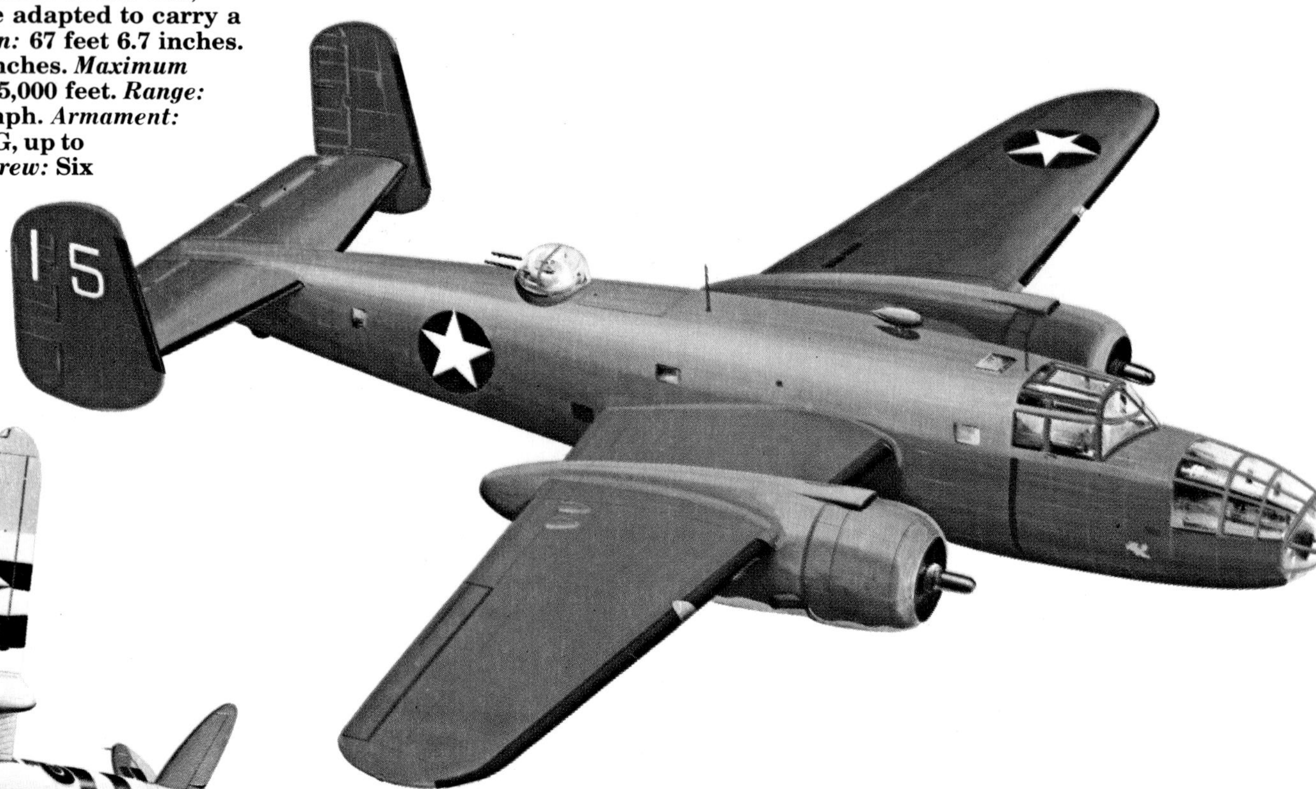

De Havilland Mosquito Mk XVIII: **A fighter-bomber version of the aircraft which was used by the RAF in almost every role from long-range bomber to night-fighter and high-speed transport.** ***Span:*** **54 feet 2 inches.** ***Length:*** **40 feet 10¾ inches.** ***Maximum speed:*** **380 mph at 13,000 feet.** ***Range:*** **1,270 miles.** ***Armament:*** **One 57-mm Molins gun, four .303-inch MG, two 500-lb bombs or eight rockets under the wing**

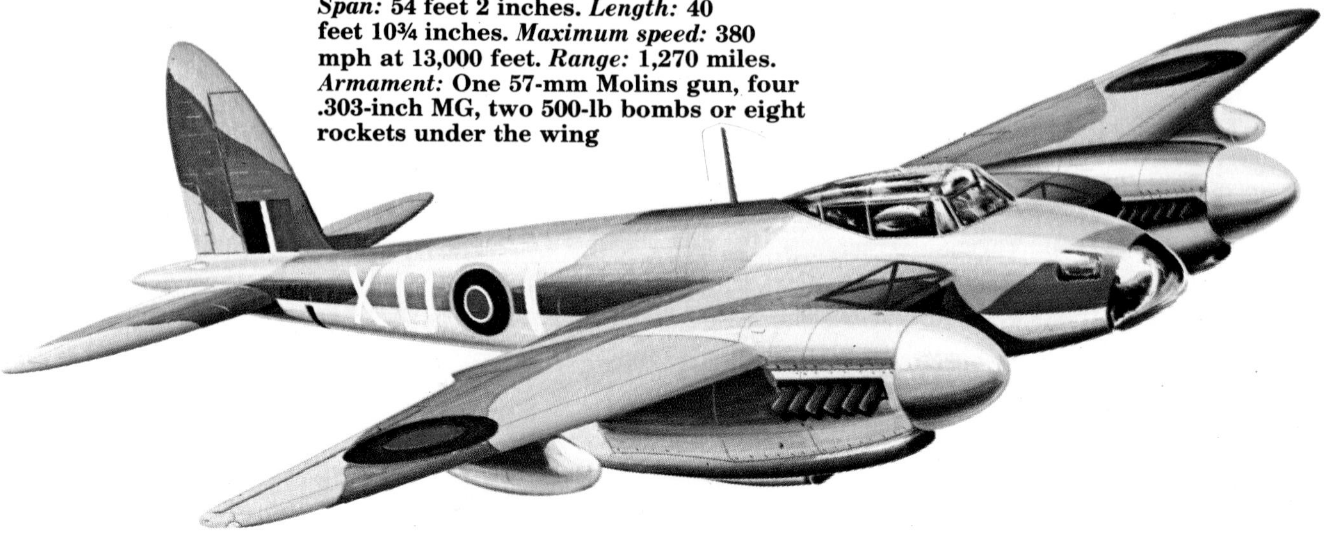

John Batchelor

the massing paraphernalia of war, while every port, large or small, on the island's coasts bristled with shipping. Wherever Britain, from the extremities of Scotland and Wales to Cornwall and the Kent coast, was less than a camp, a dump, a training ground, or any other of the multitude of activities relevant to the cross-Channel assault, it was a munitions works.

The problem of attempting to move all this was a greater hazard than the threat of the V-1s and V-2s on London and the south coast ports. The chance of massive enemy interference had to be taken.

The attitude of the 'Bomber Barons', who, in General Morgan's words 'remained obstinately aloof', manifesting many of the characteristics of a 'new élite', made it inevitable that a serious command crisis would follow upon the appointment of a supreme commander for Overlord. General Eisenhower was not slow to point out that: 'The strategic air arm is almost the only weapon at the disposal of the supreme commander for influencing the general course of action, particularly during the assault phase.'

This is a simple statement of fact, and no supreme commander worth his salt could have accepted the attitude of the strategic air force commanders, and abrogated his right to command. The command of the ground forces was in the hands of General Montgomery, and with General Bradley commanding the US 1st Army, Commander Designate of the US 12th Army Group. The great invasion fleet was under Admiral Ramsay, and it was not until April that the obstructive and obstinate Admiral King authorised the full complement of US naval resources. Without the command of the air forces in his hands the Supreme Commander would be reduced to a cipher, a mere pusher of the button, afterwards to sit back, certainly for days, possibly for weeks, with no real prospect of influencing the battle. In this context Eisenhower's statement to Churchill on March 3 that he would 'simply have to go home', and his subsequent memo to Washington, dated March 22, 'unless the matter is settled at once I will request relief from this command', lose all trace of petulance.

The fact was (and is) that the Supreme Commander in his fight with the strategic air force commanders in 1944, and to a great extent with the British Prime Minister and the Chiefs-of-Staff, emphasised the obvious truth that air, sea, and land forces had become the three prongs of a single weapon. The proud and jealous distinctions, worse than 'nationalism', between the services, were already becoming blurred. A supreme commander must command them all, and in submitting each service must lose some part of its separate identity.

Welding the air/sea/land forces

In a small way Combined Operations Headquarters had functioned as an embryo of this trend. It had welded land and sea forces into a potent combined weapon, and had often 'used' the air weapon effectively in close support, at first under Lord Louis Mountbatten, and then equally well under General Laycock.

But the stand of the strategic air force commanders, and their supporters, was not aimed solely at the Supreme Commander. Apart from the fact that they believed they knew best how to use the strategic air arm, they objected also to relinquishing some of their command power into the hands of Air Chief-Marshal Sir Trafford Leigh-Mallory, Air Commander-in-Chief, Allied Expeditionary Air Force, on the grounds that his experience in Fighter Command, which had been mainly exercised in the defence of Britain, had not fitted him for an aggressive rôle with the strategic air weapon. But primarily they feared that he – and the Supreme Commander – would use strategic air power tactically.

In fact the demands of Overlord and Pointblank, the combined bomber offensive, were certainly not mutually exclusive or incompatible. The Supreme Commander had made it clear that in seeking command of the air forces he had not the smallest intention of interfering with, for example, Coastal Command. He had no quarrel with the strategic aims pursued by the bomber commanders, as far as they went, but he and his staff must have the right to state and to press their views on the use of air power in direct relation to Overlord, and to control it, at least, in the assault stages, and now, urgently, in the last 90 days.

Coincidentally, therefore, with the rather confused command arguments, an argument raged on the best way to serve Overlord from the air. The Deputy Supreme Commander, Air Chief-Marshal Sir Arthur Tedder, became the champion and chief exponent of what was known as 'The Transportation Plan' against General Spaatz, the champion and chief spokesman of 'The Oil Plan'. The argument, at times bitter, carried also grave political implications, and was pursued in an atmosphere of 'tense anxiety' until April.

All these difficulties were resolved by the middle of April largely by the efforts of two of the most experienced airmen in the world, both of whom happened to be men of outstanding character and ability, Air Chief-Marshal Sir Charles Portal, a member of the Chiefs-of-Staff, and Tedder, Eisenhower's Deputy Commander.

Briefly, the Transportation Plan aimed at the disruption of the enemy communications, the destruction of railways, locomotives, marshalling yards, repair and maintenance facilities, roads and bridges, and the prevention of enemy reserves reaching the battlefield. This, in General Eisenhower's view, was 'the greatest contribution he could imagine' to the success of Overlord, and Tedder was his worthy champion.

Some idea of the feeling generated by this argument may be gathered from a remark made by General Spaatz to General Arnold, that he hoped 'the AEAF plan (the Transportation Plan) will be repudiated by Tedder of his own accord, thus avoiding hard feelings'.

But Tedder stuck to his guns, which were also the Supreme Commander's guns. Early in March he set about the dual tasks of reconciling the bomber commanders to the minimum command needs of the Supreme Commander, while at the same time fighting for the Transportation Plan, not only against Spaatz and Harris, but against 'the facts' produced by Air Intelligence, the doubts of 21st Army Group, and the grave misgivings of the British Prime Minister and the War Cabinet. It was one of the very few matters in regard to strategy upon which the British War Cabinet was consulted. This does not indicate that the War Cabinet was a rubber stamp, but that it had plenty of work to do without commenting on command problems, unless called upon to do so.

In the final resolution of these two important matters, the command problem, and the air targets to be adopted in support of Overlord, Sir Charles Portal acted in the rôle of 'umpire', 'chairman', 'interpreter' to the Prime Minister and the Chiefs-of-Staff, holding the balance of the arguments with great skill while retaining a powerful personal judgement and opinion. On March 9 Tedder drafted a scheme of command acceptable to Eisenhower, and on March 27, with Portal's aid, he 'supervised' the Strategic Air Command for Overlord, co-ordinating the combined air effort with Leigh-Mallory's tactical air forces. On that day, also, having won agreement for the Transportation Plan, he relieved Leigh-Mallory of responsibility in the running of it. Thus the Deputy Supreme Commander became Eisenhower's direct channel of air command for Overlord, while the Combined Chiefs-of-Staff retained the last word in strategic matters.

Eisenhower wins use of air power

This arrangement did not suit everyone, but it was the best possible in the difficult circumstances. The US Joint Chiefs-of-Staff objected to the word 'supervised', and wanted the stronger word 'directed'. The vital point was that the Supreme Commander had won the use of the air power he needed for Overlord and would retain essential control over it in the relevant period.

The target argument, waged by the main protagonists, Tedder and Spaatz, was less confused. In early March, General Spaatz produced a reasoned and carefully worked out Oil Plan, while Tedder produced his plan for the disruption of communications. This was not an attack on combined bomber offensive strategy embodied in Operation Pointblank. Eisenhower and Tedder were agreed that the destruction of the Luftwaffe bomber and fighter strength – which had continued to grow in numbers – must remain the first priority. They had no quarrel with Pointblank, as far as it went, but they were resolved to prevent the movement of enemy reserves into the battle area. Spaatz, they felt, might be right in his belief that by depriving the enemy of oil both the Luftwaffe, and almost all ground movement, would cease. They did not object to the Oil Plan, except as an alternative to their own. It was all very well for the commanders of the strategic air forces to state with conviction that the power of the enemy was being sapped at source, that at a given moment the whole 'house' would collapse, but the evidence for such an optimistic view was not conclusive. At best, it would be a nerve-racking wait as zero hour approached.

The real crux of the argument lay probably in the use of air power as an independent air weapon, and its use, as Ehrman put it, 'within the context of other operations'.

While the arguments and counter-arguments were pursued hotly throughout March both plans were virtually in operation. Pointblank, designed as an operation in support of Overlord, had been in action for a full nine months. Tedder's 'Transportation Plan' had been partially in operation since the beginning of the year. Neither plan was, therefore, wholly speculative.

The original Transportation Plan put forward in January by Allied Expeditionary Air Force Headquarters was based on an analysis by Professor Zuckerman. It called for a sustained 90-day attack directed against 72 carefully chosen targets, 39 of them in Germany and 33 in France and Belgium. The plan, constantly shorn of its targets, which were subject to constant pressures and permutations

Overwhelming air power: 'the greatest contribution to D-Day'

from air, civil, and military authorities, operated on a limited basis while the arguments were being hotly debated. The strategic views expressed by General Spaatz, Air Chief-Marshal Harris and their supporters, were that it would be quixotic and totally wrong to divert strength from the main bomber offensive at a time when it was beginning to take powerful effect; and, secondly, that railways and marshalling yards were notoriously difficult targets, and that no effective slow-down of enemy transport would be achieved in time for D-Day.

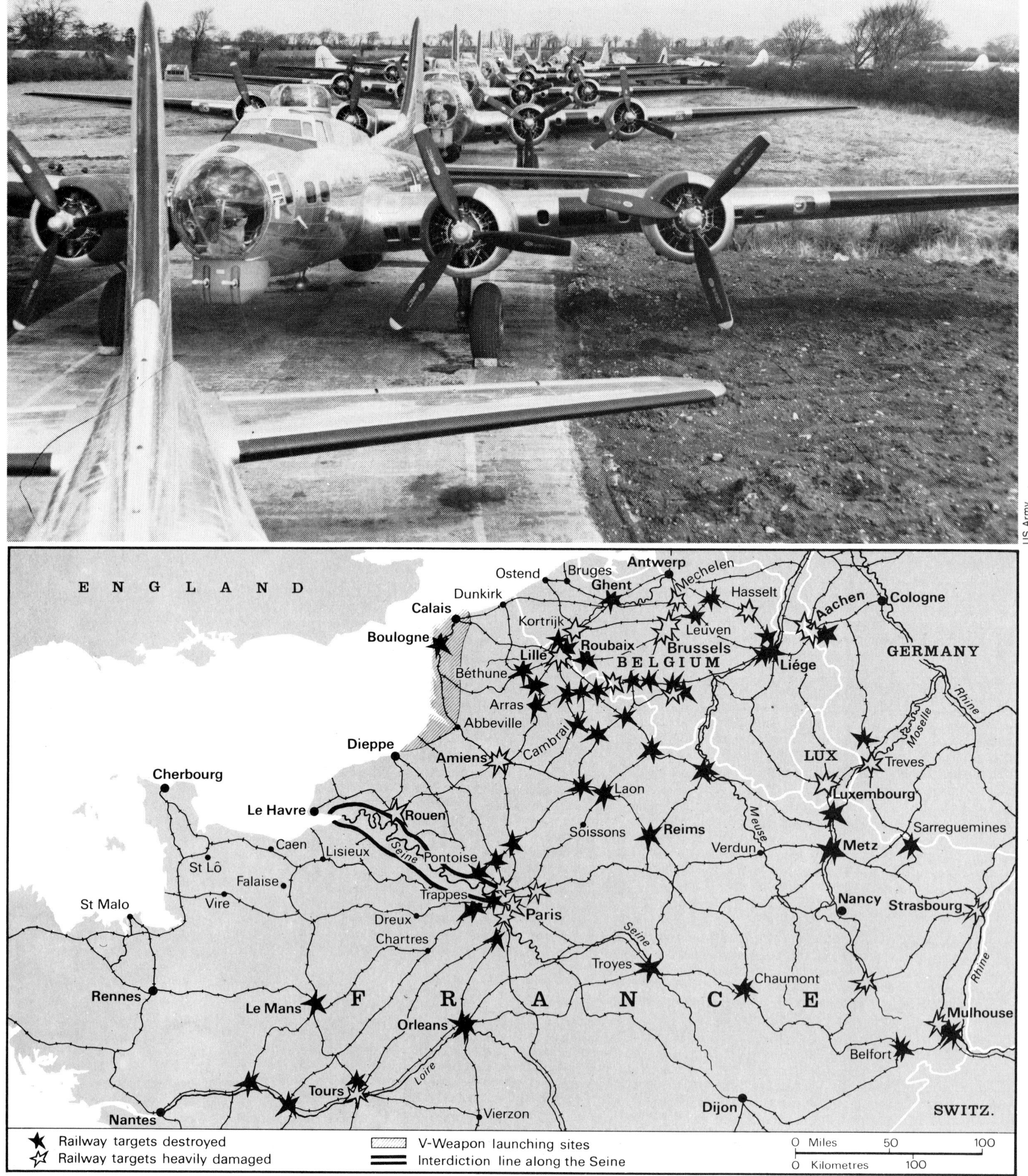

The British Chiefs-of-Staff, largely sympathetic to this view, and beset by grave fears of the consequences of heavy bombing in France and Belgium, were reluctant to clear the 'Zuckerman' targets, changed their minds constantly, and forced the AEAF to operate under grave handicaps against limited objectives.

Assessments of early results by Air Intelligence, by SHAEF G-2, and by 21st Army Group HQ, pointed to almost total failure of the effort. As late as May 9, 21st Army Group, more directly concerned in the end results than any other body, referred to the Transportation Plan, as 'pin-pricking on rail communications'. They were frankly scornful.

Never have assessments been more wide of the mark. The German communications were at the point of almost total collapse, for it was misleading simply to count trains and engines destroyed. Hundreds of engines, physically still 'in existence', were on the verge of breakdown, and the maintenance and repair facilities had sustained such a hammering, that it would prove impossible to get most of the battered trains on the move.

◁ On these two pages are shown the aim and effect of the massive Allied air offensive which General Eisenhower was to describe as: 'the greatest contribution he could imagine' to the success of Overlord. To prepare for the invasion, the Allied air forces undertook a concentrated campaign, which was so planned as to isolate the Normandy area by hitting vital railway junctions in northern France and destroying the bridges across the Seine, while seeming to prepare for an invasion in the Calais area. By D-Day, all the main objectives had been achieved: the amount of supplies reaching the troops in Normandy was minimal, while the Germans were still convinced that the attack would come further north. *(Above)* Flying Fortresses, newly arrived in Britain, await issue to combat units.

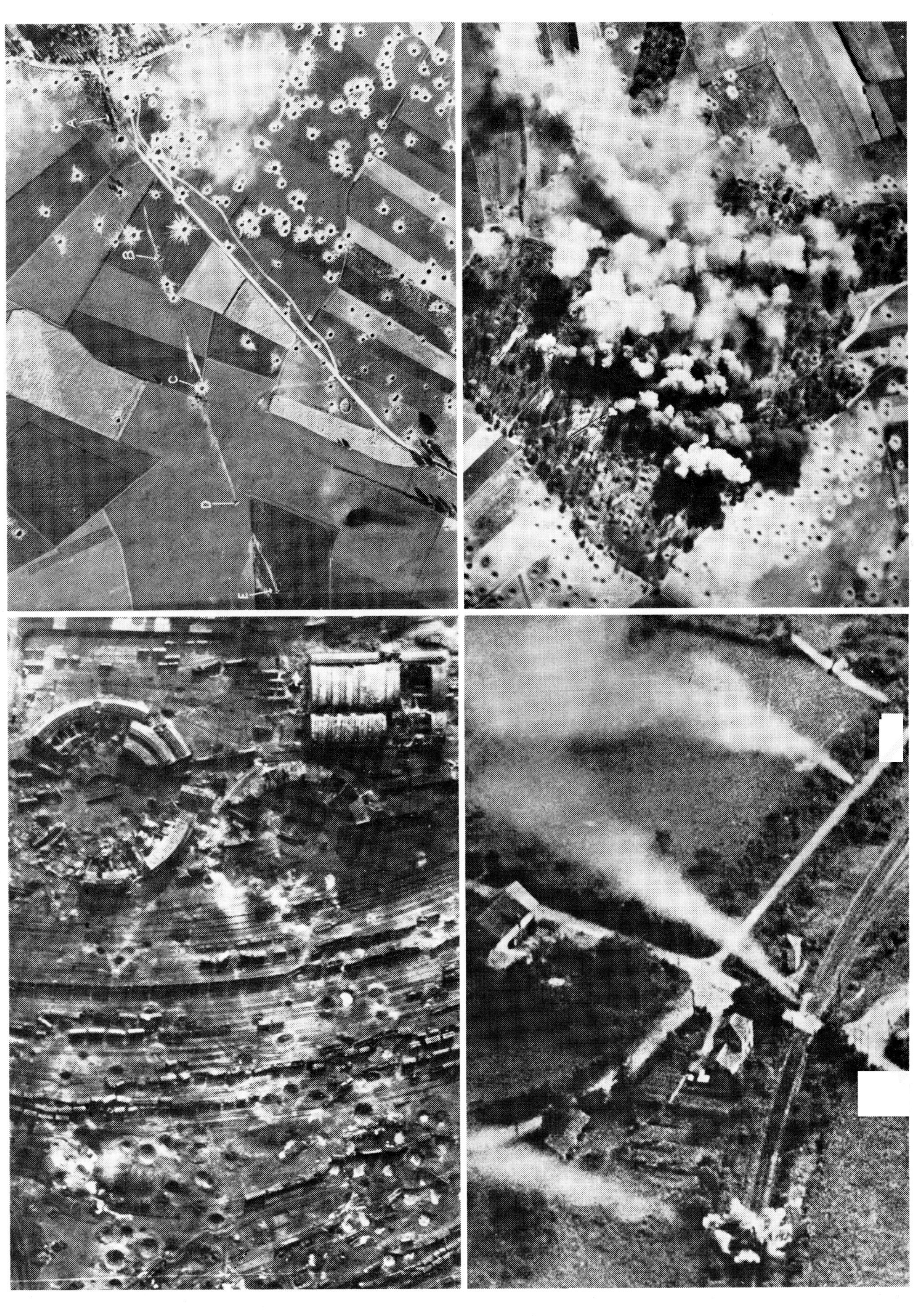

▷ The Allied Expeditionary Air Force at work: *(Top left)* The aftermath of an attack on a flying-bomb site. 'A' marks the launching ramp, and 'B', 'C', 'D', and 'E' are V-1s which crashed on launching. *(Top right)* A flying-bomb site under attack. *(Below left)* The damage at Amiens marshalling yard after a visit by Bomber Command. *(Below right)* RAF Typhoons attacking a road and rail junction.

Imperial War Museum (left and right)

Nevertheless, at the height of his argument for the Transportation Plan most of the facts seemed to argue against Tedder. He stood as firm as a rock, convinced of the correctness of his view, and that nothing else would be of direct physical aid to Overlord. But it would have taken arguments of greater potency than those put forward by Harris, Spaatz, and their Intelligence supporters to prevail against the direct and urgent desire of the Supreme Commander. The arguments of greater force concerned the fear that the French and Belgians would suffer heavy civilian casualties, which, it was believed, must inevitably follow upon intensive bombing of marshalling yards. Some authorities put the expectation of civilian casualties as high as between 80-160,000. The possibility gave Churchill, among others, grave misgivings, and Portal was forced to draw the attention of the air planners to the fact that attacks on occupied countries, which might cause heavy civilian casualties and damage, were prohibited under a ruling dated June 3, 1940.

'This is war, and people will be killed'

The War Cabinet was then consulted, and was extremely uneasy. Tedder stood his ground; questioned the estimates, and agreed to avoid routes south of Paris on the 'Grande Ceinture', and danger points like Le Bourget. Nevertheless, the fear of civilian casualties on a high scale remained a source of grave uneasiness to all concerned, but least of all, it seemed, to the French people. Major-General Pierre Koenig, commanding the French forces in Britain, in consultation with Tedder, expressed himself forcibly: 'This is war and it must be expected that people will be killed . . . We would take twice the anticipated loss to be rid of the Germans.'

But there were also difficulties in tying in the French Resistance in support of the operation. A Forced Labour Edict by the Nazis in 1943 had inspired thousands of young Frenchmen and women to 'take to the hills and woods', and from these the Maquis was formed. As saboteurs they had proved remarkably effective, and in the early stages of the air attack on the railways they were credited with the destruction of 808 locomotives against the 347 destroyed from the air. This was used as a further argument against the communications plan.

None of the difficulties had escaped Tedder. Even, he believed, if the enemy rail traffic could be reduced by 10% by D-Day it would be worth while. He and the Supreme Commander were convinced beyond a doubt that only in this way could air power make a direct contribution to Overlord.

The arguments, heart searchings, accompanied by constant changes of targets, and the inclusion of roads and bridges, continued almost up to the eve of D-Day, as also did the derogatory and derisory intelligence estimates of the effects on traffic, and of the 'load of hatred being generated in the hearts of the French people'. They were hopelessly wrong on both counts. The civilian casualties were less than 10% of the worst fears, and were suffered without rancour.

Meanwhile, on March 25, Portal called a meeting with the object of reaching a decision. There was no longer room for delay. The Air Ministry, the War Office, the Ministry of Economic Warfare, the Joint Intelligence Committee, were all represented. The Supreme Commander, his deputy Tedder, together with Leigh-Mallory, Harris, and Spaatz, attended with their staffs. The debate favoured Overlord, and with that, on March 27, the Deputy Supreme Commander co-ordinated air operations in support of Overlord, and assumed responsibility for carrying out the 'Transportation Plan'.

The British Prime Minister, however, continued to urge upon Eisenhower the need to avoid civilian casualties, and remained uneasy until the middle of May, far from sure that military implications should outweigh the possible political implications. In the end he was fully reconciled. The results were significant.

Throughout all the arguments and disagreements, covering command, strategy, and tactics, the Allied air forces met all the great variety of demands upon them, and pursued their offensive with unabated vigour, while planning and training to lift three airborne divisions simultaneously into Normandy. Even General Spaatz continued to hammer away at his oil targets, and one is inclined at times to wonder what all the fuss was about.

In March, a minor command crisis followed Leigh-Mallory's establishment of an advanced headquarters of AEAF under Air Marshal Sir Arthur Coningham to operate in direct support of the ground forces. The objections of the bomber commanders to this appointment may not have been more than a last sop to their prejudices. In spite of everything Operation Pointblank had operated for a full ten months by the eve of D-Day. Up to the end of March, with the combined bomber offensive the aims were:

- The reduction of the Luftwaffe;
- The general reduction of the German war potential;
- The weakening of the will of the German people.

In the last phases the direct demands of Overlord, and of the assault landing, Neptune, took priority with five primary tasks:

- To attain and to maintain an air situation whereby the Luftwaffe was rendered incapable of effective interference with Allied operation;
- To provide continuous reconnaissance of enemy dispositions and movements;
- To disrupt enemy communications and supply channels for reinforcement;
- To deliver offensive strikes against enemy naval forces;
- To provide airlift for airborne forces;

In the assault phase the plan was designed:

- To protect the cross-Channel movement of assault forces against enemy air attack, and to assist the naval forces to protect the assault against enemy naval attacks;
- To prepare the way for assault by neutralising the beaches;
- To protect the landing beaches and shipping concentrations;
- To dislocate enemy communications and movement control during assault.

Plastering Northern France with bombs

In addition to all these tasks a sustained attack was pressed against the flying bomb sites and rocket bases, thus to stave off the threat to the assembly areas, the massed shipping, and all the intricate preparations within range of the new weapons.

To meet these commitments Air Chief-Marshal Leigh-Mallory disposed some 5,677 aircraft of the US 9th Air Force and the 2nd Tactical Air Force of the Royal Air Force. Of these, 3,011 were medium, light, fighter, and fighter-bombers, and the remainder transport aircraft, gliders, reconnaissance, and artillery observation aircraft.

Between February 9 and D-Day these forces, aided by the heavy bombers of combined bomber offensive, attacked 80 rail and road targets with 21,949 aircraft dropping 76,200 tons of bombs. Some 51 targets were destroyed, 25 severely damaged, and slight damage was caused to the remaining four. On March 6 Bomber Command made the first heavy attack on Trappes, some 20 miles to the north of Paris, claiming 190 direct hits. The final effect revealed the inadequacy of the existing Intelligence estimates, and went some way towards justifying the claims of the air marshals that they 'felt' and 'thought' they were achieving their various objects. By D-Day railway traffic within 150 miles of the battlefield was at least 75% unusable, and the whole railway system of north-west Europe had been dislocated. Air photography, or even visual observation on the ground, failed to reveal the condition of locomotives and rolling stock still 'in existence', but often held together 'by the last cotter pin'.

Early in May, the tactical air forces opened an all-out assault on trains, railway bridges, and road bridges over the Seine below Paris. Heavy attacks were pressed on Mantes-Gassicourt, Liége, Ghent, Courtrai, Lille, Hasselt, Louvain, Boulogne, Orleans, Metz, Mulhouse, Rheims, Troyes and Charleroi. The pattern of the bombing might as easily have been designed to isolate the Pas de Calais as Normandy, and did not reveal the planned area of the Allied assault. Substantial attacks against road and railway bridges over the Loire waited upon the day. In the event, every bridge serving the battlefield was down.

Attacks on radar installations, wireless telegraphy, and navigational stations paralysed enemy signals, and made air and sea reconnaissance virtually impossible. A total of 49 coastal batteries covering the sea approaches were also attacked with some success, while the long sustained assaults on the German aircraft industry had reduced production by some 60%. It was known that more than 5,000 enemy aircraft had been destroyed in combat between the middle of November and D-Day. These facts, combined with the constant harassing of airfields, and the German losses among their trained pilots, effectively banished Luftwaffe interference from the battlefield.

Meanwhile the combined bomber offensive pursued by Harris and Spaatz steadily sapped the industrial strength of the German nation, reducing it to a meagre skeleton, yet with astonishing powers of endurance.

An important side-issue of the offensive against the railways was that 18,000 men of the Todt Organisation (the German forced labour organisation) were forced off urgent work on the strengthening of the 'Atlantic Wall' to undertake the even more urgent tasks of railway repair.

In the last weeks before D-Day German troops, many of them of low calibre, lay almost helpless under the Allied bombs by night and day.

Such is a brief glimpse of the overwhelming contribution of air power in direct support of the Normandy landings. It was enough.

STRIKE FROM THE SEA: BRITAIN'S CARRIER AIRCRAFT

Supermarine 'Seafire' Mk IIC
Developed for the carrier arm from the Mk V Spitfire fighter. The Seafire IIC was later replaced by the more sophisticated Mk III, which had fully folding wings and a superior flight performance. *Max speed:* 333 mph. *Max range:* 755 miles with drop tank. *Service ceiling:* 32,000 feet. *Armament:* two 20-mm cannon, four .303-inch machine-guns; one 500-lb bomb OR two 250-lb bombs

Fairey 'Firefly' Mk I
Fighter and reconnaissance aircraft. Most of its service with the Fleet Air Arm was in the Pacific theatre. *Crew:* two. *Max speed:* 316 mph. *Max range:* 1,300 miles. *Service ceiling:* 28,000 feet. *Armament:* four 20-mm cannon; eight 60-lb rockets OR two 1,000-lb bombs

Fairey 'Barracuda' Mk II
Torpedo-bomber and reconnaissance aircraft. The 'Barracuda's' most celebrated battle honour was the Fleet Air Arm strike against the battleship *Tirpitz*
Crew: three. *Max speed:* 228 mph. *Max range:* 686 miles. *Service ceiling:* 20,000 feet. *Armament:* two Vickers 'K' machine-guns; six 250-lb bombs OR four 450-lb depth-charges OR one 1,620-lb torpedo

RAF COASTAL COMMAND

Bristol Beaufighter night-fighter and anti-shipping strike aircraft. Armament: four 20-mm cannon, six ·303-inch machine-guns; one 2,127-lb torpedo OR one 1,650-lb torpedo and two 250-lb bombs OR eight rocket projectiles. Max speed: 320 mph. Range: 1,480 miles

The Fairey Swordfish, the veteran Royal Naval strike aircraft of the war, played a key role in the chase of the *Bismarck*. **Crew:** two or three. **Normal range:** 770 miles. **Armament:** one 1,610-lb torpedo OR one 1,500-lb mine OR eight 110-lb bombs OR six rocket projectiles; two ·303-inch machine-guns. **Max speed:** 154 mph

Bristol Beaufort Mk I—the RAF's standard torpedo-bomber for four years of the war. Some 1,120 Beauforts were completed, of which 955 were Mk Is, and Beauforts saw action in almost every theatre of the war. **Max speed:** 265 mph. **Range:** 1,035 miles. **Crew:** four. **Armament:** four ·303-inch machine-guns; up to 2,000 lbs of bombs or mines OR one 1,605-lb torpedo, carried semi-externally

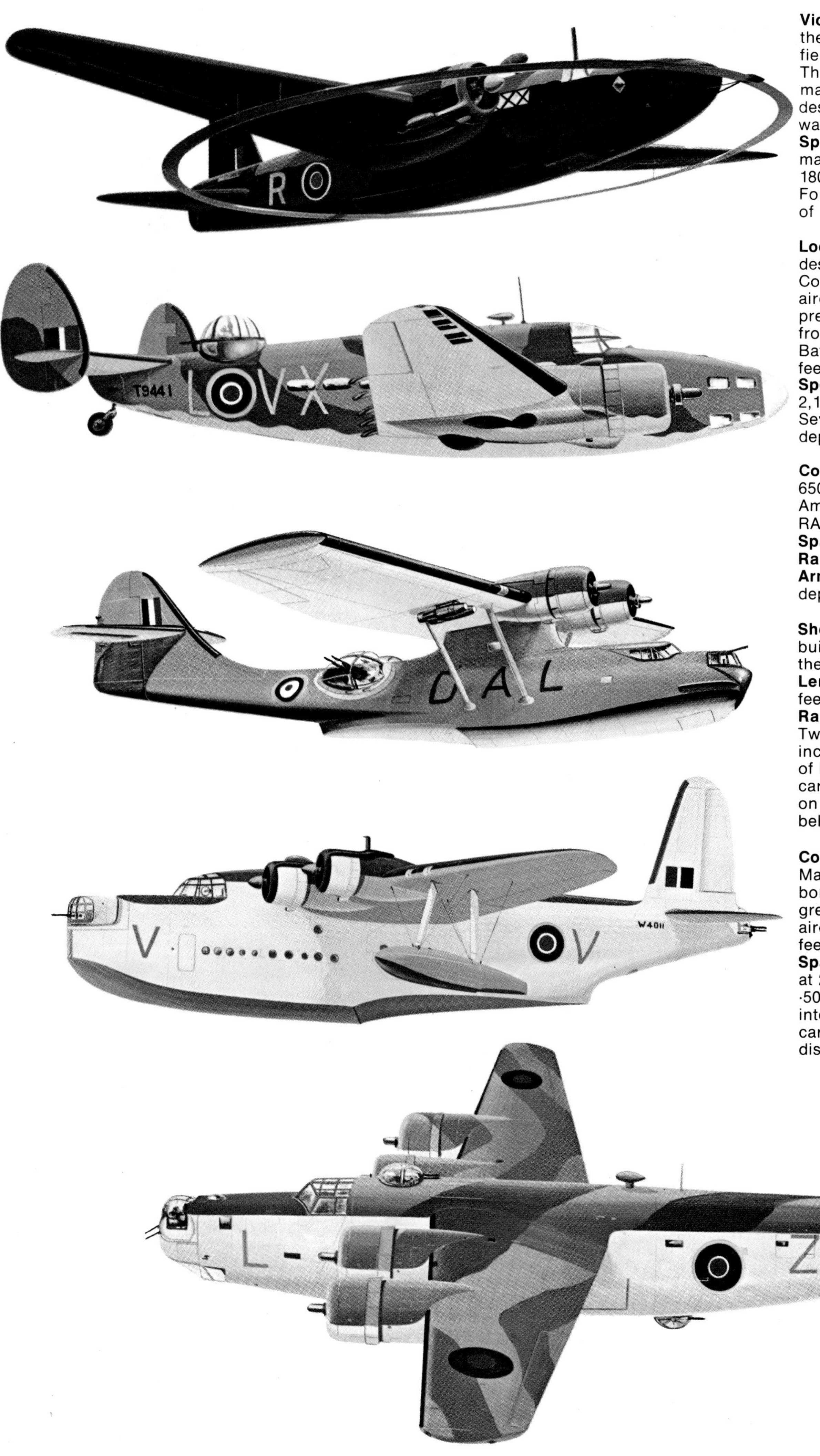

Vickers Wellington Mark I: One of the older designs which was modified for use by Coastal Command. This aircraft is fitted with the magnetic ring which was used to destroy magnetic mines in shallow waters. **Length:** 64 feet 7 inches. **Span:** 86 feet. **Speed:** 265 mph maximum. **Range:** 3,200 miles at 180 mph. **Crew:** Five. **Armament:** Four ·303-inch MG. Up to 6,000 lb of bombs

Lockheed Hudson: An American design which was in service with Coastal Command as a training aircraft before the war, and was pressed—very successfully—into front-line service for much of the Battle of the Atlantic. **Length:** 44 feet $2\frac{1}{2}$ inches: **Span:** 65 feet. **Speed:** 292 mph maximum. **Range:** 2,160 miles at 254 mph. **Armament:** Seven ·303-inch MG. Four 500-lb depth charges. **Crew:** Four

Consolidated PBY Catalina: Over 650 of this tough and dependable American design were used by the RAF. **Length:** 65 feet $1\frac{1}{4}$ inches. **Span:** 104 feet. **Speed:** 185 mph. **Range:** 3,750 miles at 130 mph. **Armament:** Six ·303-inch MG, four depth charges. **Crew:** Up to eight

Short Sunderland: Over 700 were built of this military development of the pre-war 'C' class flying boats. **Length:** 85 feet 4 inches. **Span:** 112 feet $9\frac{1}{2}$ inches. **Speed:** 212 mph. **Range:** 2,980 miles. **Armament:** Two ·50-inch and up to 12 ·303-inch machine-guns. Up to 2,000 lb of bombs or depth charges were carried internally and wound out on racks through panels just below the wing roots

Consolidated B-24 Liberator: Maritime patrol version of the bomber which was built in far greater numbers than any other US aircraft. **Speed:** 300 mph at 30,000 feet. **Length:** 67 feet 2 inches. **Span:** 110 feet. **Range:** 2,100 miles at 215 mph. **Armament:** Up to 14 ·50-inch MG, 5,000 lb of bombs internally—up to 12,800 lb could be carried on wing racks for short distances. **Crew:** 12

John Batchelor

The early experiments with jet engines and aircraft led to both Britain and Germany having jet fighters operational during the Second World War. Me 262s terrorised British bombers, while Gloster Meteors brought down several V-1 flying bombs. But against conventional aircraft the jet planes' superior speed could also be a handicap, hindering accurate fire

TOO FAST TO FIGHT

The real impetus to the development of jet aircraft was the start of the Second World War in September 1939. As country after country realised the ugly truth, industry, science and engineering teams girded for their parts in the struggle to come.

Germany had a head start, thanks to the pioneering work by Ernst Heinkel. So it should not be surprising that the world's first turbojet aircraft to be designed as a fighter from the beginning was yet another Heinkel effort, the He 280. It was also the world's first twin-jet aircraft.

Heinkel visualised a twin-engined jet fighter, with engines slung in individual nacelles under the wing, minimising the length of the intake and exhaust ducting. For ground clearance, and to avoid blasting loose huge chunks of the runway surface, he decided on tricycle landing gear, the first on a German aircraft.

Design of the He 280 started in late 1939. In March 1940, the Air Ministry awarded a contract to the Messerschmitt organisation for prototypes of a twin-engined aircraft. A few days later, Heinkel got essentially the same sort of contract.

The first prototype He 280 was completed by September, lacking only airworthy engines. Heinkel had the prototype flown first as a glider, testing basic aerodynamic characteristics. When the Heinkel HeS 8A engines were ready for flight the following spring, the airplane was already well understood.

On 2 April 1941, at Marienehe airfield, Fritz Schaefer climbed into the cockpit of the He 280. He taxied out and took off, climbing to 900 ft or so for a circle of the field. He did not attempt to retract the landing gear, or to do anything exceptional with the aircraft.

Three days later it was flown again, and demonstrated to Udet and others from the Air Ministry. Their indifference was annoying to Heinkel, who could not understand why his advanced ideas were continually rejected.

He thought the He 280 had proved its point and that it should be considered for production. So he arranged a series of tests against the Luftwaffe's top fighter of the time, the Focke-Wulf 190. It was no contest; the jet-propelled fighter outperformed the Fw 190 in every way. The Ministry bent a little, and awarded Heinkel a contract for 13 pre-production aircraft.

His designers put together a further development, with the unusually heavy armament of six 20-mm cannon, and proposed it to the Air Ministry. To everybody's surprise, the Ministry awarded a contract for the production of 300, but Heinkel's facilities, strained as they were by existing production programmes, were bypassed by this order and the He 280 was scheduled to be built by another firm.

But by then the Me 262 had flown under jet power; it appeared so promising that the Ministry cancelled the He 280.

The rocket-powered jet fighter arrived, in prototype form, in 1941. On 13 August Messerschmitt test pilot Heini Dittmar strapped himself into a prototype Me 163A, started the rocket engine, and blasted across the turf at Peenemünde-West, the experimental Luftwaffe airfield. The Me 163A was held in a climb until the fuel was burned; then Dittmar turned and began a circling letdown to a landing. It was the first flight by a rocket-powered interceptor prototype, and it began a long, frustrating and ultimately unsuccessful development programme.

It had begun some years earlier, as a project to power a tailless glider designed by Dr Alexander Lippisch. Working at the German Research Institute for Soaring (DFS), Lippisch's team had brought along the design of their DFS 194 to the point where it obviously required industrial support.

Messerschmitt was designated, and Lippisch's team went to Augsburg. The aircraft turned out well, but its rocket powerplant did not, and the DFS 194 was never flown under power. It was used instead for ground tests of the rocket.

The baulky rocket was replaced by a new design with controllable thrust, other changes were made, and the result was the Me 163A series, prototypes used for development of the interceptor version.

It was one of this first batch of 13 that Dittmar first flew in August 1941. But there was a long time between that first flight and the first operational sortie. The Me 163 did not see action until 13 May 1944, and even that attempt to seek combat was made in a development aircraft, one of the Me 163B prototypes. By the time the Luftwaffe had had production versions of the Me 163B in service, the war was running down and the visions of hundreds of the tiny rocket fighters slashing through disrupted bomber formations had been reduced to the actual-

Messerschmitt Me 163
Crew: 1 *Powerplant:* 1 Walter RII liquid-propellant rocket *Span:* 30·5 ft *Length:* 17·8 ft *Weight:* 5291 lb *Speed:* 558 mph

MOD

May 1973: 'Vintage Pair' of the RAF's Historic Flight, a De Havilland Vampire T 11, the last Vampire still flying with the RAF, and a Gloster Meteor T 7.

ity of a few sporadic intercepts and some hideous operational accidents.

A dispassionate examination of the concept led to one conclusion: it was possible to be too fast for effective combat. The Me 163s were designed to be used as interceptors of daylight bombing raids. They were to take off and climb rapidly (they could get to bomber height in less than three minutes), attack the bombers with their paired 30-mm cannon, and break away for the return to base.

In practice, the speed of the rocket fighter was so much greater than that of its bomber target that a pilot only had two or three seconds to aim and fire. It proved to be nearly impossible. The Me 163 was not suitable for combat against slow-flying bombers.

Those that did get into combat managed to shoot down a few bombers, but it was too late. The factory producing one of the essential fuel components was bombed in August 1944. Ground transportation was under constant attack, and several complete shipments of rocket fuel were lost to Allied gunnery. As winter neared, the weather worsened – and the Me 163 was not suitable for bad weather or night operations. The whole programme ground to a halt, with only a few intercepts flown against special targets such as high-altitude photo flights.

There was only one truly successful jet fighter developed and brought to operational status during the Second World War: the Messerschmitt Me 262. In spite of setbacks to the smooth development of the programme caused by such diverse factors as Hitler's dreams and bombing realities, the project maintained and even gained momentum.

It began in late 1938 with an Air Ministry contract with Messerschmitt for a twin-engine jet fighter. By March 1940, both Messerschmitt and Heinkel were told to go ahead with the development of their respective twin-jet fighters.

The first Messerschmitt prototype was completed well before its jet engines were ready for flight. The first alternative, to fit rocket engines in the nacelles for flight tests, was ruled out because the engines weren't considered safe enough.

So Messerschmitt installed a standard Junkers Jumo piston engine in the nose, and the first flight of an Me 262 was made on 18 April 1941, with a piston engine and propeller providing propulsion, and empty jet nacelles under the wings. By March of the following year airworthy jet engines were available, and on 25 March the prototype was flown on the combined power of its piston engine and the two new jets. It nearly ended in disaster for the pilot, Fritz Wendel, because both turbojets failed shortly after takeoff, and he had a tough time keeping the Me 262 in the air.

Wendel made the first flight on jet power only with the third prototype, which had been fitted with a pair of Junkers Jumo 004A-0 turbojets producing about 1850 lb of thrust each. On 18 July 1942 he took off from the hard-surfaced runway at Leipheim for a flight of about twelve minutes. He completed a second flight that day, and was delighted with the way the plane handled.

But he had had to use brakes momentarily during the takeoff roll, in order to get the tail up into the slipstream so that the elevators would be effective. The braking served to rotate the aircraft nose down and had to be done carefully, gently and at exactly the right time.

This must have been one of the reasons that Messerschmitt decided to redesign the Me 262 with a new type of landing gear – the tricycle type with nosewheel – that became the standard for all subsequent Me 262s.

Happily for the Allied cause, the decision-making machinery broke down on the Me 262 programme. Production schedules were changed almost monthly. Variations on the theme were developed on request and the Me 262 was built as a fighter, an all-weather fighter, a reconnaissance aircraft, a ground-attack aircraft, a fighter with reconnaissance capabilities, a fighter-bomber, and an interceptor with rocket booster engines in the nacelles, all in a single-seat version. Two-seat models were developed as trainers and night fighters. They were built in small batches of only a few of most of the versions, and only one model was produced in any quantity.

It was July 1944 before the Me 262 engaged in combat, the first recorded instance being an encounter with a reconnaissance Mosquito flown by Flt Lt Wall, RAF. Wall reported that an Me 262 made five passes at his Mosquito, but in each case he was able to break away and finally dove into clouds to escape his persistent adversary.

Time and the losing position of Germany caught up with the Me 262. By tremendous industrial effort, mass production of the aircraft had been achieved under mountains of difficulties. The first production aircraft had been delivered in March 1944, and by February 1945 production had peaked at 300 completed aircraft per month. Factory delivery data show that 1320 were rolled out of the doors for delivery to the Luftwaffe during the 13-month production programme.

The most famous unit to operate the Me 262 was JV 44, formed and commanded by General Adolf Galland. The unit arrived

Heinkel He 162A-2
Crew: 1 *Powerplant:* 1 BMW 003E-1, 1760 lb thrust *Span:* 23·6 ft *Length:* 29·7 ft *Weight:* 5478 lb *Armament:* 2×20-mm cannon *Speed:* 518 mph at 19,680 ft

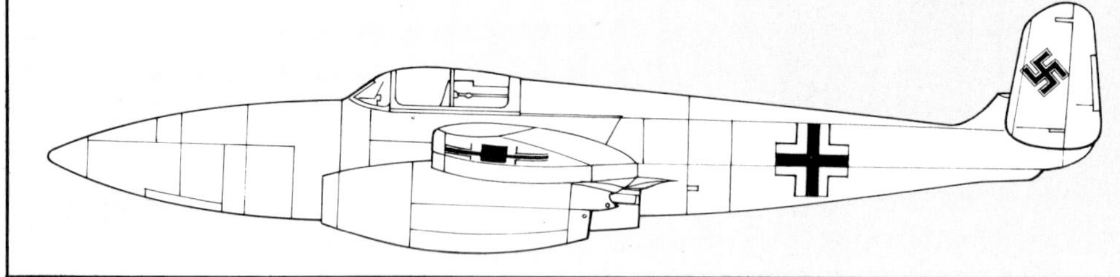

Heinkel He 280
Crew: 1 *Powerplant:* 2 HeS 8, 1100 lb thrust each *Span:* 40 ft *Length:* 34·1 ft *Weight:* 9500 lb *Armament:* 3×20-mm cannon *Speed:* 558 mph at 19,680 ft

Cockpit is a totally enclosed unit for pressurisation purposes, although no service machines were ever pressurised
Tank filler cap
Radio loop
Stabiliser adjusting motor
238-gallon tank
132-gallon auxiliary tank
Flaps
Radio
Master compass
Variable orifice 'bullet' moves in and out to vary exit area

at its base near Munich on the last day of March 1945, and operated for only about one month, finally making its sorties from the autobahn between Munich and Augsburg. But in that time, they terrorised bomber crews, made about 50 kills, and established once and for all the value of the jet fighter.

As Germany's position grew more desperate, so did attempts to develop new weapons to stave off the inevitable. One of these was the Heinkel 162, a tricky single-engined jet fighter. Its specification, issued in September 1944, called for a lightweight fighter, using an absolute minimum of strategic materials, and capable of being put into rapid mass production. It was to be flown into combat by the loyal Hitler Youth, after they had been given a brief training period on gliders.

Heinkel was awarded the contract on 30 September. By 29 October the He 162 had been designed, and construction had begun. The first prototype was flown on 6 December, with Flugkapitän Peter at the controls. One month later, the first He 162s were delivered to a test unit, and in February 1945 I/JG-1 began conversion to the type.

Few German records remain of those frantic last days, but there is at least one reported incident of combat between an He 162 and a USAAF P-51 Mustang. The jet was able to turn and climb with the Mustang, but it was much faster and had greater acceleration. The combat was inconclusive; neither claimed victory.

By the end of the war, about 275 had been built and another 800 were in various stages of assembly. It was a formidable accomplishment by the Heinkel organisation. They designed a contemporary jet fighter in one month, flew it nine weeks after starting design, and delivered 275 in less than seven months.

There was one more last-gasp defence effort to fly: the Bachem 349 Natter. Work had begun in the spring of 1944, to a specification for a target defence interceptor. Bachem's first proposal was rejected in

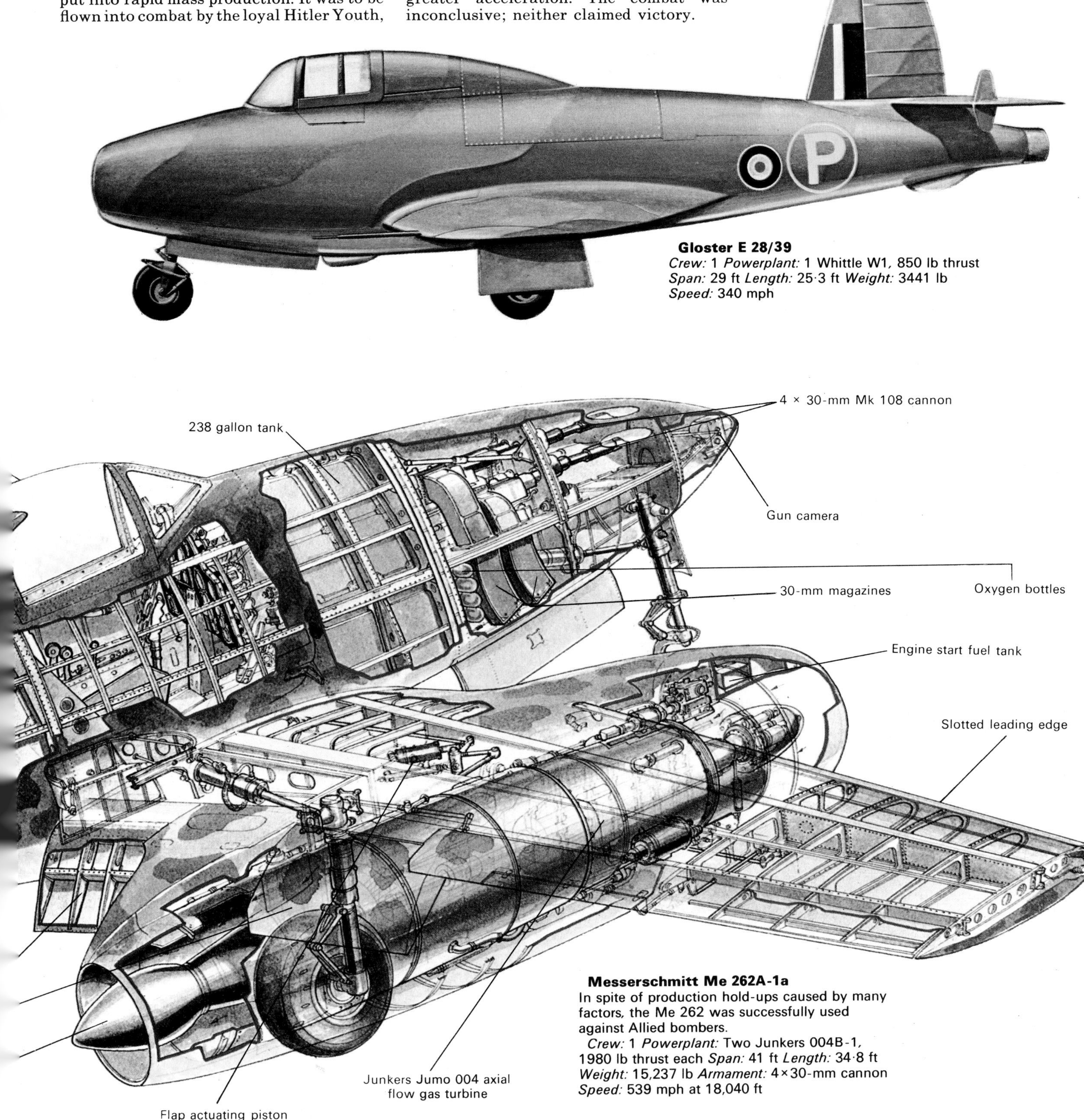

Gloster E 28/39
Crew: 1 *Powerplant:* 1 Whittle W1, 850 lb thrust
Span: 29 ft *Length:* 25·3 ft *Weight:* 3441 lb
Speed: 340 mph

Messerschmitt Me 262A-1a
In spite of production hold-ups caused by many factors, the Me 262 was successfully used against Allied bombers.
Crew: 1 *Powerplant:* Two Junkers 004B-1, 1980 lb thrust each *Span:* 41 ft *Length:* 34·8 ft
Weight: 15,237 lb *Armament:* 4×30-mm cannon
Speed: 539 mph at 18,040 ft

favour of a Heinkel design; but Erich Bachem knew the sources of power and had an interview with Heinrich Himmler. The decision of the Ministry was immediately changed to support the Bachem proposal as well.

It was a tiny wooden airframe powered by a single rocket engine, boosted by four solid-propellant rockets, launched from a vertical tower, and armed by a nose full of air-to-air rockets. The attack over, the pilot was expected to bail out. He and the valuable engine were to be saved by parachutes.

The Natter was tested as a glider in November 1944, launched unmanned in December under boost power only, and was successful in both tests. But the first piloted flight ended in disaster. On 28 February 1945 Oberleutnant Lothar Siebert, a volunteer for the test flight, was killed when the canopy came off during launch, apparently knocking him unconscious as it left. The Natter crashed out of control. But the next three manned launches were successful, and the programme moved ahead. Seven manned flights were made in all, and the production programme continued to grind out the wooden airframes which took only a few hundred man-hours each to build.

In April 1945, a squadron of 10 Natters was set up ready to launch near Stuttgart, waiting for the next bomber raid for its initiation into combat. But before the aerial assault, Allied armoured units rolled into the area, and the Natter crews destroyed their aircraft to keep them from falling into enemy hands. That was the effective end of the Natter programme.

The turbulence of war was a major factor in the establishment and cancellation of aircraft programmes. It was the beginning of war that must have been one of the events prompting the issuing of a British Air Ministry specification, E 28/39, for a single-seat fighter prototype aircraft powered by a gas turbine for jet propulsion.

Earlier, the Ministry had contracted with Power Jets, a firm headed by Frank Whittle, for development of an airworthy jet engine. Power Jets received its first Ministry support in March 1938; the engine contract was received on 7 July 1939.

The aircraft contract, issued to Gloster Aircraft on 3 February 1940, described a design based on the need for an interceptor. Top speed was to be about 380 mph, and armament was to be four machine-guns. The primary purpose of the aircraft was to obtain flight data on the engine, but it was also to be a prototype fighter.

The first run of an engine in the E 28/39 airframe was made on 6 April 1941, using an unairworthy engine. The next day, Flt Lt P E G Sayer began taxi tests at Brockworth. The plane rolled across the green field, picking up speed and slowing again as Sayer felt out the handling. Three times during the taxi runs, Sayer lifted the plane off the ground briefly. It seemed ready to fly.

The first prototype was trucked to the airfield at Cranwell, home of the RAF College where Whittle had spent his cadet days. There were practical as well as sentimental reasons for selecting that field. It had a long runway, with clear approaches, and was one of the best available fields for test work.

On 14 May Sayer repeated some of the taxi tests and planned to fly the following day. Low clouds hid the sky on the morning of May 15, but towards evening they began to lift. The camouflaged E 28/39 with Sayer in the cockpit trundled out to the starting area. There was a rising howl from the

Gloster Meteor F 3
Meteors were the only Allied jet fighters to see operational service during the Second World War.
Crew: 1 *Powerplant:* 2 Rolls-Royce Derwents, 2000 lb thrust each *Span:* 43 ft *Length:* 41 ft *Armament:* 4×20-mm cannon *Speed:* 585 mph at sea level

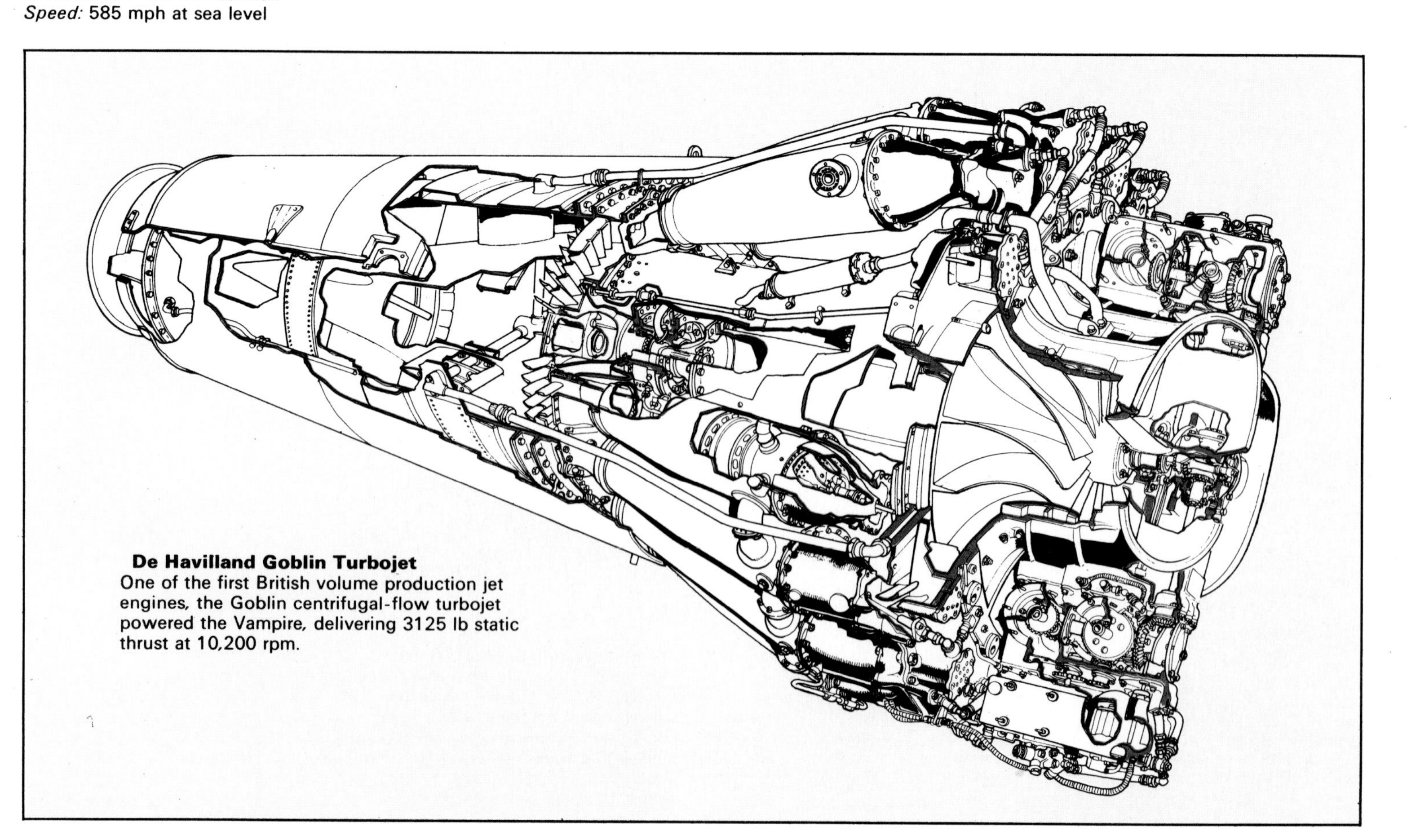

De Havilland Goblin Turbojet
One of the first British volume production jet engines, the Goblin centrifugal-flow turbojet powered the Vampire, delivering 3125 lb static thrust at 10,200 rpm.

engine, the plane began to move, and with darkness already gathering, Sayer lifted the plane off on its first flight.

He stayed aloft 17 minutes. It was the first flight ever made by a British jet-propelled aircraft.

Official support came soon. The flight programme was pushed to learn more about this new form of propulsion. Gradually the aircraft was taken to 25,000 ft and 300 mph in less than 10 hours flying.

Later, Rolls-Royce took over development of the engine, and raised its basic thrust to 1400 lb. Then the plane was flown to a maximum speed of 466 mph, and to an altitude above 42,000 ft. Gloster completed its portion of the programme in late June 1943, and turned the E 28/39 over to the care of the Royal Aircraft Establishment at Farnborough.

Britain's first true jet fighter was the Gloster Meteor, begun as an answer to specification F 9/40. It was planned as a twin-engine craft, because one engine of the type then available was hardly sufficient to obtain performance better than that of contemporary piston-engined fighters. Further, there was a supposed advantage of twin-engine reliability and safety.

The Gloster design team laid out their twin with the jet engines buried in the wings, and with the rear spars built around large holes for the jet pipes to pass through. Tricycle landing gear and a high tail were other basic decisions. Armament was to be four 20-mm cannon in the nose, and the cockpit was to be pressurised. Design began some time around August 1940.

About a year later, problems arose with the specified engines; the Power Jets W 2B engines had not been declared airworthy. One prototype was converted to take the Halford H 1 engines then in advanced development, and another to take the Metropolitan-Vickers F 2 engines. The H 1 engines were first cleared for flight, and the fifth prototype Meteor was trucked to the aerodrome at Cranwell, where Gloster pilot Michael Daunt made the first flight on 5 March 1943.

With Rolls-Royce in the engine programme, the final choice for the Meteor powerplant was the Welland W 2B, basically the Whittle/Power Jets engine. Wellands powered the first 20 production F Mk 1 Meteors, a fighter rushed into production and action near the end of the war. Issued to 616 Squadron RAF, based at Culmhead and later at Manston, they first saw action on 27 July 1944, on 'Diver' patrol against the German V-1 buzz-bombs. Sqdn Ldr Watts was the first Meteor pilot to contact one; but his guns jammed and the flying bomb continued on course. First kill of a V-1 was made on 4 August by F/O Dean, whose guns also jammed. So Dean closed the distance, eased the Meteor's wingtip under that of the V-1, and banked sharply away. The Meteor's wingtip slammed against the V-1's wing and sent it into a spiral dive and a crash in open country.

F/O Rogers, almost at the same time, was having more conventional success. His guns fired, and he became the first RAF pilot to shoot down an enemy aircraft from a jet fighter.

Britain's only other jet fighter of the war years, the de Havilland DH 100 Vampire, was very different from the Meteor. Designed to specification E 6/41, which defined an experimental aircraft rather than the fighter required by the Gloster Meteor specification of F 9/40, the Vampire started to take shape on the drawing boards at Hatfield in May 1942.

The single jet engine was enclosed in an egg-shaped fuselage, with inlets for the air at the root of each wing, and the exhaust discharging directly aft on the centre line of the egg. De Havilland designers used twin tail booms, perhaps borrowing the idea from the piston-engined Lockheed P-38 Lightning.

The Vampire was all metal, but there was one holdover from earlier DH designs; the cockpit section was constructed of a plywood and balsa sandwich material.

It was an all-DH project. The engine was the Halford H 1, designed by Maj Frank Halford and built by de Havilland. Geoffrey de Havilland, Jr, made the first flight on 30 September 1943, at Hatfield, six months after the Meteor had flown. The time differential was critical; the Meteor just barely saw action near the end of the war, but the Vampire was too late to be tested under combat conditions.

About a year earlier, the first flight of the first US jet fighter, the Bell XP-59A, had taken place. The site was a remote desert area, part of the USAAF Muroc Bombing and Gunnery Range located on a dry lake bed about 100 miles north of Los Angeles, California. (That site later became Edwards Air Force Base.)

Robert M Stanley, then chief pilot for Bell, fired up the twin General Electric I-A turbojets, which had been closely but not completely copied from the British W 2B engines. A few minutes later, on the after-

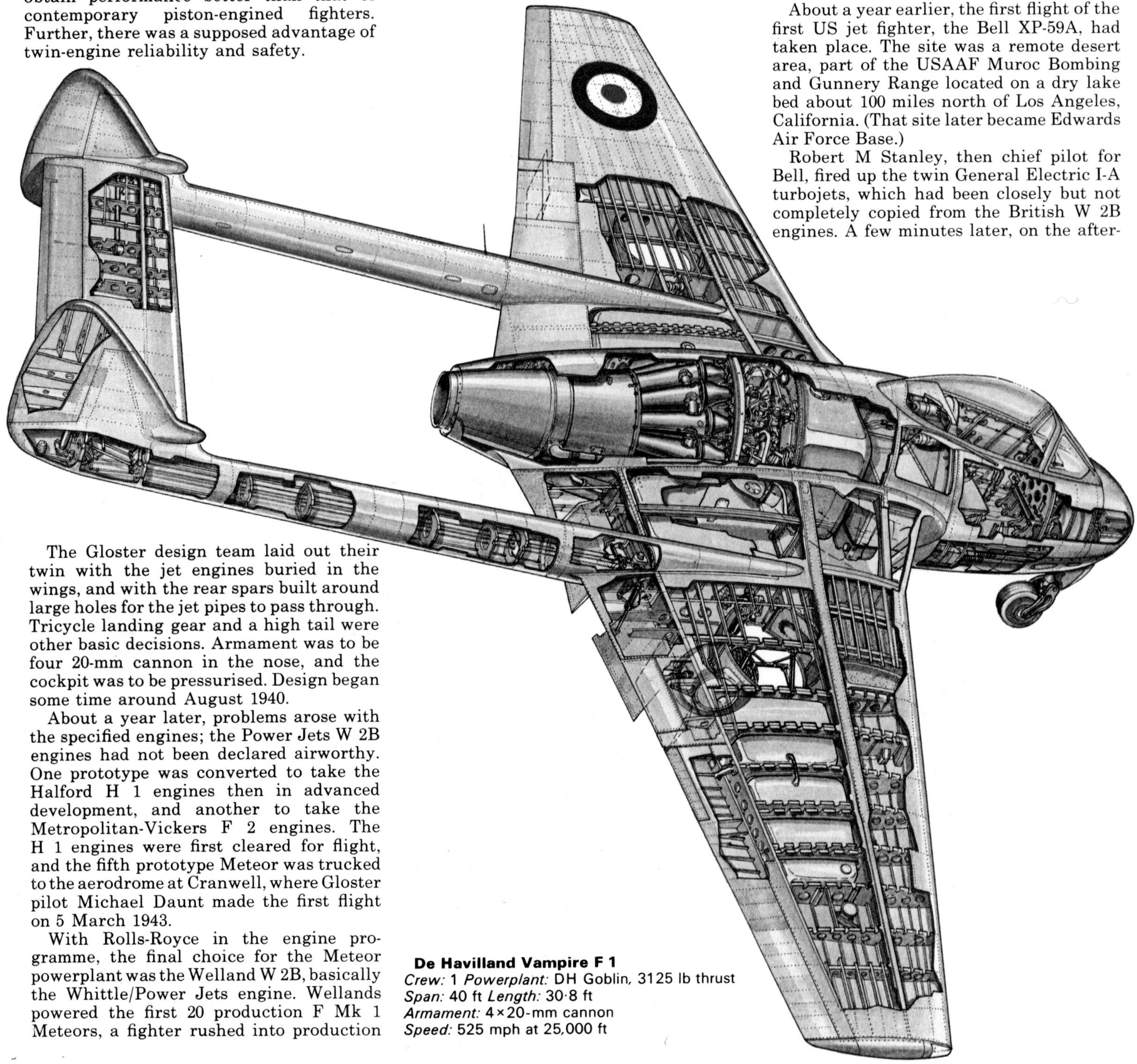

De Havilland Vampire F 1
Crew: 1 *Powerplant:* DH Goblin, 3125 lb thrust
Span: 40 ft *Length:* 30·8 ft
Armament: 4×20-mm cannon
Speed: 525 mph at 25,000 ft

noon of 1 October 1942, the XP-59A lifted off the dry lake bed into the California sky.

It would not have made such progress without British help. Major General Henry H Arnold, then Chief of the USAAC, visited Britain in the spring of 1941, saw the Whittle engine and the E 28/39, and was impressed. After follow-up meetings, it was agreed that the US should copy the Whittle engine and develop a twin-engine fighter around it. Bell were chosen as the airframe company to be responsible, and General Electric were chosen to build the engines. Bell were given eight months from the date of the contract approval to have their first aircraft ready for flight.

Construction stayed on schedule, but the timetable for GE engine deliveries slipped. They were not ready until August 1942, and they were never trouble-free. Their performance did not meet expectations, because

Smithsonian Institution Photo No A516A

Bell XP-59A Airacomet
More of a research aircraft than a service fighter, the XP-59A first flew in October 1942

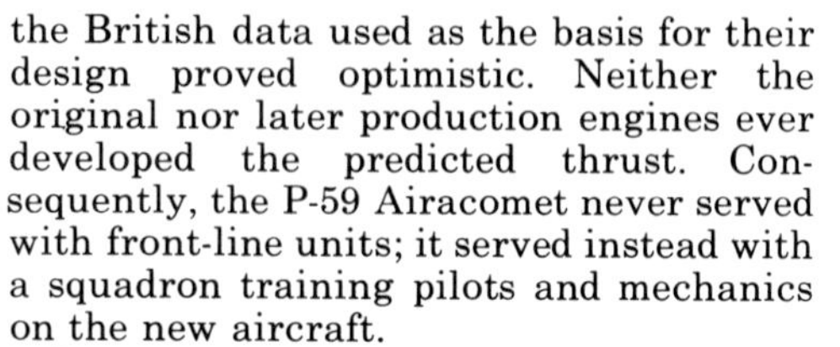

Crew: 1 *Powerplant:* 2 General Electric I-A, 1250 lb thrust each *Span:* 49 ft *Length:* 38·8 ft *Weight:* 10,450 lb *Armament:* 2×37-mm cannon *Speed:* 502 mph at 35,160 ft

the British data used as the basis for their design proved optimistic. Neither the original nor later production engines ever developed the predicted thrust. Consequently, the P-59 Airacomet never served with front-line units; it served instead with a squadron training pilots and mechanics on the new aircraft.

It was obvious early in the Bell programme that its performance was not going to be earth-shaking. Everybody had ideas about what to do, but Lockheed's Clarence L (Kelly) Johnson was to see his ideas take tangible form.

Lockheed had done earlier work on a jet fighter proposal, had been rejected, but had persisted. On one of Johnson's periodic visits to Wright Field, then the technical headquarters of the USAAF, he was asked to consider designing a jet fighter around a British engine. Within a few days the first sketches were ready, and Johnson got the go-ahead in June 1943. At the far side of the Lockheed airport at Burbank, California, a temporary building was erected, the 'Skunk Works', named after a mythical factory in the popular comic strip, 'Li'l Abner'.

The contract gave Lockheed 180 days to design, build and fly the XP-80. They beat the construction deadline and had the plane ready to go in 143 days. But the first flight was delayed by engine availability, and it was not until 9 January 1943, that Lockheed chief test pilot Milo Burcham made the first flight with the XP-80 from the dry lake bed at Muroc.

Then Lockheed had to repeat the whole performance. It was decided that the production P-80 would be powered by the new General Electric I-40 engine, based on British designs. Back to the Skunk Works went Johnson's team, to emerge 139 days later with another prototype, the XP-80A. It first flew on 11 June 1944, and by the time the war ended, 45 had been delivered to USAAF squadrons. A few had even been tested at operational bases in England and Italy, but had been kept from any area where combat might have been possible.

Early in the development of the jet fighter, the navies of Great Britain and the US had studied the new type and wondered how best to adapt it to carrier operations. In the US, the Navy Bureau of Aeronautics were sponsoring the development of a series of axial-flow turbojets by Westinghouse Electric Corp. These small-diameter engines promised much better overall installed performance than did the bulkier centrifugal-flow engines pioneered by Whittle, Rolls-Royce, and General Electric.

The Navy, Westinghouse and the McDonnell Aircraft Corp got together in early 1943 to discuss the design of a Naval fighter built around two or more of the Westinghouse engines. McDonnell designers investigated a wide range of possibilities, guided by basically conservative design policies. They checked eight-, six-, four- and twin-engined schemes and settled on the twin as the basis for their design of the XFD-1. It was to be a fighter with a defensive mission of combat air patrol at 15,000 ft above a carrier task force. Two years and a few days after the contract was signed, the first prototype XFD-1 took to the air on 26 January 1945. Two months later McDonnell received a production order.

But the war was to be over by almost two years when the first McDonnell Phantoms, redesignated FH-1, were delivered to the fleet. By then, it was apparent that the Phantoms were only an interim type serving to accumulate some fleet experience with jet fighters.

To the East, the Russians had been working for several years to develop their own rocket-powered interceptor. Two designers – Bereznyak and Isaev – planned a tiny aircraft around a single rocket engine rated at 2420 lb of thrust. They designed a conventional fighter, armed with a pair of 20-mm cannon in the nose, and intended for the same kind of mission as the Me 163.

The expected bomber raids against Russia never happened; the rocket-powered interceptor would not have been needed. But it was a fatal accident during a test flight that put an end to the development programme. The first flight had been successful. Test pilot Grigori Bakhchivandzhe flew the BI for a little longer than three minutes on its maiden trip on 15 May 1942.

It was slow development. A second plane was added, but the rocket engine proved troublesome. Only six flights were logged in ten months. Bakhchivandzhe was killed

Smithsonian Institution Photo No 75-Y844

Lockheed XP-80 Shooting Star
The USAF's first service jet, modelled on British Whittle designs, arrived too late to see combat. The sectional diagram (below left) shows the layout of the cockpit, engine and fuselage construction
Crew: 1 *Powerplant:* 1 Halford H-1, 2460 lb thrust *Span:* 36·9 ft *Length:* 32·8 ft *Weight:* 8916 lb *Speed:* 502 mph at 20,480 ft

on the seventh, a high-speed run at relatively low altitude. Witnesses saw black smoke instead of the usual short red-orange flame from the engine; the plane pitched down and began to disintegrate in the air before it crashed and exploded.

The seven airframes that had been built were scrapped along with the components for another 20 or so, on orders from the Kremlin banning all further work on rocket fighters.

Only two jet fighter projects ever got under way in Japan, and both were inspired by German developments. Japan acquired licence rights to the Me 163 and its rocket engine. But delivery of a sample Me 163 and a complete set of blueprints was not completed; the submarine carrying them to Japan was sunk. Japan received only a single rocket engine and an Me 163 manual a Japanese naval officer had brought back from a visit to Germany.

In July 1944 the Japanese Navy issued a specification for a rocket-powered interceptor. The Army joined the programme, and the first prototype of a training glider was completed by December 1944. It flew successfully, after being towed to altitude and released. But the aircraft itself, the Mitsubishi J8M1, was not as successful. The first prototype was finished in June 1945, and its first flight was scheduled for 7 July. The engine failed soon after takeoff, and the J8M1 smashed into the ground, killing Lt Cdr Toyohiko Inuzuka, the test pilot. Although production had started, and other J8M1 aircraft were available, no more flights were made before the Japanese surrender.

One of only two wartime jet fighter programmes to get under way in Japan, the Mitsubishi J8M1 Shusui *was little more than a copy of an Me 163 in Japanese markings*

Maru Magazine/Orion Press

The success of the Me 262 programme sparked Japanese interest in a twin-jet fighter, and the Navy issued an order to Nakajima for development of such a fighter, based on the German twin-jet craft but smaller. Data were limited. The turbojet engines were designed using, among other sources, photographs of the German BMW 003 turbojet. The first prototype was completed in August 1945, just days before the final bell rang for Japan. On 7 August it made its first flight from the Naval air base at Kisarazu, with Lt Cdr Susumu Tanaoha at the controls. On his second flight, Tanaoha had to abort during the takeoff run because of engine failure. It was the last attempt to fly the Nakajima J8N1 *Kikka*.

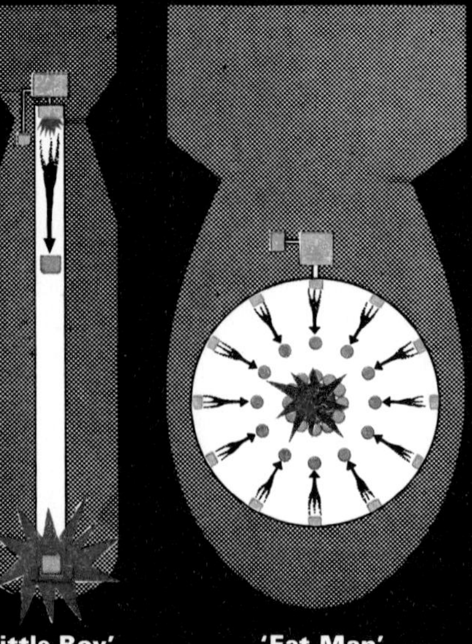
'Little Boy'
the Hiroshima bomb

'Fat Man'
the Nagasaki bomb

THE ULTIMATE WEAPON

The world still lives with the moral and political implications of the decision to drop the atomic bomb on two Japanese industrial cities, Hiroshima and Nagasaki, in 1945. The memory of the charred ruins of those cities, of the thousands of victims vaporised, shredded or burnt beyond recognition – and of those that today endure a living death from the effects of radiation – cannot be blotted from our conscience. Hopefully, the ultimate weapon will be its own ultimate deterrent

Hiroshima, the atomic desert

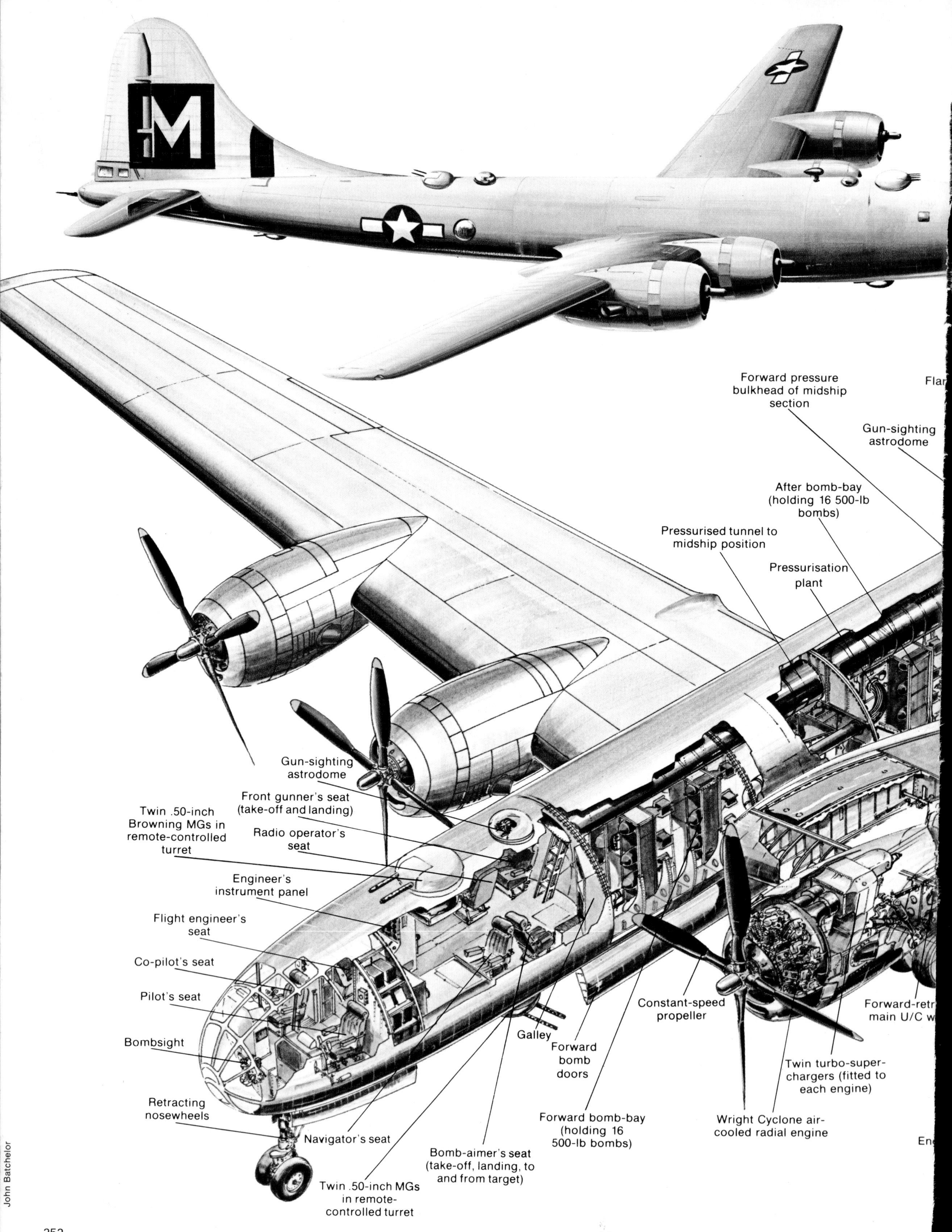

John Batchelor

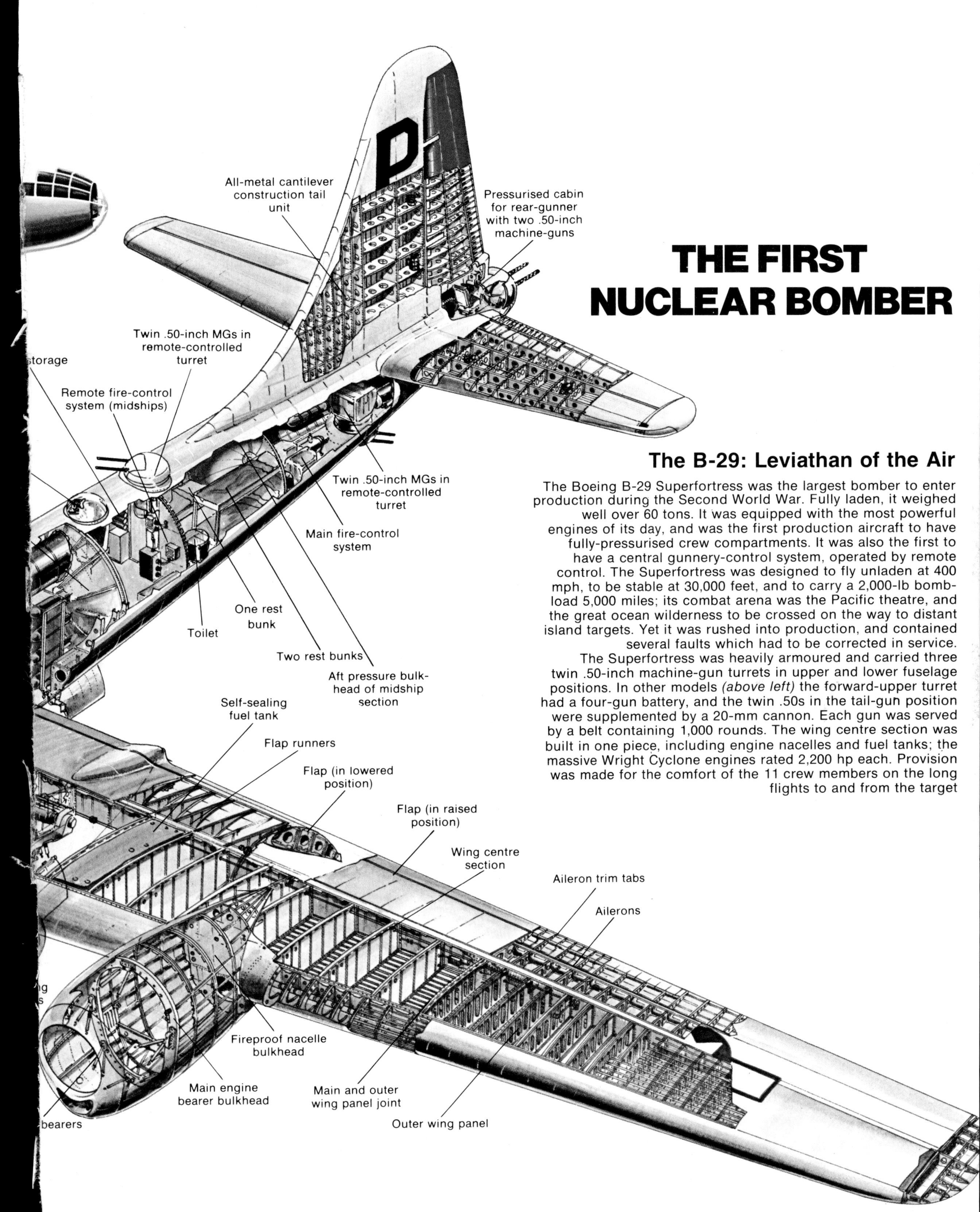

THE FIRST NUCLEAR BOMBER

The B-29: Leviathan of the Air

The Boeing B-29 Superfortress was the largest bomber to enter production during the Second World War. Fully laden, it weighed well over 60 tons. It was equipped with the most powerful engines of its day, and was the first production aircraft to have fully-pressurised crew compartments. It was also the first to have a central gunnery-control system, operated by remote control. The Superfortress was designed to fly unladen at 400 mph, to be stable at 30,000 feet, and to carry a 2,000-lb bomb-load 5,000 miles; its combat arena was the Pacific theatre, and the great ocean wilderness to be crossed on the way to distant island targets. Yet it was rushed into production, and contained several faults which had to be corrected in service.

The Superfortress was heavily armoured and carried three twin .50-inch machine-gun turrets in upper and lower fuselage positions. In other models *(above left)* the forward-upper turret had a four-gun battery, and the twin .50s in the tail-gun position were supplemented by a 20-mm cannon. Each gun was served by a belt containing 1,000 rounds. The wing centre section was built in one piece, including engine nacelles and fuel tanks; the massive Wright Cyclone engines rated 2,200 hp each. Provision was made for the comfort of the 11 crew members on the long flights to and from the target

INDEX

Compiled by Wing Commander Roger Pemberton
Page references in *italics* indicate illustrations; & between page numbers means that the text is interrupted by full-page illustrations

Aircraft are indexed individually, under their usual appellations, *e.g.* BE Series; Dakota, Douglas; DH9a; Hurricane, Hawker; Mosquito, DH; Spitfire, Supermarine. 'Engines, areo' and 'machine guns' are grouped, by nationalities, under those two headings respectively.

Abbreviations: a/c, aircraft; a.e., aero engine; A-H, Austro-Hungarian; Br, British; br, bomber; Fr, French; ftr, fighter; Ger, German; Ital, Italian; Jap, Japanese; recce, reconnaissance; Russ, Russian; US, American.

F

G

H

I

J

K

L

M

PRINTED IN BELGIUM